CYBERLAW AND E-COMMERCE

CYBERLAW AND E-COMMERCE

David Baumer
North Carolina State University

J. C. Poindexter
North Carolina State University

Boston   Burr Ridge, IL   Dubuque, IA   Madison, WI   New York   San Francisco   St. Louis
Bangkok   Bogotá   Caracas   Kuala Lumpur   Lisbon   London   Madrid   Mexico City
Milan   Montreal   New Delhi   Santiago   Seoul   Singapore   Sydney   Taipei   Toronto

McGraw-Hill Higher Education ⚡
A Division of The McGraw-Hill Companies

CYBERLAW AND E-COMMERCE

Published by McGraw-Hill, an imprint of The McGraw-Hill Companies, Inc. 1221 Avenue of the Americas, New York, NY, 10020. Copyright © 2002 by The McGraw-Hill Companies, Inc. All rights reserved. No part of this publication may be reproduced or distributed in any form or by any means, or stored in a data base or retrieval system, without the prior written consent of The McGraw-Hill Companies, Inc., including, but not limited to, in any network or other electronic storage or transmission, or broadcast for distance learning. Some ancillaries, including electronic and print components, may not be available to customers outside the United States.

This book is printed on acid-free paper.

1 2 3 4 5 6 7 8 9 0 CSI/CSI 0 9 8 7 6 5 4 3 2 1

ISBN   0–07–244120–8

Publisher: *John E. Biernat*
Sponsoring editor: *Andy Winston*
Developmental editor II: *Christine Scheid*
Marketing manager: *Lisa Nicks*
Project manager: *Jim Labeots*
Production supervisor: *Debra R. Sylvester*
Media producer: *Jennifer Becka*
Designer: *Matthew Baldwin*
Cover designer: *Joanne Schopler*
Cover image: *Ken Davies/Masterfile*
Interior design: *Matthew Baldwin*
Supplement producer: *Susan Lombardi*
Typeface: *10/12 Times Roman*
Compositor: *Interactive Composition Corporation*
Printer: *Courier Stoughton, Inc.*

Library of Congress Cataloging-in-Publication Data

Baumer, David L,
    Cyberlaw and e-commerce: security, risk management, and control / David Baumer,
   J.C. Poindexter.
       p. cm.
    Includes index.
    ISBN 0–07–244120–8 (alk. paper)
     1. Electronic commerce—Law and legislation—United States.   2. Software protection—Law and legislation—United States.
   3. Intellectual property—United States.   I. Poindexter, J. Carl (Julius Carl), 1943-   II. Title.
   KF888 .B33 2002
   343.7309′944—dc21   2001030397

www.mhhe.com

Dedicated with love and affection to Joan,
my uncomplaining and supportive wife, and to
my two sons, Erik and Paul, both of whom make me proud to be a father
—DLB

Dedicated with much love, devotion, and appreciation to my wife, Martha, and to all of our
wonderful children, Carlyle, Katherine, Taylor, and Parker
—JCP

BRIEF CONTENTS

CONTENTS

CHAPTER 9

INTELLECTUAL PROPERTY II: BASIC COPYRIGHT AND TRADEMARK LAW   257

LIST OF CASES

PREFACE

ONCE YOU ENTER YOU CAN NEVER GO BACK

In the late 1960s, Jim Morrison of the Doors invited his fans in one song to "break on through to the other side." The name of this textbook is *Cyberlaw and E-Commerce* because we want to ensure that you know that this is not a traditional Business Law or Legal Environment textbook. This text does provide comprehensive coverage of the mainstays of Business Law in its "Basic" chapters that deal with contracts and torts. Also we deal with Basic Intellectual Property Law including patent, trade secret, copyright, and trademark laws in much more detail than is provided in other Business Law and Legal Environment textbooks. The main thrust of *Cyberlaw and E-Commerce,* however, is focused on the new legal challenges that changes in technology have created for modern business managers. We have included several chapters dealing with contracting for software development, business organization of cyber companies, E-Commerce contract law, and cybertorts that are not provided by any other legal textbook for business majors, but which address some of the most pressing legal issues that will face those future managers.

Technological Innovation Changes Everything . . . Including Law

Significant changes in society are often closely followed by significant legal changes. Changes in the United States and world economies during the last 10 years are, by any measure, significant. Most of the significant changes in the United States and world economies are due to advances in technology, particularly information technology. Broadly defined, more than one third of the GDP in the United States is attributable to *information technology,* and that figure is expected to exceed half by 2006. Many of the laws that comprise the legal environment of business will change and the pace of the change is likely to be rapid. It is hoped that this book will enable business students and others involved in information technology to focus on the legal issues that have the most significant impacts on them and their businesses in the 21st Century. This book targets future managers who will be dealing with information technology in some way, but also provides sufficient treatment of traditional business law topics to enable managers to effectively make legal decisions involving contracts, tort exposure, business organization, and intellectual property.

Emphasis Is Placed on the New as Well as High-Tech

Throughout this textbook reliance is placed largely on cases that are of very recent origin, many of which deal with high-tech issues. In much of the textbook, it is assumed that students are familiar with the Internet, software and hardware capabilities, basic mathematics and statistics, and management issues. The portfolio of cases and situations that we review for business students will resemble those that business managers will face in the future and are more in sync with cases and business problems students will face in other courses than what is found in more traditional business law and legal environment texts. In their Operations Management, MIS, Finance, and many other courses, it is assumed that students know the basics of mathematics, computer technology, and other tools of successful managers. The same assumption is made in this textbook. Business students, MBAs or undergraduates, taking a law course using this textbook will be tested equivalently to those students taking other, more traditionally analytical courses, such as those mentioned above.

Constrained Optimization in Topic Coverage

In our view modern business pedagogy involves recognition that there are many issues that are basically *cross-functional*. In other words, managers in each functional area of business have had to deal with new challenges created by technology, advances in information systems, and, we believe, law. There are legal issues in every functional area of business, and many of these legal issues were hardly mentioned or not taught at all to business students 10 years ago. We are at the beginning of a new era in business and the focus in this textbook is upon the emerging legal issues that will face future managers. Given the size of this book we are dedicated to avoiding redundancy. We devote significant attention to intellectual property and little space to labor law. In most business programs, labor law and related issues are covered by the Human Resource Management courses, with little need to duplicate that coverage in a Legal Environment course. We hope that we provide an exciting and relevant presentation of the significance of law in this exciting Information Age.

WHAT IS COVERED IN *CYBERLAW AND E-COMMERCE*

Contract Law with High-Tech Applications

In this book we have eschewed much of the traditional approach to introducing business students to law. Many of the preliminary topics that receive extensive coverage in the first few chapters of Legal Environment textbooks, such as legal theory, the structure of the legal system in the United States, legal vocabulary, ethics, and social responsibility of business, are covered in limited ways in this book. After a preliminary chapter that surveys the confluence of high technology and changes in the legal system, we immerse students into a three-chapter sequence on contract law that deals with **Basic Contract Law, E-Commerce Contract Law,** and **Contracting for Software Develop-**

ment (Chapters 2, 3, and 4). As compared to most Business Law textbooks, we have fewer old "landmark" cases and more cases involving high-tech issues. In our examination of E-Commerce Contract Law we discuss UCITA, UETA, and the proposed revisions to Article 2 of the UCC. We believe that decisions made in contracting for software development are among the most important decisions that business managers must make. We provide a unique examination of that process in a chapter that features a number of real-world examples and management recommendations.

Torts, Cybertorts and Product Liability

Chapter 5 covers **Basic Tort Law.** In Chapter 6 **Cybertorts, Privacy, and Government Regulation,** we examine tort law in cyberspace. We discuss how companies use the Internet to collect personal information from customers and visitors to their websites. We also look at recent government legislation on the handling of medical and financial records and the collection of information from children. Chapter 7 discusses **Product Liability** law, incorporating recent developments including the Restatement Third of Torts. Timely high-tech issues in product liability, including warnings, state-of-the-art defenses, and design defects are covered, making use of simple mathematics inspired by Learned Hand.

Intellectual Property: Creation, Use, and Protection

Without a doubt the greatest difference between the skill set of successful managers 20 years ago and those needed today is the fact that managers, now and in the foreseeable future, manage intellectual property (IP). What was once allocated to attorneys, management in the 21st Century of IP, is now at the center of decision making. Chapter 8, **Intellectual Property I: Patent Law Basics and Trade Secret Law,** examines the modern evolution of patent law while still covering foundation issues. We mix examination of basic points of patent law with management recommendations and examples of catastrophes that have occurred from management mistakes. As with the rest of the book, virtually all of the cases in the IP chapters are quite recent. A number of high-tech human resource management issues are dealt with in the trade secret portion of Chapter 8.

Chapter 9 continues with an emphasis on the modern in **Intellectual Property II: Copyright and Trademark Basics.** This chapter offers detailed coverage of the challenges to copyright law posed by the Internet, MP3 technology, and Napster. Our experience in using much of this material in the classroom is that students respond enthusiastically to cases such as Napster and other material that they are already encountering. We also look at trademark law and domain name issues as well as at the impact of the Anticybersquatter Consumer Protection Act. Chapter 10 examines how various branches of IP law converge for the **Protection of Software.** We deal with the transformation of patent law and the increasing acceptance of software and business methods patents. Throughout the three IP chapters, we examine recent federal legislation that has channeled the direction of technological development.

Business Organization and Cyber Companies

Chapter 11 examines traditional **Business Organization,** again with an emphasis on more recent cases. We jump into cyberspace in Chapter 12 with our analysis of **Cyber Companies and Internet Agreements.** Not only does this deal with the new, high-tech start-ups such as Amazon.com and others, but it also examines the movement of traditional companies into establishment of a greater Internet presence. Companies whose main interface with the public is electronic must be concerned with different issues than are corporations operating under traditional state incorporation statutes, with a focus on local brick-and-mortar facilities. Cyber companies sign web-hosting agreements that can have greater legal impact on their mode of operations than the traditional doctrines of corporate law.

CASE SELECTION

As mentioned above, compared with most (probably all) other law books for business management majors and MBA students, our cases are more recent. They are also longer and more complicated, of necessity, because technology often plays a central role in the court resolution of such cases. Indeed, in many cases, courts seem to be focused on a detailed elaboration of what they conceive to be the essential elements of the technology under discussion and how these elements can

be analyzed with precedents that originated in simpler times. Some of these cases are used to illustrate why Congress has had to step in and enact new legislation due to existing statutes' failures to accomplish the goals of the existing legislation. Since so many of the cases in this text are of such recent origin, it is a virtual certainty that many of them will eventually be overturned or clarified by statute or subsequent court decision. Be that as it may, we believe that immersion of students in the legal issues that will be important in the future will better equip them to operate in the highly fluid legal environment that appears to be characteristic of changing times.

INTERNET INSERTS

Most of the inserts that we use come straight from the World Wide Web. Using the Internet as a library is a big part of the promise of the Internet, as much of that material is freely available to all. A number of this text's inserts are statements by advocacy groups who have definite E-Commerce ideas, for example about the enforceability of shrinkwrap agreements or privacy on the World Wide Web. Throughout, virtually all such inserts are inspired in some way by technological change that has then set off legal changes. Many of the positions taken by the authors of these inserts would have been incomprehensible 10 years ago because they deal with situations unimaginable to people living in 1990.

INTERNATIONAL PERSPECTIVE

Although we do not devote a single separate chapter to international law in this text, we do integrate an international perspective throughout the textbook. International legal aspects appear most prominently in our IP chapters, but we also discuss international approaches to privacy and database protection.

INSTRUCTOR SUPPORT MATERIALS

This book has an accompanying Instructor's Manual. The Instructor's Manual is based on notes that have been used in the course that inspired the writing of this text, Technology, Law, and the Internet. The Instructor's Manual enables an instructor who may be leery of the leap into cyberspace to make that transition with a solid outline of the material that is presented in the textbook.

The instructor's manual includes a wide variety of resources designed to facilitate instruction. It begins each chapter with an outline of the text, as well as separate, detailed teaching notes. For each chapter there are questions to stimulate class discussion, suggestions for class activities, and additional outside resources for further study. Unique to this text, we have included a list of video resources that can be used to further illustrate concepts from the text. These resources are described in enough detail to allow instructors to make informed decisions about utilizing them in class prior to researching and purchasing or renting the materials. To aid in this research, the whereabouts of these resources, along with current approximate prices are included in this section.

SUMMARY THOUGHTS

Having taught similar material for over 20 years, we have been reinvigorated by the cyberlaw explosion. We believe that the material in this textbook is so timely as to excite both instructors and students. Consequently, we view this text as the most relevant and up-to-date legal textbook for MBA and undergraduate business management students currently available. There is little doubt that knowledge of law has become increasingly significant to the success of managers, particularly those who have a substantial Internet presence or who are involved in management of technology. *Cyberlaw and E-Commerce* is a breakthrough textbook that we believe will be followed by many others in the years to come.

ACKNOWLEDGMENTS

There are several people who provided invaluable assistance in the development of this book project, but one person clearly was paramount in her support. Ms. Kimberly Eilers worked with us from the start, believed in the project, and really mothered this project until it was able to spread its wings. Kimberly formatted, edited, and corrected the proposal for this book that attracted McGraw-Hill (as well as several other publishers). Although the authors take responsibility for the contents of this book, much of the creativity in the way the material is presented is directly attributable to Kimberly.

Also we received valuable assistance from Dr. Elmer F. Baumer, retired Associate Provost from the Ohio State University. Much of Dr. Baumer's expert assistance appears in Chapter 3: Contract Law for E-Commerce: UCITA, UETA, and UCC Revisions. We used Chapter 3 as a key part of the book proposal and it is one of the defining chapters of this book. Not only did Elmer provide expert editing, but much of the research for that chapter came from Elmer's Internet excursions. Just one more example of how a father will always help a son when he gets over his head. Thank you very much!

We'd also like to acknowledge those who took the time to review our manuscript and give us comments and suggestions. We sincerely thank them for their time and opinions:

Tony Enerva—Lakeland Community College
Andrea Giampetro-Meyer—Loyola College
Debra Kleiner—St. John's University
Bruce May—University of South Dakota
Judy Spain—Eastern Kentucky University
Maurice Tonissi—Quinsigamond Community College
Tom Tuytschaevers—Northeastern University

Finally, we would like to thank Andy Winston, Sponsoring Editor, and Christine Scheid, Development Editor II, of McGraw-Hill for their encouragement, support, and guidance. Andy in particular was a great believer in this project and his enthusiasm continues to inspire us. Christine has a practical wisdom borne from bringing to life many textbooks and she had to impart a lot of that wisdom to us in the writing of this book. Thanks to both of you.

The Legal Environment of Business in the Information Age

W hile sharing an order of fries at the student union cafeteria Meg asked, "Ben, do you remember the guys who won the Management School's business plan competition here two years ago with the customer service software package?" "Sure, they had a great combination of technology and a marketing strategy," replied Ben. "I'll bet that package is making lot of money right now." Half-smiling, half-frowning, Meg said, "Yes, I think it is doing great. Unfortunately, their business plan is making the money for someone else! Apparently the guys made a marketing presentation that revealed a lot of operating details to an enterprise software company, and that company replicated the software and took it to market without any agreement with our guys. At least, that's what Greg Smith told me when I saw him at the Pub last night. He was one of the computer science guys on the team. He said there's been a lawsuit filed asking for an injunction against the pirate firm's offering the software and demanding damages. Unfortunately, he said, their lawyer has told them that their technology and marketing was better than their legal work, so he isn't sure they'll prevail in court. They're hoping to get some settlement offer, even if it's only $20,000, while the pirates make millions from their ideas."

"Gosh," said Ben, "I remember some stories similar to that from that legal environment course all of us business majors have to take. At the time, though, I figured those were such rarities I'd never run into anything like it." "Apparently, Greg and the other guys on the team thought the same thing," Meg exhorted. "He says they all wish the business majors on the team had pushed them harder to get proper nondisclosure agreements and to have all their copyrights in place before they had any discussions with possible investors in their technology."

Is this just a hypothetical scenario? Absolutely not. Both "potential" companies and existing, often well-established companies have costly experiences like the one discussed by Meg and Ben, as reflected in the actual case on the next page. You may notice that the case below concerns two of the major players in the personal computer market. The allegation by the Apple Corporation is essentially that they developed the Graphical User Interface (GUI) based on icons and that Microsoft Corporation imitated their (Apple's) GUI. Quite obviously, a lot was at stake in clarifying the legal status of the Windows operating system.

Apple Computer, Inc. v. *Microsoft Corporation*
United States Court of Appeals for the Ninth Circuit
35 F.3d 1435; 1994

CASE BACKGROUND AND FACTS

Lisa and Macintosh are Apple computers. Each has a graphical user interface ("GUI") which Apple Computer, Inc. registered for copyright as an audiovisual work. Both GUIs were developed as a user-friendly way for ordinary mortals to communicate with the Apple computer; the Lisa Desktop and the Macintosh are based on a desktop metaphor with windows, icons, and pull-down menus which can be manipulated on the screen with a hand-held device called a mouse. When Microsoft Corporation released Windows 1.0, having a similar GUI, Apple complained. As a result, the two agreed to a license giving Microsoft the right to use and sublicense derivative works generated by Windows 1.0 in present and future products. Microsoft released Windows 2.03 and later, Windows 3.0; its licensee, Hewlett-Packard Company (HP), introduced NewWave 1.0 and later, NewWave 3.0, which run in conjunction with Windows to make IBM-compatible computers easier to use. Apple believed that these versions exceed the license, make Windows more "Mac-like," and infringe its copyright. This action followed.

Notice that when the earliest version of Windows was released (Windows 1.0), Apple complained but eventually reached an agreement to license some portion of its (Apple's) GUI to Microsoft. In this case the plaintiff (the party suing) is Apple and it is suing based on its claim that its copyrighted software, the GUI's for its Lisa and MacIntosh computers, were copied by later versions of Windows. The decision of the trial court was for the defendant,

Microsoft and the opinion by Judge Rymer discusses the decision of the Ninth Circuit Court of Appeals in the Federal Court system.

OPINION BY JUDGE RYMER

Apple asks us to reverse because of two fundamental errors in the district [trial] court's reasoning. [Footnotes deleted] First, Apple argues that the court should not have allowed the license for Windows 1.0 to serve as a partial defense. Second, Apple contends that the [trial] court went astray by dissecting Apple's works so as to eliminate unprotectable and licensed elements from comparison with Windows 2.03, 3.0, and NewWave as a whole, incorrectly leading it to adopt a standard of virtual identity instead of substantial similarity.

The district court's approach was on target. In so holding, we readily acknowledge how much more complex and difficult its task was than ours. The district court had to grapple with graphical user interfaces in the first instance—and for the first time, with a claim of copying a computer program's artistic look as an audiovisual work instead of program codes registered as a literary work. In this case there is also the unusual, added complexity of a license that arguably covers some or most of the allegedly infringing works. The district court therefore had to cut new paths as it went along; we have the luxury of looking at the case at the end of the trip. From this vantage point, it is clear that treatment of Apple's GUIs, whose visual displays are licensed to a great degree and which are a tool for the user to access various functions of a computer in an aesthetically and ergonomically pleasing way, follows naturally from a long

line of copyright decisions which recognizes that works cannot be substantially similar where analytic dissection demonstrates that similarities in expression are either authorized, or arise from the use of common ideas or their logical extensions.

* * *

1. Because there was an agreement by which Apple licensed the right to make certain derivative works, the district court properly started with the license to determine what Microsoft was permitted to copy. Infringement cannot be founded on a licensed similarity. We read Microsoft's license as the district court did, to cover visual displays—not the Windows 1.0 interface itself. That being so, the court correctly decided first to identify which visual displays in Windows 2.03, 3.0, and NewWave are licensed and which are not.

2. The district court then properly proceeded to distinguish ideas from expression, and to "dissect" unlicensed elements in order to determine whether the remaining similarities lack originality, flow naturally from basic ideas, or are one of the few ways in which a particular idea can be expressed given the constraints of the computer environment. Dissection is not inappropriate even though GUIs are thought of as the "look and feel" of a computer, because copyright protection extends only to protectable elements of expression.

3. Having found that the similarities in Windows 2.03

and 3.0 consist only of unprotectable or licensed elements, and that the similarities between protectable elements in Apple's works and NewWave are de minimis, the district court did not err by concluding that, to the extent there is creative expression left in how the works are put together, as a whole they can receive only limited protection. When the range of protectable and unauthorized expression is narrow, the appropriate standard for illicit copying is virtual identity. For these reasons, the GUIs in Windows 2.03, 3.0 and NewWave cannot be compared for substantial similarity with the Macintosh interface as a whole. Instead, as the district court held, the works must be compared for virtual identity.

* * *

We therefore hold that the district court properly identified the sources of similarity in Windows and NewWave, determined which were licensed, distinguished ideas from expression, and decided the scope of Apple's copyright by dissecting the unauthorized expression and filtering out unprotectable elements. Having correctly found that almost all the similarities spring either from the license or from basic ideas and their obvious expression, it correctly concluded that illicit copying could occur only if the works as a whole are virtually identical.

QUESTIONS FOR ANALYSIS

1. Stripped to its essence, the claim advanced by the plaintiff, Apple, against Microsoft, the defendant, is that the defendant unlawfully copied its GUI. Was Apple claiming that Microsoft exactly copied it GUI or that the "look and feel" of the software was the substantially similar?

2. The court refers to unprotectable and licensed elements of Apple's GUI. What was unprotectable about its GUI? What was licensed?

3. If Microsoft had copied the source and object code of Apple's operating system, would that act have been an illegal infringement?

The fact that students, or recent graduates, make mistakes by giving away their ideas without proper legal protection does not mean that mistakes of much greater significance are not committed by more experienced and established firms. It seems clear from the *Apple* case above that the attorneys working for Apple licensed away the crown jewels of the company to Microsoft when the similarities between its operating system and Windows 1.0 first became apparent. Note, however, that instead of being chastened by its encounter with Apple regarding the earliest version of Windows, Microsoft instead made subsequent versions of Windows even more similar to the Apple operating systems. There is really no way of knowing whether the accommodating posture initially adopted by Apple emboldened Microsoft, but it is clear that Windows took off after resolving its legal difficulties with Apple in this case.

ORGANIZATION OF THE TEXTBOOK

Readers should not be troubled if they don't feel fully in command of the legal issues explored in the case above. In general, we believe immersion into the real-world legal issues involving contracts, torts, business organization, and property will better enable business students and others to link this textbook with many of the same issues they are dealing with in other business courses. We emphasize high-tech legal issues, often involving software, in each basic area of law, while also providing coverage of the traditional areas of law.

THE LEGAL ENVIRONMENT OF BUSINESS

Your company, prospective or well-established, may have world-class product development, a finance group skilled at maximizing firm value, a marketing staff that excels at product design, placement, and promotion, enlightened human resource management personnel, and highly efficient production and transportation. And, yet, the collective benefit of high skill levels in all of these functional levels can be thwarted by legal problems.

The *Apple* v. *Microsoft* case is representative of costly legal problems involving intellectual property. There are other types of legal problems involving intellectual property, along with a wide array of potential legal mine fields companies face in the areas of contracts, torts, product liability, consumer protection, employee protection, environmental law, securities regulation, credit regulation, international law, and antitrust law. Clearly, every functional area of business management entails potential legal problems that can threaten a company's financial viability. Managers should have a broad understanding of the legal restrictions and demands imposed by the law as they seek to address the demands of the business community, workers, consumers, and government.

TECHNOLOGY AND THE LAW

A major focus of this textbook is on the legal issues that frequently confront managers today, and that promise (threaten?) to do so with increasing frequency in the future as we rapidly progress from the *industrial* age of the twentieth century to the *information* age of the twenty-first century. Technological change/progress has always impacted the law and vice versa, both through changes in existing statutes and through the creation of wholly new statutes. Also the courts are an important source of legal innovation when they encounter novel legal issues created by new technology (see the Chakrabarty case below). Confronted with new technological realities, the courts have had to be innovative, adapting case law and creating new precedents in many areas of law. From the perspective of firms, like the ones visited briefly already, recent modifications of patent and copyright statutes, and of court rulings interpreting those statutes, have significantly changed the legal environment of business facing managers (particularly in high-tech businesses). Several areas of interface between technology and the law are briefly discussed below, with each of the topics visited needing further exploration.

Intellectual Property

Many companies in the information age are valued mainly for the *intellectual property* (IP) they own. Intellectual property is intangible, meaning that it has no physical existence. There are four basic forms of legal protection for IP. Some firms such as the Coca-Cola Company keep their IP in the form of *trade secrets*. Coca Cola has never applied for a patent on the formula used to make Coca Cola, but instead has relied upon keeping the formula secret from rivals (see Chapter 8). For many firms, *patents* protect

their innovations. Patent law explicitly grants to the patentee (the person receiving the patent) exclusive rights to make, use, or sell the patented process, product, machine, or composition of matter (Chapter 8). *Copyright* law provides legal protection for authors of original compositions such as books, music, and computer software (Chapter 9). Unauthorized reproductions are *infringements* and enable the copyright owner to collect damages. *Trademark* law allows manufacturers to identify their goods with a distinguishing mark and punishes infringers who deliberately or unintentionally imitate registered trademarks (Chapter 9).

Impact of Various Levels of Legal Protection

For firms that produce *computer software,* there are various possible means of using the law to protect their IP creations. These include copyright, patent, trade secret, and trademark law. On the other hand, for companies that specialize in the "production" of herbal medicines from naturally occurring substances in the Brazilian Rain Forest, IP law offers little protection (the reasons for relative lack of legal protection of discoveries of this kind are discussed in Chapter 8). Effective protection through IP law enables companies engaged in new lines of business endeavor to succeed, but lack of IP protection causes the opposite effect. Different levels of IP protections that industries receive may largely explain the growth of software-related industries relative to lack of development of life-saving new medicines derived from exotic jungle plants.

The demands for adequate legal protection of IP have severely tested the limits of pre-existing law in recent years and are, hence, stretching and blurring the boundaries of existing intellectual property law. In addition, other established branches of law from contracts to regulatory law, such as securities law, are confronted by new challenges due to technological advances. Many of the legal issues discussed below introduce topics that are dealt with in chapters later in this book.

Electronic Commerce and Contract Law

Electronic commerce (E-commerce) is growing explosively and is likely in the infancy of its growth trajectory. As with any business, a company that makes substantial E-commerce sales must rely on firm "contractual agreements" with other businesses and ordinary consumers or customers. Existing *contract* law, such as that codified in the Uniform Commercial Code (UCC), rests heavily on the notion of "objective" intent in determining whether a contract has been formed. E-commerce contracts often rely on electronic agents. Determining the "intent" of electronic agents is a non sequitur; machines do not possess "intent" to do anything. So, technical innovation and the growth of E-commerce can be expected to force extensive modification of commercial contract law in the years ahead. Samples of the extensive modifications that are likely to occur to contract law as a result of E-commerce are discussed in Chapter 3.

With regard to successfully navigating commercial linkages provided by the Internet and E-commerce, managers certainly should have knowledge of basic contract law, supplemented with recognition of the differences that operating in a technology-driven setting entails. Not surprisingly, this body of law is rapidly evolving, requiring managers to regularly update their knowledge of the legal environment in which they operate. Illustratively, significant revisions of the UCC, dealing mainly with electronic contracting and the licensing of IP for Internet applications, were on the threshold of adoption as this chapter was being written. In the future, new "uniform" laws such as the Uniform Computer Information and Transactions Act (UCITA) and the Uniform Electronic Transactions Act (UETA) may rival the UCC in significance to business managers.

Tort Law and Invasions of Privacy

A "tort" (discussed in Chapter 5) is a noncontractual interaction in which the plaintiff (the victim) is wrongfully harmed by the defendant (the alleged victimizer). Ordinarily, tort and contract law involve different issues, but in cyberspace they frequently overlap (Chapter 6). Internet companies can accomplish market research by attaching "cookies" to the browsers of visitors to their websites. Cookies, which can be used to track journeys of customers through the Internet, extract information from these visitors or customers, often without the knowledge or consent of customers. Privacy concerns abound as increased use of E-commerce and the Internet take place. Tort law, which includes invasions of privacy, has recently been augmented by a growing number of federal statutes

that make more explicit what companies can and cannot do in the way of extracting and sharing information on the Internet.

Security and Encryption

Computer system privacy and security issues have spawned the birth of an entire new industry. Increasingly firms are relying on encryption software to protect transactions and communications over the Internet. In addition, industrial espionage through computers and system invasions by pranksters, sometimes spreading viruses, has required firms to invest heavily in system security. Security measures involve the human resource department (HRM) as well as the information technology (IT) staff. Good and effective security requires a commitment from management and company employees, up-to-date security equipment and software, and technical skill in deploying and maintaining security technology. Security issues cross several branches of law including contracts, torts, and protection of intellectual property. Security systems that have descended through the ages such as personal signatures have to be radically updated for E-Commerce transactions. Reasonable security measures are required to protect trade secrets, but since more and more is at stake, what is reasonable as security measures continues to escalate.

Protection, Creation, and Use of Software

The heart and soul of technological advance in the information age is computer *software*. Seeking protection of their property rights for this new (information age) form of property, software developers have sought refuge from imitation through copyright laws since the dawning of computer development. Under the Copyright Act of 1976, Congress decided that something called "software" was properly subject to protection under the copyright laws, and placed it in the category of "literary works."[1]

Copyrights are not intended to create monopolies. Courts, subsequently, have struggled with the application to computer software of existing, pre-information age, copyright precedents. Prior to 1976 copyrights were applied to tangible media such as books, films, and the like. Courts have had to extend and modify existing case law to reflect the realities of

[1]17 U.S.C. §§ 101 and 117.

Internet Ethics We Know Your Health Affairs

Consider the following example of Internet sleuthing provided by *Consumer Reports*. The real question is not whether such activities are taking place, they are; but whether, upon graduation, you would work for one of the firms gathering such information. In addition, there are public policy questions about whether obtaining and transferring medical information should be illegal.

Does it matter? Should you be concerned? Consider the hypothetical case of Nora T. Hyde, 42, a Maryland corporate middle manager. As far as Nora knows, her colleagues at work and the bank where she's applied for a home-improvement loan have no idea she recently had a bout of early-stage breast cancer. And even her husband doesn't know that Nora has been taking antidepressant medication to help her recover her spirits after her surgery.

What Nora doesn't realize is that without her knowledge or consent, various computer databases have efficiently swept up virtually every detail of her medical history. A record of her lumpectomy went into Maryland's computerized cancer registry and also its hospital discharge dataset—along with her birth date, race, and gender.

Into the state's new outpatient Encounter Dataset went the details of her visit to the doctor for depression treatment—complete with an encrypted "unique patient identifier." Two databases, one at her neighborhood pharmacy and one at the giant pharmaceutical-benefit clearinghouse that handles drug claims for her company's health plan, also recorded her prescription for an antidepressant.

Nora's health insurance plan received notice of all these things, too, because to have her medical costs reimbursed, Nora gave blanket permission to disclose the information. Recently, the health plan signed a contract with an Internet company to put all its claims processing online and plans to protect patients' privacy with passwords and "secure sockets layer" technology.

Meanwhile, Nora spent some time visiting health websites. At a drug-company site, she filled out an online form to order a discount coupon for a medicine. The instant she typed in her name and address, automated software plugged her name and address into a big direct-mail database from which the drug company learned her age, her household income, her hobbies, and her catalog purchase history.

Nora is a fiction. But every one of the electronic databases and Internet ventures mentioned in this vignette is up and running. For the moment, most of them operate in relative isolation. The drug company website, for instance, doesn't link up with the state hospital discharge database. But before long it will be technically possible for all of these records to be cross-referenced and merged to create a cradle-to-grave picture of your health history.

"Technology now has the ability to collect a vast amount of information, and to mix and match and merge and commingle it at a level undreamed of a generation ago," says Carole Doeppers, a privacy advocate for the Wisconsin chapter of the American Civil Liberties Union. "It's out there, and everybody wants it, and it's very profitable."

This new world of digitized medical information promises some real benefits. Electronic medical records have already been shown to vastly reduce the likelihood of medical error caused by ignorance of some critical fact about a patient's health history, such as a drug allergy. Electronically transmitted prescriptions drastically reduce medication errors. In one study reported in 1999, medication errors for hospitalized patients dropped 81 percent after doctors started entering drug orders on a computer instead of by hand. Using databases to track medical outcomes yields valuable information about which treatments work best.

But, say privacy experts, the very architecture of the Internet makes it difficult—perhaps even impossible—to guarantee the confidentiality of personal health information stored or transmitted online. And for the moment, at least, the laws requiring companies even to make the attempt are few, weak, or—at the federal level—nonexistent. Until laws change, it is up to you to protect the privacy of your health information.

"If you put your medical information online," says Robert Gellman, a Washington, D.C., privacy consultant, "you're turning your private information over to the world."

Note that concerns about privacy are not restricted to the U.S. Privacy International makes annual "Big Brother" awards. According to its website, "Privacy International (PI) is a human rights group formed in 1990 as a watchdog on surveillance by governments and corporations. PI is based in London, England, and has an office in Washington, D.C. PI has conducted campaigns throughout the world on issues ranging from wiretapping and national security activities, to ID cards, video surveillance, data matching, police information systems, and medical privacy."

Source: http://www.consumerreports.org/Special/ConsumerInterest/Reports/0008med0.htm

software, wherein value lies in the patterns of electronic code that gives a software product its look, feel, and functionality. The legal issues regarding software and copyright law required the courts to make difficult choices, as copyright laws *are not intended to create monopolies* in definable product markets. As user interfaces have become more standarized, less and less of computer software programs are copyrightable. The evolution of copyright protection of software is a story that modern business managers should know well.

Increasingly software is protected by patents. It is a formidable challenge for the court system to devise tests/bases for decisions that meet both the needs of IP protection for software creators and the public's need for access to competitively provided software products. As the economy continues its trek towards more corporate wealth in the form of intangible (digital) assets, this balancing act will require a continuing evolution of IP protection law. A recent trend in IP law has been increased use of patents to protect software (see Chapter 10). Although initially resisted by the courts and the PTO, "digital" patents have become commonplace. Amazon.com has even patented its software for purchasing books online. The benefit for programmers of patenting software is that they do achieve a legal monopoly. The costs are that it is more difficult to acquire a patent than a copyright.

Other Software Issues: Contracts with Software Developers

With increasing frequency, managers in a wide array of businesses must make crucial decisions involving software. Software decisions include issues of timing and content, and are likely to rely on experience with like decisions, good and bad, made previously (Chapter 4). Contracts entered into with software vendors and consultants typically have a long list of clauses, which individually and/or collectively can have an enormous impact on the ownership of software, the application of software, and restrictions that apply to the use of software. Rather than cookie-cutter or standardized boilerplate contracts, software agreements are often business-to-business *negotiated* deals with extensive sets of terms and conditions that, unfortunately, are often a pitfall for the unwary.

Human Resource Management

Part of an effective program to protect IP is apt to involve incentives to keep secrets. Employment contracts that reward employees who invent or discover creations of value to their firms are a standard feature of IP protection efforts. Nondisclosure agreements, non-compete agreements, and other employment contract components may also be used to protect "trade secrets" and other elements of a company's intellectual property. A whole new set of issues arises when a firm outsources software development or some other process that may involve IP (Chapter 4). As illustrated by the Chapters 4 and 8 cases, loss of important IP rights can occur by oversights that could easily be avoided. Of course, HRM operations also have many other legal standards and requirements to deal with including non-discrimination standards, retirement plan funding standards, etc., which are outside the scope of this book.

A PRIMARY GOAL: LEGAL ISSUE RECOGNITION

It is essential for managers in every enterprise to be mindful of the legal pitfalls that can confront their companies. As acknowledged at the beginning of this chapter, every functional area in the business world has legal exposure. The focus of this text is on those areas of exposure that are most critical to managers in modern, technology-based, information age companies. A manager in such a company should know the basics of IP law, how to create IP protection, and how to use and maintain that protection. Modern managers should understand basic contract, tort, and property law and be able to use those concepts in Internet transactions. In the future every company will be wired to the Internet except for street vendors and even they may have some net-accessible, hand-held computer. Also in the future manager performance will depend increasingly on management of intellectual property. Companies will proliferate that have no bricks or mortar, the so-called dot.coms.

Recalling the unfortunate experience of our recent graduates discussed at the beginning of this chapter, it would be instructive to review standard IP protection concepts. Suppose Greg and his team had asked, "Before we reveal our technology to anyone outside of our group, what can we do to protect our

Employers are increasingly using high-tech solutions to discover what employees are doing on the job in ways that are not apparent to employees. Should employees be informed that the company has software to detect what they do with their computers while on the job? Should employers be allowed to monitor employee e-mail files? Should employers be able to use all the high-tech tools at their disposal to detect employee misfeasance and malfeasance? Consider the following article from the Privacy Foundation:

WORKPLACE SURVEILLANCE HEATS UP: "EMPLOYEES ARE TOAST"

Millions of employees in the United States and worldwide are now subject to electronic monitoring by employers—a stealthy trend fueled by relatively cheap technology (like mini-surveillance cameras and keystroke monitoring software) and employer paranoia about unauthorized use of e-mail and the Internet by employees. Two-thirds of major American firms now do some type of in-house electronic surveillance, and 27 percent of all firms surveyed monitor email, according to the American Management Association. Dozens of companies including Xerox, Dow Chemical, and The New York Times (and government agencies including the Central Intelligence Agency) fired and disciplined employees in 2000 because of alleged bad behavior in using the companies' communications networks. "Employees are toast," one chief privacy officer told the Privacy Foundation, noting that employers have substantial economic, legal, and now, technical clout over employees in this area.

Look for: "Workplace Privacy Rights" to become a negotiated fringe benefit, with new economy companies leading the way.

Source: http://www.privacyfoundation.org/release/top10.html

rights in this technology? Our response might have been, "Greg, let's review the basic protections of IP provided by existing law, which will include patents and copyrights." Then, later, we can add other important elements to your understanding of IP protection including adroit use of contract law.

COSTLY ERRORS AND CONSEQUENCES

The list of legal blunders that have had dramatic impacts on high-tech companies is long and rapidly growing, as evidenced by the following brief selection of notable milestones in the legal history of software systems.

Apple versus Microsoft[2]

The *Apple* v. *Microsoft* case presented above is the final chapter in a battle between two of major players in the computer industry.

Many computer experts have claimed that Apple Computer had, by far, the best operating system software for personal computers in the late 1980s and early 1990s. When the early versions of Microsoft Windows, with a similar user interface, were first being offered for sale, Apple considered legal action against Microsoft. Eventually, however, Apple signed a licensing agreement with Microsoft that it believed would maintain its market advantages in the *graphical user interface* (GUI) market. In the licensing agreement, Apple, as licensor, agreed to allow Microsoft to sell its Windows operating software, even though it made use of a GUI much like that created by Apple.

Over time, subsequent versions of Windows became more and more similar to the operating system of Apple's popular Macintosh series of PCs. Eventually, Apple brought a copyright infringement suit against Microsoft—as it attempted to protect what Apple viewed as its own IP. To Apple's horror, the court hearing the case concluded otherwise, ruling that the earlier license agreement between Apple and Microsoft effectively allowed Microsoft to imitate Apple's operating system with impunity. According to the court hearing the case, anything in Microsoft's operating software that was not covered specifically in the license agreement, was largely deemed to not be subject to copyright protection. The foundation for Microsoft's dramatic rise and Apple's lengthy decline was that

[2] *Apple Computer, Inc.* v. *Microsoft Corp.*, 35 F.3rd 1435, cert. Denied, 115 S.Ct. 1176 (1994).

favorable licensing agreement eagerly entered into by Microsoft during its infancy. More astute management and legal counsel to Apple might have led to very different histories for Apple, Microsoft, or both.

Back to Consultant-Written Software

In the 1970s and 1980s, many companies hired computer software consultants to write programs customized for their specific use. These contracts called for the consultants to write, install, and service software for the client company. Down the road, many of these companies (and business owners) discovered that the software development they had **paid for** had resulted in software packages, suitable for other firms in their industry, which were in fact being sold to competitors by the software writers. The contracts client companies had accepted made the software writers the owners of the software.

On the other hand, client companies that received the copyright for the software developed for them by the software suppliers had very little incentive to fully pay the software firms. Once the client firms had the copyrights and the software itself, they had the leverage to extract additional work from the software vendors. *Software escrow firms* provide a market solution to deal with these issues. For a fee, software escrow firms retain computer code until they are satisfied that the software vendor has done its job and until the client company has paid the vendor for the work completed. Contracts between software development firms and client firms are among the most significant that management can negotiate. Numerous court cases indicate egregious mistakes that have been made.

Better Mouse Traps Held Off the Market

In our age of rapid technological progress, many small firms have created innovative intellectual properties (including tangible products) that threaten the market success of some large and well-established companies. In the 1980s and 1990s it has not been unusual for large and successful but threatened companies to contract with smaller innovators for rights to the innovator's IP, with much of the compensation to be paid based on sales. Perhaps not surprisingly in retrospect, a number of those innovations then sat on shelves, not developed or promoted by the already-successful company. Of course, with the innovator's compensation for his or her IP tied to future sales, an absence of

sales results in very limited payments from the larger company for the elimination of a competitive threat. Competent counsel for innovators would insist on either a large licensing fee up-front or a clause requiring the larger firm to *use best efforts* to market the licensed product.

BASIC FUNCTIONS OF LAW

What is the Law?

There can be numerous definitions of law, most of which do not add importantly to the understanding of law by business management majors and those whose first, and probably only, formal exposure to law is contained in this textbook. Most would agree with a statement by Oliver Wendell Holmes that "Law is a statement of the circumstances, in which the public force is brought to bear . . . through the courts." In other words, the law is composed of rules that must be obeyed and if not, public forces, generally the police, will compel compliance. Supported by public forces, courts of law decide rights and duties of the litigants.

The law, however, is not just words on a piece of paper. The law involves much more than simply determining the meaning of words that are written in a constitution or in a collection of statutes. Law should be thought of more as a prediction about how the courts will resolve disputes. In the infamous 1896 *Plessey* v. *Ferguson* case, the U.S. Supreme Court decided that state laws requiring the separation of the races, did not offend the 14th Amendment to the U.S. Constitution, which prohibits a state from "deny[ing] to any person within its jurisdiction the equal protection of the laws."[3]

In the 1896 *Plessey* case, a Louisiana State statute required African Americans to sit separately from white people on railroad trains. In its opinion, the U.S. Supreme Court did not view requiring the races to be separated as violating the 14th Amendment to the U.S. Constitution as long as the facilities accorded to blacks and whites were equal. Thus the infamous phrase "separate but equal" was born and provided a foundation for segregationist legislation that was enacted by many states through the first half of the 20th Century.

By 1954 when *Brown* v. *The Board of Education* case appeared before the U.S. Supreme Court, it was clear that the Supreme Court was about to declare a

[3]163 U.S. 537, 16 S.Ct. 1138 (1896).

state statute requiring segregation by race in education unconstitutional under the 14th Amendment.[4] During the 58-year period between 1896 and 1954, not a single word in the 14th Amendment had changed and yet it is clear that the law had changed. If law is viewed as a prediction about how courts will resolve disputes, then it is clear that the Constitutional Law had changed sometime before the famous *Brown* case. In the *Brown* case, Chief Justice Earl Warren emphatically rejected the notion that the state of Kansas could justify the separation of the races in education under the 14th Amendment.

SOURCES OF LAW IN THE UNITED STATES

Common Law

Common law was created in England when disputes were settled in a court of law, instead of by violence. Following his victory at the Battle of Hastings in 1066, William the Conqueror laid claim to all of England. The common law first began sometime around the end of the 11th Century and was mainly used to resolve disputes between private citizens. The early courts, called the King's Courts, were an important unifying factor creating the nation-state of England. Without the common law England could have remained Balkanized like much of Western Europe for several more centuries.

Precedent

At the beginning of Norman rule, Parliament was not an important force in law making in England. There were few statutes, or laws created by a legislative body, such as a Parliament. Instead, most law was *created* through the resolution of disputes between private citizens. As an example, assume that two farmers who occupied property adjacent to each other went to court to determine who was liable when, say, a fire that started on the property of one farmer (A) crossed property lines and burned down a dwelling on the other farmer's (B) property. (See Figure 1.1.) Let us assume that the fire started because hay stacked by A on his property burst into flames due to lightning. Let us also assume that before the fire started, B warned A that hay was flammable and that if a fire started, his (B's) house was in peril.

[4]347 U.S. 483, 74 S. Ct. 686 (1954).

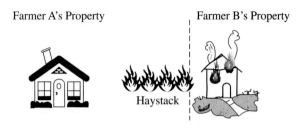

Farmer A's Property   Farmer B's Property

Haystack

Figure 1.1 **Property Line Dispute**
Clipart source: Corel

After the fire occurred, most likely B would have picked up a stick and gone over to A's house to thrash A. A in turn, knowing that this action was likely to occur, would have armed himself and perhaps called together some of his sons and brothers to aid in his defense. B would have known about A's defense preparations and would have assembled his own gang. A violent outcome wouldn't be a surprise.

Alternatively, if B knew that, at common law, whoever first breached the peace was in the wrong and instead decided to complain at court about A's behavior, the resolution of this dispute might be expected to be a peaceful one. B would be the complaining party or the *plaintiff* and A would try to defend himself as the *defendant*. If, after hearing the case, the court decided that A was in the wrong and was *negligent* in not moving the hay to a different location, this decision would create a *precedent* that could be used by other courts dealing with similarly situated parties.

If another situation subsequently occurred involving farmers C and D, who had adjacent property lines, D, the owner of the dwelling, could warn C to remove the flammable materials next to his house, citing the case between A and B. D could say that not only was C's haystack a fire hazard, but also that if a fire started and consumed his (D's) house, that C would be liable for the fair market value of the house. Of course, two cases might not be identical, even though common elements exist that can provide a tie to existing precedent (case law). Instead of hay, suppose that C had stacked logs next to the property line, close to D's house. Logs are flammable but not nearly so easily as hay. It's also likely to take more work to move logs than hay.

If the logs somehow ignited into flame and damaged D's dwelling, a trip to court is a likely result. In this situation, it's possible that the defendant could prevail, perhaps because the chance of logs igniting is so much less than with hay, so that C's actions would not be deemed negligent. The court would have to decide. With the court's decision, a new precedent would be created and this process would continue with many other variations. You might ponder a situation in which Farmer F built his house next to Farmer E's property line *after* E's hay was already sitting on the ground.

The next case deals with a much more modern situation involving patent law. See if you can determine the precedent that was established in this case.

Stare Decisis

The precedent-creating process occurs in many types of disputes among citizens. As precedents build up over a point of law, such as the responsibilities of adjacent landowners to each other, a rule of law is created that becomes like a statute. Parties knowledgeable about the line of cases, usually attorneys, can advise clients as to potential liability for various actions. As such rules of law accumulate in multiple areas of human activity, many of which involve commerce and

---

Diamond, Commissioner of Patents and Trademarks v. *Chakrabarty*
Supreme Court of the United States
447 U.S. 303 (1980)

BACKGROUND AND FACTS

A microbiologist filed a patent application relating to his invention of human-made, genetically engineered bacteria capable of breaking down multiple components of crude oil, a capability possessed by no naturally occurring bacteria. A patent examiner from the Patent and Trademark Office rejected the microbiologist's patent claim, ruling, among other things, that the bacteria, as living things, were not patentable subject matter under the Patent Act, which provides for the issuance of a patent to a person who invents or discovers "any" new and useful "manufacture" or "composition of matter." The United States Patent and Trademark Office Board of Appeals affirmed, but the United States Court of Customs and Patent Appeals ultimately reversed, holding that the fact that micro-organisms are alive is without legal significance for purposes of the patent law. The case has been appealed to the U.S. Supreme Court by Diamond, Commissioner of the Patent and Trademark Office.

OPINION: BURGER, CHIEF JUSTICE

Chakrabarty's patent claims were of three types: first, process claims for the method of producing the bacteria; second, claims for an inoculum comprised of a carrier material floating on water, such as straw, and the new bacteria; and third, claims to the bacteria themselves. The patent examiner allowed the claims falling into the first two categories, but rejected claims for the bacteria. His decision rested on two grounds: (1) that micro-organisms are "products of nature," and (2) that as living things they are not patentable subject matter under 35 U. S. C. § 101.

* * *

The Constitution grants Congress broad power to legislate to "promote the Progress of Science and useful Arts, by securing for limited Times to Authors and Inventors the exclusive Right to their respective Writings and Discoveries." Art. I, § 8, cl. 8. The patent laws promote this progress by offering inventors exclusive rights for a limited period as an incentive for their inventiveness and research efforts. [References deleted] The authority of Congress is exercised in the hope that "[the] productive effort thereby fostered will have a positive effect on society through the introduction of new products and processes of manufacture into the

economy, and the emanations by way of increased employment and better lives for our citizens."

The question before us in this case is a narrow one of statutory interpretation requiring us to construe 35 U. S. C. § 101, which provides:

"Whoever invents or discovers any new and useful process, machine, manufacture, or composition of matter, or any new and useful improvement thereof, may obtain a patent therefor, subject to the conditions and requirements of this title."

Specifically, we must determine whether respondent's micro-organism constitutes a "manufacture" or "composition of matter" within the meaning of the statute.

* * *

In cases of statutory construction we begin, of course, with the language of the statute. And "unless otherwise defined, words will be interpreted as taking their ordinary, contemporary, common meaning." We have also cautioned that courts "should not read into the patent laws limitations and conditions which the legislature has not expressed."

Guided by these canons of construction, this Court has read the term "manufacture" in § 101 in accordance with its dictionary definition to mean "the production of articles for use from raw or prepared materials by giving to these materials new forms, qualities, properties, or combinations, whether by hand-labor or by machinery." Similarly, "composition of matter" has been construed consistent with its common usage to include "all compositions of two or more substances and . . . all composite articles, whether they be the results of chemical union, or of mechanical mixture, or whether they be gases, fluids, powders or solids." In choosing such expansive terms as "manufacture" and "composition of matter," modified by the comprehensive "any," Congress plainly contemplated that the patent laws would be given wide scope.

The relevant legislative history also supports a broad construction. The Patent Act of 1793, authored by Thomas Jefferson, defined statutory subject matter as "any new and useful art, machine, manufacture, or composition of matter, or any new or useful improvement [thereof]." Act of Feb. 21, 1793, § 1, 1 Stat. 319. The Act embodied Jefferson's philosophy that "ingenuity should receive a liberal encouragement." 5 Writings of Thomas Jefferson 75–76 (Washington ed. 1871). Subsequent patent statutes in 1836, 1870, and 1874 employed this same broad language. In 1952, when the patent laws were recodified, Congress replaced the word "art" with "process," but otherwise left Jefferson's language intact. The Committee Reports accompanying the 1952 Act inform us that Congress intended statutory subject matter to "include anything under the sun that is made by man." [footnote deleted]

This is not to suggest that § 101 has no limits or that it embraces every discovery. The laws of nature, physical phenomena, and abstract ideas have been held not patentable. Thus, a new mineral discovered in the earth or a new plant found in the wild is not patentable subject matter. Likewise, Einstein could not patent his celebrated law that $E = mc^2$; nor could Newton have patented the law of gravity. Such discoveries are "manifestations of . . . nature, free to all men and reserved exclusively to none."

Judged in this light, respondent's micro-organism plainly qualifies as patentable subject matter. His claim is not to a hitherto unknown natural phenomenon, but to a nonnaturally occurring manufacture or composition of matter—a product of human ingenuity "having a distinctive name, character [and] use."

* * *

The U.S. Supreme Court ruled that Chakrabarty was entitled to a patent on a manmade, but nevertheless, living organism.

QUESTIONS FOR ANALYSIS

1. What was the precise legal issue that the Court was dealing with? Why did the examiner at the Patent and Trademark Office turn down Chakrabarty?
2. Using the reasoning of the court, should a cloned human being be patentable?

---

economic relationships between various citizens and between citizens and the state, a legal system emerges. In such a system, judges tend to follow precedents decided by other judges faced with similar facts unless underlying conditions in society change. If a judge does decide that a dispute among citizens is very similar to a dispute dealt with previously, with the court decision recorded, then the judge will most likely apply the doctrine of *stare decisis,* which means the judge has decided to stand on a previously decided case.

Overturning Precedents

Changes in technology are a major force creating the conditions for overturning precedents. At one time most landlord–tenant relationships were between land "lords" who were literally lords and tenant-farmers, who were serfs. Economically it made sense for the serfs, rather than the landlords, to be responsible for the maintenance of the leased premises. Serfs generally possessed more expertise and more incentive to maintain their dwellings in habitable condition. A precedent allocating responsibility for maintaining the leased dwellings in habitable condition became common in England and traveled to colonial courts in North America.

During the 20th century as apartments became more common, *precedents* that required tenants to look after the upkeep of the leased property became unrealistic. Slowly, but steadily, judges in virtually all the states overturned the *precedent* that required tenants to be responsible for the habitability of leased apartments. A host of other examples could be cited. Many of the changes in precedent are due to evolutions in societal mores such as views on racial segregation. Precedents enforcing conditions attached to deeds, such as prohibitions on blacks ever owing the deeded property, have been overturned by most courts as not being in the public interest (and not constitutional!).

Adoption in the United States of the Common Law Tradition

When England established the colonies, in what was later to become the United States, colonial courts used English common law as their foundation. Since the United States is a union of *sovereign* states, there are 50 bodies of common law in the U.S., in addition to the body of common law followed by federal courts based on decisions of those courts. State courts frequently, though not invariably, refer to decisions of courts made in other states for guidance and precedent reference. The fact that there are occasions when states do not follow precedents created in other states makes for anomalies among the states. Many of the most significant legal changes that have occurred in the latter half of the 20th century have been due to the "uniform" movement, which is dedicated to elimination of idiosyncrasies of state law that have built up under the common law. One of the most prominent unifying examples is the Uniform Commercial Code (UCC).

Application to Modern Law

Any court that writes an opinion on a case contributes to the common law. State trial courts as well as the U.S. Supreme Court can create common law precedents. When the U.S. Supreme Court handed down the *Plessey* v. *Ferguson* decision in 1896, it added to the common law by interpreting the 14th Amendment as *not* prohibiting separation of the races so long as the conditions for each race were equal. Later in several Constitutional decisions leading up to the famous *Brown* decision in 1954, the U.S. Supreme Court held that various state-supported, segregated law schools were not equal under the 14th Amendment because the "white" schools offered better opportunities for its students to network. Quite obviously, if the state-supported "black" law school is inferior because it offers less networking opportunities, then integrated schools are constitutionally required.

Common law is also created when the courts interpret statutes such as the antitrust laws which are written ambiguously, but which are reasonably precise in application given the common law decisions that form a history interpreting the statutes. Recently in the news, the Department of Justice charged Microsoft with "monopolization". Monopolization can only be defined in light of the previous court precedents that have occurred in other cases when large firms were similarly charged.

This process of creating common law decisions regarding the meaning of statutes occurs at both the state level and the federal level. It has been said that, "the U.S. Constitution is what the U.S. Supreme Court says it is." Such statements are a testament to the importance of common law decisions by all courts, from the trial courts to supreme courts, in both the states and at the federal level.

Constitutional Law

At the apex of the legal system in the United States are constitutions. Each state has its own constitution and our nation as a whole has the U.S. Constitution, which is the *supreme law* of the land. It is important to note that legal interpretation of the U.S. Constitution is a job for the federal courts and, ultimately, the U.S. Supreme Court. Laws, broadly defined to include state and federal statutes, regulations of administrative agencies, and other official acts taken by members of the executive branches of government, must not conflict with the U.S. Constitution. Any laws that conflict with a constitution are said to be "unconstitutional" and thus null and void. The determination of the constitutionality of other state or federal laws is a judicial function.

U.S. Constitution

Revolutionaries who had recently overthrown despotic colonial rule that was unresponsive to their wishes wrote the U.S. Constitution. Although most of the Founding Fathers were of English origin, they were also very influenced by French political philosophers such as Montesquieu and Rousseau. Together with John Locke and others among English progressives, the Founders believed in limited government and protection of certain "inalienable" rights. Rights are *inalienable* when they cannot be taken away from someone. Among the inalienable rights that the colonist/revolutionaries thought important were freedom of speech, freedom to bear arms, freedom from unreasonable searches and seizures, the right to due process, and so on. These inalienable rights are memorialized in the *Bill of Rights*, which comprises the first 10 Amendments to the U.S. Constitution.

The Importance of Freedom and Inalienable Rights

At the time the Constitution was being developed, it was clear in the minds of the Founders that the greatest threat to freedom was government. In order to protect peoples' inalienable rights from the despotism of a strong and unresponsive central government, the Founders created the *checks and balances,* which are the hallmark of government structure in the United States. The Ninth and Tenth Amendments reserve all rights not delegated to the federal government to the sovereign states and their citizens. The powers of the federal government were limited to enumerated powers, among which include the power to coin money, regulate interstate commerce, and declare war. Also included among the enumerated powers of the federal government was the power to advance science and the arts by encouraging inventors and authors and thus both patent and copyright law are federal law. The *Necessary and Proper Clause* within the U.S. Constitution allows the federal government to take steps that are not specifically enumerated among the powers of the federal government, but which are necessary and proper to achieve the enumerated powers.

Our system of dividing power between federal and state governments has been labeled *federalism.* Many of the constitutional struggles of the 20th century have involved attempts by the President and/or Congress to expand the power of the federal government. In several instances, the U.S. Supreme Court has reversed itself in ways that have allowed the federal government to take more power at the expense of state governments.

Separation of Powers

It was clearly the determination of our nation's founding fathers to prevent the emergence of an excessively powerful branch of federal government. The checks and balances established to avoid this possibility are reflected in the division of federal governmental functions into three branches: the executive, the legislative, and the judicial. To a great extent, each of these branches of government has an ability to limit the power of each of the other branches.

Under our constitution, only Congress (the legislative branch) has the power to raise taxes, but the President (executive branch) has a veto power over this right. The U.S. Supreme Court (judicial branch) can declare a law unconstitutional, but amendments to the Constitutional rulings can overturn such rulings. The president, like most chief executive officers running companies, can order actions taken. However, Congress can refuse to fund programs, agencies, and actions proposed or supported by the President. Under extreme circumstances, the Congress has the power to remove a President.

The legislative branch is further divided between two branches (Senate and House). Some specific tasks are allocated individually to each branch of Congress, while other tasks are jointly accomplished between the two branches of Congress.

Constitutional Hierarchy

The Supremacy Clause in the U.S. Constitution states that "This Constitution and the Laws of the United States, which shall be made in Pursuance thereof" and all Treaties made, or which shall be made, under the Authority of the United States, shall be the Supreme Law of the Land . . ." The impact of the Supremacy Clause is that all *state* laws, including state constitutions, are subordinate to federal law, whether the *federal* law be constitutional, statutory, or regulatory.

As long as they do not conflict with federal law, state constitutions are the supreme law within the states and laws passed by state legislatures must not be in conflict with the state constitution. State constitutions differ to a degree that prevents a generalized discussion of their nature that is applicable to all states. It is notable, however, that all 50 states have three branches of government: legislative, executive, and judicial.

Statutory Law and Legislative Bodies

A *statute* is a law passed by a legislature. Congress is an example of a legislative body as are the 50 state legislatures that function within the states. To be legal, a *state* statute must not conflict with the state or federal constitution. Federal statutes passed by Congress are unconstitutional if they conflict with the U.S. Constitution. Some states such as California are known for the significant legislation that is enacted directly by the electorate through referenda and initiatives. Proposition 209, which prohibits racial preferences by any state agency in the State of California, was made part of statutory California law by a statewide ballot.

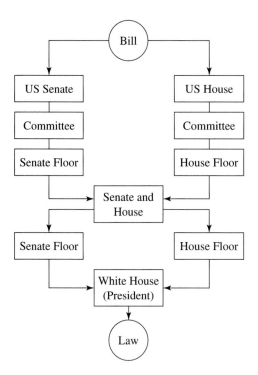

How a Bill Becomes a Law

At the federal level, *statutes* begin as *Bills* (proposed legislation) that are introduced to either the House or the Senate (note that only the House can initiate tax increases). Typically, Bills are assigned to an appropriate committee for processing. Not surprisingly, Bills often fail to emerge from the congressional committee as a consequence of lack of general support within the committee. Generally the same Bill is introduced in both the House and the Senate. However, by the time the parallel Bills are passed by each body, amendments to the Bills are apt to make them differ to a degree that requires a unifying conference

to end up with a Bill that can be acceptable to both Houses of Congress. Once passed by Congress, a Bill goes to the President for signature.

The President can *sign the Bill into law,* at which time the Bill becomes a statute. On the other hand, the President can *veto* any Bill passed by Congress. Vetoes, however, can be overridden by a two-thirds vote of both Houses of Congress. Even supported and approved by Congress and the President, a newly passed statute can be challenged in court and declared unconstitutional.

State Statutes

Similar processes take place at the state level, though there are numerous differences in detail state by state. In some states, such as North Carolina, the Governor does not have veto power. In some states, being a legislator is a full time job while, in others, the job is specifically designed for citizen-legislators who only work part time as state legislators.

States have been called 'laboratories for democracy', reflecting the fact that individual states can "experiment" with different laws that, generally, do not have national consequences. Many federal laws began as experiments at the state level. For example, federal securities (stocks and bonds) regulation was preceded by about 30 years with the state Blue Sky Laws. State Blue Sky Laws superceded common law fraud in the sale of securities and replaced it with a standard that made it much easier for *defrauded* investors to sue and get their money back in the event that the victims (the defrauded investors) cannot prove that the sellers of the securities intentionally lied in order to make the sales.

Although states have a degree of freedom for legal experimentation, differences among state laws can actually have national consequences that are detrimental

National Conference of Commissioners

The National Conference of Commissioners on Uniform State Laws is now in its 108th year. The organization comprises more than 300 lawyers, judges, and law professors, appointed by the states as well as the District of Columbia, Puerto Rico, and the U.S. Virgin Islands, to draft proposals for uniform and model laws and work

toward their enactment in their legislatures. Since its inception in 1892, the group has drafted more than 200 acts, among them such bulwarks of state statutory law as the Uniform Commercial Code, the Uniform Probate Code, and the Uniform Controlled Substances Act.

to businesses that operate in more than one state. Such businesses have to be familiar with the idiosyncrasies of state law in the various states in which they do business. To counteract the negative consequences of legal differences among the states, the National Conference of Commissioners on Uniform State Laws (*NCCUSL*) is dedicated to easing the cost of doing business by making state laws more uniform. The NCCUSL has developed a comprehensive list of areas of law for which uniform laws have been proposed. The areas of law for which the NCCUSL has enacted uniform statutes include partnerships, athletes-agents, child custody, probate, and many others. Except for the Uniform Commercial Code, most of these uniform statutes have not been adopted by all the states.

Administrative Agencies

Legislatures can define legal and illegal actions for individuals and businesses, but often a more hands-on approach has been shown to be effective. Typically, Congress or a state legislature is concerned about a specific problem such as worker safety or fraud in the securities markets. The legislative body will pass a statute that not only defines actions that are illegal, but also may create an administrative agency to enforce the statute and develop regulations consistent with the statute. Administrative agencies such as the Environmental Protection Agency (EPA), the Securities and Exchange Commission (SEC), and innumerable others develop expertise in the areas that they regulate and fashion regulations that are more detailed than a legislature's.

Regulations

Regulations from administrative agencies are by far the most voluminous source of law. When businesses complain about government red tape, it often reflects their concern that administrative agencies, particularly the ones at the federal level, create needless volumes of regulations. The Occupational Safety and Health Administration (OSHA), for example, has regulations that define how far off the floor fire extinguishers are to be (36 to 42 inches). It's likely that many businesses have a dim view of the need for such detailed regulation.

Many agencies require businesses to self-monitor and report specific activities and characteristics of the business. Typical are required reports on the racial, sexual, and age distribution of job incumbents and applicants (to Equal Employment Opportunity Commission), discharges of pollutants (to the Environmental Protection Agency), and reports of any on-the-job worker injuries (to Occupational Safety and Health Administration).

Legal Actions

Administrative agencies generally have their own courts, headed by administrative law judges (ALJs). Typically, an agency enforces its regulations through legal actions before ALJs, in procedures like those in trial courts. Administrative agencies, especially at the federal level, are highly visible to the businesses under their purview, and often influence those businesses by the threat of an investigation or other actions that would create negative publicity for such businesses. Needless to say, the legal environment for businesses is heavily influenced by the actions of administrative agencies, both at the federal and state levels.

OTHER BRANCHES OF GOVERNMENT

Judiciary

The legal environment of businesses is, of course, intimately linked to the judicial interpretation of laws, a task performed by judges. Some statutes are tightly written leaving little room for interpretation, but most statutes and some regulations of administrative agencies are sufficiently ambiguous that the parties (the government versus a business) find it more in their interests to litigate than to negotiate a settlement out of court. In many cases judges do more than just interpret the law. In some very high-profile cases such as *U.S.* v. *Microsoft,* the parties waive their rights to trial by jury and allow judges to make findings of fact. Judges also rule on motions such as requests for preliminary injunctions, which can stop actions of businesses or the government, even without a showing that one party is liable or guilty.

Executive

The President is the chief executive officer at the federal level. Over 3,000 positions in the executive branch of government are political appointees. These appointees can have a critical impact on the legal environment that businesses face. During the Reagan

Administration, James Watt was Secretary of the Interior while Bruce Babbit has occupied that position under President Clinton. These two gentlemen have radical differences in their views on stewardship and development of natural resources on government-held land. Students should appreciate that the legal environment of businesses can change significantly, even though there has not been a statutory or regulatory change, but merely a change in personnel. The President has other powers such as the right to issue *Executive Orders* that affect administrative agencies and businesses.

OTHER SOURCES OF LAW

Arbitration and International Law

Increasingly, trading partners are creating their own sets of legal constraints through arbitration agreements. In contracts that contain arbitration clauses, the parties agree that an arbitrator instead of a judge will resolve any dispute. Arbitration holds many advantages over court litigation, as it is generally viewed as faster and cheaper, along with being likely to provide damage awards that are less variable than those provided by juries of laymen. At both the federal and state levels there are statutes which require judges to respect arbitration clauses and not interfere when a contract calls for resolutions of disputes by arbitration. The delays and expense of court litigation continue to make arbitration a very attractive alternative for many businesses.

Globalization of markets has been a major force increasing the significance of international regulations in the mix of legal constraints faced by businesses. In part because the United States is a world leader in creating IP, it has pushed for international respect for IP through various conventions. There is evidence of widespread disregard for IP rights among many nations, particularly the less developed countries. In the past the United States has also pressed for free trade and lower tariffs through the General Agreement on Tariffs and Trade (GATT). GATT has given way to the World Trade Organization (WTO) which acts as a referee in trade disputes among countries.

The United States is a signatory country on the United Nations Convention on the Recognition and Enforcement of Foreign Arbitration Awards. As with domestic disputes, trading partners internationally recognize that arbitration generally is faster, cheaper, and more efficient than transcountry litigation.

International Data Transfers

Except for England, the rest of Europe does not rely on the common law tradition. Most of Europe, however, has joined together to form the European Union (EU), which has authority to enact laws that supercede the laws of individual countries. One of the most significant Directives of the EU has been the European Commission's (the governing body of the EU) Directive on Data Privacy, which went into effect in October, 1998. The legal philosophy in Europe and the EU has been much more interventionalist than in the U.S. The European Union, however, relies on comprehensive legislation that, for example, requires creation of government data protection agencies, registration of data bases with those agencies, and in some instances prior approval before personal data processing may begin.

The 1998 Directive not only protected personal data of European citizens, but also prohibited transfers of such data with other countries that did not provide protection essentially equivalent to the EU standard. The U.S., which relies on the common law for much of its data protection, does not have government data protection agencies or registration of databases with such agencies. Transatlantic data transfers were threatened by the 1998 Directive and the U.S. Department of Commerce has been working diligently to develop arrangements that satisfy the EU standards while not interfering too dramatically with the way U.S. firms that collect and transfer data do business. Database protection and transfers are discussed in some detail in Chapter 9.[5]

USEFUL LEGAL CLASSIFICATIONS

A key to understanding law is the ability to compartmentalize. For example, it makes no sense to apply criminal law concepts to civil suits. Compared with other courses in business curricula, law is not the most difficult discipline analytically. Once the type of law that applies is determined, resolution of a case becomes much easier. The following are basic classifications in law that should become second nature to students.

Substantive versus Procedural Law

The legal principles dealt with in this text are, by and large, what can be described as *substantive* law. Substantive law is concerned with laying out the rights

---

[5]Discussion of database transfers between the U.S. and the E.U. takes place at: http//www.export.gov/safeharbor/.

Public and Private Law

Public Law	Private Law
Administrative Law	Contract Law
Antitrust	Corporate Law
Constitutional Law	Nuisance Law
Criminal Law	Partnership Law
Environmental Law	Property Law
Patent and Copyright Law	Tort Law
Consumer Protection Law	Trade Secret Law

and responsibilities of the parties to a lawsuit. In the case of two farmers who have adjacent property lines, substantive law determines whether one farmer has a responsibility to the other farmer to clear out fire hazards next to the other farmer's dwelling. Substantive law addresses the question of whether states can fashion segregationist legislation in light of the 14th Amendment, which guarantees equal protection under the law. It is well worthwhile for business managers to have a solid understanding of basic substantive law.

Procedural law pertains to the rules of the contest when two parties go to court to resolve a dispute. To make a sports analogy, the winner of a football game is like the substantive winner of a court case, but the rules of the football game are akin to procedural law (and referees, who are supposed to be neutral, are like judges). Procedural law dictates how courtroom proceedings and related litigation activities take place. Parties that seek to introduce evidence that does not conform to *procedural law* requirements will be penalized by the exclusion of such evidence. Other procedural law issues pertain to motions made by either party, instructions to the jury, and a lot of other issues.

Unless you intend to represent yourself (or your company) in litigation, without the assistance of legal counsel, you don't need to learn a great deal of procedural law. Part of your job as a manager is to recognize substantive legal issues that threaten the profitability of your company. When your company is involved in litigation, it is your attorney's job to make sure your

case is not jeopardized by failing to abide by procedural law.

Public versus Private Law

Public law involves the relationship between government and citizens (including business). *Private* law resolves disputes between citizens. When a party alleges that another trading partner has breached a contract, it is private law (contract law) that is used to resolve the disputes. In public law disputes, the government is the plaintiff while the defendant is a private entity such as a business or individual.

In the public law arena, the government has often intervened and modified (corrected) free market agreements that citizens and businesses can make among themselves. Illustratively, the government has declared that employment discrimination based on race, sex, and national origin is illegal under the Civil Rights Act of 1964, subjecting companies to damage claims and other penalties for discriminatory employment conditions they permit to exist (even if they can get "voluntary" acceptance of jobs at discriminatory compensation levels).

When two companies that compete with each other agree to charge the same price, Section I of the Sherman Antitrust Law is violated. The two colluding companies are subject to sanctions, including (but not limited to) the value of damages inflicted by the companies' collusive actions. Both antitrust violations and discriminatory (by race, sex, national origin, age, or disability) employment conditions involve public law.

Civil and Criminal Law

	Civil Law		Criminal Law
Contract Law	Sale of Goods	**Misdemeanor Offenses**	Traffic Violations
	Employment Contracts		Drunk and Disorderly Conduct
	Purchase and Sale of Real Estate		Theft of Small Amounts of Property
	Lease of Intellectual Property		Theft of Computer Services
Tort Law	Battery		
	False Imprisonment	**Felonies**	Murder
	Defamation		Kidnapping
	Trespass		Child Pornography
			Burglary

Other examples of public law include criminal law, constitutional law, and administrative law that comes into play when an administrative agency takes a business to court. The table above is not exhaustive of all categories of either public or private law.

Civil versus Criminal Law

For most businesses, civil law is far more important than criminal law. Most public and private law is civil, though there are exceptions. A notable difference between civil and criminal law is that, if the defendant loses a civil case, the sanction against the defendant is generally monetary. In contrast, a defendant who loses a criminal case can be fined, but can also be imprisoned or even executed.[6] In a criminal case, the defendant is prosecuted on behalf of society or the public.

Criminal and civil procedure also differ significantly. In a criminal case, the state has the responsibility to prove *beyond a reasonable doubt* that the defendant is guilty (under substantive criminal law). In a criminal case, the defendant cannot be made to testify. Criminal cases are often subdivided into felonies and misdemeanors. Felonies are more serious offenses, in which the defendant can receive a sentence exceeding one year in jail. Misdemeanors are

less serious offenses, where the maximum imprisonment is less than one year.

In a civil case, the plaintiff tries to prove by a *preponderance of the evidence* that the defendant was responsible for a civil wrong that entitles the plaintiff to a monetary recovery or some kind of injunctive relief. The courts have resisted mathematical comparisons between *beyond a reasonable doubt* and *preponderance of the evidence,* but it is the authors' opinion that former standard is akin to Type I error of .05 or less, while the latter implies that the probability the plaintiff's version of the truth is superior to the defendant's is greater than .5. In other words, in a criminal case where the *beyond the reasonable doubt* standard is used, the jury must have a less than one in twenty chance (of Type I error) in their minds that the defendant is not guilty when the jury finds them guilty. *Preponderance of the evidence* is synonymous with the statement that "It is more likely than not that the defendant did the deeds that entitle the plaintiff to a monetary recovery."

OTHER CONSIDERATIONS

A Caution Regarding the Overlay of Ethics and Law

Students should be careful not to confuse law and ethics. Although there may be general societal agreement on an ethical issue, compliance with a generally

---

[6]In some civil cases the plaintiff seeks an injunction which is a court order directing the defendant to do or not to do something. If the defendant fails to abide by an injunction, the court can order the defendant to jail.

accepted ethical standard is optional unless the law requires compliance. Pharmaceutical companies have been accused of using Third World countries for development of drugs because their legal standards for the marketing of new drugs are less stringent than in the United States. Should a pharmaceutical company market drugs in Third World countries that have been rejected by the U.S. Food and Drug Administration? It may be considered unethical by some, but it is not illegal for a corporation to market such drugs in Third World countries. Technology certainly works to expose us to new ethical issues, as well as legal issues. With limits on pages and expertise, this book must focus primarily on legality, rather than ethics. However, it is impossible to focus a textbook on Cyberlaw issues without dealing significantly with ethical issues. Many students view the Napster case as a moral issue that pits "little" people (primarily young fans) against giant and well-represented record companies. Consider the latest turn in the Napster saga:

Law and Ethics Join Forces in Cyberspace?

Napster is a web site that has created a rift between those with IP to protect, recording artists and the Recording Industry Association of America (RIAA), and music fans. A college student, Shawn Mullins, created technology that allowed millions of website visitors to "share" their files of copyrighted songs and music. After two important legal battles went against them, Napster has recently come out with a new business plan which includes software that will allegedly filter out copyrighted material from their subscribers.

As much as anything else, the Napster case illustrates new ethical challenges that have been created by technical advances. Stripped to the essence, Napster facilitates its members to obtain copyrighted songs without paying for them. On the other hand, Napster advocates contend that record sales have actually increased since Napster began its enormous popularity. Furthermore, many Napster users have complained about high CD prices and have noted that many of the recording artists are already very well compensated for their compositions.

The following is a CNN article about the latest wrinkle in the Napster story.

NAPSTER FILTER WELCOMED BY MUSIC INDUSTRY

SAN FRANCISCO, California—The president of the Recording Industry Association of America said she believed that there had been progress in Friday's hearing on the federal injunction that could cripple the Napster song-swapping service.

Attorneys for the recording industry and Napster were back in federal court Friday, where U.S. District Judge Marilyn Hall Patel was expected to modify an injunction to essentially shut down the music file-sharing service.

Napster attorney David Boies announced in the hearing that Napster would start implementing a system over the weekend that will block users from downloading restricted artists albums and songs.

"It's important for me to give some credit to Napster today," said Hillary Rosen of the RIAA. "I think they came into court trying to be productive, I still think that they've got a way to go.

"There are things and affirmative steps they should be taking which they have resisted in court today, but they did say they wanted to work with something effective and we'll take them at that word," Rosen added.

A federal appeals court ordered the hearing last week. The three-judge panel upheld most of Patel's original injunction from last July, but ordered the judge to redraft it.

The appellate ruling was a victory for the recording industry, which claims the service violates copyright laws. The court said Patel must modify her injunction to require record labels to identify which copyrights are being violated.

Patel did not issue a new injunction Friday, but it could come at any time.

NAPSTER ATTORNEY DEFENDS SERVICE

Rosen said that Napster's admission that it could filter songs was a dramatic change in position.

"What Napster said today, which they have essentially have been denying for the last year, was that they could filter out unauthorized songs," Rosen said "You'll remember they argued before this court last year, they argued last September at the 9th Circuit

Continued from page 20

[Court of Appeals] that they couldn't. Today they have finally said what we've all known for over a year, that they absolutely can filter out unauthorized works."

Boies said Napster was adapting its system to conform with the appeals court ruling, but he believed that a jury would find that the service was not illegal.

He said Napster can block individual file names, but cannot go into the files to see if there has been a copyright violation. Boies said the appeals court put the burden of proving copyright infringement on the recording industry.

"They placed on the plaintiffs the burden of first coming forward and identifying a work that they had a copyright in, and second demonstrating that it was listed on the Napster index that is available through Napster," Boies said. "Because the court of appeals—we think—properly put that burden on the plaintiffs, we have begun by dealing with those files where the plaintiffs have met that burden."

Boies said Napster has already blocked more than 1 million song files.

Record companies want Napster to block out all files of a song or album. It has submitted a list of more than 6,500 songs it wants blocked.

FEE-BASED SYSTEM SCHEDULED FOR SUMMER

When asked about Napster's plan to settle the lawsuit for $1 billion dollars over five years, Rosen said the courts were the wrong place to settle the disputed licensing.

"The money that Napster offered they should be offering in individual discussions with individual companies," Rosen said. "There isn't an industry

license that can be granted and there won't be an industry response to a billion dollar offer."

Under the proposal, Napster would have provided guaranteed revenue of $1 billion to the major labels, songwriters and independent labels and artists over the next five years. Major labels would have received $150 million per year for a non-exclusive license, divided according to files transferred. Another $50 million per year would have been set aside for independent labels and artists to be paid out based on the volume of files transferred.

The model includes a basic membership plan for users that would cost as much as $5 per month with a limit on file transfers. A premium monthly membership would cost as much as $10 and would offer unlimited file transfers.

The Internet service is going forward with the proposed fee-based system, which it says will be in place by summer.

Napster is one of the most widely used Web sites, with 57 million registered users.

The new proposed Napster, scheduled for launch this summer, also would have limitations of 128 kilobytes per second and lower for sharing files, which would hamper both the speed and quality of music being swapped. Users also would have to pay an additional fee to burn CDs and to transfer their music to portable devices.

CNN Correspondent James Hattori contributed to this report.

Source: http://dailynews.netscape.com/dailynews/cnnnews.tmpl?story=napster.hearing.0403021930.html

SUMMARY

- The law relates to everyday experiences. Business students should be very aware of the importance of law. A legal mistake can be fatal to any business or business plan.
- The legal environment of business is rapidly changing with the rise of the Internet and the explosion of high-tech enterprises whose principal assets are in the form of *intellectual property* (IP).

- The explosion of technology and the development of E-Commerce have caused the law to change significantly, particularly in the areas of *contract* law and intellectual property law, which includes patent, copyright, trademark, and trade secret law.
- The Internet has introduced a whole new way of doing business, but traditional *tort* law continues

- to be relevant. In particular, extractions of information without the consent of users or customers can be an invasion of privacy.
- Businesses face the threat of industrial espionage and hackers bent on mischief. In response, computer security consultants use a wide variety of tools to protect businesses. Encryption is used to scramble communications to avoid interception of valuable information.
- Court protection of software is still evolving. Originally, it was thought that copyright law would be the mainstay of legal protection against unauthorized reproductions, but lately other forms of intellectual property protection, such as patents and trade secrets, have been used to legally protect software.
- The primary goal of this textbook is to enable students to recognize legal issues.
- The law is more than words on a piece of paper. It is set of rules that are enforced by public forces, generally the police. The law evolves according to societal changes and technological growth.
- The law simultaneously provides a vehicle for social change and for promoting social cohesion. In countries that are not unified legally, violence and social disruption are more common.
- The common law was created when parties to a dispute came to court for judicial resolution of conflict. The common law is built through precedents and *stare decisis*. The common law originated in England and was the court system used by the colonial courts.
- The common law continues to redefine law in a modern context adapting to changes in society and technology.
- Constitutional law sits at the apex of our legal system. A primary function of the U.S. Constitution is protection of the rights elucidated in the Bill of Rights. The Supremacy Clause in the U.S. Constitution requires that federal law will prevail in conflicts with state law.
- Statutes are laws passed by legislative bodies. In order to be enforceable, a statute must not conflict with a state constitution or with the U.S. Constitution. There are 51 legislatures in the United States, Congress and 50 state legislatures.
- Congress and the states often create administrative agencies to enforce regulatory statutes and devise regulations consistent with the regulatory statute. The largest body of law, by volume, is the accumulation regulations from administrative agencies.
- Increasingly, commercial parties are bypassing the courts through arbitration clauses. Arbitration is generally faster and cheaper than court litigation. At the international level, arbitration clauses are very common.
- It is useful to classify law into various categories. The focus of this textbook is substantive law. Other useful classifications include civil versus criminal law, and public versus private law.

BASIC CONTRACT LAW

2

Among branches of law, contract law is uniquely linked with business. It is because of the demands of business, that law in this area evolved and continues to evolve to facilitate, rather than impede, commercial practices of business. Business is an inherently risky endeavor and people in business generally seek to avoid risk. Contracts are instrumental in reducing risk and also serve to increase business efficiency.

Adam Smith pointed out in the *Wealth of Nations,* written in 1776, that as the size of markets expand, increased specialization takes place. In order to meet expanding market demands, one-person operations gave way to combinations of workers, capital, and the other basic factors of production. Within a business, the services of all factor inputs—land, labor and capital—are linked by contracts. Indeed, freedom to contract was and is regarded as a foundation for our capitalist economic system.

A common characteristic of repressive governments is that they severely limit the freedom to contract. In communist regimes suppliers of capital were prohibited from funding enterprising businesspeople,

and, as a result, inefficient state-operated enterprises continued to exist because of lack of competition. Of course, there can be legitimate reasons to truncate freedom in order to promote societal goals. Contracts that condition employment upon not being a member of a union, often called 'yellow dog' contracts, were outlawed by the Wagner Act in 1933. Securities law, regulating exchanges of stocks and bonds, requires that purchasers be given accurate information before a business owner can sell shares of ownership in his business. Much of the regulatory law that is broadly approved by most Americans, including labor, environmental, securities, and equal opportunity employment laws, involves limitations on freedom of contract.

WHAT IS A CONTRACT?

A contract is an agreement that creates a legally enforceable obligation to perform. The *Restatement of Contracts* defines a contract as a, "promise or set of promises for the breach of which the law gives a remedy, or the performance of which the law in some way recognizes as a duty."[1] In ordinary English, if you enter into a contract and then do not perform as promised, the other party to the contract can take you to court for some kind of remedy, usually in the form of money damages, which are theoretically set equal to the court estimation of damages.

Valid contracts require:

1. **an agreement,** which normally includes an **offer** and **acceptance** of that offer;
2. **consideration,** each side to the contract agrees to do something like perform services or pay money that they were not previously obligated to do;
3. **that both parties to the contract have capacity to contract,** i.e., both parties are over 18 and know what they are doing; and
4. **that performance under the contract is legal,** so each side can perform under the contract without violating a law or public policy.

It is important to recognize that not all *agreements* are *contracts*. There are a number of agreements that do not entitle the nonbreaching party to go to the court for redress. A promise to make a gift, for example, is not enforceable in court because the promise is not supported by *consideration* (discussed below). A number of agreements are illegal by statute and some are void because they are contrary to public policy. For example, a public official could agree to change her mind on an issue in return for a bribe offered by an interested party. If the public official rendered the favorable ruling, such an agreement would be void. The public official could not go to court to recover the value of the bribe. It is, therefore, important to recognize (1) what agreements rise to the level of *contract* and (2) the legal consequences of contracts.

Common Law of Contracts and the U.C.C.

This chapter will examine what is described as the *common law of contracts.* Since each state has its own common law tradition, each state has its own common law of contracts. Contracts are supposed to reduce un-

certainty by enabling businesspersons to plan, invest, and conduct business based on agreements they have with others. When the basic law of contracts varies from state to state, it adds to uncertainty. As the geographic scope of business in the United States expanded, there was increasing dissatisfaction with the "common law" of contracts that varied from state to state. The Uniform Commercial Code (UCC) was composed in response to dissatisfaction with the common law of contracts and has been adopted by all 50 states.

The impact of the UCC has been to **regularize** legal treatment of contracts in all 50 states. The UCC has been particularly effective with respect to the sale of goods (Article 2 of the UCC). The "uniform" movement has not been so successful in eradicating state by state differences in contract law regarding other transactions such as employment, property, leases, and most other areas of law where contracts are a significant part of the environment.

NOMENCLATURE OF CONTRACT LAW

Issues in contract law are discussed more efficiently when the proper terminology is used. Once a contract issue is properly classified, the rules of law that apply to that classification are relatively straightforward and understandable. Students are encouraged to (1) try to classify any particular contract issue in terms as narrow as possible and (2) to begin thinking and using the language of contract law because using the "legalese" associated with contract law will enhance issue recognition and resolution of contract problems.

Valid, Void, Voidable, and Unenforceable

A *valid* contract is a contract that is enforceable. A valid contract has the characteristics discussed above which include the option to go to court to seek redress if the other party to the contract does not perform.

A *voidable* contract is a contract that can be voided by one of the parties. A contract is voidable if there is a "victim" whose participation in the contract was induced by an unfair means. If a person was induced to sign a contract based on fraudulent misrepresentation, then the defrauded party (victim) can refuse to perform and avoid damages for breach of contract. In fact the defrauded party (victim) can sue the fraudulent party to *rescind* the contract and get their money, or other consideration (things of value), back. Other situations that enable a victim to get out of a contract without liabil-

---

[1]The American Law Institute was organized in 1923 following a study conducted by a group of prominent American judges, lawyers, and teachers known as "The Committee on the Establishment of a Permanent Organization for the Improvement of the Law." The Committee had reported that the two chief defects in American Law, its uncertainty and its complexity, had produced a 'general dissatisfaction with the administration of justice'." The ALI publishes "Restatements" of basic principles of law including the Restatement of Contract Law. Periodically, the ALI updates its Restatements.

Valid, Void, Voidable, and Unenforceable

Valid:	An enforceable contract.	void it, then it is valid. It is enforceable at the option of the victim.
Void:	A nonenforceable contract. The courts refuse to enforce it because it violates a statute or public policy.	
Voidable:	A contract that can be voided by one of the parties if he or she was a victim of unfair enticement. If a victim does not	Unenforceable: A contract where either party can decide not to go through with the contract. There is no victim in an unenforceable contract.

ity include contracts with minors, contracts that are the result of force or threat of force and several other situations discussed later in the chapter. It should be noted that, even if a party to a contract is a victim of fraud, that party may decide to go ahead with the contract, so a voidable contract has the potential of being a valid contract, at the option of the victim.

A *void* contract is a contract that courts will refuse to consider because the contract violates a statute or is against public policy. Gambling contracts, contracts between unlicensed professionals and clients, and contracts whose performance would undermine a goal of public policy are examples of void contracts. A difference between void and voidable contracts is that a voidable contract is enforceable at the option of the victim, whereas a void contract is not enforceable. Also, courts generally will not allow a party to a void contract to recover money or other consideration that may have been lost while participating in the void contract. There are, however, statutes that have been enacted to protect the public such as requirements that professionals hold appropriate licenses. Under a void contract, a victim (the intended beneficiaries of the protective statute) can generally recover monies paid to unlicensed professionals.

If a contract is *unenforceable,* either party to the contract can decide not to go through with the contract. Certain contracts must be in writing to be enforceable. Either the buyer or the seller in an oral real estate contract can decide not to perform without liability because contracts for the sale of real estate must be in writing to be enforceable. As compared to a voidable contract, if a contract is unenforceable, there is no "victim" who has the option to decide whether to go ahead with the contract or bail out. Another example of an unenforceable contract occurs when a party delays

too long before suing when a contract is breached. Under the laws of most states, a party has three years after a breach of contract to decide whether to sue. After that period, the *Statute of Limitations* will have run and the contract becomes unenforceable. An effect of bankruptcy is that contract performance requirements of the bankrupt party become unenforceable. Still, if the contract obligation of the bankrupt party is **secured,** creditors are able to recover the pledged collateral.

Bilateral and Unilateral

Most contracts are *bilateral* in the sense that a promise is *exchanged* for a promise. In a typical sales contract, a seller promises to deliver the goods by a certain date and the buyer promises to pay for the goods in the way called for in the contract. When two promises are exchanged, both parties are *promisors* with respect to the promises they make and *promisees* as to the promises made by the other party. In a breach of contract suit, it is the promisee who is suing for the failure of the other party to live up to his or her promises made in creating the contract. Bilateral contracts are the norm and the result of a bilateral contract is that both parties are legally bound to adhere to their promises.

There are some contracts that are properly termed *unilateral* because there is only one promisor in the contract. Reward contracts are typical of unilateral contracts. If Jeff posts a reward that he will pay $50 for the return of his dog, Fifi, the only way to accept that offer is to perform by finding and returning Fifi. Promisees in reward contracts are not bound to promisors, if they say they are going to look for the dog. Unilateral contracts are different from bilateral contracts in that the party making the promise is bound if the other party performs what is called for in the promise, but not vice versa. As we will see shortly, unilateral contracts often are a poor way of doing business because a promisor can withdraw his promise (or offer) at anytime before performance has been completed, thus leaving the promisee without a remedy if performance is partially completed.

Executory and Executed

A contract to be completed in the future is an *executory* contract. Contractual performance that has been performed is *executed*. Thus the two terms, executory and executed, refer to timing issues as related to performance. In a typical sales contract, at the conception of the contract (which can take place when the parties sign the contract), both parties are promising to perform certain actions in the future. At the signing of the contract, the contract is classified as an *executory bilateral* contract in which both parties are liable to the other for failure to perform as called for in the contract. Executory bilateral contracts are the norm in business transactions.

Express and Implied

An *express* contract contains an explicit agreement between the parties that there is a contract. An employment contract is an express contract because the wage or salary agreed upon is explicitly in return for work to be performed by the employee. A bid made at an auction creates an express contract if the auctioneer hammers down the gavel indicating that the bid has been accepted. Express contracts should not be confused with written contracts. Thousands of oral contracts are made everyday on stock exchanges for the purchase and sale of stock, which represents ownership in corporations, and virtually all of these contracts are express, but not written.

Some contracts are *implied* based on conduct. A contract is implied because the conduct of the parties indicates consent to be bound in a contract. If Jane felt ill and went to see a doctor, after treatment she would pass by a receptionist who would inquire about how Jane wanted to pay for the services rendered. The conduct of both parties created an implied contract. When Jane checked in with the doctor, it was implied that she would pay for medical services rendered. Implied contracts arise from routine situations that occur millions of times each day in the United States, generally without controversy. If the doctor told Jane that his services were of extraordinary value and she owed him $10,000 for just one visit, Jane would not be legally obligated to pay anywhere near that amount. Jane's visit to the doctor implied a willingness to contract, but only under reasonable terms.

Quasi-Contract

If there is no agreement between the parties, one party may, nevertheless, be able to recover from the other party based on *unjust enrichment.* Unjust enrichment is the basis for a damage award given to someone who has been economically injured as a result of a *quasi-contract* with another. Technically a quasi-contract exists when (1) the plaintiff conveys benefits to the defendant (2) in the expectation of receiving compensation, (3) the defendant knowingly receives the benefits, and (4) the transfer results in unjust enrichment for the defendant. The key factor in this theory of damages is the **knowing receipt** of benefits by the defendant. If a neighbor boy shows up to your house with a lawn mower, you raise your hand to greet him, and he starts cutting your backyard, you may not have a valid contract with the boy, but he would be entitled to collect for the fair market value of the services rendered based on quasi-contract. On the other hand, if you took a vacation and, upon your return, discovered that your lawn was recently cut by the same neighborhood boy, he would not be entitled to recovery because you did not knowingly receive the benefits.

A quasi-contract claim is often the last ditch effort of a party who cannot prove that there was a valid contract between it and another party. Several Hollywood producers and directors have been sued by writers who claim that they (the writers) gave the producers or directors ideas for movies that later became very successful. Most of these suits are unsuccessful. Art Buchwald, however, was the exception with his successful suit against the producer of the movie *Coming to America* because, apparently, he had told the producer of the idea several years before the film was produced.

Knowledge Transfers between Firms

For business students it is important to recognize that they could be on either side of a quasi-contract dispute. Many times small firms develop ideas that have tremendous market value, but lack the resources to commercialize their creations. Large and medium-sized firms are often on the lookout for partnerships with small firms that develop innovative technology or other "ideas," but need commercial development support from the more established firm(s). Of course, the small firm generally is properly reluctant to reveal its idea or new technology without some guarantee of payment, while the large firm does not want to get sued if it develops a product in the same general area but does not use the idea of the smaller firm.

Contracts by Large Firms   With this situation having become increasingly common, large firms, in particular, have developed contract language that essentially agrees to pay the small firm if their idea is used (generally if their idea is patentable), but the small firm waives its right to sue if the idea is not patentable or if the idea is not used. Small firms generally are able to require that the large firm sign a Non-Disclosure Agreement (NDA), which means that even if the large firm does not use the idea, it will not disclose the idea to oth-

ers. When meetings and contract language are not carefully planned, the result can be a messy, costly and often unproductive quasi-contract suit.

Market Alternatives   The problem of transferring knowledge between firms is sufficiently common that there are firms that specialize in combining idea people and technology with more established firms that could make use of such ideas. Knowledge Express (http://www.knowledgeexpress.com/) is a company that provides knowledge transfer services including searching "licensable technologies from corporate, government and university sources." There are a large number of firms that specialize in knowledge transfers between firms as a search of the World Wide Web will reveal, using "knowledge transfer" for terms.

Permanence Corporation, Plaintiff-Appellant, v. *Kennametal, Inc., Defendant-Appellee*
United States Court of Appeals for the Sixth Circuit
908 F.2d 98 (1990)

BACKGROUND AND FACTS

Permanence was formed by its president and majority shareholder Charles S. Baum in 1969 for the purpose of developing and exploiting certain processes developed by Baum. In the 1970s Permanence conducted research and manufactured products in the tungsten carbide field. On May 24, 1977, Permanence obtained U.S. Patent No. 4,024,902 (hereinafter "Patent 902") for a process to form an alloy by incorporating tungsten carbide into a steel matrix. The patent was entitled "metal sintered tungsten carbide composites and method of forming the same." Thus Baum was the classic inventor who forms a company and attempts to deal with a larger more established firm, Kennametal.

On February 8, 1979, Permanence executed a written agreement with defendant Kennametal, a publicly traded corporation specializing in the manufacture of tools, tooling

systems, and supplies for the metal working industry.

In the contract between the parties, Permanence granted Kennametal the non-exclusive right to the licensed patents (existing Patent 902 and patents that would issue from applications owned by Permanence) n1 for a period of 24 months subject to the non-exclusive license previously granted to Masco Corp. for Patent 902. For the non-exclusive license, Kennametal agreed to pay Permanence a consideration of a $150,000 fee and a royalty rate of 2 3/4% on the net sales price of products made by Kennametal using processes that fell under valid claims of the licensed patents. Advance royalties of $100,000 were to be paid upon the signing of the agreement for the non-exclusive license.

The agreement also provided that Kennametal would have the option to obtain the exclusive license to the patents. Kennametal agreed to pay

Permanence a second $150,000 fee and a second $100,000 in advance royalties upon the exercise of the option for an exclusive license. On February 8, 1979, the parties signed the agreement and a $150,000 up-front fee and an advance payment of royalties in the amount of $100,000 was paid to Permanence for the non-exclusive right to the patents. On February 5, 1981, Kennametal exercised its option and paid an additional $250,000 for the grant of the exclusive agency—$150,000 for the exercise of the option and a second $100,000 in advance royalties.

Seven years later on April 18, 1988, Permanence filed a one-count complaint alleging that Kennametal had breached the contract by not fulfilling an obligation to use best efforts to exploit the patents. As there was no express "best efforts" provision in the contract, plaintiff argued that the grant of an exclusive agency imposes on the licensee (Kennametal) an implied duty to use best efforts to exploit. On February 1, 1989, Kennametal moved for summary judgment, arguing that it had spent $500,000 for the use of the patented technology of Permanence and that a best efforts obligation had specifically been negotiated out of the agreement.

OPINION: CONTIE, SENIOR CIRCUIT JUDGE

The sole issue before this court on appeal is whether the district court erred in its order granting summary judgment that as a matter of law an implied best efforts obligation did not arise in the contract between the parties.

* * *

Plaintiff's legal theory that the court will imply a duty on the part of an exclusive licensee to use "best efforts" [Footnotes deleted] to bring profits and revenues into existence finds its ultimate support in the landmark opinion of Judge Cardozo, *Wood* v. *Lucy, Lady Duff-Gordon,* 222 N.Y. 88, 118 N.E. 214 (1917). There, the defendant, a fashion designer, gave the plaintiff the exclusive privilege of marketing defendant's designs. The court implied an obligation to exploit the design, although there was not an express obligation to do so in the contract, because defendant's sole revenue from the grant of the exclusive agency was to be derived from plaintiff's sale of clothes designed by defendant, and defendant was thus at plaintiff's mercy. [References deleted] In subsequent cases, an obligation to employ best efforts has generally been implied in contracts in which the only consideration for a grant of property lies in payment of royalties.

* * *

In *Maxwell* v. *Schaefer,* 381 Pa. 13, 112 A.2d 69 (1955), the Pennsylvania Supreme Court stated that since plaintiff's profits for granting the exclusive contract depended entirely on the volume of sales defendant was able to create for the product, "it may fairly be inferred that all parties to the agreement fully intended and expected [defendant] to devote reasonable effort to the promotion of [the product]." *Id.* at 72, citing *Wood* v. *Lucy, Lady Duff-Gordon,* 222 N.Y. at 90-91. Thus, under Pennsylvania law an obligation to use "best efforts" will be implied in a contract granting an exclusive agency if the plaintiff depends for its consideration solely upon sales of the licensed product.

* * *

Plaintiff concedes that there was no best efforts obligation to exploit the non-exclusive license initially granted to Kennametal for a $150,000 fee and $100,000 in advance royalties. Yet royalties (2 3/4%) were also to be paid on products manufactured under the non-exclusive license. Moreover, the royalty rate for both the exclusive license and the non-exclusive license after 24 months was contingent on whether the products manufactured by Kennametal under the patents were ones which directly competed with products sold by Masco that had been produced under the non-exclusive license previously granted to it. The fact that the relationship with Masco subsequently proved to be unproductive and did not generate royalties for Permanence does not justify imposing an implied covenant to exploit on Kennametal.

The key provisions of the contract between Permanence and Kennametal which militate against implying a covenant to use best efforts are Kennametal's obligation to pay $150,000 in order to exercise the option for the exclusive license and the $100,000 in additional advance royalties paid under the exclusive license. Courts have held that by imposing a substantial minimum or advance royalty payment, the licensor, in lieu of obtaining an express agreement to use best efforts, has protected himself against the possibility that the licensee will do nothing. Rather than leaving the licensor at the mercy of the licensee, the demand for a substantial up-front or advance royalty payment creates an incentive for the licensee to exploit the invention or patent. In the present case, Permanence received a substantial total advance payment of $250,000 for its right to the exclusive license and, unlike the licensor in the majority of cases where a duty to exploit has been implied, did not depend for its consideration solely on Kennametal's sale of products developed under the patents.

* * *

The court affirmed the decision of the trial court to grant a motion for a summary judgment, thus dismissing the case that Permanence filed against Kennametal.

QUESTIONS FOR ANALYSIS

1. According to the court in this case, under what circumstances would the licensee, the defendant Kennametal, have an obligation to use "best efforts" to sell the patent that was licensed it to it by the plaintiff, Permanence?

2. Does the plaintiff have any recourse in this case? Can the plaintiff go to another potential licensee? Why not?

3. Is this a case where the inventor's invention will stay on the shelf unless the established company, Kennamental, decides it wants to exploit the patent more fully?

CONTRACT FORMATION

There are five elements to contract formation. They are **offer, acceptance, consideration, capacity of the parties of contract,** and **legality.** If these five elements are not present, an "agreement" is not a valid contract. Each of these elements, in turn, has sub-elements. This requires us to focus narrowly on possible flaws to the validity of a contract. What is discussed next is the theory of contract formation under the common law. In practice, courts are focusing increasingly on the **conduct** of the parties to a contract and on commercial practices within the industry.

Offer

The beginning of a contract takes place with an *offer,* which is made by the *offeror.* When the offeror makes an offer, (s)he creates an opportunity for the offeree (the person to whom the offer is made) to make a contract by agreeing to the offer with an acceptance. Under the common law of contracts, an offer has three elements: *intent, certainty* and *definiteness* of terms, and it is *communicated* to the offeree.

Intent to make an offer is judged by an *objective* standard. It is immaterial whether subjectively the offeror really intended to make an offer or not, but rather intent is judged from the perspective of a hypothetical "reasonable person." The criteria the courts use, and what they ask juries to consider, is what would a reasonable person (reasonable offeree) have thought under the circumstances? If a reasonable person would have thought that the offeror intended to make an offer, then the intent element is satisfied. By using the "reasonable person" standard, the courts can bring in the circumstances under which the offer was made. If the offeror was in his office during regular business hours meeting with a possible business partner, it is more likely that an offer has been made than if the "offeror" was at a bar with a drink in hand, even though many contracts have been formed in bars.

Advertisements

It is important to distinguish intent to make an offer from an invitation to bargain. Most advertisements are interpreted by the courts as invitations to bargain unless the advertisement is very specific. Merely stating in a catalogue or an advertisement in a newspaper that a particular brand of clothes are available for sale at 20 percent off the normal price is considered a solicitation of offers. When customers arrive and offer to buy the clothes for the discounted price, the store can accept or refuse the offer. The more specific the offer, however, the more likely the courts will interpret an advertisement as an offer and a number of advertisements have been considered offers.

Internet Advertisements Are also Offers   One impact of the Internet is that the line between advertisements and legal offers has been blurred if not obliterated. On the Internet, thousands of web sites advertise their products but they also make offers that are legally binding if a customer clicks the "yes" button, signifying assent to the offer. As discussed above, the traditional view of most advertisements is that they are invitations to bargain, not legally binding offers, but on the Internet advertisements are also offers capable of creating a contract if a customer assents to the offer/advertisement.

Prior Conduct between the Parties

In many cases, intent is assumed from prior conduct or from what is common in the industry. If Jim is in the habit of hiring Jerry to accompany him on auctions to buy livestock and pays Jerry $500 per trip, an offer takes place if Jim tells Jerry to "get suited up, we are going to Kansas City for an auction." Under the circumstances, it is reasonable for Jerry to believe that Jim has made an offer to employ him for the auction in Kansas City.

Alternatively, consider the following statement by Bill: "I am considering selling my house. Would you think that $150,000 is an excessive price?" Such a statement would most likely be considered an invitation to bargain, rather than an offer in which Bill was inviting an acceptance. In order for Bill to be deemed to have the requisite intent, there has to be a showing that the offeror was doing more than just speculating out loud, which is how Bill's statement would be interpreted.

Certainty and Definiteness of Terms

At common law the offer to contract has to contain the essential terms of the contract so that the contract was reasonably **certain.** At a minimum the offer has to contain the identities of the parties to the contract, the subject matter of the contract, the price, and the quantity. In most contracts the offer actually has to contain more terms than price, quantity, the parties, and the subject matter of the contract. If a material term in the contract is missing, then the offer is incomplete. Under such circumstances, a response by the offeree filling in the missing material terms would transform the original offeror into the offeree, and the original offeree into the offerer. In analyzing contract formation, it is common for the parties to change hats from offeror to offeree.

Communication

An offer by X to sell to A does not mean that yet another party (B) can "accept" the offer. An offeree cannot accept an offer unless the offer has been **directed toward** him or her. An offer does not have to be personal to a particular offeree, as the offeror could make the offer to a class of offerees, such as potential customers who are not dealers. Nevertheless, if the offeree is unaware of the offer at the time the offeree renders performance, such as returning a pet to its owner, the offeree is not entitled to whatever compensation was promised in the offer (i.e., the reward offered for the pet's return).

Impact of the Internet   Again, with the Internet, the legal requirement that an offer be directed towards an offeree is being diminished by communication technology. An offer made on the Internet invites acceptance from, literally, anyone in the world. It is true that the same could be said of catalogs for a mail order business, but catalogs are sent to selected audiences, whereas Internet offers are easily accessible to anyone with a computer and an Internet connection.

Acceptance

The common law of contracts developed a logical model for acceptances, but that model often does not correspond to actual commercial practice. Under the common law of contracts, an acceptance possesses

---

Ben Hunt, Jr. and Jeanne B. Hunt, Husband and Wife; George W. Brown and Coweta Jean Brown, Husband and Wife v. McIlroy Bank and Trust
Court of Appeals of Arkansas
616 S.W.2d 759 (1981)

BACKGROUND AND FACTS

McIlroy Bank and Trust, filed a foreclosure suit against the defendants, alleging that appellants (the defendants) were in default on six separate promissory notes due and payable to the appellee (McIlroy Bank and Trust).[1] The appellants are Ben Hunt, Jeanne Hunt, George Brown and Coweta Brown, all of whom were doing business at S.B.H. Farms. Appellants filed a general denial, alleged a number of affirmative

[1]The appellant is the party (or parties) applying the verdict of the lower court. The appellee is the party that contesting the appeal. Sometimes both parties appeal the decision of the trial court; the defendant may appeal an adverse decision on the issue of liability, while the plaintiff may appeal the amount of damages awarded by the trial court.

defenses and counterclaimed against appellee for $750,000, contending appellants were damaged as a result of certain misrepresentations and a breach of an oral contract by the appellee to loan appellants monies. The trial court found that appellants failed to produce evidence of fraud or misrepresentation, nor was there proof of an oral agreement or contract requiring appellee to loan monies to appellants. The court dismissed appellants' counterclaim and entered judgment in favor of appellee on its complaint.

OPINION BY: GLAZE

One of appellants' points for reversal arises out of their contention that in October, 1976, the appellee, through its agricultural loan officer, Don Larkin, orally contracted to loan ap-

pellants an indefinite amount of monies which would be sufficient to build hog houses, to buy livestock and to generally finance the expansion of their existing farming operation. The appellee argues, and the trial court found, that no contractual agreement was reached between the parties because the terms discussed by the parties were so indefinite and uncertain that neither side could have performed the agreement with any degree of certainty. Since appellants are the parties who urge the existence of an oral agreement, it was incumbent upon them to show by a preponderance of the evidence the existence of such parol agreement, a breach and damages. [References deleted]

In reviewing the record before us, we keep foremost in mind two legal principles when deciding whether a valid contract was entered into by appellants and appellee in October, 1976: (1) A court cannot make a contract for the parties but can only construe and enforce the contract which they have made; and if there is no meeting of the minds, there is no contract. and (2) It is well settled that in order to make a contract there must be a meeting of the minds as to *all* terms. The essential elements of a contract were recited by the court in *Gentry* v. *Hanover Insurance Company,* 284 F.Supp. 626 (D. C. Ark. 1968), viz.: (a) competent parties, (b) subject matter, (c) legal consideration, (d) mutual agreement, and (e) mutual obligations.

After a study of the evidence presented at trial, we have no hesitancy in agreeing with the chancellor that the appellants failed to prove a contract existed between themselves and the appellee. Appellee's officer, Larkin, and appellant Ben Hunt initially discussed the financing of the expansion of the S.B.H. Farm operation, but the total amount of loan proceeds was never decided. Hunt said that at one time Larkin told him he could have up to $750,000. Larkin testified that the appellee was willing to loan in excess of $500,000, and it could have been $700,000. Both Larkin and Hunt agreed that no interest rate or repayment terms were ever agreed upon. There apparently was some discussion that long term permanent financing would be necessary, but the terms of such financing were left to future determination. Meanwhile, short term notes were signed by appellants for loan proceeds so the farm expansion could commence. Although Larkin and Hunt may have generally agreed on a course of action as to the need for financing the farm project, they never agreed on the essential, much less all of, the terms of a contract to loan monies. There is no way that a court could take the general terms discussed between Larkin and Hunt regarding an open-ended loan with no repayment provisions and be asked to enforce an agreement without filling in necessary terms essential to the formation of a contract. The subject matter of the proposed agreement was indefinite and the mutual assent and obligations were so vague as to be unenforceable.

* * *

In accordance with the foregoing, we affirm the trial court's findings and decision.

Affirmed.

QUESTIONS FOR ANALYSIS

1. The court in this case indicated that there was not a contract because the essential terms of the loan contract were not agreed upon. What terms is the court referring to?

2. In addition to lacking of meeting of the minds on the essential terms of the contract, the "agreement" was oral? Does this case suggest that the maxim, "Get it in writing" is apt for this case?

three elements: (1) the offeree must possess *intent* to be bound by the offer, (2) the acceptance must be *complete and unqualified,* and (3) it must be *communicated* to the offeror.

Intent

Intent on the part of an offeree is evaluated in the same way as for an offeror. The question that is asked is, "What would a reasonable offeror think under the circumstances?" If the words or actions of the offeree would lead a reasonable offeror to believe that the offeree intended to accept the offer, then the intent element of the acceptance is satisfied. Again the "reasonable man" standard enables juries to consider all the surrounding facts as to whether the offeror was justified in believing that the offeree intended to accept the offer.

Complete and Unqualified

Under the common law of contracts, the acceptance must be *complete* and *unqualified.* The complete and unqualified requirement has often been referred to as the *mirror image rule.* At common law, the offeree must agree to accept each and every term in the offer without qualifications. If the offeree does not accept each term in the offer, it is considered a *rejection* of the offer. If the offeree adds additional terms to the offer in his or her acceptance, it is considered a *counteroffer,* and thus, also a rejection of the original offer. When an offeree makes a counteroffer, the offeree immediately becomes the offeror with respect to the counteroffer and the offeror becomes the offeree with all roles of the parties reversed.

Dissatisfaction with the mechanistic restrictions of the common law led to substantial and continuing revisions of this rule in the Uniform Commercial Code. Commercial practice is such that in the *sale of goods* **most** acceptances by businesses are accompanied by additional terms. For all contracts that are not governed by the U.C.C., however, additional or different terms in the acceptance transforms the acceptance into a rejection of the offer and a counteroffer.

Communicated to the Offeror

In order to complete the acceptance, the offeree must communicate acceptance to the offeror. The acceptance can be mistransmitted and, as a result, there is litigation on occasion, related to the communication requirement. Under the common law of contracts, risk of loss due to mistransmission is borne by the offeror if the offeree uses:

1. the *same means of transmission* used to make the offer (if the offer does not authorize a specific means of acceptance) or
2. the *means of transmission authorized* in the offer. If an offer is made to the general public, but the offer requires acceptance by first class mail, then a faxed acceptance sent instead would not bind the offeror, because the offeree did not use the *authorized* means of acceptance.

Faxes and e-mails are fast diminishing the significance of the so-called "mailbox rule." Under the mailbox rule an *acceptance,* communicated by the authorized means of acceptance, is effective when dispatched. That is, once the acceptance **leaves the hands** of the offeree the contract is considered formed. On the other hand, a rejection is effective only when **received** by the offeror, regardless of the means used by the offeree to communicate. The mailbox rule allows for offerees to send a rejection of an offer one day, then change course and send an acceptance the next day. Under these facts a contract **would be formed** as long as the acceptance is dispatched before the offeror receives the rejection. With e-mails and faxes, however, the gap in time between dispatch and receipt is so small that the mailbox rule is no longer a significant legal issue unless the parties rely exclusively on the U.S. mail (sometimes referred to as snail mail in the digital world). Finally, the mailbox rule only applies to acceptances. All other transmissions including offers, rejections, revocations, and counteroffers are effective when received.

Termination of the Offer

A live offer is akin to a loaded gun; it may be activated or triggered by events beyond control of the offeror and thus it is a significant legal issue to determine when an offer expires or is terminated. Traditionally, there are two types of events that terminate offers: actions of the parties and operation of law.

Actions of the Parties

The common law rule is that an offeror can *revoke* an offer at anytime, even if the offeror states in the offer that it will remain open for a longer time. There are, of course, exceptions to this rule, but, in general, an offeror can withdraw an offer at any time. If the offeror revokes an offer, the revocation is effective when it is received by the offeree, which brings the mailbox rule back into play if the parties exclusively rely on surface mail. If an offeror attempts to revoke an offer, but the offeree has already dispatched an acceptance, a contract is formed if the dispatch of the acceptance occurs before the communication of the revocation to the offeree.

Exceptions

There are a few narrow exceptions to the rule that an offer can be revoked at any time. When an offeree relies to his detriment on an offer made by an offeror, then the doctrine of *promissory estoppel* makes the offer irrevocable. Promissory estoppel occurs when the offeror (1) makes an offer that the offeror knows, or should know, will be relied upon by the offeree, (2) the offer is relied upon by the offeree, (3) the reliance is detrimental to the offeree in the absence of contract performance by the offeror, and (4) injustice can only be prevented by enforcing the promise. If a rich person makes a promise to a church to donate $10,000,000 towards the construction of a hospital and the church spends $1,000,000 acquiring real estate for construction of the hospital, the church can sue to enforce the promise under promissory estoppel.[2]

If an offeree pays an offeror to keep a promise open, as in an option contract, the offeror cannot revoke the promise during the agreed time span of the option. Option contracts are common in stock market transactions, where an optionee will pay for the opportunity to buy stock at a fixed price in the future. If the price of the stock rises, the optionee will exercise the option and purchase the stock, profiting by the difference between the market price at the time of the contract and when the option is exercised. Commercial real estate option contracts also are common. Under the UCC if an offer by a merchant states that it will

---

[2]Damages under promissory estoppel would be the reliance costs of $1,000,000 rather than the $10,000,000 promised.

remain open for say 10 days, then the offer is irrevocable during that period of time (as discussed in the next chapter).

Lapse of Time   If nothing is said in the offer, the offer lapses after a *reasonable* period of time. Reasonableness in this context depends on the industry. The more volatile are price movements in the industry, the more quickly offers lapse. In the stock market, an offer without a defined time period may be deemed lapsed after 30 minutes, while an offer to buy a house may last for a week or longer if there is no statement in the offer on when the offer expires. For most transactions, it seems prudent to put in an expiration date in the offer because of the large possible consequences that can occur depending on whether or not the offer is accepted.

Rejection of the Offer   An offer terminates if the offeree rejects the offer. Counteroffers are considered rejections under the common law of contracts. If an offer states that it will remain open for 10 days and the offeree rejects the offer on day three, the offeree cannot "accept" the offer on day eight. The only way for the offer to be revived is for the offeror to make the same offer again.

Operation of Law   There are certain events that terminate offers by operation of law. These events also operate after an offer has been formed. If a legal change occurs that makes performance of the contract illegal, a *supervening illegality,* the offer is terminated. Also, if the subject matter of the contract is destroyed, the offer is terminated. Suppose Rocco, a promoter of rock concerts, makes an offer to bring in the band *ZZ Top* for a concert but, subsequent to the offer, the concert facilities are destroyed in a fire and there are no other facilities within the vicinity suitable for holding a rock concert. The offer to engage *ZZ Top* is terminated by operation of law. Similarly, *death or incapacity* of the offeror or offeree terminates the offer. The incapacity of either party could be physical or mental.

Consideration

In a word, *consideration* is the exchange element in a contract. In order to be enforceable, a promise must be supported by consideration. In contract law, a promisor makes a promise and the promisee is the recipient of the promise. If a promisor promises to pay the promisee $500 in two weeks and nothing more occurs, the promisor has promised to make a gift, which is unenforceable. In order for the promisee to legally enforce the promise, the promisee must incur a *legal detriment* in return.

Legal Detriment Theory of Consideration

There are three categories of legal detriments that qualify as consideration. First, note that the promise of the promisor to pay $500 is consideration. A promise to pay money is consideration. If the promisee promised to pay back the $500 with interest in a year, that promise would transform the promise into a *loan agreement*. If the promisee promised to perform services in return for the $500, the agreement would be an *employment* contract. If the promisee agreed not to sue the promisor in return for $500, the agreement or contract would be called a *settlement*. If a promisee agrees to pay money, perform services, or refrain from pursuing a legal claim, the promisee has incurred a legal detriment that is capable of supporting a promise by the promisor to pay money (or perform services, or settle a lawsuit).

The benefits of consideration do not have to be directed towards the promisor. If a promisor promised to pay $500 to the promisee, there would be a valid contract if the promisee agreed to tutor the children of the promisor. The benefits of a contract need not accrue to the party agreeing to pay money; instead, the benefits of the contract could be directed towards a third party. In examining the consideration element in contracts, students are advised to determine whether the party receiving the benefits of a promise has incurred a legal detriment. If the answer is yes, then the consideration element in contracts has been satisfied.

Adequacy of Consideration

In general, the courts will not consider the adequacy of consideration. The courts are not in the business of setting "fair" prices and thus, if a party to a contract strikes a poor deal, the party cannot go to the courts and claim the contract is unfair. Having said that, in egregious situations, particularly when one side is relatively uneducated, poor, and without alternatives, contracts are sometimes voided (not enforced) by courts due to *"unconscionability"*. Unconscionability is a defense against the enforcement of any contract regulated by the UCC.

Past Consideration

Jim rescues Mary from a burning building at considerable peril to his own safety. Three weeks later in gratitude for Jim's selfless gesture, Mary promises to pay Jim $10,000 for his own medical bills as well as the danger he endured to save her. Three months later Mary still has not paid Jim and his patience is wearing thin. Can Jim sue Mary for the promise she made to pay him $10,000? The answer is definitely no. Gratitude for past actions does not qualify as consideration, as the next case illustrates.

O'Neal v. *Home Town Bank of Villa Rica et al.*
Court of Appeals of Georgia
237 Ga. App. 325; 514 S.E.2d 669, (1999)

FACTS AND CASE BACKGROUND

"Banker Fred L. O'Neal originated the idea of a new community bank in Villa Rica and expended significant effort to organize it. In the course of his work he recruited organizers for the bank who allegedly promised and assured him repeatedly that he would be compensated with employment by the bank for at least three years. Near the time it was organized the bank hired O'Neal, without written agreement or formal board approval of a multi-year contract. Four months later and after Home Town Bank of Villa Rica was formed, the board voted to terminate O'Neal, as an employee at will. O'Neal sued the bank and the organizers (collectively "bank") in multiple counts: breach of contract, quantum meruit, fraud, conspiracy, breach of fiduciary duty, intentional and negligent infliction of emotional distress, attorney fees and costs, securities fraud, and defamation, both slander and libel."

"O'Neal challenges the grant of summary judgment on each count. Summary judgment is authorized only when all undisputed facts and their reasonable inferences, viewed most favorably to the nonmoving party, preclude a triable issue as to at least one essential element of the case."

CASE DECISION: BEASLEY, PRESIDING JUDGE

1. BREACH OF CONTRACT

O'Neal contends he had a three-year contract identical to the written contract of the chief financial officer, Laura Cross, with only the salary differing. The salary was to be $65,000 for the first year, $67,500 for the second, and $70,000 for the third. He deposed that the organizers promised to put the agreement in writing but never did. On the other hand, he conceded the organizers asked him to prepare a written contract, but he never presented one to them. O'Neal was hired on March 10, 1997, and was terminated on July 15.

* * *

At best O'Neal's evidence supports a finding that leading up to the formation of the bank, O'Neal and the organizers repeatedly discussed that once it was formed the bank would hire O'Neal and give him a contract similar to that of the CFO. "Unless an agreement is reached as to all terms and conditions and nothing is left to future negotiations, a contract to enter into a contract in the future is of no effect." Because the terms of the alleged three-year agreement were not nailed down, it is not enforceable.

Second, O'Neal testified that the consideration he gave in exchange for the three-year employment agreement was his past effort to organize the bank. . . . The Court reasoned that past consideration generally will not support a subsequent promise, and the situation presented was no exception. This is so in part because the purported consideration was not rendered to the bank which had yet to be established when the promotion and organization took place. These services perhaps were rendered to benefit the organizers, but as shown above the agreement with the organizers is not enforceable.

Third, "a verbal contract for services to begin in the future and continue for a year [or more] is void under the Statute of Frauds."

In sum, what remains for trial are the claims of libel and corresponding costs and fees.

Judgment affirmed in part and reversed in part.

QUESTIONS FOR ANALYSIS

1. In what way is this case similar to the first case? Were the terms of the "agreement" between the plaintiff and defendant definite?
2. The plaintiff in this case, Fred O'Neal, claimed that there was consideration to support the promises made to him by the defendant. What was the consideration that O'Neal claimed he provided?

Preexisting Duty

If a person is already obligated to do something by law or to refrain from some action because of a legal prohibition, then for that person to agree not to violate the law is not legal consideration. Allegedly, organized crime used to approach store owners and offer "protection" contracts, which meant that if the store owner did not pay the protection money, the thugs in the criminal ring would burn down the store. A promise to refrain from violating a criminal statute, however, is not valid consideration because all citizens have a *preexisting duty to obey the law*. Of course, organized crime did not and does not generally look to the courts for enforcement of agreements.

Preexisting Contractual Duty

Assume that Carol has a contract to build a house for Craig and that the contract price is $100,000. If Craig claims that a strike by brick layers makes performance at $100,000 impossible, but agrees to complete construction for a total price of $110,000, the agreement to add an additional $10,000 to the contract price lacks consideration. This is the critical issue in the next case

reviewed. In order for the $110,000 contract price to be enforceable, Carol must perform an additional assignment. Building a $50 sandbox in the rear of the house, however, would enable Carol to collect the additional $10,000. Since this is a trivial subterfuge to get around a common law rule that is long on formalism but short on content, this rule has been abolished under the UCC, which allows for modifications of existing contracts without new consideration (see next chapter).

Illusory Promises

Some promises appear to contain consideration, but do not. Such promises are often called *illusory* promises. Again, recall that the foundation for consideration is that each promisor incurs a legal detriment. If the promisor does not incur a legal detriment, meaning that the promisor makes a promise that does not bind him or her in any way, the agreement lacks consideration and thus is not a contract. A promise by Keith to purchase as much grain as he wants to from Jerry does not bind Keith to any particular quantity and thus the promise lacks consideration. Even if Jerry had worked out price, quality, and delivery terms, a promise by Keith to purchase as much as he wants to does not bind Keith in any way.

Robert Chuckrow Construction Company v. *Gough*
Court of Appeals of Georgia
159 S.E.2d 469 (1968)

CASE BACKGROUND AND FACTS

The evidence adduced on the trial of this case on May 2, 1967, shows that the plaintiff (Gough) was a subcontractor of the defendant on a construction job known as the Kinney Shoe Store, having agreed with the defendant in a written contract dated April 30, 1965, to perform carpentry work required by the drawings and specifications for that building. A part of the carpentry work was the assembly and erection of wooden trusses, which supported the roof deck on the building. By the express provisions of the written contract, Gough undertook to "provide all labor and materials, scaffolding, tools, equipment

and all other things necessary for the prosecution and completion of the work in strict accordance with the drawings and specifications and job control chart. . ."

The written contract contained the following provisions: "Subcontractor hereby assumes entire responsibility and liability for any and all damage or injury of any kind or nature whatsoever . . . to all property caused by, resulting from, arising out of, or occurring in connection with the execution of the work provided for in this contract." Gough's employees had erected approximately 38 of the trusses on May 15, 1965, when 32 of them fell off the build-

ing. On the following Monday, Gough was told by the defendant's representative to remove the fallen trusses from the building, disassemble, inspect, rebuild, and re-erect them. Gough proceeded to remove the trusses that fell, inspect, rebuild where necessary and re-erect them. He also erected the balance of the trusses required to complete the roof truss structure and completed the carpentry work on the project. He was paid by the defendant all sums owed under the written contract of April 30, 1965, together with all charges for extra work except for the costs incurred by him in connection with the fallen trusses.

OPINION BY: QUILLIAN

The question on which the decision of the present case turns is whether the evidence adduced upon the trial showed the parol contract sued upon to be an enforceable agreement. Assent of the parties to the terms of the contract and a consideration for the performance of the same are essential requisites to its validity. Where either of these elements is lacking the contract is not binding or enforceable. [References deleted]

The plaintiff, under the terms of the parol agreement, assumed no obligation or duty that he was not bound to perform under the written contract he had previously entered into with the defendant. Under both the written contract and the oral agreement the defendant assumed the obligation to erect and properly place the same number of trusses to support the decking for the roof of the building.

The Supreme Court held in *Johnson* v. *Hinson,* 188 Ga. 639, 644 (4 SE2d 561): "An agreement on the part of one to do what he is already legally bound to do is not a sufficient consideration for the promise of another." A similar pronouncement of the principle is found in *Willingham Sash &c. Co.* v. *Drew,* 117 Ga. 850 (1, 2) (45 SE 237): "Where one undertakes to perform for another service or labor for a given sum any amount paid in excess of that sum, not based upon a new consideration, is a mere gratuity . . . A employed B to build a house for the sum of $1,400. A paid the $1,400 before the completion of the house; and it becoming apparent that B would be unable to comply with the contract without suffering loss, B was told by A to estimate what sum would be necessary to complete the building, and upon being informed that $350 would be required, B was told to complete the building and this amount would be paid in addition. Under this latter arrangement B was to do only what was contemplated by the original contract. After the $1,400 had been paid and before the payment of the $350, A was served with a summons of garnishment in a suit against B, and judgment was rendered in favor of the garnishee. *Held:* (1) That the agreement to pay the additional sum of $350 was a nudum pactum. (2) That at the time of the service of the summons of garnishment the relation of debtor and creditor did not exist between A and B."

* * *

The court went on to hold that the agreement was based on a preexisting contractual obligation and therefore was not enforceable because it lacked consideration.

QUESTIONS FOR ANALYSIS

1. Explain in layman's terms why the court ruled that the defendant was not bound to pay the plaintiff extra money for the reassembled trusses?
2. What should the plaintiff have done to make the subsequent agreement binding. Hint: What does any promisee have to do to make an agreement binding?

Similarly, a promise by a promisor to perform in a certain way, coupled with the retention of the right to cancel at anytime for any reason without notice, does **not** bind the promisor. There is no consideration if the promisor does not incur a legal detriment and retention of the right to cancel at any time does not in any way curtail any activity that the promisor may have wanted to pursue. It is important to note, however, that small changes in illusory promises can create the necessary consideration for a binding contract. If the promisor promises to purchase a quantity of widgets from the promisee while retaining the right to cancel, but the promisor also promises to provide *notice* before cancelling, there is consideration. Also if the promisor promises not to cancel unless some valid reason occurs, consideration is present.

Effect of Lack of Consideration

The effect of lack of consideration is that the agreement is left unenforceable. Either party to an agreement that does not have consideration can rescind or cancel the contract. The promisor may have made a binding promise, but if the other party to the agreement did not make a promise that had consideration, the party that agreed to be bound can cancel the contract.

Capacity

Unrestricted freedom to contract assumes that both parties to a contract are capable of looking out for their own self-interest. For some people that assumption is questionable either because they are too young or are otherwise disabled mentally. In general, both parties to a contract must have legal *capacity* to contract or else the resulting contract is voidable based on incompetence (lack of capacity). When a minor or a mental incompetent uses lack of capacity to escape contractual obligations, he or she is said to *disaffirm* the contract, which is basically the same as voiding the contract.

Minors

The contractual age of capacity is 18 in most states. A contract between a minor and an adult can be voided or *disaffirmed* at the option of the minor. In other words, the minor can sign a contract, receive the consideration, such as a new CD player, and then later decide to *disaffirm* the contract and get his or her money back. If the minor has the consideration such as a CD player, he must return it, but in most states the minor's right to disaffirm is not contingent upon return of consideration. If the minor loses the consideration or the consideration is damaged or wrecked, the minor can still disaffirm. In contrast, the adult party to a contract with a minor cannot use the minor's lack of capacity and cancel or disaffirm the contract due to lack of capacity on the part of the minor.

Another Impact of the Internet   The Internet is a great equalizer. The clicks of rich and poor, great and not so great all have the same impact on machines. In face to face transactions the vendor can immediately discern that the potential buyer may not be eighteen or the legal contracting age and can demand identification. E-Commerce facilitates purchases by minors because their age is not detectable, forcing online vendors to collect more information about the purported buyer and perhaps only accepting purchases through a credit card. In spite of these precautions, Internet purchases by minors are disaffirmable as with any other contract.

Ratification

Upon turning 18, the minor still has the power to disaffirm the contract, but that option is limited to a short period of time. If the minor makes a payment on a contract after turning 18, the minor will be deemed to have *ratified* the contract. For contracts that straddle minority and majority status, once a contract is ratified it becomes a valid contract. If a minor simply does nothing after turning 18 or continues using the consideration called for under the contract, the minor loses the right to disaffirm and the contract is deemed ratified.

Exceptions

While the law of contracts is structured with the socially desirable goal of protecting minors from foolish decisions, the resulting right of minors to disaffirm can make doing business with minor customers very risky. If contracts with minors are disaffirmable at the option of the minor, then banks (which can make student loans), sports agents, and a host of others who sometimes deal with minors, will not do so. Complicating this situation, the right of minors to escape contract obligations is filled with exceptions regarding the dis-

affirmability of educational loans, insurance contracts, and agency agreements, and the exceptions allowed differ from state to state.

Most states have an exception in the case of *necessaries*. An adult party who contracts to supply a minor with **necessary** goods and services (food, clothing, shelter, and job-related products such as employment placement services and even automobiles) can recover the *fair market value* of the necessary from the minor or his parents. Even with numerous exceptions to the right to disaffirm, engaging in business transactions that require formal contracts with a minor brings considerable risk as courts are very intolerant of sharp dealing that harms a minor even if the consideration is a necessary.

Adults Who Are Incompetents

Adults can become incompetent to participate in contracts due to a number of causes. Illustratively, an adult who becomes so intoxicated with alcohol or drugs that she does not know the consequences of the contract she signs is an incompetent and thus can later disaffirm the contract. The test of incapacity due to alcohol or drugs is different than those used by the police to determine if a person is driving under the influence (DUI). A person could be legally drunk (legally incompetent) for purposes of operating a motor vehicle while still having contractual capacity. To disaffirm a contract due to intoxication, the adult must have been "totally bombed" at the time and the disaffirmance must occur within a short period of regaining sobriety.

Mental Illness   A contract with someone who has been judged incompetent by the state is void and is no contract at all. People who live at mental institutions or have guardians appointed by the state to act on their behalf are incompetents and have no capacity to contract. In some contracts, an adult can claim incapacity to contract based on temporary incapacity due to mental illness such as extreme depression, schizophrenia, or other mental disorders. The temporarily incompetent adult can disaffirm upon regaining mental faculties, or, if a guardian is appointed, the guardian can use incapacity at the time the contract was executed to disaffirm. Generally, in order to disaffirm the adult must return the contract consideration. Also be aware that the rules regarding contracts with incompetents vary from state to state.

Legality

Contracts must be *legal* to be valid. Such a statement may seem tautological but, in contract law, legality has a specific meaning that is not immediately obvious. Certainly if performance of the contract entails a violation of a statute, state or federal, the contract is void due to illegality. Among such illegal contracts that sometimes affect businesses are contracts that involve gambling, contracts between unlicensed professionals and clients, and loans with interest charges that exceed legal limits (usury laws).

Contracts Contrary to Statutes: Gambling

A state can outlaw gambling, even though it is sometimes unclear what the difference is between illegal gambling and involvement in stock market speculation and other risky ventures. Gambling, in law, involves the *creation of risk that had no prior existence* whereas speculation, hedging, and other risky ventures essentially involve transference of risk from one party to another rather than creation of risk. In a parallel vein, taking out a life insurance policy on someone who is not related to you in any way, either by family or business connections, is akin to betting on a person's life. In fact, such insurance **contracts create a risk that had no prior existence** and an incentive (sometimes called *moral hazard*) on the part of the beneficiary of the insurance contract to have the insured meet an untimely demise.

Usury Laws

Many states have usury statutes that limit the amount of interest that can be charged on various types of loans. The usury limits on interest vary from state to state and vary within states, depending on the type of loan: personal, mortgage, or business. In some states the penalty for usurious loans is forfeiture of all interest, and in some states the creditor forfeits both principal and interest for loans with interest rates that exceed legal limits.

Licensing Requirements

In all states practitioners of various professions and occupations must be licensed. Among the professions and occupations for which licenses are required are law, medicine, plumbers, beauticians, and morticians, just to name a few. For the foregoing professionals and others who are required to obtain licenses to practice, a competency exam is generally required as well as educational attainments and sometimes apprenticeships. Contracts with unlicensed professionals are illegal and void at law. A client contracting with an unlicensed professional can receive professional services and then refuse to pay the professional. The courts will not protect unlicensed professionals.

Online Distribution of Illegal Products   The Internet facilitates sales of illegal and quasi-legal products. The website Buy Steroids Online (http://www.buy-steroids-online.nu/) offers to sell anabolic steroids online in advertisements that feature bodybuilders. Other websites sell Viagra, a prescription medicine, online after a doctor examines the purchaser online and then writes a prescription. Online gambling is easily accessible through hundreds of sites, most of which are located in other countries. The anonymity of the Internet has made heretofore risky and illegal transactions a lot less risky for vendors and purchasers. Customers of illegal and quasi-legal websites should be aware that since the contracts are illegal they are void and the courts will not allow themselves to be used to obtain a return of money or other consideration. Dealing with the quasi-legal websites that peddle drugs or offer opportunities to gamble is strictly a caveat emptor (buyer beware) endeavour.

Contracts Contrary to Public Policy

Contracts that Are Unconscionable   Certain contracts have been held unconscionable and thus void at law. Some contracts are unconscionable because they are written to excuse liability for intentional actions of one party. It is common in high-risk sports activities, such as hang-gliding and bungee-jumping, for operators to secure contractual waivers of liability from participants for negligence on the part of operators or employees of the business. The operator is concerned that if someone is injured, there will be a costly and uncertain lawsuit that could cost millions if the business loses. By signing waivers of liability, customers acknowledge the risks and voluntarily assume these risks. If operators of these establishments, however, try to obtain complete waivers of liability for all actions of employees of these establishments, including intentionally harmful actions, the courts will declare the contract unconscionable.

Entities that Owe Duties to the Public   Airlines, inn-keepers, banks, and utilities are all restricted by unconscionability constraints from requiring customers to sign a contract that absolves them of liability for various acts of negligence. If a business has a duty to the public and is in some sense unavoidable, such as in the case of a common carrier (an airline),

Cevern, Inc. v. *Ferbish*
District of Columbia Court of Appeals
666 A.2d 17, (1995)

FACTS AND CASE BACKGROUND

"Cevern, Inc., the appellant, brought an action to establish a mechanic's lien on the home of appellees Robert Ferbish and Viola Stanton. Cevern sought to recoup a balance of $10,295.61 it said was owed to it for work performed under a home improvement contract with Thelma Ferbish, also an appellee, who allegedly acted as the owners' agent. Appellees counterclaimed, alleging that they had expended $43,600 to correct Cevern's work."

"On August 24, 1992, the scheduled date of trial, counsel for appellees orally moved for summary judgment, asserting that Cevern was not licensed at the time it entered into the home improvement contract. The trial judge granted the motion the next day on the ground that "[Cevern] was not a licensed contractor at the time it received payment on the home improvement contract. . . . notwithstanding the fact that [Cevern] subsequently received a valid license before the work was completed." The judge also rejected Cevern's claim for recovery in quasi-contract. At appellees' request, he dismissed without prejudice their counterclaim. On September 3, 1992, Cevern moved for reconsideration of the judgment, which the trial judge denied. Also, pursuant to a request in appellees' opposition, the judge entered judgment in their favor for $14,000, the amount counsel for appellees stated they had paid to Cevern. (To do so, the judge on his

own motion reinstated the counterclaim and deemed it amended to demand restitution)."

CASE DECISION: FARRELL, ASSOCIATE JUDGE

In entering judgment for appellees for $14,000 in restitution, the trial judge declared that, under this court's decisions, "a contract made in violation of a licensing statute that is designed to protect the public will usually be considered void and unenforceable, and the party violating the statute cannot collect monies due on a quasi-contractual basis." Therefore, since Cevern accepted an advance payment from appellees on August 31, 1990 it could recover neither in contract nor in quantum meruit. The fact that Cevern acquired a license before completing the contracted-for work, and before receiving the balance of payment therefor, did not avail it. The judge explained:

> The purpose of licensing statutes would be frustrated if recovery were permitted for work performed without a license. . . . This rationale equally applies to situations where the contract is entered before the issuance of a license, or where some of the preliminary work is done before a license is issued, and a balance of the work is completed after the license has issued. . . . Such a "straddle" arrangement would also run afoul of the underlying rationale for the statutory and

regulatory scheme in this area of the law.

In the District of Columbia it is a principle of long standing that an illegal contract, made in violation of a statutory prohibition designed for police or regulatory purposes, is void and confers no right upon the wrongdoer. This rule applies to a breach, a prohibitory regulation enacted to protect the public. . . . Therefore, we have oft held that receipt of payment by an unlicensed contractor before completion of the work under the contract violates the home improvement regulations and renders the contract void and unenforceable, even on a quasi-contractual basis.

* * *

The judgment of the Superior Court is *Affirmed*.

QUESTIONS FOR ANALYSIS

1. Is the court saying that the plaintiff cannot recover because he is not licensed, or that he was not licensed at the time the contract was signed?

2. At the time of the contract, did it matter that the defendant, who had paid Cevern $14,000, was also participating in an illegal contract? Are licensing statutes tilted towards the nonlicensed party in contract law? Why do you think that this tilt may be true? What is the purpose of the licensing statutes?

then contracts that negate liability for negligence are unconscionable. As an example, airlines are prohibited from absolving themselves of liability for lost luggage, although there are statutory caps on liability per piece of luggage. If the contents of their luggage are especially valuable, customers are encouraged to pay more for insurance to alert the airlines that their luggage is especially valuable, and to provide notice that extra precautions should be undertaken in its handling.

Disparities in Education and Access to Resources
Contracts are sometimes declared unconscionable on an *ad hoc* basis. This can occur if the bargain is especially *unfair* and if one of the parties to the contract is much less educated and sophisticated, while the other party makes use of high-powered attorneys and fine print in contracts to surprise the other party. Courts and even state legislatures have intervened, in some cases, to prevent unpleasant surprises for the less educated party by prohibiting fine print warranty disclaimers (warranty disclaimers are discussed in the next chapter).

Contracts in Restraint of Trade   A legacy from English common law is court determination to closely scrutinize trade restraints. A *covenant not to compete* is sometimes contained in employment contracts. Employment contracts that prohibit ex-employees from ever working in an industry upon terminating employment are considered unreasonable trade restraints and thus unconscionable. Employers and others can enforce contracts that have covenants not to

compete, but these clauses must be limited in time and space. For highly skilled programmers, a computer company may be able to enforce a prohibition on the programmer working for a rival within two years of separation of employment. Covenants not to compete also often accompany the sale of a company by which the owner(s) of the company being purchased agree not to set up a rival firm for a period of time in a certain area.

Geographic Dimensions of Cyberspace   Covenants not to compete were traditionally enforceable only if limited in time and space. A measuring stick as to the geographic limits of the covenant was the area where the ex-employer actually makes sales. With the World Wide Web, all firms with a website literally are (1) advertising to the world and (2) can make sales throughout the world. Also since so much work is electronic, the need for employees to come to a central location is attenuated. An ex-employee with valuable trade secrets could work for a nearby rival of his former employer while being physically located out of state and perhaps out of the jurisdiction of the courts in the former employer's state.

General Commercial Packaging, Inc., Plaintiff-Appellant, v. *TPS Package Engineering, Inc.*
United States Court of Appeals for the Ninth Circuit
126 F.3d 1131 (1997)

BACKGROUND AND FACTS
General Commercial Packaging (General Commercial) provides packing and crating services to businesses in Florida and California. It was hired by its long-standing customer, Walt Disney Companies (Disney), to package materials for transport to the new EuroDisneyland, and sought a subcontractor to help with the work in California. General Commercial ultimately chose defendant TPS Package Engineering (TPS).

To protect its business relationships with Disney and other California customers, General Commercial required TPS to sign a

contract containing the following provision before beginning work on the EuroDisneyland Project:

TPS agrees, that during the term of this contract, and for one year after termination of this contract, that neither TPS nor any of its employees will back-solicit or otherwise deal directly with Walt Disney Companies, its affiliates and subsidiaries, or any other company which G.C.P. Inc. has introduced to and contracted with TPS to perform packing and crating subcontracting services. TPS agrees that any work it directly

provides to or performs for any G.C.P. Inc. client without G.C.P. Inc. involvement or approval will result in a sales commission automatically and retroactively applied to all such transactions of 25% of Gross Invoice to the client payable in full from TPS to G.C.P. Inc.

Within a period of one year after signing a contract with plaintiff, General Commercial Packaging, defendant began dealing directly with the Disney Corporation. The plaintiff sues for breach of the covenant not to contract with Disney.

OPINION: PER CURIAM

Under California law, "every contract by which anyone is restrained from engaging in a lawful profession, trade, or business of any kind is to that extent void." Cal. Bus. & Prof. Code § 16600. Although TPS raised no objection to the clause which precluded it from dealing directly with Disney—thereby cementing a highly profitable subcontracting relationship with General Commercial—it now claims that section 16600 renders its promise void. TPS reads section 16600 to nullify "every part of every contract that restricts a person from pursuing, in whole or in part, any trade, business or profession." [Reference deleted] The contract it signed, TPS concludes, is invalid because it prohibits TPS from infiltrating Disney's corner of the packing and shipping market.

We rejected this strict interpretation of section 16600 in *Campbell* v. *Board of Trustees of Leland Stanford Junior Univ.*, 817 F.2d 499 (9th Cir. 1987). The plaintiff in *Campbell*, a psychologist responsible for developing a widely used career counseling test, signed a contract with Stanford University promising not to engage in any activities that might "injure the sale of" the test. *Id.* at 501. In deciding whether the contract violated section 16600, we stated:

> Even though the California
> Legislature rejected the

common-law rule that "reasonable" restraints of trade are generally enforceable, it did not make all restrictions unenforceable. . . . "While the cases are uniform in refusing to enforce a contract wherein one is restrained from pursuing an entire business, trade or profession . . . , where one is barred from pursuing only a small or limited part of the business, trade or profession, the contract has been upheld as valid."

* * *

General Commercial's contract with TPS is therefore valid unless it "completely restrains" TPS from plying its trade or business. In considering this question, we recognize that a contract does not have to impair a party's access to every potential customer to contravene section 16600. Because most businesses cannot succeed with only a handful of customers, a contract can effectively destroy a signatory's ability to conduct a trade or business by placing a substantial segment of the market off limits. This explains why courts have been less tolerant of contracts that prohibit employees from soliciting all of their former employers' customers.

TPS has never disputed General Commercial's claim that the con-

tract "does *not* prohibit TPS from engaging in the crating and packing business.' Nor could it. The agreement only precludes TPS from dealing with Disney and those other firms which General Commercial "has introduced to *and* contracted with TPS to perform packing and crating subcontracting services." Apart from Disney, TPS was not barred from soliciting work from any firm with which it had a prior relationship. The contract thus only limits TPS's access to a narrow segment of the packing and shipping market.

The district court's order granting TPS's motion for summary judgment on Count I of its complaint is reversed. The breach of contract claim is remanded to the district court for consideration of any remaining defenses which TPS may have raised.

QUESTIONS FOR ANALYSIS

1. Since this covenant not to compete was ruled legal, what kind of covenant not to compete would fail the criterion laid out by this California Court?
2. Why would the courts treat a covenant not to compete differently if it applied to a business as opposed to an employee? What situation are the courts concerned about?

GENUINENESS OF ASSENT

Freedom of contract is not respected when the agreement is tainted by proof that the agreement was obtained as a result of mistake, fraud, misrepresentation, undue influence, or duress. The effect of showing that the agreement is tainted is that the contract becomes voidable at the option of the injured party. Thus, fraud, for example, can be used as a *defense* in a breach of contract suit by the defendant, claiming that he is not going to perform because he was induced into the con-

tract only because the plaintiff lied to him. Often victims of fraud sue to *rescind* a contract so that they can get back their money or other consideration transferred. On the other hand, if the victim of fraud decides to go ahead with the contract, the defrauding party must perform or risk a lawsuit.

Mistake

If both parties to a contract are mistaken as to a material fact, either party can void the contract. In order for a mistake to be voidable, the mistake must be mutual, or must be an error about which one party knows or should have known that the other party is mistaken. In one famous "classic" case from history, both parties to a sales contract involving cotton believed that the cotton would arrive in England from Bombay, India on board of a ship called the *Peerless*.[3] Unknown to each party, there were two ships named *Peerless* that left Bombay within a few months of each other. When the first *Peerless* arrived, the buyer purchased his cotton but when the second *Peerless* arrived, the seller sued because the buyer refused to purchase the contracted-for cotton. The buyer was able to escape contractual liability by showing that the parties to the contract had made a mutual mistake about two *Peerless* ships.

Construction contracts on major projects are often formed when general contractors are asked to submit bids. If six contractors submitted bids, five of which were between $900,000 and $1.1 million, but one bid was $100,000, it is fairly obvious that the last bid was due to a typing mistake. The owner of the construction site could not snap up the $100,000 bid because he would have known, or should have known, that the contractor had made a mistake.

Fraud and Misrepresentation

Fraud takes place when one party to a contract knowingly lies about an important fact to the other party who reasonably relies on those lies and suffers damages as a result. Although there are various definitions of contractual fraud, most would agree that if the plaintiff showed the following, he would have proved fraud:[4]

1. **Misrepresentation of an important fact.** Fraud takes place when the fraudulent party says something that relates to the contract that is not true. Students should distinguish false statements of fact from **opinions** about a future event. In general, opinions are not the basis for fraud. **Professional opinions,** however, can be a foundation for fraud. If an attorney offers an opinion about the legal impact of a document and that opinion is false, fraud can exist if the other elements of fraud are present.
2. **Scienter.** This is knowledge that the statements made are false.

3. **Intent to defraud.** The purpose of the lies (knowing misrepresentations of material facts) was to induce the other party to enter into a contract.
4. The nonfraudulent party **reasonably relied** on the fraudulent statements. If the alleged victim of fraud does not take the ordinary precautions of businesspeople, then the courts will not bail out an allegedly defrauded party to a contract.
5. The fraud is the **proximate cause** of the victim's **damages.** As discussed earlier, proximate cause is legal causation, which takes place when damages are reasonably foreseeable and there is a direct link between the fraud and the victim's damages.

If fraud is shown, the contract involving fraud is voidable at the option of the victim and the victim can sue for damages. If **misrepresentation** is shown (fraud without the intent elements, 2. and 3. above), the contract is voidable, but a suit for damages is not allowed. If Nancy, the owner and seller of a house, asserts that the foundation of the house is sound, while knowing that subsidence (the foundation is sinking) is taking place, she has committed fraud. If Nancy was unaware of the subsidence and states that the foundation of her house is intact, she has made an innocent misrepresentation. If a buyer relied on her sincere belief that the foundation was sound, the buyer could get his money back when the subsidence was detected. If the misrepresentation by Nancy was not innocent, the buyer may be able to recover for other expenses associated with the purchase of the house and lost opportunities elsewhere.

Duress

A contract that is the result of force, threat of force, threat of criminal prosecution, or blackmail is voidable at the option of the victim. Note that a contract that is the result of the threat of civil litigation is a valid *settlement*. In some cases an agreement between the parties is tainted by economic blackmail. Economic blackmail can take place when a large corporation has more than one contract with another, smaller firm that has cash flow problems. Courts have allowed duress as a defense in economic blackmail cases when the large firm extracted a harsh bargain in subsequent contracts by threatening to withhold valid cash payments in the current contract.

---

[3]Court of Exchequer, England, 1864. 159 Eng. Rep. 375.

[4]Note that the elements of contractual fraud are the same as for tortious fraud or deceit.

Undue Influence

There are certain relationships that require one party not to take advantage of the other party. For example, attorneys are supposed to put the interest of their clients above their own in business transactions. In many family situations, a stronger party has a duty to not take advantage of a weaker party, particularly if the weaker party is ill or is much less educated or sophisticated. Undue influence makes a contract voidable at the option of the weaker party if (1) the bargain is objectively unfair, (2) the stronger party owed a fiduciary duty to the weaker party or the weaker party was in a weakened mental state and (3) the weaker party had no access to outside counsel. In order to negate charges of undue influence, particularly when dealing with family members, a person should insist that the family member see an outside attorney or accountant. Professionals who have business dealings with clients similarly should insist that the client consult a nonaffiliated financial advisor before contracting with a client.

WRITING REQUIREMENTS AND THE STATUTE OF FRAUDS

Most contracts are enforceable even though they are not in writing. There are six types of contracts, however, and these contracts are **'important'** contracts that must be in writing to be enforceable. These six types of contracts, listed below, should be thought of as exceptions to the general rule that oral agreements can be valid contracts, provided the agreement can be proved by a preponderance of the evidence in court. The following contracts are not enforceable unless they are in writing:

1. *Surety contracts,* in which a surety promises a creditor that if a covered debtor does not pay the amount owed on a loan, that he, the surety, will make the payment. Bonding companies, which are often required in government contracts, are sureties.
2. Contracts in which an *executor to a will agrees to be personally liable* for the debts of the deceased.
3. Contracts, which by their terms, *cannot be performed within one year.* For example, a two-year employment contract cannot be performed within one year.

4. *Marriage contracts,* including prenuptial agreements, must be in writing. Marriage contracts are not so significant nowadays with the demise of dowries, but prenuptial agreements are increasingly common.
5. Any contract significantly involving *real estate* including sales, mortgages (real property is collateral for a loan), easements, drilling rights, and insurance contracts.
6. Contracts involving the *sale of goods* when the sales price exceeds *$500.* This is a UCC rule. Under proposed revisions to the UCC, the new limit will be $5,000.

Exceptions to the Exceptions

The general rule is that oral contracts are enforceable as long as the terms of an agreement can be proved. The six types of exceptional contracts listed above must be in writing, but there are exceptions to these six categories. If the elements of *promissory estoppel* are present, promises made with respect to one of these six categories are still enforceable. Notable among other exceptions that apply to the six **important** contracts are:

1. In a surety contract, if the surety orally promises the debtor that he (the surety) will pay the debtor's debt to the creditor, the *creditor* can enforce this oral promise made by the surety (as a third-party beneficiary of the contract, discussed below).
2. In some states there is part performance exception to oral contracts for the sale of real estate. If the buyer takes possession of the real estate, makes significant improvements to the land and buildings, and/or pays some or all of the purchase price, then an oral sale of real estate is an enforceable contract.
3. Under the UCC there are three exceptions to the rule that contracts for the sale of goods whose price in total exceeds $500 must be in writing.

Parity between Paper and Electronic Records?
Increasingly, business is being conducted online and an issue has arisen as to whether electronic records are to be treated the same as paper records. This topic is very controversial and is discussed in some detail in the next chapter. The short answer is generally "yes," but there are numerous exceptions in which electronic records are not given the same legal effect as paper records.

Sufficiency of the Writings

If writing is required, the writing does not have to be on one piece of paper. The courts have pieced together contracts that consisted of letters, internal memoranda, invoices, and purchase orders. Increasingly, electronic records have parity with paper records (see Chapter 8). At a minimum the writings must identify the parties to the contract, the subject matter of the contract, the price, the quantity, and all other material terms. The relevant common law rule is mechanistic in its application of the need for writings, while the UCC is liberal in supplying missing terms from **prior conduct** of the parties, **trade usage,** and the **UCC gap-fillers.** *UCC gap-fillers* include reasonable terms as to when money is due, delivery terms, risk of loss terms, and other material terms that may not appear in the writings.

Parol Evidence Rule

Whether a writing is required or not, if there is a written contract, the *parol evidence rule* operates to exclude outside or extrinsic evidence. If, for example, in a contract suit, one party claims that the other party orally assured him that "the company never enforces the warranty disclaimers in boldface print near the signature line," evidence of such an oral statement would be excluded under the parol evidence rule. The parol evidence rule also excludes outside writings that are in conflict with a written contract. If the parties want to exclude all outside evidence, it is common for a contract to include an *integration* clause that states that the complete agreement between the parties is contained within the four corners of the written agreement.

Even with integration clauses, outside or parol evidence is not excluded if the extrinsic evidence is submitted to clear up incomplete or ambiguous agreements, or if the parol evidence is submitted to prove fraud or other taints on the agreement. Without an integration clause, evidence of a trade usage or prior course of dealing is admissible to courts and juries in understanding what the parties agreed to in the written contract. To avoid court usage of such extraneous evidence, integration clauses are used.

PERFORMANCE AND DISCHARGE OF CONTRACTUAL OBLIGATIONS

In most cases, the contractual obligations of both parties to a contract are discharged without liability by the performances called for in the contract. For contracts involving the sale of goods, the required performance is governed by the UCC perfect tender rule (discussed in the next chapter). For all other contracts, a less than perfect performance can entitle the promisor to the contracted for consideration (generally money) minus the cost of repair. In a construction contract, if there are minor discrepancies between performance called for in the contract and that which is offered, the builder is entitled to the contract price minus the costs incurred by the owner to make the house conform to what was called for in the contract.

If the performance offered by a party fails in the *essential purpose* of the contract, then such performance amounts to a *material* breach. In a construction contract if the house is so poorly constructed that the building inspector will not issue a certificate of occupancy certifying that the dwelling is fit for human inhabitation, then the builder has failed in the *essential* purpose of the contract. In some cases, late performance is considered a material breach. If the promisee wants to make clear beforehand that late performance is a material breach, the promisee should insist on a time-is-of-the essence clause. Whether performance offered by the promisor constitutes *substantial performance,* which fulfills the essential purpose of the contract, or whether a material breach has occurred is for juries to decide. If the promisor materially breaches a contract, the obligation of the promisee to pay money to the promisor is eliminated.

Delegation of Duties

For the vast bulk of contracts, the promisor is a business and responsibility for performing is *delegated* to employees. In general, all contractual duties can be delegated to employees or others who are willing to perform the duties called for in the contract. In some contracts, the special skills of the promisor are the reason the contract was formed, in which case the duties of the promisor cannot be delegated. Again, a promisee that does not want ambiguity on this topic can simply insert a clause in the contract that prohibits delegations because of the special skills of the promisor. Star athletes and featured entertainers possess unique skills that cannot be delegated. If a promoter contracted with Eminem to perform at an outdoor stadium, Marshall Mathers (Eminem's "real" name) could not delegate his promise to perform to a local "garage" band.

The party to whom the duties of the contract are delegated is the delegatee. If performance is unsatisfactory, the promisee cannot sue the delegatee for breaching the contract because there is no privity of contract between the parties. The promisee can only look to and sue the delegator, who is generally the employer of the delegatee.

Assignment of the Benefits of a Contract

If Jack buys a car from Smith Automobiles, he probably would want to "finance" the purchase, paying for the car in installments. Smith Automobiles may have expertise in selling cars, but may be reluctant to evaluate the creditworthiness of Jack as well as service the loan, incur collection expenses, etc. It is common for automobile dealerships to assign their installment sales contracts to banks or other financial institutions. The bank or other financing institution will pay a discounted cash amount to the car dealership, then assume responsibility for collecting the loan.

In a typical installment sales contract, the seller becomes an assignor when he accepts money from a financial institution in return for the assignment. As assignee, the "bank" is responsible for *notifying* the purchaser that payments are to be made to it, not to the car dealership. Suppose the car malfunctions and the purchaser claims that it wants the car repaired first before continuing to make payments on the car. In general, assignees (banks) take the benefit of the contract subject to defenses that the purchaser had against the seller (assignor). In other words, if the purchaser had a defense against the seller, that defense is good against the assignee.

In general the benefits of any contract can be assigned as long as the obligations of the promisor/obligor (often a purchaser) are not increased by the assignment. Also assignments are prohibited when the promisor/obligor is required to perform personal services for the promisee. A manservant may be willing to serve an English aristocrat, but that same servant may object to serving a rock star whose lifestyle is much different. An assignee steps into the shoes of the assignor, which means that if the purchaser/obligor does not live up to his obligations, the assignee can sue for breach of contract.

Third Party Beneficiaries

If the purpose of a contract is to benefit a third party, the promisor who fails to perform can be sued by either the promisee or the third party beneficiary. If Jim divorces Mary and, as part of the divorce settlement, promises to pay for his daughter Jenny's college edu-

cation, then when Jenny graduates from high school, she is the intended beneficiary of the contract between Jim and Mary. If Jim does not pay for Jenny's college education, either or both Mary or Jenny could sue Jim. In the divorce settlement, Jenny was a *donee* beneficiary, indicating that Jim was intending to make a gift to Jenny. In other cases, the third party beneficiary is owed money by the promisee and the promisor has promised to pay or perform services for the *creditor* beneficiary.

In many contracts, a third party is *incidentally* benefited by performance by the promisor. For example, if a fertilizer company makes timely deliveries to a plant nursery, a beekeeper located up the road will benefit, because his bees will expend less energy obtaining nectar for honey-making. However, since the purpose of the contract between the fertilizer company and the plant nursery was not to benefit the beekeeper, the beekeeper, as an *incidental* beneficiary, would have no standing to sue if the fertilizer company did not deliver as promised.

Discharge of Contractual Obligations

Material Breach

As mentioned above, if one party to a contract materially breaches the contract, the contractual obligations of the other party are discharged. If an employee fails to show up for work, the employer does not have to pay the employee. In some cases, a promisor knows in advance that he is not going to perform on a contract and announces to the other party that performance is unlikely. Such behavior is characterized as an *anticipatory breach* and it too discharges the other party from contractual obligations. The victim of an anticipatory breach can sue immediately (for breach of contract) while terminating any performance called for under the contract, or the nonbreaching party could encourage the other party to reconsider and perform as promised.

Rescission

Sometimes both parties to a contract decide that they want to end the contract. If both sides still have promises to fulfill, then they can agree to cancel the contract and each side will have consideration because they are both giving up something of value (the right to receive the benefit of performance from the other party). If only one party to a contract has promises to fulfill, then there must be consideration for the agreement to cancel that performance. The consideration requirement could be satisfied by the promisor agreeing to perform some trivial task, in return for the agreement by the promisee not to sue for failure to perform.

Note further that "victims" (minors, defrauded parties, mistaken parties) in voidable contracts can sue to rescind a contract, thus relieving them of their obligation to perform. The motivation behind rescission is to return the parties to the positions they occupied before the contract was formed. In ordinary English, most suits to rescind voidable contracts are suits by victims (of say fraud) to recover lost consideration, generally money.

Novation

Imagine a contract between A and B. A novation occurs when A agrees that the previous contract with B is now a contract between A and C. An effect of a novation is that A can no longer sue B, once A has agreed to look to C for performance. Novations are common when businesses are formed. Suppliers and creditors initially require personal signatures of the lead shareholders in a newly formed business. As the business establishes itself and its creditworthiness, creditors and suppliers will accept a substitution of the obligations of the original shareholders (the Bs in this contract) for those of the newly formed business (C).

Accord and Satisfaction

It is common in business that contractual expectations may not be realized while a contract is in existence. Rather than suing, or walking away from the contract, the parties may negotiate a new *accord*. When the terms of that new accord are performed, a *satisfaction* takes place. Contract modifications are common and the only legal pitfall that occasionally accompanies the recontracting is that there must be consideration for contract modifications.[5] With an accord and satisfaction the same (original contracting) parties make a new agreement whereas, with a novation, new parties agree to abide by the same (old) contract.

Discharge by Operation of Law

The same factors discussed above in relation to termination of an offer are present after a contract has been formed to terminate contractual obligations. A promisor's obligations under a contract are discharged

---

[5]Under the UCC, contracts can be modified without consideration.

without liability if, subsequent to formation, the promisor dies, becomes incapacitated, declares bankruptcy, or performance is declared illegal due to a change in the law.

Discharge Due to Impossibility

Closely related to discharge by operation of law is discharge due to *impossibility*. In fact, there are several legal excuses under **impossibility** that overlap with operation of law. According to some sources, a legal change subsequent to formation of a contract that makes performance illegal creates a discharge due to impossibility. Other legal excuses due to impossibility include war, Acts of God, incapacity, or death of the promisor. Under the UCC, more excuses for not performing are allowed under the concept of *impracticability*.

Objective Impossibility   Under either standard it is important to distinguish the comment, "I cannot perform" from, "It cannot be accomplished." Only the latter statement can be the foundation for the legal excuse of impossibility. Under both concepts it is assumed that the promisor has made a good faith attempt to perform, but circumstances beyond his control have made performance impossible, or at least extremely difficult. These circumstances are to be distinguished from ordinary price changes or weather changes that are normal risks of doing business.

When the promisor is allowed to escape contractual liability by claiming impossibility, the expectations of the promisee are dashed. When the defendant in a contract case tries to show impossibility, courts are being asked to decide whether the particular event, a strike, war, a legal change, was a risk that the promisee was willing to bear at the start of the contract. If the answer is yes, then the promisor will be able to escape liability. To avoid legal surprise, the parties can insert clauses into a contract that make explicit what risks the promisee is willing to bear. Often the parties to a contract make use of a *force de majure* clause, which excuses performance in the event of war, legal change, and Acts of God. Obviously, these clauses could be tailored to particular contracts.

Discharge Due to the Occurrence or Nonoccurrence of a Condition

Parties to a contract can condition performance on events that are within or outside the control of the

Be Careful What You Sign

An abusive broker can cause you to take a margin loan without knowing it—and you'll still have to repay. Maybe you didn't want to buy that particular stock. Maybe you never intended to borrow. Maybe the loan was technically illegal. Tough luck. That loan is yours. Even if you noticed the loan immediately and ordered the broker to desist, your objection won't count unless you file it in a very particular way (for the secret, read on).

Anyway, that's the current state of the law. "Consumer protection" for margin borrowers is a joke. You can even be sued by the Securities Investor Protection Corp. (SIPC), which you probably thought would leap to your defense.

This brings me to Judy and Arnold Hyman of Boynton Beach, Fla., now retired. The Hymans used to own three dry-cleaning stores. For years they've kept their money in mutual funds.

But then their sons, Mark and Bill, decided to try day trading for a living. They hitched up with Cygnet Securities in Waldwick, N.J., and imagined they could do low-risk trading with high returns. Bill, 37, told his folks it would be a big help if they opened Cygnet accounts for him to trade. They did, in 1995. They didn't invest a penny of their retirement savings; they just signed the papers. "You'd do anything for your children," Judy Hyman says.

Fast forward to 1997. Cygnet failed. George Swan, Cygnet's owner, agreed to let the National Association of Securities Dealers bar him from the securities business for making unauthorized trades in customers' accounts. W S. Clearing, Inc., the firm that handled Cygnet's back-office business, failed too. In 1998 the owner of W S. Clearing, William Saydein, settled with the Securities and Exchange Commission on a charge of misappropriating clients' money.

As usual, SIPC stepped in to clean up the failed firms—replacing cash or securities (up to $500,000) that the firms might have stolen or lost. SIPC also collects any money the firms are owed—including (without pity) customers' unpaid margin loans.

So it came to pass that in January 1998, SIPC sued the Hymans for more than $1 million in margin loans. "What loans?" the stunned Hymans cried. "Your loans," SIPC said—loans that turned up in their accounts. Similar suits were filed in nine other cases.

It wasn't son Bill's day trading that did the Hymans in. They discovered instead that George Swan had been buying huge amounts of a little-known stock called Data Race for his clients and himself. It was done on borrowed money At first Swan's purchases drove up the price. But eventually Data Race declined and Cygnet collapsed.

Here's where the real margin lesson starts. At a small brokerage firm you don't borrow from the firm itself. You borrow from the clearinghouse-in this case W S. Clearing. SIPC says that W. S. wasn't to blame for the Data Race mess; it only lent money, which it should get back.

When you're on margin, you have a virtually ironclad contract to repay, says securities-law professor Steve Thel of Fordham University in New York. You can't default by saying you didn't understand the loan (you should stay home at night, reading the confirmation slips your broker sends). Nor does it matter if the broker borrowed more than the margin rules allow. You owe the money! Maybe you can charge your broker with fraud. Still, you owe the clearinghouse!

Ways out: There are only two possible ways out.

First, the margin loan might be erased if the trade was fraudulent and the clearinghouse was directly involved. This line of attack was taken by the Hymans' attorney, Thomas Harris of Irvine, Calif. He lost the case and has appealed.

You might also escape if you watch every single transaction that your broker makes and protest immediately—in writing—if you object (phoned objections don't count). The letter might get the trade reversed. If the broker ignores you, however, you'll still have to cover the loan. Hard to believe, but true. As for the Hymans, there's no way they could have tracked the blizzard of trades in their accounts.

Even writing a letter isn't as straightforward as it sounds. Cygnet client Howard Jahre of New York City sent Cygnet a written protest before it failed, saying he hadn't authorized the Data Race trades. In its lawsuit, however, SIPC brushed the letter off. Says SIPC: you have to write to the clearinghouse directly, not just to your broker. Who tells investors that? And the letter will work as a legal defense only if your margin contract allows it, says retired securities lawyer Charles Rechlin of Sullivan & Cromwell in Los Angeles.

Source: Excerpt from "Something New in Market Risk," *Newsweek;* New York; Jun 5, 2000; Jane Bryant Quinn. Author of "Making the Most of Your Money".

The Opera Company of Boston, Inc., Appellee, v. The Wolf Trap Foundation for the Performing Arts, Appellant
United States Court of Appeals for the Fourth Circuit
817 F.2d 1094 (1987)

BACKGROUND AND FACTS

This suit between the parties arises under a contract between the plaintiff The Opera Company of Boston, Inc. (Opera Company) and the defendant The Wolf Trap Foundation for the Performing Arts (Wolf Trap) by which the Opera Company for its part agreed to give four "fully staged orchestrally accompanied [operatic] performances to the normally recognized standards" of the Opera Company. Wolf Trap, in turn, for its part under the contract was obliged to make the above payments and also to furnish the place of performance including an undertaking "to provide lighting equipment as shall be specified by the Opera Company of Boston's lighting designer."

Both parties to the contract apparently performed all their obligations under the contract through the operatic performance on June 14. These performances had been fully sold as well as had [one] remaining performance on June 15. During this final day, the weather was described as hot and humid, with rain throughout the day. Sometime between 6:00 and 6:30 p.m. a severe thunderstorm arose causing an electrical power outage. As a result all electrical service in the Park, in its roadways, parking area, pathways and auditorium were out. Conferences were had among representatives of the Park Service and that of Wolf Trap. The Park Service recommended the immediate cancellation of the performance and advised Wolf Trap if the performance were not cancelled, it disclaimed any responsibility for the safety of the people who were to attend as well as those who were to perform. It was the Park Service's view that a prompt cancellation was necessary to enable the parties to leave the park safely and to prevent others from coming. Wolf Trap agreed and the performance was cancelled.

While some of these discussions were being carried on a representative of the Opera Company was present but she took no part in the decision to cancel, though she voiced no objection. Since the performance was cancelled, Wolf Trap failed to make the final payment under the contract to the Opera Company. Five years after the cancellation, the Opera Company filed this suit to recover the balance due under the contract.

OPINION: RUSSELL, CIRCUIT JUDGE

The single question on appeal is whether this dismissal of Wolf Trap's defense of impossibility of performance was proper. The resolution of this issue requires a review of the doctrine of impossibility. We proceed first to that review.

III

The doctrine of impossibility of performance as an excuse or defense for a breach of contract was for long smothered under a declared commitment to the principle of sanctity of contracts. This rationale for constrained application of the doctrine was expressed by the United States Supreme Court in *Dermott* v. *Jones* (2 Wall.), 69 U.S. 1, 8, 17 L. Ed. 762 (1864):

> The principle which controlled the decision of the cases referred to rests upon a solid foundation of reason and justice. It regards the sanctity of contracts. It requires parties to do what they have agreed to do. If unexpected impediments lie in the way, and a loss must ensue, it leaves the loss where the contract places it. If the parties have made no provision for a dispensation, the rule of law gives none. It does not allow a contract fairly made to be annulled, and it does not permit to be interpolated what the parties themselves have not stipulated.

* * *

A shorter statement of the new rule is given in *Mishara Const.* [**19] *Co., Inc.* v. *Transit-Mixed Con. Corp.,* 365 Mass. 122, 310 N.E.2d 363, 367 (1974) in which the court said: "It is implicit in the doctrine of impossibility (and the companion rule of 'frustration of purpose') that certain risks are so unusual and have such severe consequences that they must have been beyond the scope of the assignment of risks inherent in the contract, that is, beyond the agreement made by the parties." . . .

It is now recognized that "A thing is impossible in legal contemplation when it is not practicable; and a thing is impracticable when it can only be done at an excessive and unreasonable cost." (citing authorities) The doctrine ultimately represents the ever-shifting line, drawn by courts hopefully responsive to commercial practices and mores, at which the community's interest in having contracts enforced according to their terms is outweighed by the commercial senselessness of requiring performance. When the issue is raised, the court is asked to construct a condition of performance based on the changed circumstances, a process which involves at least three reasonably definable steps.

Applying the law as above stated to the facts of this case, we conclude, as did the district judge, that the existence of electric power was necessary for the satisfactory performance by the Opera Company on the night of June 15 . . . The district judge, however, refused to sustain the defense because he held that if the contingency that occurred was one that could have been foreseen reliance on the doctrine of impossibility as a defense to a breach of contract suit is absolutely barred. As we have said, this is not the modern rule and he found that the power outage was foreseeable. In this the district judge erred. Foreseeability, as we have said, is at best but one fact to be con-

sidered in resolving first how likely the occurrence of the event in question was and, second whether its occurrence, based on past experience, was of such reasonable likelihood that the obligor should not merely foresee the risk but, because of the degree of its likelihood, the obligor should have guarded against it or provided for non-liability against the risk. This is a question to be resolved by the trial judge after a careful scrutiny of all the facts in the case. The trial judge in this case made no such findings. The cause must be remanded for such findings. In connection with that remand, the parties may be permitted to offer additional evidence on the matters in issue.

* * *

The judgment herein must, therefore, be vacated and the action remanded

to the district court to make findings, based on a statement of reasons, whether the possible foreseeability of the power failure in this case was of that degree of reasonable likelihood as to make improper the assertion by Wolf Trap of the defense of impossibility of performance.

QUESTIONS FOR ANALYSIS

1. According to the Court of Appeals, if an event was foreseeable, could that event, nevertheless, make the performance qualified for the impossibility defense?
2. If an event is foreseeable and there is no allocation of risk, then if the event occurs, the promisor must have impliedly assumed that risk. Is that logic consistent with the case logic as explained by the U.S. Court of Appeals?

---

parties to the contract. If Mary makes an offer to Peter, "You will have a job working for me if you graduate from college this spring," a *condition precedent* for hiring Peter has been established—namely, that he graduate from college during the spring. If Peter should fail to graduate from college during the spring, Mary's obligation to hire Peter is eliminated.

Reflecting a *condition precedent* that is outside of the control of the parties, Henry may tell George that he will have a job working in the White House if presidential candidate B beats candidate G. Obviously, Henry's obligation to hire George is based on a condition that is outside the control of either party to the contract.

When a *condition subsequent* occurs, the promisor's obligation to perform also ceases. If Henry tells Sam that "you have a job at my store as long as you always show up to work sober," Henry's obligation to employ Sam ceases if Sam shows up to work drunk.

As discussed at the start of the chapter, most contracts are executory bilateral agreements. In executory bilateral contracts, both parties are promisors and promisees. An effect of this relationship is that obligations for both parties to perform are **concurrent.** If one party defaults on the agreed-upon performance, it releases the other party from having to perform. In a

typical sales contract, the buyer must pay some money immediately as a down payment. If the buyer does not pay the down payment, the seller does not have to deliver the goods. If the buyer pays the down payment but the seller does not deliver the goods, then the obligation of the buyer to pay the rest of the balance due ceases.

CONTRACTUAL REMEDIES

Most contract remedies award money to compensate for the breach of a valid contract. In rare instances, there are other remedies that involve injunctions or specific performance requirements. In contrast to tort remedies, intent is not a factor in determining damages. In other words, the amount of damages awarded does not depend on whether the breaching party attempted to perform and failed or deliberately defaulted on the contract.

Monetary Damages

Compensatory Damages

The legal underpinning for **damages** (money awards) in contract cases in general is the intent to compensate the nonbreaching party for the losses incurred as a result of the breach of contract. Typically, damages awarded are inadequate to fully compensate the non-breaching party because attorney fees are not added for a successful plaintiff unless there is a clause in the contract awarding the winning party in contract litigation attorney fees and court costs. Of course, damages must be proved with reasonable certainty and courts are notably conservative in the requirements of proof. So, lost profits generally are not recoverable for new businesses that do not have a track record upon which to base damages.

In a typical sales contract breach situation, the damage award would involve the difference between the market price and the contract price of what the contract called for delivering, multiplied times the contract quantity, plus some recovery for incidental expenses associated with making an additional sale or purchase. If the market price is rising, typically the seller will be the defaulting party so it is damages to the purchaser that equal:

$$D = (P_m - P_k) * Q_k$$

where D is damages, P is price, Q is quantity, and m and k stand for market and contract, respectively. If the buyer defaults, the order of P_m and P_k would be reversed.

Reliance and Restitution Damages

In some contracts the nonbreaching party also incurs costs that were incurred due to reliance upon the breaching party performing its contract obligations. When there is adequate proof, reliance costs can be recovered. Reliance costs are more often recovered by a plaintiff in a promissory estoppel case which is explicitly based on the detrimental reliance costs incurred by the promisee. When the nonbreaching party sues as a result of a breach, that party can recover *restitution* expenses which is the consideration given to the breaching party before the breach takes place. Also, in voidable contracts, if the victim sues to rescind the contract, the victim is basically suing for restitution expenses to recover consideration given to the other party. Finally, in quasi-contract suits, the plaintiff is suing for restitution to prevent the *unjust enrichment* of the breaching party.

Consequential Damages

In some contracts, breach will entail unusual expenses that are not typical of such contracts. Consider, for example, a common carrier contract. It is a breach of contract for the carrier, say an airline, to lose a passenger's luggage. Damages for lost luggage are fixed to an amount ($750) determined by statute. In some cases, however, the value of the customer's luggage and/or goods in the luggage exceed $750. In such cases, to avoid the $750 limitation on possible recovery, it is incumbent upon the customer to inform the airline that his or her luggage or its contents are especially valuable. Moreover, such a concerned passenger would likely face an increased insurance charge on his or her luggage, which would further put the carrier on notice to be particularly careful. Consequential damages are recoverable in contract cases of this sort so long as the breaching party was reasonably aware of the extra expenses (consequential damages) associated with a breach, but the burden is upon the nonbreaching party to *notify* the breaching party if the expenses of loss are not reasonably foreseeable.

Liquidated Damages

Proving damages is inherently uncertain and juries and judges can become confused when accountants and economists argue about variable costs, fixed costs, and other minutiae. If damages are difficult to estimate, as they are with late performance in a road construction contract, the parties can agree in advance as to a formula for calculating damages. With *liquidated damages* clauses the parties stipulate in advance a formula for calculating damages, and such clauses are enforceable as long as they are reasonable. If the damage formula in a liquidated damages clause is excessive, the courts will label it a *penalty* and refuse to enforce it.

Punitive Damages

In contrast to the approach of tort law, the **intent** of the breaching party is not an issue in determining damages under contract law. There can be punitive damages in connection with a breach of contract but only if a tort also has occurred. So, for example, a defective product that breaches a warranty could also inflict a tort and, if the plaintiff can show the defendant displayed a reckless disregard for the safety of the public, punitive damages may be awarded (e.g., a pharmaceutical company that conceals adverse information about a new product in order to gain approval from the Food and Drug Administration, only to have that new product cause injuries or death, will be a target for suits asking for both compensatory and punitive damages). Punitive damages have also been awarded in insurance cases and in cases involving contracts dealing with the handling of corpses. Except for these infrequent exceptions, punitive damages are not typically a focus of contract law disputes.

Mitigation of Damages

The nonbreaching party in a contract case has an obligation to mitigate damages as much as is reasonable. If the nonbreaching party is a landlord, the landlord has an obligation to rent out the premises (assuming a willing tenant can easily be located), even though the previous tenant breached the lease. If an employee has been wrongfully discharged in contravention of an employment contract, the employee would nevertheless have an obligation to take a job offer from another employer. For both the landlord and the ex-employee, there are reasonableness constraints on the obligation to mitigate damages. An executive who is wrongfully fired from her job does not have to respond to a Help Wanted placed in the front window of the local McDonald's outlet to have a claim for lost compensation. A landlord who is willing to rent out his basement apartment to college coeds does not have to rent to a member of the Hells Angels to have a claim for lost rents.

Other Remedies

The remedies discussed below are "*equitable*" remedies, which means they are issued at the discretion of the presiding judge. In order to obtain an equitable remedy, the petitioning party must not be engaging sharp dealing. Since equitable remedies are discretionary with the judge, "in order to obtain equity, the party must act equitably." Both the equitable remedies of injunctions and specific performance are appropriate when monetary damages are inadequate to compensate the plaintiff for the total costs of the breaching party's behavior.

Injunctions

As with all injunctions, the plaintiff must show that (1) she is likely to succeed on the merits when the case comes to trial and (2) that irreparable harm is taking place so that the defendant must be stopped from further breaches of contract. Suppose that McCloud Dairy has a set of customers who rely upon it to de-liver milk every three days. Since milk cannot be stored easily, establishing a milk supply that is reliable is of paramount importance to retail outlets such as grocery stores. Assume that there are other potential suppliers of milk, but that McCloud has been able to keep its customers because it is reliable in delivering milk.

Now, suppose that a repair shop that serviced the trucks of McCloud Dairy deliberately slowed down its maintenance schedule in order to extract a higher price from McCloud. Suppose further that the repair shop had physical custody of the milk trucks. Under the facts it is clear that (1) the repair shop breached its repair contract with the dairy and (2) that irreparable harm might occur to McCloud unless the trucks were released immediately, given the value customers attach to reliability in timely wholesale milk distribution. Under these facts, a court in a breach of contract case would issue an *injunction* ordering the release of McCloud's trucks immediately.

Specific Performance

In some cases, the consideration in a contract is unique and there are no market alternatives that are available at reasonable prices. Real estate, works of art, and family heirlooms are all examples of consideration that cannot be reproduced on the market. In these cases, the nonbreaching party does not want a monetary award so much as it wants the actual consideration that was the subject matter of the contract. Specific performance is an appropriate remedy when the court can supervise the contract with a minimum of effort. If the breaching party had contracted to sell real estate that has special appeal to the purchaser, the court may be willing to issue an order to the seller to transfer the deed. The transferring of deeds is a relatively uncomplicated affair with recorded results that are easily verified. Not all contracts are so amenable to specific performance requirements.

Mark McGwire's batting skills are also unique consideration and no one during the 1990s was able to hit as many home runs in the major leagues as "Big Mack." If McGwire refused to play for the St. Louis Cardinals even though that is called for in his employment contract, the courts would not order specific performance because they do not want to get into the business of supervising McGwire's performance on a baseball diamond.

SUMMARY

- A contract is an agreement that creates a legally enforceable obligation to perform.
- Since each state has its own common law tradition, each state has its own common law of contracts. Contracts are supposed to reduce uncertainty by enabling businesspersons to plan, invest, and conduct business based on agreements they have with others. When the basic law of contracts varies from state to state, it adds to uncertainty.
- The impact of the UCC has been to **regularize** legal treatment of contracts in all 50 states.
- A *valid* contract is a contract that is enforceable. A *voidable* contract is a contract that can be voided by one of the parties. A *void* contract is a contract that courts will refuse to consider because the contract violates a statute or is against public policy. If a contract is *unenforceable,* either party to the contract can decide not to go through with the contract.
- Most contracts are *bilateral* in the sense that a promise is *exchanged* for a promise.
- A promise that has been performed is a promise that has been *executed.*
- An *express* contract contains an explicit agreement between the parties that there is a contract. A contract is implied because the conduct of the parties indicates consent to be bound in a contract.
- If there is no agreement between the parties, one party may, nevertheless, be able to recover from the other party based on *unjust enrichment* (sometimes called *quantum meruit*).
- Large firms, in particular, have developed contract language that essentially agrees to pay the small firm if their idea is used (generally if their idea is patentable), but the small firm waives its right to sue if the idea is not patentable or if the idea is not used.
- There are five elements to contract formation. They are **offer, acceptance, consideration, capacity of the parties to contract,** and **legality.**
- There are three categories of legal detriments that qualify as consideration. If a promisee agrees to pay money, perform services, or refrain from pursuing a legal claim, the promisee has incurred a legal detriment that is capable of supporting a promise by the promisor to pay money (or perform services, or settle a lawsuit). Gratitude for past actions does not qualify as consideration.
- Some promises appear to contain consideration, but do not. Such promises are often called *illusory* promises.
- The contractual age of capacity is 18 in all states. A contract between a minor and an adult can be voided or *disaffirmed* at the option of the minor.
- Adults can become incompetent to participate in contracts due to a number of causes: intoxication or mental illness. However, a person could be legally drunk (legally incompetent) for purposes of operating a motor vehicle while still having contractual capacity.
- Contracts must be *legal* to be valid.
- Certain contracts have been held unconscionable and thus void at law. Some unconscionable contracts are in categories such as contracts that purport to excuse liability for intentional actions of one party.
- Fraud takes place when one party to a contract knowingly lies about an important fact to the other party who reasonably relies on those lies and suffers damages as a result.
- Fraud, for example, can be used as a *defense* in a breach of contract suit by the defendant, claiming that he is not going to perform because he was induced into the contract only because the plaintiff lied to him.
- If both parties to a contract are mistaken as to a material fact, either party can void the contract.
- A contract that is the result of force, threat of force, threat of criminal prosecution, or blackmail is voidable at the option of the victim.
- There are six types of contracts that must be in writing to be enforceable: surety contracts, executor to a will agrees to be personally liable, if cannot be performed within one year, marriage contracts, real estate, and sale of goods in excess of $500.
- There are six important exceptions to mandatory written contracts.
- Whether a writing is required or not, if there is a written contract, the *parol evidence rule* operates to exclude outside or extrinsic evidence.

- If the performance offered by a party fails in the *essential purpose* of the contract, then such performance amounts to a *material* breach.
- Discharge of contractual obligations can be due to: material breach, rescission, novation, accord and satisfaction, by operation of law, and discharge due to impossibility.

- Most contract remedies award money to compensate for the breach of a valid contract. In rare instances, there are other remedies that involve injunctions or specific performance requirements. Monetary damages can be: compensatory, restitution, consequential, liquidated, punitive, and mitigating.

CURRENT AND FUTURE CONTRACT LAW FOR E-COMMERCE

INTRODUCTION: POTENTIAL FOR CHAOS OR UNIFORM TREATMENT

The Internet is a wonderland that can be enjoyed by the young, old, and those in-between. It is also, however, a vast commercial market where many contracts are formed every second. The Internet and E-Commerce have created new situations that have generated sweeping proposals for fundamental changes in contract law. In many ways, however, E-Commerce has created what Yogi Berra might have described as deja vu all over again for commercial contract law. During the first half of the 20th Century, when many U.S. businesses expanded their geographic scope, there was a tremendous desire for *uniform* treatment of contracts for the sale of goods throughout the U.S. That same dynamic is now occurring in E-Commerce. There is a general recognition of the desirability of uniform contract law to govern E-Commerce, but to date that does not exist, though there are extensive proposals for reform of contract law on the Internet as we will see in this chapter.

As we know from the previous chapter, the *common law* of contracts evolved from cases and precedent. As a consequence, each state had its own unique contract law based on the cases and precedents in that state. When most companies were small and sold most of their output intrastate, the fact that each state had slightly different contract laws was not a major commercial inconvenience. As companies grew larger, dissatisfaction with 50 unique bodies of contract law became more evident, *particularly in the sale of goods.* Companies based in New York that were selling goods nationwide had to be prepared to defend themselves against claims in every state in which they had sales because, if the company sold direct to purchasers in another state, *minimum contacts* (and jurisdiction) were established. So, if a customer in North Dakota claimed their vacuum cleaner did not work properly, they could sue the New York vacuum cleaner company for breach of contract in North Dakota, taking advantage of any peculiarities of North Dakota contract law. Even less palpable contacts with buyers in other states, such as owning an office, directing advertisements, or hiring sales representatives in another state, satisfied the minimum contacts jurisdiction test. Eventually, dissatisfaction with contract differences across states led to the passage of the Uniform Commercial Code (UCC) by all 50 states during the 1950s and 1960s. The impact of the UCC was to increase certainty on the part of interstate sellers and so facilitate interstate commerce.

With a focus on contract law applicable to product sales, the UCC does not apply to the many other forms of contract law not involving the sale of goods. This includes contracts for employment, real estate, and, indeed, most other transactions. For many of these (nonproduct) transactions, state by state differences in contract (and other branches of) law still exist. For the past 100 years a group of judges and attorneys, concerned with differences among the states in various branches of law have formed the National Conference of Commissioners of Uniform State Laws (NCCUSL). The NCCUSL is dedicated to reducing or eliminating state by state differences in many areas of law from child adoptions to trade secret protection.[1] The major project of the NCCUSL lately has been development of uniform contract law for the Internet. NCCUSL has developed and revised the Uniform Computer Information Transactions Act (UCITA) and the Uniform Electronic Transactions Act (UETA). Also the NCCUSL has proposed significant revisions of the UCC to accommodate E-Commerce. All three of these proposals for change are discussed below.

Overview

There are four major issues related to E-Commerce contract law that are addressed in this chapter. The list is not exhaustive. There are other E-Commerce contract law issues that undoubtedly will surface in the future and are present currently. In the interim, the four issues discussed below have been the subject of much controversy and legal resolution of these issues is not clear at this point. The four issues we look at are:

1. **Parity between Electronic and Paper Records.** The prospect of treating *electronic records* the same as *paper records* is opposed by many groups who are advocates of consumer interests. "Record" is the term now used to replace "document" or "writing".
2. **Enforceability of Shrinkwrap, Clickwrap, and Boxtop Licenses.** There are significant contract formation issues associated with shrinkwrap, clickwrap, and boxtop licenses and terms of contracts that are added after a buyer has agreed to purchase a product subject to such licenses.
3. **Attribution Procedures.** With electronic (mouse click) purchases, a vendor needs secure

mechanisms to be assured that the order that they have received is legitimate. Accompanying concerns revolve around the conditions under which a vendor can sue a person for an order received online.
4. **Digital Signatures and Certificates.** With standard paper contracts, signatures have operated to uniquely identify parties to a contract. Obviously, that's a problem in E-Commerce transactions. Recent legislation by Congress attempts to provide several acceptable substitutes to traditional signatures in electronic commerce, but not without remaining concerns.

Uniform Commercial Code

During the first part of the 20th Century, dissatisfaction with differences in contract law among the states in the sale of goods led to the composition and passage of the Uniform Commercial Code. As the name indicates, the UCC deals with commercial contracts, and for purposes of this book, it deals exclusively with the sale of goods. When U.S. companies began selling to customers located in many different states, the demands for uniform contract treatment became more intense and work began on the Uniform Commercial Code. Dissatisfaction with the status quo was so universal that all 50 states have adopted the UCC.[2]

Still, there are many *commercial* transactions not subject to the UCC including those associated with service contracts and licenses of information. Since computer services, including management of information systems and information technology, have become increasingly important, the beneficial impact of the UCC has lessened. Hence, a return to the "bad old days" of state-by-state differences in contract law is a concern of the business and legal communities. To deal with this unpleasant reversal of progress, an ambitious set of new "uniform" laws has been proposed, but has not yet been enacted by most states. It should be noted, too, that there is considerable resistance from some consumer groups to the adoption of these new "uniform" acts. Later in the chapter we give "equal time" to the opposition to these uniform acts. Readers are better able to appreciate the opposition after we delve into the main body of the proposals for E-Commerce contract law.

Also note that, in some cases, computer software has been treated as a good for purposes of the UCC

---

[1]To appreciate the scope of their activities, visit the NCCUSL website at www.nccusl.org.

[2]The only state that has adopted UCC with some significant differences is Louisiana, which has a continental law tradition.

Getting Acquainted with the Law

UCC	Universal Commercial Code—applies to anything dealing with interstate commerce
Article 2	The sale of goods
Article 2B	Electronic transactions
Section 2-207	Additional terms
Section 2-210(a)	Legal recognition of electronic records and authentications
Section 2-212	Forming contracts electronically
NCCUSL	National Conference of Commissioners on Uniform State Laws
UCITA	Uniform Computer Information Transactions Act
Section 212	Efficacy and Commercial Reasonableness of the Attribution Procedure
Section 213	Determining Attribution
Section 214	Electronic Error: Consumer Defenses
UETA	Uniform Electronic Transaction Act (proposed)
Section 103	Applies to electronic records and signatures for commerce purposes
Section 104	Excludes transactions covered by other laws
Section 106	Electronic signatures are valid
Section 204	Legal recognition of electronic records

---

in the same way that a book is a good. The contents of a book are intellectual property of an author, but the book itself is classified as a book (a good). In some cases the courts have made the same analogy with computer software as illustrated by the *Advent* case below.

UCC Revisions: Proposed Article 2 Subpart 2B Electronic Records and Intent

Article 2 of the UCC, which governs the sale of goods, has been rewritten and is in the process of being reenacted to accommodate E-Commerce. Under the proposed revisions to Article 2 of the UCC, a new Subpart B: *Electronic Transactions* has been added to Article 2 to make clear that it is the controlling law with regard to *electronic sales* of goods.[3] Proposed Section 2-210 (a) (of Subpart B), Legal Recognition of Electronic Records and Authentications, declares that electronic records are to be treated the same as other records (written documents) germane to contracts. This is a bone of contention between the NCCUSL and attorneys representing consumer groups. The

[3]The proposed Revised Article 2 and Subpart B are located at http://www.nccusl.org/draftingprojects.htm#cc2.

NCCUSL wants parity between electronic records and paper records, while consumer groups cite numerous situations in which electronic records fail to protect consumers as well as paper records do.

Proposed Section 2-212 (of Subpart B) states that contracts can be formed with the aid of electronic agents "even if no individual is aware of its receipt [of an electronic message]." These two changes, (1) legal recognition of electronic records and (2) contract formation when one or both sides to the contract are electronic agents, are also present when electronic contracts are formed *not* involving the sale of goods, as we shall see immediately below. Proposed Article 2 of the UCC (which deals with the sale of goods), UCITA, and UETA all agree that electronic records should be given equal weight with paper records and that contracts can be formed electronically when one or both of the parties is represented by software and electronic agents.

The Uniform Computer Information Transactions Act

In trying to address the many challenges posed to the UCC by E-Commerce, the Commissioners at the NC-CUSL decided not to revise the UCC with respect to

Group Approves Controversial Software Law

A U.S. group that works to unify state laws today overwhelmingly approved a controversial proposal to adopt common licensing rules for software and other information technology transactions that critics contend would hold IT companies hostage to the whims of software vendors. The Uniform Computer Information Transactions Act (UCITA) was voted on during a meeting in Denver of the National Conference of Commissioners on Uniform

State Laws (NCCUSL), a private group of more than 300 lawyers, judges and law professors. Under NCCUSL guidelines, draft legislation has to be approved by a majority of states present when votes are taken, and that majority must include representatives from at least 20 states.

Source: Excerpt from: July 29, 1999, Jack McCarthy and Nancy Weil, IDG News Service\Boston Bureau www.nccusl.org/.

the *licensing* of computer information as had originally been proposed. Instead of completing a new section of the Uniform Commercial Code, the authors have renamed the *proposed uniform statute* the **Uniform Computer Information Transactions Act** (UCITA). The scope of UCITA includes *computer software, multimedia interactive products, computer data and databases, Internet and online information.* For example, UCITA deals with the lease of computer information, which occurs whenever you "purchase" software. Most people are aware that a purchaser of software is actually purchasing the *right to use* the software within the constraints of the software license. You can "purchase" software at a store or online but there are restrictions in most licenses that prevent you from copying the software and reselling it to several friends.

Procedural Steps Required for Implementation of UCITA

UCITA will not be part of the UCC but, instead, is being put forward separately by the National Conference of Commissioners on Uniform State Laws (see www.nccusl.org).[4] With this approach, the Uniform Law Commissioners will attempt to have each state enact UCITA as a stand-alone statute that will uniformly regulate a category of computer law applicable to certain transactions. To date UCITA has been adopted by only two states, Virginia and Maryland. UCITA is the source of considerable controversy as

groups purporting to represent consumers and business interests, particularly high-tech business interests, have a number of concerns over UCITA content.

By design, UCITA will cover licenses of computer software, but the sale on goods in the Internet will still be subject to the UCC.[5] As with the UCC, UCITA is a substantive, gap-filling statute. If the parties to a contract do not have a particular term in the contract regarding an issue such as implied warranties, UCITA supplies that term. For example, if nothing is said in the contract licensing the software to a purchaser about implied warranties, UCITA requires that, "a licensor that is a merchant with respect to computer programs of the kind warrants: (1) to the end user that the computer program is fit for the ordinary purposes for which such computer programs are used; . . . "[6] This is the UCITA equivalent to the UCC's implied warranty of merchantability.[7] A draft of UCITA is available at www.law.upenn.edu/bll/ulc/ulc_frame.htm.

In the absence of laws dealing specifically with computer-conducted commerce, courts in the past have dealt with cases involving computer transactions by applying the UCC. The fit between the UCC and computer software disputes is often deficient, as the next case indicates.

---

[4]The National Conference of Commissioners on Uniform State Laws has as its primary objective, fostering statutory uniformity across state lines. The success of the NCCUSL varies. All 50 states have adopted the UCC but in other areas of law, state adoptions are far less than unanimous. Among the state laws for which the NCCUSL has proposed model laws are corporate law, uniform partnership law, and many others. In 1999 there were over 30 proposed "uniform" state laws including the Uniform Parentage Act, the Uniform Probate Code, and the Uniform Athlete-Agent Act among others.

[5]See Section 103 of UCITA, which excludes any transaction involving the sale of goods for which the primary purpose of the sale is the goods and not transfer of information.

[6]Section 403 (a)(1) of UCITA.

[7]The implied warranty of merchantability under the UCC Section 2-314 reads as follows, "(2) Goods to be merchantable must be at least such as

   a. pass without objection in the trade under the contract description; and
   b. in the case of fungible goods, are of average quality with the description; and
   c. are fit for the ordinary purposes for which such goods are used; and . . . "

There are several other characteristics that are listed as being part of the implied warranty of merchantability under the UCC.

Advent Systems Limited v. *Unisys Corporation*
United States Court of Appeals, Third Circuit
925 F.2d 670 (1991)

FACTS AND CASE BACKGROUND

Plaintiff, Advent Systems Limited, is engaged the production of software for computers. In 1986 the company had developed an electronic document management system (EDMS), which was the result of substantial research and development efforts. Defendant, Unisys Corporation, manufactures computers and was interested in selling the EDMS software in the U.S. Advent and Unisys signed two contracts, one a distribution contract and the other an outline of an overall agreement, called Heads of Agreement. The agreements called for Advent to supply software and hardware while Unisys was supposed to head up marketing and distribution efforts. Following the agreement, Unisys had difficulty selling EDMS. Unisys attempted to sell the system to Arco (an oil giant) but was unsuccessful. The relationship between the parties soured in part because Unisys was reorganizing. Advent sued for breach of contract and claimed economic damages. At the trial court [district court], a jury awarded Advent $4.5 million in a breach of contract claim. Defendant, Unisys, appeals claiming that the contract involved the sale of goods and thus was governed by the UCC. Since the UCC requires an explicit quantity term in order to sue for damages, Unisys claims that Advent's suit should be dismissed.

OPINION: WEIS, CIRCUIT JUDGE

II. SOFTWARE AND THE UNIFORM COMMERCIAL CODE

The district court ruled that as a matter of law the arrangement between the two parties was not within the Uniform Commercial Code and, consequently, the statute of frauds was not applicable. As the district court appraised the transaction, provisions for services outweighed those for products and, consequently, the arrangement was not predominantly one for the sale of goods.

The Distribution Agreement begins with the statement, "Unisys desires to purchase, and Advent desires to sell, on a nonexclusive basis, certain of Advent hardware products and software licenses for resale worldwide." Following a heading "Subject Matter of Sales," appears this sentence, "(a) Advent agrees to sell hardware and license software to Unisys, and Unisys agrees to buy from Advent the products listed in Schedule A." Schedule A lists twenty products, such as computer cards, plotters, imagers, scanners and designer systems.

Advent was to invoice Unisys for each product purchased upon shipment, but to issue separate invoices for maintenance fees. The cost of the "support services" was set at 3 percent "per annum of the prevailing Advent user list price of each software module for which Unisys is receiving revenue from a customer." Services included field technical bulletins, enhancement and maintenance releases, telephone consultation, and software patches, among others. At no charge to Unisys, Advent was to provide publications such as installation manuals, servicing and adjustment manuals, diagnostic operation and test procedures, sales materials, product brochures and similar items. In turn, Unisys was to "employ resources in performing marketing efforts" and develop "the technical ability to be thoroughly familiar" with the products.

In support of the district court's ruling that the U.C.C. did not apply, Advent contends that the agreement's requirement of furnishing services did not come within the Code. Moreover, the argument continues, the "software" referred to in the agreement as a "product" was not a "good" but intellectual property outside the ambit of the Uniform Commercial Code.

Because software was a major portion of the "products" described in the agreement, this matter requires some discussion. Computer systems consist of "hardware" and "software." Hardware is the computer machinery, its electronic circuitry and peripheral items such as keyboards, readers, scanners and printers. Software is a more elusive concept. Generally speaking, "software" refers to the medium that stores input and output data as well as computer programs. The medium includes hard disks, floppy disks, and magnetic tapes.

In simplistic terms, programs are codes prepared by a programmer that instruct the computer to perform certain functions. When the program is transposed onto a medium compatible with the computer's needs, it becomes software.

The increasing frequency of computer products as subjects of commercial litigation has led to controversy over whether software is a "good" or intellectual property. The Code does not specifically mention software.

In the absence of express legislative guidance, courts interpret the Code in light of commercial and technological developments. The Code is designed "[t]o simplify, clarify and modernize the law governing commercial transactions" and "[t]o permit the continued expansion of commercial practices." As the Official Commentary makes clear:

> This Act is drawn to provide flexibility so that, since it is intended to be a semi-permanent piece of legislation, it will provide its own machinery for expansion of commercial practices. It is intended to make it possible for the law embodied in this Act to be developed by the courts in the light of unforeseen and new circumstances and practices.

* * *

Computer programs are the product of an intellectual process, but once implanted in a medium are widely distributed to computer owners. An analogy can be drawn to a compact disc recording of an orchestral rendition. The music is produced by the artistry of musicians and in itself is not a "good," but when transferred to a laser-readable disc becomes a readily merchantable commodity. Similarly, when a professor delivers a lecture, it is not a good, but, when transcribed as a book, it becomes a good.

That a computer program may be copyrightable as intellectual property does not alter the fact that once in the form of a floppy disc or other medium, the program is tangible, moveable and available in the marketplace. The fact that some programs may be tailored for specific purposes need not alter their status as

"goods" because the Code definition includes "specially manufactured goods."

The topic has stimulated academic commentary with the majority espousing the view that software fits within the definition of a "good" in the U.C.C.

Applying the U.C.C. to computer software transactions offers substantial benefits to litigants and the courts. The Code offers a uniform body of law on a wide range of questions likely to arise in computer software disputes: implied warranties, consequential damages, disclaimers of liability, the statute of limitations, to name a few.

The importance of software to the commercial world and the advantages to be gained by the uniformity inherent in the U.C.C. are strong policy arguments favoring inclusion. The contrary arguments are not persuasive, and we hold that software is a "good" within the definition in the Code.

The relationship at issue here is a typical mixed goods and services arrangement. The services are not substantially different from those generally accompanying package sales of computer systems consisting of hardware and software.

* * *

In this case the contract's main objective was to transfer "products." The specific provisions for training of Unisys personnel by Advent were but a small part of the parties' contemplated relationship.

The compensation structure of the agreement also focuses on

"goods." The projected sales figures introduced during the trial demonstrate that in the contemplation of the parties the sale of goods clearly predominated. The payment provision of $150,000 for developmental work which Advent had previously completed was to be made through individual purchases of software and hardware rather than through the fees for services and is further evidence that the intellectual work was to be subsumed into tangible items for sale.

We are persuaded that the transaction at issue here was within the scope of the Uniform Commercial Code and, therefore, the judgment in favor of the plaintiff must be reversed.

QUESTIONS FOR ANALYSIS

1. If UCITA is adopted by all the states it will govern transactions such as those in this case. Do we really need UCITA if, as the court indicates above, the UCC is an understandable body of contract laws that applies in every state?

2. The court analogizes computer software to a book. Writing the book is not the production of a good but the book itself is surely a good and thus subject to the UCC. The court also uses the example of a laser disk that contains music. Are books and disks on the one hand and computer software on the other hand completely analogous?

Uniform Electronic Transaction Act

The NCCUSL is also proposing the Uniform Electronic Transaction Act (UETA), the text of which is available at the same website (http://www.law.upenn.edu/library/ulc/uecicta/eta1197.htm). According to Section 103 of the UETA, "this Act applies to electronic records and electronic signatures generated, stored, processed,

communicated or used for any purpose in any commercial or governmental transaction." Section 104, however, excludes from the coverage of UETA the transactions that are subject to other law including UCITA. The essence of the UETA is contained in Section 201: Legal Recognition of Electronic Records. According to subsection (a), "a record may not be denied legal effect, validity or enforceability solely because it is in the form of an electronic record." Subsection (b) indicates that, "[I]f a rule of law requires a record to be in writing, or provides consequences if it is not, an electronic record satisfies that rule." The bottom line is that e-mails could supply evidence of a written agreement that is required by the Statute of Frauds, noted above, UETA's treatment of the *effect of electronic records* is the same as is proposed in both, Section 2B of the proposed revisions of the UCC and UCITA.

As MEMORANDUM

John M. McCabe
Legislative Director/Legal Counsel
jmmccabe@nccusl.org

Memo to: Interested Parties

Subject: The Uniform Electronic Transactions Act and Consumers

The Internet is the marketplace for the 21st Century, but it is a marketplace where the principal advantage belongs to the buyer and the borrower, not the seller or the lender. It is a marketplace without borders. Every seller and every lender must compete with their counterparts in every part of the world. It is capitalism and price competition in its most merciless form. Consumers receive understandable comparative information on price and other terms of deals in nanoseconds. Do you want to buy a car? On the "Net" the best price and best financing deal are a keystroke away. You may also ask other consumers about their experiences with the model that you may want to buy in the nearest chat room or bulletin board. There is no place for sellers and lenders to hide on the Internet, and the power it gives to consumers is extraordinary and unprecedented.

80 million people in the United States are online. They have reached into their wallets to do their business there. Online retail sales, alone, rose to an estimated $20 billion from almost zero in 1999. Businesses spent an additional $109 billion buying from each other in the same year. By 2003, estimates suggest on-line retail sales of $144 billion and business sales of $1.3 trillion. Consumers like electronic transactions for their convenience and speed, and because they can comparison shop as never before. They are voting with their modems and buying with a click. It is an unstoppable tide.

The Uniform Electronic Transactions Act (UETA), approved by the National Conference of Commissioners on Uniform State Laws in 1999, was drafted to eliminate any doubt concerning the enforceability of electronic transactions, whether in the form of retail Internet trans-

actions, electronic credit transactions, electronic data interchange or e-mail usage. UETA is designed to put electronic transactions on a par with paper transactions.

Concerns have been raised in consumer circles about electronic consumer transactions; fears about the unknown impact upon consumers engaged in this new marketplace. The arguments are as follows: electronic transactions are unfamiliar; they take place too quickly; consumers won't find all the terms of a deal before signing on to it; there may be new opportunities for fraud.

UETA responds to these concerns, but not by confining consumer transactions to the paper world. The paper world prevents consumers from obtaining the best information for making good choices. That is why much consumer law is concerned with disclosure of information— disclosure that often defeats itself because the consumer does not get information in understandable forms. The Internet is disclosure with a vengeance. There is also fraud in the paper world, made easier by consumer inability to obtain and process information about cost-effective choices. UETA does not confine consumer transactions to the paper world because that does not benefit consumers.

It is important to make sure that the rules which validate electronic transactions do not burden those who are unprepared for electronic transactions. UETA applies only to transactions in which the parties have agreed to do business with each other, electronically. For an electronic record to be effective, it must be capable of being retained by the recipient. The sender of a record cannot inhibit the ability of the recipient to print or store the electronic record. Simply put, electronic records and signatures may not be imposed on anybody, but particularly those who do not have computers or access to them.

UETA recognizes the existence of computer programs used by sellers and lenders to automate their transactions. It makes it clear that those who use such programs, called "electronic agents," are bound to contracts made by those "electronic agents." UETA provides a special remedy in the event an "electronic agent" makes an error.

—Continued on page 62

As MEMORANDUM   *Continued from page 61*

Of course, the main consumer benefit from UETA is its contribution to the level playing field. All the substantive legal rules, including those for consumer protection, apply in the electronic marketplace as they do in the traditional, paper-bound marketplace. A sale remains a sale. A credit transaction remains a credit transaction.

"Under no circumstances should electronic commerce operate independently from existing legal systems," says Patricia Brumfield Fry, chair of the UETA drafting committee. "While every estimate of growth of electronic commerce has been exceeded in a matter of months, the power of the consumer in dealings with merchants has kept pace. Until it is shown that specific needs have arisen online, the electronic market should be dealt with on a par with existing markets. UETA assures consumers the protections and safeguards which have been developed through the decades, and lets them take full advantage of the benefits of electronic commerce.

Relationship between Proposed Section 2B of the UCC, UCITA and UETA

UETA is a procedural statute that applies to a transaction as long as the parties to the contract agree to use electronic commerce for that transaction. Both revised Article 2 of the UCC (Section 2B) and UCITA are substantive statutes that supply terms to contracts when such terms in the contract are absent.[8] UETA deals comprehensively with E-Commerce and contract law, while the revised Article 2 of the UCC deals mainly with the sale of goods, which may involve E-Commerce but may not. NCCUSL staff who are developing revisions of Article 2 of the UCC and those composing UETA and UCITA have made efforts to coordinate the three acts so that the same behavior under the three acts has the same legal consequences. Also there are a number of categories of laws that are excluded from the coverage of UETA including laws relating to real estate transactions, trusts, other than testamentary trusts, Articles 3, 4, 4A, 5, 6, 7, 8, or 9 of the Uniform Commercial Code, and other more recent statutes which address the use of electronic records. This list of exclusions under UETA is not exhaustive.

[8]Comments to Revised Article 2-207 reads as follows: "Fourth, gaps in agreements where a contract is formed are filled by 'terms' supplied by or incorporated from the UCC."

Uniform Electronic Transactions Act: Consumer Nightmare or Opportunity?

Consumers Union West Coast Regional Office. Prepared: 8/23/99

[Author's note: This article was written while the California proposal was still in bill form. It has since been enacted. All of the protections described here are now part of the California UETA.]

1. Should a lender be allowed to send a foreclosure notice only to an email address that is five years old?
2. If a consumer needs a paper copy of a disclosure or contract notice sent by email, should the consumer have to pay a fee to get a copy of that notice?
3. Should a salesperson be able to sign a consumer up to receive all future notices by email when the consumer does not own a computer?
4. If a law requires that a certain type of contract be in writing, should a record of a phone call satisfy that requirement?
5. Should utility shutoff warnings go only to an email address that might be shared within a family and checked primarily by the children?

Are the consumer warning bells going off in your head? Well, all of these scenarios and more will be permitted by

Continued from page 62

the new Uniform Electronic Transactions Act (UETA). UETA is coming soon to your state legislature.

WHAT IS UETA?

UETA is a uniform law approved July 1999 by the National Conference of Commissioners on Uniform State Laws (NCCUSL).[1] If adopted by state legislatures, UETA will elevate electronic records and signatures to the same legal status accorded paper records and hand-written signatures. UETA is grounded on three premises:

- That most state law requirements for a writing can be satisfied by an electronic record, including an email.
- That most state law requirements for a signature can be satisfied by an electronic signature.
- That, in most cases, the parties to a contract can agree to any form of electronic communication.

UETA'S UNDERLYING PREMISES ARE PROBLEMATIC

Often, however, these premises do not apply in consumer contracts. The first premise will be true in only some consumer situations. An electronic record may be just as good as a written record for an inexpensive transaction that is completed in a short time. On the other hand, a consumer entering into a five-year car loan or a 30-year mortgage needs the note and contract in a form which he or she can keep. Home computers are replaced every few years, and previously downloaded contracts are unlikely to be copied over to a new system. Change-of-terms notices for a service provider operating only on the Internet probably can be delivered by email, but a notice that your car is being recalled for a safety problem should arrive in the mail.

The first premise also assumes that email arrives at least as reliably as regular mail, which is contrary to the experience of many consumers. Consumers currently may change email addresses more frequently than they move. Those with email addresses seem to check them either far more frequently or far less frequently than their

[1]The full text of UETA, with official commentary, can be downloaded from: http://www.law.upenn.edu/library/ulc/ulc_frame.htm
The above address will take you to the NCCUSL Drafts of Uniform and Model Acts Official Site page. Click on the Final Acts link, which will take you to the NCCUSL Final Acts page. Scroll through the Index on this page and choose the Uniform Electronic Transactions Act link, which will take you to the UETA Final Draft link at the bottom of the page.

daily check of the regular mail. In addition, an Internet email provider may go out of business, leaving a consumer with no choice but to obtain a new email address.

As to the second premise, an electronic signature does not always fully serve the purposes of a written signature. Where there is a risk of forgery, a written signature may provide additional safeguards because it may be harder to forge than a purported electronic signature. An electronic click made at home may not serve the purpose of emphasizing the seriousness or the particular risks of a transaction as well as a written signature.

The third premise of UETA is reflected in the broad deference it gives to the autonomy of contracting parties. It defers to the agreement without distinguishing between negotiated agreements and standard form contracts or contracts of adhesion. This approach could give wide latitude to drafters of standard form contracts to define and impose the conditions of electronic communication.

For example, UETA adopts the principle that each party should be able to determine when it will receive information electronically, and when it wishes to insist on receiving a paper communication. This sounds good in theory, but in practice it allows one-sided contracts. UETA also allows an on-line seller to insist on sending all information to the consumer electronically. The seller, however, can require that the consumer communicate any complaints, refund requests, billing disputes or other communications to the same company only by regular mail.

Here is another example of a perverse effect created by UETA's rule of autonomy to contracting parties. UETA contains definitions of both "sent" and "received." According to these provisions, material is "sent" when it enters a computer system or a server that is outside the control of the sender. Further, that information is "received" when it enters the recipient's computer. These definitions contain loopholes. A message is received even when the recipient cannot open or read it; or when the message was automatically discarded by a junk mail filter. The definitions nevertheless do capture the basic idea that something is received when it gets to you or to a place where you can retrieve it.

UETA permits the parties to the contract to vary these definitions so that "sent" and "received" can be redefined to be anything. Under UETA, a web seller could define information to have been received by the buyer at the

—Continued on page 64

Uniform Electronic Transactions Act: Consumer Nightmare or Opportunity?

Consumers Union West Coast Regional Office. Prepared: 8/23/99   *Continued from page 63*

moment that the seller posts that information to its own web site—even if the customer is not aware of its posting.

OTHER DRAWBACKS OF UETA

- Permits using a paper contract followed by an electronic change in the terms of that paper contract.
- Permits using email to substitute for legal requirements to provide a paper notice even when the consumer has not been doing business with the company by email.
- Permits an electronic signature to be made to a paper record.
- Exposes consumers to the risk that notices with a legal or contractual effect will be sent only to a rarely checked email address.
- Exposes consumers to the risk that notices with a legal or contractual effect will be considered received even if the consumer is unable to open or read them, or if the notice is automatically discarded by a junk mail filter.
- Permits a party to redefine "sent" and "received" so that both are satisfied merely by posting a notice to a website.
- Allows a record of a telephone call to substitute for a written record.[2]
- Fails to include a right to a free, written copy of a contract or notice delivered electronically.
- Lacks a rule stating that an electronic record is not considered delivered if it is delivered in a form which cannot be opened and read by the recipient.
- Offers no unfettered right on the part of the consumer to revoke an authorization to communicate electronically and revert to paper communication. (The consumer may revoke the authorization with respect to future transactions, but not for the initial transaction).

[2]UETA defines an electronic record to include information that is either inscribed on a tangible medium or that is stored in an electronic or other medium and is retrievable in perceivable form. A telephone call that is tape-recorded or digitally retrievable is an electronic record under this definition.

- Lacks a statutory restriction on the use of old email addresses.[3]

CHALLENGES FOR CONSUMERS ABOUND

Electronic commerce has pluses and minuses for consumers. For those consumers who have access to the Internet, on-line shopping holds out the promise of increased price competition and selection. At the same time, electronic commerce also offers some new opportunities for sellers to hide contract terms, posting them in ways that make the consumer unlikely to find or read them, or even sending the terms only after payment. UETA also produces some new opportunities for scam artists, e.g., by allowing a seller to switch to electronic communication after a paper contract has been signed. For the creative and criminal mind, UETA offers few limits.

UETA was introduced in California before it was finalized as a uniform act. Some important improvements for consumers were added to the California version.[4] These improvements are absent from the uniform version which will be offered in other state legislatures. Legislators, consumers, consumer law enforcement officials, consumer advocates, and others should consider insisting upon both the California changes and other improvements to UETA before it moves forward in their states.

* * *

[The article continues with several more proposals for change.]

Source: Excerpt information: This article appeared in the July/August issue of *NCLC Reports,* Credit & Usury Edition. Prepared by: Gail Hillebrand, Consumers Union of U.S., West Coast Regional Office, San Francisco, CA 94103.
Phone: 415-431-6747 Fax: 415-431-0906
Email: hillga@consumers.org.
Please contact us at http://www.consumersunion.org/contact.htm.

[3]Even in a five-year car loan or a 30-year mortgage, UETA would allow the creditor to keep using the same email address whether or not there is any reason to believe that address is still good. UETA does contain a limited restriction on the use of bad addresses if the email bounces back to the sender.
[4]The full text of the California's UETA bill, SB 820, can be found at: http://www.sen.ca.gov/htbin/testbin/ca

As noted above, the UCC (the current version and the proposed revisions) and UCITA are substantive gap-fillers in contract law. If the contract between two parties (businesses or end users) is silent on a point of law, such as responsibility for the risk of loss for mis-

transmission of an electronic response (say the consumer clicks on the wrong button), the aforementioned statutes will govern unless the parties agree on a different provision. If businesses or customers do not like the outcomes provided by the aforementioned statutes, they are free, with very few limitations, to fashion their own contract terms. A major criticism of UCITA and the other E-Commerce contract revisions is that they treat consumers and businesses as equals in terms of negotiating contracts—in fact, most vendors on the Internet offer contract terms to consumers on a "take it or leave it" basis.

The Electronic Records Debate

A major thrust of proposals for E-Commerce contract law is to provide electronic records with parity to paper records. The least controversial of the three proposed revisions (Revised Article 2B, UCITA, and UETA), UETA has been attacked by the widely respected Consumers' Union. To date 40 states have adopted UETA. Needless to say, promoters of UETA, including the NCCUSL, are hoping for a 50-state adoption.[9] The position of the Consumers Union is reflected in the state-

[9]Twelve more states have introduced UETA to their state legislatures.

ment above, which has been excerpted from their website at www.consumerunion.org/contact.htm.

Response of the NCCUSL

The NCCUSL maintains a legislative list of how many states have adopted their proposed uniform laws along with explanations of why states should adopt these uniform laws. The included article insert is a recent NCCUSL statement of its position on why all states should adopt UETA. In light of the two previous articles, consider the confusion generated by the following case because of the ambiguous status of electronic records. If electronic records are treated the same as paper records, then consumers are bound by paragraphs buried in subscriber agreements, which are regularly ignored by most people. If consumers are not bound by membership agreements, then vendors would be reluctant to enter into agreements with customers because customers would not be bound and limitations of liability (discussed below) would not be enforceable.

In Re RealNetworks, Inc., Privacy Litigation
United States District Court, N.D. Illinois, Eastern Division
2000 WL 631341 (N.D.Ill.) (2000)

FACTS AND CASE BACKGROUND:
(IN THE WORDS OF THE COURT)

Plaintiffs Michael Lieschke, Robert Jackson, and Todd Simon (collectively, the "Plaintiffs"), both on behalf of a class of Illinois plaintiffs and individually, brought suit against Defendant RealNetworks, Inc. ("RealNetworks") under federal and common law. Plaintiffs allege trespass to property and privacy, claiming that RealNetworks' software products secretly allowed RealNetworks to access and intercept users' electronic communications and stored information without their knowledge or consent. Previously, this Court considered and granted RealNetworks' motion to stay this matter and enforce arbitration, finding that the End User License Agreement (the "License Agreement") required arbitration of this

dispute. Subsequently, this Court allowed Intervenor David Keel (the "Intervenor") to file his additional arguments in support of Plaintiffs' opposition to arbitration in order to raise certain arguments not presented to the Court when it decided the arbitration issue. It is these arguments that the Court presently addresses.

RealNetworks offers free basic versions of two products, RealPlayer and RealJukebox, for users to download from RealNetworks' site on the World Wide Web. These products allow users to see and hear audio and video available on the Internet and to download, record, and play music.

Before a user can install either of these software packages, they must accept the terms of RealNetworks' License Agreement, which appear on the user's screen. Paragraph 10 of

the Agreement includes the following clause:

> This License Agreement shall be governed by the laws of the State of Washington, without regard to conflicts of law provisions, and you hereby consent to the exclusive jurisdiction of the state and federal courts sitting in the State of Washington. Any and all unresolved disputes arising under this License Agreement shall be submitted to arbitration in the State of Washington.

Defendant cites this clause as binding authority for its assertions that arbitration is required. Intervenor, on the other hand, argues that this clause does not operate to require arbitration for several reasons. First, Intervenor contends that the License Agreement, including the arbitration requirement, does not constitute a "writing." Second, Intervenor claims that Ninth Circuit decisional law controls the construction of the arbitration provision and dictates that the arbitration clause be read narrowly to preclude enforcement in this action. Finally, Intervenor argues that the arbitration provision is unenforceable because it is unconscionable.

OPINION BY: KOCORAS, J

Although national policy encourages arbitration of disputes, submission to arbitration is consensual, not coercive. Thus, a court cannot force a party to arbitrate unless that party has entered into a contractual agreement to do so.

* * *

I. WRITING REQUIREMENT

Intervenor claims that the License Agreement, including the arbitration provision, does not constitute a writing as required by the Federal Arbitration Act (the "FAA") and the Washington Arbitration Act (the "WAA") in order to be enforced. According to Intervenor, the License Agreement is an electronic agreement, and electronic agreements do not satisfy the "written" agreement provisions of the FAA and the WAA. Moreover, Intervenor asserts that even if some electronic agreements are acceptable, RealNetworks' electronic agreement is not because a user cannot print or save it. RealNetworks does not dispute that the arbitration provision must be written in order to be enforceable. Rather, RealNetworks argues that its License Agreement, including the arbitration provision, constitute a writing and that it may be printed and saved.

Both the Intervenor and RealNetworks agree that Congress intended the FAA to apply only to written contracts. Because the terms in the statute must be given their plain meaning and do not explicitly allow

for an "electronic" agreement, Intervenor reasons that an electronic communication cannot satisfy the writing requirement, but only a written one can. However, this only begs the question, what is a written agreement? Although contract terms must be given their plain and ordinary meaning, the Court is unconvinced that the plain and ordinary meaning of "writing" or "written" necessarily cannot include any electronic writings.

Courts frequently look to dictionaries in order to determine the plain meaning of words and particularly to examine how a word was defined at the time the statute was drafted and enacted. The FAA was enacted in 1925. As now, words had several different definitions. In relevant part, at the time, Webster's Dictionary defined "writing" as:

1. The act or art of forming letters or characters on paper, wood, stone, or other material, for the purpose of recording the ideas which characters and words express, or of communicating them to others by visible signs.
2. Anything written or printed; anything expressed in characters or letters. See *WEBSTER'S DICTIONARY* (1913).

Webster's defined "written" as the participle of write, which it defined as:

To set down, as legible characters; to form the conveyance of meaning; to inscribe on any material by a suitable instrument; as, to write the characters called letters; to write figures.

A legal dictionary at the time provided that "The word 'written,' used in a statute, may include printing and any other mode of representing words and letters." See Pope, Benjamin, W., *Legal Definitions,*

Callaghan and Co. (1920). Thus, although the definition of a writing included a traditional paper document, it did not exclude representations of language on other media. Because electronic communications can be letters or characters formed on the screen to record or communicate ideas by visible signs and can be legible characters that represent words and letters as well as form the conveyance of meaning, it would seem that the plain meaning of the word "written" does not exclude all electronic communications. That being said, the Court does not now find that all electronic communications may be considered "written." Rather, the Court examines the contract at issue in this action and finds that its easily printable and storable nature is sufficient to render it "written."

The Court rejects Intervenor's contention that the License Agreement is not printable and storable. Intervenor asserts that RealNetworks affirmatively inhibits users from printing or storing the License Agreement by failing to provide a conspicuous "print" or "save" button on the pop-up License Agreement window. However, Intervenor is incorrect in its assertions because the License Agreement may rather easily be printed and is automatically stored on the user's hard drive despite the absence of the "print" and "save" buttons. In fact, there exists more than one way to print the License Agreement. First, before the user has even accepted the License Agreement, the user can right click his mouse over the text of the License Agreement, select all, and copy and paste it onto any word processing program. Since using the right click function is too specialized for Intervenor, he even has the option to simply click and drag the cursor over the text of the License Agreement in order to highlight it and then copy and paste the License Agreement onto any word processing program. Moreover, users have yet another way of printing the License Agreement. After a user accepts the License Agreement, it is automatically downloaded and saved to the user's hard drive. The user can then click on the License Agreement, listed separately as either "RealJukeBox License Agreement" or "RealPlayer License Agreement," depending on the product, and easily print out either agreement from the file pull down menu. Thus, Intervenor's assertion that the License Agreement cannot be saved, retrieved, or printed is incorrect. Moreover, once installed, the License Agreement is not hidden, as Intervenor claims, but is listed as prominent and separate icons under "Real" on the "Start" menu. Although any computer use can be intimidating, the process of printing the License Agreement is no more difficult or esoteric than many other basic computer functions, and the melodrama and over exaggeration with which Intervenor describes the alleged impossibility of printing the License Agreement is disingenuous.

Finally, Intervenor points to Congress' present day discussions about electronic communications in arguing that the FAA's and WAA's writing requirement cannot be satisfied by an electronic communication. However, the modern congressional discussions that Intervenor points to do not serve as evidence of Congress' intent when it enacted the FAA in 1925. That Congress may now, with some hindsight on the advance of electronic communication, explicitly provide for written and electronic agreements in new legislation, does not mean that Congress in 1925 excluded electronic communications from the category of written communications by not explicitly providing for it. Rather, "New words may be designed to fortify the current rule with a more precise text that curtails uncertainty." Modern Congress' discussions indicate that it was, in fact, the "uncertain" legal effect of an electronic record or an electronic signature that prompted Congress to consider the "Electronic Signatures in Global and National Commerce Act," to which Intervenor cites. Moreover, it seems that the License Agreement would, nevertheless, constitute a writing even for purposes of Congress' discussions today because the License Agreement may be printed and stored.

Thus, the License Agreement, including the arbitration provision, is a written agreement.

* * *

The court went on to find for the defendant, holding that the End User License Agreement (EULA) effectively barred a suit in court because of the arbitration clause.

QUESTIONS FOR ANALYSIS

1. The court sought to limit the precedential value of this case by stating that they were not holding that all electronic records satisfy writing requirements. Was the fact that the EULA was easily printable a factor in the court's decision that the electronic writing satisfied the writing requirement under the Federal Arbitration Association?
2. Is the result in this case just the kind of event that the Consumers Union was warning against in their article above? Do you read End User License Agreements?

CHALLENGES TO CONTRACT LAW CREATED BY THE INTERNET AND E-COMMERCE

Formation of Contracts: Common Law

The common law theory of contracts presupposes that an offeror manifests (1) intent to make an offer, (2) that contains certain terms that are reasonably definite, and (3) that the offer is communicated to the offeree. The offeree also is assumed to manifest intent to be bound by certifying assent to the terms in the offer (see http://www.law.cornell.edu/ucc/ucc2-206.text.html for UCC definitions of offer and acceptance).

The aforementioned basic principles of contract law must be substantially modified to deal with the commercial realities of Internet transactions. Sometimes *intent* must be gleaned from electronic agents that operate based on artificial intelligence. Signatures are generally used in written contracts to memorialize intent and yet signatures are not easily facilitated on the Internet, though there is something called "*digital signatures*" that will be discussed below. Intent is just one of the thorny issues that has had to be dealt with in attempting to meld traditional contract law with E-Commerce. As discussed above, both UCITA and revised Article 2 of the UCC allow intent to be *inferred* from the operations of electronic agents, and signatures (called authentications) can occur with a response to an invitation to click to accept.

Electronic Data Interchange

Electronic Data Interchange (EDI) is a closed system in which one company's computer communicates with another computer from a different company. EDI

Invesco Funds Group No Longer Wants the Mail Carrier to Stand between It and New Mutual-Fund Customers

Denver-based Invesco said it will become the first mutual-fund company to allow investors to open new fund accounts entirely over the Internet ... The move represents a quantum leap in the development of mutual-fund transactions on the Internet. In the past, the fund industry has been criticized as slow in embracing the Web. For instance, while large fund companies Fidelity Investments and Vanguard Group permit investors to fill out fund-account applications on the Web, a new account still can't be opened without customers first printing out the Internet forms and mailing them in with a personal check.

No Signature Here

The primary hurdle preventing full-transaction capability on the Web: the need for an investor's signature. A signature gives a fund-account authentication and also authorizes the firm to move assets from the investor's bank account to the fund account. As a result, many fund companies have been waiting for digital signatures to be available on the Internet before launching new accounts online.

Without signatures, "it seems it could make things a little more open to misinterpretation," warns Jim Folwell, an analyst at fund consulting firm Cerulli Associates in Boston. 'It gives the fund company one less legal leg to stand on.' But Invesco, a $30 billion-under-management unit of Amvescap, has decided to circumvent the signature barrier by not requiring one at all. Jon Pauley, Invesco's vice president of electronic commerce, says the firm will provide new investors with electronic consent firms and a series of passwords and other devices to ensure that the opening of a new account is secure. New money for accounts opened over the Web will be drawn directly from an investor's bank account, and fund shares will be priced at the end of that day. He declined to reveal other details, citing competitive concerns.

Source: August 26, 1999, Pui-Wing Tam and David Franecki, "Invesco to Allow Investors To Open Accounts Online," *THE WALL STREET JOURNAL* http://interactive.wsj.com.

is closed because it is not accessible by outsiders, as is a website on the World Wide Web. EDI has proved to be a very efficient means of doing business between two large companies that have a large volume of business that is expected to continue for an indefinite duration. Consider an apparel manufacturer such as one of the famous clothing brand names—maybe Calvin Klein. Suppose the Calvin Klein Company has an EDI contract with J.C. Penny. When inventories of Calvin Klein products become low, J.C. Penny's computers contact Calvin Klein's computers and request shipments of the appropriate replacements. The EDI between these two computers creates legally binding contracts even though there is no individualized attention from human agents of either side of the agreement. There is, however, an overall EDI agreement that deals with terms of the contracts, essentially an agreement to agree in the future. EDI orders (contracts) for the replacement inventory items described are formed electronically without human intervention and are legally enforceable based on whichever of the current UCC or the Revised Section 2B applies to the transaction.

Contract Formation Issues Involving Computer Software

It is virtually impossible to browse the Internet without encountering offers. Indeed, the opening frames shown by Internet Service Providers (ISPs), such as America OnLine (AOL), are accompanied by legally binding offers to contract. The offeror in this case is a company whose offer is out there for all to see. If the member uses search engines, (s)he will be exposed to banners that include additional offers to sell various products. The offer is electronic, though prospective customers could print it out. There is a question as to what the offer actually is, however. Assume that the offeror is trying to sell software that recognizes human voices or a digital camera. There are generally both narrative and various visual descriptions of the product(s) and the prospective customer is invited to purchase the product on-line. Often the seller will request credit card information to effect the sale, but generally other methods of payment are accepted such as checks or money orders.

The following case shows the consequences of consent online. The plaintiffs in this case effectively had to travel to the State of Washington to bring suit against Microsoft because of a forum clause buried deep in the "agreement" they had entered with Microsoft. As with the previous case, important legal rights are contained in End User Agreements.

Additional Terms and Acceptances with a Click

Under the common law of contracts an acceptance must be *complete* and *unqualified,* meaning that the offeree agrees to each and every term in the offer and does not add additional terms. If the offeree adds additional terms in the acceptance or requests a change in the offer, the offeree has made a counter offer and becomes the offeror. In the past, the absolutist approach of the common law of contracts clashed with commercial practice that often involved company forms such as invoices (from the seller) and purchase orders (from the buyer) that each contained contract terms. When the UCC was enacted, it specifically allowed for additional terms in the acceptance and that allowance has been continued under the proposed revisions under Article 2 (Section 2-207).

Steven J. Caspi v. *The Microsoft Network, L.L.C.*
Superior Court of New Jersey, Appellate Division
323 N.J.Super. 118, 732 A.2d 528 (1999)

FACTS AND CASE BACKGROUND

Plaintiffs are subscribers of Microsoft Network (MSN), an online computer service. Two of the plaintiffs reside in the State of New Jersey. The plaintiffs allege fraud and breach of contract on the part of MSN, claiming that they were victimized by negative option billing, which means that the plaintiffs were charged with paying for software unless they took action to say they did not want the software. Plaintiffs sue in state court in New Jersey and defendants (MSN) cite a forum selection clause, which is part of the subscribers' contracts with MSN. The forum selection clause requires that lawsuits against MSN must be litigated in the State of Washington.

OPINION: KESTIN, J.A.D.

We are here called upon to determine the validity and enforceability of a forum selection clause contained in an on-line subscriber agreement of the Microsoft Network (MSN), an on-line computer service. The trial court granted defendants' motion to dismiss the complaint on the ground that the forum selection clause in the parties' contracts called for plaintiffs' claims to be litigated in the State of Washington. Plaintiffs appeal. We affirm.

The amended class action complaint in 18 counts sought divers relief against two related corporate entities, The Microsoft Network, L.L.C. and Microsoft Corporation (collectively, Microsoft). Plaintiffs asserted various theories including breach of contract, common law fraud, and consumer fraud in the way Microsoft had "rolled over" MSN membership into more expensive plans. Among the claims was an accusation that Microsoft had engaged in "unilateral negative option billing," a practice condemned by the attorneys general of 21 states, including New Jersey's, with regard to a Microsoft competitor, America Online, Inc. Under the practice as alleged, Microsoft, without notice to or permission from MSN members, unilaterally charged them increased membership fees attributable to a change in service plans.

The four named plaintiffs are members of MSN. Two reside in New Jersey; the others in Ohio and New York. Purporting to represent a nationwide class of 1.5 million similarly aggrieved MSN members, plaintiffs, in May 1997, moved for multi-state class action certification.

Shortly thereafter, defendants moved to dismiss the amended complaint for lack of jurisdiction and improper venue by reason of the forum selection clause which, defendants contended, was in every MSN membership agreement and bound all the named plaintiffs and all members of the class they purported to represent. That clause, paragraph 15.1 of the MSN membership agreement, provided:

> This agreement is governed by the laws of the State of Washington, USA, and you consent to the exclusive jurisdiction and venue of courts in King County, Washington in all disputes arising out of or relating to your use of MSN or your MSN membership.

Plaintiffs cross-moved, inter alia, to strike a certification submitted in support of defendants' motion to dismiss and to compel the deposition of the certificant.

*   *   *

Before becoming an MSN member, a prospective subscriber is prompted by MSN software to view multiple computer screens of information, including a membership agreement which contains the above clause. MSN's membership agreement appears on the computer screen in a scrollable window next to blocks providing the choices "I Agree" and "I Don't Agree." Prospective members assent to the terms of the agreement by clicking on "I Agree" using a computer mouse. Prospective members have the option to click "I Agree" or "I Don't Agree" at any point while scrolling through the agreement. Registration may proceed only after the potential subscriber has had the opportunity to view and has assented to the membership agreement, including MSN's forum selection clause. No charges are incurred until after the membership agreement review is completed and a subscriber has clicked on "I Agree."

The trial court observed:

> Generally, forum selection clauses are prima facie valid and enforceable in New Jersey. New Jersey courts will decline to enforce a clause only if it fits into one of three exceptions to the general rule: (1) the clause is a result of fraud or "overweening" bargaining power; (2) enforcement would violate the strong public policy of New Jersey; or (3) enforcement would seriously inconvenience trial. The burden falls on the party objecting to enforcement to show that the clause in question fits within one of these exceptions. Plaintiffs have failed to meet that burden here.

Judge Fitzpatrick correctly discerned that:

> New Jersey follows the logic of the United States Supreme Court

decision in *Carnival Cruise Lines* v. *Shute,* 499 U.S. 585, 111 S.Ct. 1522, 113 L.Ed.2d 622 (1991). * * * In *Carnival,* cruise ship passengers were held to a forum selection clause which appeared in their travel contract. The clause enforced in *Carnival* was very similar in nature to the clause in question here, the primary difference being that the *Carnival* clause was placed in small print in a travel contract while the clause in the case sub judice was placed on-line on scrolled computer screens.

The trial court opinion went on to analyze plaintiffs' contentions:

> Plaintiffs' consent to MSN's clause does not appear to be the result of fraud or overweening bargaining power. In New Jersey, fraud consists of (1) material misrepresentation of a past or present fact; (2) knowledge or belief by the declarant of its falsity; (3) an intention that the recipient rely on it; (4) reasonable reliance by the recipient; and (5) resulting damages. Plaintiffs have not shown that MSN's forum selection clause constitutes fraud. The clause is reasonable, clear and contains no material misrepresentation.
>
> Further, plaintiffs were not subjected to overweening bargaining power in dealing with Microsoft and MSN. The Supreme Court has held that a corporate vendor's inclusion of a forum selection clause in a consumer contract does not in itself constitute overweening bargaining power. In order to invalidate a forum selection clause, something more than merely size difference must be shown. A court's focus must be whether such an imbalance in size resulted in an inequality of bargaining power that was unfairly exploited by the more powerful party.
>
> Plaintiffs have shown little more than a size difference here. The on-line computer service industry is not one without competition, and

therefore consumers are left with choices as to which service they select for Internet access, e-mail and other information services. Plaintiffs were not forced into a situation where MSN was the only available server. Additionally, plaintiffs and the class which they purport to represent were given ample opportunity to affirmatively assent to the forum selection clause. Like *Carnival,* plaintiffs here "retained the option of rejecting the contract with impunity." In such a case, this court finds it impossible to perceive an overwhelming bargaining situation.

* * *

After reviewing the record in the light of the arguments advanced by the parties, we are in substantial agreement with the reasons for decision articulated by Judge Fitzpatrick. We reject as meritless plaintiffs' arguments on appeal that the terms of the forum selection clause do not prevent plaintiffs from suing Microsoft outside of Washington or, alternatively, that the forum selection clause lacks adequate clarity. The meaning of the clause is plain and its effect as a limiting provision is clear. Furthermore, New Jersey's interest in assuring consumer fraud protection will not be frustrated by requiring plaintiffs to proceed with a lawsuit in Washington as prescribed by the plain language of the forum selection clause. As a general matter, none of the inherent characteristics of forum selection clauses implicate consumer fraud concepts in any special way. If a forum selection clause is clear in its purport and has been presented to the party to be bound in a fair and forthright fashion, no consumer fraud policies or principles have been violated. Cf. id. at 63-64, 606 A.2d 407. Moreover, as a matter of policy interest and apart from considerations bearing upon the choice-of-law provision in the forum selection clause, plaintiffs have given us no reason to apprehend that the nature and scope of consumer fraud protections afforded by the State of Washington are materially different or less broad in scope than those available in this State.

QUESTIONS FOR ANALYSIS

1. How many students who are members of various online services carefully read their membership agreements?
2. Note that just because MSN is part of a very large corporation,

that the court did not agree it was evidence of unfair bargaining power. What additional fact may have tipped the scale in favor of the defendants? *Hint:* Suppose there was only online service such as MSN.

In fact, the proposed Section 2-207 of the UCC makes it easier (than in the current Article 2 of the UCC) to include additional terms in the contract that were not in the offer. Proposed Section 2-207(b) states that, "if a contract is formed by offer and acceptance and the acceptance is by a record containing terms additional to or different from the offer . . . the terms of the contract include:

1. terms in the records [offer and acceptance] of the parties to the extent that they agree;
2. nonstandard terms, whether or not in a record, to which the parties have otherwise agreed;
3. standard terms in a record supplied by a party to which the other party has expressly agreed; and

4. terms supplied or incorporated under any provision of the UCC."

Under the current Article 2, *additional terms* in the acceptance were not part of the contract if these terms *materially altered* the contract.[10] When the new Article 2 is passed, additional terms in the acceptance will be part of the contract even if they materially alter the contract. The bottom line is that additional terms in the acceptance are firmly established in commercial practice and the UCC. The following case illustrates the difficulties of applying "old" UCC law to E-Commerce transactions.

[10]Section 2-207(2) "Between merchants such terms become part of the contract unless:
. . . . (b) they materially alter it; or," . . .

Step-Saver Data Systems, Inc. v. *Wyse Technology*
U.S. Court of Appeals, 3rd Circuit
939 F.2d 91, (1991)

FACTS AND CASE BACKGROUND

Step-Saver was among the leaders in value-added retailing for International Business Machines (IBM). Step-Saver developed multi-user capabilities within micro-computer technology, which meant that purchasers could buy fewer computers because all the computers are linked together. After evaluating its needs, Step-Saver selected a multi-user operating system from TSL called Multilink Advanced. Step-Saver used monitors manufactured by Wyse Technology and computers by IBM.

The software Step-Saver was selling was supposed to operate with an operating system by Microsoft (MS-DOS) or software developed by Step-Saver. The target audience was law and medical offices. Almost from the start, dissatisfied customers complained that Multilink Advanced did not operate as warranted.

In the TSL's software there was a boxtop license that purported to be the complete understanding between the parties (TSL and licensees of its software) and a disclaimer of all express and implied warranties.

The boxtop license gave purchasers 15 days to return the software, otherwise they were bound by the terms in the boxtop license. Based on the language in the boxtop, TSL moved for, and was granted, a motion for a directed verdict.

OPINION: WISDOM, JUDGE
II. THE EFFECT OF THE BOX-TOP LICENSE

The relationship between Step-Saver and TSL began in the fall of 1984 when Step-Saver asked TSL for information on an early version of the

Multilink program. TSL provided Step-Saver with a copy of the early program, known simply as Multilink, without charge to permit Step-Saver to test the program to see what it could accomplish. Step-Saver performed some tests with the early program, but did not market a system based on it.

In the summer of 1985, Step-Saver noticed some advertisements in *Byte* magazine for a more powerful version of the Multilink program, known as Multilink Advanced. Step-Saver requested information from TSL concerning this new version of the program, and allegedly was assured by sales representatives that the new version was compatible with 90 percent of the programs available "off-the-shelf" for computers using MS-DOS. The sales representatives allegedly made a number of additional specific representations of fact concerning the capabilities of the Multilink Advanced program.

Based on these representations, Step-Saver obtained several copies of the Multilink Advanced program in the spring of 1986, and conducted tests with the program. After these tests, Step-Saver decided to market a multi-user system which used the Multilink Advanced program. From August of 1986 through March of 1987, Step-Saver purchased and resold 142 copies of the Multilink Advanced program. Step-Saver would typically purchase copies of the program in the following manner. First, Step-Saver would telephone TSL and place an order. (Step-Saver would typically order 20 copies of the program at a time.) TSL would accept the order and promise, while on the telephone, to ship the goods promptly. After the telephone order, Step-Saver would send a purchase order, detailing the items to be purchased, their price, and shipping and payment terms. TSL would ship the order promptly, along with an invoice. The invoice would contain terms essentially identical with those on Step-Saver's purchase order: price, quantity, and shipping and payment terms. No reference was made during the telephone calls, or on either the purchase orders or the invoices with regard to a disclaimer of any warranties. Printed on the package of each copy of the program however, would be a copy of the boxtop license. The boxtop license contains five terms relevant to this action:

1. The boxtop license provides that the customer has not purchased the software itself, but has merely obtained a personal, nontransferable license to use the program.
2. The boxtop license, in detail and at some length, disclaims all express and implied warranties except for a warranty that the disks contained in the box are free from defects.
3. The boxtop license provides that the sole remedy available to a purchaser of the program is to return a defective disk for replacement; the license excludes any liability for damages, direct or consequential, caused by the use of the program.
4. The boxtop license contains an integration clause, which provides that the boxtop license is the final and complete expression of the terms of the parties' agreement.
5. The boxtop license states: "Opening this package indicates your acceptance of these terms and conditions. If you do not agree with them, you should promptly return the package unopened to the person from whom you purchased it within 15 days from date of purchase and your money will be refunded to you by that person."

The district court, without much discussion, held, as a matter of law, that the boxtop license was the final and complete expression of the terms of the parties' agreement. Because the district court decided the questions of contract formation and interpretation as issues of law, we review the district court's resolution of these questions *de novo*.

Step-Saver contends that the contract for each copy of the program was formed when TSL agreed, on the telephone, to ship the copy at the agreed price. The boxtop license, argues Step-Saver, was a material alteration to the parties' contract which did not become a part of the contract under UCC § 2-207. Alternatively, Step-Saver argues that the undisputed evidence establishes that the parties did not intend the box top license as a final and complete expression of the terms of their agreement, and, therefore, the parol evidence rule of UCC § 2-202 would not apply . . .

To understand why the terms of the license should be considered under § 2-207 in this case, we review briefly the reasons behind § 2-207. Under the common law of sales, and to some extent still for contracts outside the UCC, an acceptance that varied any term of the offer operated as a rejection of the offer, and simultaneously made a counteroffer. This common law formality was known as the mirror image rule, because the terms of the acceptance had to mirror the terms of the offer to be effective. If the offeror proceeded with the contract despite the differing terms of the supposed acceptance, he would, by his performance, constructively accept the terms of the "counteroffer", and be bound by its terms. As a result of these rules, the terms of the party who sent the last form, typically the seller, would become the terms of the parties' contract. This result was known as the "last shot rule."

The UCC, in § 2-207, rejected this approach. Instead, it recognized that, while a party may desire the terms detailed in its form if a dispute, in fact, arises, most parties do not expect a dispute to arise when they first enter into a contract. As a result, most parties will proceed with the transaction even if they know that the terms of their form would not be enforced. The insight behind the rejection of the last shot rule is that it would be unfair to bind the buyer of goods to the standard terms of the seller, when neither party cared sufficiently to establish expressly the terms of their agreement, simply because the seller sent the last form. Thus, UCC § 2-207 establishes a legal rule that proceeding with a contract after receiving a writing that purports to define the terms of the parties' contract is not sufficient to establish the party's consent to the terms of the writing to the extent that the terms of the writing either add to, or differ from, the terms detailed in the parties' earlier writings or discussions. In the absence of a party's express assent to the additional or different terms of the writing, section 2-207 provides a default rule

that the parties intended, as the terms of their agreement, those terms to which both parties have agreed, along with any terms implied by the provisions of the UCC.

The reasons that led to the rejection of the last shot rule, and the adoption of section 2-207, apply fully in this case. TSL never mentioned during the parties' negotiations leading to the purchase of the programs, nor did it, at any time, obtain Step-Saver's express assent to the terms of the boxtop license. Instead, TSL contented itself with attaching the terms to the packaging of the software, even though those terms differed substantially from those previously discussed by the parties. Thus, the boxtop license, in this case, is best seen as one more form in a battle of forms, and the question of whether Step-Saver has agreed to be bound by the terms of the boxtop license is best resolved by applying the legal principles detailed in section 2-207.

* * *

The court decided that since Section 2-207 applied, the additional terms in the boxtop license were part

of the contract only if the parties agreed to the additional terms or if those terms did not materially alter the contract. The court ruled that the warranty disclaimers did, in fact, materially alter the contract and, thus, that they did not become part of the contract—TSL's boxtop agreement with warranty disclaimers had no contractual standing.

QUESTIONS FOR ANALYSIS

1. If TSL was only willing to sell the software with the warranty disclaimers, how, realistically, could it have communicated this information to its purchasers? If most of the contracts were agreed to over the phone, how many customers would be willing to listen to long-winded discussions of warranty disclaimers?
2. Would the result have been different in this case if TSL sought to limit liability to replacement of defective copies, rather than disclaiming all warranties? Is a limitation of liability a material alteration of the contract?

When Additional Terms in the Acceptance (or Offer) Are Enforceable

When the customer signifies willingness to purchase an item online, he or she is often confronted with additional terms of the "offer". Among these terms are various clauses regarding warranties, return policies, reproductions or duplications of the product if it is software and other "fine print". The purchaser is cautioned that assent to purchase the item means that the purchaser agrees to each term in the fine print. These terms are often called "clickwrap" agreements and their enforceability is crucial to the transaction, particularly if the item is purchased over the Internet. In effect, the offer to sell is accompanied by terms that are not apparent to the purchaser before the decision to purchase is made. Much the same situation occurs if software is

purchased over the counter at a retail outlet at a computer store. In a "shrinkwrap" agreement, the customer is bound by the terms of the contract even though the customer cannot know what many of the terms are until she has paid her money and breaks open the (shrink) wrapping around the CDs or diskettes that contain the software program. A "boxwrap" (or boxtop) agreement has similar characteristics in that the consumer can only discover the terms of the contract by opening the box and reading the terms of the contract, usually at the bottom of the box next to the product.

The *Hill* case, directly below, illustrates the need for customers to read boxtop agreements and respond promptly. Note that there is no requirement for an arbitration clause to be highlighted among the clauses in the boxtop agreement.

Issues Surrounding Clickwraps

The enforceability of clickwrap agreements raises two fundamental issues of contract law—formation and assent.

The formation of a contract between buyer and seller typically occurs before the buyer takes possession of the goods. The buyer and seller negotiate the terms of the sale, often memorializing their understanding in a written agreement, and then the goods are tendered. By contrast, when a consumer purchases software that displays a clickwrap agreement at the time of installation, the consumer has already purchased the product and is being asked to consent to the contract that purportedly memorializes their agreement. In this case, the question becomes "is the contract formed at the moment of purchase or later when the buyer assents to the terms of the clickwrap agreement?" Consumers have argued that such agreements are unconscionable because the parties lack the opportunity to bargain over or modify the terms of the agreement.

Clickwrap agreements also challenge our understanding of the manifestation of the buyer's assent. A contract is traditionally enforceable when the parties sign an agreement. In a clickwrap scenario, however, the buyer consents not with a written signature but with the click of a mouse. Is this sufficient to bind the buyer to the terms of the clickwrap agreement?

Source: August 11, 1998, Richard Raysman and Peter Brown, "Clickwrap License Agreements," *New York Law Journal.* http://prod01.ljextra.com/internet/0811clickwrap.html

Rich and Enza Hill v. *Gateway 2000, Inc.*
U.S. Court of Appeals for the Seventh Circuit
105 F.3d 1147 (1997)

FACTS AND CASE BACKGROUND

Rich and Enza Hill purchased a Gateway 2000 computer based on a phone conversation from a representative of Gateway. When the box containing the computer arrives, there are additional terms in the box which Gateway claims are part of the contract. The Hills were given 30 days to decide whether they are bound by the terms or whether they want to return the computer.

Among the additional terms in the box is an arbitration clause. The arbitration clause requires that all disputes regarding performance of the Gateway 2000 computer are subject to being arbitrated and that the customer does not have the right to pursue a remedy in court. The Hill's complain that the arbitration clause was not prominent and that they should not be bound by terms of a contract that they did not know about when they agreed to the contract.

OPINION: EASTERBROOK

One of the terms in the box containing a Gateway 2000 system was an arbitration clause. Rich and Enza Hill, the customers, kept the computer more than 30 days before complaining about its components and performance. They filed suit in federal court arguing, among other things, that the product's shortcomings make Gateway a racketeer (mail and wire fraud are said to be the predicate offenses), leading to treble damages under RICO for the Hills and a class of all other purchasers. Gateway asked the district court to enforce the arbitration clause; the judge refused, writing that "the present record is insufficient to support a finding of a valid arbitration agreement between the parties or that the plaintiffs were given adequate notice of the arbitration clause." Gateway took an immediate appeal, as is its right.

The Hills say that the arbitration clause did not stand out: they concede noticing the statement of terms but deny reading it closely enough to discover the agreement to arbitrate, and they ask us to conclude that they therefore may go to court. Yet an agreement to arbitrate must be enforced "save upon such grounds as exist at law or in equity for the revocation of any contract." A contract need not be read to be effective; people who accept take the risk that the unread terms may in retrospect prove unwelcome. Terms inside Gateway's box stand or fall together. If they constitute the parties' contract because the Hills had an opportunity to return the computer after reading them, then all must be enforced.

ProCD, Inc. v. *Zeidenberg* [citation omitted] holds that terms inside a box of software bind consumers who use the software after an opportunity to read the terms and to reject them by returning the product. Likewise, *Carnival Cruise Lines, Inc. v. Shute* enforces a forum-selection clause that was included among three pages of terms attached to a cruise ship ticket. *ProCD* and *Carnival Cruise Lines* exemplify the many commercial transactions in which people pay for products with terms to follow; *ProCD* discusses others. The district [**4] court concluded in *ProCD* that the contract is formed when the consumer pays for the software; as a result, the court held, only terms known to the consumer at that moment are part of the contract, and provisos inside the box do not count. Although this is one way a contract could be formed, it is not the only way: "A vendor, as master of the offer, may invite acceptance by con-

duct, and may propose limitations on the kind of conduct that constitutes acceptance. A buyer may accept by performing the acts the vendor proposes to treat as acceptance." [Citation omitted] Gateway shipped computers with the same sort of accept-or-return offer ProCD made to users of its software. ProCD relied on the Uniform Commercial Code rather than any peculiarities of Wisconsin law; both Illinois and South Dakota, the two states whose law might govern relations between Gateway and the Hills, have adopted the UCC; neither side has pointed us to any atypical doctrines in those states that might be pertinent; *ProCD* therefore applies to this dispute.

The decision of the district court is vacated, and this case is remanded

with instructions to compel the Hills to submit their dispute to arbitration.

CONCLUSION

The decision of the District Court that the Hills could proceed in the federal courts was reversed because the Circuit Court of Appeals held that the arbitration clause was enforceable.

QUESTIONS FOR ANALYSIS

1. When, according to the court of appeals, did the customer accept the offer of the seller?
2. Is it commercially feasible for a sales representative to read (and be prepared to explain) the fine print over the phone?
3. Are this case and the previous case consistent?

Modern Contract Law: Layers of Terms

The distinctions between the specifics of many e-contracts and traditional requirements for valid contracts should be clear. In E-Commerce, *intent* is presumed by the electronic offer made by the vendor. The offeree's intent to assent to the terms of the contract provided by the offeree is manifested by a *click* from the customer or even by the operation of an electronic agent. As we have seen, the offeree often cannot know the terms of contract until after physical transfer of the product has occurred. In effect, the buyer learns what he or she has assented to after paying money and receiving the product. Once these conditions have been satisfied, the legal question becomes, "Is the customer bound by terms of an agreement that he or she learns about after purchase?" The answer is yes provided several conditions are met. These include:

1. The customer must be given *clear notice* of the additional terms, which must be written in understandable English.
2. The customer must be given *clear notice as to what constitutes acceptance*. Acceptance could be manifested by a click at the appropriate button, breaking the wrapping around software, or by choosing not to return a product in a specified time interval.

3. The customer must have an *opportunity to inspect the terms* in the wrap agreement.
4. The customer has an *unqualified right to return the merchandise* for a full refund if the customer does not agree to the terms contained in the clickwrap, shrinkwrap, or boxwrap.
5. The customer cannot be bound by *terms that are unconscionable* in light of ordinary commercial standards.

Much software can be purchased over the Internet and, when such purchases occur, the buyer is technically a licensee and not owner of the software so that UCITA applies. The software vendor (really a licensor) will generally have terms in the contract restricting what the licensee can do with the software. Examples are provided by the *Hill* and *Step-Saver* cases above. ZDNet has a clickwrap agreement for its software (e.g., http://www.zdnet.com/filters/terms/). There have been several cases that illustrate the enforceability of clickwrap agreements (as well as shrinkwrap and boxwrap). The evolution of these cases shows that the courts are increasingly receptive to the enforceability of these agreements.

UCITA explicitly deals with additional terms in comments to **Section 210. Adopting Terms of Records.** In Comment 3, the composers of UCITA make the following observation, "In ordinary commercial practice, while some contracts are formed and their terms fully defined at a single point in time, many commercial transactions involve a rolling or layering process. An agreement exists, but terms are clarified or created over time. That principle is acknowledged in various portions of original Article 2 of the U.C.C." The comments go on to cite Section 2-207 of the U.C.C. "that later records presented to the other party are treated as proposed modifications or confirming memorandum only in cases of 'a proposed deal which in commercial understanding has in fact been closed.'"

According to the UCITA comments to the same section, "Often, the commercial expectation is that terms will follow or be developed after performance begins. While some courts seem to hold that an initial agreement per se concludes that contracting as a single event notwithstanding ordinary practice and expectations that terms will follow, other courts recognize layered contract formation and term definition, correctly viewing contracting as a process, rather than as a single event." The bottom line is that the trend that began in Section 2-207, which recognizes the possibility of additional terms in the acceptance, is fully endorsed and accentuated in UCITA. Following commercial practice, after a deal is struck, additional terms dealing with warranty, maintenance, and other standard provisions are added to the contract, "without having to consider all such terms in the first interaction of the automated contracting system."

IDENTITY PROBLEMS: WHO IS ACCEPTING?

With click-on acceptances, the advantage of unique signatures is lost. Clearly the vendor has a difficult time determining whether the clicker (the person clicking the acceptance dot) is the offeree to whom the offer was made. The critical issue is whether there is a contract when fraud or mistake is present in interactions between computers and between computers and individuals. Note first, that the default provisions of UCITA and revised Article 2 can be modified by agreement in the contract. In other words, the parties to a contract can decide among themselves who bears the risk of mistransmission. Certainly in most EDI contracts, risk of mistransmission provisions are standard clauses and resulting losses are allocated by agreement to the sender, the sendee, or a combination

of both. The risk of E-Commerce fraud or mistake can be reduced if the parties have a prior relationship, which makes identification of purchasers much more reliable. Certainly, there are instances in which it is the vendor who must assume the losses associated with fraudulent clicks. If the clicker is a minor, the vendor is subject to having the contract disaffirmed. There are other risks borne by the vendor when fraud or mistake is present, especially if the goods are sent.

Costs and Benefits of Gathering Information about Visitors to a Website

One mechanism used by vendors to prevent fraud is the use of passwords. The vendor can gain experience by asking for information from customers, who may become "members" of the vendor's website. Passwords can be used as a substitute for signatures, but the liability for unauthorized use of a password is borne by the customer.

A raft of issues arises from the gathering of information about customers because such information is valuable—Internet vendors can make money selling such information to other vendors. The issue of sales of marketing information to third parties and possible invasions of privacy is discussed in some detail in Chapter 6. Quite certainly, vendors have a legitimate interest in gathering sufficient information about website visitors to prevent fraud. Once they gather that information on customers, such information can be and in many cases has been used in ways not anticipated by website visitors.

ATTRIBUTION PROCEDURES AND CONSUMER DEFENSES

According to Section 102(5) of UCITA "'Attribution Procedure' means a procedure established by law, administrative rule, or agreement, or a procedure otherwise adopted by the parties, to verify that an electronic event is that of a specific person or to detect changes or errors in the information. The term includes a procedure that requires the use of algorithms or other codes, identifying words or numbers (passwords), encryption, callback or other acknowledgment, or any other procedures that are reasonable under the circumstances." Translated into English, it means a procedure for attributing to a specific individual a specific electronic event such as ordering software over the Internet.

Bill to Give E-Signatures Legal Weight

Everyone's banking on e-commerce to give the economy a boost—and Congress is doing its part to help make it happen. The Internet Growth and Development Act of 1999 (HR 1685) is a catch-all bill intended to make the Internet a thriving medium, according to Rep. Rick Boucher (R-Virginia, NINTHNET@mail.house.gov), the bill's sponsor. Boucher's bill would, among other things, give digital signatures the same legal weight as paper-based signatures, and it would require Websites to post notice of their policies regarding the use of personal information. Boucher seems to have lumped several pet projects into the bill; the resulting hodgepodge probably has little chance of being passed into law.

Source: *PC World,* Sep99, Vol. 17 Issue 9, p33, 2p, 1c, Furger, Robert, "Washington Tackles Internet Law".

Attribution in the Absence of Special Arrangements

We can view attribution in two cases, with the second by far being the preferred situation for legitimate vendors. In case one, attribution, in the absence of any special arrangement, requires the person relying on attribution to prove it.[11] In other words, if a vendor receives an order for an item from a customer and bills the customer, the vendor has the burden of showing that the customer placed the order if the customer denies responsibility. Section 213(a) of UCITA states that,

> [An electronic event] is attributed to a person if it was the act of that person or its electronic agent, or the person is otherwise bound by it under the law of agency or other law. The party relying on attribution . . . has the burden of establishing attribution.

As pointed out by Professor Nimmer, just because the vendor has the burden of establishing attribution, does not mean all is lost. If the vendor has evidence that the goods ordered were shipped to the website visitor's address and goods are found on the premises of the visitor, the burden of proof is probably met. Professor Nimmer suggests that shifting the burden of proof is more difficult when the items ordered are computer information or services.

Attribution When a Reasonable Procedure Is Used

If the attribution procedure is reasonable, then the person pointed to by the attribution procedure must pay for the software or other product ordered, unless the person can show that they did not order the products. Section 214 of UCITA requires that an *attribution procedure* be commercially reasonable and defines commercial reasonableness "in light of the purposes of the procedure . . . " In other words, a vendor must have a procedure for determining who the purchaser is and that procedure must be reasonable in light of the importance of the transaction. Similar provisions exist in both UETA and the UCC. According to the Reporter's notes for UCITA, "[t]he general requirement of commercial reasonableness is that the procedure be a commercially reasonable method of identifying the party as compared to other persons, . . ." The Reporter goes on to note that vendors are not required to use "state of the art procedures."

The Importance of Signatures

At common law signatures are made valid in a number of ways. They can occur through agents, stamps, printed signatures, or engraved signatures. With EDI, the overall agreement between the partnering companies effectively substitutes for signatures. The UCC is even more liberal in accepting as a signature, "any symbol executed or adopted by a party with present intention to authenticate a writing." According to Section 102(6) of UCITA, authenticate means:

A. to sign, or

B. otherwise to execute or adopt a symbol or sound, or to use encryption or another process with respect to a record, with intent of authenticating person to:
   i. identify that person; or
   ii. adopt or accept the terms or a particular term of a record that includes or is logically

---

[11]See Professor Raymond Nimmer, Contract Law in Electronic Commerce, paper presented at The New Media Conference, Sponsored by the Practicing Law Institute, New York, (January, 2000).

"Business Bureau Seeks Input on Internet Ethics"

The Better Business Bureau of Utah is encouraging local businesses to share their ideas about ethical business practices for the growing online marketplace.

Proposals collected from Utah businesses will be considered for inclusion within a code of preferred business practices for merchants doing business on the Internet. The Code of On-line Business Practices is being prepared by BBBOnLine, a program of the Council of Better Business Bureaus.

Source: "Business Bureau seeks input on Internet ethics," Enterprise/Salt Lake City, 06/21/99, Vol. 28 Issue 52, p9.

---

associated with, or linked to, the authentication, or to which a record containing the authentication refers.

UCITA addresses using technology to substitute for signatures that are unique to individuals. Signing a document is allowed to authenticate intent to contract, but other ways such as encryption are contemplated as a means of substituting for signatures.[12]

Attribution under UETA and UCITA

Under Section 1-108(a) of UETA, "[a]n electronic record or electronic signature is attributable to a person if it was the act of the person. The act of the person may be proved in any manner, including a showing of the efficacy of any security procedure applied to determine the person to which the electronic record or electronic signature was attributable." Section 1-108(b) indicates that, "[T]he effect of an electronic record or electronic signature attributed to a person under subsection (a) is determined from the context and surrounding circumstances at the time of its creation, execution, or adoption, including the parties' agreement, if any, and otherwise as provided by law." If a purchaser gives her name and credit card number to execute a purchase, that combination of acts is likely to be adequate attribution by that person.

Who is signing is discussed in Section 213 of UCITA. As stated above, subsection (a) of Section 213 reads, "An electronic event is attributed to a person if it was the act of that person or its electronic agent, . . . The party relying on attribution of an electronic event to another person has the burden of establishing attribution." The section goes on to state that, "if there is an attribution procedure between the parties with respect to an electronic event,

the following rules apply:

1. The effect of compliance with an attribution procedure established by other law or administrative rule is determined by that law or rule.

2. In all other cases, if the parties agree to or otherwise knowingly adopt, after having had an opportunity to review the terms of an attribution procedure to verify the person from which an electronic event comes, the record is attributable to the person identified by the procedure, if the party relying on that attribution satisfies the burden of establishing that:
   A. the attribution procedure is **commercially reasonable;** (boldface added)
   B. the party accepted or relied on the electronic event in good faith and in compliance with the attribution procedure and any additional agreement with or separate instructions of the other party; and
   C. the attribution procedure indicated that the electronic event was that of the person to which attribution is sought."

In other words, except if there is a law established by a governmental body that provides otherwise for attribution, the vendor can rely on *commercially reasonable* attribution procedures as long as the other qualifications are present, which include assent of both parties to the attribution procedure. Of course it is the vendor who normally sets up the attribution procedure and is the party in charge of securing assent of the other party (generally a customer). Assent is generally secured by clicking a dot on a website signifying assent.

Sally is interested in purchasing a book from Amazon.com. Sally participates in supplying Amazon information about herself as well as a credit card number. Sally orders the book and her credit card is debited the purchase price of the book. Sally is liable for the value of the book even if she claims that she did not

---

[12]Encryption is discussed in more detail later on in the chapter.

order the book. She would have the burden of proof to show she did not order the book.

Electronic Errors and Consumer Defenses under UCITA

If the consumer makes an error by clicking on the wrong dot, and if there is no reasonable method for immediate detection and/or correction of this error, "the consumer is not bound by an electronic message that the consumer did not intend and which was caused by an electronic error, if the consumer, . . . "[13] does several things upon learning of the error or the reliance by the other party [the vendor], whichever occurs first:

1. notifies the other party of the error; and
2. causes delivery to the other party of all copies of the information [generally software] or pursuant to reasonable instructions from the other party, delivers to another person or destroys all copies; and
3. has not used or received any benefit from the information or caused the information or benefit to be made available to a third party.

In ordinary English, the consumer is required to act promptly when (s)he discovers an error. Suppose the consumer was ordering 10 video games from a website that featured such games, but, inadvertently, the consumer typed in 110 for quantity. Upon discovering the error, the consumer must promptly notify the vendor, return the unordered merchandise, and not use it or gain advantage, and not allow others to do the same. The same consumer defenses apply to UETA, which is the overlay for Article 2 of the UCC.

CRYPTOGRAPHY

For decades, cryptography has been used to disguise communications that may be intercepted. Cryptography has been applied to the various means of electronic communications including telex, fax, electronic funds transfers, and EDI. Each of the foregoing are generally closed systems, not accessible by the general public, but are subject to interception by a saboteur or spy who has detailed knowledge of the underlying technology. During World War II, U.S. intelligence spent considerable resources trying, ultimately successfully, to crack codes used by the Japanese to encrypt the transmission of orders that directed their military operations.

With the advent of the Internet, communications are open and much more susceptible to interception. Cryptography is the science of transforming data to hide its content and prevent unauthorized modification or use. The "key" to encrypted communications is a decoding mechanism that should be kept secret. The sender of the sensitive data encrypts the data (sometimes called "plaintext") using a key to make the message unintelligible to interceptors. The intended recipient has a key that enables him or her to decrypt the message and make it intelligible again. In some cases the keys of the sender and recipient are the same but, increasingly, encryption is accomplished with asymmetric keys, some "public" and some "private."

Commweb is a website (www.commweb.com) that supplies definitions of words and concepts in use on the Internet. Commweb discusses and defines *cryptography* in the following manner:

> The conversion of data into a secret code for transmission over a public network. The original text, or plaintext, is converted into a coded equivalent called ciphertext via an encryption algorithm. The ciphertext is decoded (decrypted) at the receiving end and turned back into plaintext.
>
> The encryption algorithm uses a key, which is a binary number that is typically from 40 to 128 bits in length. The greater the number of bits in the key (cipher strength), the more possible key combinations and the longer it would take to break the code. The data is encrypted, or "locked," by combining the bits in the key mathematically with the data bits. At the receiving end, the key is used to "unlock" the code and restore the original data.

Secret Key versus Public Key

> There are two cryptographic methods. The traditional method uses a secret key, such as the DES standard. Both sender and receiver use the same key to encrypt and decrypt. This is the fastest method, but transmitting the secret key to the recipient in the first place is not secure.
>
> The second method is public-key cryptography, such as RSA, which uses both a private and a public key. Each recipient has a private key that is kept secret and a public key that is published for everyone. The sender looks up the recipient's public key and uses it to encrypt the message. The recipient uses the private key to decrypt the message. Owners never have a need to transmit their private keys to anyone in order to have their messages decrypted, thus the private keys are not in transit and are not vulnerable.
>
> Sometimes, both DES and RSA are used together. DES provides the fastest decryption, and RSA provides a convenient method for transmitting the

[13]UCITA Section 214(b).

What Is the Role of the United States Government in Cryptography?

The U.S. government plays many roles in cryptography, ranging from use to export control to standardization efforts in the development of new cryptosystems. Recently the government has taken an even bigger interest in cryptography due to its ever-increasing use outside of the military. The U.S. government plays a much larger role in cryptography than any other government in the world.

In the past, the government has not only used cryptography itself, but has cracked other country's codes as well. A notable example of this occurred in 1940 when a group of Navy cryptanalysts, led by William F. Friedman, succeeded in breaking the Japanese diplomatic cipher known as Purple.

In 1952, the U.S. government established the NSA (The National Security Agency), whose job is to handle military and government data security as well as gather information about other countries' communications. Also established was NIST, The National Institute of Standards and Technology, which plays a major role in developing cryptography standards.

During the 1970s, IBM and the U.S. Department of Commerce—more precisely NIST (then known as NBS, The National Bureau of Standards)—developed along with NSA the Data Encryption Standard, DES. This algorithm has been a standard since 1977, with reviews leading to renewals every few years. The general consensus is that DES will not be strong enough for the future's encryption needs. During the next few years, NIST will be working on a new standard, AES, the Advanced Encryption Standard, to replace DES. It is expected that AES will remain a standard well into the 21st century.

Currently there are no restrictions on the use or strength of domestic encryption (encryption where the sender and recipient are in the U.S.). However, the government regulates the export of cryptography from the U.S. by setting restrictions on how strong such encryption may be. Cryptography is dealt with as an item in the International Trade in Arms (ITAR) bill, and is considered for those purposes to be munitions.

Source: http://www.rsa.com/rsalabs/faq/html/1-6.html

---

secret key. Both the DES-encrypted text message and the secret key needed to decrypt it are sent via the RSA method. This is called a *digital envelope*.

Cryptography methods change as computers get faster. It has been said that any encryption code can be broken given enough computer time to derive all of the permutations. However, if it takes months to break a code, the war could be won or lost, or the financial transaction consummated well before coded transmissions are translated for prying eyes. Of course, as computers get faster, keys must get longer and the algorithms become more complex to stay ahead of the game. See *DES*,[14] *RSA*,[15] *digital signature, digital certificate,* and *steganography*.

The secret method uses the same key to encrypt and decrypt. The problem is transmitting the key to the recipient in order to use it. The public key method uses two keys. One kept secret and never transmitted, and the other made public. Very often, the public key method is used to safely send the secret key to the recipient so that the message can be encrypted using the faster secret key algorithm.

---

[14]**DES** (**D**ata **E**ncryption **S**tandard) A NIST-standard secret key cryptography method that uses a 56-bit key. DES is based on an IBM algorithm which was further developed by the U.S. National Security Agency. It uses the block cipher method which breaks the text into 64-bit blocks before encrypting them. There are several DES encryption modes. The most popular mode exclusive ORs each plaintext block with the previous encrypted block.

DES decryption is very fast and widely used. The secret key may be kept a total secret and used over again. Or, a key can be randomly generated for each session, in which case the new key is transmitted to the recipient using a public key cryptography method such as RSA.

Triple DES is an enhancement to DES that provides considerably more security than standard DES, which uses only one 56-bit key. There are several Triple DES methods. EEE3 uses 3 keys and encrypts 3 times. EDE3 uses 3 keys to encrypt, decrypt, and encrypt again. EEE2 and EDE2 are similar to EEE3 and EDE3, except that only 2 keys are used, and the first and third operations use the same key. See *encryption algorithm, cryptography, RSA,* and *Fortezza*.

[15]**RSA** (1) (**R**ivest-**S**hamir-**A**dleman) A highly-secure cryptography method by RSA Data Security, Inc., Redwood City, CA, (www.rsa.com). It uses a two-part key. The private key is kept by the owner; the public key is published.

Data is encrypted by using the recipient's public key, which can only be decrypted by the recipient's private key. RSA is very computation intensive; thus it is often used to create a digital envelope, which holds an RSA-encrypted DES key and DES-encrypted data. This method encrypts the secret DES key so that it can be transmitted over the network, but encrypts and decrypts the actual message using the much faster DES algorithm.

RSA is also used for authentication by creating a digital signature. In this case, the sender's private key is used for encryption, and the sender's public key is used for decryption. See *digital signature*.

The RSA algorithm is also implemented in hardware. As RSA chips get faster, RSA encoding and decoding add less overhead to the operation. See *cryptography* and *digital certificate*.

DIGITAL SIGNATURES

In many cases authenticating an electronic signature is not an issue because the transacting parties have a pre-existing relationship and the parties have means of determining who the other party is when contracting. The vendor in such cases has access to a good bit of information about the potential purchaser including name, address, credit card numbers, and other information. One means of verifying that the person on the other side of the transaction is the person he purports to be is to use passwords. In other cases, however, the vendor would prefer more certainty with regard to the identity of the party on the other end of an electronic communication. They can achieve this with a digital signature system that functions like a notary. Notaries verify signatures by requiring the signatory to show identification and sign documents in their presence. When notaries put their stamps on documents, there is increased evidence that the signer is in fact the person the other party expected to sign the document.

According to Commweb a digital signature is:

> An electronic signature that cannot be forged. It is a computed digest of the text that is encrypted and sent with the text message. The recipient decrypts the signature and recomputes the digest from the received text. If the digests match, the message is authenticated and proved intact from the sender.

Signatures and Certificates

A digital signature ensures that the document originated with the person signing it and that it was not tampered with after the signature was applied. However, the sender could still be an impersonator and not the person he or she claims to be. To verify that the message was indeed sent by the person claiming to send it requires a digital certificate (digital ID) which is issued by a certification authority. See *digital certificate*.

According to the same source (Commweb) a digital certificate is:

> The digital equivalent of an ID card used in conjunction with a public key encryption system. Also called *digital IDs,* digital certificates are issued by trusted third parties known as certification authorities (CAs) such as VeriSign, Inc., Mountain View, CA, (www.verisign.com), after verifying that a public key belongs to a certain owner. The certification process varies depending on the CA and the level of certification. Drivers' licenses, notarization and fingerprints are examples of documentation required.

The digital certificate is actually the owner's public key that has been digitally signed by the CA. The digital certificate is sent along with an encrypted message to verify that the sender is truly the entity identifying itself in the transmission. The recipient uses the public key of the CA, which is widely publicized, to decrypt the sender's public key attached to the message. Then the sender's public key is used to decrypt the actual message.

The most vulnerable aspect of this method is the CA's private key, which is used to digitally sign a public key and create a certificate. If the CA's private key is uncovered, then false digital certificates can be created. See *digital signature* and *PKI*.

The digital certificate contains the following data:

> owner name, company and address
> owner public key
> owner certificate serial number
> owner validity dates
> certifying company ID
> certifying company digital signature

Commweb provides an example to assist (bewildered) readers:

> The sender uses a one-way hash function to compute a small digest of her text message. Using her private key, she encrypts the digest, turning it into a digital signature. The signature and the message are then encrypted using the recipient's public key and transmitted. The recipient uses his private key to decrypt the text and derive the still-encrypted signature. Using his public key, he decrypts the signature back into the sender's digest and then recomputes a new digest from the text message. If the digests match, the message is authenticated. See *digital envelope* and *MAC*.

In cyberland, the role of notary is taken by Certification Authorities (CAs). At the time of signature, the role of a CA is to verify the identity of the online signatory. Typically, CAs offer different levels of security and also offer fraud insurance.[16] At the lowest level of security, the CA will verify that indeed the purchaser has the e-mail address indicated. At the highest level of security, the CA will have the sender of information physically come into one of its offices and show identification. The highest level of security is essentially what a notary does on a routine basis using paper records. In some states there already is

---

[16]See e.g., VeriSign at http://www.verisign.com

legislation on digital signatures while in others, there is no legislation at present. Lack of uniformity among the states, of course, creates an unsatisfactory situation when what is legal in one state may not be legal in another state. Federal legislation, described below, is a predictable result. A problem with federal legislation, however, is that more and more of contract law, which traditionally has been state law, is now becoming federal.

The American Bar Association has taken the position that if a CA complies with its own procedures, it should not be liable if the sender (signer) is fraudulent. CAs also offer insurance to consumers against cyber break-ins. Currently, if a message is encrypted and others obtain the key, there is *unlimited liability* that is borne by the recipient of the information who is often a customer. The loss of credit cards and ATM cards does not carry unlimited liability unless the consumer is exceptionally negligent. It is reasonable to expect legislation limiting liability on this point in the not too distant future. Hopefully the legislation will be federal so that uniform treatment of the same transaction can occur anywhere in the United States.

Millennium Digital Signature Act

Congress recently passed and the President signed the Millennium Digital Signature Act (MDSA). The MDSA is federal legislation that will apply to all states. The MDSA allows people to transact business online using digital signatures. The MDSA does not narrowly define digital signatures as exclusively making use of cryptography as described above. Instead the MDSA allows for a variety of methods to effectuate digital

signatures including:

1. A simple password entered into a form on a web page. The website would have to issue the password, or confirm that it belongs to a certain person.
2. Hardware like thumbprints, or retinal scanning devices, or electronic pads or styluses, that plugs into personal computers. Information from such a device would be sent over the Internet to a business, which would then keep it on file as proof of authenticity for future activities.
3. Third-party services that use software to generate encrypted keys that can be attached to e-mail messages or tamper-proof electronic documents. This is essentially the same service described in the discussion above regarding digital signatures, cryptography, and certfication authorities. The third party holds the identity of the two parties and can then use encryption software to ensure that only the two parties involved in a contract can obtain and sign the document, whether on a web page or an e-mail.

The MDSA was scheduled to take effect on October 1, 2000. The bill allows for a variety of technologies to create digital signatures because, at this date, it is not clear which technology will be adopted by the free market as the most efficient method. In any event, there is a clear perception that technology needs to be developed that will imitate the effect of signatures on pieces of paper to reduce fraud. The net result of the MDSA is to make it much easier for businesses and consumers to agree to binding contracts electronically. More legislation and technological developments are likely in this area as E-Commerce continues to expand.

SUMMARY

- E-Commerce is currently plagued by some of the same problems that led to the passage of the UCC. In the absence of uniform legislation, state-by-state differences are inevitable with respect to E-Commerce. State-by-state differences in E-Commerce contract law is widely viewed as undesirable.
- To deal with this problem, a number of uniform bills have been proposed including UCITA, UETA, and revisions to Article 2 of the UCC (Subpart B).

- The thrust of these uniform acts is to create legal parity between paper records and electronic records. There is considerable resistance by consumer groups to this parity and progress towards passage of UCITA , UETA, and revised Article 2 has been slow.
- The UCITA covers licenses of computer software but does not cover the sale on goods on the Internet. The scope of the UCITA includes computer software, multimedia interactive products,

computer data and databases, and Internet and on-line information.

- The UETA deals comprehensively with E-Commerce and contract law. The UCC covers the sale of *goods,* which does not necessarily involve E-Commerce.

- The basic principles of contract law are modified to deal with Internet transactions. Intent is inferred from the operations of electronic agents and "signatures" can occur with a response to an invitation to click to accept.

- EDI contracts can be formed electronically without human intervention.

- Surfing the Internet most likely means that you will encounter opportunities for binding offers to contract.

- The revised Section 2-207 of the UCC makes it easier to include additional terms in contracts that are not in the offers.

- *Clickwrap agreements* are additional terms in an agreement that may involve warranties, return policies, reproductions, and other "fine print."

- *Shrinkwrap agreements* bind the customer to the terms in the contract even though the customer cannot know what many of the terms are until the software, CD, or diskette is purchased.

- The customer is bound by the terms of an agreement that he or she learns about after purchase when the customer has been given clear notice of the additional terms, clear notice as to what constitutes acceptance, an opportunity to inspect the terms in the wrap agreement, and an opportunity to return the goods if the customers objects to the additional terms.

- With click-on acceptances, if the clicker is a minor, the vendor is subject to having the contract disaffirmed.

- If a person, or his or her agent, commits an electronic act, then the event is attributed to that person. The burden of establishing attribution falls on the party relying on attribution of an electronic event, unless a commercially reasonable attribution procedure is agreed to by both parties and is used.

- The consumer is not bound to an agreement made in error by clicking the wrong dot if the consumer notifies the other party of the error, returns the misordered merchandise, and does not use it to gain advantage.

- The identification process must be commercially reasonable.

- *Certification Authorities* verify the identity of the online signatory. The American Bar Association has indicated that if a CA complies with its own procedures, it should not be liable if the sender is fraudulent.

- The Millennium Digital Signature Act is federal legisation that allows E-Commerce trading partners to create legally binding, electronic signatures.

4

CONTRACTING AND LICENSING SOFTWARE

It is difficult to imagine managing a company today without becoming involved in consequential software decisions. The importance of software is evident in every business function and most day-to-day activities. Nearly every firm uses specialized software in its payroll department. If the firm has a CFO (Chief Financial Officer), he or she most certainly employs specialized financial software to make financial projections and probably the firm has a good deal of computer interaction with the company's bank via more software. Manufacturing firms rely heavily on specialized software for inventory control, billing, shipping, and other mission-critical functions. Some firms that develop new products make use of CAD (computer aided design) software to develop and refine their product ideas. Indeed, virtually every department in modern companies relies on computer software, much of which is customized to company needs and specifications.

Use of software by a firm involves a classic "make or buy" decision; a firm can hire programmer-employees to compose its software or it can hire the services of an outside firm. There are critically important legal issues involved when a firm resolves its "make or buy" software decision. Frustrated

expectations, often followed by costly litigation, have been commonplace when decisions managers make in this area are "uninformed". In this chapter we consider three scenarios for a firm acquiring the software it needs or wants. These are:

1. A firm hires employees or an outside firm to *create* software for it;
2. A firm *contracts* with a software vendor of copyrighted and trademarked software for installation of their software, but some of the terms in the license agreement are *negotiable;* and
3. A software vendor sells a customer firm mass-market copies of its software under licenses *that are not negotiable.*

BENEFITS AND COSTS

Creating Your Own Software

As future managers, students should be aware of the critical issues that arise when decisions concerning software are being made. The most "hands-on" situation occurs when the firm hires its own employees to create software that is totally customized to the needs

---

Seven Rules to Live By in Licensing Software

Please see article at http://www.computerworld.com/cwi/story/0,1199,NAV63-128-1357-1367_STO41906,00.html "Rules to live by in licensing software" Computerworld; Framingham; Mar 20, 2000; Joe Auer.

Additional Readings:
http://developer.apple.com/mkt/swl/
"Software Licensing"; Apple Computer, Inc, Software Licensing M/S 198-SWL 2420 Ridgepoint Drive, Austin, TX 78754.
http://www.globetrotter.com/art5.htm
"Software Licensing Flexibility Complements the Digital Age", Copyright © 1994; Fenwick & West & Sandy J. Wong.
http://slashdot.org/yro/00/01/12/217259.shtml
"Software Licensing, 2001" Slashdot, January 14, 2000; Michael Sims.

---

of the firm. The decision to hire employees to create original software, however, may be inefficient because there's no need to reinvent wheels—software nearly as good as that which is "custom" developed for a client firm (or even better!) may be commercially available at far less than the cost of hiring and paying employees to develop newly created software.

Becoming a Licensee

Having software created or licensed by an outside firm involves negotiating a software license either from a software developer or from an established software vendor. Bringing in an outside firm creates a host of legal issues that requires informed decision-making by managers. Many terms within software licenses are negotiable and the optimal license varies from firm to firm. Many well-known software vendors become franchisors and their contact with end users is accomplished through franchisees. Because of the "baggage" of franchise law, which has special protections for franchisees in many states as well as FTC regulations at the federal level, many software vendors in the business-to-business (commonly referred to as B to B) market refer to their distributors as "partners."

An example of these quasi-franchise arrangements is provided by Hyperion e-Business software (www.hyperion.com). At their website, Hyperion offers software that assists businesses in planning, reporting, analysis, and modeling. According to the company, "Hyperion has joined forces with over 300 partners that are recognized in their fields of expertise, including System Integration, Tools, Applications, Data Integration, Distributors, Platform, Service and Education. Hyperion Alliance Partners can work with you to create or identify integrated solutions to maximize your

business success." Among the partners of Hyperion are Brio Technology, Arthur Anderson, and Doubleclick. The copyright to Hyperion software is owned by the company but its contact with clients is often accomplished through its partners, who often also carry software of their own and from other software vendors. For example, one of Hyperion's partners is Balrae, which also carries copyrighted software from the Lawson company. In addition, Balrae customizes software for its clients and sometimes brings in assistance from third party software developers. Obviously, client firms should be prepared to sort through the structure and legal liabilities associated with alliances and partnerships of software developers.

Buying Software Off the Shelf

In the case of reliance on mass distribution software, there is no opportunity to negotiate terms and conditions of licenses. The license is made available for a price on "a take it or leave it" basis. The enforceability of mass distribution licenses is an issue that requires attention to detail. Courts are willing to enforce mass distribution license restrictions, but only if the customer or end user has a fair chance to evaluate the terms of the license and a chance to get a refund in the event that they do not agree with these terms.

Microsoft Corporation sells a very popular software program, called Office, which includes word processing, spreadsheets, presentation software, and other elements. The terms of trade for Office purchasers (really licensees) are spelled out at the Microsoft website (www.microsoft.com/info/cpyright.htm). The terms of this license are not negotiable given the huge number of customers for this very popular software package. According to

Microsoft, "The Software is made available for downloading solely for use by end users according to the License Agreement. Any reproduction or redistribution of the Software not in accordance with the License Agreement is expressly prohibited by law, and may result in severe civil and criminal penalties. Violators will be prosecuted to the maximum extent possible."

Making Decisions about Software

The decision to acquire software necessarily involves a number of legal issues. At its core, most business software makes use of proprietary information in some way. Even if the software a company adopts is not customized to that company, it is likely that at least some of the software requires the assistance of a consulting firm for installation and trouble-shooting in the event that the system malfunctions. When one firm asks another firm to assist in the creation, installation, or maintenance of software, the expectations of the parties regarding appropriate procedures, schedules, performance results, etc., should be established as unambiguously as possible.

A FIRM DECIDES TO CREATE ITS OWN SOFTWARE

Using Employees to Create Software and the Relevance of Copyright Ownership

If a firm chooses to hire *programmer-employees* to develop software for its needs, then the issue of ownership of the software created is relatively simple. Software is copyrightable, meaning that the company can prevent others from copying (or otherwise reproducing or distributing) its software without the firm's permission. Software is *owned* by the party that owns the copyright. Unauthorized reproduction of copyrighted software is called *infringement,* enabling the copyright owner to go to court and collect damages from infringers and to obtain *injunctions* prohibiting the production of additional copies.

If the composer of the software is an employee, that person's **employer** is automatically the **owner** of the copyright. Since damages are greater in the event of an infringement from a copyright that is registered with Copyright Office in Washington D.C., it often makes sense to in fact register copyrightable software. The costs ($30) are minimal and copyrights are routinely granted to applicants without the extensive scrutiny that is characteristic of patent applications. Copyright law and the benefits of owning a copyright are discussed extensively in Chapter 9.

Employees versus Independent Contractors

Most firms do not have a need for a staff of computer programmers on a long-term, full-time basis, but may have periodic needs for the services of programmers. When programmers are hired to write software for a firm, however, their status as employees or *independent contractors* can be a source of litigation. Certainly if the programmer(s) have already formed a firm and bid on the job, they will be considered independent contractors. There are situations, however, when it is unclear whether the programmers are employees or independent contractors. The resolution of this issue is significant because **programmers who develop software for another company are the owners** of any software they develop, *unless a clause* in the contract that was used to hire them **assigns** the copyrights to the software they develop to the hiring firm.

Autonomy of the Programmers

Courts have developed a lengthy list of factors that may be relevant in determining whether someone hired by a firm is an employee or an independent contractor. However, two factors seem to determine most decisions. In general, courts will look to *control* and to how the employer treats the employee with respect to *taxes and benefits*. With employees, the employer typically can tell them **what** to do and **how** to do it. Independent contractors typically maintain autonomy over their methods of operations such that, while employers can assign tasks to them, they do not tell them *how* to perform these tasks. For example, an employer may tell an outside computer consulting firm what functions it expects a software product to perform, but probably would allow the vendor computer firm to select the programming language of the source code.

The Importance of Tax Status

Courts also are strongly influenced by the manner in which an employer treats those they contract with vis à vis the government. Courts will look at whether taxes are withheld, whether contributions are made to the state unemployment compensation fund, and whether benefits are provided. Courts will not allow a firm to take one position on the status of those they hire

---

"Managing in the new millennium"

Companies can become involved with outside workers in disputes over intellectual property. Full-time employees and consultants hired to create software, for instance, are bound by different intellectual property laws. The employee's work product is automatically a "work for hire" that is owned by the employer, but the consultant will own that work product unless he or she assigns it to the company in a signed document. Many companies have been forced to pay substantial amounts to former consultants to buy ownership rights to software they had paid the consultant to create. If your company uses outside software developers, here are some actions you can take to avoid this painful scenario.

Use a standard proprietary information and inventions agreement that:

1. Spells out the worker's duties to protect the rights of your company, third-party suppliers and customers, and his or her former employer concerning confidential and proprietary information;
2. Assigns to the company all work product he or she creates that is related to the company business, results from work performed for the company, or uses company resources;
3. Says that he or she has no conflicting work from third parties; and

4. Lists, where possible, all prior inventions and original works of authorship the person has made before the engagement.

Your company also should conduct entrance and exit interviews in which the interviewer emphasizes the worker's responsibilities to the company. At the exit interview, collect keys, computers, cell phones, documents, and other items belonging to the company. Terminate access codes to computer systems, E-mail, and voice mail. Minding the legal P's and Q's with your workforce aids productivity and avoids costly exposures.

Source: From "Managing in the New Millennium," by Susan H. Nycum, January 3, 2000. Copyright © 2000 by CMP Media Inc., 600 Community Drive, Manhasset, NY 11030, USA. Reprinted from *INFORMATIONWEEK* with permission.

Additional readings:

http://www.utsystem.edu/ogc/intellectualproperty/ippol.htm
"U.T. System Intellectual Property Policy".

http://www.fplc.edu/tfield/plfip/plfipCom.htm#III.A.
"Intellectual Property: The Practical and Legal Fundamentals", Franklin Pierce Law Center; Thomas G. Field, Jr.

http://www.fenwick.com/pub/ip_audit.htm#14
"Acquiring and Protecting Technology: The Intellectual Property Audit", Publications © 1992; David L. Hayes.

---

with the IRS and then renounce that position when it comes to copyright ownership. If the firm does not withhold taxes on a programmer, then the firm is indicating to the IRS that the programmer is not an employee. When the issue of ownership of copyrights surfaces, the company will be bound by the position it took on tax issues with respect to whether the programmer is an employee or an independent contractor.

Prominent among other criteria that courts have used for determining whether a person is an independent contractor or employee are such factors as (1) who supplies the tools, (2) the degree of training possessed by the worker, and (3) whether the duration of employment is tied to completion of a job or is indefinite. In general, independent contractors supply their own tools, are highly trained prior to engagement and are often licensed, and, finally, usually are hired by the job. The following case deals with many of these issues. Management should never

make mistakes like those made in this case by Island Swimming Sales.

Ex-Employees and Trade Secrets

In light of the discussion above, it would appear that using employees to develop software would serve to protect and preserve intellectual property for the company's exclusive use. That picture is clouded, however, when employee turnover is considered. Employees and ex-employees are subject to agreements that prohibit them from disseminating trade secrets of their employer or ex-employer. There can be disputes, however, as to what constitutes a trade secret. General skills developed on the job by employees cannot be trade secrets. Firm-specific skills can be trade secrets, but if those skills become generally known in the industry, what was once a trade secret becomes a general skill and thus not protectible.

Aymes v. *Bonelli, dba, Island Swimming Sales, Inc.*
United States Court of Appeals, Second Circuit
(980 F.2d 857, 1992)

FACTS AND CASE BACKGROUND

In May 1980, Aymes was hired by Jonathan Bonelli, the president and chief executive officer of Island Swimming Sales, Inc., to work as a computer programmer. Island operated a chain of retail stores selling swimming pools and related supplies. Aymes, who received a graduate degree from Cornell University's School of Engineering in 1981, worked with Island's computer systems from 1980 to 1982.

During that period, Aymes created a series of programs called "CSALIB" under the general direction of Bonelli, who was not a professional computer programmer. CSALIB was used by Island to maintain records of cash receipts, physical inventory, sales figures, purchase orders, merchandise transfers, and price changes. There was no written agreement between Bonelli and Aymes assigning ownership or copyright of CSALIB. Aymes does contend, however, that Bonelli made him an oral promise that CSALIB would only be used at one computer in one Island office.

Aymes did most of his programming at the Island office, where he had access to Island's computer hardware. He generally worked alone, without assistants or coworkers, and enjoyed considerable autonomy in creating CSALIB. This autonomy was restricted only by Bonelli who directed and instructed Aymes on what he wanted from the program. Bonelli was not, however, sufficiently skilled to write the program himself.

Although Aymes worked semi-regular hours, he was not always paid by the hour and on occasion presented his bills to Bonelli as invoices. At times, Aymes would be paid by the project and given bonuses for finishing the project on time. It is undisputed that Aymes never received any health or other insurance benefits from Island. It is similarly undisputed that Island never paid an employer's percentage of Aymes's payroll taxes and never withheld any of his salary for federal or state taxes. In fact, Aymes was given an Internal Revenue Service 1099 Non-Employee Compensation form instead of the standard employee W-2 form.

Aymes left Island in September 1982 when Bonelli unilaterally decided to cut Aymes's hours. Aymes considered this to be a breach of an oral agreement he allegedly made with Bonelli. At the time Aymes left, Island owed him $14,560 in wages. Aymes also requested payment for multi-site use of CSALIB. When he became persistent in his demands for compensation, however, Bonelli insisted that he sign a release for his rights to CSALIB in order to receive the back earnings. Aymes refused to sign and was not paid.

On March 12, 1985, Aymes registered CSALIB in his own name with the United States Copyright Office. On March 21, 1985, Aymes filed a complaint against Bonelli and Island in the United States District Court for the Southern District of New York (MacMahon, J.), alleging copyright infringement under the Copyright Act of 1976 and various state claims.

After a lengthy series of pre-trial motions, the copyright infringement claims were bifurcated from the pendent state claims and the case was reassigned. On September 10, 1991, a bench trial was conducted by the district court (Martin, J.) on the copyright infringement claim with Aymes appearing pro se. On September 24, 1991, the district court found that, contrary to Aymes's contention, Bonelli never agreed to limit Island's right to use or modify CSALIB. The district court further held that Aymes had no copyright over CSALIB because the program was a "work made for hire," which meant that the authorship belonged to Island under 17 U.S.C. § 201(b) (1988). Accordingly, the court dismissed Aymes's copyright infringement claim.

Aymes now appeals.

OPINION: ALTIMARI,
CIRCUIT JUDGE

Under the Copyright Act of 1976, copyright ownership "vests initially in the author or authors of the work." 17 U.S.C. § 201(a) (1988). Although the author is generally the party who actually creates the copyrightable work, the Act provides:

In the case of a work made for hire, the employer or other person for whom the work was prepared is considered the author for purposes of this title, and, unless the parties have expressly agreed otherwise in a written instrument signed by them, owns all of the rights comprised in the copyright.

Id. § 201(b). The Act defines a work made for hire as: "(1) a work prepared by an employee within the scope of his or her employment; or (2) a work specially ordered or commissioned for use . . . if the parties expressly agree in a written instrument signed by them that the work shall be considered a work made for hire." Id. § 101.

It is undisputed that Aymes and Bonelli never signed a written agreement assigning ownership rights in

CSALIB. We must therefore consider whether the program was a work prepared by Aymes as an employee within the scope of his employment. If so, CSALIB qualifies as a "work made for hire" whose copyright belongs to Island as Aymes's employer.

The Copyright Act does not define the terms "employee" or "employment," and, consequently, the application of these terms is left to the courts. In *Reid,* the Supreme Court addressed the question of when an individual is an employee under the work for hire doctrine.[1] Relying extensively on the legislative history of the Copyright Act, the Court concluded that to "determine whether a work is for hire under the Act, a court first should ascertain, using principles of the general common law of agency, whether the work was prepared by an employee or an independent contractor." The Court then set forth the factors to be used in making this determination:

In determining whether a hired party is an employee under the general common law of agency, we consider the hiring party's right to control the manner and means by which the product is accomplished. Among the other factors relevant to this inquiry are the skill required, the source of the instrumentalities and tools, the location of the work; the duration of the relationship between the parties, whether the hiring party has the right to assign additional projects to the hired party; the extent of the hired party's discretion over when and how long to work; the method of payment; the hired party's role in hiring and paying assistants; whether the work is part of the regular business of the hiring party; whether the hiring party is in business; the provision of employee benefits, and the tax treatment of the hired party.

[1]*Community for Creative Non-Violence v. Reid,* 490 U.S. 730, 104 L. Ed. 2d 811, 109 S. Ct. 2166 (198).

I. APPLICATION OF THE *REID* TEST

The district court applied the *Reid* test thoroughly, factor-by-factor. The court's factual findings as to the presence or absence of the *Reid* factors cannot be disturbed unless clearly erroneous. We begin our analysis by noting that the *Reid* test can be easily misapplied, since it consists merely of a list of possible considerations that may or may not be relevant in a given case. *Reid* established that no one factor was dispositive, but gave no direction concerning how the factors were to be weighed. It does not necessarily follow that because no one factor is dispositive all factors are equally important, or indeed that all factors will have relevance in every case. The factors should not merely be tallied but should be weighed according to their significance in the case.

Some factors, therefore, will often have little or no significance in determining whether a party is an independent contractor or an employee. In contrast, there are some factors that will be significant in virtually every situation. These include: (1) the hiring party's right to control the manner and means of creation; (2) the skill required; (3) the provision of employee benefits; (4) the tax treatment of the hired party; and (5) whether the hiring party has the right to assign additional projects to the hired party. These factors will almost always be relevant and should be given more weight in the analysis, because they will usually be highly probative of the true nature of the employment relationship.

In contrast, in the instant case the district court gave each factor equal weight and simply counted the number of factors for each side in determining that Aymes was an employee. In so doing, the district court overemphasized indeterminate and thus irrelevant factors having little or no bearing on Aymes's case. Because

we find that the *Reid* test was not intended to be applied in a mechanistic fashion, we review each of the factors and consider their relative importance in this case. We begin by addressing those factors bearing most significantly in our analysis.

a. The Right to Control The district court did not specifically address whether Aymes or Island Swimming had the right to control the manner of CSALIB's creation. Even without a specific finding, it is clear from the record that Bonelli and Island had the right to control the manner in which CSALIB was created. Aymes disputed Bonelli's purported skill at programming, but even without such knowledge Bonelli was capable of directing Aymes on CSALIB's necessary function. Aymes was not working entirely alone. He received significant input from Bonelli in programming CSALIB, and worked under programming limitations placed by Bonelli. Consequently, this factor weighs heavily in favor of finding that Aymes was an employee.

b. The Level of Skill The district court found that although Aymes's ability as a programmer required skills "beyond the capacity of a layman, it required no peculiar expertise or creative genius." We disagree. Aymes's work required far more than merely transcribing Bonelli's instructions. Rather, his programming demanded that he use skills developed while a graduate student at Cornell and through his experience working at a family run company. Other courts that have addressed the level of skill necessary to indicate that a party is an independent contractor have held architects, photographers, graphic artists, drafters, and indeed computer programmers to be highly-skilled independent contractors. . .

We therefore conclude that the district court erred in relying on

Aymes's relative youth and inexperience as a professional computer programmer. Rather, the court should have examined the skill necessary to perform the work. In this case, Aymes was clearly a skilled craftsman. Consequently, this factor weighs heavily in his favor.

c./d. The Employee Benefits and Tax Treatment

The district court found that Aymes received no employee benefits from Island, but disregarded this factor as merely being an indication that Aymes was an employee who worked "off the books." It is undisputed that Aymes was not provided with health, unemployment, or life insurance benefits. Similarly, it is uncontested that Island did not pay a share of Aymes's social security taxes and did not withhold federal or state income taxes.

The failure of Island to extend Aymes any employment benefits or to pay any of his payroll taxes is highly indicative that Aymes was considered an outside independent contractor by Island. Indeed, these two factors constitute virtual admissions of Aymes's status by Bonelli himself. Moreover, they also point out a basic inequity in Aymes's treatment. Island benefitted from treating Aymes like an independent contractor when it came to providing benefits and paying a percentage of his payroll taxes. Island should not in one context be able to claim that Aymes was an independent contractor and ten years later deny him that status to avoid a copyright infringement suit.

These two factors are given even greater weight because they are undisputed in this case. During the ten years in which this case has been litigated, all the other issues have been hotly contested. But for purposes of benefits and taxes, Island definitely and unequivocally chose not to treat Aymes as an employee. Island deliberately chose to deny Aymes two basic attributes of employment it presumably extended to its workforce. This undisputed choice is completely inconsistent with their defense.

The importance of these two factors is underscored by the fact that every case since *Reid* that has applied the test has found the hired party to be an independent contractor where the hiring party failed to extend benefits or pay social security taxes. . .

* * *

f. Remaining Factors

The remaining factors are relatively insignificant or negligible in weight because they are either indeterminate or inapplicable to these facts. It is important to address them each individually, however, to show why they are relatively insignificant. Although none carries much weight, they are addressed in order of their relative importance in this determination.

* * *

A review of this analysis shows that the significant factors supporting Island's contention that Aymes was an employee include Island's right to control the means of CSALIB's creation and Island's right to assign other projects. The significant factors supporting Aymes's argument that he was an independent contractor include: the level of skill needed to create CSALIB; the decision of Island not to offer him benefits; and his payment of his own social security taxes. The other factors were either indeterminate, because they were evenly balanced between the parties, or of marginal significance, because they were inapplicable to these facts.

Examining the factors for each side in terms of their importance, we conclude that the only major factor strongly supporting Island is that it directed the creation of the program. Island did reserve the right to assign Aymes other projects, which is a major factor, but under these facts this was not necessarily inconsistent with an independent contractor relationship. Supporting Aymes's argument that he was an independent contractor, however, are several important factors—his skill, and the tax and benefit factors—that outweigh the elements supporting Island. The other factors outlined in *Reid* are either indeterminate or of negligible importance, and cannot outweigh the significance we attach to Island's choice to treat Aymes as an independent contractor when it was to Island's financial benefit. Now that this treatment is no longer to Island's benefit, the company must still adhere to the choice it made.

On balance, application of the *Reid* test requires that we find Aymes to be an independent contractor when he was creating CSALIB for Island. Consequently, we hold that CSALIB is not a work for hire. Aymes therefore owns the copyright as author of the program.

QUESTIONS FOR ANALYSIS

1. What did the district court do wrong in its determination as to whether the Aymes was an employee or an independent contractor?

2. The court in this case found that Aymes was an independent contractor in spite of the fact that Bonelli exerted a good deal of control over Aymes's work. The court seems to make a moralistic determination that if Bonelli treated Aymes as an independent contractor for tax purposes, that "the company must adhere to the choice it made." Is the court saying that if the company files a Form 1099 on someone, that that person is necessarily an independent contractor, but if the company provides benefits and withholds taxes, the person may or may not be an employee?

In the *Hogan* case, immediately following, employees signed agreements that stipulated that certain Software, developed by the employer and disclosed to them, was a trade secret. However, when employment terminated, these employees disclosed and used the Software, claiming that the Software was no longer a trade secret because other firms and programmers in the industry possessed the skills to reproduce this Software even though they did not work for Hogan. In other words, the employees claimed that their former employer could not bind them to its list of what is a trade secret when skill levels outside the firm had *evolved* to the point where skills that were formerly specialized, became general. Since there had been conceptual growth in the industry, what was formerly a trade secret (the Software) was no longer a trade secret because the court found that others, who did not work for the employer, now possessed skills sufficient to reproduce software with the same functionality.

Hogan Systems, Inc. v. Cybresource Int'l., Inc.
United States Court of Appeals, 5th Circuit
158 F.3d 319 (1998)

Facts and Case Background

Hogan Systems, Inc. ("Hogan") is the developer and owner of copyrighted data processing software used by major banks worldwide. Such software—including the source code, object code and related documentation for Hogan's Umbrella System and the other programs at issue in this case (the "Software")—was stipulated to be a trade secret. Hogan owns the copyright in the Software. Hogan maintains that since the early 1980's, it has required its employees to sign a confidentiality agreement—agreeing not to disclose or use the Software and related secrets without Hogan's express written consent. Hogan requires its licensees to maintain the confidentiality of the Software and related trade secrets as well. Hogan does not sell the Software to third parties, but instead licenses it to its customers. Norwest is one of the many major banks that are Hogan licensees.

Case Decision: STEWART, Circuit Judge

Hogan entered into an initial license (the "Initial License") with Norwest in 1980, permitting Norwest's use of the Software. Hogan suggests that in the Initial License Agreement,

Norwest stipulated to the trade secret status of the Software, and agreed not to distribute or disclose the Software to third parties. The Initial License was non-assignable.

The four individual defendants/appellees, David Boehr, Douglas Paradowski, James Helms, and Michael Greene (together the "Individual Defendants"), are former employees of Hogan who terminated their employment on various dates between September 29, 1995 and July 15, 1996. During their employment at Hogan each of the four signed substantially similar confidentiality agreements (the "Confidentiality Agreements") with Hogan, containing identical commitments concerning the restricted use and non-disclosure of Hogan's trade secrets and confidential materials. Each of the Confidentiality Agreements indicates that the employee's general skill, knowledge, and experience is not encompassed by the confidentiality obligation.

Following his departure from Hogan, Greene formed Cybresource International, Inc., ("Cybresource") an independent service organization ("ISO") at which Boehr, Paradowski, and Helms later became employees. In anticipation of a symbiotic relationship with Hogan, Greene signed

a Professional Services Agreement (the "Cybresource–Hogan Agreement") with Hogan dated October 18, 1995. In that Agreement, Hogan alleges that Cybresource stipulates to the trade secret status of the Software and related processes, technical mastery, and ideas of Hogan. Hogan insists that Cybresource pledged that its representatives would keep Hogan's proprietary information secret, and that they would not copy or otherwise use the information except as expressly authorized by Hogan in the performance of the Cybresource–Hogan Agreement. These promises and stipulations expressly survive any termination of the Cybresource–Hogan Agreement.

* * *

B. Trade Secrets

Hogan also appeals the district court's decision to grant summary judgment upon Hogan's misappropriation of trade secrets claim and its breach of contract claim. The district court's decision was based upon its finding that the information Hogan complained about was not a trade secret, but rather was "general knowledge, skill, and experience" that the Individual Defendants garnered as a result of their former employment with Hogan, and which their Confidentiality Agreements with Hogan recognized as not being a trade secret. On appeal, Hogan submits that the summary judgment evidence proves that the Individual Defendants have acquired specialized knowledge about the process and structure of the Software that they are now exploiting to their own commercial advantage.

In order for information to be a trade secret, it must not be generally known or readily ascertainable by independent investigation. See, e.g., *Rugen* v. *Interactive Business Systems, Inc.,* 864 S.W.2d 548, 552. Here, Hogan stipulated to the fact that many individuals in the field obtain comparable abilities and expertise without ever being employed by Hogan. We thus disagree with Hogan's argument and affirm the district court's decision.

QUESTIONS FOR ANALYSIS

1. This case illustrates that naming a skill developed by an employee a trade secret does not make it so. Do you think that there was a way for the plaintiff to have avoided competition with its former employees?
2. Can you think of any other agreements that survive termination of the underlying contract? Should there be a reasonableness time limit on nondisclosure agreements just as there is on covenants not to compete?

Copyright Act and Works for Hire

If copyrightable software is developed by an employee within the employee's scope of employment, the Copyright Act allocates the copyright to the employer.[2] If software is developed for a firm by independent contractors, then the independent contractor owns the software, although the client firm can use the software developed for them by the independent contractors. There are several potentially unfavorable consequences (for the hiring firm) if the software is owned by the independent contractor, including the following:

1. The hiring (or client) firm may be limited in its right to independently develop upgrades. Upgrades are considered *derivative works.* The right to create derivative works is exclusively possessed by copyright owners according to the Copyright Act.[3] The continuation of the *Aymes* case below (*Aymes II*) suggests that client firms are not limited in their upgrades as long as there is no *external* (outside the firm) use of the upgrades.
2. Virtually the same software can be sold to rivals of the hiring firm. Since development costs have already been incurred by the independent contractors (software developers), they can afford to sell copies (and/or near copies) of the software developed for a fraction of the contract price they charged the original hiring firm.

Aymes I above illustrates a high level of Court support for the rights of software creators. However, the scales of justice are not tilted entirely in favor of software writers. The following case demonstrates solid court support for reasonable rights for client firms. This case, *Aymes II,* clarifies the Court's earlier position and makes clear that purchasers of software have virtually unlimited rights to modify the software they paid for, so long as they do not distribute it externally.

Joint Authorship

From the perspective of the independent contracting firm, there are significant legal pitfalls for the unwary, too. If the hiring firm participates extensively in development of software, it may achieve the status of *joint author*. According to the Copyright Act, when several parties work together to create a single work in which individual contributions are inseparable, the parties become joint authors.[4] As a joint author, the hiring firm would be entitled to share in royalties that the independent contractor receives from licenses to other firms for use of the software created. Notice in the case above that the defendant, Bonelli, claimed to be a joint author of the software created for him by Aymes. The court did not buy that argument, however.

Transfer of Ownership and Assignment Clauses

If programmers hired to create software for a client firm are independent contractors (and most are), then it is likely that the hiring firm will want to include an

---

[2]Section 101(C)(1) of the Copyright Act defines a work for hire as, "a work prepared by an employee within his or her scope of employment."
[3]Section 106 Exclusive Rights of Copyrighted Works (2) indicates an exclusive right of a copyright owner is "to prepare derivative works based upon copyrighted works".

[4]Copyright Act Section 101.

Aymes v. *Bonnelli (II)*
United States Court of Appeals for the Second Circuit
(47 F.3d 23)

FACTS AND CASE BACKGROUND: (IN THE WORDS OF THE COURT)

On the first appeal, we reversed the judgment of the district court and remanded for further proceedings. Aymes, 980 F.2d at 865. We held that under Community for Creative Non-Violence v. Reid, 490 U.S. 730, 104 L. Ed. 2d 811, 109 S. Ct. 2166 (1989), Aymes as a matter of law was an independent contractor, rather than Island's employee. We therefore found that, as author of the program, Aymes owned the copyright, and we remanded for a determination of Aymes's infringement claim. We noted, however, that based on the district court's earlier findings, it appeared "unlikely" that Aymes would prevail. An additional issue that required consideration on remand was whether Bonelli was a "joint owner" of the copyright under 17 U.S.C. § 201(a) because of his contribution to its creation.

OPINION: PRATT, CIRCUIT JUDGE

Aymes contends that the defendants' modifications to CSALIB constituted copyright infringement under 17 U.S.C. § 106 because he, as the owner of the copyright to CSALIB, had the exclusive right to prepare derivative works. 17 U.S.C. § 106 provides:

Subject to sections 107 through 120, the owner of [a] copyright under this title has the exclusive rights to do and to authorize any of the following:

1. to reproduce the copyrighted work in copies or phonorecords;
2. to prepare derivative works based upon the copyrighted work;

17 U.S.C § 106(1) & (2) (1977)

In this case, Island does not dispute that it altered CSALIB and thereby created a "derivative work" from the original CSALIB program that Aymes developed for Island. See 17 U.S.C. § 101 (defining "derivative work" as "a work based upon one or more preexisting works," including "any . . . form in which a work may be recast, transformed, or adapted"). Unless excused by another statutory provision, Island's modification would constitute an infringement of Aymes's copyright . . .

There is another statutory provision, however, § 117, which provides:

Limitations on exclusive rights: Computer programs

Notwithstanding the provisions of section 106, it is not an infringement for the owner of a copy of a computer program to make or authorize the making of another copy or adaption of that computer program provided:

1. that such a new copy or adaption is created as an essential step in the utilization of the computer program in conjunction with a machine and that it is used in no other manner, or
2. that such new copy or adaptation is for archival purposes only and that all archival copies are destroyed in the event that continued possession of the computer program should cease to be rightful. Any exact copies prepared in accordance with the provisions of this section may be leased, sold, or otherwise transferred, along with the copy from which such copies were prepared, only as part of the lease, sale, or other transfer of all rights in the program. Adaptations so prepared may be transferred only with the authorization of the copyright owner. (Amended December 12, 1980, Public Law 96-517, § 10(b), 94 Stat. 3028).

17 U.S.C. § 117 (EMPHASIS ADDED)

Defendants contend their rights are determined by this section, rather than § 106, because (1) they are "the owner[s] of a copy of a computer program" and (2) they made modifications "as an essential step in the utilization of CSALIB." As to the defendants' first claim, as the district court noted early in this litigation, "the plaintiff cannot realistically dispute the fact that he sold defendants the computer program and that defendants are therefore the rightful owners of the program." True, the district court erroneously viewed Aymes as an employee; but even as an independent contractor, Aymes was paid by Island to design a program specifically for Island's use, and for those efforts he earned in excess of $70,000. Island, therefore, had a right to use the program for its own business purposes.

As to Aymes's second contention, an "owner of a copy of a computer program" is authorized to make a "new copy or adaption [if it] is created as an essential step in the utilization of the computer program . . . and . . . it is used in no other manner." 17 U.S.C. § 117(1). Section 117 was implemented to follow "the recommendations of the National Commission on New Technological Uses of Copyrighted Works [the "CONTU"] with respect to clarifying the law of copyright ownership of computer software." . . . ("Congress adopted CONTU's suggestions and amended the Copyright Act").

The CONTU issued a final report ("Contu Report"), Final Report of the National Commission on New Technological Uses of Copyrighted Works 30 (1978), which recommended that congress amend the copyright law so that a rightful possessor of a copy of a computer program would be able to make certain copies and adaptions of the program without infringing the program's copyright. The Contu Report states that "persons in rightful possession of copies of programs [should] be able to use them freely without fear of exposure to copyright liability." Contu Report at 31. Buyers should be able to adapt a purchased program for use on the buyer's computer because without modifications, the program may work improperly, if at all. No buyer would pay for a program without such a right.

Bonelli and Island, as rightful owners of a copy of CSALIB, did not infringe upon Aymes's copyright, because the changes made to CSALIB were necessary measures in their continuing use of the software in operating their business. 17 U.S.C. § 117(1) (1992). The modifications here fall easily within the contemplation of Contu:

> Because of a lack of complete standardization among programming languages and hardware in the computer industry, one who rightfully acquires a copy of a program frequently cannot use it without adapting it to that limited extent which will allow its use in the possessor's computer. The copyright law, which grants to copyright proprietors the exclusive right to prepare translations, transformations, and adaptions of their work, should no more prevent such use than it should prevent rightful possessors from loading programs into their computers. Thus, a right to make those changes necessary to enable the use for which it was both sold and purchased should be provided.

Contu Report at 32.

* * *

Nor does it appear that the modifications to the program were for any purpose other than Island's internal business needs. The original program made provisions for late charges, and Island did alter CSALIB to keep it current from year to year and to maintain the viability of the original software when Island upgraded its computer to accommodate successive generations of IBM systems. In this connection, the Contu Report also comments:

> The conversion of a program from one higher-level language to another to facilitate use would fall within this right [of adaption], as would the right to add features to the program that were not present at the time of rightful acquisition . . . . Again, it is likely that many transactions involving copies of programs are entered into with full awareness that users will modify their copies to suit their own needs, and this should be reflected in the law . . . . Should proprietors feel strongly that they do not want rightful possessors of copies of their programs to prepare such adaptions, they could, of course, make such desires a contractual matter.

Contu Report at 13-14 (emphasis added) quoted in *Foresight Resources,* 719 F. Supp. at 1009.

Although at the time the parties entered into an agreement for the creation of CSALIB they orally agreed that the program would be used on one Island computer, the district court found that the oral agreement had not been breached. Moreover, both parties knew that modifications would be essential for the continued functioning of the program on an upgraded computer system, and that, in fact, the system was continually being upgraded in order

to keep up with Island's growth. Until this lawsuit Aymes never sought to prohibit others from making modifications to the programs, although for some time he had been aware that Island had hired another programmer to convert and modify CSALIB. Indeed, Aymes was present and raised no objection while some of the modifications were being made by Island's employees.

Finally, there is no merit to Aymes's suggestion that defendants infringed his copyright because they used the programs in an unauthorized manner and for an external purpose. *Foresight Resources,* 719 F. Supp. at 1009; Apple Computer, 594 F. Supp. at 621. The district court found that Island used CSALIB for internal business purposes only and did not distribute the program to its subsidiaries. These findings are not clearly erroneous. Nor is there evidence that the modified program was marketed, manufactured, distributed, transferred, or used for any purpose other than Island's own internal business needs. See Id. ("the copy authorized by Section 117 must be made only for the owner-user's internal use").

We have considered Aymes's other contentions and find them to be similarly without merit.

QUESTIONS FOR ANALYSIS

1. Does this opinion mean that since Bonelli can modify the CSALIB software to work with upgraded operating systems and computer equipment, that Bonelli could resell these adaptations to other firms?
2. What did the court suggest that Aymes should have done if he wanted to prevent Bonelli from modifying the CSALIB without permission. Do you suspect that such prohibitions would be standard terms in license agreements?

assignment clause in its contract for software development. An assignment clause typically would transfer ownership of the copyright for the software to the hiring firm. Without an assignment clause, the hiring firm is at the mercy of the independent contractors with respect to upgrades, copies, and distribution of the software. In the absence of specific provisions in a written contract, the hiring firm has an *implied* right to use the application software it paid for. The hiring firm has the right to make an archival (backup) copy of the software, but does not have the right to sell or license to others the software it paid for in its contract with the software developer.

Adverse Interests

After customized software is created for a firm, the interests of the software consulting firm and its client are directly opposite. The client, or hiring firm, wants the software for itself and wants to prevent the software from coming into possession of its rivals. The software-consulting firm, however, possesses a potentially valuable asset once the contract with its client has been completed. If the software firm has possession and ownership of the software code, it is a good bet that rivals of the client firm in the same industry have the same needs for software and are willing to pay for that software. Since reproduction of software is virtually costless, the software development firm can make potentially very substantial profits selling copies of the software to other firms, even at prices of 1/5 to 1/10 of the original contract price. Note, further, that a hiring firm with no assignment clause or other restrictions on the actions of the software development firm could be worse off than if it did not hire the software firm at all. Its rivals can gain a competitive advantage by acquiring a valuable input (the software) at a fraction of the cost paid by the hiring firm.

Toolbox Codes

Although the interests of software consultants and their client firms may be adverse with respect to the final product, namely the application software that is *customized* to the needs of the client firm, the interests of the two firms may or may not be adverse with respect to *toolbox codes*. Toolbox codes are standard components of most software products, including user interfaces, shopping carts for E-Commerce sites, and other familiar conventions used in software products. It makes no sense for software firms to create essentially identical components of software for different

clients. Software consultants who are able to take their tools (codes that can be plugged in to produce pull-down menus, etc.) with them upon completion of a job are better able to complete their contracts for less money. A reasonable split of ownership between software consulting firms and client firms typically results in the client firm getting the copyright on the application software while the software firm is entitled to retain its toolbox in the form of software code that can be used on other jobs. Knowledgeable software firms also will insist that they retain ownership of tools that they took to the job.

However, the client firm also clearly has an interest in the software consultant's toolbox codes. The client firm may anticipate a need to modify or upgrade the software package in the future or may even intend to resell the software. Success in either of these endeavors is likely to involve mixing and switching toolbox codes. Without a license for full and unrestricted use of the needed toolbox codes, the client firm is vulnerable to a copyright infringement suit brought by the software firm, particularly if the client firm is reselling the software and, in effect, going into competition with the software firm.

So, in addition to obtaining a *copyright* on a final application product, the hiring firm may also want to negotiate for a *license agreement* with respect to the toolbox codes needed for servicing and modifying that software product. The terms of the license are negotiable, with the ideal from the client firm's perspective being a perpetual, nonexclusive worldwide license to use the tools in the toolbox. Such a license will allow the client firm to upgrade its software internally or possibly with the services of another software development company. By obtaining a license to the toolbox codes, the hiring firm breaks its dependent tie to the original software development company and moves to an improved bargaining position in subsequent contract negotiations.

What Happens When Ownership of Software Is Retained by the Software Firm

In many instances, a client firm is not in a position to negotiate the terms of many of the elements of a contract with a software vendor. If the software-consulting firm is providing applications based on popular software products such as those put out by SAS, ORACLE, and Lawson, the parent companies of these successful commercial applications packages are simply not going to transfer ownership of customized versions of their software to small and medium-sized businesses.[5] When the software installation contract is complete, the client firm becomes a *licensee* of the owners of the software, which may be the software consulting firm or may be, and this is more likely, a parent company with whom the software consulting firm is a franchisee or partner.

In many cases, the client firm has no residual interest in the software other than use in its business and therefore, from its perspective, whether it is a licensee or owner of the software is irrelevant. The client firm wants to use the functionality of the software, but does not contemplate being in the business of distributing or subleasing the software to other firms.

Client Firm as Licensee

In the limit, a very broad license of software approaches ownership. If a client firm is entitled to a perpetual, transferable, irrevocable, fully-paid-for license with an unqualified right to sublicense and/or modify, then the client firm may be in a stronger legal position than if it is the copyright owner. With a very broad license, the licensee has all the benefits of ownership and perhaps less of the burdens. The copyright owner may be called upon to defend the copyright in the event of an infringement, a burden not shared by the licensee. Of course, the client firm, as licensee, would want a prohibition on sales or licenses of the software by the consulting firm (the licensor) to rivals of the client firm.

Protection of Competitive Advantage

As described above, a client firm can certainly harm its position in the market by contracting with a computer software firm without appropriate safeguards. In particular, if the software firm retains the copyright to the customized software and is not prohibited from reselling the software, the client firm's rivals can obtain the same, or possibly improved, software at a much-reduced price. To avoid such disasters and to protect competitive advantage, the hiring firm should insist on the following from an outside software vendor:

1. An assignment clause that assigns ownership of the software in the form of a copyright to the client firm, but, failing that,

2. If the client firm is unable to obtain the copyright on the software developed by the consultant, then the hiring firm should obtain as broad a license as possible so that the hiring firm can modify, sublicense, and resell the software they "paid for", and

3. At a minimum the software-consulting firm must agree not to market the same or similar software to rivals of the hiring firm. If the software firm does not agree to this provision, then it is possible that the client firm will, in effect, be subsidizing software development for its rivals.

4. To further protect its competitive advantage, the hiring firm should insist that the software consultant **not** display its (the client firm's) software at trade shows or to other firms. In addition, the software should be identified as a trade secret and the software firm should be prohibited in the contract from talking about, selling, or licensing the client firm's software. Such prohibitions on disclosure are often called *Non-Disclosure Agreements* (NDAs).

Confidentiality Issues Between Software Consultants and Client Firms

Nondisclosure Agreements and Trade Secrets

In software development contracts, there are two important aspects of NDAs. First, there is the software itself, which the client firm can legitimately identify as a trade secret and, which consequently, the software vendor firm is required to keep secret. Trade secrets, which are discussed in more detail in Chapter 8, have been described as: (1) Information that is used in business and (2) derives value because it is secret from the competition and (3) is subject to reasonable efforts by the firm holding the trade secret to keep it secret.[6] Clearly, customized software can be claimed as a trade secret, entitled to trade secret protection. If such software is copyrighted, the Copyright Office allows for registration without an accompanying full disclosure of the computer code, which would make that code available to the public, hence to rivals of the firm that made or bought the software.[7] So, trade secret law can be used **with** copyright law to provide more protection

---

[5]Each of these firms is well-known in the B to B software market. SAS, Oracle, and Lawson can be accessed at their websites: www.SAS.com, www.Oracle.com, and www.Lawson.com, respectively.

[6]This description of trade secrets is largely taken from the Uniform Trade Secrets Act, which has been adopted in 40 states.
[7]See Circular 61 of the U.S. Copyright Office, "Copyright Registration for Computer Programs".

for the IP in software than either branch of law could provide separately.

Due Diligence Still Required by Client Firm

Another important dimension of NDAs required of outside computer consultants deals with knowledge of the client's business gained while customizing and installing software. In most cases, it would be physically impossible to conduct business while shielding software-providing firms from all trade secrets or other sensitive information. Software installation itself is quite disruptive to normal business activity, but to try to accomplish customization and installation, while also protecting trade secrets from view, is apt to be highly disruptive of the ongoing conduct of business and, hence, highly inefficient. To avoid such disruptions, it is commonplace for firms to require NDAs of software vendors, installers, and service providers. It is notable that obtaining an NDA from a software consultant does not mean that the hiring firm can discharge its security force and procedures. Even though the software consultant signs an NDA, the hiring firm must still use **reasonable measures** to protect the secrecy of its trade secrets and would have an obligation to question irregular behavior by the software consulting firm or its employees. Failure by the client firm to protect against subterfuge by the software firm could result in a declaration that its negligence resulted in the loss of trade secrets with an accompanying denial of any remedy against others who might be using its software.

Other Contractual Protections

Intellectual Property Indemnification

In the hiring of an outside software vendor, it is prudent for the hiring firm to require the software consulting firm to agree to the following:

1. If the copyright to the software is assigned to the hiring firm, that use of the software will not amount to an infringement of other copyrights or patents.
2. In the contract with the software consulting firm, a statement that creation and installation of its work will not constitute an infringement of any "intellectual property rights of any third persons including, but not limited to, copyrights, patents, and trademarks."[8]

An indemnification clause requires the indemnifying firm (the software developer) to step in and defend the indemnified firm (the client firm) from infringement suits by third parties regarding use of the software provided by the software firm, i.e. an indemnification clause requires the indemnifier to step in and defend the lawsuit, paying for the legal fees and for damages if the indemnified firm is found liable. If the client firm is the target of a suit, there is a pretty good chance that the software firm committed fraud by appropriating (a legal term for stealing without paying) code from some other firm's software. Even if the software firm is committing fraud by making the noninfringement promise, an intellectual property indemnification clause remains important to the client firm as it negates claims by third parties with superior rights to the software (copyright, patent holders, trademark owners) that any infringement was *willful*. In copyright and patent infringement suits, damages awarded are significantly lower if the defendant "innocently" infringed. By requiring an indemnification clause, the client firm can assert it was unaware of any wrongdoing by the software developer.

Limitations of Liability or Insurance?

Most software development companies seek to limit their liability for coding errors or other mistakes made in the installation of software. Typical language limiting liability may state that the software development firm is not liable for:

> "special, consequential, incidental, indirect or punitive loss, damage or expenses (including but not limited to lost profits, savings, data, loss of facilities, or equipment, or the cost of recreating lost data) regardless of whether arising from breach of contract, warranty, tort, strict liability or otherwise, even if it has been advised of their possible existence or if such losses, damages, or expenses were reasonably foreseeable. Any action by either party must be brought within two (2) years after the cause of action arose."[9]

Another clause commonly used in capping damages associated with software installation is a limit on liability that is equal to the contract price scheduled to be paid by the client firm.

Note that, even with limitations of liability, software development firms have potential liability. Client firms often negotiate the language in limitations of

---

[8]Language taken from an actual software development contract. Name of company is being withheld by request of the company.

[9]Language taken from an actual software development contract. Name of company is being withheld by request of the company.

liability so that the software firms are liable for some contingencies which they are warned about, such as the importance of timely performance. However, software development firms are notorious for having very few tangible assets that can be attached to satisfy an adverse judgment. So, it is possible for contractual agreements to provide little protection from injury actually suffered by a client firm. A limitation of liability for mistakes by programmers that far exceeds the assets of the computer consultants is an academic exercise with no real significance. If the software-consulting firm does have substantial financial assets, then they are likely to negotiate aggressively to limit their liability for mistakes made in the source or object code.

An alternative is for the client firm to insist that the software development firm carry *errors and omissions insurance*. Established and reputable computer consulting firms should be able to obtain insurance policies that pay out in the event of mistakes by the programmers or other company staff. If the computer consultant works for a firm that has virtually no financial assets and cannot obtain errors and omissions insurance, then discussing a limitation of liability clause is a waste of time.

Source Code Retention

Computer consulting firms are young firms in a young industry, a recipe for considerable instability. Given the possible instability of many computer consulting firms, client retention of the source code for applications software can be an important issue in software development contracts. A hiring firm that will pay for software development certainly does not want that source code, which it will pay for, to become available to rivals at all, much less at vastly reduced prices. This would appear to justify a client firm demanding that all source code be turned over to it as that code is developed. There is, however, an equally compelling counterpoint. If the hiring firm retains a copy of the source code throughout the contract, the leverage the software firm enjoys in dealing with a client firm is very low. An unscrupulous client (hiring) firm that has copies of the source code can refuse to pay the software consulting firm until it has performed all that was called for in the contract and then some. In most software contracts between software firms and client firms unexpected events take place. The software may or may not do all the software firm claimed it could do, or the client expected it to do, at the start of the contract.

Consider a software package that can do 97 percent of what was claimed, but which would require very substantial expenses for modifications that would accomplish the remaining (relatively minor) functions discussed when the software installation was contracted. Suppose, too, that the software can be used to perform some tasks that were not recognized at the start of the contract. If the client firm retains the source code, then it could refuse to make payments to the software developer unless the software firm incurred some very heavy expenses in return for modest increases in functionality. On the other hand, a computer consultant who absconds with the source code, can leave a client firm with software that was 90 percent installed when all or most payments were received, but totally unusable. From the perspective of the client firm, considerable protection is provided by requiring the software firm to turn over source code on a daily basis as it is developed (certainly "frequent," if not daily).

Source Code Escrow Provisions   Given the huge bargaining advantages held by the party that possesses the source code for a software package, an arrangement has emerged that creates a more level playing field for both parties in the form of commercial "software code escrow" companies. Source code (software) escrow firms are third parties that are brought into software development contracts to supervise performance of the software contract and to provide software code holding services. An escrow firm collects contract payments from a client firm and receives and stores source code from the client's software consulting firm. With the escrow firm as intermediary, the software firm does not get paid until the client firm indicates that performance is satisfactory, while the client firm does not get the software's source code until the software firm has been paid. Under these restrictions, both parties have an incentive to satisfactorily complete a contract for software development and installation.

National Software Escrow, Inc. (NSE) is a source code escrow company located near Cleveland Ohio.[10] According to the company, "NSE, which has been providing source code escrow services to varied industry sectors since 1986, acts as a neutral third party and holds a copy of the source code in an offsite storage facility for the life of the license agreement for the benefit of both the Software Developer and Software

---

[10]National Software Escrow, Inc., is available at http://www.nationalsoftwareescrow.com.

User." NSE offers Three and Two party escrow agreements. In the Three-Party Escrow agreement, NSE manages an agreement between the licensor (software developer) and Licensee (user firm). In Two-Party Escrow agreements an agreement between the software developer and NSE is drawn up so that multiple users can be brought into software license agreements that have no (unpleasant) surprises for any of the parties.

Contract Pricing Choices

When two firms enter into a software development contract, misunderstandings, disputes, friction, and conflicts appear to be inevitable. Commonplace disputes focus on disagreements regarding what was to be provided (what functions, what interface characteristics, what processing speed and efficiency) and on what price was to be paid for what. To minimize the likelihood of such disagreements, great care is required in the construction of contracts, with a great deal of attention in contracts focused on pricing. Pricing agreements generally take one of two forms—a *fixed price* contract or *a time and materials* contract.

Fixed Price Deliverable Work

In this type of software development contract, the software firm gets paid based on completion of the contracted assignment. The contract price is fixed and does not vary according to the amount of time that it takes to develop and install the software. The client firm has some assurance of the ultimate price while the software firm can make significant profits if the time to installation completion is less than anticipated. Since the software firm does not get paid based on the number of hours it devotes to the software assignment, it does not have an incentive to drag its feet in order to get paid more. Such a contract shifts the risk of underestimating the difficulty of the job to the software-consulting firm. Software firms will hedge their risk by bidding higher on fixed price deliverable jobs so that they have some slack if they made a mistake on any aspect of the job. Frequently, however, client firms will ask for changes in the contractual performance specifications, which requires both parties to agree on a *change order*. Change orders, and the resulting increases in the contract price, provide an opportunity for software firms to recoup some of the money lost on an underbid contract.

Time and Materials Project

In this type of contract, the risk of an underbid contract is borne by the client firm. Clients pay for cost overruns so the software firm is probably willing to work for less on a per-hour basis. Most of the risk is borne by the client in this type of contract because many thousands of dollars can be expended without achieving the performance standards that both parties intended.

A problem to be resisted in time and materials projects is creeping specification. After the software developer begins to ask the client questions and show solution possibilities, the client firm may request a lot more functionality in its contract with the software developer. Oftentimes it is the software developer that suggests 'Cadillac' software, when standard software would do just as well. A good project manager is aware of the problems associated with creeping specifications and the need to document any price changes in the original software contract. Software developers should be warned that they will not be paid for changes that are orally agreed upon with a representative of the client firm. Either the change is made pursuant to a change order, that is in writing and agreed to by both sides, or the software firm proceeds at its own risk (of not getting paid for the extra time it puts in adding functionality to the software).

Security Concerns and Dispute Resolution Mechanisms

Other disputes arise over security concerns. A software developer must understand the client firm's business intimately and the intrusions attendant to developing that understanding are bound to be resented by some within the client business. Information that the client firm regards as sacred may be the same type of information that the software development firm is exposed to in many other assignments. Employees of software development firms may be somewhat free-wheeling, whereas the client firm may be much more security conscious.

Given the nature of the relationship between a software development firm and the client firm, it is very often desirable that dispute resolution mechanisms be specified in the contract to avoid precipitous and likely unproductive litigation. This is desirable no matter what the source of potential disagreement is, whether pricing, product characteristics, security concerns, or some other issue.

Arbitration and Choice of Law Clauses

Litigation can provide a remedy in a court of law for a software developer that has not been paid completely, or for a client firm that did not receive software that possessed the functionality it believes is called for in the contract. In the fast-paced world of high-tech, however, to wait for a minimum of a year or more even before the nonbreaching party gets its day in court, is typically a very unsatisfactory outcome. "Justice delayed is justice denied" is a frequently re-cited maxim in law, which certainly can apply when software developers and client firms lock horns in a contractual dispute.

A combination of *mandatory arbitration* and *choice of law* clauses provide a superior private remedy in many cases.[11] Arbitration clauses can have a number of benefits. First, the firms can agree on a short statute of limitations (or period to file a complaint), say one or two months. If the allegedly aggrieved party does not file for an arbitrator during that time period, then the issue is moot. In addition, the wait for an arbitrator is far less than in court liti-gation, often as little as a month or less. An arbitra-tor could make a timely ruling on a disputed issue without delays that could "kill" most projects be-tween two companies if the same dispute went to court. A third benefit stems from the fact that arbitra-tors are usually very knowledgeable in the applica-tion field that is the focus of arbitration, eliminating the need to bring a judge up to speed in a technical area. This reduces the amount of "time in court" and its attendant costs for lawyers and experts. Further-more, knowledgeable arbitrators will not yield unrea-sonable awards or verdicts. Fourth, the decision of an arbitrator is ***final, binding and not appealable,*** except in very rare instances involving bribery or lack of consent to the arbitration. Appeals processes, you should know, are very expensive. Fifth, both federal and state courts are bound by statutes that require the courts to enforce judgments (or awards) of arbitrators.[12]

Additional certainty takes place if a *choice of law* clause is included in the contract. Since a software-consulting contract is considered a service contract, it will not be subject to the UCC, which brings back the problem of differences in contract law among the states as a factor causing additional complexity and uncertainty in the resolution of disputes. Without a specific clause in the contract, it is most likely that the laws of the state where the contract is performed will control, but determining where performance takes place can be problematic. The client company can be located in one state while development of most of the source code could take place in another state. Given the ease of Internet transmissions, precise geographic determination of where the contract is being executed seems beside the point. Yet, important legal conse-quences depend on this determination. Rather than leaving this important issue to chance, the parties should agree to a choice of law clause.

Summary of Software Development Contracts

As with many areas of law, a little planning goes a long way in the development of software contracts. Firms that hire programmers should be aware of the consequences of hiring independent contractors ver-sus hiring programmers as employees. If independent contractors are used, ownership of copyrighted soft-ware must be clearly addressed along with any restric-tions that may be placed on either the hiring firm and/or the software development firm with respect to subsequent use and distribution of the software. Given the frequency with which disputes are occurring in software contracts, such contracts should include mechanisms for resolving ambiguous legal issues and for specifying the location of and nature of dispute resolution.

NEGOTIATING BUSINESS-TO-BUSINESS LICENSES

Business-to-business licenses for existing (copy-righted) software products generally involve negoti-ated contract clauses within the license agreements that are tailored to fit the individual transaction. In contrast to the situation(s) addressed above, existing software typically has already been developed, copy-righted, and trademarked. The terms of negotiated licenses depend on more factors than can be captured in a general discussion of licensing. So the following discussion is necessarily general, and differences among actual license agreements may overwhelm the similarities.

---

[11]For this first book, we probably need to provide some way that brings the students up to speed with respect to arbitration.
[12]At the federal level, the Federal Arbitration Act allows for arbitration to resolve disputes involving all Acts of Congress that do not specifically prohibit arbitration. Similar statutes exist at the state level.

A Few Tips

Please see this article:
http://www.computerworld.com/cwi/story/0,1199,NAV63-128-1357-1367_STO46789,00.html
"Is it your software? Or the outsourcer's?" *Computerworld;* Framingham; Jul 10, 2000.

Additional readings:
http://www.bellgully.co.nz/publications/presentations/ak981420793.html
"Negotiating and designing an effective Outsourcing Contract—A practical legal view", Presentation by Wayne Hudson - 19 May 1998.
http://www.logica.com/globe/globe09/outsourcing.html
"Look before you leap", *Logica,* Issue 9-1999; Logica Globe.

Form of the License

Most business-to-business software licenses are *non-exclusive,* meaning, of course, that the software vendor (the licensor) can license the same software to other firms (who are licensees). In addition, almost all software licenses are *nontransferable* by the licensee so that the licensee does not become a sublicensor in competition with the licensor. In addition, the use made of software will generally be restricted to the *normal operations* of the licensee so that the licensee cannot sell or rent to other firms access to the software. Licensees can generally insist that the license be *irrevocable* so long as the license fees are paid and the other restrictions of the license are not breached.

Number of Permitted Users and Use Agreements

Many companies are affiliated with other companies as subsidiaries, sister corporations, joint venturers, long-term strategic allies, and so forth. Many of these affiliates may have physical access to the facilities of the licensee. Specifying permitted users is often imperative if the licensor wants to maximize fees. If the license grants unlimited use to permitted users, then restricting permitted users from those firms that are very closely aligned with the licensee enables the licensor to collect more fees than a license that states nothing about permitted users.

On the other hand, if license fees are based on *use* of the software, then the number of permitted users is irrelevant. When license fees are based on use, the licensor gets paid each time a licensee uses the software, so restricting permitted users is not in the interest of the licensor. Software packages with use-based billing incorporate counting mechanisms, metering either the number of uses or minutes used. Westlaw is an online legal library supported by software and used by law firms. Westlaw bases its charges on the number of minutes the licensee uses its product. Once a user at the site of the licensee's business gets online with the Westlaw software, the charges begin, whether the user is a secretary, paralegal, attorney, or an attorney from another firm. Westlaw is not interested in restricting its product to only a few specified users at the site of the licensee's business.

License Restrictions and Fee Structures

If license fees are not based on number of *minutes* the software is used or number of *times* the software is used, then the license should restrict the use of the software or fees collected by a licensor will rapidly erode. Licensees must be restricted from distributing the software in the form of subleases, assignments, transfers, etc., to third parties. It is also common for a license to prohibit modification, disassembly, and reverse engineering of the software. Furthermore, the software vendor may have bundled its software with licensed software from another vendor that may also have specific restrictions.

License fees can be based on several different criteria. A **Per-User** license restricts use of the software to a limited number of users at the purchaser's site. The restriction can be based on concurrent users at any one time or can be based on the aggregate number of users regardless of when the software is used. **Site-Based** licenses restrict use of the software to a particular location or equipment, though the number of users at the site is not limited. Finally, the license may restrict the **number of copies** that the licensee is entitled to install at its location. Software vendors generally would be expected to seek to maximize license fees and to select a fee structure that will accommodate users while generating the desired fees. Since the fee structure of vendors often is not negotiable, users can only select from the fee choices offered that one which best enables them to realize the functionality of the software for the cheapest price. Regardless of what the license states, under the Copyright Act, users are entitled to make at least one archival copy.[13] The Copyright Act also requires that licensees destroy their archival copies at the termination of a license.

Acceptance Date

Few firms are willing to pay large software license fees unless they are convinced that the software offered will work properly with their computers, data, and information systems. Vendors typically allow a testing period before the licensee is required to pay the annual license fee. License fees may be paid in installments depending upon the achievement of certain benchmarks. Separate fees may be required by contract according to specific events such as when the software is physically delivered, when it is installed, when staff is trained to use it, and when it is put into actual operation. Licensors, of course, want short and well-defined testing periods before a final acceptance is required. Licensees want a longer testing period to make sure that the software delivers the functionality that the vendor claims. Licensees also want a complete refund if the software is not accepted. The parties need a clear agreement on acceptance criteria (preferably prior to contracting) to determine whether the licensee is entitled to reject the software after installation.

Warranties

There is a wide variance in software warranties. A licensor naturally wants to minimize its obligations while licensees want extensive guarantees. Software licenses are not regulated by the UCC, so the *perfect tender* rule does not apply. The perfect tender rule allows buyers to reject goods or performance unless it perfectly conforms to what is called for in the contract. Even though the perfect tender rule is not in effect, it is common for the vendor to warrant that the software will *substantially* conform to the documentation that accompanies the software. Without the word

"substantially" the vendor is risking breach of warranty and rejection of the software because of a few minor "bugs" in the software. At a minimum, the vendor should warrant that the software does not infringe any other copyright or patent and that it is free from viruses and other disabling codes. In addition, if sales brochures and other materials make promises about the capabilities of the software, that information should be included among the warranty terms. Vendors that try to disclaim all warranties, express and implied, while at the same time making extensive claims about the capabilities of their software in their sales brochures, run substantial risk that the warranty disclaimers will be disregarded.

Timing Issues

It is common for a license agreement to extend beyond the accompanying warranty period. The warranty may expire after 90 days, 6 months, or a year on a software license that lasts several years. After the warranty expires, malfunctioning software is the responsibility of the licensee, but the vendor generally provides for service work and/or upgrades on the software for a fee. Not all aspects of the warranty need expire at the same time. It is common for the *replacement of defective parts* portion of the warranty to expire long before the warranty against viruses or disabling code expires. The latter two warranties tend to be perpetual.

Remedies under Warranty

Remedies for breach of warranty are typically limited by the software vendor to replacement or repair of defective products. Warranty disclaimers are common and generally are stated in boldface type so that there will not be any question on the part of users as to what they are entitled to in a breach of warranty suit. It is important to note that **unless warranty remedies are expressly limited or disclaimed, then users are entitled to sue for both compensatory and consequential damages.** Furthermore, if the warranty remedy fails in its essential purpose, the user will not be limited to replacement of parts but instead can sue for monetary damages to its business. If the warranty expires before the testing period for the software can reasonably be completed, then the courts will find that the warranty remedy fails in its essential purpose as occurred in the case below.

---

[13]Section 117(2) of the Copyright Act.

Chatlos Systems, Inc. v. *National Cash Register Corporation*
U.S. District Court, New Jersey
479 F.Supp. 738 (1979)

FACTS AND CASE BACKGROUND

In the spring of 1974 the plaintiff (Chatlos) was becoming overwhelmed by data and was in the market for assistance from a computer company. Long, a salesman from National Cash Register (NCR), recommended that Chatlos acquire a computer known as NCR 399 Magnetic Ledger Card (MAG). Long represented that the 399 MAG could accomplish six functions: Accounts Receivable, Payroll, Order Entry, Inventory Deletion, State Income Tax, and Cash Receipts. The contract was signed on July 11, 1974. Because Chatlos could not get credit to finance the purchase of the computer, NCR sold the computer to a bank which then leased the computer to Chatlos. Under the lease, Chatlos was obligated to pay the bank $70,162.09. The payroll function did not become functional until March of 1975. By January 1, 1976, the system was still not operational and NCR sent new technicians to Chatlos. By March of 1976 the system was still not working and in June of that year Chatlos asked that the lease be cancelled and that the computer be removed from their premises. A series of meetings took place during July and August of 1976 as NCR officials requested another opportunity to make the system work. By September of 1976 the system still was not performing four of the six functions that NCR claimed the system could accomplish. The court ruled that this transaction was a sale of goods, which meant that Article 2 of the UCC applied. The contract Chatlos had with NCR contained an exclusive remedy clause that limited NCR's obligation on any software malfunction to within

60 days of delivery. Furthermore, there was a limitation of liability clause that excluded liability for all consequential damages.

OPINION: WHIPPLE, SENIOR DISTRICT JUDGE

A two-step process is necessary in order to fully consider the initial question of damages herein. The first inquiry must be to determine the value of the goods if they had been as warranted. This is not the "market value" since that term is conspicuously absent from s 2-714(2). The appropriate starting place is the $70,162.09 the plaintiff indebted itself to pay the bank for the computer system. It includes the amount the defendant received, the sales tax, together with the interest charges under the lease arrangement. [Footnote Deleted] The $5,621.22 paid by the plaintiff for the service contract is added because it was an inseparable element of the entire transaction. The Court finds the total value of the computer system if it had been as warranted to be $75,783.31.

The value of what was accepted must be deducted from the $75,783.31. Plaintiff's expert testified that the value of the hardware presently located at CSI is between $5,000.00 and $7,000.00. Taking the average, the Court finds the present value to be $6,000.00. An additional element must be calculated; the value of the payroll function which plaintiff admits was used from March 1975 until October 1976. Since neither plaintiff nor defendant presented any evidence of this value, the Court will assign a value as follows. The payroll function was one of the six that *745 were promised, therefore, it is reasonable to recognize this benefit

as one-sixth of the value if as warranted, or one-sixth of $75,783.31. This equals $12,630.55. The sum of the two adjustments is $18,630.55. When this figure is deducted from $75,783.31 the $57,152.58 result is the amount to which plaintiff is entitled as the direct measure of damages for breach of warranty, before discussion of incidental and/or consequential damages.

NCR maintains that an effective limitation on recovery of consequential damages appears in the System Services Agreement. The written warranties previously discussed conclude that "NCR's obligation is limited to correcting any error in any program as appears within 60 days after such has been furnished." (Plaintiff's ex. 30-c, 30-d; Def. 81, 82) Later language in the System Services Agreement states, "in no event shall NCR be liable for special or consequential damages from any cause whatsoever." These phrases clearly attempt to limit the purchaser's remedy to having any error corrected within sixty days after the appropriate programs are furnished. Since four of the six functions were never furnished, the attempted limitation falls squarely within N.J.S.A. 12A:2-719(2) which provides that:

Where circumstances cause an exclusive or limited remedy to fail of its essential purpose, remedy may be had as provided in this Act.

Uniform Commercial Code Comment 1 following N.J.S.A. 12A:2-719 states:

(I)t is of the very essence of a sales contract that at least minimum adequate remedies be available. If the parties intend to conclude a contract for sale within this Article they must accept the legal consequences that there must be at least a fair quantum of remedy for breach of the obligations or duties outlined in the contract. Thus any clause purporting to modify or limit the remedial provisions of this Article in an unconscionable manner is subject to deletion and in that event the remedies made available by this Article are applicable as if the stricken clause had never existed. Similarly, Under subsection (2), where an apparently fair and reasonable clause because of circumstances fails in its purpose or operates to deprive either party of the substantial value of the bargain, it must give way to the general remedy provision in this Article. (emphasis supplied)

This reasoning has been adopted by several courts. In *Beal* v. *General Motors,* 354 F.Supp. 423 (D.Del. 1973) a motion to strike allegations of consequential damages was denied, despite an apparently valid exclusive remedy clause. There the district court noted that:

(t)he purpose of an exclusive remedy of replacement or repair of defective parts, whose presence constitute a breach of an express warranty, is to give the seller an opportunity to make the goods conforming while limiting the risks to which he is subject by excluding direct and consequential damages that might otherwise arise. From the point of view of the buyer the purpose of the exclusive remedy is to give him goods that conform to the contract within a reasonable time after a defective part is discovered. When the warrantor fails to correct the defect as promised within a reasonable time he is liable for a breach of that warranty. . . . The limited, exclusive remedy fails of its purpose and is thus avoided under s 2-719(2),

whenever the warrantor fails to correct the defect within a reasonable period. (citations omitted) (emphasis added)

Because NCR never furnished four of the six promised functions, their attempted limitation of remedy failed of its essential purpose. CSI was thereby deprived of the substantial value of its bargain. For these reasons NCR is liable for consequential and incidental damages as provided for in N.J.S.A. 12A:2-714(3) and defined in N.J.S.A. 12A:2-715.

* * *

Incidental and consequential damages are defined as follows:

1. Incidental damages resulting from the seller's breach include expenses reasonably incurred in inspection, receipt, transportation and care and custody of goods rightfully rejected, any commercially reasonable charges, expenses or commissions in connection with effecting cover and any other reasonable expense incident to the delay or other breach.
2. Consequential damages resulting from the seller's breach include:
   a. Any loss resulting from general or particular requirements and needs of which the seller at the time of contracting had reason to know . . . .

* * *

The plaintiff has offered exhibits and testimony to substantiate their claim for these damages. The first loss to be considered is what plaintiff calls increased labor cost for accounting, inventory, sales, and executive salaries. These costs largely occurred after September 1976 and are

disallowed with an important exception. Having found NCR expressly warranted that CSI would save labor costs by implementation of the 399/656 Disc, and that warranty having been breached, it is necessary to compensate plaintiff for the consequential costs.

It was estimated that by implementation of the NCR computer system, CSI would save the cost of two employees whose services would no longer have been needed. NCR knew this was a major reason CSI entered the transaction. The United States Supreme Court has determined that: Damages are not rendered uncertain because they cannot be calculated with absolute exactness. It is sufficient if a reasonable basis of computation is afforded, although the result be only approximate . . . *Eastman Kodak Co.* v. *Southern Photo Materials Co.,* 273 U.S. 359, 379, 47 S.Ct. 400, 405, 71 L.Ed. 684 (1926). From the proofs it appears the cost for each employee of this type was $15,000 annually. Therefore plaintiff is entitled to the cost (for eighteen months) for each of the employees receiving $15,000 per year, a total of $45,000.

Plaintiff also seeks damages for executive salaries for the time devoted to working with NCR. These are reasonable with the exception of the time spent by Mr. Chatlos. As Chief Executive Officer he assumed the risk of all corporate problems and is not entitled to reimbursement of compensation by NCR. The expenses for the Plant Operations Manager (12% Of salary for twenty-six weeks or $2,620.00) and the Chief Bookkeeper (30% Of salary for the eighteen month period or $5,107.20) are reasonable. Plaintiff is therefore awarded $7,727.20. See *Clements Auto Company* v. *Services Bureau Corp.,* supra.

Plaintiff also seeks losses in profits for excesses and deficiencies in inventory. These were a consequence of the failure of the inventory deletion and order entry functions to operate. This was another major reason CSI entered into the transaction. Plaintiff presented evidence (plaintiff's ex. 52) and testimony to show lost profits because of excess inventory in 1975 totaling $5,080.95. Similarly for 1976 CSI showed a deficiency in inventory causing a profit loss of $3,325.24. When adjusted to include only the eighteen-month period these figures are reduced to $4,234.13 for 1975 and $2,216.83 for 1976, a total of $6,450.96. CSI paid $1,750.00 for a manual inventory system which could not perform the functions as well as a computer system. Plaintiff is entitled to the $1,750.00 in addition to $6,450.96 for profit losses.

CSI will receive the cost of various supplies purchased in an attempt to make the computer function. Evidence disclosed this amount to be $1,433.00. Moreover, plaintiff is entitled to the cost of the space occupied by the machine. Testimony revealed a formula for the annual rental; the cost per square foot multiplied by the measured size of the computer. After adjusting the figure to include only the eighteen months, plaintiff is entitled to $1,197.00.

Plaintiff's requests for the value of the space occupied by Mr. Hicks, cost of the powerline, and for maintenance of the area where the computer was kept, are denied. Mr. Hicks was trying to make it operate, the powerline was needed for the payroll function to be performed, and maintenance would have been done whether the machine worked or not.

* * *

The court concluded that the plaintiffs were entitled to consequential damages of $63,558.16 in addition to $57,152.76 which was the difference between what was offered in the contract and what the plaintiff received. Note that the original contract price was about $75,000 so that the defendant lost more money on this contract than they expected to make if the contracted had gone ahead as planned.

QUESTIONS FOR ANALYSIS

1. The opinion indicates that the remedy allowed in the contract between Chatlos and NCR "failed in its essential purpose." Does this case provide a lesson for contracts drawn up by large companies such as NCR that are so one-sided that the courts refuse to enforce limitations?

2. How would you define "consequential damages"? What are some of the components of consequential damages that are elucidated near the end of the court opinion?

Warranty Disclaimers versus Limitations of Liability

A warranty disclaimer exists when the vendor specifically disclaims express and implied warranties in clear and unambiguous language. The following language disclaims all warranties except those that the vendor is willing to back:

> THE WARRANTIES SET FORTH ABOVE ARE IN LIEU OF ALL OTHER WARRANTIES, WHETHER STATUTORY, EXPRESS OR IMPLIED (INCLUDING ALL WARRANTIES OF MERCHANTABILITY AND FITNESS FOR A PARTICULAR PURPOSE AND ALL WARRANTIES ARISING FROM COURSE OF DEALING OR USAGE OF TRADE).

Limitations of Liability

A limitation of liability occurs when a firm warrants, or guarantees, a product but seeks to limit its liability for the consequences of breach of warranty. In the case of software, the vendor may warrant or guarantee that the software will substantially conform to the descriptions contained in the documentation that accompanies the software. If the software does not perform as described, the vendor seeks to limit liability by special language that limits liability for breach of warranty. The following is typical:

> VENDOR'S TOTAL LIABILITY SHALL NOT EXCEED THE LICENSEE FEE PAID BY LICENSEE WITH RESPECT TO THE SOFTWARE PRODUCT ON WHICH SUCH LIABILITY IS BASED. IN NO EVENT SHALL VENDOR BE LIABLE FOR ANY INDIRECT, SPECIAL, INCIDENTAL, CONSEQUENTIAL, PUNITIVE OR EXEMPLARY DAMAGES ARISING OUT OF OR IN CONNECTION WITH THIS AGREEMENT OR ANY ACTS OR OMISSIONS ASSOCIATED THEREWITH OR RELATING TO THE USE OF THE SOFTWARE LICENSE HEREUNDER, WHETHER SUCH CLAIM IS BASED ON BREACH OF WARRANTY, CONTRACT, TORT OR OTHER LEGAL THEORY.

As we have seen from the *Chatlos* case, limitations of liability will not always be enforced. As between businesses, the courts are much more willing to enforce limitations of liability so long as they are not unconscionable. Unconscionability, however, is more readily invoked in contracts between businesses and consumers, because it is presumed that businesses are more sophisticated than ordinary consumers.

Relevance to Sale of Goods Contracts

It may also be prudent for the software vendor to specifically limit liability for breach of warranties that they are making. A software vendor is likely to specifically disclaim liability for consequential damages. Under the UCC (Section 2-791(3)), limiting liability for personal injury in the case of consumer goods is considered prima facie evidence of unconscionability and thus unenforceable. In the past software vendors could absolutely limit liability for consequential damages, including personal injury, because (1) malfunctions of most software did not cause personal injury and (2) most software was sold separately and thus not subject to 2-719(3) of the UCC. Software is now an increasingly ubiquitous feature of many tangible physical products sold to consumers, such as appliances, communications equipment, medical equipment, and even airplanes and automobiles. If a consumer appliance malfunctions because of a software failure, the transaction would be governed by the UCC and 2-719(3) would apply. If 2-719(3) applies, limitations of liability for personal injury for a consumer good would not be enforceable and thus a software designer could be liable for consequential damages.

Third Party Software

Increasingly, software vendors are selling products that include other (third party) vendors' software packages embedded in the complete package being provided. In such situations, the software vendor selling to end users as a licensee and end users are sublicensees. Vendors who are reluctant to warrant software they have not developed can limit their liability by making some or all of the following warranty disclaimers:

1. Not Error Free: VENDOR DOES NOT WARRANT THAT THE SOFTWARE WILL OPERATE WITHOUT INTERRUPTION OR WILL BE ERROR-FREE.
2. Results: VENDOR DOES NOT WARRANTY THE RESULTS OBTAINED BY ANY USE OF THE SOFTWARE.
3. Modification: THE FOREGOING WARRANTIES WILL BE RENDERED NULL AND VOID IF THE LICENSEE MODIFIES OR USES THE SOFTWARE IN AN UNAUTHORIZED MANNER.

A commercial licensee should at least insist that the warranties made by third-party vendors, whose software is embedded or bundled with other software licensed by the package-selling vendor, will be passed through to the licensee so that the licensee can take advantage of them. In general, licensees should recognize what is taking place when the software vendor will not stand behind software that it is licensing. A software vendor in this role is telling users that, if the software malfunctions, they (users) will have to chase down a remote software firm with whom the user has no privity of contract to pursue warranty remedies. As software users in the high-tech world have become increasingly sophisticated, they generally have demanded guarantees with regard to whom is responsible for fixing, repairing, or replacing software (or hardware) that does not function properly. The prospect of contacting a new firm (a third-party vendor) when software does not perform as advertised is not inviting. The third-party vendor firm can always claim that its software works fine, and that it is the software of the other software vendor that is the problem. The bottom line is that software licensees should insist that the warranties provided by software vendors apply to all the software the vendors are licensing. If software vendors disclaim any responsibility for third-party software, end users (licensees) should be aware of the risk of having each provider denying responsibility for malfunctioning software.

Source Code Escrow
Object Code Transfers

Most software is programmed in source code that is readable by humans such as HTML, COBOL, C++, and Visual Basic. When a software vendor actually transfers software to a licensee, it usually has been converted to object code, which consists of 1s and 0s, and is not readable by humans. The transformation of the computer code from source to object is a protection mechanism. When the licensed program is in the form of object code its secrets are safe unless it is decompiled, which normally will be prohibited by the license. Decompilation occurs when the object code is transformed back into source code, which is readable and capable of being modified by licensees. With the computer program in the form of object code, licensees' computers can operate the program, but it is very difficult for licensees to modify or repair *their* software.

Legal Risks Borne by Licensees

Licensees can become very dependent on license(s) with software vendor(s). Depending on the software and the business of the licensee, licensed software can be crucial to operations of the entire company. Since technology doesn't stand still in any area of business, it is certain that there will be a need at some point in the future to update licensed software and configure it with other upgrades. Licensees have a stake in gaining access to the licensed software in case the vendor becomes *bankrupt, goes out of business, or ceases to support the software.*

A logical solution to these risks is placement of a duplicate copy of a high value computer program with a source code escrow company. Certain events can be deemed release points that allow the licensee access to the source code of the licensed software. Vendors will not normally offer source code escrow as part of a license agreement. However, since such arrangements have become fairly common in software development contracts, particularly where there is a large-scale software implementation, vendors will generally allow buyers to negotiate provisions for the protection of the licensee. Typically, vendors will insist that licensees bear the costs of any source code escrow service and will seek to limit the triggering events to those few described above (bankruptcy, etc.). Of course, once a licensee obtains the source code for licensed software, it is in a position to modify and repair that software without the aid of the licensor/vendor.

Human Resource Management Issues

Large-scale software implementations typically require a project team of licensor employees to work on site at the location of the licensee. Occasionally, friction between employees of the licensee and those of the licensor becomes an issue. It is prudent for the licensee to have a clause inserted within the license giving it the right to demand replacement of any staff of the licensor who create problems with the licensee's employees. The staff replacement clause should emphasize that the decision to replace must be nondiscriminatory with respect to race, sex, age, disability, and any other protected class. At many universities, government offices, and in some cities and states, *sexual orientation* is also a protected class.

Antiraiding Provisions   Another human resource management risk is that the installation team of the licensor will do such a good job in installation of the software and on accompanying training on its use that the licensee will make offers for the services of project team members. Because of this risk, licensors often require an antiraiding or solicitation clause in a license agreement. The duration of such antiraiding provisions can extend beyond the life of accompanying licenses. As with all trade restraints, such antiraiding provision must be **reasonable** to be enforceable, which means that they must be limited in time and geographic scope. If an antiraiding clause in a contract prohibiting a licensee from employing an employee of the licensee for, say, three years after an installation is completed, that clause most likely would be considered an unreasonable trade restraint and, thus, unenforceable. Case law provides guidance with regard to allowable limits on trade restraints of this kind.

Summary of Business to Business Licenses

There are numerous legal issues that managers of companies that undertake large-scale software installations should resolve based on knowledge of the law. Software vendors will certainly be cognizant of legal issues that could affect their business and client companies should be knowledgeable with respect to what aspects of software licenses are negotiable. As businesses continue to adopt the latest in information technology, software choices will be among the most important decisions made by management. Skillful negotiation of software contracts is a must.

Until UCITA (discussed in Chapter 3) is passed by state legislatures, there will not be uniform contract law regarding the licensing of computer information. Courts have had to borrow concepts from Article 2 of the UCC and Article 2A of the UCC (which deals with leases) as well as adapt prior rulings to unprecedented situations created by advances in technology. Until uniform legislation passes in this area, software vendors will probably insist on choice of law provisions that reduce legal uncertainty.

MASS DISTRIBUTION LICENSES

When software is "sold" retail, the number of customers precludes individualized contact negotiations. Since there are significant costs of individually negotiating with customers about software licenses, the same license is offered to each customer, whether that customer is a company or a consumer. From the point of view of software vendors, an important legal issue is whether the provisions and restrictions contained in the mass distribution licenses are *enforceable*. In Chapter 3 we examined the issue of *procedural* challenges to x-wrap licenses. In this section, we examine challenges to the *content* of x-wrap licenses.

Typical Terms in a Mass Distribution License

As described above, the "purchaser" of software is not actually purchasing ownership of anything, but is more properly classified as a licensee. The software vendor is actually a licensor and, since mass distribution software is sold to numerous customers, the transaction costs of individually negotiating with customers are prohibitively high. Customers are offered the right to license the software on a "take it or leave it" basis. Typical of the statements and restrictions contained in "x-wrap" licenses are the following terms, among others:

1. The customer has not purchased the software, but merely has obtained a personal, nontransferable license to use the program. Authors' note: obviously, the intent in this statement is to prevent customers from making copies of the software and distributing to others, thus denying the licensee additional fees for the software.
2. The "x-wrap" license disclaims all express and implied warranties, except for the warranty that the disk is free of defects. Authors' note: the software vendor is willing to guarantee that the software is as described in the manual, but does

not assume liability for any harm that may occur because the software malfunctions.
3. The x-wrap license provides that the sole remedy available to the purchaser is return of the defective disk for replacement.
4. The x-wrap license contains an *integration* clause, which provides that the x-wrap license is the final and complete expression of the terms of the parties' agreement.
5. The x-wrap license contains a statement that opening the shrinkwrap (or box or clicking in an Internet transaction) indicates agreement with these terms and that if the purchaser does not agree with these terms, the purchaser must return the software within a relatively short period of time, such as 15 to 30 days.

ENFORCEABILITY OF X-WRAP LICENSES: CHALLENGES BASED ON CONTENT

Getting courts to enforce such restrictions has been a chore for vendors. First there is a procedural issue which concerns whether the customer has a fair opportunity to examine the terms in the x-wrap agreement. After procedural fairness tests have been satisfied, there is another hurdle for software vendors to mount, which is a requirement that the content of the x-wrap agreements not be **unconscionable.** In the *Brower* case immediately below, the plaintiffs took issue with the terms of an x-wrap agreement (in this case, a box-top agreement that accompanied the defendant's computer packages).

Tony Brower et al. v. *Gateway 2000, Inc.*
676 N.Y.S.2d 569
(N.Y.App.Div., 1998)

FACTS AND CASE BACKGROUND

This is a class action lawsuit in which plaintiffs are consumers who purchased computers and software products from defendant through a direct-sales system, by mail or telephone order. The plaintiffs are seeking compensatory and punitive

damages for, inter alia, breach of warranty, breach of contract, false advertising and deceptive sales practices based upon their alleged inability to access the around-the-clock technical support. In this case the plaintiffs learned of the terms of the contract only after making the

decision to purchase Gateway computers. Among the clauses in the box-top license agreement was an arbitration clause requiring arbitration of any "dispute or controversy arising out of or relating" to the agreement, with the arbitration to be held in Chicago before the International

Chamber of Commerce (ICC). The effect of this clause was to foreclose consumers' right to go to court if they were unhappy with the product and, furthermore, to require that they go to Chicago if they wanted to pursue arbitration. In addition, consumers had to pursue their arbitration remedies under the rules of the International Chamber of Commerce and pay the ICC fees.

OPINION: MILONAS, J. P.

First, the [trial] court properly rejected appellants' argument that the arbitration clause was invalid under UCC 2-207. Appellants claim that when they placed their order they did not bargain for, much less accept, arbitration of any dispute, and therefore the arbitration clause in the agreement that accompanied the merchandise shipment was a "material alteration" of a pre-existing oral agreement. Under UCC 2-207 (2), such a material alteration constitutes "proposals for addition to the contract" that become part of the contract only upon appellants' express acceptance. However, as the court correctly concluded, the clause was not a "material alteration" of an oral agreement, but, rather, simply one provision of the sole contract that existed between the parties. That contract, the court explained, was formed and acceptance was manifested not when the order was placed but only with the retention of the merchandise beyond the 30 days specified in the Agreement enclosed in the shipment of merchandise. Accordingly, the contract was outside the scope of UCC 2-207.

In reaching its conclusion, the IAS Court took note of the litigation in Federal courts on this very issue, and, indeed, on this very arbitration clause. In **Hill v Gateway 2000** (105 F3d 1147, *cert denied;* 118 S.Ct. 47), plaintiffs in a class action contested the identical Gateway contract in dispute before us, including the

enforceability of the arbitration clause. As that court framed the issue, the "[t]erms inside Gateway's box stand or fall together. If they constitute the parties' contract because the Hills had an opportunity to return the computer after reading them, then all must be enforced." The court then concluded that the contract was not formed with the placement of a telephone order or with the delivery of the goods. Instead, an enforceable contract was formed only with the consumer's decision to retain the merchandise beyond the 30-day period specified in the agreement. Thus, the agreement as a whole, including the arbitration clause, was enforceable.

* * *

Finally, we turn to appellants' argument that the IAS Court should have declared the contract unenforceable, pursuant to UCC 2-302, on the ground that the arbitration clause is unconscionable due to the unduly burdensome procedure and cost for the individual consumer. The IAS Court found that while a class action lawsuit, such as the one herein, may be a less costly alternative to the arbitration (which is generally less costly than litigation), that does not alter the binding effect of the valid arbitration clause contained in the agreement . . .

As a general matter, under New York law, unconscionability requires a showing that a contract is "both procedurally and substantively unconscionable when made" (*Gillman v Chase Manhattan Bank,* 73 NY2d 1, 10). That is, there must be "some showing of 'an absence of meaningful choice on the part of one of the parties together with contract terms which are unreasonably favorable to the other party' (*Matter of State of New York v Avco Fin. Servs.,* 50 NY2d 383, 389). The *Avco* Court took pains to note, however, that the purpose of this doctrine is not to re-

dress the inequality between the parties but simply to ensure that the more powerful party cannot "'surprise'" the other party with some overly oppressive term.

As to the procedural element, a court will look to the contract formation process to determine if in fact one party lacked any meaningful choice in entering into the contract, taking into consideration such factors as the setting of the transaction, the experience and education of the party claiming unconscionability, whether the contract contained "fine print," whether the seller used "high-pressured tactics" and any disparity in the parties' bargaining power . . . None of these factors supports appellants' claim here. Any purchaser has 30 days within which to thoroughly examine the contents of their shipment, including the terms of the Agreement, and seek clarification of any term therein (e.g., *Matter of Ball [SFX Broadcasting], supra,* at 161). The Agreement itself, which is entitled in large print "Standard Terms and Conditions Agreement," consists of only four pages and 16 paragraphs, all of which appear in the same size print. Moreover, despite appellants' claims to the contrary, the arbitration clause is in no way "hidden" or "tucked away" within a complex document of inordinate length, nor is the option of returning the merchandise, to avoid the contract, somehow a "precarious" one. We also reject appellants' insinuation that, by using the word "standard," Gateway deliberately meant to convey to the consumer that the terms were standard within the industry, when the document clearly purports to be no more than *Gateway's* "standard terms and conditions."

With respect to the substantive element, which entails an examination of the substance of the Agreement in order to determine whether the terms unreasonably favor one party . . . we do not find that the possible inconvenience of the chosen site (Chicago) alone rises to the level of unconscionability. We do find, however, that the excessive cost factor that is necessarily entailed in arbitrating before the ICC is unreasonable and surely serves to deter the individual consumer from invoking the process (see *Matter of Teleserve Sys. [MCI Telecommunications Corp.]*, 230 AD2d 585, 594, *lv denied* App Div, 1st Dept, Sept. 30, 1997, 1997 NY App Div LEXIS 10626). Barred from resorting to the courts by the arbitration clause in the first instance, the designation of a financially prohibitive forum effectively bars consumers from this forum as well; consumers are thus left with no forum at all in which to resolve a dispute. In this regard, we note that this particular claim is not mentioned in the *Hill* decision, which upheld the clause as part of an enforceable contract.

While it is true that, under New York law, unconscionability is generally predicated on the presence of both the procedural and substantive elements, the substantive element alone may be sufficient to render the terms of the provision at issue unenforceable (see *Gillman* v *Chase Manhattan Bank, supra,* at 12; *Matter of State of New York* v *Avco Fin. Servs., supra,* at 389; *State of New*

York v *Wolowitz,* 96 AD2d 47, 68). Excessive fees, such as those incurred under the ICC procedure, have been grounds for finding an arbitration provision unenforceable or commercially acceptable (see, e.g., *Matter of Teleserve Sys. [MCI Telecommunications Corp.], supra,* at 593–594).

Thus, we modify the order on appeal to the extent of finding that portion of the arbitration provision requiring arbitration before the ICC to be unconscionable and remand to Supreme Court so that the parties have the opportunity to seek appropriate substitution of an arbitrator pursuant to the Federal Arbitration Act (> 9 U.S.C. S 1 et seq.), which provides for such court designation of an arbitrator upon application of either party, where, for whatever reason, one is not otherwise designated (> 9 U.S.C. S 5).

* * *

The court held that the provision in the Gateway contract that required customers complaining about defective products to pay fees to International Chamber of Commerce to obtain a ruling from an arbitrator was unconscionable and thus unenforceable. The remedy portion of the Gateway contract was thus declared unenforceable and the customers were entitled to obtain the services

of an arbitrator pursuant to the Federal Arbitration Act without the need to pay the ICC fees. There was no mention in the court's decision as to whether aggrieved customers had to travel to Chicago to appear before an arbitrator.

QUESTIONS FOR ANALYSIS
1. What is the difference between procedural and substantive unconscionability? What kind of unconscionability was present in this case?
2. It would be useful for students to identify the terms in the agreement between Gateway and consumers that the court considered not unconscionable. In fact, the court "blessed" every term in the agreement, except for the requirement to appear before the International Chamber of Commerce. That included the requirement for purchasers to come to Chicago to litigate their rights before the arbitrator. Do you think it is fair for a large computer company to require customers dissatisfied with the performance of their products to make a trip to Chicago to appear before an arbitrator?

Business-to-Business Mass Market Licenses

Mass-market licenses are the subject of controversy, both procedurally and substantively. For consumers to have to travel several states to complain before an arbitrator about defective merchandise that costs between $1,000 and $4,000 seems to be pushing the envelope. Given the number of sales made by mass marketeers, efficient litigation planning seems reasonable, but consumers are also expecting to have a fair and reasonably accessible remedy if the merchandise or software is defective. In the next case involving two businesses, allegedly defective software was licensed to a contracting firm that seriously underbid a contract as a result of the software. The

license agreement excluded liability of the licensor for consequential damages against a charge, by the licensee (in this case the contracting firm), that the exclusion of consequential damages was unconscionable. The court in the following case rejected the argument that an exclusion of consequential damages between two businesses was substantively unconscionable. It is probably accurate to say that the courts will leave undisturbed license agreements between two businesses, but are more protective of consumers in mass-market license sales. The following case is quoted at length because it deals with many of the software issues that we have examined in both Chapters 3 and 4.

M.A. Mortenson Company, Inc., Petitioner, v. Timberline Software Corporation and Softworks Data Systems, Inc., Respondents
Supreme Court of Washington
998 P.2d 305 (2000)

FACTS AND CASE BACKGROUND

The plaintiff Mortenson is a nation-wide construction contractor with corporate offices located in Kirkland, Washington. Defendant Timberline is a software developer while Softworks is an authorized dealer for Timberline. Since 1990 Mortenson has used Timberline's Analysis software to assist in its preparation of bids. Mortenson had used Medallion, an earlier version of Bid Analysis but in early 1993 Mortenson installed a new computer operating system in its Washington office. Reich, president of Softworks, was contacted after Mortenson discovered that Medallion did not work after the new operating system was installed. Reich informed Mortenson that a newer version of Bid Analysis, Precision, was compatible with its new operating system. Mortenson ordered several copies of the new software through a purchase order which indicated that Softworks would also provide assistance in installing the software. Reich signed the purchase order, ordered the Precision software from Timberline, and received the software from Timberline. The software contained a shrinkwrap license that called for users to read the terms of the license and indicated that if they did not agree with the terms of the license, they could get a complete refund. Under a separate heading the license agreement contained a Limitation of Remedies and Liability clause which specifically excluded liability for consequential damages.

In the presence of Mortenson employees, Reich installed the Precision software and claimed that it worked. Mortenson then used the software to prepare a bid on a major construction contract called the Harborview Medical Center. The software allegedly malfunctioned a few times and gave error messages including: "Abort: Cannot find alternate." Mortenson received this message 19 times before submitting a bid generated by the software. Mortenson was awarded the Harborview Medical Center contract and then discovered that the software (Precision) had underbid by approximately $2 million. In response to the suit filed by Mortenson against Timberline, Timberline admitted that there was a bug in their software that could have caused the underbid. Other customers of Timberline had reported similar difficulties.

Timberline moved for a summary judgment claiming that its limitation of liability barred Mortenson's claim for consequential damages due to an underbid on the Harborview Medical Center. Mortenson claims that the limitation of liability clause in the license agreement was unconscionable.

OPINION BY: SUPREME COURT OF WASHINGTON, EN BANC

TERMS OF THE CONTRACT

Mortenson next argues even if the purchase order was not an integrated contract, Timberline's delivery of the license terms merely constituted a request to add additional or different terms, which were never agreed upon by the parties. Mortenson claims the additional terms did not become part of the contract because they were material alterations. Timberline responds that the terms of the license were not a request to add additional terms, but part of the contract between the parties. Timberline further argues that so-called "shrinkwrap" software licenses have been found enforceable by other courts, and that both trade usage and course of dealing support enforcement in the present case.

"(1) A definite and reasonable expression of acceptance or a written confirmation which is sent within a reasonable time operates as an acceptance even though it states terms additional to or different from those offered or agreed upon, unless acceptance is expressly made conditional on assent to the additional or different terms.

"(2) The additional terms are to be construed as proposals for addition to the contract. Between merchants such terms become part of the contract unless:

"(a) the offer expressly limits acceptance to the terms of the offer;

"(b) they materially alter it; or

"(c) notification of objection to them has already been given or is given within a reasonable time after notice of them is received.

"(3) Conduct by both parties which recognizes the existence of a contract is sufficient to establish a contract for sale although the writings of the parties do not otherwise establish a contract. In such case the terms of the particular contract consist of those terms on which the writings of the parties agree, together with any supplementary terms incorporated under any other provisions of this Title."

There, Step-Saver, a value added retailer, [FN8] placed telephone orders for software and confirmed with purchase orders. The manufacturer then forwarded an invoice back to Step-Saver. The software later arrived with a license agreement printed on the packaging. Finding the license "should have been treated as a written confirmation containing additional terms," the Third Circuit applied U.C.C. section 2-207 and held the warranty disclaimer and limitation of remedies terms were not part of the parties' agreement because they were material alterations. Mortenson claims Step-Saver is controlling, as "virtually every element of the transaction in the present case is mirrored in Step-Saver." We disagree.

A "value added retailer" evaluates the needs of a particular group of potential computer users, compares those needs with the available technology, and develops a package of hardware and software to satisfy those needs.

First, Step-Saver did not involve the enforceability of a standard license agreement against an end user of the software, but instead involved its applicability to a value added retailer who simply included the software in an integrated system sold to the end user. In fact, in Step-Saver the party contesting applicability of the licensing agreement had been assured the license did not apply to it at all. Such is not the case here, as Mortenson was the end user of the Bid Analysis software and was never told the license agreement did not apply.

Further, in Step-Saver the seller of the program twice asked the buyer to sign an agreement comparable to their disputed license agreement. Both times the buyer refused, but the seller continued to make the software available. In contrast, Mortenson and Timberline had utilized a license agreement throughout Mortenson's use of the Medallion and Precision Bid Analysis software. Given these distinctions, we find Step-Saver to be inapplicable to the present case. We conclude this is a case about contract formation, not contract alteration.

We also note the contract here, unlike the contract in Step-Saver, was not "between merchants" because Mortenson does not deal in software.

RCW 62A.2-204 states:

1. A contract for sale of goods may be made in any manner sufficient to show agreement, including conduct by both parties which recognizes the existence of such a contract.
2. An agreement sufficient to constitute a contract for sale may be found even though the moment of its making is undetermined.
3. Even though one or more terms are left open a contract for sale does not fail for indefiniteness if the parties have intended to make a contract and there is a reasonably certain basis for giving an appropriate remedy.

(Emphasis added.)

Although no Washington case specifically addresses the type of contract formation at issue in this case, a series of recent cases from other jurisdictions have analyzed shrinkwrap licenses under analogous statutes.

In *ProCD*, which involved a retail purchase of software, the Seventh Circuit held software shrinkwrap license agreements are a valid form of contracting under Wisconsin's version of U.C.C. section 2-204, and such agreements are enforceable unless objectionable under general contract law such as the law of unconscionability. The court stated, "[n]otice on the outside, terms on the inside, and a right to return the software for a refund if the terms are unacceptable (a right that the license expressly extends), may be a means of doing business valuable to buyers and sellers alike."

In *Hill*, the customer ordered a computer over the telephone and received the computer in the mail, accompanied by a list of terms to govern if the customer did not return the product within 30 days. Relying in part on *ProCD*, the court held the terms of the "accept-or-return" agreement were effective, stating, "[c]ompetent adults are bound by such documents, read or unread." *Hill,* 105 F.3d at 1149 (emphasis added). Elaborating on its holding in *ProCD,* the court continued:

The question in *ProCD* was not whether terms were added to a contract after its formation, but how and when the contract was formed—in particular, whether a vendor may propose that a contract of sale be formed, not in the store (or over the phone) with the payment of money or a general "send me the product," but after the customer has had a chance to inspect both the item and the terms. *ProCD* answers "yes," for merchants and consumers alike.

(emphasis added)

Interpreting the same licensing agreement at issue in *Hill,* the New York Supreme Court, Appellate Division concluded shrinkwrap license terms delivered following a mail order purchase were not proposed additions to the contract, but part of the original agreement between the parties. The court held U.C.C. section 2-207 did not apply because the contract was not formed until after the period to return the merchandise.

We find the approach of the *ProCD, Hill,* and *Brower* courts persuasive and adopt it to guide our analysis under RCW 62A.2-204. We conclude because RCW 62A.2-204 allows a contract to be formed "in any manner sufficient to show agreement . . . even though the moment of its making is undetermined," it allows the formation of "layered contracts" similar to those envisioned by *ProCD, Hill,* and *Brower.* We, therefore, hold under RCW 62A.2-204 the terms of the license were part of the contract between Mortenson and Timberline, and Mortenson's use of the software constituted its assent to the agreement, including the license terms.

The terms of Timberline's license were either set forth explicitly or referenced in numerous locations. The terms were included within the shrinkwrap packaging of each copy of Precision Bid Analysis; they were present in the manuals accompanying the software; they were included with the protection devices for the software, without which the software could not be used. The fact the software was licensed was also noted on the introductory screen each time the software was used. Even accepting Mortenson's contention it never saw the terms of the license, as we must do on summary judgment, it was not necessary for Mortenson to actually read the agreement in order to be bound by it.

Furthermore, the U.C.C. defines an "agreement" as "the bargain of the parties in fact as found in their language or by implication from other circumstances including course of dealing or usage of trade or course of performance. . . ." RCW 62A.1-201(3) (emphasis added). Mortenson and Timberline had a course of dealing; Mortenson had purchased licensed software from Timberline for years prior to its upgrade to Precision Bid Analysis. All Timberline

software, including the prior version of Bid Analysis used by Mortenson since at least 1990, is distributed under license. Moreover, extensive testimony and exhibits before the trial court demonstrate an unquestioned use of such license agreements throughout the software industry. Although Mortenson questioned the relevance of this evidence, there is no evidence in the record to contradict it. While trade usage is a question of fact, undisputed evidence of trade usage may be considered on summary judgment.

As the license was part of the contract between Mortenson and Timberline, its terms are enforceable unless "objectionable on grounds applicable to contracts in general. . . ."

ENFORCEABILITY OF LIMITATION OF REMEDIES CLAUSE

Mortenson contends even if the limitation of remedies clause is part of its contract with Timberline, the clause is unconscionable and, therefore, unenforceable.

Limitations on consequential damages are generally valid under the U.C.C. unless they are unconscionable. Whether a limitation on consequential damages is unconscionable is a question of law. "Exclusionary clauses in purely commercial transactions . . . are prima facie conscionable and the burden of establishing unconscionability is on the party attacking it." American Nursery Prods. If there is no threshold showing of unconscionability, the issue may be determined on summary judgment.

Washington recognizes two types of unconscionability—substantive and procedural—which we will now address in turn.

1. Substantive Unconscionability

Mortenson asserts Timberline's failure to inform it of the "defect" in the software prior to its purchase renders the licensing agreement substantively unconscionable.

" 'Substantive unconscionability involves those cases where a clause or term in the contract is alleged to be one-sided or overly harsh. . . .' " " 'Shocking to the conscience', 'monstrously harsh', and 'exceedingly calloused' are terms sometimes used to define substantive unconscionability."

As an initial matter, it is questionable whether clauses excluding consequential damages in a commercial contract can ever be substantively unconscionable. Even if the doctrine is applicable, however, the clause here is conscionable because substantive unconscionability does not address latent defects discovered after the contracting process.

In Tacoma Boatbuilding, the Western District of Washington considered whether a contractual clause limiting consequential damages was substantively unconscionable under Washington law, where mechanical problems developed in several boat engines after the contracting process. Like Mortenson, the purchaser in Tacoma Boatbuilding argued because the product did not work properly, the limitation clause was unconscionable. The court rejected this theory:

Comment 3 to [U.C.C.] § 2-719 generally approves consequential damage exclusions as "merely an allocation of unknown or undeterminable risks." Thus, the presence of latent defects in the goods cannot render these clauses unconscionable. The need for certainty in risk-allocation is especially compelling where, as here, the goods are experimental and their performance by nature less predictable.

Tacoma Boatbuilding, 28 U.C.C. Rep. Serv. at 35 (citation omitted)
We find the result in Tacoma Boatbuilding an accurate analysis of Washington's law of substantive unconscionability and adopt it here. In a purely commercial transaction, especially involving an innovative

product such as software, the fact an unfortunate result occurs after the contracting process does not render an otherwise standard limitation of remedies clause substantively unconscionable.

An example of the proper focus of the substantive unconscionability doctrine is found in *Brower* v. *Gateway 2000, Inc.* There, a shrinkwrap software license similar to the license in the present case included a mandatory arbitration clause, which required the use of a French arbitration company, payment of an advance fee of $4,000 (half which was nonrefundable),

significant travel fees borne by the consumer, and payment of the loser's attorney fees. The *Brower* court found this clause substantively unconscionable.

In contrast, Timberline's consequential damages clause, when examined at the time the contract was formed, does not shock the conscience in the manner of the *Brower* mandatory arbitration clause; it is not substantively unconscionable.

CONCLUSION

Mortenson has failed to set forth any material issues of fact on the issue of

contract formation, and has also failed to make a threshold showing of unconscionability sufficient to avoid summary judgment.

We affirm the Court of Appeals, upholding the trial court's order of summary judgment of dismissal and denial of the motions to vacate and amend.

GUY, C.J., SMITH, MADSEN, TALMADGE, IRELAND, JJ., and BROWN, J.P.T., concur.

SANDERS, J. (dissenting).

SUMMARY

- It is difficult to overstate the importance of software decisions.
- Firms can *make* or *buy* software. Each decision has its own critical legal implications.
- If a firm decides to make its own software using employees, the firm owns the software. Using employees to create software has the fewest legal issues, but may be economically inefficient.
- Software is owned by the owner of the copyright for the software. The copyright owner can sell, reproduce, distribute, or prepare derivative works with respect to copyrighted software.
- Copyrights do not require registration with the Copyright Office in Washington D.C., but registration gives the copyright owner significant legal rights in the event of litigation.
- Programmers hired to compose software for a firm can be *employees* or *independent contractors*. If the firm does not withhold payroll taxes and exerts little control over development of the software, those hired are most likely independent contractors.
- Independent contractors, hired to compose software, are the copyright owners of that software. The firm hiring independent contractors to compose software must have an *assignment clause* in the contract to obtain ownership of the copyright.

- There are significant negative legal consequences that occur if the hiring firm cannot get the copyright to software it paid for.
- In many instances, a firm hiring software developers cannot get copyright ownership, so the firm should strive to negotiate a license to use the software that meets the needs of the hiring firm.
- Part of the license that the hiring firm negotiates with the software developer should serve to prevent the software developer from selling similar or identical software to rivals of the hiring firm.
- *Toolbox codes* are software codes that are composed by the software developer to create standard command structures and user interfaces such as those that provide for shopping carts in webpage software.
- A well-designed license allows the client (or hiring) firm to make unfettered use of the software it contracted for. In addition, the hiring firm, as licensee, should insist that the software development firm be bound by *nondisclosure agreements* in order to protect its trade secrets.
- The hiring firm should insist on an *indemnification clause* in the contract with the software developer. Such an indemnification clause should guarantee that the software sold by the software vendor firm will not infringe copyrights, patents, and trademarks owned by other firms. If the hiring firm is

sued by a third party for infringement, the software developer is bound by the indemnification clause to step in and defend the hiring firm and pay damages if the suit is lost.

- It is common for software developers to make use of clauses in their contracts with client firms that limit their liability in a number of ways. Such clauses are called *limitations of liability.*

- Control of source code provides a firm with tremendous leverage. If the client firm does not have their software's source code, it can be left with unusable software if something happens to the software developer. If the client firm does have the source code, its incentive to pay the software developer is attenuated. Licensees may use this leverage to extract extra work from the software developer.

- *Software escrow firms* maintain control of software code until a job is completed. With a software escrow arrangement, the client firm will not get the code until the software developer has been paid. The software developer does not get paid until the escrow company is satisfied that the software has been properly installed and is functioning according to specifications.

- Software developers contract for payment based on *fixed price* contracts or *time and materials* contracts. With a fixed price contract, the risk of underbidding is borne by the software developer. In a time and materials contract, the risk of underestimating the amount of time necessary to create and install software is borne by the hiring firm.

- In time and materials contracts, client firms should resist creeping specification. All additions to the contract should be accompanied by *change orders* that both parties agree to.

- Disputes often arise between software developers and client firms. Given the slowness of court litigation and its public nature, firms should make use of *arbitration* and *choice of law* clauses. Arbitration clauses require disputes to be sent to an arbitrator. Decisions of arbitrators are not appealable unless very unusual events occur such as fraud. Choice of law clauses allow the parties to have some certainty as to which state's laws will apply.

- Business to business licenses for existing software typically contain a number of clauses that enable both parties to achieve their objectives. The licensor (software vendor) will typically insist that the license is nonexclusive and nontransferable, so that the licensee does not compete with the software vendor. The licensee can rely on clauses that make its license irrevocable as long as it does not violate the terms of the license agreement.

- Licensees can generally select among various fee structures and use limitations. Among the typical restrictions are limitations on the number of permitted users and precise definitions of who is a permitted user. If licensors are paid by number of minutes or number of times that their software is used, they will not be concerned about limiting numbers of users.

- Large-scale installations of software often contain a testing period and a negotiable acceptance date. Licensees desire extensive testing before acceptance while licensors desire just the opposite.

- Warranties are legal promises that describe what the software vendor is guaranteeing about its product(s). Sales brochures may become part of the contract, resulting in the vendor being bound by promises it makes in its advertising materials.

- Virtually all software vendors seek to limit liability for warranties that they make. Common limitations include the disclaimer of all implied warranties and limitations on liability for consequential damages, including lost profits. It is also common for software vendors to limit total liability to the amount paid under the contract by the licensee.

- As more products make use of software, software vendors could become liable for malfunctioning tangible physical products governed by the UCC. Section 2-719 prohibits limitations of liability for breaches of warranties in the case of personal injury caused by consumer goods.

- Software vendors are increasingly involved in bundling their own software with software owned by other (third-party) vendors. It is common for software vendors to seek to limit their liability for third-party software.

- Given the potential for liability with bundled, third-party software, software vendors may insert clauses that limit liability by stating that the vendor is not claiming the software is error-free, the software will not guarantee results, and all warranties will be declared null and void if the software is tampered with or modified.

- Software escrow arrangements can protect software licensees. Certain events, such as bankruptcy of the software vendor, can trigger release of the software code to licensees so that they are not stuck with software that cannot be upgraded or modified.

- Large-scale software installations also involve human resource management issues. Licensees typically have the power to exclude troublesome employees of the software vendor, subject to general nondiscrimination limitations. In parallel fashion, software vendors make use of antiraiding clauses that prevent licensees from hiring employees away from the vendors for significant periods of time after installation of the software.

- *Mass distribution software* generally comes with licenses that are not negotiable because of the large number of licensees.
- The enforceability of mass distribution software licenses depends on a number of procedural safeguards that are discussed in a previous chapter.
- Courts have refused to enforce some parts of mass distribution software licenses based on unconscionability. Unusual clauses that place inordinate burdens on licensees in the event of malfunctioning products are declared unconscionable. Disclaimers of implied warranties must be conspicuous, in boldface print, near the signature line.

TORTS: WRONGS AND THEIR REMEDIES

A *tort* is a *wrong*. It can be a spoken wrong or an act (action), or a nonaction (carelessness) that is wrong, with *injury* inflicted on a person or property. The typical remedy for torts is compensatory monetary *damages* (the defendant pays the plaintiff for the injuries inflicted due to the tort), though other court remedies in the form of punitive damages may also be possible.

A tort is a violation of duties required by society on all parties as a matter of law and is separate from the duties required by contract, which are voluntarily assumed by the contracting parties. So, a tort is a noncontractual interaction in which one party (who may become a defendant) wrongfully harms another party (who may be a plaintiff in a resulting lawsuit). As is quite likely apparent to you, there are many ways in which one party can do wrongful harm to another by act or the failure to act. Consequently, there are many forms of torts that are readily recognizable as grounds for legal action.

LIABILITY

A typical tort case involves two parts: the plaintiff first must show that he or she has been the victim of a civil wrong and secondly, the plaintiff has the requirement to show what his or her damages are. Torts are classified into categories that have relevance to the damages phase of tort litigation:

- If the tort is classified as *intentional,* then the plaintiff may be entitled to both compensatory and punitive damages, the latter of which could exceed compensatory damages by several orders of magnitude.
- A second category of torts is those based on *negligence* of the defendant. In a tort based on negligence, the defendant is being sued, not because she intended to harm the plaintiff, but because she was insufficiently careful in view of the surrounding circumstances.
- The last category of torts is *strict liability* torts, which involve liability without a showing of fault. If a defendant engages in high-risk activities such as using dynamite in construction, the defendant is liable for all resulting damages even if there is no showing that the defendant was negligent or careless in any way.

In tort litigation, if the plaintiff cannot establish that the defendant was liable, then there is no point in going on to the damages phase of the litigation. For students, understanding tort law is much easier if the tort is classified into one of the three categories above because the standards of proof and damages vary depending on the category of tort.

DAMAGES

Compensatory Damages

Damage awards in tort cases can take several forms. The general theory of damages in tort is that the defendant should compensate the plaintiff for the wrongful harm caused. Compensatory damages can be straightforward when property is damaged, but are subject to much more controversy when the damages involve personal injury or wrongful death. Juries arrive at highly variable rulings when the plaintiff's injuries involve loss of a limb or life. Also, juries may exhibit a pro-plaintiff bias, particularly when the defendant is obviously a wealthy corporation.

Punitive Damages

In the event of injury due to fraud or to actions that can be considered to be *intentional* wrongdoing, additional monetary awards, referred to as *punitive* or *exemplary damages,* may be imposed by a court in order to punish the defendant and provide incentives for avoidance of like future wrongs. Although some sort of intent is necessary for a jury to award punitive damages, that term can be extended to mean that the defendant exhibited a reckless disregard for public safety as when, for example, a corporation weighs profits against human life in designing products. Punitive damage awards that are four to five times the compensatory damage award are not uncommon.

Other Remedies

In addition to damage awards for civil torts, courts may issue *injunctions* to prohibit acts that are viewed as wrongful. Sometimes damages awarded in a tort case are *nominal*—they are modest in amount (e.g., $1) and are intended as symbolic recognition of the wrong done, though substantial harm may not have been done.

TORT OVERVIEW

In this chapter we develop basic principles of tort law, which are applied in the next chapter to cyberspace and other situations in which new technology has created pressure for or resulted in recent legal changes in tort law. In Chapter 7: *Product Liability*, tort law is applied to high-tech products that again are creating pressure for change, especially products that use software.

INTENTIONAL TORTS

An intentional tort occurs if there is intent by the defendant to engage in the act that results in injury, even if the injury suffered is not intended. There are many torts that involve physical trespass on another, such as assault, battery, and false imprisonment, but these torts are not generally relevant in business and are not the focus of the tort discussions in this textbook. Instead, we focus on intentional torts that are more common in business and which are facilitated by advances in technology. For the plaintiff to sustain an *intentional* tort claim, the plaintiff has to convince a jury or judge that:

- the defendant knew what he (she) was doing and
- the defendant knew or should have known the possible consequences of the action taken.

What is legal intent?   If the plaintiff claims that the defendant intentionally inflicted severe emotional distress (discussed below) on her by stalking her over the Internet, the defendant cannot defend his actions by saying that he did not know that his actions harmed the plaintiff emotionally. Under these facts (1) the defendant knew what he was doing (stalking) and (2) knew, **or should have known,** that his cyberstalking would cause severe emotional distress. On the other hand, most traffic accidents occur because one party to the accident was careless on the road. Even though some blame is rightfully attributed to the negligent driver, in most traffic accidents there is no evidence that the defendant intended to harm the plaintiff.

Intentional Infliction of Emotional Distress

It is a civil wrong to intentionally inflict emotional distress on another person. Intentional infliction of emotional distress is a tort that is increasingly being used in novel situations, such as a sexual harassment or cyberstalking.

The tort, intentional infliction of emotional distress, is conduct so extreme and outrageous that it results in severe emotional distress to another person. The conduct must be outrageous to a reasonable person, beyond the bounds of decency in a civilized society, and must result in far more than mere indignation and annoyance. Courts have held that embarrassment, humiliation, anger, fear, and worry can be indicators of severe mental distress. Certainly, if the victim sought medical help following the defendant's actions, it would be evidence of severe emotional distress.

A business making harassing phone calls to a delinquent customer on a regular basis after midnight may be found liable for the emotional distress caused, while the same phone calls during normal waking hours may be liability-free. Collection agencies are often defendants in intentional infliction of emotional distress cases and high-pressure sales operations also are targets for such cases. Another group of typical defendants for this tort are practical jokers, whose "jokes" cross the line and cause severe emotional distress because of outrageous behavior. In addition, victims of sexual harassment are frequently plaintiffs in intentional infliction of emotional distress cases, in part because the statute of limitations (time for filing the suit) under the Civil Rights Act is short (six months).

Leta Fay Ford v. Revlon, Inc.
Supreme Court of Arizona
(153 Ariz. 38, 734 P.2d 580) (1987)

FACTS AND CASE BACKGROUND

Leta Fay Ford had worked for Revlon, Inc., for 10 years, working her way up from a clerical position to a buyer position. In October 1979, Revlon hired Karl Braun as the new manager for the purchasing department, making him Ford's supervisor. On April 3 of 1980, Braun invited Ford to dinner "to discuss business." At dinner, business soon turned to Braun's personal interest in Ford. At the end of dinner, as Ford started to leave, she was ordered by Braun to sit down, that she was not going anywhere, and that he planned to spend the night with her. Ford rejected these advances and was told by Braun that "you will regret this." Ford testified that immediately afterward, her working relationship with Braun was strained and uncomfortable.

A month later, on May 3, Revlon held its annual service awards picnic. At the picnic, Braun followed Ford around most of the day and, at one point, pressed close to her and graphically described his intent to have sex with her. Later in the day, Braun grabbed Ford in a chokehold as she came out of the restroom, fondled her

with his other hand as he continued holding her, and repeated his intentions. A friend of Ford's jerked Braun's arm loose and Ford wrenched herself free and ran away from Braun. This day's event prompted Ford to initiate a series of meetings with numerous members of Revlon management to report her complaints and ask for relief. The recipients of her presentations, protests, and requests for help included the Phoenix Revlon controller, the personnel manager for the clerical and technical group in the Phoenix plant, the personnel manager for executives, the director of personnel at the Phoenix plant, a human resources manager "trouble shooter" in Revlon headquarters, the vice-president of industrial relations and operations, and others.

This series of interactions continued from May until December and into the next year. In various meetings, Ford was visibly shaken and very emotional. During this May to December sequence, Braun had continued his harassment of Ford, calling her into his office and telling her that he wanted to destroy her, that so long as she worked for him she was never

going to go anywhere, refusing to let her sit down while in his office, requiring her to stand in his office while he stared at her, without conversation, etc. During the time of the harassment, Ford developed high blood pressure, a nervous tic in her left eye, chest pains, rapid breathing, and other symptoms of emotional stress, and went to a physician about her condition. On February 23, 1981, Ford submitted a written request for a transfer out of the purchasing department. On February 24, Braun placed Ford on a 60-day probation because of her allegedly poor work performance.

On February 25, Ford had another meeting with Revlon management personnel regarding her harassment. At this meeting, she submitted a handwritten complaint that read, in part:

> "I want to officially register a charge of sexual harassment and discrimination against K. Braun. I am asking for protection from Karl Braun. I have a right to be protected. I am collapsing emotionally and physically and I can't go on."

After this meeting, Ford was told that Braun's actions would be investigated and that he would be closely watched. Not until 3 months later, on May 8, was a report on Ford's charges written—a report that corroborated Ford's charge of sexual assault and that recommended that Braun be censured. On May 28, nearly 14 months after Ford's initial complaint, Braun was issued a letter of censure from Revlon. In October of 1981, Ford attempted suicide. On October 5, Revlon terminated Braun. In April of 1982, Ford sued Braun and Revlon for assault and battery, and for intentional infliction of emotional distress. At trial, two written personnel policies were admitted as evidence. One policy dealing with employee complaints indicated that "Any employee who has a complaint about any aspect of . . . employment is entitled to have the complaint heard, investigated and, if possible, resolved." Legitimate complaints were to be dealt with as quickly and fully as possible according to this policy. A second written policy defined sexual harassment in accordance with the Equal Employment Opportunity Commission (EEOC) guidelines and provided that personnel executives who were made aware of allegations of sexual harassment are responsible for investigating promptly, fully, and with the highest degree of confidentiality, and for taking . . . actions to deal with alleged violations or for referring them to higher authority for disposition.

At trial, the jury found Braun liable for assault and battery, but not for intentional infliction of emotional distress. The jury found Revlon liable for intentional infliction of emotional distress but not liable for assault and battery. The jury assessed damages of $100 in compensatory damages and $1,000 in punitive damages against Braun.

The jury assessed damages of $10,000 in compensatory damages and $100,000 in punitive damages against Revlon.

Revlon appealed this decision and the Court of Appeals reversed the judgement of the trial court against Revlon. The Appeals Court indicated that since Braun (as agent) was found not guilty of intentional infliction of emotional distress, then Revlon (as principal) could not be found guilty. The Supreme Court granted review because its members disagreed with this limitation on the liability of Revlon.

OPINION OF THE COURT: IN BANC

The court of appeals held that Revlon could not be liable for intentional infliction of emotional distress if Braun was not liable. Per the appeals court, Revlon's liability is inextricably tied to the acts of Braun. Since Braun's acts did not constitute intentional or reckless infliction of emotional distress, then the inaction of Revlon on Ford's complaint certainly could not reach that level.

We disagree. Admittedly, when the master's liability is based solely on the negligence of his servant, a judgment in favor of the servant is a judgment in favor of the master. When the negligence of the master is independent of the negligence of the servant, the result may be different.

* * *

In a case factually similar to this one, the U.S. Court of Appeals for the Fourth Circuit recognized that a corporation could be liable for intentional infliction of emotional distress because its supervisor was aware of the sexual harassment of an employee by a manager and failed to stop it even though the underlying harassment might not rise to the level of either assault and battery or intentional infliction of emotional

distress. We believe Revlon's failure to investigate Ford's complaint was independent of Braun's abusive treatment of Ford.

* * *

The three required elements for the tort of intentional infliction of emotional distress are: first, the conduct of the defendant must be "extreme" and "outrageous"; second, the defendant must either intend to cause emotional distress or recklessly disregard the near certainty that such distress will result from his conduct; and third, severe emotional distress must indeed occur as a result of defendant's conduct. We believe that the conduct of Revlon met these requirements. First, Ford made numerous Revlon managers aware of Braun's activities at company functions. Ford did everything that could be done, both within the announced policies of Revlon and without, to bring this matter to Revlon's attention. Revlon ignored her and the situation she faced, dragging the matter out for months and leaving Ford without redress. Here is sufficient evidence that Revlon acted outrageously.

Second, even if Revlon did not intend to cause emotional distress, Revlon's reckless disregard of Braun's conduct made it nearly certain that such emotional distress would in fact occur. Revlon knew that Braun had subjected Ford to physical assaults, vulgar remarks, that Ford continued to feel threatened by Braun, and that Ford was emotionally distraught . . .

Third, it is obvious that emotional distress did occur. Ample evidence, both medical and otherwise, was presented describing Ford's emotional distress . . .

We also note that Revlon had set forth a specific policy and several guidelines for the handling of sexual harassment claims and other employee complaints, yet Revlon recklessly disregarded these policies and guidelines. Ford was entitled to rely on the policy statements made by Revlon . . .

* * *

We hold that Revlon's failure to take appropriate action in response to Ford's complaint of sexual harassment by Braun constituted the tort of intentional infliction of emotional distress. The decision of the court of appeals is vacated. The judgment of the trial court is reinstated.

QUESTIONS FOR REVIEW

1. Explain the Supreme Court's rationale in holding that Revlon (the principal) was liable for the tort of outrage when Braun (the agent) was not.

2. Suppose the jury had held Braun liable for intentional infliction of emotional distress. Do you think it would be possible in that case for the Supreme Court to conclude that Revlon was not also liable?

3. Explain and illustrate three elements that must be present for the tort of outrage to occur.

A New Form of Intentional Infliction of Emotional Distress: Cyberstalking

The tort of intentional infliction of emotional distress requires a showing by the plaintiff that the defendant has engaged in extreme and outrageous behavior that causes severe emotional distress. See if you think that the following fits that definition:

CYBERSTALKING BY J.A. HITCHCOCK
VOLUME 17, ISSUE 4 • JULY/AUGUST 2000

Four years ago, the word cyberstalking hadn't been coined yet. No one knew what to call it; some called it online harassment, online abuse, or cyber-harassment. And we're not talking two people arguing with each other or calling each other bad names. There were incidents where it had gone beyond an annoyance and had become frightening. As more and more incidents became known and victims reached out to law enforcement for help, all they received were either blank stares or were told to turn off their computer. States didn't have laws in place to protect victims, and their harassers kept up the harassment, which escalated sometimes to real-life stalking situations.

What is cyberstalking? It's when an online incident spirals so out of control it gets to a point where a victim fears for his or her life.

CASE EXAMPLE 1

In 1999, "Nanci" went into a Worcester, Massachusetts, romance chat room. Another chatter commented that he did not like her username. She defended herself and soon the two began arguing with each other in the chat room. But the argument didn't end. Each time Nanci tried to log onto the chat room, her harasser was there, waiting for her, and became more aggressive. At one point, he told her he'd hired someone else in the chat room to beat her up; another time he posted information he'd found out about her online—who her father was and where she lived—then said he wouldn't be happy until she was "6 feet under the ground."

Justifiably horrified, Nanci went to her local police, who basically laughed at her and told her there was nothing to be done. Yes, even with the implied death threat. The harasser became more aggressive and began e-mailing or Instant Messaging Nanci, telling her what kind of car she was driving, where she'd been earlier that day, and the name of her daughter. Nanci went to the State Police, the county District Attorney, then the State Attorney General. Each one pointed fingers at the other, claiming they couldn't help her, but that the other department should.

Nanci finally hired a lawyer, filed a civil suit, then contacted local media. When she appeared in court with TV journalists following her, the DA backed down and began helping her. Charges were finally filed against her cyberstalker, and a trial date has been set for later this year. "Cyberstalking often receives a low priority in computer crime cases," says Greg Larson, vice president of Internet Crimes, Inc. "Police departments usually have limited manpower for computer crimes, so in importance, these cases seem to be put on the back burner until a serious incident occurs."

Source: http://www.infotoday.com/lu/jul00/hitchcock.htm

Invasion of Privacy

As a matter of Constitutional Law, privacy from *governmental* intrusions is recognized under the Fourth Amendment, which provides protection against unreasonable searches and seizures. Although not explicitly found in the text of the Constitution, the *Roe* v. *Wade* decision, which prevents states from prohibiting abortion, is based on a Constitutional notion of privacy.[1] Tort law protects this right against a number of specific forms of invasion of privacy, *by private individuals*. It is important to recognize that governmental and private invasions of privacy are evaluated under different standards. Tort law protects against the following:

1. **Commercial use** of someone's name or likeness without permission,
2. **Intrusion into a person's solitude** by illegally searching their premises or belongings, by bugging or wire-tapping their residence, by the unauthorized intrusion into their financial records, etc.,
3. **Public revelation** of information that **places a person in a false light,** such as by attributing to a person ideas not held or actions not taken by that person,
4. **Public revelation of facts** about a person that **a reasonable person would find repugnant**. The revelation of abuse of alcohol or drugs, or the revelation of information regarding a private citizen's sex life or financial affairs could result in court action.

Each of the four items listed immediately above are considered *invasions of privacy,* though they refer to different types of actions by defendants.

Reasonable expectations of privacy   The courts use a notion of a *reasonable expectation of privacy* to determine if a possible tort occurs (or a violation of the Fourth Amendment). If it is reasonable for a person to expect privacy, as with what they do behind closed doors in a bathroom or a bedroom, then the courts will protect that interest. Public figures, such as a president, a senator, a police chief, or a movie star make their livings by attracting attention to themselves and, as a result, have very limited protection from invasions of privacy. For public figures, courts have

concluded that the public's right to information takes primacy over bruised egos of public figures. Facts that are part of the public record may also be repeated without fear of liability.

Commercial Use of Someone's Name or Likeness without Permission: Misappropriation

Commercial use of someone's name or likeness is traditionally lumped together with other invasions of privacy, but this invasion of privacy is really a misappropriation, a wrongful taking of a property right owned by another without compensation or permission. Some years back, a Port a John company sold its products with the slogan, "Heeere's Johnny", the classic introduction for the popular talk show host Johnny Carson. Carson successfully sued the company for using a phrase associated with Johnny Carson's show. Increasingly, courts have ruled that celebrities have a property right in their name or likeness, which may persist in some cases after their death. The Elvis Presley estate has been able to successfully sue "Elvis" impersonators and other uses of the "King's" name or likeness unless royalties are paid.

On-the-Job Privacy Issues

One of the battlegrounds where invasions of privacy have surfaced is the workplace. New advances in technology have given employers abilities to monitor employee performance and to snoop into other areas which many employees consider "private." Litigation has taken place over cameras in the workplace, which may include bathrooms and dressing rooms—areas where drug transactions sometimes take place. In addition, employers have required that employees take drug tests as well as intrusive psychological tests. Phone calls and e-mails are routinely monitored and in some cases polygraph tests have been administered.

Drug Testing
Private Employees   As a condition of employment, private employers in virtually all states can require employees to take drug tests that may involve urine, blood, or hair samples. The Fourth Amendment does not apply to private employers, leaving them relatively unfettered in their drug testing activities. Some employers administer a progression of drug tests that

---

[1]*Roe* v. *Wade,* U.S. Supreme Court, 410 U.S. 959 (1973).

are increasingly accurate (and expensive). If an employee fails the first test, he or she is generally required to retest using procedures that are more precise. In some states, there are restrictions on testing employees after they have been hired. These states generally require employers to have *probable cause* to retest an employee after they have already been hired. Probable cause is generally established when there is on-the-job evidence of erratic behavior, which indicates possible drug use, or if there are precipitous declines in productivity.

Public Employees When the employer is a governmental entity, courts have held that drug testing **is a search** for Fourth Amendment purposes. Generally, the Fourth Amendment requires a showing of probable cause. Hence, to require testing a governmental employer must have good reason to believe that an individual employee is impaired. Given the transparent disparity of treatment between employees who work for public versus private employers, the courts have decided that there are a number of exceptions that allow for drug testing of public employees, even without a showing of individualized probable cause. At this point, the courts are engaging in ambiguous balancing tests when evaluating testing of public employees for substance abuse. The more serious the potential threat is to public health and safety, the more nonindividualized drug tests of public employees are allowed. Those who carry guns on the job, as police do, can be tested without a showing of individualized probable cause. Public employees who work in public transportation have been tested for drugs in the aftermath of train wrecks, even though there is no individualized showing of probable cause to indicate that a particular employee is a substance abuser.

Polygraph Testing

Polygraph testing (lie detectors) has been used by employers to detect employee theft and for other purposes, such as determining whether the employee has criminal tendencies. Many labor groups have petitioned government, state and federal, to end the unrestricted use of polygraphs on the job. In general, employer requirements for employees to take polygraph tests have been outlawed under the Employee Polygraph Protection Act of 1988.

The Employee Polygraph Protection Act was a direct response to the frequency of inappropriate uses of polygraphs by employers. Prior to this Act, prospective employees were often quizzed about matters unrelated to job performance. As a result of the Act, polygraph testing has been largely eliminated. There are, however, exceptions to the Polygraph Protection Act. Illustratively, when an employee is accused of stealing, polygraph testing is permissible, but must be administered according to specific documented procedures. Employers can also use polygraph testing on employees who work in security jobs, but again with specific procedural requirements.

Psychological Testing and Counseling

Some states, like California, specifically protect the right of privacy in their constitution. In California there have been cases in which questions on job interview questionnaires have been ruled too intrusive. Most of these cases relate to situations in which prospective applicants must answer questions about matters totally unrelated to the job, such as ones asking about sexual preferences. Employers should carefully consider whether getting the answers to intrusive questions, particularly those that do not clearly relate to job performance, are really worth the effort.

Many employers offer employees job counseling to deal with personal problems. In some cases, substance abuse, marital problems, and other sensitive issues are discussed in counseling sessions. If the counselor is an employee of the firm, employees who go to such counselors *should not assume* that counseling sessions are totally confidential unless the company makes a promise to that effect. Many employment-related decisions are made as a result of consultations with job counselors who are employees as well. Indeed, employees have been fired as a result of disclosures made to counselors provided by employers.

On-the-Job Monitoring by Employers

Employers have increasing capabilities of monitoring employee activity on the job and are using these capabilities. There have been abuses when employers have used their monitoring abilities to view members of the opposite sex in situations where the employees (invariably female) had a reasonable expectation of privacy. New technology, especially software, gives employers the ability to monitor on-the-job productivity for word processors and others whose jobs make heavy use of computer programs. Cameras are also common at many work sites, allowing the monitoring of physical activities. Software has been developed that tracks where employees travel on the Internet and is able to report to employers whether the employee has been visiting "adult" sites on the job. Numerous workers have lost their jobs or have been reprimanded as a result of on-the-job Internet cruising.

Inform Employees of What Will Be Monitored

In general, there are no federal or state laws that prohibit employer monitoring of employees. In some cases, employer monitoring of employees can be an *unreasonable intrusion* into the private affairs of the employee (and thus an actionable tort for invasion of privacy), particularly if the monitoring is not related to job performance. Employers who monitor employees by camera, through software, or by other means should inform employees of that fact for at least two good reasons:

- First, informing employees that they are subject to monitoring may curb the objectionable behavior that is the target of monitoring.
- Second, employees who have been informed of the monitoring will have a reduced expectation of privacy, thus undercutting any employee tort claim based on an unreasonable intrusion into the private affairs of another.

Clearly there are occasions when employer monitoring of employees is an invasion of privacy that becomes legally actionable. There have been cases in which employers have "rewarded" male employees by giving them the opportunity to view, through hidden cameras, dressing rooms of female employees. The women in these cases clearly had a reasonable expectation of privacy and the monitoring was not for the purpose of preventing on-the-job drug abuse or any other job-related reason.

Phone Calls and E-mail

Congress passed the Omnibus Crime Control and Safe Streets Act in 1968. This act regulated on-the-job wiretapping by employers for a number of years. Under this act, employers were prohibited from tapping telephone conversations of employees on the job unless:

- The telephone monitoring was during the regular course of business, or

- The employee had consented to the employer's telephone monitoring.

These exceptional permissions were so broad that employers had no trouble monitoring phone conversations of employees as a matter of course. Even though courts have often been hostile to employer monitoring of employee conversations, prudent managers have been able to insulate themselves from liability by simply informing employees that a condition of employment is acceptance of employer monitoring of phone conversations. Moreover, at least one court has held that, even if employers tell employees that their e-mails will remain confidential, employees do not have a reasonable expectation of privacy with respect to e-mails that are sent on the job.[2]

Electronic Communication and Privacy Act

In 1986 Congress passed the Electronic Communication and Privacy Act (ECPA) that amended the 1968 Omnibus Crime Act. The ECPA allows employers the same access to e-mails that it allows them to telephone conversations on the job, along with the same exceptions. Hence, informing employees of possible e-mail monitoring insulates employers from liability for engaging in that monitoring. Of course, if employers expect computers assigned to their workers to be used only for company related purposes, and not for private (e-mail) conversations, employees should be informed of that expectation. Proper warnings reduce claims that employees have an expectation of privacy with respect to e-mails. The protections of ECPA were extended not just to e-mail, but also to cellular and wireless phones, so that using scanners to intercept conversations using this technology was made a criminal act (in the same way that the Omnibus Crime Act made wiretapping telephone conversations criminal years ago). The bottom line is that employers can monitor phone and e-mail conversations on the job by informing employees that their phone or e-mail conversations are subject to monitoring.

Defamation

A First Amendment right to freedom of speech does not extend to making *untrue* statements to *third parties*, spoken or written, that are *harmful* to an individual's *reputation*. The law provides a remedy against

---

[2]*Bill McLaren v. Microsoft Corp.,* 1999 WL 339015 (Tex.App.-Dallas).

Bill McLaren, Jr. v. *Microsoft Corporation*
Court of Appeals of Texas, Dallas
(1999) WL 339015

FACTS AND CASE BACKGROUND

McLaren was an employee of Microsoft Corporation. In December 1996, Microsoft suspended McLaren's employment pending an investigation into accusations of sexual harrassment and "inventory questions." McLaren requested access to his electronic mail to disprove the allegations against him. According to McLaren, he was told he could access his e-mail only by requesting it through company officials and telling them the location of a particular message. By memorandum, McLaren requested that no one tamper with his Microsoft office workstation or his e-mail. McLaren's employment was terminated on December 11, 1996.

Following the termination of his employment, McLaren filed suit against the company alleging as his sole cause of action a claim for invasion of privacy. In support of his claim, McLaren alleged that . . . Microsoft had invaded his privacy by "breaking into" some or all of the personal folders maintained on his office computer and releasing the contents of the folders to third parties. According to McLaren, the personal folders were part of a computer application created by Microsoft in which e-mail messages could be stored. Access to the e-mail system was obtained through a network password. Access to personal folders could be additionally restricted by a "personal store" password created by the individual user. McLaren created and used a personal store password to restrict access to his personal folders.

McLaren concedes in his petition that it was possible for Microsoft to "decrypt" his personal store password. McLaren alleges, however, that "[b]y allowing [him] to have a personal store password for his personal folders, [McLaren] manifested and [Microsoft] recognized an expectation that the personal folders would be free from intrusion and interference." McLaren characterizes Microsoft's decrypting or otherwise "breaking in" to his personal folders as an intentional, unjustified, and unlawful invasion of privacy.

OPINION: ROACH, JUSTICE

Texas recognizes four distinct torts, any of which constitutes an invasion of privacy:

1. Intrusion upon the plaintiff's seclusion or solitude or into his private affairs;
2. Public disclosure of embarrassing private facts about the plaintiff;
3. Publicity which places the plaintiff in a false light in the public eye;
4. Appropriation, for the defendant's advantage, of the plaintiff's name or likeness.

[Citations deleted throughout] At issue in this case is whether McLaren's petition states a cause of action under the first recognized tort. There are two elements to this cause of action: (1) an intentional intrusion, physically or otherwise, upon another's solitude, seclusion, or private affairs or concerns, which (2) would be highly offensive to a reasonable person. When assessing the offensive nature of the invasion, courts further require the intrusion to be unreasonable, unjustified, or unwarranted. This type of invasion of privacy is generally associated with either a physical invasion of a person's property or eavesdropping on another's conversation with the aid of wiretaps, microphones, or spying.

In his petition and on appeal, McLaren contends the fact that the e-mail messages were stored under a private password with Microsoft's consent gave rise to "a legitimate expectation of privacy in the contents of the files."

In *Trotti*, the court considered the privacy interest of an employee in a locker provided by the employer to store personal effects during work hours. The court began its analysis by recognizing that the locker was the employer's property and, when unlocked, was subject to legitimate, reasonable searches by the employer. The court further reasoned:

"This would also be true where the employee used a lock provided by [the employer], because in retaining the lock's combination or master key, it could be inferred that [the employer] manifested an interest both in maintaining control over the locker and in conducting legitimate, reasonable searches."

But, the court concluded, when, as in *Trotti*, an employee buys and uses his own lock on the locker, with the employer's knowledge, the fact finder is justified in concluding that the "employee manifested, and the employer recognized, an expectation that the locker and its contents would be free from intrusion and interference."

McLaren urges that the locker in *Trotti* is akin to the e-mail messages in this case, "only the technology is different." We disagree. First, the locker in *Trotti* was provided to the employee for the specific purpose of storing personal belongings, not work items. In contrast, McLaren's workstation was provided to him by Microsoft so that he could perform the functions of his job. In connection with that purpose and as alleged in McLaren's petition, part of his workstation included a company-owned computer that gave McLaren the ability to send and receive e-mail messages. Thus, contrary to his argument on appeal, the e-mail messages contained on the company computer were not McLaren's personal property, but were merely an inherent part of the office environment.

Further, the nature of a locker and an e-mail storage system are different. The locker in *Trotti* was a discrete, physical place where the employee, separate and apart from other employees, could store her tangible, personal belongings. The storage system for e-mail messages is not so discrete. As asserted by McLaren in his petition, e-mail was delivered to the server-based "inbox" and was stored there to read. [Footnotes deleted] McLaren could leave his e-mail on the server or he could move the message to a different location. According to McLaren, his practice was to store his e-mail messages in "personal folders." Even so,

any e-mail messages stored in McLaren's personal folders were first transmitted over the network and were at some point accessible by a third-party. Given these circumstances, we cannot conclude that McLaren, even by creating a personal password, manifested—and Microsoft recognized—a reasonable expectation of privacy in the contents of the e-mail messages such that Microsoft was precluded from reviewing the messages.

Even if we were to conclude that McLaren alleged facts in his petition which, if found to be true, would establish some reasonable expectation of privacy in the contents of his e-mail messages sent over the company e-mail system, our result would be the same. We would nevertheless conclude that, from the facts alleged in the petition, a reasonable person would not consider Microsoft's interception of these communications to be a highly offensive invasion. As set forth in McLaren's petition, at the time Microsoft accessed his e-mail messages, McLaren was on suspension pending an investigation into accusations of sexual harassment and "inventory questions" and had notified Microsoft that some of the e-mails were relevant to the investi-

gation. Accordingly, the company's interest in preventing inappropriate and unprofessional comments, or even illegal activity, over its e-mail system would outweigh McLaren's claimed privacy interest in those communications. We overrule the second point of error.

We affirm the trial court's judgment.

QUESTIONS FOR ANALYSIS

1. Of the four invasions of privacy, what kind of invasion was McLaren alleging took place in this case?

2. What is the significance of the claim made by McLaren that he had an expectation that his e-mail messages would remain private because he stored them in a personal locker?

3. Does this case stand for the proposition that employee purses can be searched? What are its implications for the monitoring of bathrooms and dressing rooms? Was it important that McLaren's e-mails were used on the job and were the subject of the charges against him by a female co-worker?

persons who make false and defamatory statements of fact about others. Violating this required standard of conduct orally is the tort of *slander* while breaching this duty in writing is **libel.** In a business setting, making false statements about a company's products, its business practices or other business matters are equally wrongful (this tort is sometimes called product disparagement).

Must be seen or heard by third parties   An essential element of a defamation claim is the *publication* of the false statement(s) to a *third party*. Accusing your partner of stealing company assets in a private conversation is not defamation, while telling your accountant that this has occurred is (if the charge is not factual). Making false statements to a third party, having such

statements overheard by a third party even if they are addressed to the alleged offender, having your secretary type notes or a letter containing your charges, or airing such claims in an Internet communication can make you a defendant in a defamation suit. Whatever the medium, anyone who repeats (replicates) a defamatory statement is also liable for defamation damages even if the source of the statement is cited.

Publisher or Distributor Liability?   Defamation creates liability not only for an author who writes a libelous article, but also for the publisher of that story. Thus, not only was the author of a story that falsely claimed Carol Burnett was drunk at an event liable for libel, but liability also extended to the *National Enquirer* that published the article. On the other hand,

---

"Privacy and the Prying Eyes of Cyberspace"

Case-by-case decision making makes it difficult to formulate e-business policies that limit exposure to privacy claims while simultaneously capitalizing on profit opportunities in the marketplace for consumer data. What is highly offensive in Topeka might not offend in Los Angeles. Establishing national and international policies on privacy is reduced to guesswork when local standards of reasonableness and offensiveness are involved. The Internet is a global—not a local—marketplace.

With the spotlight on heightened government scrutiny of consumer privacy on the Internet, scholars, privacy groups and consumer advocates have proposed several ideas to protect consumer privacy, including the following:

- All e-businesses of every kind should disclose their privacy policies, and if the policy changes after the consumer has reviewed and accepted it, the consumer should have an opportunity to reconsider his or her acceptance and opt out of the changes. As part of every privacy policy, consumers should be able to opt out of any sharing of their information.
- The standard for data collection in e-commerce should be "minimization," i.e., the information collected from consumers should be limited to that required for the specific transaction. Any request for additional information should be plainly marked "optional" so the consumer is aware he or she is not required to provide it.
- Consumer opt-out methods should be largely troublefree to use, meaning they should not require consumers to write letters, linger in voice-mail purgatory or have to click through to multiple pages to express their preferences. Likewise, opt-out selections should be valid until revoked or changed by the consumer, and not expire.
- The standard for information sharing (unless otherwise agreed by the consumers) should prevent the sharing of information for purposes unrelated to the original transaction in which the data was collected.
- E-businesses should obtain meaningful, informed consent from consumers for information sharing. Meaningful consent excludes "take-it-or-leave-it" policies, requirements for acceptance of the policy to gain access to the Web site and any consent not written in plain English.
- All consumers should be able to learn the identity of those with whom their information has been shared, and to learn exactly what has been shared. These two rights taken together are sometimes referred to as a "right of access." In the same vein, consumers should be provided a mechanism for correcting mistaken information in their data files or in any data transmitted to others.

Excerpt source: "Privacy and the prying eyes of cyberspace;" *Mortgage Banking*; Washington; Apr 2000; Andrea Lee Negroni.

---

newsstands and grocery stores that distributed the *National Enquirer* were not liable because the courts have ruled that they do not have responsibility to monitor and censor libelous material. Internet Service Providers (ISPs) such as Mindspring and AOL rebroadcast libelous remarks made by users, thus increasing the potential damage from those remarks. The question of ISP liability for defamatory remarks made by users is taken up in the next chapter.

Slander versus Libel

At common law certain kinds of spoken statements are considered slanderous per se (i.e., as a matter of law). These include statements that a person has a socially unacceptable communicable disease, that a person has committed improprieties while engaging in a profession or trade, that a person has committed a serious crime or been imprisoned for such a crime, or a statement that an unmarried woman is unchaste. For such statements, a finding that these statements were made and published to third parties is sufficient to result in a judgment for damages because these statements are **presumed** harmful to one's reputation.

In the absence of such per se slander violations, a victim of slander is not entitled to monetary damages unless there is proof of "special damages." The plaintiff must prove actual economic or monetary losses to be entitled to collect any damages. In contrast to slanderous statements, libelous (written) statements are viewed by the court system as having more enduring and broad circulation, and are assumed to more likely reflect deliberation on the part of the defendant. As such, a defendant who libels another is liable for damages without the plaintiff having to prove any specific injury.

Could This Be You?

Mary, in Hagerstown, Maryland, is having an online chat room conversation with an Internet acquaintance, Susan, in Los Angeles. In this typed conversation, Mary observes that her newly promoted boss "drinks to the point of intoxication, comes to work in that state, and is having an affair with a sales representative that works for her." Does this statement constitute defamation? Is it slander or libel? What if Mary had simply indicated that she found her new boss to be ". . . a thoroughly unpleasant and obnoxious person." Is that slander or libel? Is it actionable? What issues are introduced because these statements were made on the Internet as opposed to in person or in a letter?

Recall that spoken defamatory statements are slander, and that only selected slanderous statements (those that are slander *per se*) merit damages without proof of specific monetary or economic injury. Mary's statement describing her view of her boss's character traits is not likely even to be viewed by a court as slander (being merely the expression of an opinion, not a statement of alleged facts). Moreover, even if it were viewed as slanderous, since it is not one of the statement forms that is

slander *per se*, no damages could be expected unless Mary's boss could prove specific economic injury.

On the other hand, the factual allegations in the first statement above attributed to Mary threaten damage to the boss's reputation and even the possibility of damage to her career. This would be slander per se if the statement were viewed as spoken, with no need for the maligned boss to prove any specific economic injury to collect defamation damages.

In reality, courts appear to be treating Internet "conversations" as equivalent to written documents, as the chat room public exchange described above is potentially viewable by large numbers of Internet users, can be electronically stored, downloaded, printed, etc. Hence, any defamatory statement published online constitutes libel. So, a defamatory statement of fact online is compensable with monetary damages even if, as a spoken statement, it would not constitute slander per se. Even in written form, however, an opinion regarding the obnoxious nature of the boss (to Mary) would likely not be actionable.

Source: Example provided by the authors.

Defenses to Defamation

In the United States, *truth* is the fail-safe antidote to defamation claims. So, if a defendant in a defamation suit can prove that the allegedly defamatory statement of fact is actually true, no tort has been committed. Note that truth is an affirmative defense, which means that the defendant would have the burden of proof in establishing that the plaintiff was in fact guilty of the things attributed to him or her by the defendant.

Absolute Privilege Another defense to defamation claims is based on *privilege*. In certain settings, such as legislatures and courtrooms, there is **absolute** *privilege*—statements made by attorneys and judges during a trial are exempt from defamation claims as are statements made by legislators during legislative debates (even if statements are made maliciously with full knowledge that they are untrue)! This *privileged speech* standard views court and legislative personnel as dealing with public interest matters in which there should be no limitation or restriction of full and free expressions and statements.

Qualified Privilege There also are circumstances in which there is more restricted *qualified privilege*. If statements are made in good faith, with absence of malice, and communicated only to those who have a legitimate reason for receiving the information provided, the source of such statements is exempt from defamation claims. So, providers of letters of recommendation for jobs or for college admissions, managers who provide work performance evaluations, and other sources of like documents enjoy protection from defamation claims conditional upon their privilege not being abused. Not surprisingly, many defamation suits arise from workplace statements, most often stemming from unfavorable job evaluations and unfavorable references for new jobs. Also there is federal legislation protecting credit bureaus if they make a mistake as long as they act promptly once the mistake is pointed out. Under the Fair Credit Reporting Act, credit bureaus are required to reinvestigate errors that are pointed out to them by people who claim their credit histories are being misreported. If the credit bureau reinvestigates and decides not to change its data on the person, that person's version of events must be included in the credit report also.

Public Figures As was the case with invasion-of-privacy issues, public figures are less shielded than private citizens from defamatory statements. To expect recovery in a defamation suit, a public figure must be able to prove that the defendant knew a published statement was false or exhibited a reckless disregard for the truth. This additional proof requirement is often called *legal malice*. Publishers (of newspapers, magazines, etc.), who are often targets of defamation suits, attempt to protect themselves by having two or more independent sources for potentially troublesome articles.

Richard G. Godbehere et al. v. *Phoenix Newspapers, Inc. et al.*
Supreme Court of Arizona
(162 Ariz. 335, 783 P.2d 781) (1989)

FACTS AND CASE BACKGROUND
In the Spring and summer of 1985, newspaper publishers in the Phoenix, Arizona area printed over 50 articles, editorials, and columns about local law enforcement. The publications stated that the plaintiff law enforcement officers and employees engaged in illegal activities, staged narcotics arrests to generate publicity, illegally arrested citizens, misused public funds and resources, committed police brutality, and generally were incompetent at law enforcement. Sheriffs, deputies, and civilian employees of the sheriff's office brought libel and invasion of privacy action against the newspapers. Plaintiffs alleged that the publications were false, damaged their reputations, harmed them in their profession, and caused them emotional distress.

In the Maricopa County, Arizona Superior Court, all invasion of privacy claims were dismissed. Plaintiffs appealed and the Court of Appeals affirmed the trial court's verdict. Plaintiffs then appealed to the Arizona Supreme Court.

OPINION OF THE COURT: FELDMAN, SUPREME COURT VICE CHIEF JUSTICE
We granted this review to determine whether Arizona should recognize a cause of action for false light

invasion of privacy, and if so, what the proper standard should be.

* * *

In 1890, Samuel Warren and Louis Brandeis published an article advocating the recognition of a right to privacy as an independent legal concept . . . [T]hey also described how courts used contract and property law to protect thoughts, ideas, or expressions from wrongful appropriation. Warren and Brandeis contended these were nothing more than 'instances and applications of a general right to privacy.' Hence, they supported recognition of the right 'to be let alone.'

* * *

In 1960, Dean Prosser concluded that four separate torts had developed under the right of privacy rubric: (1) intrusion on the plaintiff's seclusion or private affairs; (2) public disclosure of embarrassing private facts; (3) publicity placing the plaintiff in a false light in the public eye; and (4) appropriation of the plaintiff's name or likeness for the defendant's advantage . . . In 1977, the Restatement [of Torts] adopted Prosser's classification. Although each tort is classified under invasion of privacy, they "otherwise have almost nothing in common except that each represents an interference with the right of the plaintiff 'to be let alone.'"

* * *

False light invasion of privacy . . . protects against the conduct of knowingly or recklessly publishing false information or innuendo that a 'reasonable person' would find 'highly offensive.' . . . Thus, we believe the tort action for false light invasion of privacy provides protection against a narrow class of wrongful conduct that falls short of 'outrage,' but nevertheless should be deterred. . . . Unless the interest in protecting privacy rights is outweighed by the interest in protecting speech, . . . we see no reason not to recognize an action for false light invasion of privacy.

* * *

FREE SPEECH CONSIDERATIONS
As in defamation, a public official in a false light action must always show that the defendant published with knowledge of the false innuendo or with reckless disregard of the truth. . . . In *Hustler Magazine, Inc.* v. *Falwell*, . . . the Supreme Court held that a public figure plaintiff must prove . . . actual malice in order to recover for intentional infliction of emotional distress. Although *Hustler* was an intentional infliction case, the language used by the Court is so broad that it applies to any tort action relating to free speech, particularly 'in the area of public debate about public figures.' Additional protection for free speech comes from the principle that

protection for privacy interests generally applies only to private matters . . . Suffice it to say that in this case, where we deal with publications concerning public officers performing public duties, the first amendment controls

* * *

IS FALSE LIGHT AVAILABLE IN THIS CASE?

Finally, publishers contended that even if we recognize false light actions, the action does not lie in this case. They argue that not only do the publications discuss matters of public interest, but plaintiffs have no right of privacy with respect to the manner in which they perform their official duties. We agree.

We have specifically held that the right of privacy does not exist 'where the plaintiff has become a public character . . .' In addition, privacy rights are absent or limited 'in connection with the life of a person in whom the public has a rightful interest, [or] where the information would be of public benefit.' . . . It is difficult to conceive of an area of greater public interest than law enforcement. . . . Therefore, we hold that there can be no false light invasion of privacy action for matters involving official acts or duties of public officers.

Consequently, we adopt the following legal standard: a plaintiff cannot sue for false light invasion of privacy if he or she is a public official and the publication relates to performance of his or her public life or duties.

We do not go so far as to say, however, that a public official has no privacy rights at all and may never bring an action for invasion of privacy. Certainly, if the publication presents the public official's private life in a false light, he or she can sue under the false light tort, although actual malice must be shown.

The Supreme Court has held that 'the public official designation applies at the very least to those among the hierarchy of government employees who have, or appear to the public to have, substantial responsibility for or control over the conduct of government affairs.' . . . The sheriff and the deputies here are public officials.

The publications at issue concern the discharge of their public duties and do not relate to private affairs. Therefore, plaintiffs have no claim for false light invasion of privacy.

We affirm the trial court's dismissal of the false light claim.

QUESTIONS FOR REVIEW

1. Newspapers in Pheonix obviously published materials that were highly critical of local law enforcement. Arizona courts appear to be endorsing this activity. Compose a short essay describing the benefits for a democratic society of having a press that is free to engage in such activities.
2. If the newspapers had written equally critical articles about a local owner of a chain of fast food restaurants, who then sued for false light invasion of privacy, would the court outcome have been different? Why?
3. What would have been different if the published materials delved into the private lives of the Sheriff, deputies, etc.?

"Libel and Slander on the Internet"

The Internet creates an interesting twist to the challenge of interpreting the law of defamation; the question currently vexing the legal community is whether electronic communication is libel or slander.

Because slander is more difficult to prove, defendants in Internet defamation actions prefer to be held to the slander standard, while plaintiffs prefer to bring a libel suit. This begs the question: Is electronic communication more like print or speech?

Although many users instinctively feel the Internet is a form of publication (witness the evolution of e-zines, e-journals, and protocols for scholarly citation of Internet references), the courts continue to wrestle with whether something on a Web page or BBS is spoken or published. And since defamation law is primarily state law, 50 court systems are confronting the problem with 50 different legal perspectives.

Interestingly, this same issue arose when television and radio became popular. Since people spoke on radio and television, the courts initially sought to apply slander standards to broadcast defamation. The courts eventually recognized the breadth of exposure and resulting damage from broadcast defamation was akin to published defamation, and began to apply libel standards to broadcast defamation.

While the broadcasting standard may eventually apply to Internet defamation, in the short term there will still be dispute as to whether potential plaintiffs can pursue legal actions under libel or slander standards. The final resolution to this debate may eventually require legislative intervention.

Source: Excerpt from: "Libel and, Slander on the Internet," Association for Computing Machinery. *Communications of the ACM,* New York; Jun 2000; *Anthony M Townsend; Robert J Aalberts; Steven A Gibson.*

FRAUDULENT MISREPRESENTATION, CONVERSION, AND TRESPASS TO LAND

Remembering that torts are acts and forms of conduct that can also be criminal, a focus on misrepresentation, conversion, and trespass will complete our journey through intentional torts. This section also involves a shift from a focus largely on intentional torts against people to intentional torts against property.

Fraudulent Misrepresentation (Deceit)

Out of ignorance, statements may be made that misrepresent reality. *Fraudulent misrepresentation* (or just *fraud*), however, involves intent, as it is the deliberate misrepresentation of *facts* in order to gain an advantage. More than salesmanship or business "puffery" is required to establish fraudulent misrepresentation. So, a salesman's claim that his company's used cars are the absolute best available could not be fraud, because they are basically opinions, not facts. It is fraud, however, to sell used cars with rolled back speedometers while misrepresenting the true mileage on the cars sold. It is fraud to knowingly sell real estate that has a toxic waste deposit on it that the buyer has no knowledge of. It is fraud to sell a warehouse with a leaking roof while representing the building as leak-free. It would also be fraud for an attorney to attempt to involve you in a tax avoidance scheme that the attorney knows or has reason to know is illegal.

Generally, to establish damages for fraudulent misrepresentation, the following elements are required:

1. a misrepresentation of facts material to the issue at hand
2. with knowledge that the "facts" presented are false or with "reckless disregard for the truth,"
3. intent to induce reliance on the misrepresented facts,
4. a reasonable reliance on the misrepresented facts on the part of the injured party, and
5. actual damages that occur as a result of reliance on the misrepresentation.

While representing only a small proportion of all such transactions, there are clearly fraudulent misrepresentation problems affecting Internet transactions. This is true both of ordinary sales transactions in which sellers collect for goods offered on the Internet but never deliver the goods and also of financial investment transactions in which alleged brokers induce people to invest in companies that either don't exist or which have little value. Unfortunately for victims of Internet fraud, the recovery of damages is often difficult or impossible as the offending party is likely to be geographically remote and hard to even identify.

Students should be mindful that the elements of the tort of deceit or fraud are the same as those for contractual fraud. It is a tort to deceive someone in a noncontractual situation, such as obtaining entrance to a bar using a fake ID, and it is also a crime. It is a crime to obtain property under false pretenses, such as by offering goods for sale, collecting the money and absconding with the money without delivering the product.

Defenses against damage awards in fraudulent misrepresentation cases involve efforts to undermine one or more of the claimed elements necessary for imposing damages. So, a defendant can be expected to attempt to show that there was no misrepresentation of known facts, that there was no attempt to induce the plaintiff to rely on facts provided, that it was unreasonable for the plaintiff to in fact rely on information provided, and that no actual damages occurred as a result of the fraud, even if all other elements are as indicated by the plaintiff.

Wrongful Takings and Intermeddling

Conversion

Conversion is the taking and/or using of someone else's personal property without permission and without justification. Cars, boats, planes, stereos, art, jewelry and countless other items can be converted. If Jim goes into another student's dorm room and without permission takes his stereo to set up and enjoy in his own room, Jim has committed the tort of conversion and can be liable to the victim for the full (fair market) value of the stereo. Of course, under separate criminal law, Jim has stolen the stereo and is subject to criminal prosecution. With civil tort law, the victim doesn't have to wait for criminal prosecution, but can pursue damage recovery on his own. So, conversion is the civil side of theft.

Intent is not necessarily an element in conversion. If an individual **mistakenly** believes that he or she is entitled to personal property items taken, there is still conversion. If an individual unknowingly buys stolen goods, that buyer is guilty of conversion in spite of absence of knowledge that the goods were stolen. Damages in conversion cases are equal to the value of the converted property, but the defendant is entitled to that property. It is also important to recognize that acts far less serious than criminal theft can constitute conversion. Even temporary exercises of dominion or control over the personal property of another can be conversion, so being clumsy in a store and knocking over a lamp could meet the requirements.

Defenses against conversion claims would include efforts to show the personal property in possession of the defendant is not the missing property, that the plaintiff has no ownership right in the property superior to that of the defendant, or that the property was taken out of necessity—I took the horse to care for it as the owner was abusing the animal and letting it starve to death. It is also a defense to claim the exercise of control over the personal property was so slight that a conversion did not take place.

Trespass

Trespass occurs when, without consent, an individual goes onto another's property (land) or interferes with the rights of the owner of personal property to the exclusive possession, use and enjoyment of that property. In the eyes of the law, land and improvements to land (such as buildings) are *real property* while all other items owned (money, cars, furniture, etc.) are *personal property*.

Trespass to Real Property

A trespass to land occurs when a person, without permission, goes on over or under another's land, causes something else to intrude onto another's land, remains on the land when asked to leave, or permits anything to remain on the land. So, it is a tort to walk on your neighbor's land without permission, you may not lawfully dam the creek that runs through your pasture and cause a lake to form on your upstream neighbor's corn field, you can't legally drive your SUV through the neighbor's tulip bed, spray his house with a hose, or build a barn partly on his property. It is permissible to fly over property you don't own so long as you maintain minimum altitudes as required by aviation regulations.

Liability of Landowners to Trespassers

Under old common law, a trespasser was liable for damages to property and generally could not claim damages for any injuries sustained on another's property. Modern standards are considerably changed and "reasonable duty" is the typical standard today. Landowners do not have the right to deter trespassers with surprising, life-threatening traps such as spring guns that are set off when burglars attempt to enter a dwelling. An auto salvage yard owner is expected to post signs indicating the presence of "junkyard" guard dogs. Homeowners are liable to children for injuries or death sustained by trespassing children drawn to the "attractive nuisance" of a swimming pool, a storage building, or some other enticing object on the home owner's property. It does remain possible for a property owner to remove a trespasser from property owned, or to hold a trespasser on that property for a **reasonable** amount of time awaiting the arrival of police, and not be liable for assault and/or battery or false imprisonment so long as only **reasonable force** is employed.

Defenses against a trespass charge include a showing that the supposed property owner did not, in fact, own and/or have the right to possess the property. Also it is a defense to show that there was good and just cause for the trespass—e.g., it was necessary to relieve a situation that was dangerous to someone else or to the public at large. It is defense to retrieve personal property owned by the trespasser such as repossessions of cars so long as violence does not occur.

Trespass to Personal Property

Trespass to personal property involves intentional and wrongful interference with the owner's possession or use of personal property. Hiding your roommate's sleeping bag, preventing him from camping out to be in line for a basketball ticket allocation, is a trespass to personal property. Proof that a trespass is justified serves as a defense. So, an auto repair shop can hold a customer's car after repairs are completed if the customer hasn't paid for the repair.

Damage Considerations   Court awards for trespass to personal property are often zero because they are based on any difference in the fair market value of the personal property before and after the trespass. Trespass to personal property is often also a conversion and, since damages are higher under conversion, it is preferred by most plaintiffs. Even though damages for trespass to personal property are generally less than those for conversion, trespass to personal property is a tort and victims of torts are entitled to obtain injunctions from the courts for continuing violations. The ability to petition the courts for an injunction is particularly relevant in cyberspace.

Trespass in Cyberspace   Cyberspace has allowed for dramatic expansions of second-hand sales. Shrewd shoppers who heretofore had to scour garage sales and

Torts		
Intentional Torts	Infliction of emotional distress, invasion of privacy, and defamation.	Defenses for defamation include absolute privilege, qualified privilege, and public figure.
	Fraudulent misrepresentation, conversion, and trespass to land, trespass to personal property, misappropriation.	Defenses for conversion include proving that the plaintiff has no superior property right or the property was taken out of necessity. Defenses against trespass include showing that the property owner did not have the right to possess the property or the trespass was a necessity.
Negligence	The following four elements must be present for liability: (1) duty of care, (2) breach of duty, (3) measurable damage, (4) proximate cause.	Defenses include assumption of risk, contributory negligence, or intervening cause.

flea markets to obtain bargains now regularly use Internet auction sites such as eBay.com. eBay, however, is not the only auction site and, indeed, the value of an auction site is directly related to its size. In other words, more buyers and sellers will come to a website the greater the number of options available.

Aggregators are websites that electronically assimilate and organize the offerings and bids from several auction sites simultaneously. Aggregators make use of software robots that perform searching, copying, and retrieving functions that consume large amounts of the processing and storage capacity of the auction sites and can cause the auction website to "crash." Auction websites such as eBay specifically prohibit many of the functions that aggregators use to collect information at their sites to make their sites more attractive to their subscribers. Is making use of a public website in this manner a trespass? Although the following case gave a definitive answer to eBay and Bidder's Edge, the law in this area is not well established.

EBAY, Inc., Plaintiff, v. BIDDER'S EDGE, Inc., Defendant
United States District Court for the Northern District of California
100 F. Supp. 2d 1058 (2000)

BACKGROUND AND FACTS

eBay is an Internet-based, person-to-person trading site. eBay offers sellers the ability to list items for sale and prospective buyers the ability to search those listings and bid on items. The seller can set the terms and conditions of the auction. The item is sold to the highest bidder. The transaction is consummated directly between the buyer and seller without eBay's involvement. A potential purchaser looking for a particular item can access the eBay site and perform a key word search for relevant auctions and bidding status. eBay has also created category listings which identify items in over 2500 categories, such as antiques, computers, and dolls. Users may browse these category listing pages to identify items of interest.

Users of the eBay site must register and agree to the eBay User Agreement. Users agree to the seven-page User Agreement by clicking on an "I Accept" button located at the end of the User Agreement. The current version of the User Agreement prohibits the use of "any robot, spider, other automatic device, or manual process to monitor or copy our web pages or the content contained herein without our prior expressed written permission."

eBay currently has over 7 million registered users. Over 400,000 new items are added to the site every day. Every minute, 600 bids are placed on almost 3 million items. Users currently perform, on average, 10 million searches per day on eBay's database. Bidding for and sales of items are continuously ongoing in millions of separate auctions.

A software robot is a computer program which operates across the Internet to perform searching, copying and retrieving functions on the websites of others. A software robot is capable of executing thousands of instructions per minute, far in excess of what a human can accomplish. Robots consume the processing and storage resources of a system, making that portion of the system's capacity unavailable to the system owner or other users. Consumption of sufficient system resources will slow the processing of the overall system and can overload the system such that it will malfunction or "crash." A severe malfunction can cause a loss of data and an interruption in services.

Bidder's Edge (BE) is a company with 22 employees that was founded in 1997. The BE website debuted in November 1998. BE does not host auctions. BE is an auction aggregation site designed to offer on-line auction buyers the ability to search for items across numerous on-line auctions without having to search each host site individually. As of March 2000, the BE website contained information on more than 5 million items being auctioned on more than one hundred auction sites. BE also provides its users with additional auction-related services and information. The information available on the BE site is contained in a database of information that BE compiles through access to various auction sites such as eBay. When a user enters a search for a particular item at BE, BE searches its database and generates a list of every item in the database responsive to the search, organized by auction closing date and time. Rather than going to

each host auction site one at a time, a user who goes to BE may conduct a single search to obtain information about that item on every auction site tracked by BE. It is important to include information regarding eBay auctions on the BE site because eBay is by far the biggest consumer-to-consumer on-line auction site.

On November 9, 1999, eBay sent BE a letter reasserting that BE's activities were unauthorized, insisting that BE cease accessing the eBay site, alleging that BE's activities constituted a civil trespass and offering to license BE's activities. eBay and BE were again unable to agree on licensing terms. As a result, eBay attempted to block BE from accessing the eBay site; by the end of November, 1999, eBay had blocked a total of 169 IP addresses it believed BE was using to query eBay's system. BE elected to continue crawling eBay's site by using proxy servers to evade eBay's IP blocks.

The parties agree that BE accessed the eBay site approximately 100,000 times a day. eBay alleges that BE activity constituted up to 1.53 percent of the number of requests received by eBay, and up to 1.10 percent of the total data transferred by eBay during certain periods in October and November of 1999 and alleges damages between $40,000 and $70,000 due to the demands made on their system by BE's software robots.

eBay now moves for preliminary injunctive relief preventing BE from accessing the eBay computer system based on nine causes of action: trespass, false advertising, federal and state trademark dilution, computer fraud and abuse, unfair competition, misappropriation, interference with prospective economic advantage and unjust enrichment. However, eBay does not move, either independently or alternatively, for injunctive relief that is limited to restricting how BE can use data taken from the eBay site.

Opinion by: RONALD M. WHYTE, U.S. Dist. Court Judge

According to eBay, the load on its servers resulting from BE's web crawlers represents between 1.11 percent and 1.53 percent of the total load on eBay's listing servers. eBay alleges both economic loss from BE's current activities and potential harm resulting from the total crawling of BE and others. In alleging economic harm, eBay's argument is that eBay has expended considerable time, effort and money to create its computer system, and that BE should have to pay for the portion of eBay's system BE uses.

* * *

If BE's activity is allowed to continue unchecked, it would encourage other auction aggregators to engage in similar recursive searching of the eBay system such that eBay would suffer irreparable harm from reduced system performance, system unavailability, or data losses. BE does not appear to seriously contest that reduced system performance, system unavailability or data loss would inflict irreparable harm on eBay consisting of lost profits and lost customer goodwill. Harm resulting from lost profits and lost customer goodwill is irreparable because it is neither easily calculable, nor easily compensable and is therefore an appropriate basis for injunctive relief. Where, as here, the denial of preliminary injunctive relief would encourage an increase in the complained-of activity, and such an increase would present a strong likelihood of irreparable harm, the plaintiff has at least established a possibility of irreparable harm.

* * *

BE correctly observes that there is a dearth of authority supporting a preliminary injunction based on an ongoing to trespass to chattels. In contrast, it is black letter law in California that an injunction is an appropriate remedy for a continuing trespass to real property. [References deleted] If eBay were a brick and mortar auction house with limited seating capacity, eBay would appear to be entitled to reserve those seats for potential bidders, to refuse entrance to individuals (or robots) with no intention of bidding on any of the items, and to seek preliminary injunctive relief against noncustomer trespassers eBay was physically unable to exclude. *** The court concludes that under the circumstances present here, BE's ongoing violation of eBay's fundamental property right to exclude others from its computer system potentially causes sufficient irreparable harm to support a preliminary injunction.

* * *

Trespass to chattels "lies where an intentional interference with the possession of personal property has proximately caused injury." Trespass to chattels "although seldom employed as a tort theory in California" was recently applied to cover the unauthorized use of long distance telephone lines. Specifically, the court noted "the electronic signals generated by the [defendants'] activities were sufficiently tangible to support a trespass cause of action." Thus, it appears likely that the electronic signals sent by BE to retrieve information from eBay's computer system are also sufficiently tangible to support a trespass cause of action.

In order to prevail on a claim for trespass based on accessing a computer system, the plaintiff must establish: (1) defendant intentionally and without authorization interfered with plaintiff's possessory interest in the computer system; and (2) defendant's unauthorized use proximately resulted in damage to plaintiff.

A. BE's Unauthorized Interference

eBay argues that BE's use was unauthorized and intentional. eBay is correct. BE does not dispute that it employed an automated computer program to connect with and search eBay's electronic database. BE admits that, because other auction aggregators were including eBay's auctions in their listing, it continued to "crawl" eBay's web site even after eBay demanded BE terminate such activity.

* * *

BE argues that it cannot trespass eBay's website because the site is publicly accessible. BE's argument is unconvincing. eBay's servers are private property, conditional access to which eBay grants the public. eBay does not generally permit the type of automated access made by BE. In fact, eBay explicitly notifies automated visitors that their access is not permitted. "In general, California does recognize a trespass claim where the defendant exceeds the scope of the consent." *Baugh* v. *CBS, Inc.,* 828 F. Supp. 745, 756 (N.D. Cal. 1993).

Even if BE's web crawlers were authorized to make individual queries of eBay's system, BE's web crawlers exceeded the scope of any such consent when they began acting like robots by making repeated queries. Moreover, eBay repeatedly and explicitly notified BE that its use of eBay's computer system was unauthorized. The entire reason BE directed its queries through proxy servers was to evade eBay's attempts to stop this unauthorized access. The court concludes that BE's activity is sufficiently outside of the scope of the use permitted by eBay that it is unauthorized for the purposes of establishing a trespass.

* * *

B. Damage to eBay's Computer System***

eBay is likely to be able to demonstrate that BE's activities have diminished the quality or value of eBay's computer systems. BE's activities consume at least a portion of plaintiff's bandwidth and server capacity. Although there is some dispute as to the percentage of queries on eBay's site for which BE is responsible, BE admits that it sends some 80,000 to 100,000 requests to plaintiff's computer systems per day. Although eBay does not claim that this consumption has led to any physical damage to eBay's computer system, nor does eBay provide any evidence to support the claim that it may have lost revenues or customers based on this use, eBay's claim is that BE's use is appropriating eBay's personal property by using valuable bandwidth and capacity, and necessarily compromising eBay's ability to use that capacity for its own purposes.

* * *

Bidder's Edge, its officers, agents, servants, employees, attorneys and those in active concert or participation with them who receive actual notice of this order by personal service or otherwise, are hereby enjoined pending the trial of this matter, from using any automated query program, robot, web crawler or other similar device, without written authorization, to access eBay's computer systems or networks, for the purpose of copying any part of eBay's auction database. As a condition of the preliminary injunction, eBay is ordered to post a bond in the amount of $ 2,000,000 to secure payment of any damages sustained by defendant if it is later found to have been wrongfully enjoined. This order shall take effect 10 days from the date on which it is filed.

Questions for Analysis

1. Explain precisely the nature of the trespass to personal property that eBay alleged was occurring as a result of BE's activities.
2. Why was the court unconvinced that, because eBay's website is publicly accessible, it could not be trespassing?

Misappropriation

Another tort that is becoming increasingly used by plaintiffs is misappropriation. Traditionally misappropriation was a remedy used by firms whose trade secrets were wrongfully taken by other firms, ex-employees, and others who obtained access to the trade secrets. More recently, there have been misappropriation suits based on the right of publicity, the right to control use of someone's name or likeness and other intangible property rights that do not fit in any of the traditional IP categories of patent, copyright, or trademark. Suppose a company reports news "hot" off the wire, such as a play-by-play account of a basketball game whose rights are "reserved" to those who have permission of the league for broadcast? Consider the following case.

The National Basketball Association v. Motorola, Inc. doing business as Sports Trax, Defendant
United States Court of Appeals for the Second Circuit
105 F.3d 841 (1997)

BACKGROUND AND FACTS

The facts are largely undisputed. Motorola manufactures and markets the SportsTrax paging device while STATS supplies the game information that is transmitted to the pagers. The product became available to the public in January 1996, at a retail price of about $200. SportsTrax's pager has an inch-and-a-half by inch-and-a-half screen and operates in four basic modes: "current," "statistics," "final scores" and "demonstration." It is the "current" mode that gives rise to the present dispute. In that mode, SportsTrax displays the following information on NBA games in progress: (*i*) the teams playing; (*ii*) score changes; (*iii*) the team in possession of the ball; (*iv*) whether the team is in the free-throw bonus; (*v*) the quarter of the game; and (*vi*) time remaining in the quarter. The information is updated every two to three minutes, with more frequent updates near the end of the first half and the end of the game. There is a lag of approximately two or three minutes between events in the game itself and when the information appears on the pager screen.

SportsTrax's operation relies on a "data feed" supplied by STATS reporters who watch the games on television or listen to them on the radio. The reporters key into a personal computer changes in the score and other information such as successful and missed shots, fouls, and clock updates. The information is relayed by modem to STATS's host computer, which compiles, analyzes, and formats the data for retransmission. The information is then sent to a common carrier, which then sends it via satellite to various local FM radio networks that in turn emit the signal received by the individual SportsTrax pagers.

Although the NBA's complaint concerned only the SportsTrax device, the NBA offered evidence at trial concerning STATS's America On-Line ("AOL") site. Starting in January 1996, users who accessed STATS's AOL site, typically via a modem attached to a home computer, were provided with slightly more comprehensive and detailed real-time game information than is displayed on a SportsTrax pager. On the AOL site, game scores are updated every 15 seconds to a minute, and the player and team statistics are updated each minute.

The district court dismissed all of the NBA's claims except the first—misappropriation under New York law.

OPINION BY: WINTER CIRCUIT JUDGE

The issues before us are ones that have arisen in various forms over the course of this century as technology has steadily increased the speed and quantity of information transmission. Today, individuals at home, at work, or elsewhere, can use a computer, pager, or other device to obtain highly selective kinds of information virtually at will. *International News Service* v. *Associated Press,* 248 U.S. 215, 63 L. Ed. 211, 39 S. Ct. 68 (1918) ("INS") was one of the first cases to address the issues raised by these technological advances, although the technology involved in that case was primitive by contemporary standards. INS involved two wire services, the Associated Press ("AP") and International News Service ("INS"), that transmitted news stories by wire to member newspapers. Id. INS would lift factual stories from AP bulletins and send them by wire to INS papers. INS would also take factual stories from east coast AP papers and wire them to INS papers on the West Coast that had yet to publish because of time differentials. The Supreme Court held that INS's conduct was a common-law misappropriation of AP's property.

With the advance of technology, radio stations began "live" broadcasts of events such as baseball games and operas, and various entrepreneurs began to use the transmissions of others in one way or another for their own profit. In response, New York courts created a body of misappropriation law, loosely based on INS, that sought to apply ethical standards to the use by one party of another's transmissions of events.

* * *

We hold that the surviving "hot-news" INS-like claim is limited to cases where: (*i*) a plaintiff generates or gathers information at a cost; (*ii*) the information is time-sensitive; (*iii*) a defendant's use of the information constitutes free-riding on the plaintiff's efforts; (*iv*) the defendant is in direct competition with a product or service offered by the plaintiffs; and (*v*) the ability of other parties to free-ride on the efforts of the plaintiff or others would so reduce the incentive to produce the product or service that its existence or quality would be substantially threatened.

* * *

The district court's injunction was based on its conclusion that, under New York law, defendants had unlawfully misappropriated the NBA's property rights in its games. The district court reached this conclusion by holding: (*i*) that the NBA's misappropriation claim relating to

the underlying games was not preempted by Section 301 of the Copyright Act; and (*ii*) that, under New York common law, defendants had engaged in unlawful misappropriation.

* * *

We conclude that Motorola and STATS have not engaged in unlawful misappropriation under the "hot-news" test set out above. To be sure, some of the elements of a "hot-news" INS-claim are met. The information transmitted to SportsTrax is not precisely contemporaneous, but it is nevertheless time-sensitive. Also, the NBA does provide, or will shortly do so, information like that available through SportsTrax. It now offers a service called "Gamestats" that provides official play-by-play game sheets and half-time and final box scores within each arena. It also provides such information to the media in each arena. In the future, the NBA plans to enhance Gamestats so that it will be networked between the various arenas and will support a pager product analogous to SportsTrax. SportsTrax will of course directly compete with an enhanced Gamestats.

However, there are critical elements missing in the NBA's attempt to assert a "hot-news" INS-type claim. As framed by the NBA, their claim compresses and confuses three different informational products. The first product is generating the information by playing the games; the

second product is transmitting live, full descriptions of those games; and the third product is collecting and retransmitting strictly factual information about the games. The first and second products are the NBA's primary business: producing basketball games for live attendance and licensing copyrighted broadcasts of those games. The collection and retransmission of strictly factual material about the games is a different product: e.g., box-scores in newspapers, summaries of statistics on television sports news, and real-time facts to be transmitted to pagers. In our view, the NBA has failed to show any competitive effect whatsoever from SportsTrax on the first and second products and a lack of any free-riding by SportsTrax on the third.

QUESTIONS FOR ANALYSIS

1. What element of the plaintiff's claim of misappropriation did the court hold was missing?
2. What circumstances did the court suggest would be a misappropriation? Suppose instead that the AOL technology improves to the point where there are no delays in transmission of the scores and other "stats."
3. Suppose that AOL adds a voice component to its transmissions. Would transmissions make what AOL and SportTrax do a misappropriation of the NBA game?

NEGLIGENCE

Differing from the array of intentional torts dealt with above, torts (wrongs) involving *negligence* are not the result of *intent* but are harms that can be viewed as occurring by accident or by mistake. With negligence, an individual or business engages in actions or conduct that is not intended to harm another but which, unfortunately, does. Quite often, the lack of intent does not

free the negligent partly of responsibility (liability) for the harm caused. A "but it was an accident" plea could be expected to prompt the familiar refrain, "Tell it to the judge."

Liability for injury/damage suffered through negligence arises when the following four elements exist:

1. The defendant owes a *duty of care* to the plaintiff,

2. The defendant *breaches* that duty of care by negligence,
3. The plaintiff suffers *measurable damage,*
4. The defendant's negligence is the *proximate cause* of the injury.

Duty of Care

Tort law applies the *reasonable person standard* in determining what the duty of care is. The court system, as agent for "society," views a reasonable person as someone who is prudent, careful, honest, and skilled at avoiding causing injury to others. It is presumed that individuals have a **duty of care** for others and that a reasonable person would live up to a reasonable **standard of care** when interacting with others. Reasonable persons do not engage in reckless behavior. They obey speed limits, make sure that floors in stores are not slippery, and screen employees who work with minors to make sure they are not child molesters. In other words, tort law requires reasonable persons to take reasonable precautions against reasonably foreseeable risks.

Causation or Proximate Cause

For a defendant to be liable in a negligence case, causation must be established. The standard test for the fact of causation is the "but for" test—"but for Mr. Smith running a red light and hitting plaintiff's car, the plaintiff would not have suffered the (work) disability that has reduced his earning capacity by $1 million." A problem exists with this causation test, however, in its potential for extending the links of causality (hence, liability) to relatively remote actions.

It could be argued that "But for Mr. Smith's Rolex losing time, getting him off to a late start for an impor-tant meeting, he would not have been speeding, would not have lost control of his car, and would not have injured the plaintiff." Can Mr. Smith (and/or his lawyer) conclude that the Rolex company is responsible for Mr. Smith's injury? Not likely. A court would ask if the faulty watch was the *proximate cause* (the legal cause) of Mr. Smith's injury (instead of his choice to speed), doubtless concluding that it was Mr. Smith's choice to speed (Mr. Smith's own negligence) that resulted in plaintiff's injuries.

Foreseeability

In many cases, whether a defendant is living up to his or her duty of care responsibility depends upon whether or not the event of injury from the defendant's conduct would be *foreseeable* by a reasonable person. You shouldn't be surprised to find that a court, adhering to the reasonable person standard, would conclude that truck drivers have a duty of care for other users of roads, that running a red light might *reasonably* be expected to result in collisions with other vehicles, and that the collision of the cement truck with the car alluded to above was, indeed, the cause of plaintiff's costly injuries. In like fashion, courts are likely to find the necessary elements for damages in negligence cases whenever it is reasonably foreseeable that the defendant's careless or reckless actions could result in injuries. It is reasonably foreseeable that a restaurant that serves "undercooked" meat and has no system for checking to make sure such events do not occur is liable for the reasonably foreseeable consequences.

The following case illustrates the application of proximate cause and how it provides limits on liability when bizarre situations occur, even though the defendant, were negligent in carrying out their duties.

Juliette P. Shipley et al. **v.** *Budd Services, Sumitomo, et al.*
Court of Appeals of North Carolina
(525 S.E.2d 847) (2000)

FACTS AND CASE BACKGROUND
Sumitomo Electric Lightwave Corporation is a global technology company with facilities in numerous locations around the world. Its Research Triangle (North Carolina) facility relied on Budd Services to provide security and to limit facility access to employees and visitors with proper access cards. In April of 1994, a disgruntled former employee entered the Sumitomo facility using an old "temporary" access card that he still had from his initial employment and shot five people, including

himself. He and two of the workers died. A number of suits were filed against Sumitomo and Budd Services by workers and families of those killed.

After the settlement of numerous claims, Juliette Shipley sought damages from Budd, claiming that Budd was negligent and that Budd's negligence caused her to suffer severe emotional distress with an attendant loss of earning capacity and other injuries. According to the plaintiff's pleadings, while Budd Services had gotten the former employee's worker security badge, it had not gotten a temporary access card that the gunman used to get into the Sumitomo facility. According to the plaintiff's suit, the security company should have tracked temporary access cards and, with an accurate record of cards issued, should have required the return of the employee's access card when his employment terminated eight months prior to the shooting spree.

In the Durham County, N.C. Superior Court, summary judgment was entered in favor of the defendant, Budd Services, decreeing that Budd Services had no liability for any emotional distress injury suffered by the plaintiff.

OPINION OF THE COURT: MARTIN, APPEALS COURT JUDGE

[Plaintiff] seeks damages from Budd for emotional distress suffered by reason of Budd's negligence. Plaintiff . . . alleges that Budd negligently performed its contractual duty to provide security at Sumitomo, and this negligence caused her to suffer severe emotional distress. The issue presented by her appeal is whether it was reasonably foreseeable that she would suffer emotional distress as a result of Budd's negligent failure to retrieve a temporary access card from [the gunman] and to otherwise prevent his entry into the Sumitomo

plant. We hold that it was not and affirm the entry of summary judgment in favor of Budd.

* * *

An action for the negligent infliction of emotional distress has three elements: (1) defendant engaged in negligent conduct; (2) it was reasonably foreseeable that such conduct would cause the plaintiff severe emotional distress; and (3) defendant's conduct, in fact, caused plaintiff severe emotional distress . . . The plaintiff must show that the distress suffered was "a proximate and foreseeable result of the defendant's negligence."

* * *

In her complaint, plaintiff Shipley alleges that 'as a direct and proximate result of the negligence by Budd Services, Inc., resulting in the shootings . . . and his attempt to kill Juliette Shipley, Ms. Shipley suffered severe emotional distress.'

* * *

Thus, the enquiry in the present case must focus on whether Shipley's emotional distress was a foreseeable and proximate result of Budd's negligence.

* * *

. . . In this case we hold that the emotional distress suffered by Shipley was not a reasonably foreseeable consequence of any negligent conduct on Budd's part. Viewed in the light most favorable to plaintiff Shipley . . . , the evidence shows that Budd . . . negligently failed to retrieve [the access] card from [the gunman] after his employment at Sumitomo terminated, allowing [him] to gain entry to the factory where he killed two people and injured several others. The evidence permits a reasonable inference that plaintiff Shipley was at least one of [his] targets.

* * *

These facts are sufficient to support a finding that Budd engaged in negligent conduct, and that plaintiff Shipley suffered severe emotional distress. However, these facts do not support an inference that Shipley's emotional distress was a reasonably foreseeable result of Budd's negligent acts; Budd's negligence in failing to retrieve the access card and Shipley's emotional distress are simply too attenuated to support a finding of reasonable foreseeability . . . The possibility that (1) defendant's negligence in failing to retrieve the temporary access card (2) would combine with [the ex-employee's] rage against his former employer (3) to result in a workplace shooting (4) which would cause Shipley to suffer emotional distress, was, like the situation in Sorrells, 'too remote to permit a finding that it was reasonably foreseeable.' Therefore, an essential element of plaintiff's claim is nonexistent and summary judgment in favor of Budd must be affirmed.

QUESTIONS FOR ANALYSIS

1. Can you imagine facts that would make the security firm liable for negligent infliction of emotional distress? Aren't security firms hired precisely to deal with these freaky situations when an employee loses control of his actions?

2. Why is it important that there be reasonable limits to liability? Suppose a car mechanic did a negligent job and George's car would not start and so he had to get a cab, but the cab driver was drunk and George was killed in an accident. Is it not true that, but for the car mechanic's negligence, George would still be alive? Is it not true that applying the "but for" test, there would be a lot more litigation and people would have to be extraordinarily cautious?

Duties of Landowners/Property Owners

A few states, including California, expect owners of property to exercise *reasonable care* to protect anyone who comes onto the property owned from injury. Most jurisdictions, however, adhere to a common law tradition that has maintained different classes of liability exposure for different classes of property incursions.

Duties to Trespassers

Under common law, anyone who enters a landowner's property without consent is a *trespasser*. With occasional exceptions, in a common law jurisdiction the property owner owes the trespasser no duty of care to warn of dangerous conditions unless the doctrine of attractive nuisance applies. Hence, a street person who falls into the property owner's septic tank that had been left open for cleaning has no viable claim for ruined clothes or any other injury, unless the condition that resulted in injury is deemed to be the result of *gross misconduct* on the part of the property owner. A property owner is also liable for intentionally injuring a trespasser.

The protection from liability to trespassers generally is voided if the trespassers do not have an adult capacity for reason and if they are attracted to something on the property that results in foreseeable exposure to risk of injury. So, if a toddler who wanders into your yard to get to your unfenced swimming pool falls into that pool and drowns, you are liable. Likewise, you are liable for injuries to kids who are attracted to your barn where a rope from a second floor loft provides thrilling rides down. The traditional label for man-made structures that provide this liability exposure is *attractive nuisance*.

Licensees and Business Invitees

Anyone who comes on your property with permission, including a social guest, is a *licensee* (and you, the property owner, are the licensor who licensed your guest to come onto your property). Licensees are entitled to warnings of **hidden** dangers (contamination in your swimming pool, inadequate supports for the upstairs deck where you are entertaining, etc.). A *business invitee* is entitled to even more protection from risks than licensees. A business invitee is anyone who is invited onto your place of business or home for business purposes. Landowners have an obligation to warn of dangerous conditions that they knew about, or should have known about. *Slip and fall* injury cases are frequent occurrences for retail businesses. If it can be argued that an injury occurred because the store was not diligent enough in discovering dangerous conditions (the slippery floors) and providing warnings, then the case will go to a jury. Historically, juries have been sympathetic to customers and so, if the case is not dismissed before trial, a handsome settlement for the plaintiff is quite possible.

In the following case the plaintiff was injured by an Act of God, i.e., lightning. The fact that the actual instrument that injured plaintiff was not in control of the defendant does not necessarily mean that the defendant is not liable if the harm was foreseeable and precautions could have been taken by the defendant to lower the probability of injury.

Spencer Van Maussner et al. v. *Atlantic City Country Club et al.*
Superior Court of New Jersey, Appellate Division
(299 N.J. Super. 535, 691 A.2d 826) (1997)

FACTS AND CASE BACKGROUND

At 7:30 A.M. on Sunday, March 28, 1993, plaintiff, a longstanding member of the Atlantic City Country Club, arrived at the Club with three friends who regularly played golf together. The sky was overcast with misty conditions. It was drizzling rain at 8:00 A.M. when the Club's starter directed the foursome to begin play. As the foursome played the first two holes, the drizzle turned into a downpour, which subsided when they began play on their third hole. After one of the players hit his approach shot on this hole, the group observed a lightning bolt. The players and their caddies decided to return to the clubhouse, about a half mile away at this point, to seek shelter.

There were no man-made shelters on the course and plaintiff put up his umbrella to avoid the rain as he headed for the clubhouse. While the group was en route to the clubhouse, there was a second lightning bolt that struck plaintiff. One of the foursome immediately went to the clubhouse for help while another remained with Mr. Maussner and provided CPR until the police and medics arrived. According to members of the foursome, the Club caddie master and the Club pro arrived at about the same time as the police. During this time, lightning continued to appear in the sky.

Plaintiff filed a complaint in the Superior Court of Camden County, New Jersey, seeking damages for the injuries sustained from the lightning strike. Defendants filed an answer to this complaint alleging that the Club and its owners were under no duty to protect plaintiff from a lightning strike and that plaintiff's injuries were the result of an act of God. Defendants moved for summary judgment dismissal of this suit asserting that plaintiff had not "met his burden of establishing that defendants created or maintained a dangerous condition on the golf course."

The trial court granted defendant's request for summary judgment. Maussner then appealed.

DISCUSSION AND OPINION: KLEINER, JUDGE, APPELLATE DIVISION

The issue raised is whether golf course operators owe a duty of care to their patrons to protect them from lightning strikes. Plaintiffs . . . appeal from the entry of an order granting summary judgment to defendants. In their appeal, plaintiffs contend that the trial court erred in summarily concluding that the owners and operators of a golf course owed no duty to golfers to protect them from lightning strikes. According to plaintiffs, a lightning strike on a golf course is a foreseeable risk that must be addressed by the owners of the course where various means of protection are feasible. Plaintiffs maintain that the dismissal of this case . . . denied them the opportunity to ascertain who bore the responsibility for failing to implement proper safety procedures at defendant's club.

Defendant's in this case indicated that they had a number of policies in place to protect their patrons including:

"Monitored the weather channel and was in constant communication with the weather station."

"Signs were posted at the Country Club instructing members of its evacuation plan and how to proceed if inclement weather struck during play . . ."

Club members were warned about the general risks of lightning by a notice from Don Siok, the Club golf pro, and a U.S.G.A. poster, which were both posted in the locker room. The notice from Siok advises golfers that:

WEATHER CONDITIONS SOMETIMES NECESSITATE OUR GOLF COURSE EVACUATION PLAN TO BE IMPLEMENTED. WHEN AUTHORIZED PERSONNEL ADVISE YOU TO COME IN OFF THE COURSE, IT IS IMPERATIVE THAT YOU DO SO. OUR WEATHER MONITORING SYSTEM . . . ADVISES US OF DANGEROUS ELEMENTS IN THE AREA AND GIVES US TIME TO CLEAR THE COURSE TO INSURE YOUR SAFE EVACUATION. THE U.S.G.A. RECOMMENDS YOU REACT IMMEDIATELY TO A DANGEROUS SITUATION AND TO SEEK SHELTER IF YOU FEEL DANGER FROM LIGHTNING OR STORM IS IMMINENT.

"As described by the Club, their evacuation plan, which entailed Club employees retrieving golfers on the course at the first notice of thunder or lightning . . . Defendants also maintained that golfers were encouraged

to retreat to nearby private homes in the event of a severe storm."

The Club also contended that it had " . . . consulted the National Weather Service on the morning of the incident and . . . there were no warnings that lightning was possible."

The Club did not possess any equipment for detecting lightning, had not installed any audible warning devices, nor had they erected any shelters on the course.

* * *

Plaintiff claimed and presented evidence that " . . . notices were not placed in the locker room until after he was struck by lightning . . . Plaintiff and his friends . . . denied any knowledge that they would be welcome at these [neighboring] homes."

Plaintiff " . . . opined that if the Club's evacuation plan worked as the Club stated that it did, the Club employees would have arrived earlier than they did." Plaintiff also stated that the Club "had no shelter anywhere on the course at the time of this incident other than the clubhouse . . . [and that] . . . other golf courses in the area have shelters along the course and siren or horn systems for warning golfers of a change in the weather."

* * *

Plaintiff offered the expert analysis of a golf course consultant (Berger) who concluded that the Club:

1. did not use available lightning detection equipment;
2. did not make proper use of various weather reporting services;
3. did not provide shelter at convenient spots throughout the course;
4. did not have an effective evacuation plan; and
5. did not adequately warn golfers of the hazards of lightning.

Berger concluded that "but for these failures, this incident and the serious injuries sustained by Spencer Van Maussner on March 28, 1993 were preventable."

*   *   *

The question of how far a golf course's obligation towards its patrons should extend has been addressed by one commentator [Professor Flynn] who argues that the liability of golf courses should be assessed in light of the U.S.G.A. guidelines. As pointed out by Professor Flynn, The major governing bodies of golf throughout the world proscribe the following rule: "As there have been many deaths and injuries from lightning on golf courses, all clubs and sponsors of golf course competitions are urged to take every precaution for the protection of persons against lightning."

Professor Flynn suggests that reasonable care requires golf course operators to place conspicuous signs warning golfers of the dangers of lightning and indicating the proper response to a lightning storm. Also, . . . a golf course operator should use 'a siren and golf course marshals or other personnel to warn golfers of approaching lightning and to usher golfers to safety.' Flynn states that 'most golf courses have voluntarily adopted these precautionary steps or have involuntarily adopted these . . . steps at the urging of the golf course insurer.' [Flynn] states that 'golf courses that choose to provide weather shelters should construct lightning-proof weather shelters.' . . . Flynn concludes his analysis of 'reasonable care' by suggesting that high-tech automatic lightning protection systems may be required as a way to discharge a golf course's duty to its patrons but notes that such devices vary in cost and in their reliability.

*   *   *

Although a foreseeable risk is the indispensable cornerstone of any formulation of a duty of care, not all foreseeable risks give rise to duties . . . Traditionally, premises liability has been governed by the common law distinctions between trespassers, licensees, and invitees. The property owner was deemed to owe a different duty of care to a person on his or her land depending upon the category into which that person fit. Under this common law analysis, an 'owner or possessor of property owes a higher degree of care to the business invitee because that person has been invited on the premises for purposes of the owner that often are commercial or business related' . . . To such an invitee, a landowner owed a 'duty of reasonable care to guard against any dangerous conditions on his or her property that the owner either knows about or should have discovered.'

*   *   *

Traditionally, an act of God is the cause of an accident if it is a purely natural force that 'could not have been prevented by any amount of foresight and pains and care reasonably to be expected of [a defendant].'

Under New Jersey law, a plaintiff can recover from a defendant even where the defendant's negligence coincides with an act of God . . . '[A] defendant is not relieved from liability where there is proof of his negligence, combined with some independent or foreseeable intervening cause which occasions the harm.' . . . "We have held it to be long-settled that 'when there has been a finding of wrongdoing which is an efficient and cooperative cause of the mishap, the wrongdoer is not relieved from liability by proof that an act of God was a concurring cause." . . . The act of God defense, in and of itself, does not exculpate defendant. Further analysis requires that we examine 'basic fairness under all of the circumstances in light of considerations of public policy.'

CONCLUSIONS

1. We find that when a golf course has taken steps to protect golfers from lightning strikes, it owes the golfers a duty of reasonable care to implement its safety precautions properly . . .

2. Our holding has the following consequences. All golf courses have a duty to post a sign that details what, if any safety procedures are being utilized by the golf course to protect its patrons from lightning. If a particular golf course uses no safety precautions, its sign must inform golfers that they play at their own risk and that no safety procedures are being utilized to protect golfers from lightning strikes. If, however, a golf course chooses to utilize a particular safety feature, it owes a duty of reasonable care to its patrons to utilize it correctly . . . If a golf course has an evacuation plan, the . . . plan must be posted; if a golf course uses a siren or horn system, the golfers must be able to hear it and must know what the signals mean; and if the golf course uses a weather forecasting system, it must use one that is reasonable under the circumstances.

*   *   *

This matter is reversed and remanded for proceedings not inconsistent with this opinion. [The court remanded the case back to the trial court to determine if the defendant was liable for the plaintiff's injuries using the criteria discussed in the opinion.]

QUESTIONS FOR ANALYSIS

1. What kind of "industry standards" for golf courses would be relevant to the question of the duty of care the

country club owed the plaintiff in this case? Would the country club have been better off to have a policy of offering no protection from lightning to its patrons? Explain why or why not.

2. How does the existence of U.S.G.A. recommendations complicate your answer to this question? Is a lightning strike of a particular golfer foreseeable? Are lightning strikes on golf courses foreseeable?

3. Does the foreseeability of lightning strikes as you've described it have implications for the policies golf course operators should follow on lightning protection?

4. If a golfer who was warned not to be on a golf course is struck by lightning while playing in spite of the warning and order to leave, would the golf course have liability?

5. Under common law, what class of "visitor" to golf course property would this person be? What duty of care is owed to this class of person?

Duties of Professionals

A significant concern to professional service providers, including doctors, lawyers, engineers, and accountants is the standard of care that they are expected to meet in their delivery of services to their customers. A member of a learned profession is held responsible for meeting the standards of the profession in the delivery of services. Malpractice cases are negligence cases in which it is contended that such standards have not been met, breaching the practitioner's duty of care to an injured party. If a professional holds herself out as a specialist within a profession, then she will be held to the standards of specialists within the field. In this regard, a brain surgeon is held to a higher standard of care and treatment for head injuries than that expected of a general practitioner in medicine.

Negligence Per Se

In some classes of negligence torts, statutes serve to establish standards of conduct/action so that no court determination of what a reasonable person would do is required to establish liability. When a state or the federal government sets a safety rule (statutory or regulatory) and a defendant violates the rule, there is no issue as to whether the defendant acted reasonably—clearly she did not. If Mary is driving 65 in a 55 MPH zone and an accident occurs, Mary is liable *per se* because she broke a safety law that is the proximate cause of the plaintiff's injuries.

Res ipsa Loquitur

In the lengthy list of torts discussed above, there is a presumption of innocence on the part of the defendant unless and until the plaintiff can prove (by a preponderance of the evidence) the elements of liability. However, some injurious wrongs may be viewed as so obvious that it becomes the duty of a defendant to disprove what appears to be obvious. The Latin phrase above, *res ipsa loquitur*, is literally translated as "the thing speaks for itself." Res ipsa loquitur is applicable when the instrumentality causing the injuries was totally in control of the defendant and those injuries would not normally have taken place, but for negligence on the part of the defendant. If the doctrine applies, the burden of proof shifts to the defendant and the case will normally go to a jury.

In some cases, mistakes by professionals are obvious as when doctors amputate the wrong limb or attorneys miss important deadlines that prejudice their clients' cases. If Sally, with serious circulatory problems in her left leg, goes into a hospital to have that leg amputated, only to wake up post-operatively to discover that the surgeon has removed her right leg, it can be presumed that there was negligence on the part of the surgeon (and perhaps other members of the "service" provider). Clearly, with Sally asleep from anesthesia, the surgeon **had control** of the situation that resulted in injury and it is apparent that the injury would not normally have occurred **but for negligence.** Torts that reflect this combination of elements require defendants to disprove their negligence.

Defending Liability in Negligence Suits

As plaintiffs seek to establish liability in tort cases by proving that the elements of the tort claims are facts, defendants just as vigorously defend themselves against the determination that they are liable. There are a number of specific forms of defense that are important in tort claims. Included in our discussion below are superseding or intervening cause, assumption of risk, contributory negligence, comparative negligence, and Good Samaritan protections.

Superseding or Intervening Cause

Even when a wrongful action with potential to harm another has occurred, the chain of causation between wrongful act and liability for injury can be broken by an *intervening* event or condition. Derrick, driving without keeping a close lookout, hits a pedestrian in a crosswalk, knocking the pedestrian against a guardrail at the edge of the road. Unfortunately, a storm has just downed a power line a short distance away, charging the guardrail with current. The pedestrian is killed by the electric charge.

In this situation, Derrick would be liable for any injuries suffered as the direct result of his car's impact with the pedestrian, but would not be responsible for the death from electrocution. The deadly electrical charge was an unforeseeable **intervening** event that **superseded** the car's impact as the cause of the **wrongful death.**

Assumption of Risk

Anyone who *voluntarily* enters into an activity or situation that is foreseeably risky, then suffers injury of the type that might be anticipated, can be banned from any recovery for injury by an **assumption of risk** defense. So, a plaintiff who sues a downhill skiing facility for her broken leg is likely to run into an assumption of risk defense. Skiing is known to be risky and skiers voluntarily assume this risk by paying money and ascending the slopes. It should be noted that this defense does not apply if artificial conditions such as manmade structures on a slope create conditions that are unusually hazardous—conditions that the skier (customer) could not reasonably foresee, but which the facility operator knew or should have known existed. In high-risk sports it is prudent for the operator of the facility to have customers sign forms that acknowledge awareness of the risk and that these risks are voluntarily assumed by the customers. Be wary, though, that a signature acknowledging risk assumption does not prevent liability for a hazardous condition that the customer would not have reason to know about!

Contributory Negligence

Under traditional common law, *contributory negligence* by the plaintiff is an affirmative defense against a claim of *negligence* by the defendant, with certain specific exceptions. If a plaintiff's own negligence *contributed* to his or her injury, that plaintiff is barred from establishing liability on the part of the defendant. The standards used regarding whether the plaintiff was contributorily negligent are the same as that applied to evaluate whether the defendant was negligent, the reasonable person standard.

The contributory negligence defense standard results in harsh consequences for injured parties because there is no mechanism for allocating blame on a percentage basis. As long as the defendant can show that the plaintiff's negligence contributed in any way to her injuries, the plaintiff is barred from any recovery even though most of the fault for the accident lies with the defendant. The harshness of the contributory negligence doctrine has caused all but five states to abandon it in favor of comparative negligence.

Comparative Negligence

Most states have switched from a contributory negligence to a comparative negligence standard, with damages in the simplest case allocated in proportion to the responsibility (fault) of the parties for the injuries sustained. Hence, in the situation above where a court had determined that a fair value for compensation of an injured pedestrian's injuries was $300,000, if the plaintiff pedestrian was found to be one third (33 percent) responsible for the accident and injury, and the defendant two thirds (67 percent) responsible, the court would award $200,000 (two thirds of the $300,000) to the plaintiff with the defendant liable for that sum.

Often this standard is modified, with a partial comparative negligence scale imposed that is likely to include a fault threshold for establishing liability. The threshold might involve a **50 percent rule.** With a 50 percent rule, damages are awarded on a simple comparative negligence basis as long as the plaintiff is less than 50 percent at fault. However, if the plaintiff's "contributory" share of responsibility is 50 percent or more, the defendant is held free of liability for any injury suffered by the plaintiff.

Good Samaritan Statutes

Willard is at a baseball game when he has a heart attack. A doctor attending the game runs to his car for his medical bag and goes to Willard's aid, before any rescue vehicle can arrive. In spite of the rescuing doctor's effort to resuscitate Willard, and those of the rescue squad, things go badly for Willard and he dies. Willard's wife sues the doctor, claiming mistakes in the emergency care he provided (i.e., negligence). The threat of lawsuit provides a strong incentive to not provide such aid. Recognizing this problem, most states have adopted *Good Samaritan* statutes. According to these statutes, if someone **aids** another in need, the injured party is barred from a claim of negligence (but not reckless behavior) against the rescuer.

STRICT LIABILITY

Intentional torts and torts attributable to negligence each involve actions where the defendant is **at fault** for the conduct which caused the injury. In the former case, the fault is motivated by a desire to harm while, in the latter case, fault is attributable to carelessness. There is another category of torts, called *strict liability,* for which liability for injury is imposed for a reason or reasons other than fault—even when a high degree of care to avoid injuries is exerted.

Strict liability is associated with activities that are inherently risky to the public (others) even when reasonable care is taken. The law considers it fair and just that there be compensation for injuries when the defendant chooses to engage in such activities. For example, putting on fireworks displays, using explosives for earth excavation or demolition, crop-dusting, storing hazardous wastes, harboring wild animals, and other abnormally dangerous activities bring exposure to strict liability.

The most prominent application of strict liability occurs in connection with product liability—the liability borne by sellers when they sell defective products to the public. That topic is discussed in detail in Chapter 7.

SUMMARY

- *A tort* is a *wrong*. It can be a spoken or written wrong, an act (action), or a nonaction (carelessness) that is wrong, with *injury* inflicted on a person or property.
- Damages are awarded in the form of nominal, compensatory, or punitive. Torts are commonly classified as (1) intentional, (2) unintentional, or (3) strict liability torts, depending on the intentions of the defendant. For an intentional tort claim to have merit before a court, it must be true that: the defendant knew what he (she) was doing and knew or should have known the possible consequences of the action taken.
- Intentional infliction of emotional distress, is conduct so extreme and outrageous that it results in severe emotional distress to another person.
- Tort law protects against a number of forms of invasion of privacy including: (1) commercial use of someone's name or likeness without permission, (2) intrusion into a person's solitude by illegally searching their premises or belongings, by bugging or wire-tapping their residence, by the unauthorized intrusion into their financial records, etc., (3) by the public revelation of information that places a person in a false light, such as by attributing to a person ideas not held or actions not taken by that person, (4) by the public revelation of facts about a person that a reasonable person would find repugnant.
- An essential element of a defamation claim is the *publication* of the false statement(s) to a *third party*. The law provides a remedy against persons who make false and defamatory statements of fact about others. Violating this required standard of conduct orally is the tort of *slander* while breaching this duty in writing is *libel.*
- Defenses to defamation suits are the truth, absolute privilege, qualified privilege, and some public figure claims.
- *Fraudulent misrepresentation* (or just *fraud*) involves intent, as it is the deliberate misrepresentation of *facts* in order to gain an advantage.
- Generally, to establish damages for fraudulent misrepresentation, the following elements are required: (1) a misrepresentation of facts material to the issue at hand, (2) with knowledge that the "facts" presented are false or with "reckless disregard for the truth," (3) intent to induce reliance on the misrepresented facts, (4) a reasonable reliance on the misrepresented facts on the part of the injured party, and (5) actual damages that occur as a result of reliance on the misrepresentation.
- *Conversion* is the taking and/or using of someone else's personal property without permission and without justification.
- *Trespass* occurs when, without consent, an individual goes onto another's property (land) or interferes with the rights of the owner of personal property to the exclusive possession, use and

enjoyment of that property. In the eyes of the law, land and improvements to land (such as buildings) are *real property* while all other items owned (money, cars, furniture, etc.) are *personal property*.

- With negligence, an individual or business engages in actions or conduct that is not intended to harm another but which, unfortunately, does. Quite often, the lack of intent does not free the negligent party of responsibility (liability) for the harm caused.

- Liability for injury/damage suffered through negligence arises when the following four elements exist: (1) The defendant owes a *duty of care* to the plaintiff, (2) the defendant *breaches* that duty of care by negligence, (3) the plaintiff suffers *measurable damage,* (4) The defendant's negligence is the *proximate cause* of the injury.

- Anyone who comes on your property with permission, including a social guest, is a *licensee* (and you, the property owner, are the licensor who licensed your guest to come onto your property). Licensees are entitled to warnings of **hidden** dangers (contamination in your swimming pool, inadequate supports for the upstairs deck where you are entertaining, etc.).

- A member of a learned profession is held responsible for meeting the standards of the profession in the delivery of services. Malpractice cases are negligence cases in which it is contended that such standards have not been met, breaching the practitioner's duty of care to an injured party.

- In some classes of negligence torts, statutes serve to establish standards of conduct/action so that no court determination of what a reasonable person would do is required to establish liability. This is called negligence per se.

- Res ipsa loquitur is applicable when the instrumentality causing the injuries was totally in control of the defendant and those injuries would not normally have taken place, but for negligence on the part of the defendant. If the doctrine applies, the burden of proof shifts to the defendant and the case will normally go to a jury.

- Defenses to negligence suits include superseding or intervening cause, assumption of risk, contributory negligence, comparative negligence, and Good Samaritan protections.

- *Strict liability* is a category of torts. It is when liability for injury is imposed for a reason or reasons other than fault—even when a high degree of care to avoid injuries is exerted.

6

CYBERTORTS, PRIVACY, AND GOVERNMENT REGULATION

Chapter 5 provided coverage of basic tort law and an array of mostly "traditional" applications of tort law. As we saw, tort law casts a broad shadow, encompassing a wide variety of personal harms. In fact, torts cover a territory so wide that it is difficult to write a brief and concise description of exactly what tort law is. Generally, however, we've seen that torts involve an unwelcome intrusion on some protected personal right—the right to privacy of person and/or property, the right to personal safety, the right to expect a reasonable standard of care from professionals, the right to a safe and nonhostile work environment, the right to sanctity of contracts, etc. In addition, for tort liability such intrusions must result in some injury, which can be physical, psychological, or economic.

The recent explosive growth of electronic interconnectedness and E-commerce have doubtless created a large volume of new potential tort exposures. With increasing dependence on electronic links for the conduct of communications and business transactions, the impact of even a brief server shutdown can be very substantial. Injury (economic or otherwise) invites litigation, with new applications of tort law to be expected. Commerce, even down to decision making, is now heavily dependent on software. If software fails

to live up to the users' expectations, there may be injury and, hence, a desire for tort injury recovery (this topic is discussed in more detail in Chapter 7). Also, our new technologies have created new and novel methods of storing and communicating important information, simultaneously creating opportunities for new ways of intruding on the privacy of such information—hence, on the rights of individuals—an invitation for tort claims.

From basic and traditional tort law we know that businesses have broad concerns for tort liability for defamation, both written and oral. This chapter begins with an extension of our knowledge regarding defamation in a wired world, then continues with an array of new and novel applications of privacy law, necessitated by modern, cyberworld developments.

DEFAMATION AND THE INTERNET

By way of review, defamation requires a showing by the plaintiff that the defendant (1) made untrue statements that (2) were published or reproduced in some way and (3) harmed the reputation of the plaintiff. If the plaintiff is a public figure and the defendant is the

149

media, the plaintiff must also show that the defendant knew the statements made were false or else had a reckless disregard for the truth. Traditionally, publishers have been held liable for the defamatory writings of authors they publish, but bookstores have not been held liable for selling books that are defamatory.

Computer-based electronic communication (particularly e-mail) has become an integral component of communication and information transmission throughout the world. This is a form of communication that allows the cheap and efficient transport of information to any site in the world, with information transmitted to another individual, another individual company, or to a "mass" audience. Some transmissions are sent from computers owned and operated by the sender, and some are sent from company-owned computers by a company employee. There has been considerable concern regarding liability exposure for what is sent electronically, with companies (that own computers) and internet service providers (ISPs) rightly concerned that they can be the target for lawsuits in the event of transmission of defamatory statements—e.g., a single defamatory message could result in a tort suit against an employer.

As reviewed in basic torts and as reflected in the Restatement (Second) of Torts, ". . . one who repeats or otherwise republishes defamatory matter *is subject to liability as if he had originally published it.*" [emphasis added]. Hence, when defamatory material is duplicated, there is a potential for newspapers, journals, and magazines to face tort liability for printed information. Since such information producers have the opportunity to know the content of the material being published, they have a duty to avoid the publication of defamatory information and are subject to the same liability as the original authors of that information. On the other hand, liability has typically not been imposed on distributors of written documents such as newsstands, bookstores, and like sales outlets, libraries, etc. Distributors are clearly distinct from publishers and if their duty to know the content of what they are distributing were to approach the duty of publishers to know the content of what they are publishing, it would severely reduce freedom of expression.

Liability of Bookstores versus Publishers

In *Smith* v. *California* the U.S. Supreme Court considered the case of a bookstore that was convicted of violating a Los Angeles city ordinance that outlawed possession of obscene writings or books.[1] Note that this 1959 case does not deal with defamation but, instead, with the issue of whether a bookstore is subject to the same liabilities as a publisher for carrying defamatory materials or whether a distinction between the two is made.

In the *Smith* case, the book in issue was one of many thousands available for sale in this bookstore and no evidence indicated that the bookstore owner or other personnel had reviewed the book. Upon consideration of the strict liability ordinance at issue, the Supreme Court reasoned that ". . . by dispensing with any requirement of knowledge of the contents of the book on the part of the seller, the ordinance tends to impose a severe limitation on the public's access to constitutionally protected matter." Since it is unreasonable to expect a bookstore owner/operator to review and be familiar with everything a bookstore sells, the ordinance would impede the sales of all books, both obscene and not obscene.

Based on the First Amendment, the Supreme Court overturned the conviction of the bookstore in *Smith* that was carrying obscene materials and, through its opinion, endorsed the application of a clear distinction between publishers and distributors in determining defamation liability. Based on this distinction, *distributors* of written works that contain defamatory content are shielded from liability unless they know or should have known (have reason to know) the injurious nature of the content of the work(s) they have sold. Courts have continued to rely on this distinction as they have been confronted with defamation claims stemming from Internet messaging.

In marked contrast to the decision rendered in the case "*Cubby, Inc.* v. *Compuserve, Inc.,*" in *Stratton Oakmont, Inc.* v. *Prodigy Service,* the same service, an ISP, **was** held liable for defamatory materials that appeared on a bulletin board it sponsored. In an effort to distinguish itself from other ISPs, Prodigy marketed itself as a family-oriented ISP. As a result of the *Stratton* case, the apparent consequences of supervising the content of what appears on its server is that an ISP **is liable** for defamatory material that appears on bulletin boards it purports to supervise.

In the aftermath of *Stratton,* there appeared to be serious liability consequences associated with an ISP supervising the content of what appeared on the server. Many organizations, including most universities, now

---

[1]*Smith* v. *State of California,* 361 U.S. 147 (1959).

Cubby, Inc. v. *Compuserve, Inc.*
United States District Court, S.D. New York
776 F.Supp. 135 (S.D. NY 1991)

FACTS AND CASE BACKGROUND

CompuServe develops and provides computer-related products and services, including CompuServe Information Service ("CIS"), an online general information service or "electronic library" that subscribers may access from a personal computer or terminal. Subscribers to CIS pay a membership fee and online time usage fees, in return for which they have access to the thousands of information sources available on CIS. Subscribers may also obtain access to over 150 special interest "forums," which are comprised of electronic bulletin boards, interactive online conferences, and topical databases.

One forum available is the Journalism Forum, which focuses on the journalism industry. Cameron Communications, Inc. ("CCI"), which is independent of CompuServe, has contracted to "manage, review, create, delete, edit and otherwise control the contents" of the Journalism Forum "in accordance with editorial and technical standards and conventions of style as established by CompuServe."

One publication available as part of the Journalism Forum is *Rumorville USA* ("*Rumorville*"), a daily newsletter that provides reports about broadcast journalism and journalists. *Rumorville* is published by Don Fitzpatrick Associates of San Francisco ("DFA"), which is headed by defendant Don Fitzpatrick. CompuServe has no employment, contractual, or other direct relationship with either DFA or Fitzpatrick; DFA provides *Rumorville* to the Journalism Forum under a contract with CCI. The contract between CCI and DFA provides that DFA "accepts total responsibility for the contents" of *Rumorville*. The contract also requires CCI to limit access to *Rumorville* to those CIS subscribers who have previously made membership arrangements directly with DFA.

CompuServe has no opportunity to review *Rumorville's* contents before DFA uploads it into CompuServe's computer banks, from which it is immediately available to approved CIS subscribers. CompuServe receives no part of any fees that DFA charges for access to *Rumorville*, nor does CompuServe compensate DFA for providing *Rumorville* to the Journalism Forum; the compensation CompuServe receives for making *Rumorville* available to its subscribers is the standard online time usage and membership fees charged to all CIS subscribers, regardless of the information services they use. CompuServe maintains that, before this action was filed, it had no notice of any complaints about the contents of the *Rumorville* publication or about DFA.

OPINION: LEISURE, DISTRICT JUDGE

A. THE APPLICABLE STANDARD OF LIABILITY

Plaintiffs base their libel claim on the allegedly defamatory statements contained in the *Rumorville* publication that CompuServe carried as part of the Journalism Forum. CompuServe argues that, based on the undisputed facts, it was a distributor of *Rumorville*, as opposed to a publisher of the *Rumorville* statements. CompuServe further contends that, as a distributor of *Rumorville*, it cannot be held liable on the libel claim because it neither knew nor had reason to know of the allegedly defamatory statements. Plaintiffs, on the other hand, argue that the Court should conclude that CompuServe is a publisher of the statements and hold it to a higher standard of liability.

Ordinarily, "'one who repeats or otherwise republishes defamatory matter is subject to liability as if he had originally published it.'" . . . With respect to entities such as news vendors, bookstores, and libraries, however, "New York courts have long held that vendors and distributors of defamatory publications are not liable if they neither know nor have reason to know of the defamation." . . .

The requirement that a distributor must have knowledge of the contents of a publication before liability can be imposed for distributing that publication is deeply rooted in the First Amendment, made applicable to the states through the Fourteenth Amendment. "[T]he constitutional guarantees of the freedom of speech and of the press stand in the way of imposing" strict liability on distributors for the contents of the reading materials they carry. In *Smith*, the Court struck down an ordinance that imposed liability on a bookseller for possession of an obscene book, regardless of whether the bookseller had knowledge of the book's contents. The Court reasoned that

"Every bookseller would be placed under an obligation to make himself aware of the contents of every book in his shop. It would be altogether unreasonable to demand so near an approach to omniscience." And the bookseller's burden would become the public's burden, for by restricting him the public's access to reading matter would be restricted. If the contents of bookshops and periodical stands were restricted to material of which their proprietors had made an inspection, they might be depleted indeed.

* * *

With respect to the *Rumorville* publication, the undisputed facts are that DFA uploads the text of *Rumorville* into CompuServe's data banks and makes it available to approved CIS subscribers instantaneously. [Footnotes deleted] CompuServe has no more editorial control over such a publication than does a public library, bookstore, or newsstand, and it would be no more feasible for CompuServe to examine every publication it carries for potentially

defamatory statements than it would be for any other distributor to do so.

* * *

Technology is rapidly transforming the information industry. A computerized database is the functional equivalent of a more traditional news vendor, and the inconsistent application of a lower standard of liability to an electronic news distributor such as CompuServe than that which is applied to a public library, bookstore, or newsstand would impose an undue burden on the free flow of information. Given the relevant First Amendment considerations, the appropriate standard of liability to be applied to CompuServe is whether it knew or had reason to know of the allegedly defamatory *Rumorville* statements.

* * *

For the reasons stated above, CompuServe's motion for summary judgment to is granted on all claims asserted against it.

QUESTIONS FOR ANALYSIS

1. What is the standard of liability for libel? What three things must the plaintiff show in order to recover?

2. What is the difference in liability for libel among authors, publishers, and distributors? In this case is the court saying that it pays for an ISP to be deliberately ignorant of what is taking place in its chat rooms and forums?

Stratton Oakmont, Inc. v. *Prodigy Services Company*
Supreme Court, Nassau County, New York
1995 WL 323710 (1995)

CASE BACKGROUND AND FACTS

As in the previous case, the defendant, PRODIGY, maintains an electronic bulletin board called "Money Talks." PRODIGY also advertises that it is a family-oriented ISP and reserves the rights to remove objectionable material from its operations, including electronic bulletin boards. The plaintiff claims that he was libeled in "Money Talks" and that PRODIGY is also liable as distributor of defamatory material.

OPINION: STUART L. AIN, JUSTICE

Plaintiffs commenced this action against PRODIGY, the owner and operator of the computer network on which the statements appeared, and

the unidentified party who posted the aforementioned statements. The second amended complaint alleges ten (10) causes of action, including claims for *per se* libel. On this motion, "in order to materially advance the outcome of this litigation" (Zamansky affidavit, par. 4), plaintiffs seek partial summary judgment on two issues, namely:

1. whether PRODIGY may be considered a "publisher" of the aforementioned statements; and,

2. whether Epstein, the Board Leader for the computer bulletin board on which the statements were posted, acted with actual and apparent authority as PRODIGY's

"agent" for the purposes of the claims in this action.

By way of background, it is undisputed that PRODIGY's computer network has at least two million subscribers who communicate with each other and with the general subscriber population on PRODIGY's bulletin boards. "Money Talks," the board on which the aforementioned statements appeared, is allegedly the leading and most widely read financial computer bulletin board in the United States, where members can post statements regarding stocks, investments and other financial matters. PRODIGY contracts with bulletin Board Leaders, who, among other things, participate in board discussions and undertake promotional efforts to encourage usage and increase users. The Board Leader for "Money Talks" at the time the alleged libelous statements were posted was Charles Epstein.

PRODIGY commenced operations in 1990. Plaintiffs base their claim that PRODIGY is a publisher in large measure on PRODIGY's stated policy, starting in 1990, that it was a family-oriented computer network. In various national newspaper articles written by Geoffrey Moore, PRODIGY's Director of Market Programs and Communications, PRODIGY held itself out as an online service that exercised editorial control over the content of messages posted on its computer bulletin boards, thereby expressly differentiating itself from its competition and expressly likening itself to a newspaper. [References deleted]

In one article PRODIGY stated:

"We make no apology for pursuing a value system that reflects the culture of the millions of American families we aspire to serve. Certainly no responsible newspaper does less when it chooses the type of advertising it publishes, the letters it prints, the degree of nudity and unsupported gossip its editors tolerate."

* * *

Let it be clear that this Court is in full agreement with Cubby . . . Computer bulletin boards should generally be regarded in the same context as bookstores, libraries and network affiliates. [Reference deleted] It is PRODIGY's own policies, technology and staffing decisions which have altered the scenario and mandated the finding that it is a publisher.

PRODIGY's conscious choice, to gain the benefits of editorial control, has opened it up to a greater liability than CompuServe and other computer networks that make no such choice. For the record, the fear that this Court's finding of publisher status for PRODIGY will compel all computer networks to abdicate control of their bulletin boards incorrectly presumes that the market will refuse to compensate a network for its increased control and the resulting increased exposure. Presumably PRODIGY's decision to regulate the content of its bulletin boards was in part influenced by its desire to attract a market it perceived to exist consisting of users seeking a "family-oriented" computer service. This decision simply required that to the extent computer networks provide such services, they must also accept the concomitant legal consequences. In addition, the Court also notes that the issues addressed herein may ultimately be preempted by federal law if the Communications Decency Act of 1995, several versions of which are pending in Congress, is enacted. [Reference Deleted]

* * *

The aforementioned testimony by PRODIGY employees and documentation generated by PRODIGY, together with the Guidelines themselves, cannot be disputed by PRODIGY and leave no doubt that at least for the limited purpose of monitoring and editing the "Money Talks" computer bulletin Board, PRODIGY directed and controlled Epstein's actions. In reaching this conclusion the Court has taken care not to rely on any testimony by Epstein, inasmuch as it is the conduct of the principal which must create the impression of authority, not the conduct of the agent. [Reference deleted] Based on the foregoing, the Court holds that Epstein acted as PRODIGY's agent for the purposes of the acts and omissions alleged in the complaint.

QUESTIONS FOR ANALYSIS

1. What novel issues on defamation claims were brought before the courts by the emergence of the Internet as a high volume communications medium?
2. Describe, prior to the trial of this case, how effective you believe existing case law was as a guide to court decisions in Internet defamation cases?
3. Exactly why was the decision in *Cubby* so different from the decision in *Stratton Oakmont?*

make it clear that they **do not supervise** the content of what appears on web space they provide for faculty and staff. At the bottom of this text's authors' web pages is the following legend supplied by North Carolina State University: *"The material on this page is not endorsed, sponsored, provided, on or behalf of North Carolina State University."* This legend is NC State's attempt to deflect liability for defamation by faculty and staff following the *Stratton* case.

When powerful interests are exposed to unforeseen legal liability, Congress often comes to the rescue. In no small way, the chink in the armor of Internet service providers exposed by the *Stratton* decision sped the creation of provisions in the **Communications Decency Act of 1996** aimed at undoing the chilling effect on editorial control of that decision. Of course, the focus of the CDA was also to reduce the exposure of children to adult and raunchy material on the Internet, which is precisely what the ISP in *Stratton* was trying to do.

The Communications Decency Act of 1996 (CDA)

With a clear intent of protecting ISPs from liability exposure as the reward for trying to police content, Congress penned Section 230 (C) of the CDA which provides that no ". . . provider or user of an interactive computer service shall be treated as the publisher or speaker of any information provided by another information content provider." In this provision, Congress rejected the notion of classifying ISPs as publishers in the event of defamation claims. In support of the desirability of ISPs exercising a degree of editorial control without that effort opening the door to liability exposure, Congress strictly limited the liability for defamatory material of ISPs if they had policies and practices aimed at restricting the Internet publication of materials the ISP viewed as obscene, lewd, lascivious, filthy, excessively violent, harassing, or otherwise objectionable, whether or not such material is constitutionally protected.

If the *Stratton* precedent was to hold sway in subsequent court decisions, Congress clearly feared that the disincentives for ISP policing of content would aid and abet the spread of objectionable Internet content. Congress explicitly indicated that one of the objectives of the CDA was to overrule the *Stratton* decision and any other similar decisions that treated ISPs as publishers or speakers of content that was not their own. Congress also explicitly preempted inconsistent state laws, in effect reestablishing *Cubby* as the prevailing doctrine, allowing ISPs to exercise a degree of broad editorial control without being subject to a publisher's strict liability. As a result of the CDA, an ISP will not be legally punished by being subjected to possible defamation suits if the ISP tries to clean up content on its server. The following case is illustrative of that principle.

Kenneth M. Zeran v. America Online, Inc.
United States Court of Appeals for the Fourth Circuit
129 F.3d 327 (1997)

FACTS AND CASE BACKGROUND

In this case, an unidentified person posted a message on an AOL bulletin board advertising "Naughty Oklahoma T-Shirts." The posting described the sale of shirts featuring offensive and tasteless slogans related to the April 19, 1995, bombing of the Alfred P. Murrah Federal Building in Oklahoma City. Those interested in purchasing the shirts were instructed to call "Ken" at Zeran's home phone number in Seattle, Washington. As a result of this anonymously perpetrated prank, Zeran received a high volume of calls, comprised primarily of angry and derogatory messages, but also including death threats. Zeran could not change his phone number because he relied on its availability to the public in running

his business out of his home. Later that day, Zeran called AOL and informed a company representative of his predicament. The employee assured Zeran that the posting would be removed from AOL's bulletin board but explained that as a matter of policy AOL would not post a retraction. The parties dispute the date that AOL removed this original posting from its bulletin board.

Over the next four days, an unidentified party continued to post messages on AOL's bulletin board, advertising additional items including bumper stickers and key chains with still more offensive slogans. During this time period, Zeran called AOL repeatedly and was told by company representatives that the individual account from which the

messages were posted would soon be closed. Zeran also reported his case to Seattle FBI agents. By April 30, Zeran was receiving an abusive phone call approximately every two minutes.

Zeran first filed suit on January 4, 1996, against radio station KRXO in the United States District Court for the Western District of Oklahoma. On April 23, 1996, he filed this separate suit against AOL in the same court. Zeran did not bring any action against the party who posted the offensive messages. After Zeran's suit against AOL was transferred to the Eastern District of Virginia, AOL answered Zeran's complaint and interposed 47 U.S.C. § 230 as an affirmative defense. AOL then moved for judgment on the pleadings pursuant to Federal Rules of Civil Procedure. The district court granted AOL's motion, and Zeran filed this appeal.

OPINION: WILKINSON, CHIEF JUDGE

I.

"The Internet is an international network of interconnected computers," currently used by approximately 40 million people worldwide. One of the many means by which individuals access the Internet is through an interactive computer service. These services offer not only a connection to the Internet as a whole, but also allow their subscribers to access information communicated and stored only on each computer service's individual proprietary network. AOL is just such an interactive computer service. Much of the information transmitted over its network originates with the company's millions of subscribers. They may transmit information privately via electronic mail, or they may communicate publicly by posting messages on AOL bulletin boards, where the messages may be read by any AOL subscriber.

II. A.

Because § 230 was successfully advanced by AOL in the district court as a defense to Zeran's claims, we shall briefly examine its operation here. Zeran seeks to hold AOL liable for defamatory speech initiated by a third party. He argued to the district court that once he notified AOL of the unidentified third party's hoax, AOL had a duty to remove the defamatory posting promptly, to notify its subscribers of the message's false nature, and to effectively screen future defamatory material. Section 230 entered this litigation as an affirmative defense pled by AOL.

The company claimed that Congress immunized interactive computer service providers from claims based on information posted by a third party.

The relevant portion of § 230 states: "No provider or user of an interactive computer service shall be treated as the publisher or speaker of any information provided by another information content provider." . . . By its plain language, § 230 creates a federal immunity to any cause of action that would make service providers liable for information originating with a third-party user of the service. Specifically, § 230 precludes courts from entertaining claims that would place a computer service provider in a publisher's role. Thus, lawsuits seeking to hold a service provider liable for its exercise of a publisher's traditional editorial functions—such as deciding whether to publish, withdraw, postpone or alter content—are barred.

The purpose of this statutory immunity is not difficult to discern. Congress recognized the threat that tort-based lawsuits pose to freedom of speech in the new and burgeoning Internet medium. The imposition of tort liability on service providers for the communications of others represented, for Congress, simply another form of intrusive government regulation of speech. Section 230 was enacted, in part, to maintain the robust nature of Internet communication and, accordingly, to keep government interference in the medium to a minimum. In specific statutory findings, Congress recognized the Internet and interactive computer services as offering "a forum for a true diversity of political discourse, unique opportunities for cultural development, and myriad avenues for intellectual

activity." It also found that the Internet and interactive computer services "have flourished, to the benefit of all Americans, *with a minimum of government regulation.*" Congress further stated that it is "the policy of the United States . . . to preserve the vibrant and competitive free market that presently exists for the Internet and other interactive computer services, unfettered by Federal or State regulation."

* * *

Section 230 . . . plainly immunizes computer service providers like AOL from liability for information that originates with third parties. Furthermore, Congress clearly expressed its intent that § 230 apply to lawsuits, like Zeran's, instituted after the CDA's enactment. Accordingly, we affirm the judgment of the district court.

QUESTIONS FOR ANALYSIS

1. Based on the Zeran case, what is the basis for liability for an ISP?
2. Does it now appear that an ISP is a "publisher" or a "distributor"?
3. What impact does the Zeran case have on courts' reliance of a distinction between "publishers" and "distributors" in defamation liability cases?
4. Does an ISP have a strong incentive to police the content on its servers? Explain why or why not.
5. As an individual or business owner subject to Internet defamation, whom would you sue? What are your chances for recovery?

Employer Exposure to Defamation Liability

Current court interpretation of the CDA appears to free ISPs from liability in defamation suits, even if they have knowledge or should have had knowledge of the defamatory material, unless the ISP itself is the information content creator. In light of this standard, what should be expected with regard to employer liability exposure when an employer gives employees access to e-mail and Internet services? Consider the possible plight of a job applicant who is pursuing an executive position with your company. After what appears to have been a satisfactory job interview, one member of your company's executive hiring committee sends a disparaging (and untrue) e-mail message about the job candidate that circulates throughout the company, including to those who make the decisions on job offers. The job applicant, who has friends in the company, is given a copy of the e-mail, but is not given the job he had applied for. It certainly wouldn't be surprising in this situation to find a defamation lawsuit filed which includes your company as a defendant.

The CDA, as applied in the *Zeran* and some subsequent cases, prohibits defamation suits against providers or users of interactive computer services for defamatory statements made by third parties. Would an "employer" (as opposed to an AOL, a PRODIGY, a CompuServe, etc.) enjoy immunity from liability as a provider of a server that gives its employees access to communications? That is, would an employer have to be construed to be a "provider or user" of an "interactive computer service"? If so, this would leave just the individual who was the creator of the message as the only target for recovery from economic injury. In such a situation, the employer would not be liable based on the theory of vicarious liability for the actions of an employee. In effect, the CDA would shield employers from activity that would otherwise be defamation.

Independent of Internet developments, states are increasingly limiting liability of employers towards employees, ex-employees, and prospective employees. Such suits are notoriously laced with acrimony and facts are hard to come by. In response, most states have statutes that require the injured party (the employee, past, current, and prospective) to show not only that the statements made about him or her were false, but that the source of the defamatory remarks knew the statements were false, or had a reckless disregard for the truth. These statutes would mean, in the e-mail example above, that if the writer of the defamatory e-mail had some basis for believing that the material he put in the e-mail, then the suit against him and his employer would be dismissed. If a former employee had been discharged for theft by the former employer and the e-mail reported that fact, then the prospective employer could escape liability for defamation even if the prospective employee actually did not steal from his former employer.

PRIVACY, CYBERTORTS, AND FEDERAL AND STATE REGULATION

Overview

Americans have always had a high regard for privacy. Arguably, one of the critical factors igniting the Revolution against England was the lack of respect for privacy of the Colonials shown by authorities answering to the King of England. Certainly, the Fourth Amendment to the Constitution reflects the pervasive fear that colonial Americans had of government—in the case of this Amendment, that they would be subjected to unreasonable searches and seizures. The Fourth Amendment basically requires governmental authorities to obtain a search warrant before conducting a search of citizens. In order to get a search warrant, governmental authorities must show "probable cause" that a crime has been committed before a neutral magistrate or judge. Probable cause is shown when the police officer or other governmental official seeking a search warrant reveals evidence that makes it more likely than not that a crime has taken place.

Public vs. Private Intrusions

Although the Constitution provides protection against governmental intrusions, it does not provide protection against privacy intrusions by private entities. In fact, except in a few state constitutions, privacy, per se, is not constitutionally protected in the United States at the state or federal level. Most of the privacy concerns that have surfaced in connection with Internet transactions are concerns about the nonconsensual extraction of personally identifiable information *by private sources*. As these concerns have become more evident, Congress has responded with a panoply of new federal statutes. In addition, state common law tort claims for invasion of privacy can be potent forces aiding Internet participants in their attempts to limit snooping.

We must note that surreptitious tracking and information-gathering efforts using cookies (discussed below) is not limited to private entities. Recently, it came to light that Barry McCaffery, drug czar for the Clinton Administration, approved use of cookies to digitally track visitors to the National Drug Control Policy Office website. The article "Drug Control and the Use of Cookies" below appeared in the *Washington Post* in the year 2000.

Reasonable Expectation of Privacy

In discussing objectionable invasions of privacy, courts generally work with a concept that has been labeled, "reasonable expectation of privacy." In general, with a number of exceptions, if the government intrudes into an area where a citizen has a reasonable expectation of privacy, the government needs a search warrant. Courts also use the reasonable expectation of privacy concept when evaluating whether behavior by private entities is tortious, that is it constitutes a common law tort that protects individuals from

Drug Control and the Use of Cookies

News that the White House drug control office is secretly placing digital bugs on the computers of people who visit one of its Web sites caused an uproar yesterday, prompting White House Chief of Staff John D. Podesta to order the practice stopped. Podesta also demanded an explanation from Barry R. McCaffrey, director of the National Drug Control Policy Office, for how the practice of monitoring traffic through dropping electronic "cookies" on the hard drives of Web visitors began, White House officials said.

The surreptitious tracking by one of its own agencies was especially embarrassing to the White House, because it contradicts privacy policies that the Clinton administration is advocating for the private sector.

The Scripps-Howard News Service reported that cookies—a fairly simple computer code—were being slipped without notice on computers to monitor the effectiveness of an online anti-drug campaign.

The ad campaign worked in much the same way as other advertising that is linked to Web search engines. When Web users typed in certain key words relating to drugs, a banner ad would pop up on the screen inviting them to click on www.freevibe.com, an anti-drug site run by the drug control office. If people clicked on the site, a cookie was dropped onto their hard drives. The cookie's code allows the advertiser to see how the user entered the site, and what pages were entered once there.

The use of cookies without notice or permission is a controversial, though commonplace, practice in the private sector. The Federal Trade Commission has sought greater authority to set and enforce privacy standards, and Vice President Gore recently has made privacy an increasingly prominent campaign theme.

In a statement, White House press secretary Joe Lockhart said the drug control office had not tracked visitors by name or otherwise identified them. But he emphasized that West Wing officials "learned for the first time" yesterday about the office's use of cookies, and pledged, "We will take all steps necessary to halt these practices now."

Don Maple, who helps run the media campaign for the drug control office, said that officials there had believed the use of cookies was defensible. The office's advertising is placed by Ogilvy & Mather, which in turn contracted with DoubleClick Inc., the leading Internet advertising company. DoubleClick placed the cookies and reported the data back to Ogilvy & Mather, he said.

"The idea was that our advertising buyers wanted and needed a tool to decide where to place their banner ads," Maple said, adding that only "anonymous gross-number data" about Web visits were collected in what the drug control office believed was a way of determining whether it was spending its money wisely.

"We discovered we had underestimated the sensitivity of the White House to this practice," Maple said. He pledged that the contractors "would destroy whatever data" have been collected.

McCaffrey's operation stirred objections from civil libertarians a year after reports that the drug control office allowed TV networks to fulfill their obligation for public service advertising if they agreed to run programs with a government-approved anti-drug message. This time, he will also face questions from Congress. Rep. W.J. "Billy" Tauzin (R-La.) is sending a letter voicing strong opposition to the use of cookies and demanding an

—Continued on page 158

Drug Control and the Use of Cookies *Continued from page 157*

explanation of how they came to be used, his spokesman Ken Johnson said yesterday.

While the drug control office knew about the cookies used on freevibe.com, Maple said the office learned only this week after news inquiries that cookies were also being dropped by the Web server for another site run by the office, this one aimed at parents and called theantidrug.com. That practice too is being halted, he said.

The drug control office's use of cookies was discovered by privacy advocate Richard M. Smith, who said he found it earlier this year while doing research on the privacy practices of health-related Websites.

DoubleClick has become one of the most reviled companies in the online world among privacy advocates, who have attacked its use of Internet cookies and more advanced technologies to monitor consumer behavior. The firm says the practice allows Web ads to be more tailored for advertisers and consumers alike, and that information is not shared. "It is totally anonymous. It is not used for profiling. It is the property of that site and it is not shared with anyone else," said Josh Isay, director of public policy and government affairs for DoubleClick.

Smith said that none of his research proves that DoubleClick or the drug policy office has been spying on Americans, only that the technology would allow either to do so. "The problem is . . . DoubleClick is gathering all this information about us that's really none of their business . . . they're creating databases that could be interesting to law enforcement down the road."

Source: © 2000 *The Washington Post.* Reprinted with permission. By John F. Harris and John Schwartz; *Washington Post* Staff Writers; Thursday, June 22, 2000; p. A23.

Additional Readings:
http://www.epic.org/privacy/internet/cookiegate_pr.html
"Privacy Advocates Call on Congress to Investigate 'Cookiegate'," Electronic Privacy Information Centre.
http://www.apbnews.com/newscenter/breakingnews/2000/06/22/drugcookies0622_01.html
"White House Backs Down on Anti-Drug 'Cookies'", June 22, 2000; APBNEWs.com, James Gordon Meek.
http://www.findarticles.com/m0NEW/2000 June 21/62877127/p1/article.jhtml
"Administration Will Stop Collecting Drug User Info Online", June 21, 2000; NEWSBYTES, David Mcguire.
http://www.idgnet.com/crd banner 192064.html
"U.S. Antidrug Site Dealing Cookies", June 21, 2000; The Standard, Keith Perine.

---

unreasonable intrusions into their solitude or private affairs. In other words, their reasonable expectations of privacy are violated.[2]

In the physical world, people have a reasonable expectation of privacy when they go to the bathroom. A hidden camera in a bathroom would be regarded as an invasion of privacy because people have a reasonable expectation of privacy when they shut the door in a bathroom. The same applies to conversations with doctors, psychiatrists, and financial counselors; people expect these conversations to remain confidential. On the other hand, if a person can be observed naked from a location in which the photographer is not trespassing or using telescopic lenses, that person cannot object when his or her bare derriere is displayed in a tabloid.

In the cyberworld, opportunities for intrusions into private affairs are magnified. The following case illustrates the perils of giving out information to ISPs. In general unencrypted information distributed over the Internet is vulnerable to interception or unintended secondary use. The case makes it clear that the Internet is not a place where a person should have a reasonable expectation of privacy.

The case on page 157 basically follows precedents set in other cases regarding the subpoena of information that was voluntarily provided to parties participating over the Internet in some way. Since such information is freely made available to parties participating on the Internet, does it make sense to require the government to obtain a subpoena before they launch an investigation? Why not simply establish a precedent that there is no expectation of privacy on the Internet, particularly in light of surveys indicating that over 80 percent of Internet users do not believe their transmissions are secure.

Examples of Objectionable Intrusions That Occur on the Internet

On the Internet, there are several types of intrusions that many find objectionable and which are potentially tortious. The three objectionable intrusions discussed

---

[2]Common law torts of invasion of privacy are discussed in some detail in Chapter 5.

United States of America v. Hambrick
U.S. District Court, W.D. Virginia
55 F.Supp.2d 504, (1999)

FACTS AND CASE BACKGROUND

Scott Hambrick sought to suppress information obtained by the government in a criminal prosecution. Mr. Hambrick claims his Fourth Amendment rights were violated because personal information was obtained from his Internet Service Provider (ISP). Mr. Hambrick disclosed information to the ISP (MindSpring) including his Internet surf name, Blowuinva. The implication of this case is that information revealed to one party in connection with an Internet transaction can be obtained by the government as long as they have a search warrant.

OPINION: JAMES H. MICHAEL, JR., JUDGE

Although Congress is willing to recognize that individuals have some degree of privacy in the stored data and transactional records that their ISPs retain, the ECPA is hardly a legislative determination that this expectation of privacy is one that rises to the level of "reasonably objective" for Fourth Amendment purposes. Despite its concern for privacy, Congress did not provide for suppression where a party obtains stored data or transactional records in violation of the Act. Additionally, the ECPA's concern for privacy extends only to government invasions of privacy. ISPs are free to turn stored data and transactional records over to nongovernmental entities. ("[A] provider of electronic communication service or remote computing service may disclose a record or other information pertaining to a subscriber to or customer of such service . . . to any person other than a

governmental entity."). For Fourth Amendment purposes, this court does not find that the ECPA has legislatively determined that an individual has a reasonable expectation of privacy in his name, address, social security number, credit card number, and proof of Internet connection. The fact that the ECPA does not proscribe turning over such information to private entities buttresses the conclusion that the ECPA does not create a reasonable expectation of privacy in that information. This, however, does not end the court's inquiry. This court must determine, within the constitutional framework that the Supreme Court has established, whether Mr. Hambrick's subjective expectation of privacy is one that society is willing to recognize.

* * *

The court finds the defendant's implicit argument that certain information in cyberspace should be private requires careful consideration. Legal scholars and Congress have noted the ubiquity of cyberspace in the lives of all Americans. The members of our society increasingly live important parts of their lives through the Internet. Cyberspace is a non-physical "place" and its very structure, a computer and telephone network that connects millions of users, defies traditional Fourth Amendment analysis. So long as the risk-analysis approach of Katz remains valid, however, this court is compelled to apply traditional legal principles to this new and continually evolving technology. In so doing, the court must deny Mr. Hambrick's motion to suppress.

When Scott Hambrick surfed the Internet using the screen name "Blowuinva," he was not a completely anonymous actor. It is true that an average member of the public could not easily determine the true identity of "Blowuinva." Nevertheless, when Mr. Hambrick entered into an agreement to obtain Internet access from MindSpring, he knowingly revealed his name, address, credit card number, and telephone number to MindSpring and its employees. Mr. Hambrick also selected the screen name "Blowuinva." When the defendant selected his screen name it became tied to his true identity in all MindSpring records. MindSpring employees had ready access to these records in the normal course of MindSpring's business, for example, in the keeping of its records for billing purposes, and nothing prevented MindSpring from revealing this information to nongovernmental actors. Also, there is nothing in the record to suggest that there was a restrictive agreement between the defendant and MindSpring that would limit the right of MindSpring to reveal the defendant's personal information to nongovernmental entities. Where such dissemination of information to nongovernment entities is not prohibited, there can be no reasonable expectation of privacy in that information.

Although not dispositive to the outcome of this motion, it is important to note that the court's decision does not leave members of cybersociety without privacy protection. Under the ECPA, Internet Service Providers are civilly liable when they reveal subscriber information or the contents of stored communications to the government without first requiring a warrant, court order, or subpoena. Here, nothing suggests that MindSpring had any knowledge that the facially valid subpoena submitted to it was in fact an invalid subpoena. Had MindSpring revealed the information at issue in this case to the government without first requiring a subpoena, apparently valid on its face, Mr. Hambrick could have sued MindSpring. This is a powerful deterrent protecting privacy in the online world and should not be taken lightly.

The defendant's motion to suppress also embraces evidence found in his home pursuant to a residence search warrant. The defendant contends that because the residence search warrant was supported by an affidavit reciting evidence allegedly protected as to the defendant by his right to privacy, the court likewise must suppress the materials seized from his home. As this court has found that the MindSpring materials are not so protected, the predicate for this motion to suppress the materials seized from the defendant's home

fails, and therefore the court does not suppress such materials.

QUESTIONS FOR ANALYSIS

1. Does this case stand for the proposition that what you tell one person or company on the Internet can be subpoenaed by federal and state authorities?
2. What protection does the Electronic Computer Protection Act provide?

"Revenge of the Cookie Monsters"

"By now, you've heard of Internet 'cookies' and realize they're not just a tasty midnight snack. In the world of Cyberspace, a cookie is a small string of text that a Web server dumps on your hard drive. Designed to enhance the browsing experience, this mechanism contains bits of information that reveal which sites you've visited and what you did there. For example, if you visit a site that requires a sign-on, cookies leave data to ensure you'll have to key it in only once. They also form the basis of the shopping-cart concept in electronic commerce, allowing you to leave the site and return later to find the items you originally selected in your cart. According to Jason Catlett, president of Junkbusters Corp., a site developed to enforce a surfer's 'right to be let alone,' the information obtained through cookies could be subpoenaed or sold. Once your identity becomes known to a single company listed in your cookie file,

other companies could have access to your information. Although Catlett admits that we haven't seen specific damage performed by cookies, he believes the potential is obvious and dangerous. Besides, they can take up space on your hard drive.

Source: "Revenge of the Cookie Monsters," Brown, Monique R.; Muhammad, Tariq K. *Black Enterprise,* May 98, Vol. 28 Issue 10, p 42. Copyright 1998. Reprinted with permission *Black Enterprise* Magazine. All rights reserved.

Additional Readings:
http://www.junkbusters.com/ht/en/cookies.html
"How Web Servers' Cookies Threaten Your Privacy", Junkbusters.

http://news.cnet.com/news/0-1005-200-1534533.html
"DoubleClick Accused of Unlawful Consumer Data Use", January 28, 2000; Sandeep Junnarkar Staff Writer, CNET News.com.

http://www.usatoday.com/life/cyber/tech/cth211.htm
"Activists Charge DoubleClick Double Cross", 06/07/00; Will Rodger, USATODAY.com.

below are prominent, but this limited selection is by no means exhaustive. It is objectionable when:

1. Information is collected about someone without their knowledge or consent.
2. Companies on the Internet maintain websites, but do not have a privacy policy or do not follow their own privacy policies.
3. Websites collect, store, or transmit sensitive information about a person's finances, medical records, or engage in the collection of information from children.

There are a host of electronic intrusions that many regard as objectionable, and we will consider responses to such intrusions from both the legislative and judicial branches of government. Most of the statutes that we examine will be federal statutes, but it is important to keep in mind that privacy law is based on state common law claims, which can vary significantly from state to state.

PRIVACY ON THE NEW FRONTIER OF CYBERSPACE

It's quite clear that cyberspace, the developing Global Information Infrastructure (GII) in more formal terms, provides the most efficient mechanism for information transfers ever envisioned. Already, the GII can capture, transfer, process, and store information and make that information accessible faster and less expensively (more efficiently) than any alternative system. Moreover, the potential is currently being realized for dramatic increases in cyberspace speeds, information storage capacities, and processing power.

A wide array of social, economic, and political transactions already take place in cyberspace, ranging from online, remote medical diagnoses to shopping for flowers; from researching legal treatises to finding movie guides; from communicating with family members and friends in remote locations to casting your e-mail vote in public opinion surveys. In these and a myriad of other applications, cyberspace is widely viewed as having the capacity to vastly improve human lives in every corner of the world. At the same time, the enormous information acquisition, transfer, and processing power of cyberspace is viewed by many as exposing us all to more frequent and more pernicious invasions of our privacy than we have experienced in any other era.

Cyberspace privacy concerns are shared by academics and the general public alike. In surveys conducted by the Graphic, Visualization & Usability Center, Internet privacy has been listed as the primary concern of survey respondents, with the vast majority indicating a desire for new Internet privacy laws.[3] These results are echoed in other survey data. Academic journals, ranging from law reviews to computer applications publications, devote large shares of their printed pages to privacy issues.

Generalized Invasions of Privacy on the Internet

The Federal Trade Commission (FTC) was established in 1914 to combat "unfair and deceptive trade practices." The activities of the FTC are wide-ranging, and oversight of many Internet activities comes within its purview. At this point, the FTC has identified numerous practices that are prevalent among firms operating on the Internet as "deceptive." A number of these are discussed in the *Geocities* case below.

According to the FTC there are five principles of **Fair Information Practices** which are:

Notice/Awareness—consumers should be notified as to who is gathering data from them and the uses that will be made of that data.

Choice/Consent—consumers should consent to any secondary use for the data. There should be opt-in and opt-out provisions.

Access/Participation—consumers should have the right to contest the accuracy of the data collected.

Integrity/Security—there should be managerial mechanisms in place to guard against loss, unauthorized access, or disclosures of the data.

Enforcement/Redress—there should be remedies available to victims of information misuse. The FTC envisions self-regulation by industry groups, private rights of action based on invasion of privacy, and government enforcement as in the *Geocities* case below.

It is the goal of the FTC that every website adhere to the Fair Information Principles listed above. At a minimum the FTC will consider litigation against any website that violates its own promises made at its website.

As a background to the *Geocities* case, consider the following statistics compiled by the FTC in its report to Congress entitled "Privacy Online: Fair Information Practices in the Electronic Marketplace."[4] According to the FTC, based on a random sample of 324 websites on the Internet, 97 percent of the websites collect personal information and personal identifying information, but only 62 percent post a privacy policy. With regard to implementation of the FTC Fair Information Principles, only 55 percent of the websites

[3]GVU's 8th WWW User Survey (1997) http://www.gvu.gatech.edu/user_surveys/survey-1997-10/.

[4]The Report was issued May 2000.

provide notice that qualifies according to FTC standards, which requires that a website post a Privacy Policy, indicate what personal information is collected, describe how the site uses that information, and reveal whether the information is disclosed to third parties. Fifty percent of the websites in the survey provided consumer choice, allowing users to opt out of the data collection. Forty-three percent of the websites in the survey provided consumers access to information gathered about them and 55 percent had a statement about the security measures the website takes to insure the integrity of the information collected from interception by others. Only 20 percent of the websites implemented all four (notice, choice, access, and security) of the FTC Fair Information Principles listed above.

Data Collection and Computers

A hallmark of civilized society is the compilation of data about its citizenry. In developed countries, notably the United States, information is collected about people from the date of their birth to the date of their death and beyond. For most people in the United States medical records are routinely collected and stored as are recordings of real estate transactions, tax records, school grades, license plates, and the list goes on and on. Until recently, the bulk of the personally identifying records that were collected were stored as paper records. Although there have always been embarrassing disclosures that threatened careers or proved a person was a liar, the work of digging up records in paper form was by no means trivial. Computerization of records has changed all that. With appropriate software, a skilled operator can aggregate and parse enormous volumes of data so that comprehensive profiles of large numbers of individuals can be assembled.

Ironically, a great deal of personal information is gathered and stored by government sources, then made available to private users whose intentions are not always benign. Car insurance companies have been able to tap into Department of Motor Vehicle information, using the information obtained to justify rate increases to insured customers. Adopted children now make use of records that mothers were assured at the time of adoption would forever remain private. In some states there have been situations where predatory men seeing an attractive woman in a car have copied down the car license plate number, contacted the Department of Motor Vehicles, and from that source obtained the woman's address.

Internet Data Collection and Cookies

The pervasive expansion of the Internet has been accompanied by escalating concerns about personal privacy. There are websites and software that promise the ability to unearth all kinds of information about co-workers, relatives, and others, including criminal records, credit reports, health records, and other data.[5] Ordinary transactions between consumer and businesses online are threatened by "identity thieves" who intercept Internet transmissions and accompanying credit card numbers. As the Hambrick case above illustrates, there is no reasonable expectation of privacy for information that is given to Internet businesses.

In the minds of many, the "cookies" introduced earlier in this chapter pose the greatest threat to internet privacy. According to one website, named "Cookie Central,"

> Cookies are a very useful tool in maintaining state variables on the Web. Since HTTP is a "stateless" (non-persistent) protocol, it is impossible to differentiate between visits to a web site, unless the server can somehow "mark" a visitor.[6] This is done by storing a piece of information in the visitor's browser.
>
> This is accomplished with cookies. Cookies can store database information, custom page settings, or just about anything that would make a site individual and customizable. An analogy I like to use is that cookies are very much like a laundry "claim-check" of sorts. You drop something off, and get a ticket. When you return with the ticket, you get that same something back.

In technical terms, Cookie Central states that,

> A cookie is simply an HTTP header that consists of a text-only string that gets entered into the memory of a browser. This string contains the domain, path, lifetime, and value of a variable that a website sets. If the lifetime of this variable is longer than the time the user spends at that site, then this string is saved to file for future reference.

Although cookies have capabilities that are not objectionable and enhance efficiency on the Internet, the

---

[5]http://www.sfxserve.co.uk/Homepage/ecomm2u/CyberSpy.html.
[6]This website is an AOL recommendation, which answers frequently asked questions about cookies. See http://www.cookiecentral.com/faq/#1.1.

Bill McLaren, Jr. v. Microsoft Corporation
Court of Appeals of Texas, Dallas
(1999) WL 339015

FACTS AND CASE BACKGROUND

McLaren was an employee of Microsoft Corporation. In December 1996, Microsoft suspended McLaren's employment pending an investigation into accusations of sexual harrassment and "inventory questions." McLaren requested access to his electronic mail to disprove the allegations against him. According to McLaren, he was told he could access his e-mail only by requesting it through company officials and telling them the location of a particular message. By memorandum, McLaren requested that no one tamper with his Microsoft office workstation or his e-mail. McLaren's employment was terminated on December 11, 1996.

Following the termination of his employment, McLaren filed suit against the company alleging as his sole cause of action a claim for invasion of privacy. In support of his claim, McLaren alleged that . . . Microsoft had invaded his privacy by "breaking into" some or all of the personal folders maintained on his office computer and releasing the contents of the folders to third parties. According to McLaren, the personal folders were part of a computer application created by Microsoft in which e-mail messages could be stored. Access to the e-mail system was obtained through a network password. Access to personal folders could be additionally restricted by a "personal store" password created by the individual user. McLaren created and used a personal store password to restrict access to his personal folders.

McLaren concedes in his petition that it was possible for Microsoft to "decrypt" his personal store password. McLaren alleges, however, that "[b]y allowing [him] to have a personal store password for his personal folders, [McLaren] manifested and [Microsoft] recognized an expectation that the personal folders would be free from intrusion and interference." McLaren characterizes Microsoft's decrypting or otherwise "breaking in" to his personal folders as an intentional, unjustified, and unlawful invasion of privacy.

OPINION: ROACH, JUSTICE

Texas recognizes four distinct torts, any of which constitutes an invasion of privacy:

1. Intrusion upon the plaintiff's seclusion or solitude or into his private affairs;
2. Public disclosure of embarrassing private facts about the plaintiff;
3. Publicity which places the plaintiff in a false light in the public eye;
4. Appropriation, for the defendant's advantage, of the plaintiff's name or likeness.

[Citations deleted throughout] At issue in this case is whether McLaren's petition states a cause of action under the first recognized tort. There are two elements to this cause of action: (1) an intentional intrusion, physically or otherwise, upon another's solitude, seclusion, or private affairs or concerns, which (2) would be highly offensive to a reasonable person. When assessing the offensive nature of the invasion, courts further require the intrusion to be unreasonable, unjustified, or unwarranted. This type of invasion of privacy is generally associated with either a physical invasion of a person's property or eavesdropping on another's conversation with the aid of wiretaps, microphones, or spying.

In his petition and on appeal, McLaren contends the fact that the e-mail messages were stored under a private password with Microsoft's consent gave rise to "a legitimate expectation of privacy in the contents of the files."

In *Trotti*, the court considered the privacy interest of an employee in a locker provided by the employer to store personal effects during work hours. The court began its analysis by recognizing that the locker was the employer's property and, when unlocked, was subject to legitimate, reasonable searches by the employer. The court further reasoned:

> "This would also be true where the employee used a lock provided by [the employer], because in retaining the lock's combination or master key, it could be inferred that [the employer] manifested an interest both in maintaining control over the locker and in conducting legitimate, reasonable searches."

But, the court concluded, when, as in *Trotti*, an employee buys and uses his own lock on the locker, with the employer's knowledge, the fact finder is justified in concluding that the "employee manifested, and the employer recognized, an expectation that the locker and its contents would be free from intrusion and interference."

McLaren urges that the locker in *Trotti* is akin to the e-mail messages in this case, "only the technology is different." We disagree. First, the locker in *Trotti* was provided to the employee for the specific purpose of storing personal belongings, not work items. In contrast, McLaren's workstation was provided to him by Microsoft so that he could perform the functions of his job. In connection with that purpose and as alleged in McLaren's petition, part of his workstation included a company-owned computer that gave McLaren the ability to send and receive e-mail messages. Thus, contrary to his argument on appeal, the e-mail messages contained on the company computer were not McLaren's personal property, but were merely an inherent part of the office environment.

Further, the nature of a locker and an e-mail storage system are different. The locker in *Trotti* was a discrete, physical place where the employee, separate and apart from other employees, could store her tangible, personal belongings. The storage system for e-mail messages is not so discrete. As asserted by McLaren in his petition, e-mail was delivered to the server-based "inbox" and was stored there to read. [Footnotes deleted] McLaren could leave his e-mail on the server or he could move the message to a different location. According to McLaren, his practice was to store his e-mail messages in "personal folders." Even so, any e-mail messages stored in McLaren's personal folders were first transmitted over the network and were at some point accessible by a third-party. Given these circumstances, we cannot conclude that McLaren, even by creating a personal password, manifested—and Microsoft recognized—a reasonable expectation of privacy in the contents of the e-mail messages such that Microsoft was precluded from reviewing the messages.

Even if we were to conclude that McLaren alleged facts in his petition which, if found to be true, would establish some reasonable expectation of privacy in the contents of his e-mail messages sent over the company e-mail system, our result would be the same. We would nevertheless conclude that, from the facts alleged in the petition, a reasonable person would not consider Microsoft's interception of these communications to be a highly offensive invasion. As set forth in McLaren's petition, at the time Microsoft accessed his e-mail messages, McLaren was on suspension pending an investigation into accusations of sexual harassment and "inventory questions" and had notified Microsoft that some of the e-mails were relevant to the investigation. Accordingly, the company's interest in preventing inappropriate and unprofessional comments, or even illegal activity, over its e-mail system would outweigh McLaren's claimed privacy interest in those communications. We overrule the second point of error.

We affirm the trial court's judgment.

QUESTIONS FOR ANALYSIS

1. Of the four invasions of privacy, what kind of invasion was McLaren alleging took place in this case?
2. What is the significance of the claim made by McLaren that he had an expectation that his e-mail messages would remain private because he stored them in a personal locker?
3. Does this case stand for the proposition that employee purses can be searched? What are its implications for the monitoring of bathrooms and dressing rooms? Was it important that McLaren's e-mails were used on the job and were the subject of the charges against him by a female co-worker?

---

primary concern about cookies is that they allow information to be extracted from web browsers without the consent of web-users. Cookies allow websites to track where you have traveled in cyberspace from the time you leave the cookie-placing website until your return to that website. While cookies have a number of uses, their primary function is the recording of click-streams—that is, tracking what sites you have clicked on (visited) since you last visited the cookie-placer. Clickstreams are the information marketers want because they can then select targeted advertising for goods they think you may want based on your clickstreams.

Cookies and Privacy

There is no doubt that clickstream information is valuable to firms that market goods and services over the Internet. Until recently, many users were unaware of cookies and the fact that information was being extracted from browsers. As publicity about cookies has increased, sophisticated Internet travelers have retaliated by disabling cookies on their browsers. In many instances, websites have responded with software that denies entry to browsers' whose cookies are disabled. Lately, some firms have been able to link information gathered by cookies with real people and not just with their computers. Scanner data in grocery stores are linked to individuals, and such data, combined with clickstream data derived from cookies, dramatically expands personally identifying marketing information that is (1) relatively cheap to gather once the systems are set up and (2) is not dependent on consent of those from whom the information is collected. Needless to say, marketers are interested in more information about customers.[7]

It appears that, to most Internet users, the most objectionable aspect of cookies is the involuntary nature of the information extraction. If Internet travelers were informed about the presence of cookies, the fact that information is being extracted, the uses for that information, and had an opportunity to refuse to give the information without being excluded from a lot of the sites on the Internet, fewer objections would be heard. The authors' casual perusal of privacy statements on websites suggests that the notices about privacy policies are becoming more detailed and the use or nonuse of cookies is often discussed. Notwithstanding these evolutionary developments, the threat of government regulation is looming. Three areas of privacy have been addressed extensively by recent statutory and regulatory measures. These are: **childrens'** privacy, privacy of **medical records,** and privacy of **financial records.** Each of these areas is discussed in some detail below.

Ethical Expectations

With the power of today's software, the potential for unscrupulous behavior by companies that have websites on the Internet is evident. Some would regard the following practices as unethical:

- collecting information without informing the customer;
- secondary use of personally identifiable data;
- not having a privacy statement;
- not having a means to correct inaccuracies;
- not having a means to opt out of the system, if the consumer does not want personal data transmitted or sold to third parties;
- soliciting entrants to a contest with the intent of gathering information from applicants.

In addition to being viewed as unethical, many of the practices listed are being attacked as unfair and decep-

tive trade practices, which the FTC has the authority to halt. In the following case on page 166, the defendant was accused of many of the abuses listed above.

Reproduced on page 166 is the current (August, 2000) privacy policy of Geocities, which is owned by Yahoo!, an Internet company that facilitates searches. Notice that Yahoo! does collect personally identifiable information about members and that it uses cookies. Yahoo! claims to be Truste Certified, which means that the privacy guarantees Yahoo! makes about use of information that is acquired from visitors to their website are monitored and verified by a third party, Truste. There is no doubt that Yahoo!'s privacy policy has been shaped by the *Geocities'* decision.

USE OF PRIVATE INFORMATION, FRAUD, AND IDENTITY THEFT

As discussed in Chapter 3, UCITA, UETA, and revised Subpart B of Article 2 of the UCC require vendors to develop commercially reasonable attribution procedures in order to make their click-on contracts enforceable. Commercially reasonable attribution procedures often entail the collection of personal information about the purchaser such as name, address, phone numbers, credit card numbers, e-mail addresses, and other information. The goal behind this collection of data is to identify who is responding to the offer made by a vendor at its website and, according to both UCITA and UETA, that identification process must be commercially reasonable. Once data are collected, however, their subsequent use is a source of controversy.

Identity Theft

A serious current problem on the Internet is *identity theft*. According to the FTC, your identity can be stolen by "co-opting your name, Social Security number, credit card number, or some other piece of your personal information. In short, identity theft occurs when someone appropriates your personal information without your knowledge to commit fraud or theft. The FTC lists several ways in which identity thieves work:

- They open a new credit card account, using your name, date of birth, and Social Security number. When they use the credit card and don't pay the

---

[7]It is probably true that there is some disclosure when you get your scanner card in a grocery store that the store will be using that information in various ways.

Federal Trade Commission [File No. 982-3015]
Geocities; Analysis to Aid Public Comment
Thursday, August 20, 1998
*63 Federal Register 44624 AGENCY: Federal Trade Commission

FACTS AND CASE BACKGROUND

The Federal Trade Commission (FTC) is charged with responsibility for identifying and prohibiting unfair and deceptive trade practices. The *Geocities* case gave the FTC an opportunity to address several issues dealing with the use of information gathered by an Internet website. Among the issues addressed in this case are the acquisition, use, and sale of identifying personal information without the customer's consent. The FTC identified three deceptive trade practices, which Geocities agreed in this consent decree to cease and desist: (1) that the defendant, Geocities, gathered and sold information on members, which Geocities promised would not be sold or distributed; (2) that the defendant collected optional information which it claimed would not be sold to third parties, but in fact was sold; and (3) that they collected personally identifiable information from children without their parents' knowledge or consent.

CASE DECISION

Part I of the proposed order prohibits Geocities from making any misrepresentation about its collection or use of personal identifying information from or about consumers, including what information will be disclosed to third parties and how the information will be used. The order defines "personal identifying information" as including but not limited to "first and last name, home or other physical address (e.g.

school), e-mail address, telephone number, or any information that identifies a specific individual, or any information which when tied to the above becomes identifiable to a specific individual."

Part II of the proposed order prohibits Geocities from misrepresenting either the identity of a party collecting any personal identifying information or the sponsorship of any activity on its website.

Part III prohibits Geocities from collecting personal identifying information from any child if Geocities has actual knowledge that the child does not have a parent's permission to provide the information. The order defines "child" as ages twelve and under.

Parts IV and V of the order are designed as fencing-in provisions to prevent violations of consumers' information privacy in the future. Part IV orders Geocities to post a clear and prominent notice on its website explaining Geocities' practices with regard to its collection and use of personal identifying information. The notice must include the following:

a. What information is being collected;
b. Its intended use(s);
c. The third parties to whom it will be disclosed;
d. How the consumer can obtain access to the information; and
e. How the consumer can have the information removed from Geocities' databases.

The notice must appear on the Web site's home page and at each location on the site at which such information is collected, although the collection of so-called "tracking" information need only be disclosed on the home page.

Part IV includes a "safe harbor" provision that deems a specified procedure to be in compliance with this Part. It would allow Geocities to post a Privacy Notice on its home page along with a clear and prominent hyperlink to that notice at each location on the site at which personal identifying information is collected. The hyperlink would be accompanied by the following statement: NOTICE: We collect personal information on this site. To learn more about how we use your information click here.

QUESTIONS FOR ANALYSIS

1. The FTC has already issued a number of regulations regarding games and sweepstakes in non-Internet settings. Does it make sense for the FTC to apply general principles of prohibiting deceptive trade practices in both Internet and non-Internet locations.

2. Do you think that this type of consent decree is a way for the government to regulate the content of websites? Why aren't the common law remedies of contract fraud and the tort of deceit likely to be adequate protection?

Yahoo! Privacy Policy

Yahoo! takes your privacy seriously. Please read the following to learn more about our privacy policy. Also, please read our *Children's Privacy Policy* to learn more about how we treat personally identifiable information collected from children.

NOTICE: Go to the website http://www.ftc.gov/bcp/ conline/pubs/online/sitesee/index.html **for important information about safe surfing from the Federal Trade Commission.**

WHAT THIS PRIVACY POLICY COVERS

This Privacy Policy covers Yahoo!'s treatment of personally identifiable information that Yahoo! collects when you are on the Yahoo! site, and when you use Yahoo!'s services. This policy also covers Yahoo!'s treatment of any personally identifiable information that Yahoo!'s business partners share with Yahoo!.

This policy does not apply to the practices of companies that Yahoo! does not own or control, or to people that Yahoo! does not employ or manage. In addition, this policy does not apply to *Yahoo! Broadcast* or to *WebRing,* which have their own privacy policies.

INFORMATION COLLECTION AND USE

Yahoo! collects personally identifiable information when you register for a Yahoo! account, when you use certain *Yahoo! products or services,* and when you enter *promotions or sweepstakes.* Yahoo! may also receive personally identifiable information from our business partners.

When you register with Yahoo!, we ask for your name, email address, birth date, gender, zip code, occupation, industry, and personal interests. Once you register with Yahoo! and sign in to our services, you are not anonymous to us.

Yahoo! also automatically receives and records information on our server logs from your browser including your *IP address,* Yahoo! *cookie* information and the page you requested.

Yahoo! uses information for three general purposes: to customize the advertising and content you see on our pages, to fulfill your requests for certain products and services, and to contact you about specials and new products.

INFORMATION SHARING AND DISCLOSURE

Yahoo! will not sell or rent your personally identifiable information to anyone.

Yahoo! will send personally identifiable information about you to other companies or people when:

We have your consent to share the information;

We need to share your information to provide the product or service you have requested;

We need to send the information to companies who work on behalf of Yahoo! to provide a product or service to you. (Unless we tell you differently, these companies do not have any right to use the personally identifiable information we provide to them beyond what is necessary to assist us.);

We respond to subpoenas, court orders or legal process; or

We find that your actions on our websites violate the *Yahoo! Terms of Service,* the *Yahoo! GeoCities Terms of Service,* or any of our usage guidelines for specific products or services.

COOKIES

Yahoo! may set and access Yahoo! *cookies* on your computer.

Yahoo! allows *other companies* that are presenting advertisements on some of our pages to set and access their cookies on your computer. Other companies' use of their cookies is subject to their own privacy policies, not this one. Advertisers or other companies do not have access to Yahoo!'s cookies.

Yahoo! uses *web beacons* to access our cookies within our network of websites and in connection with Yahoo! products and services.

YOUR ABILITY TO EDIT AND DELETE YOUR ACCOUNT INFORMATION AND PREFERENCES

Yahoo! gives you the ability to edit your *Yahoo! Account Information* and preferences at any time, including whether you want Yahoo! to contact you about specials and new products.

You may request deletion of your Yahoo! account by sending an email to *account-remove@yahoo-inc.com.* Please *click here* to read about what information may possibly remain in our archived records after your account has been deleted.

SECURITY

Your Yahoo! Account Information is password-protected for your privacy and security.

—Continued on page 168

Yahoo! Privacy Policy   *Continued from page 167*

In certain areas Yahoo! uses industry-standard SSL-encryption to protect data transmissions.

CHANGES TO THIS PRIVACY POLICY

Yahoo! may edit this policy from time to time. If we make any substantial changes we will notify you by posting a prominent announcement on our pages.

QUESTIONS OR SUGGESTIONS

If you have questions or suggestions complete a *feedback form* or send an email to *privacypolicy@yahoo-inc.com*.

If you feel that your inquiry has not been satisfactorily addressed, you should contact *TRUSTe,* an independent privacy organization.

Source: Reproduced with permission of Yahoo! Inc. © 2000 by Yahoo! Inc. YAHOO! and the YAHOO! logo are trademarks of Yahoo! Inc. https://www.truste.org/validate/361**TRUSTe Certified** Yahoo! is TRUSTe-certified. This certification applies to all English-language sites under the Yahoo.com domain.

---

bills, the delinquent account is reported on your credit report.

- They call your credit card issuer and, pretending to be you, change the mailing address on your credit card account. Then, your imposter runs up charges on your account. Because the resulting bills are being sent to the new address, you may not immediately realize there is a problem.
- They establish cellular phone service in your name.
- They open a bank account in your name and write bad checks on that account.

Privacy Policy of Egghead.com

Personal data of the kind described immediately above is a valuable informational commodity that has market value. Most Internet users do not realize that visiting a website may be the foundation for calls from telemarketing firms a few months later. Having bought some flowers on the Internet, a consumer may later be contacted in various ways by representatives of gift stores trying to peddle crystal glasses or some other complementary product. As the practice of selling information obtained in the course of Internet transactions is resented by many Internet users, many Internet vendors have privacy policies that allow their site users/customers to choose not to have any information about them disseminated. An example of a privacy policy is provided by Egghead.com, which sells software, hardware, and other high-tech products online at their website (www.Egghead.com). On page 169

we examine the privacy and security policies of Egghead.com

The article, written in italics, is from the Egghead.com Privacy Policy Statement. The parts not written in italics are the authors' comments on the Egghead.com Privacy Policy Statement. The first part of the Egghead.com Privacy Statement makes guarantees to combat fear of identity fraud.

FTC Regulations Regarding Children's Sites

According to the Federal Trade Commission (in 1998), the application of Fair Information Practice principles requires special adaptations when the target audience is children.[8] Noting that there are extensive federal and state laws that protect children from alcohol, tobacco, and pornography, as well as laws that require parental consent, the FTC has its own set of child-oriented regulations. The FTC states that the following practices appear contrary to the Federal Trade Commission Act, which prohibits unfair and deceptive trade practices:

> It is a deceptive practice to represent that a site is collecting personal identifying information from a child for a particular purpose (e.g. to earn points to redeem a premium), when the information will also be used for another purpose that parents would find material, in the absence of a clear and prominent disclosure to that effect; and

---

[8]www.ftc.gov/reports/privacy3/fairinfo.htm

Your Credit Card is Safe with Egghead.com—we guarantee it!

*Y*our browser and Egghead.com's secure server encrypt confidential information during transmission, ensuring that transactions stay private and protected. Egghead.com guarantees the safety of your credit card information in the following manner: if any unauthorized use of your credit card occurs as a result of your credit card purchase from Egghead.com, simply notify your credit card provider in accordance with its reporting rules and procedures. If, through no fault of your own, your credit card company finds credit card fraud but does not waive your entire liability for unauthorized charges, Egghead.com will reimburse you for the remaining liability, up to a maximum of fifty dollars U.S. ($50.00) per card. This guarantee applies to purchases made using Egghead.com's secure server (https: protocol).

Egghead.com has privacy policies regarding:

USE OF YOUR EMAIL ADDRESS

If you provide us with your email address, register as a customer, or make a purchase from us, we will occasionally send you email with recommendations or notices of new products and prices. This email may include paid advertisements from third parties. To block future email of this type, simply follow the instructions at the bottom of the message. Separately, we send email to keep you informed about the status of your orders. These messages cannot be blocked, except for the outbid notification. You may elect to turn this off on the Account Update page.

The last sentence in the Egghead.com **Use of Your Email Policy** is an opt-out option, which is consistent with (2) (discussed above) among the FTC's Fair Information Principles.

Consistent with (1) on the FTC's Fair Information Principles, Egghead.com (immediately below) discusses generally its policy regarding sharing of information that you supply to Egghead.com. It is also clear from the discussion below that Egghead.com claims that it will not sell information you provide to third parties. Any information that is given to third parties is given to them solely for the purposes of completing the transaction and third parties are prohibited by contract from reselling personally identifying information.

SHARING OF INFORMATION

During the Egghead.com registration process, we ask you to provide us with contact information, such as name, billing address, shipping address, email address, telephone number and a valid credit card number. We use this information to verify your account when you order.

Egghead.com identifies your bids only by your initials, city and state, country, or user name if you choose to provide one. We do not sell, rent or share any customer information, except for transactions involving third parties. In such cases, we provide only the information required to complete the transaction. By contract, the third party is not permitted to sell, rent or share this information.

Your visitor and user information is aggregated for the purpose of reporting to advertisers. However, in these situations, we do not disclose to these entities any information that could be used to personally identify you, such as your name, customer number, password, credit card number, or transaction history.

Another area of concern on the Internet is legitimacy of contests and games. There is a strong suspicion by many that the real purpose of the contests and games is to gather valuable marketing information about those entering the contest. Generally to enter the contest, participants have to complete a form online that reveals a lot of personal information. So great is the skepticism regarding these contests and games that Egghead.com has placed a lot of safeguards in its privacy policy, including a pledge of no sales of the information to third parties and an ability to opt out if that information is transferred to third parties.

SOLICITED INFORMATION

You may occasionally see contests, surveys, and other features of our website that ask you to provide us with information. When you choose to respond to these requests, the information you offer may be used for several reasons, including the uses set out in the sections above. We will also provide information to third parties as necessary to meet prize fulfillment or other aspects of any contest or similar offering. If we intend to use your personal information for any other purpose, we will notify you and give you a chance to opt out before responding to our survey, contest form, or other request. Additionally, you may choose not to respond or participate in any survey, contest, or other request.

We do not sell, rent or share your customer information, except for transactions involving third parties. In such cases, we provide only the information necessary to complete the transaction. By contract, third parties are not permitted to sell, rent or share this information.

—*Continued on page 170*

Your Credit Card is Safe with Egghead.com—we guarantee it!   *Continued from page 169*

Egghead.com tries to put a positive spin on cookies in their statement about them.

COOKIES

Egghead.com uses software tags called "cookies" to identify customers when they visit our site. They help us understand your buying preferences and customize our service to your needs. By understanding which areas of

the site you visit, cookies allow us to present information, products and specials that are of personal interest to you. Our goal is to save you time and make your shopping experience unique. The information we collect with cookies is not sold, rented or shared with any outside parties.

Source: www.Egghead.com.

It is likely to be an unfair practice to collect personal identifying information, such as a name, e-mail address, home address, or phone number, from children and to sell or otherwise disclose such identifying information to third parties, or to post it publicly online, without providing parents with adequate notice and an opportunity to control the collection and use of the information through prior parental consent.

In essence, the FTC report indicates that it will prosecute sites that collect information from children without parental notice and consent. The FTC indicates that the notice required should explain in sufficient detail what the website is offering in the way of e-mail, message boards, chat rooms, and other services such as web pages. These standards make websites legally vulnerable if they do not provide adequate notices. Certainly, pornographic websites generally have prominent notices that those entering the site must be at least 18 years old.

The Children's Online Privacy Protection Act (COPPA), 1998

The Children's Online Privacy Protection Act (COPPA) applies to websites that are either directed to children or to websites for which the operator knows that personal information is collected from children. COPPA requires notices with regard to what information is collected, how the information is to be used, and the operator's disclosure practices to third parties. Besides the required notice, COPPA requires a verifiable parental consent before information can be collected from children. For purposes of COPPA, children are defined as those who are under 13. In

addition, a website cannot condition a child's participation in giveaways and games on the provision of information. Finally, COPPA requires websites to establish reasonable procedures to protect the confidentiality, security, and integrity of the personal information collected. Under COPPA, sites that serve children are expected to protect access to stored data of e-mail addresses or other personal information about children from hackers who may be pedophiles.

Financial Records: The Gramm–Leach–Bliley Act, 1999

The Gramm–Leach–Bliley Act is largely directed towards deregulating some activities of the banking industry. Title V of the Act, however, deals with Privacy and Disclosure of Nonpublic Personal Information. Title V declares that, "It is the policy of the Congress that each financial institution has an affirmative and continuing obligation to respect the privacy of its customers and to protect the security and confidentiality of those customers' nonpublic personal information." In furthering that policy, Title V requires each agency that has authority over financial institutions to fashion regulations that—

- Insure the security and confidentiality of customer records and information, and
- Provide protection against any anticipated threats or hazards to the security or integrity of those records, and
- Protect against unauthorized access to or use of such records or information.

Section 502 of the Act prohibits a financial institution from disclosing to a third party any nonpublic personal information, "unless such financial institution provides or has provided to the consumer a notice that complies with section 503." The concern expressed in Section 502 is that customer nonpublic information will be given out to third parties for marketing purposes without customer consent. Section 502 requires that customers be clearly informed before their nonpublic information will be given to third parties and that customers have an opportunity to opt out of such disclosures. Finally, Title V prohibits a financial institution from disclosing account numbers or similar access numbers including credit card information to "unaffiliated third parties for use in telemarketing, direct mail marketing, or other marketing through electronic mail to the consumer." Title V does not prohibit a financial institution from giving out an account number of a customer to a credit bureau.

Medical Records: The Health Insurance Portability and Accountability Act (HIPAA) of 1996

When Congress passed the Health Insurance Portability and Accountability Act (HIPAA) of 1996, there were a number of situations that gained widespread publicity concerning workers who could not afford to change jobs because health insurers at the new employer would not pay for "pre-existing" medical conditions. HIPAA basically made it illegal for health insurers to deny coverage for pre-existing medical conditions, and that part of the statute has been a big success.

The other part of HIPAA that has attracted increasing attention is protection of the privacy of medical records. At this point the scenario has become familiar. Computerization of medical records has made them increasingly easy to store and distribute. There have been a number of instances in which medical records have been sold to (or otherwise obtained by) third party marketers (see box on page 172). Women who are prescribed antinausea drugs during pregnancy are suddenly inundated with ads from companies selling maternity clothes. There also have been cases of disclosures of medical records that are clearly inappropriate and that have led to extreme embarrassment. Patients have not been assured that when they gave out medical information it would not end up in the hands of vendors or others who are not in any way connected with their treatment.

HIPAA called for Congress either to enact privacy legislation by August of 1999 or, failing that, to empower the Department of Health and Human Services (HSS) to fashion its own regulations. Congress did not act, so HSS issued regulations that were scheduled to become law in April of 2001. The basic principle behind HSS's regulations is that nonconsensual secondary use of personally identifying medical records is illegal, though there are a number of exceptions to this rule which we will discuss. HIPAA regulates healthcare providers, insurance companies, and HMOs, among others. Transfers of medical information between "covered" entities (healthcare providers, insurers, and HMOs) for the purposes of furthering treatment, payments, or healthcare operations are legal under HSS regulations. All other transfers of medical records require consent of patients, with a number of specific exceptions. The following list of such exceptions is not exhaustive. A nonconsensual transfer of medical records is allowed if it is used by:

- Public health authorities for purposes of preventing the outbreak of communicable diseases.
- Medical researchers who have a panel that reviews the need for personally identifying medical information. The costs of obtaining consent from patients for medical records is often prohibitive for medical researchers.
- Law enforcement pursuant to an investigation. Although there is some language about probable cause, a search warrant is not required for law enforcement to examine medical records stored by a medical facility regulated by HIPAA.
- Officials performing oversight for purposes of determining whether the provision of medical services are being efficiently delivered and whether fraud and abuse are taking place.

There are eight other exceptions that are listed by HSS through which nonconsensual secondary use of medical records can take place. Although the protection of medical records under HIPAA may seem leaky, it represents a significant improvement over the prior situation where the rules regarding medical records were not at all clear.

Not concerned about the privacy of your medical records? Consider the following article:

Are Your Medical Records Private?

A Boston technology firm is surreptitiously tracking computer users across the Internet on behalf of pharmaceutical companies, a practice that demonstrates the limits of a recent agreement to protect the privacy of Web surfers.

By invisibly placing ID codes on computers that visit its clients' World Wide Web sites, Pharmatrak Inc. can record consumers' activity when they alight on thousands of pages maintained by 11 pharmaceutical companies. For example, the company can tell when the same computers download information about HIV, a prescription drug or a company's profits from different sites.

Pharmatrak officials say the information they collect about browsing habits enables participating drug companies to compare and improve their Websites. They don't collect names and don't intend to, they say.

But they claim they can predict whether visitors are consumers, physicians, journalists or government officials, based on where they come from and what they access.

And the company's Website also suggests that it has plans to identify people. "In the future, we may develop products and services which collect data that, when used in conjunction with the tracking database, could enable a direct identification of certain individual visitors," it says, adding that they would never take advantage of such information.

Industry and federal officials applauded last month's agreement by DoubleClick, Engage and other online advertising services to give computer users more choice about when they're monitored. But Pharmatrak doesn't have to abide by the agreement because it isn't an advertiser.

Privacy advocates complain the company is acting inappropriately by monitoring computer users, with no notification, as they browse through sensitive health-care information.

"It's all hidden and it's across Websites," Richard M. Smith, a software engineer and chief technology officer of the Privacy Foundation, a nonprofit group in Denver, said of Pharmatrak's activities. "It's getting very close to that line of what nice people don't do."

Michigan's attorney general's office has warned G.D. Searle & Co., a part of Pharmacia Corp., that it faces a lawsuit for allowing Pharmatrak to monitor computer users without proper notification.

"They've taken stealth to a new low. . . . It is a classic example of corporate surveillance," said Michigan Attor-

ney General Jennifer M. Granholm. "There's no way your average computer user has any idea."

Pharmacia spokeswoman Claudia R. Kovitz said Pharmacia treats information about visitors with great care and does not receive any personally identifiable information from Pharmatrak. She acknowledged that Pharmacia Websites did not post privacy policies until late last month and still do not mention Pharmatrak.

"As Internet technology rapidly advances, and as legal and ethical guidelines evolve, we have been developing, and will continue to develop, increasingly comprehensive privacy policies based on best practices in our field," she said.

Michael Sonnenreich, Pharmatrak founder and chief executive, said people worried about privacy can set their browsers to alert them to Pharmatrak "cookies"—small strings of computer code that serve as a unique identifier. "If they file a suit like that, they are idiots," he said about the threatened action by Michigan authorities. People should know "they're using an open access means of communication."

Sonnenreich, a D.C. resident and Washington Opera board member, added: "We are absolutely rock solid protecting the integrity and privacy of these people."

Pharmatrak officials acknowledge they do not post privacy policies at client Websites stating how the company collects and uses information. But they said there's no need because they don't have the technical ability or intention to collect names. The company recently acknowledged on its Website that it sets "cookies."

Virtually unknown outside the drug industry, Pharmatrak is a subsidiary of Sonnenreich's holding company, Glocal Communications Ltd. Glocal also owns Agritrak, a fledgling operation that will provide similar services to "agri-biotech" companies.

Pharmatrak relies on the same sort of techniques to tag computers that created controversy for Internet advertising services. It places "cookies" on users' computers from a distance through software code on Web pages called a "Web bug"—a process that is invisible unless a browser is specifically set to alert a user.

Sonnenreich said the company shares the information it collects in aggregate monthly reports to Pfizer Inc., Pharmacia, SmithKline Beecham PLC, Glaxo Wellcome PLC, Aventis Pharmaceuticals Inc., Novartis Pharmaceuticals Corp., American Home Products Corp., Hoffmann-La Roche Inc. and three other drug companies that have agreed to collaborate.

Continued from page 172

Sonnenreich said the company can help clients compare how computer users behave at their Websites relative to those operated by competitors.

"Determining, for example, whether the greatest number of visitors come from Europe, Asia or the U.S., and whether they are principally from government, academia, or other commercial organizations will show whether a company is reaching its designated target audiences efficiently," Pharmatrak's Website says.

"Equally, a sudden drop or increase over time from a particular audience such as a government body is a signal well worth heeding."

The company offers an array of other services, including one called Netwatcher. Using a sophisticated search engine, Netwatcher scours the Web for any mention of client companys' executives, products and financial matters.

The search is far more powerful than Yahoo and Google, relying on thousands of keywords to root out information, company officials said. For now, Pharmatrak focuses on material posted to Websites. In the future, it may also sift through online chat rooms.

Company officials compared their word matching program to systems operated by the National Security Agency and the Central Intelligence Agency. "It's a customized intelligence search engine," Sonnenreich said. "I'm sure the government does the same thing."

Sonnenreich declined to share details. But he said companies have used the reports to respond to remarks made about a company executive and its products. In the future, companies will be able to follow up on rumors circulated by competitors, or protests planned by groups such as Greenpeace or the Sierra Club, he said.

"Any negative reports that appear on the Internet are highlighted early enough to allow the company to rectify the situation before the issue becomes a full-blown problem requiring the services of the legal department," the company literature says.

Janlori Goldman, director of the Health Privacy Project at Georgetown University, is not comforted by the company's reassurances. She worries that such stealthy scrutiny will dissuade people from using the Web to find out helpful information about health care.

"This is analogous to having hidden cameras and spies tracking people's movements and communication on the Web," Goldman said. "The lack of privacy rules on the Web is the number one barrier to people getting better health-care information, because they're afraid."

Source: © 2000 The Washington Post Company. Reprinted with permission. Robert O'Harrow Jr.; *Washington Post* Staff Writer; Tuesday, August 15, 2000; p. E01.

Additional Readings:
http://www.security-informer.com/english/crd seci_227862.html
"Privacy lawsuit filed against Pharmatrak", August 22, 2000; James Evans, IDG News Service\Boston Bureau.
http://boston.internet.com/news/article/0,1928,2001_440821,00.html
"Privacy II: California Man Sues Pharmatrak", August 18, 2000, Gavin McCormick, boston.internet.com.
http://www.seacoastonline.com/news/8_16_sb2.htm
"Firm Tracks which Medical Information Consumers Access", August 16, 2000; Associated Press, Seacoastline.

European Union and Privacy

The nations of the European Union (EU) have banded together to enact legislation that maintains strict governmental protection for privacy. By and large, the United States relies on voluntary industry codes for the protection of privacy, whereas the EU regards voluntary industry codes as deficient. In addition to governmental codes on privacy, the EU Data Protection Directive forbids transmission of data between member nations and others where privacy protection is inadequate.[9] At present according to EU standards of privacy protection, regulation in the United States is in-adequate. There is concern that literal application of the European Data Protection Directive could cause considerable interruption of data transmissions between the U.S. and the EU nations. The U.S. had until the end of 1999 to remedy its privacy laws before the impact of the EU Directive was to take place, but at the time of this writing, negotiations between the EU and the U.S. Department of Commerce were still taking place.[10]

The U.S. Department of Commerce released its privacy regulations in April of 1999 and, then, issued

---

[9]See http://www2.echo.lu/legal/en/dataprot/directiv/directiv.html which contains the EU Data Protection Directive.

[10]See the website article, "EU to U.S.: Privacy Rules Not Good Enough". http://www.thestandard.com/articles/article_print/0,1454,4289,00.html

clarifications to these regulations one-month later in May.[11] The outcome of the dialogue between the U.S. and the EU regarding the adequacy of database protection is uncertain. The thrust of privacy regulations developed and promoted by the Department of Commerce is to fashion "safe harbors" that U.S. companies could adhere to that would also satisfy EU privacy requirements. Presumptively, if a U.S. company adheres to the regulations of the Department of Commerce, those regulations would be known by the EU to comply with their Data Protection Directive.

"E.U. Privacy Directive Is Threat to Banks"

"When it comes to banks, the impact could be a disruption of data flow between Europe and the United States. For instance, a U.S. bank that offers credit cards in Germany may not be able to process the transactions in the United States. Similarly, a German customer buying goods in New York may not be able to use his German-issued credit card. Authorization for the purchase must come from a computer system in Europe, and the question arises whether it is permissible to transfer the personal information to the United States, said Swire, the author of a book on the European date protection directive—'None of Your Business: World Data Flows, Electronic Commerce and the E.U. Privacy Directive' with co-author Robert Litan—to be released later this month by the Washington-based Brookings Institution."

"Business lending and loan syndication will also be affected. Banks taking part in a syndication will want to see the underlying documents, which may contain personally identifiable information. 'Once again it is hard to see how transfers out of Europe of personal information would be permitted under the directive,' said Swire. Although he adds that for some transactions it may be possible to get consent in advance from each person named in the documents transferred to the third country."

"When it comes to investment banking, a wide range of transactions include personally identifiable information and many international transactions involve the sharing of information between American and European offices of one or more banks. 'The discussion here shows major potential problems with respect to market analysis and especially hostile takeovers,' said Swire. 'The directive may also create obstacles to the ability of European firms to raise money for the United States.'"

Source: From "E.U. Privacy Directive Is Threat to Banks," by Claire Chapman, *Thomson's International Banking Regulator,* October 5, 1998, Vol. 10, Issue 38, p. 1.

Additional Readings:
www.dss.state.ct.us/digital/eupriv.html
"Fact Sheet on the European Union Privacy Directive", John D. Woodward, Jr., Esq. & Gary Roethenbaugh.

http://www.ipmag.com/dailies/980629.html
"EU Directive on Privacy May Hinder E-Commerce" August/September 1998; IP Magazine, Al Gidari and Marie Aglion.

http://www.llrx.com/congress/061500.htm
"The EU Privacy Protection Directive and the U.S. Safe Harbor", May 15, 2000; LLRX.com; Carol M. Morrissey.

SUMMARY

- The significance of tort claims stemming from Internet activities may supercede that of traditional torts as commercial as well as personal activities move to the web.
- One important tort that involves Internet activities and that already has a significant litigation history is defamation.
- In a defamation suit, the plaintiff must show the defendant made false statements about him or her, that the false statements were heard by third parties, and that the false statements harmed his or her reputation.
- Not only is the author of defamatory comments liable, but also one who repeats or republishes defamatory comments is liable.
- Internet Service Providers have been targets of defamation suits.
- Initially, ISPs were viewed like bookstores and, thus, not subject to liability as distributors of defamatory material that appeared on their servers.

---

[11]At this writing, it is unclear whether the regulations proposed by the Department of Commerce will satisfy the EU. See
http://www.ita.doc.gov/ecom/menu.htm.

- In one defamation decision (Stratton), however, an ISP was viewed by the court as a publisher because it claimed to *supervise* content and, thus, was responsible for and **liable for** defamatory material that appeared on its server.
- Section 230 of the Communications Decency Act of 1996 bars suits that place ISPs in the same legal position as publishers, protected from liability for materials provided by third parties.
- Employers are also increasingly being shielded from liability for defamation unless there is evidence that the employer knew the statements about its employee or former employee were false or had a reckless disregard for the truth.
- If employers provide a server, they may be able to qualify for *server (ISP) immunity* under the CDA.
- The law provides remedies for invasions of privacy both by the government and private sources.
- The Fourth Amendment protects against governmental invasions of privacy. For most searches, search warrants are required, which means that the government must show probable cause before a neutral magistrate that it is likely that a crime has been committed.
- It is an actionable tort for a defendant to invade an area where a plaintiff has a reasonable expectation of privacy.
- Information communicated to ISPs is not protected by the reasonable expectation of privacy of the subscriber.
- There are numerous actions that have been taken by websites to collect information from visitors without their knowledge or consent. Furthermore much of that information is collected for resale to other firms.
- Many websites do not have privacy policies and yet 97 percent of websites collect identifying information.
- Many websites collect information from children or transmit sensitive medical and financial information. As a result government regulation has taken place.
- There are many potential invasions of privacy on the job that do not involve the Internet.
- By and large, *drug testing* by private firms is legal and, increasingly, public employers can test for drugs without establishing individualized probable cause.

- With very few exceptions, *polygraph testing* by employers is illegal.
- *Intrusive questioning* in testing administered by employers has inspired lawsuits based on invasions of privacy.
- In general there is little federal regulation of on-the-job monitoring of employees by employers.
- Employers are potentially liable when they invade employees' *reasonable expectations of privacy.* Employers can negate invasion of privacy suits by informing employees that they will be monitored and explain how they will be monitored.
- Congress has given statutory protection to employee phone calls and e-mails. Two major exceptions exist—when monitoring is done within the regular course of business or when employees consent to the monitoring.
- In one case, a court has held that employees do not have reasonable expectations of privacy when e-mails are stored on company computers (Microsoft won that one).
- The Federal Trade Commission has elucidated five principles of fair information practices that include: Notice, Choice, Access, Integrity, and Redress.
- A huge amount of personally identifying information is stored by public and private sources.
- A particularly troublesome practice is the placement of *cookies* on web browsers by websites. Using cookies, information is extracted without knowledge or consent of website visitors.
- In some high-profile cases websites have not followed guarantees made to visitors regarding their own practices with respect to the gathering of information and the use of that information.
- Privacy policies at websites are increasingly common and detailed. The effect of a privacy policy is that companies that do use cookies can claim that visitors were informed of the cookies and of the use of the information extracted using cookies and other information gathering instruments.
- With growth of the Internet, the incidence and significance of *identity theft* have risen. Identity theft occurs when someone has obtained personally identifiable information about you in order to impersonate you.
- The threat of identity theft has inspired websites to make additional investments in security in order to guarantee that transmissions between them and customers are secure and are not intercepted.

- The FTC has special concerns about the extraction of information from children. Children can be manipulated by adults into revealing information that their parents would not want revealed.
- The Children's Online Privacy Protection Act of 1998 makes it illegal to gather information from children without prior approval from parents.
- The Gramm–Leach–Bliley Act of 1999 prohibits banks and other financial institutions from revealing nonpublic financial information to third parties unless they have informed their customers and given them opportunity to opt out of such disclosures.

- The Health Insurance Portability and Accountability Act of 1996 outlaws distribution of personally identifiable medical information unless it is for the purpose of treatment, payment, or operations, with some important exceptions for public health, medical research, and law enforcement, among others.
- The European Union has stronger protection for the privacy of personal records than the United States and their Date Protection Directive prohibits sharing of data with countries that do not subscribe to their standards. Negotiations between the EU and the U.S. Department of Commerce are ongoing.

PRODUCT LIABILITY IN A HIGH-TECH ENVIRONMENT

OVERVIEW

It is difficult to overestimate the costs of high-profile product liability lawsuits. One need only recall Dow-Corning breast implants, asbestos, DES, and the Ford Pinto (discussed below) cases to realize that large corporations can lose profitability and even be forced out of business or into bankruptcy when their products have defects that harm people. As more and more products make use of high technology, the problem of hidden product defects, not anticipated by manufacturers, will become more prevalent. Already warning signals are sounding for cell phones, products that make use of software such as medical diagnostic equipment, recreational products in "extreme" sports, and increasingly sophisticated firearms. There is little doubt that if some of the aforementioned products are found to have defects, that liability for sellers will be very expensive.

PRODUCT LIABILITY LAW ENCOMPASSES MANY AREAS AND LEVELS OF LAW

Product liability law has always been a complex combination of state and federal law. In addition, product liability law can be based on contract, tort, or regulatory law. Much of product liability law is **state law.** To illustrate, if a product defect/liability suit is based on a breach of warranty, then the UCC governs. The UCC, of course, is part of state law. Most product liability suits are based on tort law, which is also based on state common law, though there have been some codifications of tort law in the form of Restatements, which will be discussed below. While the majority of product liability cases are dealt with under state law, this is not always the case. There are many products that are subject to **federal regulatory standards** originating from the Consumer Product Safety Commission, the Food and Drug Administration, and other regulatory agencies. A question of preemption of state law frequently surfaces when a plaintiff sues under *state* law and the defendant defends by claiming that it has complied with all *federal* regulations relating to the design and performance of the product.

Product Liability Law Continues to Evolve To develop a firm understanding of the application of product liability law to high-tech products, it is helpful to know a bit about the evolution of product liability, which has been created from an enormous historical volume of cases that, not surprisingly, has involved

---

Product Liability and Ethics

*I*n the U.S., many people are very weight conscious and seemingly cannot lose weight long term without some pharmaceutical assistance. Several weight-loss products, however, have had side effects that are serious or life-threatening. Does the desire for profits by pharmaceutical companies cause them to overlook possible risks? Those who took certain weight-loss drugs are now possible plaintiffs in a product liability lawsuit. Consider the following web page from the law firm of Duffus & Melvin:

Fenfluramine was thought to bring about weight loss by increasing the brain chemical serotonin, which controls satiety, or a feeling of fullness. Phentermine, which acted on another brain chemical, dopamine, increased the body's metabolism and was thought to have a role in reducing the minor side effects caused by Fenfluramine, such as drowsiness. New studies find evidence that both Pondimin and Redux increased risk of heart valve damage.

Two new studies were recently released, which confirm that fen/phen and Redux increased the risk of heart valve damage. Those who took these drugs for longer than 3 months or in high doses appear to be particularly at risk. According to one study, heart valve damage occurred in 22.7% of obese patients who took the appetite-suppressants between 1994 and 1997.

Source: Web Page at:
http://www.injurync.com/fenphen_combination.htm

---

different kinds of products. In addition to having some historical perspective on the bases for product liability law, responsible managers also should be aware of reform efforts in product liability law, both at the federal and state levels.

Much Product Liability Law Involves Economics and Ethics As Well As Law   Manufacturers are generally well aware of the costs of changing product designs. In general, design changes that add to safety also cost money and thus have an impact on price. With added costs virtually all products can be made safer but the resulting increase in price may price the product out of the market. Product liability involves ethical dilemmas as well. Suppose a pharmaceutical drug is not approved by the U.S. Food and Drug Administration, but other (possibly Third World) countries do not consider the drug unsafe? Is it ethical for a U.S. pharmaceutical firm to sell drugs that are unapproved to outlets in other countries, while earning very high profits?

Downside Risks Cannot Be Completely Eliminated Through Contract Law

Vendors of high-tech products generally are quite cognizant of potential liability for products that malfunction. In some cases, their *contractual* liability for products that do not perform as warranted or advertised can be lessened or negated by warranty disclaimers of liability and limitation of liability clauses that cap possible damages. These warranty disclaimers and limitations of liability (discussed in part in Chapters 3 and 4) are generally enforceable against trading partners, whether they be other businesses or, with some important qualifications, against ordinary consumers. Generally, courts respect freedom of contract and vendors, who are very aware of the potential for costly suits, skillfully draw up contracts that protect their downside risk.

However, no matter how skillfully vendors draw up contracts, there is substantial legal liability exposure for selling products that have what courts determine to be "defects." Tort liability for defective products exists regardless of whether a user has entered into a contractual relationship with the vendor. A product can be defective because it is improperly **manufactured,** or **designed,** or because the **warnings** on the product are **inadequate.** The principles of tort liability apply regardless of the presence of contracts, and there are important limitations on freedom of contract that further expose sellers to liability.

Constraints on Contractual Liability Limits on Consumer Products

As discussed in Chapter 2, under the UCC warranty limitations of liability are treated as *unconscionable* when the product is a *consumer good* and the seller attempts to limit liability for *personal injury.* UCC Section 2-719(b)(3) indicates that "Limitation of consequential damages for injury to the person in the case of consumer goods is prima facie unconscionable but

---

Jury Awards Rising: Study

Sharp increases in jury awards in product liability and medical malpractice cases are fueling increases in the size of all personal injury awards, according to a new study.

The median amount of compensatory damages awarded by juries in personal injury cases rose 7% in 1998 to $50,000 from $46,695 in 1997, according to the 1999 edition of "Current Award Trends in Personal Injury," published earlier this month by Jury Verdict Research of Horsham, Pa. The study analyzes only awards and not the amounts paid to plaintiffs at settlement, which often can be considerably lower.

Contributing to the increase were a 137 percent jump in the median compensatory award in product liability cases and a 46 percent rise in the median in medical malpractice cases.

Source: Excerpt from: "Jury Awards Rising: Study"; *Michael Bradford; Business Insurance,* Chicago; May 1, 2000; Vol. 34, Iss. 18; pg. 1, 2 pgs.

Additional source: "Civil-Case Plaintiffs Had Winning Year in '96"; *Lynna Goch; Best's Review,* Oldwick; Nov 1999; Vol. 100, Iss. 7; Property/casualty insurance edition; pg. 114, 1 pgs.

Additional Source: "Under Attack"; *Barbara Bowers; Best's Review,* Oldwick; Feb 2000; Vol. 100, Iss. 10; pg. 56, 2 pgs.

---

limitation of damages where the loss is commercial is not."

Magnuson-Moss Act

Note, also, the impact of the Magnuson-Moss Act, which requires sellers to classify all *written* warranties as either "Full" or "Limited". The Magnuson-Moss Act prohibits sellers from disclaiming *implied warranties* during the period when a written warranty is in force. Therefore unless a seller makes a conspicuous disclaimer that their products are being sold "As Is", the seller is prohibited from disclaiming the UCC implied warranty of merchantability, if the seller has a written warranty in place. As long as the implied warranty of merchantability is in force, sellers cannot limit their liability for defective products sold to consumers that result in personal injury. **Under U.S. law, then, no contract can totally shield vendors from liability to consumers, users, and third parties that may be injured by defective products.**

Importance of Tort Law as Alternative to Contract Law

Victims of defective products can employ tort law to seek redress in court. Note that in many product liability cases, the victim sues based on *both* tort and contract law. Although punitive damage awards are generally unavailable in contract law, *tort* plaintiffs are entitled to recover punitive damages if they can show that the seller had a reckless disregard for public safety or for its customers. It is also important to note that juries can be very sympathetic to victims of defective products. In many cases, victims are horribly injured or die as result of an allegedly defective product. Combine this with the fact that jurors relate more to ordinary consumers than they do to corporations, large or small, and the consequences are often predictable. If a product defect case goes to trial, company defendants lose in a sizeable percentage of cases and the resulting damage awards on occasion can be staggering. In most cases, a company will settle if the case survives motions to dismiss and other motions launched by manufacturers to prevent the case from going to trial or going to a jury.

PRODUCT LIABILITY BASED ON NEGLIGENCE

In general, the ordinary principles of negligence apply to malfunctioning products **if it is reasonably foreseeable** that a product defect could harm groups of people. If a vendor sells products (drugs and medical equipment) that are used to anesthetize patients undergoing medical operations and those products are defective, it is reasonably foreseeable that someone will die or be injured as a result. Patients in an operating room are entitled to recover from sellers of defective products regardless of any contractual relationships that vendors may have with hospitals or doctors. Similarly, vendors of software used by businesses may limit recoveries by business for malfunctioning software, but those agreements do not limit third parties from pursuing the software firm for injuries that are reasonably foreseeable.

Consider the following clause that frequently appears in software development contracts:

VENDOR'S TOTAL LIABILITY SHALL NOT EXCEED THE LICENSEE FEE PAID BY LICENSEE WITH RESPECT TO THE SOFTWARE PRODUCT ON WHICH SUCH LIABILITY IS BASED. IN NO EVENT SHALL VENDOR BE LIABLE FOR ANY INDIRECT, SPECIAL, INCIDENTAL, CONSEQUENTIAL, PUNITIVE OR EXEMPLARY DAMAGES ARISING OUT OF OR IN CONNECTION WITH THIS AGREEMENT OR ANY ACTS OR OMISSIONS ASSOCIATED THEREWITH OR RELATING TO THE USE OF THE SOFTWARE LICENSE HEREUNDER, WHETHER SUCH CLAIM IS BASED ON BREACH OF WARRANTY, CONTRACT, TORT OR OTHER LEGAL THEORY.

The language is quite broad in its attempt to negate possible liability, but no contract between two parties can waive possible tort claims of third parties who do not agree to these restrictions. If software is supplied to an automobile manufacturer and a defect in the software causes an accident (say the left turn signal is turned on when the dials on the dash indicate the right turn signal is on), the software developer and automobile manufacturer are liable to injured customers if they were negligent in testing the car with the software. Travel agents have software that links them with airlines and hotels. If such software contained defects that resulted in stranded travelers, the software developers may be subject to suit by the customers, even if they have negated liability to the travel agency by contract.

Negligence Claims Generally

In any claim based on negligence, the plaintiff, the injured party, must show that:

1. the defendant had a *duty* to the plaintiff,
2. the defendant *breached* that duty,
3. the breach of that duty was the *proximate* (or legal) *cause* of the plaintiff's injury, and
4. the plaintiff's *injuries* were of a kind recognized at law.

In law, actors have an obligation to use reasonable care whether they are manufacturing and selling products, or whether they are driving a motor vehicle. If it is reasonably foreseeable that failure to use reasonable care

will result in harm to another person, then defendants breach their duty to the plaintiff when they fail to use reasonable care. Sellers of products, especially high-tech products, have duties of care to customers, users, and third parties, such as bystanders. These duties include the requirement to use reasonable care in inspection, design, warnings, manufacturing and testing of the products they sell to the public.

Inspection and Testing

Manufacturers, sellers, and others may be liable to customers if their failure to make reasonable inspections of their product(s) results in harm to consumers, users, or third parties. Modern product liability law began with the *McPherson* case in which an automobile manufacturer was held liable to a consumer for failure to make reasonable inspections of tire spokes for one of its automobiles.[1] Since that time, there have been a number of cases that have been tried based on the claim that a defendant manufacturer failed to perform a reasonable inspection. Also many high-tech firms are involved in consulting services where failure to make reasonable inspections and tests are sources of potential liability. Of course, targets of product liability suits will mount vigorous defenses to seek to prevent or limit damage recoveries. Some of the difficulties of suing based on a negligence claim are illustrated by the *American Red Cross* case (discussed below) involving blood transfusions in the early 1980s.

Compliance with Government Regulations

Often, in failure-to-inspect cases, compliance with government regulations plays a critical role in determining whether the defendant's failure to inspect is negligence. If an inspection is mandated by a government safety regulation, then failure to inspect, where this is a showing that the failure to inspect is the proximate cause of the plaintiff's injuries, means that the defendant is liable per se. The defendant cannot claim that its failure to inspect was reasonable behavior when government has made a policy decision that an inspection is required. On the other hand, suppose that a firm has made all inspections that are required by the government or that it operates in a market where there are no inspections required by law? Can a firm defend

---

[1]*McPherson* v. *Buick Motor Co.*, 111 N.E. 1050 (N.Y. 1916).

itself by claiming that it made all the inspections that were required by law? The defense of compliance with all applicable required government inspections is a strong defense, but it is not an absolute defense as we will see in several cases below.

There are, indeed, many cases in which firms selling products have been successfully sued even though they complied with all applicable governmental regulations. Firms that sell meats and poultry are subject to suit if they sell contaminated products even though the company has complied with all of USDA's inspection procedures. Many drugs that have been approved by the Food and Drug Administration have been held defective, in part because juries found that the company did not adequately test for side effects of the drugs. In the case of DES, an antinausea drug that was prescribed for pregnant women, there was ample evidence that the drug companies concealed evidence of possible adverse reactions to the drug by test subjects. The fact that a pharmaceutical company has complied with all of the FDA's requirements on a product does not mean that the company has no further obligations to inspect or test that product.

Preemption of State Law?

As mentioned above, product liability suits are generally initiated under state law, either contract or, more likely, tort law. The products that are the subject of these suits are often regulated by a federal agency. So, a question that arises is whether federal regulation of the product preempts state law. In general, federal regulatory law sets **minimum** safety standards and does not preempt product liability suits in state courts based on tort or contract claims. There have been some cases in which the prevalence of federal regulatory standards has preempted state product liability claims. In most cases, preemption has not been an effective defense. In the famous *Cipollone* case involving the adequacy of warnings for cigarettes, the U.S. Supreme Court held that the warnings of the Surgeon General did preempt a state common law suit in which the plaintiff claimed the warnings were not adequate.[2] In this case, however, the Supreme Court concluded that plaintiffs were not preempted from suing the tobacco companies based on fraud. Although such imprecision drives businesses to distraction, all that can be definitively said is that the more comprehensive is a set of federal regulatory standards, the more likely state law is preempted by those standards.

Industry Practices

A parallel situation exists when industry standards are considered. If a product liability defendant does not comply with customary industry standards with respect to warnings and safety features, it is more likely that a jury will find for the plaintiff, again assuming there is a connection between the plaintiff's injuries and adherence to industry safety standards. In the Ford Pinto case discussed below, most car makers (firms in the industry) placed gas tanks in front of the rear axle for added protection in the event of a rear end collision. When this evidence was presented to a jury in a case involving a rear end collision in which one plaintiff died and another was horribly burned, the jury returned a verdict of $125 million in favor of the plaintiffs.[3]

There have been a number of cases in which the defenses of the defendants were that they complied with all applicable safety measures taken by firms selling similar products in the industry. In several cases, courts have made it clear that compliance with industry safety standards is not the final word on what constitutes reasonable safety measures. In some cases, courts have ruled that industry safety standards have lagged behind what is reasonable.

Case law, then, makes it clear that compliance with government regulations and/or industry practices does not *absolutely* insulate a firm from a product liability claim based on failure to adequately inspect or test the product. Sellers of products, particularly complicated, high-tech products, have a duty to *discover* hidden dangers in the design of a product and this is mainly accomplished by inspections and testing. There is, however, a **reasonableness** limitation in the requirement to inspect or test, so that companies are not absolute insurers of their products from all possible harm to consumers. In general, compliance with all government regulations in the industry weighs heavily in favor of the seller as does the conducting of tests and inspections that are customary in the industry. Many of the issues we have addressed—industry standards, government regulation, and the obligation to conduct reasonable inspections—are important in the next case.

---

[2]*Cipollone* v. *Liggett Group, Inc.*, 505 U.S. 504 (1992).

[3]In the *Ford* v. *Grimshaw* case, discussed below, the $125 million punitive damage award of the jury was reduced to $3.5 million on appeal.

John Doe, et al. v. American National Red Cross DBA Maryland Red Cross Chesapeake Region
United States District Court, D. Maryland
866 F.Supp. 242 (1994)

FACTS AND CASE BACKGROUND

On January 12, 1984, a young male donated a unit of blood at a mobile Red Cross collection station in the American Red Cross's Washington, D.C. Region. On or about February 3, 1984, Jane Doe was admitted to Doctors' Hospital in Prince George's County suffering from severe anemia. She received the unit of blood that had been donated on January 12. In March 1989, the donor of the blood died from AIDS. His physician reported the death to the Maryland Department of Health and Mental Hygiene, which, in turn, informed the Red Cross. In October 1990, Jane Doe's blood tested positive for the HIV virus in two separate tests. On October 23, 1990, she was diagnosed with esophageal candidiasis, an AIDS-defining illness. Eighteen months later, on May 1, 1992, Jane Doe died. Her death certificate lists AIDS as among the causes of death.

This action has been brought by John and Melanie Doe, the brother and daughter of Jane Doe. They allege that the Red Cross's negligence resulted in the death of Jane Doe. Specifically, they assert that the Red Cross was negligent because (1) it did not perform the Hepatitis B Core Antibodies Test as a surrogate test for detecting AIDS, (2) it did not screen donors by asking direct questions about their sexual history and (3) it did not provide adequate warnings of the fatal risk of transfusion-related AIDS. Discovery has now been completed, and the Red Cross has moved for summary judgment.

OPINION: J. FREDERICK MOTZ

The parties agree that the ultimate issue presented in this case is whether the Red Cross met "the standard of care, skill and diligence that a reasonable [blood bank] would use under the same or similar circumstances." . . . [footnotes deleted] They also agree, at least implicitly, that if the standard of care by which the Red Cross's conduct is to be measured is established by the industry practice and government regulations that were prevailing in January 1984, the Red Cross is entitled to the summary judgment that it seeks. There is no evidence in the record that the Red Cross's actions that are complained of were contrary to any contemporaneous industry practice or applicable government regulation. To the contrary, the uncontradicted evidence is that the Red Cross's actions were in conformity with both.

* * *

Plaintiffs contend, however, that this is not dispositive. According to them, the Red Cross can be held liable if there is sufficient evidence from which a jury could reasonably conclude that the industry effectively controlled the government regulators and "unduly lagged in the adoption of new and available devices."

* * *

Plaintiffs' evidentiary support for their surrogate testing claim is scant. They rely primarily upon documents and testimony that suggests that by January 1984 it was generally accepted that AIDS was transmissible by blood. Evidence of that fact alone, however, is far from sufficient to sustain plaintiffs' burden. What plaintiffs must demonstrate is that the failure to adopt surrogate testing in response to the increasing recognition of the transmissibility of AIDS by blood was negligent. On that point plaintiffs have presented virtually no evidence at all.

Moreover, the record proves that the Red Cross, other members of the blood banking community and government regulators articulated concerns about implementing surrogate testing, including the cost of such testing and its detrimental effect upon the blood supply. No reasonable inference can be drawn from the record that these concerns were anything but legitimate, and however those concerns may be resolved in hindsight, a factor of the time necessary to resolve them must be inserted into the equation when determining whether the industry had "unduly lagged in the adoption of new and available devices." Here, viewing the evidence most favorably to plaintiffs, all that can be said is that blood bankers and government regulators did not immediately follow the approach that plaintiffs' experts believed should have been followed. There is no evidence that blood bankers and government regulators were not struggling in good faith with issues of unknown dimension or that they were not reasonably attempting to chart what were then highly uncertain seas.

* * *

For these reasons I find that the Red Cross is entitled to the summary judgment that it seeks. A separate order granting its motion is being entered herewith.

QUESTIONS FOR ANALYSIS

1. If the facts were exactly the same except for the date, would

a blood transfusion recipient *today* be able to successfully sue Red Cross if they contracted the AIDS virus from a blood transfusion? What has changed between now and 1984?

2. Do industries have an obligation to immediately adopt possible life-saving tests, regardless of the costs?

3. Does this case support the proposition that if a company

is in compliance with applicable governmental regulations and industry safety standards it is insulated from suit?

Negligence in Manufacturing

Both in times past and today, a person injured by a defective product could make the claim that the manufacturer was negligent in the manufacture of the product. The plaintiff could show that the defendant did not adhere to industry standards for quality control in the manufacture of the product and, that, if the defendant had employed quality control measures customary within the industry, the plaintiff would not have been injured. The burden of proof borne by plaintiffs is heavy in this kind of case because it requires the plaintiff to discover such failures within the defendant's production facilities, a daunting task in most cases. In the first place, manufacturers have greater access to information about what goes on at their facilities than do plaintiffs. Moreover, employees at the manufacturer's plant may find it in their self-interest to conceal evidence. Experts will often differ on what is reasonable within the industry and juries are ill-equipped to make such technical judgments.

In some cases, however, showing that a manufacturer was negligent is straightforward. As with inspections and testing, if a manufacturer fails to adhere to a government safety regulation in production and proximate cause is shown, the defendant is negligent per se. The Consumer Product Safety Commission requires manufacturers of lawnmowers to install back flaps. If a child is injured by having his toes mangled while using a lawn mower that does not have a back flap, a manufacturer would be held negligent per se in the manufacture of the lawnmower. Most manufacturers, however, fully comply with all applicable government regulations, so having to prove negligence in manufacturing remains a very large burden for injured parties.

Strict Liability in Tort

Shortcomings of Contract Remedies and Negligence Standards Following the *McPherson* decision in the early part of the last century, courts became increasingly hostile to manufacturers' attempts to

shield themselves from liability for defective products, particularly when personal injury was involved. Manufacturers would advertise safety features such as shatterproof windshields in cars, but the contracts that purchasers signed would not allow them to recover for the resulting injuries when windshields shattered.[4] Generally these contracts allowed car owners only the replacement of the defective windshield, cold comfort to a car owner whose face was seriously lacerated by flying glass. If consumers relied upon tort law for any additional damage claims, they had to show not only that the product contained a defect, but also that the manufacturer was negligent in inspecting, testing, or assembling the product. In many cases, the manufacturer could claim that it was not negligent in the manufacture of the product because its quality control statistics exceeded the industry average, even though the individual product sold to the plaintiff was defective resulting in harm to plaintiff.

Strict Liability in Tort   In a series of cases that have been both widely applauded and criticized, courts have moved towards strict liability in tort for product liability cases. Strict liability means liability without fault, though there are some defenses available to sellers and manufacturers in product liability claims. Product liability has evolved to the following standard: "If you sell a product that has a defect and that defect is the proximate cause of a user's injuries, you are liable for the resulting damages." A number of economic and social policy reasons have been developed to justify product liability rules:

- First, manufacturers and sellers know their products better than consumers and this is particularly true as products have become increasingly complicated.
- Second, manufacturers are in a better position to redesign product to make them safer.

[4]*Baxter v. Ford Motor Company,* 168 Wash. 456 (1932).

- Third, placing liability on manufacturers spreads risk and makes the price of the product reflect its true costs to society, including costs of injuries to users.

In the next case, the court's resistance to a manufacturer's attempts to shield itself from liability for a malfunctioning consumer product is clear-cut.

Greenman v. Yuba Power Products, Inc.
Supreme Court of California
377 P.2d 897 (1963)

FACTS AND CASE BACKGROUND

Plaintiff brought this action for damages against the retailer and the manufacturer of a Shopsmith, a combination power tool that could be used as a saw, drill, and wood lathe. He saw a Shopsmith demonstrated by the retailer and studied a brochure prepared by the manufacturer. He decided he wanted a Shopsmith for his home workshop, and his wife bought and gave him one for Christmas in 1955. In 1957 he bought the necessary attachments to use the Shopsmith as a lathe for turning a large piece of wood he wished to make into a chalice. After he had worked on the piece of wood several times without difficulty, it suddenly flew out of the machine and struck him on the forehead, inflicting serious injuries. About 10 1/2 months later, he gave the retailer and the manufacturer written notice of claimed breaches of warranties and filed a complaint against them alleging such breaches and negligence.

After a trial before a jury, the court ruled that there was no evidence that the retailer was negligent or had breached any express warranty and that the manufacturer was not liable for the breach of any implied warranty. Accordingly, it submitted to the jury only the cause of action alleging breach of implied warranties against the retailer and the causes of action alleging negligence and breach of express warranties against the manufacturer. The

jury returned a verdict for the retailer against plaintiff and for plaintiff against the manufacturer in the amount of $65,000. The trial court denied the manufacturer's motion for a new trial and entered judgment on the verdict. The manufacturer and plaintiff appeal. Plaintiff seeks a reversal of the part of the judgment in favor of the retailer, however, only in the event that the part of the judgment against the manufacturer is reversed.

OPINION: TRAYNOR

Plaintiff introduced substantial evidence that his injuries were caused by defective design and construction of the Shopsmith. His expert witnesses testified that inadequate set screws were used to hold parts of the machine together so that normal vibration caused the tailstock of the lathe to move away from the piece of wood being turned permitting it to fly out of the lathe. They also testified that there were other more positive ways of fastening the parts of the machine together, the use of which would have prevented the accident. The jury could therefore reasonably have concluded that the manufacturer negligently constructed the Shopsmith. The jury could also reasonably have concluded that statements in the manufacturer's brochure were untrue, that they constituted express warranties, and that plaintiff's injuries were caused by their breach.

* * *

A manufacturer is strictly liable in tort when an article he places on the market, knowing that it is to be used without inspection for defects, proves to have a defect that causes injury to a human being. Recognized first in the case of unwholesome food products, such liability has now been extended to a variety of other products that create as great or greater hazards if defective.

* * *

We need not recanvass the reasons for imposing strict liability on the manufacturer . . . The purpose of such liability is to insure that the costs of injuries resulting from defective products are borne by the manufacturers that put such products on the market rather than by the injured persons who are powerless to protect themselves. Sales warranties serve this purpose fitfully at best. In the present case, for example, plaintiff was able to plead and prove an express warranty only because he read and relied on the representations of the Shopsmith's ruggedness contained in the manufacturer's brochure. Implicit in the machine's presence on the market, however, was a representation that it would safely do the jobs for which it was built. Under these circumstances, it should not be controlling whether plaintiff selected the machine because of the statements in the brochure, or because of the machine's own appearance of excellence that belied the defect lurking beneath the surface, or because he merely assumed that it would safely do the jobs it was built to do. It should not be controlling whether the details of the sales from manufacturer to retailer and from retailer to plaintiff's wife were such that one or more of the implied warranties of the sales act arose . . . To establish the manufacturer's liability it was sufficient that plaintiff proved that he was injured while using the Shopsmith in a way it was intended to be used as a result of a defect in design and manufacture of which plaintiff was not aware that made the Shopsmith unsafe for its intended use.

* * *

The judgment is affirmed.

QUESTIONS FOR ANALYSIS

1. What is the difference in proof required for a plaintiff to recover in a product liability case when negligence is alleged and when breach of warranty is alleged? Is there any difference in law between strict liability and breach of warranty in terms of what must be proved in court?
2. What is the legal implication of making the determination that the defendant is strictly liable in tort for a defective product? How does strict liability in tort significantly expand the potential liability of sellers?
3. Was the defect in this case a manufacturing defect or a design defect?

RESTATEMENTS OF TORTS: SECOND AND THIRD

Restatements are simply that, restatements of what learned judges and attorneys in an area of law view as **the common law** at the time. Section 402A is one of the most widely cited and influential sections of the Restatement Second of Tort law.[5] Section 402A of the Restatement Second of Torts states that:

1. One who sells any product in a defective condition unreasonably dangerous to the user or consumer or to his property is subject to liability for physical harm thereby caused to the ultimate user or consumer, or to his property, if
   a. the seller is engaged in the business of selling such product, and
   b. it is expected to and does reach the consumer without substantial change in the condition in which it was sold.
2. The rule stated in Subsection 1 applies although
   a. the seller has exercised all possible care in the preparation and sale of his products, and
   b. the user or consumer has not bought the product from or entered into any contractual relation with the seller.

Even though the Restatements do not have the legal status of a state or federal statute, most judges freely quote from and adhere to the Restatements. They are a good predictor of how courts will resolve legal disputes involving torts. Since the Restatement Second was published in 1977, courts have extensively used it as the standard for liability in product liability cases. Publication of Restatement Third in 1998 has not undermined the vitality of Section 402A of the Restatement Second.

What Section 402A of the Restatement of Torts Covers

Sellers Are Liable, Not Just Manufacturers

Note at the onset that Section 402A places liability on *sellers,* not just the company that makes the products which, in most cases, is a manufacturer. A consumer electronic product that blows up in the face of a consumer would generate liability for the manufacturer, the distributor (assuming it was a different business), and the retailer. The fact that the product is sold in a box and the box specifically states, **DO NOT OPEN,** does not absolve distributors and retailers who had no opportunity to inspect the product prior to sale. Those companies farther down the marketing chain, such as retailers, can file a cross-claim or a third party interpleader against the manufacturers saying, in effect, "While we may be technically liable, the manufacturer is primarily liable and the plaintiff should collect first from the manufacturer." In most states, retailers can direct that court-awarded damages be collected first from manufacturers but, if the assets of the manufacturer are insufficient, retailers and distributors may have to pay damages. There have also been suits against suppliers of components to manufacturers that

---

[5] The Restatement Second was published in 1977. Unless otherwise designated, we discuss the widely applied Restatement Second of Torts and then look at the changes brought about by the 1998 Restatement Third of Torts.

have been successful. The main point is that all *sellers* in the marketing chain are potentially liable to consumers if the product is sold in a defective condition.

Not All Sellers Are Covered by Section 402A   Section 402A limits liability to sellers who are regularly in the business of selling such products. Section 402A does not apply to *consumers* who are selling a product secondhand, but does apply to sellers who are in the business of selling "used" goods such as cars, but only with respect to replacements or repairs that are found to be defective. Also sellers are absolved from liability if the product is tampered with farther down the marketing chain. A drug company would not be liable for drugs that were removed from a retailer's shelf and later replaced after the drugs were laced with cyanide. Tampering is considered an affirmative defense, which means that manufacturers would have the burden of proving that their products were tampered with after they shipped the product.

Damages That Are Recoverable
Wrongful Death
Section 402A indicates that sellers are liable to users and consumers for physical harm attributable to defective products that are sold. In some cases, the harm is death, which of course requires a valuation of the plaintiff's life. Depending on the state, the plaintiff in a wrongful death case may be the decedent, the decedent's estate or his or her survivors.

Factors the Courts Take Into Account in Wrongful Death Awards   There are substantial statewide variations in wrongful death statutes but, depending on the state, the plaintiff can generally recover for the present value of lost future earnings, minus various deductions, again that vary from state to state, plus values for lost services and other considerations. In many states, the award for lost earnings in a wrongful death is the present value of earnings less what the decedent would have consumed him or herself. In most states, survivors can recover for services that the decedent would have performed around the house. There may be recovery for loss of society, companionship, love and affection, and for pain and suffering. Present value computations take into account the age, gender, and education of the decedent. When there are no punitive damage awards, wrongful death suits for young people in their early 20s typically result in values in the range of one to four million dollars.

Personal Injury
If a plaintiff dies as a result of a defective product, he or she can recover for pain and suffering before death. In personal injury cases not involving death, the plaintiff can also recover for pain and suffering as well as for mental conditions, such as depression, that are tied to the plaintiff's injuries. Damages are greatest for plaintiffs who are permanently injured and who require long term health care including in-house monitoring and therapy by health-care professionals. Such damage awards often can exceed those recoverable for wrongful death victims. Even when the plaintiff does not require long-term monitoring and treatment, difficult valuation questions arise when there is loss of a limb, eye, or bodily function.

Property Valuation
Section 402A also allows for property recoveries, but this rule is not followed in all states. As a general rule, if a plaintiff's property is damaged, he or she is entitled to recover any diminution in the fair market value of the property. For most property, determining fair market value is relatively straightforward. However, determining the value of a small business, for which stock is not publicly traded, is much more difficult. Because small businesses are risky, projected lost future profits may be heavily discounted. In recent years, there have been a large number of .coms and high-tech businesses that have zoomed from having little revenue and no profits to market valuations and IPOs in the millions and even billions. If a defective product kills or incapacitates the owner–operator of a small high-tech business, determining the fair market value of the business owned by the plaintiff is very difficult. Such a business may end up significantly undervalued or overvalued, with a variance of value estimates that is likely to be very high. Of course, expert witnesses, usually economists or accountants, are often enlisted by each party to provide their opinions to the jury in estimating the value of businesses (or lost future earnings).

Punitive Damages
A claim based on Section 402A does not require a showing of fault or intent. If there is no showing of intent to harm, then technically there should be no recovery for punitive damages, which normally requires a showing of some kind of intent. Few companies sell products to intentionally harm their customers, but there have been a number of product

liability cases in which the defendant had to pay punitive damages. If the courts or juries decide that the behavior of the company showed *a reckless disregard for the safety of customers or the general public* then, in some states, the intent requirement is satisfied for the purpose of punitive damage awards (see the Ford Pinto case below). Increasingly, state legis-latures have responded to calls by business groups for limitations on punitive damage awards. Although several variations have been tried, by 1997 over 30 states had some kind of constraints on court awarded punitive damages. The following case illustrates how large punitive damage awards had become in one state, in the 1990s.

BMW of North America v. *Gore*
U.S. Supreme Court
517 U.S. 559, (1996)

FACTS AND CASE BACKGROUND

In 1983, the American distributor of a German automobile manufacturer adopted a nationwide policy that cars which were damaged in the course of manufacture or transportation to dealers would be repaired and sold as new, without advising dealers that any repairs had been made, if the repair costs did not exceed 3 percent of the suggested retail price. In 1990, a customer purchased one of the manufacturer's cars for $40,750.88 from an authorized dealer in Birmingham, Alabama. Prior to the car's transport to the dealer, the car had been partially repainted at the distributor's vehicle preparation center at a cost of $601.37, which was about 1.5 percent of the car's suggested retail price. The customer drove the car for approximately 9 months without noticing any flaws in its appearance before taking the car to an independent automobile detailing shop. The proprietor of the shop detected evidence that the car had been repainted and informed the customer.

Thereafter, the customer brought an action in an Alabama trial court against the distributor and alleged that the failure to disclose that the car had been repainted constituted suppression of a material fact. At trial before a jury, the customer claimed that (1) his actual damages were $4,000, in that the value of one of the manufacturer's repainted cars was approximately 10 percent less than the value of a new car that had not been damaged and repaired; and (2) a punitive damages award of $2 million would provide an appropriate penalty, using the $4,000 actual damages estimate, in that since 1983, the manufacturer had sold as new 983 cars which had been repainted at a cost of more than $500 per vehicle, including 14 in Alabama.

OPINION: STEVENS

No one doubts that a State may protect its citizens by prohibiting deceptive trade practices and by requiring automobile distributors to disclose presale repairs that affect the value of a new car. But the States need not, and in fact do not, provide such protection in a uniform manner. Some States rely on the judicial process to formulate and enforce an appropriate disclosure requirement by applying principles of contract and tort law. Other States have enacted various forms of legislation that define the disclosure obligations of automobile manufacturers, distributors, and dealers. The result is a patchwork of rules representing the diverse policy judgments of lawmakers in 50 States.

*   *   *

We think it follows from these principles of state sovereignty and comity that a State may not impose economic sanctions on violators of its laws with the intent of changing the tortfeasors' lawful conduct in other States. Before this Court Dr. Gore argued that the large punitive damages award was necessary to induce BMW to change the nationwide policy that it adopted in 1983. But by attempting to alter BMW's nation-wide policy, Alabama would be infringing on the policy choices of other States. To avoid such encroachment, the economic penalties that a State such as Alabama inflicts on those who transgress its laws, whether the penalties take the form of legislatively authorized fines or judicially imposed punitive damages, must be supported by the State's interest in protecting its own consumers and its own economy. Alabama may insist that BMW adhere to a particular disclosure policy in that State. Alabama does not have the power, however, to punish BMW for conduct that was lawful where it occurred and that had no impact on Alabama or its residents. Nor may Alabama impose sanctions on BMW in order to deter conduct that is lawful in other jurisdictions.

*   *   *

Elementary notions of fairness enshrined in our constitutional jurisprudence dictate that a person receive fair notice not only of the conduct that will subject him to punishment, but also of the severity of the penalty that a State may impose. Three guideposts, each of which indicates that BMW did not receive adequate notice of the magnitude of the sanction that Alabama might impose for adhering to the nondisclosure policy adopted in 1983, lead us to the conclusion that the $2 million award against BMW is grossly excessive: the degree of reprehensibility of the nondisclosure; the disparity between the harm or potential harm suffered by Dr. Gore and his punitive damages award; and the difference between this remedy and the civil penalties authorized or imposed in comparable cases. We discuss these considerations in turn.

* * *

RATIO

The second and perhaps most commonly cited indicium of an unreasonable or excessive punitive damages award is its ratio to the actual harm inflicted on the plaintiff. See *TXO,* 509 U.S. at 459; *Haslip,* 499 U.S. at 23. The principle that exemplary damages must bear a "reasonable relationship" to compensatory damages has a long pedigree. Scholars have identified a number of early English statutes authorizing the award of multiple damages for particular wrongs. Some 65 different enactments during the period between 1275 and 1753 provided for double, treble, or quadruple damages. Our decisions in both *Haslip* and *TXO* endorsed the proposition that a comparison between the compensatory award and the punitive award is significant.

* * *

In *Haslip* we concluded that even though a punitive damages award of "more than 4 times the amount of compensatory damages" might be "close to the line," it did not "cross the line into the area of constitutional impropriety." 499 U.S. at 23–24. *TXO,* following dicta in *Haslip,* refined this analysis by confirming that the proper inquiry is "'whether there is a reasonable relationship between the punitive damages award and *the harm likely to result* from the defendant's conduct as well as the harm that actually has occurred.'" *TXO,* 509 U.S. at 460 (emphasis in original), quoting *Haslip,* 499 U.S. at 21. Thus, in upholding the $10 million award in *TXO,* we relied on the difference between that figure and the harm to the victim that would have ensued if the tortious plan had succeeded. That difference suggested that the relevant ratio was not more than 10 to 1.

The $2 million in punitive damages awarded to Dr. Gore by the Alabama Supreme Court is 500 times the amount of his actual harm as determined by the jury. Moreover, there is no suggestion that Dr. Gore or any other BMW purchaser was threatened with any additional potential harm by BMW's nondisclosure policy. The disparity in this case is thus dramatically greater than those considered in *Haslip* and *TXO.*

* * *

The judgment is reversed, and the case remanded for further proceeding not inconsistent with this opinion.

QUESTIONS FOR ANALYSIS

1. What did the U.S. Supreme Court think of the argument by the plaintiff that he was suing on behalf of 983 other similarly situated plaintiffs who were "victimized" by the same policy?
2. Why didn't the U.S. Supreme Court set an upper limit on the ratio of punitive damages to compensatory damages? Referring to a previous case, what ratio between punitive and compensatory damages did the U.S. Supreme Court indicate was "close to the line"?

STRICT LIABILITY AND PRODUCT DEFECT

The essence of Section 402A is that sellers are liable without fault. The fact that a seller has exerted reasonable or even extraordinary care in the sale of the product is irrelevant. If the product is sold in a *defective condition that makes it unreasonably dangerous,* liability on the part of the seller is established. The impact of Section 402A is that it is no longer necessary for a consumer to establish that the seller or manufacturer was negligent. If the manufacturer produces a product that has a defect, or a seller sells a defective product, and the other conditions for tort liability are satisfied, such as proximate cause and damages, then the defendant is liable for the resulting damages.

What Is a Product Defect?

The question then becomes in most product liability cases, what is a product defect? The courts have classified three types of defects, which we discuss in turn: *manufacturing, design,* and *inadequate warnings.*

Manufacturing Defects

Manufacturing defects are the least controversial among the three types of defects in products. In general, manufacturing defects are caused by mistakes at a factory. Unless something is very wrong, manufacturing defects are usually quite rare. Manufacturing defects typically are the cause when parts fall off a machine, making the machine unreasonably dangerous. Consider a chain saw as an example. A chain saw operator could be seriously injured if the hand grip is loose, allowing the operator's hand to come in contact with the moving chain saw blade.

Consumer Expectations Test

It is relatively easy to give examples of manufacturing defects, it is more difficult to formulate a conceptual criteria for "defective". One definition can be formed by using a variant of the *consumer expectations test,* i.e., by asking how an ordinary consumer would expect the product to perform. Ordinary consumers expect a bicycle to stop when the brakes are applied. If a consumer purchases a bicycle, gives it to one of her children, and an accident takes place because the brakes were not properly installed, the manufacturer would undoubtedly fail the consumer expectations test. Still, the consumer expectations test can be ambiguous and is capable of abuse, even though the Restatement of Torts Second indicates that a product is *unreasonably dangerous* (defective) if it is "dangerous to an extent beyond that which would be contemplated by the ordinary consumer who purchases it, with the ordinary knowledge common to the community as to its characteristics." Plaintiff's attorneys, whose clients are often dead or horribly maimed, can simply ask the jury whether "you expect to be in the condition of my client as a result of using the defendant's product."

Manufacturing Defect: Does the Product Conform to the Manufacturer's Product Design?

A more precise test of whether the product possesses a manufacturing defect is to ask, "does the product in question *depart* from the manufacturer's intended design?"[6] If the answer is yes, then a manufacturing defect has been established. In other words, if the design of the product calls for certain screws to be set in a particular location and, in fact, the screws are not there and the consumer is injured as a result of the screws not being in their intended position, a manufacturing defect is established. Using the manufacturer's intended design test requires a plaintiff to show the manufacturing defect with some precision.

Design Defects

Design defects are likely to be a more serious problem for sellers than manufacturing defects. With a manufacturing defect, most likely only a very few products are affected; just the defectively manufactured products that somehow got through the company's quality control tests. When a product is judged to have a *design defect,* all of the products are capable of generating liability because, as would be claimed by plaintiffs, the **design** of the product is unreasonably dangerous. Not surprisingly, in design defect cases very large class action suits are common. In such cases, the combination of attorney fees, damage awards, and bad publicity can bankrupt even large corporations.

Casualties of Product Liability Suits Based on Design Defects

There have been a number of products in high-profile cases that have been judged to have design defects. The drug DES, which was used as an antinausea drug for pregnant women, also resulted in higher rates of cancer for daughters of mothers who took the drug.[7] The IUD (Interuterine Device, a contraceptive device) was defectively designed according to the courts, because it caused women to become sterile as well as contributing to other medical problems.[8] Ford Pintos were judged to be defectively designed because they had a tendency to burst into flames when struck from the rear. Silicon breast implants have been the subject of design defect lawsuits, though virtually all of the scientific evidence suggests that there is no link between the implants and the ailments the female plaintiffs have complained of.[9] Similarly, allegations are being made about links between cell phones and brain cancer, again, in spite of the fact that the evidence of a scientific link between the two is sparse.[10]

Consumer Expectations Test, Again

Again, the consumer expectations test can be used to define a design defect by simply asking whether an ordinary consumer would expect to be in the condition of the plaintiff as a result of using the defendant's product? If the answer is no, then the product does not pass the consumer expectations test. Assume that you

---

[6]Section 2(a) of the 1998 version of the Restatement of Tort Law.

[7]*Collins v. Eli Lilly Co.,* 116 Wis.2d 166, 342 N.W.2d 37 (1984).
[8]*Coursen and Cook v. A. H. Robins Company,* 764 F.2d 1329 (1985).
[9]*In re Silicone Gel Breast Implants Products Liability Litigation* (N.D.Ala. 1993) 837 F. Supp. 1128.
[10]Cell Phones and Brain Tumors: A Bad Connection? http://www.prnews. com/cgi-bin/ . . . story/03-29-2000/0001177305& EDATE=.National Brain Tumor Foundation (www.braintumor.org).

are driving a relatively cheap car, you are hit from the rear, and the gas tank explodes. The jury in a sequel suit could be asked, "Would you expect the gas tank to blow up and burn over 80 percent of your body when struck in the rear by a vehicle going 25 MPH?" The question asked (by the plaintiff's attorney) is intended to have an obvious negative answer. It also can be expected to elicit a desire in jury members to sanction the party responsible for the affront to reasonable consumer expectations. The hypothetical facts assumed above were largely evident in the *Ford Pinto* case listed below.

Richard GRIMSHAW, Minor v. *Ford Motor Company*
Court of Appeal, Fourth District, Division 2, California
174 Cal.Rptr. 348 (1981)

FACTS AND CASE BACKGROUND

A 1972 Ford Pinto hatchback automobile unexpectedly stalled on a freeway, erupting into flames when it was rear ended by a car proceeding in the same direction. Mrs. Lilly Gray, the driver of the Pinto, suffered fatal burns and 13-year-old Richard Grimshaw, a passenger in the Pinto, suffered severe and permanently disfiguring burns on his face and entire body. Grimshaw and the heirs of Mrs. Gray (Grays) sued Ford Motor Company and others. Following a six-month jury trial, verdicts were returned in favor of plaintiffs against Ford Motor Company. Grimshaw was awarded $2,516,000 compensatory damages and $125 million punitive damages; the Grays were awarded $559,680 in compensatory damages. On Ford's motion for a new trial, Grimshaw was required to remit all but $3 1/2 million of the punitive award as a condition of denial of the motion.

OPINION: TAMURA

In 1968, Ford began designing a new subcompact automobile which ultimately became the Pinto. Mr. Iacocca, then a Ford vice president, conceived the project and was its moving force. Ford's objective was to build a car at or below 2,000 pounds to sell for no more than $2,000.

Ordinarily marketing surveys and preliminary engineering studies precede the styling of a new automobile line. Pinto, however, was a rush project, so that styling preceded engineering and dictated engineering design to a greater degree than usual. Among the engineering decisions dictated by styling was the placement of the fuel tank. It was then the preferred practice in Europe and Japan to locate the gas tank over the rear axle in subcompacts because a small vehicle has less "crush space" between the rear axle and the bumper than larger cars. The Pinto's styling, however, required the tank to be placed behind the rear axle leaving only 9 or 10 inches of "crush space"—far less than in any other American automobile or Ford overseas subcompact. In addition, the Pinto was designed so that its bumper was little more than a chrome strip, less substantial than the bumper of any other American car produced then or later.

* * *

CRASH TESTS

The crash tests revealed that the Pinto's fuel system as designed could not meet the 20-mile-per-hour proposed standard. Mechanical prototypes struck from the rear with a moving barrier at 21 miles per hour caused the fuel tank to be driven forward and to be punctured, causing fuel leakage in excess of the standard prescribed by the proposed regulation. A production Pinto crash tested at 21 miles per hour into a fixed barrier caused the fuel neck to be torn from the gas tank and the tank to be punctured by a bolt head on the differential housing. In at least one test, spilled fuel entered the driver's compartment through gaps resulting from the separation of the seams joining the rear wheel wells to the floor pan. The seam separation was occasioned by the lack of reinforcement in the rear structure and insufficient welds of the wheel wells to the floor pan.

THE COST TO REMEDY DESIGN DEFICIENCIES

When a prototype failed the fuel system integrity test, the standard of care for engineers in the industry was to redesign and retest it. The vulnerability of the production Pinto's fuel tank at speeds of 20 and 30-miles-per-hour fixed barrier tests could have been remedied by inexpensive "fixes," but Ford produced and sold the Pinto to the public without doing anything to remedy the defects . . . Equipping the car with a reinforced rear structure, smooth axle, improved bumper and additional crush space at a total cost of $15.30 would have made the fuel tank safe in a 34 to 38-mile-per-hour rear-end collision by a vehicle the size of the Ford Galaxie. If, in addition to the foregoing, a bladder or tank within a tank were used or if the tank were protected with a shield, it would have been safe in a 40 to 45-mile-per-hour rear impact. If the tank had been located over the rear axle, it would have been safe in a rear impact at 50 miles per hour or more.

* * *

Some two weeks before this case went to the jury, the Supreme Court in *Barker* v. *Lull Engineering Co.* (1978) 20 Cal.3d 413 [143 Cal.Rptr. 225, 573 P.2d 443, 96 A.L.R.3d 1], formulated the following "two-pronged" definition of design defect, embodying the "consumer expectation" standard and "risk-benefit" test: "First, a product may be found defective in design if the plaintiff establishes that the product failed to perform as safely as an ordinary consumer would expect when used in an intended or reasonably foreseeable manner. Second, a product may alternatively be found defective in design if the plaintiff demonstrates that the product's design proximately caused his injury and the defendant fails to establish, in light of the relevant factors, that, on balance, the benefits of the challenged design outweigh the risk of danger inherent in such design." (Id., at p. 432.) The "relevant factors" which a jury may consider in applying the *Barker* "risk-benefit" standard include "the gravity of the danger posed by the challenged design, the likelihood that such danger would occur, the mechanical feasibility of a safer alternative design, the financial cost of an improved design, and the adverse consequences to the product and to the consumer that would result from an alternative design." (Id., at p. 431.) Under the risk-benefit test, once the plaintiff makes a prima facie showing that the injury was proximately caused by the product's design, the burden shifts "to the defendant to prove, in light of the relevant factors, that the product is not defective."

* * *

The court referred to the fact that numerous California decisions have recognized this fact by making it clear "[that] a product may be found defective in design even if it satisfies ordinary consumer expectations, if through hindsight the jury determines that the product's design embodies 'excessive preventable danger,' or, in other words, if the jury finds that the risk of danger inherent in the challenged design outweighs the benefits of such design." (Id., at p. 430.) Thus, the risk-benefit test was formulated primarily to aid injured persons. The instant case was submitted solely on the consumer expectation standard because the trial had been virtually completed before the *Barker* decision was rendered in which our high court for the first time articulated the risk-benefit standard of design defect.

* * *

PUNITIVE DAMAGES

Ford contends that it was entitled to a judgment notwithstanding the verdict on the issue of punitive damages on two grounds: First, punitive damages are statutorily and constitutionally impermissible in a design defect case; second, there was no evidentiary support for a finding of malice or of corporate responsibility for malice. In any event, Ford maintains that the punitive damage award must be reversed because of erroneous instructions and excessiveness of the award.

* * *

Ford argues that "malice" as used in section 3294 [of the California Code] and as interpreted by our Supreme Court in *Davis* v. *Hearst* (1911) 160 Cal. 143 [116 P. 530], requires *animus malus* or evil motive—an intention to injure the person harmed—and that the term is therefore conceptually incompatible with an unintentional tort such as the manufacture and marketing of a

defectively designed product. This contention runs counter to our decisional law. As this court recently noted, numerous California cases after *Davis* v. *Hearst, supra,* have interpreted the term "malice" as used in section 3294 to include, not only a malicious intention to injure the specific person harmed, but conduct evincing **"a conscious disregard of the probability that the actor's conduct will result in injury to others."** [emphasis added].

* * *

The interpretation of the word "malice" as used in section 3294 to encompass conduct evincing callous and conscious disregard of public safety by those who manufacture and market mass produced articles is consonant with and furthers the objectives of punitive damages. The primary purposes of punitive damages are punishment and deterrence of like conduct by the wrongdoer and others. (Civ. Code, § 3294; *Owen, supra,* pp. 1277, 1279–1287; *Mallor & Roberts, supra,* pp. 648–650.) In the traditional noncommercial intentional tort, compensatory damages alone may serve as an effective deterrent against future wrongful conduct but in commerce-related torts, the manufacturer may find it more profitable to treat compensatory damages as a part of the cost of doing business rather than to remedy the defect.

* * *

Applying the above precepts to the instant case, Ford has failed to demonstrate prejudice from the claimed defect in the instructions on malice. When the instructions are read as a whole, the jury could not possibly have interpreted the words "conscious disregard of its possible results" to extend to the innocent conduct depicted by Ford. The term "motive and willingness . . . to injure" and the words "wilful," "intentional," and "conscious disregard" signify *animus malus* or evil motive.

* * *

Ford's final contention is that the amount of punitive damages awarded, even as reduced by the trial court, was so excessive that a new trial on that issue must be granted. Ford argues that its conduct was less reprehensible than those for which punitive damages have been awarded in California in the past; that the $3 1/2 million award is many times over the highest award for such damages ever upheld in California; and that the award exceeds maximum civil penalties that may be enforced under federal or state statutes against a manufacturer for marketing a defective automobile. We are unpersuaded.

* * *

In determining whether an award of punitive damages is excessive,

comparison of the amount awarded with other awards in other cases is not a valid consideration. [references deleted] Nor does "[the] fact that an award may set a precedent by its size" in and of itself render it suspect; whether the award was excessive must be assessed by examining the circumstances of the particular case. [references deleted] In deciding whether an award is excessive as a matter of law or was so grossly disproportionate as to raise the presumption that it was the product of passion or prejudice, the following factors should be weighed: The degree of reprehensibility of defendant's conduct, the wealth of the defendant, the amount of compensatory damages, and an amount which would serve as a deterrent effect on like conduct by defendant and others who may be so inclined. Applying the foregoing criteria to the instant case, the punitive damage

award as reduced by the trial court was well within reason.

* * *

QUESTIONS FOR ANALYSIS

1. Which party, the plaintiff or Ford Motor Company, wanted articulation of the risk-benefit test for the design defect part of the jury instructions? Why did the court reject this argument by Ford as a basis for overturning the judgment?

2. On what basis were the plaintiffs able to have the jury consider the "intent"? What is the significance of "intent" in product liability cases? Can a plaintiff recover punitive damages without a showing of intent?

3. Why did Ford argue that the $3.5 million punitive damage award was excessive? What was the court's answer?

Restatement Third of Torts: Definition of a Design Defect

A definition used by courts and the 1998 version of the Restatement of Torts is that a design is defective "when the foreseeable risks of harm posed by the product could have been reduced or avoided by the adoption of a reasonable alternative design, and failure to use the alternative design renders the product not reasonably safe." Implicitly, the 1998 version of the Restatement of Torts incorporates a tradeoff between "foreseeable risks" and the costs of an "alternative design." Generally, foreseeable risks include loss of human life and personal injury. The costs of alternative designs refers to additional costs borne by the manufacturer. Although tradeoffs between lives and profits or costs are repugnant to most people, such tradeoffs are contemplated when courts and juries evaluate whether a product is defectively designed.

Foreseeable Use versus Intended Use

Notice that the 1998 Restatement definition of a design defect does not require that the product be used

for its *intended* use in order for it to have a design defect. At one time, when faced by lawsuits based on crashworthiness, automobile manufacturers claimed that their designs were not defective just because they were not crashworthy. Even though customers, users, and bystanders were hurt or killed in crashes at relatively low speeds, automobile manufacturers claimed that automobiles were not intended to be crashed against other vehicles or immovable objects.

The 1998 Restatement definition of a design defect places emphasis on whether the use of a product is *foreseeable,* and not whether the use was the *intended* use. If the use is foreseeable, then the product must be designed to guard against such foreseeable harm, or there should be a warning that adequately apprises consumers of these risks. Warnings are required even if the harm comes from uses of the product that are not intended by the manufacturer. For example, airplane glue is intended by sellers to be used to assemble model airplanes. It is known, however, that some children abuse airplane glue and get high sniffing it. It is common for sellers of model airplane glue to provide conspicuous warnings against sniffing the glue.

Determining Design Defects

It is difficult for juries to make decisions regarding design defects because they do not possess the technical expertise to make such judgments. Generally, given the fact that plaintiffs are often injured or dead, if the product design of the defendant fails in any respect, the design will be deemed defective. There are a number of criteria that have been used in design defect cases, some of which are relatively easy to apply while others are much more difficult. Note that ultimately all products are capable of being used in an unsafe manner and that warnings are commonplace for most products sold today. For many pharmaceutical drugs, prescription and nonprescription, a small booklet of warnings accompanies sale of the product. Television commercials also mention warnings of possible side effects of pharmaceutical drugs, and pharmacists offer to discuss drugs when they are purchased. Note further that, in general, if a dangerous use is *apparent* then the obligation of manufacturers to provide warnings is lessened. Knives are known to cut flesh. So a silverware manufacturer can sell a sharp knife without pointing out that it is dangerous to play games with sharp knives.

Industry Practice and Government Regulation

In some cases, design defects are relatively easy to determine. If a manufactured good falls below *industry standards* with respect to safety features, it is relatively easy for a jury to conclude that the product was unreasonably dangerous by reason of a defective design. As with the damages phase of a products liability case, expert witnesses are often called in by each side to try to explain what safety features are common within the industry and whether the defendant's product did or did not meet those standards. In addition to the *Ford Pinto* case discussed above, there have been other vehicular product liability cases that involved placement of gas tanks, airbag deployment, inappropriate openings of hatchbacks, and tires that separate without warning, as was alleged in the recent *Firestone Tire* cases.

Also, for many products the government requires safety features. The Consumer Product Safety Commission, the National Highway Transportation Safety Administration, and the Food and Drug Administration all issue regulations that apply to particular products and to classes of products. Products for which designs or performance do not conform to government-mandated requirements are unreasonable per se. However, as noted above, products with designs that do comply with all government standards in the area can, nevertheless, be deemed defective.

A Sample Government Regulation Regarding Design of a Product

The Consumer Product Safety Commission has issued a number of regulations regarding consumer products. For automatic garage doors, they have issued the following regulation, which has to do with the return of the door when it encounters an obstruction. A garage door that does not conform to this regulation has a design defect per se.

> PART 1211—SAFETY STANDARD FOR AUTOMATIC RESIDENTIAL GARAGE DOOR OPERATORS—Table of Contents Subpart A—The Standard Sec. 1211.7 Inherent entrapment protection requirements. (*a*) Except for the first 1 foot (305 mm) of travel as measured over the path of the moving door operating member, both with and without any external entrapment protection device functional, a downward moving residential garage door operator shall initiate reversal of the door within 2 seconds of contact with the obstruction as specified in paragraph (*b*) of this section. After reversing the door, the door operator shall return the door to and stop at the full upmost position, unless a control is actuated or an inherent entrapment circuit senses an obstruction to stop the door during its upward travel. Compliance with this paragraph shall be tested in accordance with paragraphs (*b*) through (*g*) of this section.

The apparent intent of this government regulation (written in excellent "bureaucratize") is to prevent injury or death when a garage door collides with a person, a pet, etc. The formidable complexity of government regulations is a challenge that many producers encounter in designing their products. It is often not at all easy to tell what is permitted and not permitted by government regulations.

The Learned Hand Test

For many products there are no applicable government design regulations. Even if there are government-mandated design standards, compliance with those design standards does not totally insulate the manufacturer from a suit based on a design defect. For the product features that the manufacturer has discretion over, there are often situations where tradeoffs exist between safety and cost. Learned Hand was a highly respected U.S. Circuit Court judge who developed and applied what has become known as the *Learned Hand* test which is often applied in design defect cases. The Learned Hand test is actually a negligence test, but the consequence of failing the Learned Hand test is the imposition of *strict liability* on a company that has produced a product that causes harm to consumers.

A Little Math Can Help

Again, citing the language of the Restatement Third of Torts, a *design* defect is said to occur when "the foreseeable risks of harm posed by the product could have been reduced or avoided by the adoption of a reasonable alternative design, and failure to use the alternative design renders the product not reasonably safe." The bare bones replication of the Learned Hand test is based on three variables which are: P (the probability that the particular design selected by the manufacturer will result in harm), L (the liability or magnitude of the harm, i.e., the seriousness of the injury to consumers) and B (the burden of safety costs or an alternative design). Essentially, according to the Learned Hand Test a product design is defective when:

$$\Delta P \times L > B.$$

In words, a product design is defective when ΔP, the expected *change* in the probability that an accident will occur with this particular design, times L, the liability associated with the accidents or harm, exceeds B, the costs of utilizing an alternative product design that eliminates ΔP times L. Note further that the Learned Hand test assumes that every product design will be associated with some accidents and injury. The focus of the Learned Hand test is upon ΔP times L, not P times L. So, application of the Learned Hand test involves comparing the defendant's actual design of the product and its attendant costs (ΔP times L) with the costs of creating an alternative design (B).

Application to the Ford Pinto Case

The *Ford Pinto* case is instructive. Ford had the option of placing the gas tank in one of two locations. In location 1, the gas tank was placed behind the rear axle and more exposed in the event of collision. In location 2, the gas tank would have been placed in front of the rear axle, but this would have required additional costs per vehicle of about $11. In location 1, relative to location 2, Ford engineers estimated that there would be 180

additional deaths due to rear end collisions in which the gas tanks would be ruptured and ignite. Also the engineers at Ford estimated that there would be 180 additional burn victims and 2,100 additional vehicles would be destroyed. Thus ΔP equals 180 deaths, 180 burn victims, and the fair market value of 2,100 vehicles.

L is the liability associated with each additional ΔP. Thus Ford engineers had to value human life and injury costs. In 1974, they valued each burn victim who died at $200,000 and each burn victim who lived at $67,000. Inserting these values for the variables, Ford engineers estimated the value of $\Delta P \times L$ at about $45,000,000. Each vehicle using location 1 saved Ford $11, but Ford sold 11 million Pintos so that B, total savings using location 1 were $121 million (and, thus, the $125 million dollar punitive damage award in the *Grimshaw* case above was not a coincidence). Ford selected location 1.

Many people are repelled by unvarnished application of the Learned Hand test. Particularly objectionable is the placing of a dollar value on human life. Some object to the whole notion of valuing human life and also believe that corporations should not be in the position of playing God with lives and profits. Setting aside for the moment these moral issues, another way of looking at this case is to carefully examine the variables and their assumed values. Note that the $200,000 figure used by Ford engineers to value human life is particularly suspect. If wrongful death damage awards at the time averaged say $1,000,000 per victim, then Ford would fail the Learned Hand test and the design would be deemed defective, because the value of L, which should have been $1,000,000 times ΔP would have exceeded B ($121 million).

Law, Ethics, and Reality

Inescapable Tradeoffs   As to the claim that it is never okay to value human life and that corporate profits are irrelevant when human life is involved, morality may clash with harsh reality in courts as well as in other settings. Again, relying on the *Pinto* case, we can analyze a bit more deeply some of the inescapable aspects of that harsh reality. To begin with, we certainly would agree that location 1 for the gas tank in the *Ford Pinto* case may be associated with higher predicted deaths due to rear end collisions. However, it doubtless is also true that for location 2 there would be some rear end collisions that would have resulted in precisely the same types of injuries and deaths. In order to really enhance the protection that Pinto occupants would need to

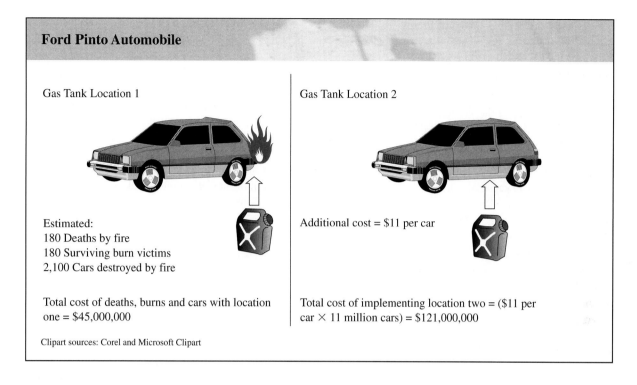

Ford Pinto Automobile

Gas Tank Location 1

Estimated:
180 Deaths by fire
180 Surviving burn victims
2,100 Cars destroyed by fire

Total cost of deaths, burns and cars with location one = $45,000,000

Gas Tank Location 2

Additional cost = $11 per car

Total cost of implementing location two = ($11 per car × 11 million cars) = $121,000,000

Clipart sources: Corel and Microsoft Clipart

shield them from getting burned up in a rear end collision, it's possible that four inches of armor plate should be added. Four inches of armor plate weighs a lot and is expensive. In order to carry the extra weight around probably a larger engine would be necessary. The combined effects of these changes would be to dramatically increase the cost of the Pinto. The target audience for Pintos was college students and the changes listed above would likely increase the cost of the Pinto to a level exceeding the budget capacity of college students.

Statistical Lives   We could continue the discussion of the consequences of trying to totally insure that no one ever dies from a rear end collision in a Pinto, but the point should be apparent that tradeoffs between cost and lives are inescapable. Suppose that, instead of 180 additional burn victims, Ford engineers had estimated that there would be two additional burn victims and that it would cost $110 per vehicle more to have the gas tank in location 2? Is Ford obligated to incur over one billion in additional costs to possibly save two "statistical" lives.[11] There are ancillary consequences of raising the costs of the Pinto such as more

pedestrians and bicyclists, which may cause additional deaths from collisions with cars.

In determining whether a design is defective, the new Restatement repeatedly makes use of the word, "reasonable." A reasonableness standard is of course a negligence standard. If the design is unreasonable, then the defendant seller is liable. Among the factors that the Restatement Third suggests should be taken into account when determining whether a design is reasonable are the following (in boldface):

1. **The magnitude and probability of foreseeable risks of harm.**

These factors are simply L and P in the Learned Hand formula.

2. **Instructions and warnings accompanying the product.**

Instructions and warnings are discussed below.

3. **The nature and strength of consumer expectations regarding the product, including expectations arising from product portrayal and marketing.**

The Restatement incorporates consumer expectations, but only as one factor in deciding whether the design of a product is defective and, seemingly, based on the way the product is marketed and advertised.

[11]What Ford engineers did is estimate ΔP, the expected additional deaths associated with the location of the gas tank, but whether two or 180 will actually die as a result of a rear end collision is indeterminable.

4. **The relative advantages and disadvantages of the product as designed and as it alternatively could have been designed. Evaluation of relative advantages may consider:**
   a. **The likely effects of the alternative design on production costs.**
   b. **The effects of the alternative design on product longevity, maintenance, repair and aesthetics.**

4. a. and b. are clearly *B* in the Learned Hand formula, the burden of an alternative product design.

   c. **The range of consumer choice.**

If the product is unique and there are no close substitutes, then courts are less critical of product design issues because there is nothing to compare the design to. Also safety benchmarks are more difficult to establish when there are no comparable products. Finally, if the product is truly unique, attacking the product design may cost the public the positive functionality associated with the product.

In the next case, some of the concepts we have developed are employed in order to determine whether the design of the defendant's truck was defective.

Jack LINDSEY, Executor of the Estate of Grace C. Lindsey, Deceased v. *Navistar International Transportation Corp.*
United States Court of Appeals for the Eleventh Circuit
150 F.3d 1307; 1998

CASE BACKGROUND AND FACTS

The tragic facts are simple enough. On September 5, 1989, Otis Madison was driving southbound on U.S. Highway 441 in Oconee County, Georgia, operating a Navistar tractor hauling an empty flatbed trailer. In front of Madison's truck, a vehicle had stopped while waiting to turn left onto County Road 267. Although the truck driver had at least a few hundred feet of unobstructed visibility, Madison, who was traveling at approximately sixty miles per hour and had an extensive record of speeding violations, did not begin reacting to the situation in front of him until much closer to the intersection. Had Madison's reaction been more timely, or had he been operating the truck within the posted speed limit, Madison could have brought the truck to a stop without a collision.

Unfortunately, however, when Madison finally did begin braking, he hit the brakes hard, and the rear axle locked up. The tractor started to skid, eventually crossing the center line dividing the lanes. Tommy Ballard, who was proceeding northbound on 441 and whose pickup truck was grazed along the entire left

side by the tractor, described the vehicle by stating that the cab of the truck was facing "directly straight to me." A bystander whose attention was called to the wreck when he heard tires "hollering on the pavement" turned to look and saw that the tractor–trailer had jackknifed, a term used to refer to the clockwise or counter-clockwise rotation of the trailer away from the tractor. The jackknifed tractor–trailer, which had crossed the center line on a two-lane highway, smashed into Grace Lindsey, who had been driving behind Ballard going northbound on 441. Immediately after the accident, Mrs. Lindsey was moaning. She responded to questions by shaking her head, but she did not speak. An ambulance took Mrs. Lindsey to the hospital, where she died from her injuries soon thereafter. Mrs. Lindsey was thirty years old when she died. She was survived by her husband, and two sons, who were two-and-a-half years and four months old at the time of her death.

Defendant–appellant Navistar International Transportation Corporation ("Navistar") appeals from a judgment for plaintiffs–appellees

Jack Lindsey individually and as executor of the estate of his late wife Grace C. Lindsey, entered after a bench trial in this product liability action for damages resulting from the jackknifing of a tractor–trailer manufactured by International Harvester Company, Navistar's corporate predecessor. Navistar contends that the district court erred in finding that the tractor was defective, in concluding that the alleged defect was a proximate cause of the accident in question, and in awarding allegedly excessive damages to plaintiffs–appellees.

OPINION: MARCUS

Contending that the tractor involved in the accident was defective and unreasonably dangerous because the design of the brake system increased the likelihood of a "jackknifing" wreck under the foreseeable circumstances of hard braking while pulling an empty or lightly loaded trailer, plaintiffs–appellees filed suit in state court in Fulton County, Georgia. Navistar removed the case to federal court and promptly moved for summary judgment, arguing that the federal regulation pertaining to truck-braking systems, 49 C.F.R. § 571.121, **preempted** plaintiffs–appellees' state law tort claims. [Emphasis added] The district court granted Navistar's motion and entered judgment for Navistar. Plaintiffs–appellees appealed. Following oral argument, this Court concluded that the federal regulation did not preempt plaintiffs–appellees' state law tort claims and reversed the district court.

* * *

[At trial] The district court, however, agreed with plaintiffs–appellees that the tractor was defective because it was manufactured without a manual limiting valve. As noted, a manual limiting valve basically allows the driver to reduce the brake force to the rear wheels manually when operating a vehicle in a lightly loaded or empty condition. This adjustment prevents the rear wheels from locking up before the front wheels during a sudden stop and thus avoids the conditions that result in jackknifing. Thus, the district court reasoned that "if the tractor in this case had been equipped with a manually adjustable limiting valve, which had been properly set by the driver to adjust the brakes for pulling an empty trailer, then the tractor's rear wheels would not have locked before the front wheels and the vehicle would not have jackknifed." Further finding that at the time the tractor in this case was manufactured, manual limiting valves were readily available on the American market at a cost of less than one hundred dollars per truck, the district court determined that the lack of a manual limiting valve on the tractor in question constituted a defect.

Accordingly, the district court awarded plaintiffs–appellees damages, including $100,000 for Mrs. Lindsey's pain and suffering, $5,000,000 for the "intangible" value of Mrs. Lindsey's life, and funeral and medical expenses in the amount of $8,361.38, for a total award of $5,108,361.38. Navistar appeals this judgment.

* * *

Turning first to the factual issues, Georgia law . . . employs a risk-utility analysis in determining whether a particular design is defective . . . The risk-utility analysis, which incorporates the concept of "reasonableness" (i.e., whether the manufacturer acted reasonably in choosing a particular product design, given the probability and seriousness of the risk posed by the design, the usefulness of the product in that condition, and the burden on the manufacturer to take the necessary steps to eliminate the risk), essentially requires the court to balance the risks inherent in a product design against the utility of the product so designed . . . In performing this analysis, there is no finite set of factors to be reviewed, although the Supreme Court of Georgia has suggested several important considerations, including the following:

1. The usefulness of the product;
2. The gravity and severity of the danger posed by the design;
3. The likelihood of that danger;
4. The avoidability of the danger, i.e., the user's knowledge of the product, publicity surrounding the danger, or the efficacy of warnings, as well as common knowledge and the expectation of danger;
5. The user's ability to avoid danger;
6. The state of the art at the time the product is manufactured;
7. The ability to eliminate danger without impairing the usefulness of the product or making it too expensive; and
8. The feasibility of spreading the loss in the setting of the product's price or by purchasing insurance.

* * *

In short, the district court order reflects that the trial judge thoroughly considered all applicable *Banks* [a previous case that established a product liability precedent in Georgia] factors in ruling that the lack of the manual limiting valve constituted a defect in the Navistar tractor. Accordingly, we hold that, on this record, the district court's factual finding that the absence of the manual limiting valve constituted a defect was not clearly erroneous.

We next address Navistar's legal argument that its tractor–trailer's lack of a manual limiting valve could not have been a defect because 49 C.F.R. § 393.48 [a regulation promulgated by the National Highway Transportation Safety Agency (NHTSA)] prohibited tractor–trailer makers from equipping their vehicles with manual limiting valves at the time the vehicle in question was manufactured. NHTSA, as the delegee of the Secretary of Transportation, is charged with the responsibility of regulating motor vehicle safety through the promulgation of national safety standards. Similarly, the Office of Motor Carrier Safety (formerly known as the Bureau of Motor Carrier Safety ("BMCS")), also pursuant to delegation from the Secretary of Transportation, has authority to prescribe requirements for the "safety of operation and equipment" of trucks operated by motor carriers. Standards issued by NHTSA and BMCS apply to "all employers, employees, and commercial motor vehicles, which transport property or passengers in interstate commerce."

Navistar argues that 49 C.F.R. § 393.48, promulgated by the BMCS, "expressly addresses devices that, like the manual limiting valve at issue, reduce braking power to one axle."

* * *

Referring to the regulation's exceptions to permit devices that "reduce or remove" braking force under certain circumstances, Navistar argues that the requirement that "all brakes . . . must at all times be capable of operating" must be read to prohibit even devices that merely reduce braking force or re-proportion braking force between the axles, except as specified in sections (b)(1) and (b)(2) of the regulation. Because a manual limiting valve re-proportions braking force among the axles by reducing braking force to the rear axle, Navistar continues, it violates the general prohibition of the regulation and does not fall into one of the specified exceptions.

The problem with Navistar's proposed interpretation is that it reads provisions into the regulation that are not there. The plain language of the general rule merely requires that, at all times, all brakes must be "capable of operating"—that is all. It does not state that all brakes must at all times be capable of operating at their high-

est capacity. The manual limiting valve does not render the brakes incapable of operating; it merely re-proportions braking force between the axles by reducing braking force to the rear axle. Indeed, the record shows that a tractor–trailer's braking system is "capable of operating" more effectively when the manual limiting device is properly employed.

* * *

We therefore conclude that, on this record, the district court did not err in finding that the lack of a manual limiting valve in the tractor–trailer in question constituted a defect which was the proximate cause of Mrs. Lindsey's death, and further, that the district court did not err in awarding $5,000,000 for the intangible value of Mrs. Lindsey's life.

Accordingly, the judgment of the district court must be, and is, AFFIRMED.

QUESTIONS FOR ANALYSIS

1. What type of defect is the plaintiff claiming affected the defendant's product? Explain. Do you see the footprints of the Learned Hand test in the factors that the District Court took into account in determining whether a design defect was present?

2. Why do you suppose that the plaintiff is suing the truck company rather than the driver of the truck?

3. What is the preemption that the defendant claims prevents a state court from ruling that there was a design defect in the defendant's truck? Can a state court rule that a product has a design defect when the defendant claims that it is just complying with regulation from a federal regulatory agency?

Inadequate Warnings

The third type of product defect is the lack of adequate warnings and/or instructions. According to the Restatement (Third of Torts), "A product is defective because of inadequate instructions or warnings when the foreseeable risks of harm posed by the product could have been reduced or avoided by the provision of reasonable instructions or warnings by the seller and the omission of the instructions or warnings renders the product not reasonably safe."

The Restatement lists four factors that are guides in determining whether the warnings are adequate:

1. Gravity and risks posed by the product,
2. The content and comprehensibility of the warnings,
3. The intensity of the expression, and
4. The characteristics of the user group.

In determining the adequacy of warnings, note that the now-familiar variables, ΔP and L, comprise the first factor. If the risk of harm is great and the harm associated with the risk is serious, then it is imperative for the manufacturer to provide a warning that is compre-

hensible to the expected user group. The more serious the harm, the more intense the warning should be. Pictures may be effective in supplementing written warnings, particularly if the target group for a product is children or people who may not speak or read English, such as immigrants. There have been many cases in which the language used in the warning or the location of the warning was judged inadequate.

Relationship to Product Design

The adequacy of warnings is conditionally related to product design. Prudence suggests that a manufacturer should make a product as safe as possible, while still retaining the functionality of the product. A manufacturer cannot simply design its products and provide a barrage of warnings. On the other hand, a comment to Section 402A of the Restatement Second indicates that, "Where warning is given, the seller may reasonably assume that it will be read and heeded; and a product bearing such a warning which is safe for use if it is followed, is not in defective condition nor is it unreasonably dangerous." As discussed above, the 1998 Restatement criteria for product design is just a

"An Ounce of Prevention May Be Worth Millions in Legal Costs"

If, after a product has been sold, a company learns about a new and significant risk of harm that might stem from the use or misuse of its product, that situation could create a post-sale duty to warn people about how to avoid that risk.

The factors are outlined in the new Restatement. In a nutshell, efforts should be undertaken to warn if the risk of danger is serious and likely to confront many people, the users of the product are not likely to know about the risk, and a warning can be communicated that would be likely to prevent harm.

Manufacturers should develop a company-wide protocol on this subject. All persons who would be in a position to learn about information that might prompt a post-sale duty to warn or might have to act on such information should be aware of the protocol. Persons who might be in a position to take action when necessary also should be aware of the protocol. Serious problems arise in companies when the left hand does not know what the right hand is doing. Corporate executives ultimately must make the decision about whether action should be taken, but the decision can be sound only if the information the executives receive is complete and accurate.

WHAT ABOUT RECALL?

When the UPLA [Uniform Products Liability Act] was created, it was decided that it was not the obligation of tort law to create a duty to recall a product. Recall obligations were to be placed in the regulatory agency with oversight authority. Having juries in random decisions in different jurisdictions determine whether products should be recalled was and is unsound public policy. Most subsequent case law supported the UPLA decision that tort law should not create an independent duty to recall.

In the few situations in which post-sale warnings would be ineffective to prevent serious harms, a duty to recall could arise, even if a government agency has not ordered one (see *Bell Helicopter Co.* v. *Bradshaw* 1979). This case law appears isolated in nature and lacking sound rationale.

The Reporters of the new Restatement agreed in general with the UPLA and decided that there should be no duty to recall a product unless the recall was mandated by an authorized government agency (Restatement of the Law of Torts 1997, 11). The new Restatement does permit liability to be imposed, however, when a company decides on its own to recall a product but then fails to act as a "reasonable person" in the circumstances.

Source: Excerpt from: "Continuing Duty to Warn: An Opportunity for Liability Prevention or Exposure"; *Victor E. Schwartz*; *Journal of Public Policy & Marketing,* Ann Arbor; Spring 1998; Vol. 17, Iss. 1; pg. 124, 3 pgs.

Additional Source: "The Nature and Impact of the Restatement (Third) of Torts: Products Liability (Section) 10: Post-Sale Duty to Warn"; *Debra L. Slifkin; Federation of Insurance & Corporate Counsel Quarterly,* Iowa City; Winter 2000; Vol. 50, Iss. 2; pg. 153, 22 pgs.

Additional Source: "Apocalypse Now? Post-Sale Duty to Warn"; *Anonymous; Defense Counsel Journal,* Chicago; Oct 1999; Vol. 66, Iss. 4; pg. 591, 6 pgs.

---

modified application of the Learned Hand formula, with a little courtesy extended to consumer expectations. However, once the Learned Hand test has been passed, manufacturers are still potentially liable for foreseeable harm to users even if that harm only occurs when the product is being misused. Once a warning is given, however, the Restatement Comment to Section 402A suggests that manufacturers are not liable to those who ignore the warnings.

Obligation to Warn about Foreseeable but Nonobvious Risks

As briefly addressed earlier, if the risk of harm from a product is obvious, then there is no obligation to warn. Razors are commonly known to cut flesh and hammers are a well-known hazard to fingers. There is no need for manufacturers to warn about such obvious risks.

Manufacturers are, however, obligated to warn about foreseeable risks of harm that could have been reduced by adequate warnings. The Restatement obligates sellers to warn about *foreseeable* risks and not necessarily about risks that may occur when the product is being used for its *intended* use. Gasoline is not intended to be swallowed, nor glue sniffed, and yet these misuses of these products are foreseeable, so warnings against such uses are required. In general, manufacturers have an obligation to warn about foreseeable risks even when those risks only occur when the product is being misused. A benefit, from the point of view of manufacturers, is that when warnings are ignored, users are less likely to recover a damage award if they are injured because **an adequate warning establishes the foundation for assumption of risk defense** (discussed on next page).

Must You Warn about Risks That Are Unforeseeable?

Finally, if a user of the product is harmed while misusing a product in ways that are not reasonably foreseeable, the manufacturer is not liable. In one bizarre case, a distraught woman sought to end her life by locking herself into the trunk of a Ford automobile and starving to death.[12] After residing in the trunk for

some time, the woman decided she didn't want to kill herself in that way anymore but could not get out of the trunk. Eventually someone discovered her in the trunk and she avoided death. Later she sued the Ford Motor Company claiming that they should have had an inside latch in the trunk. The court rejected this contention.

The following case shows just how technical the courts are in making judgments about the adequacy of warnings. Also note that the victim in this case is a six-year-old. Most six-year-olds do not read warnings.

[12]*Daniell v. Ford Motor Co., Inc.,* 581 F.Supp. 728 (1984).

Thomas H. Hisrich, Administrator of the Estate of Diana Zhang, Plaintiff–Appellant,
v. *Volvo Cars of North America, Inc.*
United States Court of Appeals for the Sixth Circuit
2000 U.S. App. LEXIS 22239; 2000 FED App. 0292P (6th Cir.) August 31, 2000, Decided

FACTS AND CASE BACKGROUND

The events in this case arise from an April 22, 1993, accident in which a Volvo 850 driven by Ke Ming Li struck the rear end of a 1986 Volkswagen Golf. Li was driving home when she failed to stop as the Volkswagen in front of her slowed to make a left turn. Li engaged her brakes, but the Volvo 850 struck the rear end of the Volkswagen at low speed, causing the Volvo 850's driver and front-passenger airbags to deploy. Li's six-year-old daughter, Zhang, was in the front-passenger seat of the Volvo 850 and was not wearing seat belt restraints. As the passenger-seat airbag deployed, the airbag and the airbag's module cover forcefully struck Zhang in the head and upper portion of her body, propelling the unrestrained child into the interior roof of the vehicle. Zhang died two days after the accident as a result of her injuries. Although Zhang was not wearing seat restraints, the parties stipulate that if the airbag had not deployed, Zhang would not have sustained her fatal injuries.

Plaintiff alleged that the Volvo 850's airbag system was defective in both its design and manufacture and in its warnings and instructions. The jury returned a verdict for Volvo, which plaintiff appeals, claiming that the district court erred by failing to instruct the jury on both the failure-to-warn defect standard and the consumer-expectation defect standard for products liability under Ohio law.

OPINION: R. GUY COLE, JR.

The jury trial began on February 22, 1999. Plaintiff presented evidence concerning the design and testing of the Volvo's airbag system. In addition, plaintiff also produced evidence concerning Volvo's knowledge of the risk to unbelted children and small adults from airbag deployment. At the close of evidence, plaintiff requested a jury instruction for defective warning or instruction pursuant to Ohio Rev. Code Ann. § 2307.76 (Anderson 1998), based on the evidence developed at trial. The trial court denied plaintiff's requested instruction, finding that the

evidence did not support the instruction. Specifically, the court found that defendants had rebutted the presumption that Li would have heeded the warnings or instructions. The district court also rejected plaintiff's proposed jury instruction on the consumer-expectation test for determining a design defect pursuant to Ohio Rev. Code Ann. § 2307.75 (Anderson Supp. 2000). The court held that "airbags in passenger automobiles are not a subject to which consumers could have reasonable expectations."

* * *

Defendants contend that plaintiff failed to establish a failure-to-warn claim. The Ohio legislature has codified products liability law with respect to defects due to inadequate warnings or instructions. **See** Ohio Rev. Code Ann. § 2307.76(A)(1). In pertinent part, the Ohio statute provides that:

(1) [A product] is defective due to inadequate warning or instruction at the time of marketing if, when it left the

control of its manufacturer, both of the following applied:

(a) The manufacturer knew or, in the exercise of reasonable care, should have known about a risk that is associated with the product and that allegedly caused harm for which the claimant seeks to recover compensatory damages;

(b) The manufacturer **failed to provide the warning or instruction that a manufacturer exercising reasonable care would have provided concerning that risk,** in light of the likelihood that the product would cause harm of the type for which the claimant seeks to recover compensatory damages and in light of the likely seriousness of that harm.

* * *

In the present case, plaintiff clearly established sufficient evidence to support the instruction under § 2307. 76(A). **See** Ohio Rev. Code Ann. § 2307.76(A)(1) (requiring that the "manufacturer failure to provide the warning or instruction that a manufacturer exercising reasonable care would have provided concerning that risk, in light of the likelihood that the product would cause harm of the type" for which recovery is sought). The parties stipulated that the airbag deployment caused the harm, Zhang's injury and subsequent death. Most importantly, on cross-examination by plaintiff's counsel, Volvo's lead designer, Bengt Shultz, who testified on behalf of the

defendants, admitted that "Volvo didn't need to test [airbags] for children" because "[Volvo] knew it would hurt children and adults if you were sitting up near it . . . when it deployed." Shultz also testified that Volvo knew that severe injuries could result to children and that front-seat passengers were often unrestrained. Further, Shultz's testimony established that this known risk was not expressly stated in the instruction manual or vehicle warnings provided by Volvo. Thus, the evidence established that defendants knew of a risk that was associated with their product, specifically the risk to the safety of unrestrained small adults and children when the airbag deploys. Given the breadth of factual findings that would allow a jury to find that a warning is inadequate, plaintiff established a genuine issue of fact on the adequacy of the warnings actually given.

Although Volvo repeatedly established that the vehicle contained a door warning sticker, owner's manual warnings, and even a videotape provided to new Volvo 850 owners which contained a warning concerning the proper placement of children in the vehicle, the testimony of Volvo's design witness, Shultz, established knowledge of a specific danger—the risk to children and small adults positioned near the airbag as it deployed—that was not expressed in a warning. Indeed, the trial court noted Volvo's knowledge of existing risk in denying defendants "superseding cause" jury instruction. The trial court stated that "it is clear . . . that Volvo definitely foresaw the possibility of individuals being unbelted in the front seat of the car, specifically the passenger side," and that based on Volvo's knowledge the court could not say that Volvo should not have foreseen

the risk associated with airbag deployment. Thus, sufficient evidence was adduced at trial to support the instruction on failure-to-warn under § 2307.76.

* * *

Because there is sufficient evidence that Volvo knew of a specific risk associated with the normal use of the product by small adults and children and evidence that this explicit risk was not part of the warnings or instructions under § 2307.76, we find that the district court abused its discretion by failing to instruct the jury on the failure-to-warn theory of liability . . . Moreover, we decline to decide that defendants' warnings were adequate as a matter of law. Accordingly, we **REVERSE** the district court's judgment denying the failure-to-warn instruction and **REMAND** for a new trial.

QUESTIONS FOR ANALYSIS

1. What is the legal impact in Ohio when a manufacturer fails to warn or fails to give an adequate warning? Is the court saying that the six-year old deceased would have heeded a warning about airbags, if one is given?

2. What is the responsibility of parents in this case? Notice that the deceased was not wearing a seat belt? Is it plausible to believe that the parents would disregard the requirement to wear seat belts but would heed a warning with respect to airbags?

3. What is the significance of the fact that apparently Volvo was aware of the risks of deploying airbags to children and small adults?

Defenses Available to Manufacturers and Sellers in Product Liability Cases

Misuse of Product, Ignoring Warnings, and Assumption of Risk

Most states allow *misuse* of the product as a defense in product liability cases. Often misuse of the product occurs in connection with ignoring warnings, but ignoring warnings is not essential to the misuse defense. In the absence of any warnings, if a consumer drives a motor vehicle at an excessive rate of speed or in hazardous driving conditions and a crash results, the consumer is unlikely to recover. If a manufacturer of tires for automobiles places a warning on its products that they are not to be inflated beyond 35 pounds per square inch and a user inflates them to 60 pounds per square inch, then has a blowout, the manufacturer can claim that the user misused the product and assumed the risk by ignoring the warning.

Obvious Risks   For an obvious risk, there is no need for the manufacturer to place a warning. If a user is aware of an obvious risk and voluntarily *assumes that risk,* the user gives manufacturers an assumption-of-risk defense if the user is harmed by the product. The function of warnings on products is to make nonobvious risks obvious. If a user ignores a warning, and heeding the warning would have prevented the harm, then he or she has assumed the risk and cannot

---

Recommendations for Marketers

When promoting and/or enhancing product design for additional consumption, the starting point for marketers is to look at the characteristics of the consumer segments being targeted. Commentators have suggested that target market decisions should include an ethical component regarding the potential vulnerability of segment members. Research has shown that consumers feel that targeting vulnerable segments is unethical, particularly if the products are dangerous or of questionable value. Inappropriate targeting strategies could result in negative publicity, including boycotts.

The pervasive theme of this analysis is that marketers must consider not only the intended uses of their products as stated by product designers, but also how people will overuse them, particularly in light of product advertising and labeling. This perspective is now discussed in terms of designing products and their warnings. While we agree that physical design issues, including the development of guards and safety devices, should precede the creation of warnings, we believe the overall product design should fully integrate warnings into the total offering.

For more than forty years safety experts have argued that the primary steps in developing safe products are to eliminate hazards from products or to provide safety devices. Only then should warnings and instructions become relevant. The three safety priorities established in 1955 by the National Safety Council are:

Principle 1: Hazard Elimination. If practical, design the hazard out of the product, workplace, job or facility via engineering means.

Principle 2: Safety Guards, Enclosures. If a hazard cannot be eliminated, guard against it or use safety design techniques to reduce risks.

Principle 3: Safety Warnings and Instructions. If the hazard cannot be guarded against, warn or instruct the user about the danger under reasonably foreseeable conditions of service and commerce.

Our analysis suggests adding a fourth principle:

Principle 4: Advertising and Labeling. In addition to proper warnings and instructions, advertising and labeling should not explicitly or implicitly encourage dangerous product overuse.

Source: Excerpt from: "Excessive Consumption: Marketing and Legal Perspectives"; *Karl A Boedecker; American Business Law Journal,* Austin; Winter 1999; Vol. 36, Iss. 2; pg. 301, 25 pgs.

Additional Source: "Changing Times"; *Maryellen Cicione; Industrial Distribution,* New York; May 1999; Vol. 88, Iss. 5; pg. H4, 3 pgs.

Additional Source: Effects of Product Liability Laws on Small Business: An Introduction to International Exposure through a Comparison of U.S. and Canadian Law; *Tipton F McCubbins; Journal of Small Business Management,* Milwaukee; Jul 1998; Vol. 36, Iss. 3; pg. 72, 7 pgs.

successfully sue. Because of fear of lawsuits, based on precedents that have occurred, most products are loaded with warnings, as manufacturers are motivated to err on the side of safety. Users of hairspray are warned not to use the product near an open flame even though the risk is obvious to most people. Consumers are warned not to swallow household cleaning products such as Drano and Comet. Purchasers of pharmaceutical drugs are warned about a plethora of possible side effects and of dangerous combinations with other drugs and alcohol.

Prominent Defenses

Even though there is significant overlap between the defenses of: (1) Misuse of the Product, (2) Ignoring Warnings, and (3) Assumption of Risk, each defense is separate and does not rely on a combination of the other two.

- Even without warnings, a misuse of a product can take place that would absolve sellers of liability if harm took place. There are no warnings on automobiles not to exceed speed limits, but a user could not recover from the manufacturer if she was driving at 100 miles per hour on a rainy day and the car crashed.
- As discussed above, a manufacturer is entitled to assume that users will not ignore warnings that are reasonably apparent. Users who ignore warnings and are hurt are not entitled to recover against manufacturers if the harm they incurred would have been avoided had they heeded the warning, regardless of whether users fully appreciated the risks of ignoring the warning.
- Assumption of risk requires that the user (1) was aware of the risk and (2) voluntarily chose to assume the risk. Experienced truck drivers who light up a cigarette while fueling have assumed the risk of the resulting consequences. At most gas stations, of course, there are prominent warnings not to smoke near where gasoline is being dispensed.

In many cases when the facts are not in dispute, the defendant is able to show that it is entitled to avoid liability based on the undisputed facts that the plaintiff misused the product, ignored a warning, or assumed the risk. The impact of these defenses is that the case is dismissed before it ever gets to trial.

Tampering

Manufacturers can use *tampering* as a defense if they can show that a product was safe when it left their hands but was altered or tampered with by someone farther down the marketing chain, or even by consumers. A famous case involving Tylenol took place some years ago when a demented individual took the product from the shelves, laced it with cyanide, and later placed it back on the shelves. The poisoned pills caused the deaths of several unsuspecting customers. Since that time virtually all manufacturers of over-the-counter drugs have packaged their products in tamper-resistant containers with warnings not to purchase or use the product if the seals have been broken. At this point, it would probably be a design defect not to sell over-the-counter drugs in tamper-resistant containers because the chance of tampering is now foreseeable. The main point is that, if a manufacturer can establish that the product was safe when it left its control and was damaged by another company, a third party, or a consumer, when injuries take place, the manufacturer has a tampering defense available.

Government Contractor Defense

If a manufacturer designs a product that conforms to a government contract, such as a weapon or an aeronautical vehicle, and the product harms a user or bystander as a result of a design defect, the manufacturer can defend itself by claiming that it is not responsible for the design of the product.

State of the Art Knowledge

Manufacturers have an obligation to test their products and to discover possible risks associated with them. In some cases, when hidden risks only become apparent long after a product is sold, a defense available to manufacturers is that they did not know and that there was no reasonable way of knowing of these risks because of the state of science at the time. This defense is generally effective, but there have been instances in which courts have held that companies have obligations to go out and push back the bounds of ignorance on the subject. There have been a number of contraceptive products that rendered women unable to bear children after use and the courts have indicated that the producers should have discovered these risks.[13] The precedents for contraceptive products have been

---

[13]In a case cited above, the A.H. Robins company is still being sued for the IUD which has not been sold in the United States for more than a decade.

sufficiently intimidating that American firms have virtually ceased new product development in that area. The recent "morning after" products, such as RU 486, have all been developed by European firms.

Proposals for Tort Reform of Product Liability Laws

Proposals to Make Product Liability Law Federal

There are a number of areas of product liability law that are difficult to justify. First, tort law is state law and compliance with the laws of one state does not insulate manufacturers from suit in another state over exactly the same transaction. Plaintiffs' attorneys are adept at selecting states whose courts are known to be more "pro-consumer." Attempts to federalize tort law were resisted by former President Clinton, a law school graduate and a recipient of significant campaign contributions from groups of trial lawyers. Attorney fees in some large class action product liability cases involving tobacco, breast implants, and guns have been in the hundreds of millions of dollars.

Caps on Punitive Damages

Business groups are also concerned about punitive damages and have proposed punitive damages caps on multiples of compensatory damage awards. In the *Gore* case above, a jury awarded $2,000,000 in punitive damages when compensatory damages were $4,000. A number of states have enacted limits on punitive damage awards, but success has been limited because plaintiffs often can select the state in which to begin a suit. If a plaintiff wins an attractive verdict in one state, the Full Faith and Credit Clause enables the plaintiff to carry the successful verdict to other states. In several states, supreme courts have thrown out statutory limits on punitive damages as being unconstitutional.

Joint and Several Liability

Under the Restatement, all *sellers* are jointly and severally liable. The impact of joint and several liability is that, if a business is only tangentially involved in the sale of a defective product, it is nevertheless potentially liable for the entire amount of damages. If the manufacturer goes bankrupt, retailers, distributors, and service companies have to pay plaintiffs, even though their culpability is marginal. As damage awards continue to escalate, pressure from business groups for reform continues. Of course, the resistance of trial attorneys and "consumer" groups to tort reform also continues.

Application of Product Liability Law to Software Products

When software first emerged as a major class of products in the U.S. economy, a number of courts treated software as though it was a tangible physical product, thus giving the UCC jurisdiction over the contract aspects of software transactions. As time went on, however, courts recognized that "sales" of software programs were not sales but licenses, calling for development of a software UCC. Dissatisfaction with treating computer programs as physical products led to the adoption of the UCITA by the NCCUSL. As discussed in Chapter 3, the NCCUSL is now trying to get all 50 states to pass UCITA so that computer information transactions will be treated uniformly across the United States. To date, that effort has not been a success since only two states have adopted UCITA.

Implications of a Negligence Standard

In tort law, services have traditionally been subject to a negligence standard. If a supplier of services creates a foreseeable risk and does not take reasonable precautions, that supplier is potentially liable to those who are bearing the risk created by the supplier. Medical doctors, accounting and law firms have all been subject to lawsuits for supplying services that fell below the standards of their professions. Computer programmers supply services, much like accountants do, so it would seem that they should be subject to the same standards. Of course, trading partners of computer programmers can waive their right to sue or can agree to damage caps for malpractice. Such clauses are very common in software development contracts. Liability to third parties, however, is unaffected by agreements software developers make with their clients, so programmers are exposed to liability for negligence when they create foreseeable risks and their work falls below industry standards.

Strict Liability for Software Products?

Given the prevalence and significance of reliance on software in the U.S. economy, it is legitimate to ask whether software programs that do not produce results as advertised (i.e., that contain defects) should be held to a strict liability standard. Of course, not all software should be lumped together; writing customized software is very similar to consulting services offered by accountants and there is no move toward a strict liability standard for accountants. Over-the-counter software, however, is a lot like the purchase of a tangible physical product for which strict liability applies, suggesting that software should be judged under a strict liability standard. Under that standard, of course, a showing of negligence is not required for a plaintiff to prevail in court. Courts have not crossed this line so far, but exceptions could creep into legal precedents the same way they did in the case of poisons, food, and drugs during the turn of the 20th century, when vendors of these products became subject to strict liability for defects in products that have serious public health effects.

Software That Has Large Impacts on Health and Safety

Software that directly affects the health and safety of large numbers of people, such as software used in transportation, may be viewed as subject to a "negligence" standard. However, courts could easily make the negligence standard of reasonable care so stringent that it resembles a strict liability standard. Already, there are debates on whether medical doctors can rely on expert (software) systems to treat patients *and* also on whether they can ignore the recommendations of these systems. As advances in medicine continue, questions will arise as to the legal status of expert systems that may be out of date. Until now, computer programmers have not been subject to strict liability for their products. That could quickly change when the first spectacular failure occurs, such as a major train wreck that is directly attributable to a programming error in software that controls train movements.

Suppliers of Hardware and Employers

Repetitive motion injuries have become a serious threat to the well-being of workers. Many repetitive motion injuries are suffered by workers who operate computers. According to the Occupational Safety and Health Administration (OSHA), repetitive motion injuries account for 1/3 of all days lost due to on the job injury.[14] In his final days in office, President Clinton promulgated new regulations for OSHA entitled Ergonomic Standards. In typical regulatory agency fashion, OSHA's proposed regulation is long and complicated.[15] Without going into excessive detail, the heart of the proposal is that employers covered by the standard would be required to establish a "full ergonomics" program to deal with musculoskeletal disorders (MSDs). The main features of the OSHA Ergonomic program are:

a. Management Leadership and Employee Participation;
b. Hazard Information and Reporting;
c. Job Hazard Analysis and Control;
d. Training;
e. "MSD Management," and
f. Program Evaluation.

After its election, the Bush Administration rescinded the Ergonomic Standards, citing excessive costs imposed on industry.

Keyboard Design   The design of keyboards has been the target of a number of lawsuits by workers claiming to be victims of repetitive motion injuries. The claim is made that manufacturers are aware of the ergonomic dangers associated with standard keyboards, and that more ergonomically suitable designs are available. Also plaintiffs claim they should have been warned about possible repetitive motion injuries. To date, keyboard design suits have not been successful, in part because of difficulties of proof and also because there is little evidence that workers would have changed their behavior if warnings had been evident on the keyboards. After all, one might ask, is a secretary going to claim that he or she would not have done their job had they been warned about possible repetitive motion injuries?

Future of Product Liability Law

It is likely that some product liability reform will take place in spite of vigorous opposition by trial attorneys and consumer groups. However, there will not be a retreat back to the time when plaintiffs had to prove that defendants were negligent. Instead, the focus of product liability cases will continue to be upon determining whether the product in question contained a "defect." In cases where a manufacturing defect is alleged, the

---

[14]OSHA has announced it proposed new Ergonomic Standards that state in the introduction that what it terms musculoskeletal disorders (MSDs) are now the largest form of on-the-job injury and account for one third of all dollars spent by companies on workers compensation. See http://www.osha-slc.gov/ergonomics-standard/overview.html.

[15]OSHA is not alone in its long-winded regulations that spell out in excruciating detail what is required by the new, proposed regulation. The proposed regulations are 610 pages long.

difficulties of determining whether there is a defect will continue to be less than when a design defect is alleged. Design defects potentially affect large numbers of people and, therefore, will be contested with more intensity. It seems clear that exclusive reliance on a subjective consumer expectations test is unwarranted and, in some cases, can lead to excessive damage awards. Of course, opinions can and do differ.

Reducing Uncertainty

It is highly desirable to reduce uncertainty as to what manufacturers can do to avoid design defects. Clearly, if manufacturers' products fall below the safety standards customary in their industry, they should expect to have trouble convincing a jury that their products are not defective. Just as clearly, if products do not comply with government safety regulations, their design is defective per se. In the areas where manufacturers have some discretion, it seems clear that a trade-off of costs and safety is unavoidable, with an extra margin for safety a wise choice. Currently, the EPA values human life at $4 million when they set safety standards for pollution in the air. The EPA weighs costs to industry versus loss of life and diseases when establishing ambient air quality standards. Firms should be able to do the same thing, but not effectively if they undervalue human life. All designs of products have costs and benefits. Products that may harm or kill some people may also possess functionality that could save far more lives than it takes. In more and more cases, manufacturers are providing warnings for the foreseeable uses and misuses of their products.

State-of-the-Art Defense

Manufacturers should be experts on the qualities of their products. They have a duty to test for possible hidden risks even though such testing is expensive. Manufacturers do not, however, possess Godlike qualities to predict what science will turn up in the future. Unless there are extraordinary circumstances, manufacturers should be able to rely on existing science in designing their products. If, after their products are in the stream of commerce, scientists discover that this or that product can lead to increased risk of cancer or other chronic diseases after extensive exposure to the product, charging manufacturers with liability for a design defect can be expected to lead to less innovation in the future.

Reform at the Federal Level

As a final matter, note that state product liability laws may be preempted by federal legislation. If federal legislation is enacted, it seems likely that caps on damage awards, particularly punitive damage awards, will be part of the package. Also federal legislation will probably provide more guidance on the issue of design defects. If federal legislation is not enacted, we will most likely continue to see suits alleging damages in the hundreds of millions and even billions of dollars. Statewide efforts at reform will face tough challenges. Some state supreme courts are hostile to any limitations on traditional rights to sue and to any damage award caps. Even if state legislatures do pass such legislation, and the laws pass muster in state courts, plaintiffs' attorneys can select which states to initiate suits in so as to maximize recoveries. It seems inevitable that many large suits involving high-tech products will occur in the future. The ability of juries to evaluate design defects in high-tech products is questionable, exposing manufacturers/producers to a high level of uncertainty in the outcomes of litigation.

SUMMARY

- High-profile *product liability* cases are a fact of life in the U.S. economy.
- Business liability for defective products cannot be eliminated by contracts. Third parties are not bound by agreements between vendors and purchasers. Also there are limits on freedom of contract that further expose vendors to liability for defective products.
- A defective product that is the *proximate cause* of a plaintiff's injuries brings liability for a tort which exists regardless of the contractual relationship between the parties.
- When a vendor sells a product, the ordinary rules of negligence apply. If negligence of a vendor creates a foreseeable risk to third parties, the vendor is liable in tort.
- Manufacturers are liable to customers and others when they are negligent in *inspecting and testing* their products for defects and hidden dangers.

- Failure to comply with government performance and design regulations makes a manufacturer liable per se for its products. Compliance with government regulations in performance and design does not, however, insulate manufacturers from liability for defective designs except when federal regulation is so extensive that state law is preempted.
- In general, industry practices provide a benchmark for safety features for a product. Failure of a manufacturer to meet industry standards for safety is strong proof that the design of the product is defective. As with government regulations, however, adherence to industry standards does not ensure that a company will not be sued for a defective product design.
- A manufacturer is liable to victims if it is negligent in manufacturing a product that causes injury.
- Because of the difficulty of proving negligence in manufacturing, product liability law only requires a showing that the product was defective when sold. It is not necessary to show fault on the part of the seller as long as there is a showing of a connection between the product defect and the resulting harm to the plaintiff. This is the strict liability standard.
- Section 402A of the Restatement Second of Tort Law is often used to define a product defect.
- Section 402A applies to sellers as well as manufacturers.
- Victims of defective products can sue for compensatory damages for *wrongful death,* including claims for pain and suffering, lost future income, fair market value of lost property and *punitive damages* when there is a showing of *intent* or of *gross disregard for the safety of the public.*
- There are three types of product defects: *manufacturing, design,* and *failure to warn.*
- Manufacturing defects exist when a product does not conform to product specifications.
- Design defects exist in products if they do not conform to government safety regulations or industry standards with respect to design. Manufacturers are expected to design products so that there is a reasonable relationship between safety features and possible harm from use or misuse of products.
- Courts make use of *consumer expectations* tests for both manufacturing and design defects.

- Manufacturers have a duty to make products safe for *foreseeable uses,* even if the foreseeable use is not the intended use by the manufacturer.
- Manufacturers have a *duty to warn* about *hidden risks* that they knew or should have known are in their products. Warnings must be reasonable and comprehensible to intended users. The reasonableness or adequacy of warnings depends on the severity of the risks, the intensity of the warnings, and the characteristics of intended users.
- Manufacturers are obligated to warn about foreseeable risks even though the risk may occur only when the product is being misused. As long as the risk associated with the product is foreseeable, manufacturers have a duty to warn.
- Among the defenses available to manufacturers are *misuse* of the product, *ignoring warnings,* and *assumption of risk.* These defenses frequently overlap one another. When consumers misuse products they are frequently ignoring warnings— a result is that they have assumed the risks of the possible resulting harm.
- Other defenses available to manufacturers include *tampering, government contractor defense,* and *state-of-the-art defense.* If a product is tampered with after it left the manufacturer, the manufacturer is not liable. The same is true if the design of the product was dictated by the government. The state of the art defense is not absolute, although in general manufacturers can successfully claim that they did not know of the risk because no one knew of the risk.
- Proposals for product liability reform focus on supplanting state law with a federal law, eliminating joint and several liability, and placing caps on punitive damage awards.
- The impact of product liability on software products is unclear. Vendors are liable when it can be shown that they are negligent in software coding, although this liability may be to third parties and not contracting partners. Strict liability has not been imposed on vendors of software as yet.
- In the future product liability law will be faced with three significant issues: will product liability continue to be governed by state law, or will it be supplanted by federal law, and what is the future of the state-of-the-art defense? If these issues were addressed, the uncertainty facing manufacturers would be significantly lessened.

INTELLECTUAL PROPERTY I: BASIC PATENT AND TRADE SECRET LAW

Management of intellectual property (IP) is no longer "just a lawyer's thing." Today, managers in companies of all sizes must be cognizant of the basics of IP law in their daily decision making. Mistakes in management of IP are legendary and are the frequent focus of articles in newspapers and other periodicals, of the courts, and increasingly in the training of future managers. Consider the following situations:

1. The company you work for is an aggressive leader in high-tech and has a large staff of scientists and engineers who have made important contributions in their disciplines. Many of these staff members regularly attend academic and trade expositions where scientific papers are presented.
2. You are considering an important product launch, but the market acceptance of the product is questionable. You hire an outside firm to conduct market research.
3. Many of your employees are young software engineers who are much in demand. Most of these employees expect to work for several

employers during their careers and some also anticipate heading up their own firm in the not-too-distant future.

Each of the foregoing confronts "management" with the potential for significant IP protection problems, as each of these situations creates opportunities for specialized knowledge, techniques, product ideas, etc., to escape from the control of your company. Recognition of IP issues is essential for managers who want to manage effectively. Decisions to apply for patents, to rely on trade secrets, or to apply combination strategies to IP protection are *management* decisions. Lawyers can be useful by pointing out the costs and benefits of alternative choices, but, ultimately, IP decisions are management decisions. The success of managers is increasingly tied to their success at managing IP. Many managers of smaller firms have limited budgets that prevent them from consulting their attorneys on every IP decision that has to be made. Whether this is or is not the case, knowledge of the basics of IP law should be part of the skill set that modern managers possess.

Some Historical Background on Legal Protection of Inventors

The Social Contract

The Framers of the U.S. Constitution were heavily influenced by John Locke who believed that government and citizens should form a basic "social contract" that laid out what each entity would be entitled to do. The idea behind the social contract was that, at least theoretically, "society" would negotiate with the government and the realms of each would be agreed upon. Society might agree that the government would serve to protect citizens from each other, resulting in the adoption of laws against criminal behavior such as burglary and the creation of mechanisms (such as police forces) for applying penalties to those who violate laws. According to this view, however, in dealing with crime, the government would not be allowed to trample upon individual rights. Hence, a citizen would not be compelled to testify against himself and therefore we have the Fifth Amendment in the U.S. Constitution. According to the Lockian view of the world, which heavily influenced the Founding Fathers, citizens possessed certain "inalienable" rights that should not be taken from them regardless of whether they were suspects in a criminal case or not.

In the arena of commerce, an important component of the social contract between government and society would call for government to encourage activities that promote the interests of society, especially when the conditions that foster those activities cannot be established by individuals. The granting of a temporary monopoly to inventors is a governmental activity that strongly encourages innovation. It is very difficult for an individual person or organization to create and maintain a monopoly without the assistance of government.

As early as the late 1700s, influential citizens in the collection of colonies that was to become the United States were aware of the need to protect and encourage the creation of intellectual property. Article 1, Section 8 of the U.S. Constitution contains enumerated (or delegated) powers of the federal government. Among those powers are the power to "promote the progress of science and useful arts, by securing for limited times to authors and inventors exclusive rights to their respective writings and discoveries." Also the federal government was given the right to "regulate commerce with foreign nations and among the several states." Among the first Acts of the U.S. Congress was adoption of the Patent Act of 1790.

Steps along the Way

To understand the basic bargain that exists in the United States between inventors and the public, it is helpful to have a sense of the legal philosophy that dominated the construction of our legal framework. Fear of a strong central government led to the *federalist system* that reserved to the states and citizens **all powers not delegated (or specifically enumerated)** to the federal government. The powers delegated to the federal government are limited in number. Patent law was, however, turned over to the federal government, so it is subject to the actions of Congress and the President.

With very few exceptions, patent law is entirely federal law and, hence, is not subject to the authority of state laws or state courts. The states, however, are not precluded from protecting intellectual property, which may or may not be patentable. State protection of intellectual property is primarily accomplished through trade secret law, which essentially outlaws certain kinds of competition among companies. When states try to protect the act of inventing, however, federal courts are almost certain to strike down the state statute, as the case on the facing page illustrates.

State Trade Secret Laws

Trade secret law is based on a body of common law that predates the Constitution. Although each state has its own common law tradition, 40 states have adopted the Uniform Trade Secret Act (UTSA). According to Section 1 of the UTSA, a trade secret,

> "means information, including a formula, pattern, compilation, program, device, method, technique or process, that: (i) derives independent economic value, actual or potential, from not being generally known to, or not being readily ascertainable by proper means by, other persons who can obtain economic benefits from its disclosure or use, and (ii) is the subject of efforts that are reasonable under the circumstances to maintain its secrecy."

The UTSA definition indicates that the subject matter of a trade secret could be very broad, but that it is not part of the public domain, has value because it is not in the public domain, and that the possessor of the trade secret is using reasonable security measures to keep it

The University of Colorado Foundation, Inc. **v.** *American Cyanamid Company*
United States Court of Appeals for the Federal Circuit
196 F.3d 1366; 1999

FACTS AND CASE BACKGROUND

In 1997, The University of Colorado sought damages for fraudulent nondisclosure, patent infringement, and copyright infringement for Cyanamid's and Dr. Ellenbogen's alleged infringements of the vitamin and mineral supplement called Materna, which the University and Drs. Allen and Seligman (Doctors) allegedly took part in researching and developing. The University and the Doctors sought restitution and disgorgement of Cyanamid's profits from sales of reformulated Materna. The University also sought equitable title to the '634 patent for Materna and sought to have the Doctors named as the inventors in the '634 patent under 35 U.S.C. § 256 (1994).

OPINION: RADER, CIRCUIT JUDGE

Following a bench trial, the district court found that the Doctors invented the Materna reformulation and that Dr. Ellenbogen was not an inventor of that composition. To determine inventorship, the district court applied state common law, rather than federal patent law. Based on its inventorship finding, the court held Cyanamid liable to the University for both fraudulent nondisclosure and unjust enrichment.

* * *

A. Two types of preemption are asserted in this case. First, this court must determine whether federal patent law preempts the University's claims under state law of fraudulent nondisclosure and unjust enrichment. Second, this court must determine whether federal patent law preempts the district court's use of a state common law standard of inventorship to find that the Doctors were the inventors of the Materna refor-

mulation. This court applies its own law to determine whether federal patent law preempts state law.

"Under the Supremacy Clause, it has been settled that state law that conflicts with federal law is without effect." Field preemption is found when state law regulates conduct in a field that Congress intends the federal government to occupy exclusively. Conflict preemption is found when the application of state law produces a conflict with the requirements, protections, prohibitions, or policies of federal law.

* * *

However, this court notes the following errors in the district court's damages determination. The district court found that Cyanamid's fraudulent nondisclosure "deprived [the University] of financial opportunities and prestige [it] would have enjoyed had their doctors been credited with the invention, and harmed Drs. Allen and Seligman both personally and professionally." However, the record shows that the Doctors intended to, and did, freely share their research results to allow Cyanamid to make and sell an improved Materna formulation. Neither the Doctors nor the University sought to obtain a patent covering the Materna reformulation, and the University has never been in the business of manufacturing or marketing prenatal vitamins. Finally, Cyanamid did not attempt to enforce the '634 patent against the University. Therefore, even assuming that the Doctors were the sole inventors of the Materna reformulation (a fact to be determined upon remand), the only financial opportunity that the University could have lost was the payment for an assignment of ownership rights in the '634

patent or a license from the University to sell the reformulated product at the time the patent issued.

If the court finds that the Doctors jointly invented the reformulated product with Dr. Ellenbogen, the financial opportunity that the University could have lost was the payment that Cyanamid would have made to secure the Doctors' cooperation in filing the required documents with the PTO, such as oaths and declarations. Because federal patent law allows joint owners to practice a patented technology without accounting to the other co-owners, Cyanamid would not have needed to acquire ownership of the patent or licenses thereunder. However, in that case, the University would have been within its rights to license others under the '634 patent or to produce and sell products thereunder. Thus, the district court could find that Cyanamid would have also paid the University for either an assignment of the University's ownership interest in the '634 patent or an exclusive license thereunder. Either arrangement would have assured Cyanamid the exclusivity, which they enjoyed during the life of the '634 patent.

By declining to seek a patent in their own right, the Doctors and the University chose to forego the opportunity to gain prestige associated with the inventorship of such a patent. Instead they presumably were satisfied with the prestige associated with publication of a journal article detailing their research. Furthermore, the University submitted no evidence showing that the Doctors suffered any loss of prestige as a result of Dr. Ellenbogen being named as the inventor in the '634 patent. Therefore, the University did not prove that by naming

Dr. Ellenbogen as the inventor in the '634 patent, Cyanamid deprived the Doctors or the University of any prestige.

Consequently, even if the Doctors were inventors of reformulated Materna under federal patent law, Cyanamid may be held liable pursuant to the fraudulent nondisclosure claim, but only for the payment that Cyanamid would have made to secure the Doctors' cooperation in filing the required documents with the PTO, an assignment of ownership rights and/or an exclusive license from the University.

* * *

The district court also held Cyanamid liable to the University for unjust enrichment. Cyanamid does not argue that the district court erred in any findings under its unjust enrichment analysis. Therefore, this court does not review those findings. This court notes, however, that a

defendant who uses a benefit provided by the plaintiff in an unauthorized and unfair manner may be liable in Colorado for unjust enrichment. However, as noted before, federal patent law preempts the district court's common law inventorship standard. Like the fraudulent nondisclosure claim, unjust enrichment hinges on the finding that the Doctors invented reformulated Materna. Thus, this court vacates the unjust enrichment liability as well.

* * *

CONCLUSION

This court vacates the district court's decision that the Doctors, and not Dr. Ellenbogen, invented the reformulation of Materna, and consequently vacates the court's fraudulent nondisclosure and unjust enrichment decisions. Because these liability decisions cannot stand, the damages awards are necessarily also vacated.

QUESTIONS FOR REVIEW

1. What is meant by federal preemption? Is the court saying that state law was in conflict with federal patent law or that the entire area of law relating to inventorship when patents are involved is exclusively governed by federal law?
2. What are the possible damages that the University may be able to recover in this case? In order to make a damage determination, what must the District Court determine on remand?
3. University staff and equipment were used to develop the patent for reformulated Materna? Why was the University precluded from recovering damages for unjust enrichment?
4. Is it fair to say that the University was in effect penalized for not applying for a patent?

---

secret.[1] Since the subject matter of trade secrets is quite extensive, and since trade secret law has potent protective power, inventors often face a choice of which mechanism(s) to use to protect their inventions—patent law or trade secret law.

Patent Law: The Basic Bargain between Inventors and Society

According to Section 101 of the Patent Act, "Whoever, invents or discovers any new and useful process, machine, manufacture, or composition of matter, or any new and useful improvement thereof, may obtain a patent therefor, subject to the conditions and requirements of this title." Section 101 indicates that to obtain a patent, the inventor must invent or discover something *new and useful*. In other words, the inventor must *add* to the body of knowledge that exists in the United States at the time. Since inventions are to be

encouraged, inventors are rewarded by patent law for *adding* to scientific knowledge by inventing something new and useful. Section 154 (a)(1) of the Patent Act provides the reward for inventors whose inventions are patented. According to this Section, every patent shall grant to the patentee the right to exclude others from **making, using, offering for sale, or selling the invention** (along with some other rights to exclude imports from foreign countries that are made using patented processes).[2]

What Does the Patentee Receive?

In ordinary English, an inventor who is awarded a patent is granted a legal *monopoly*. The patentee is given the right to exclude competition from selling (or

---

[1]The term "public domain" refers to what is known in society in each and every field, even though no one person is familiar with more than a small part of the public domain.

[2]The actual text of Section 154(a)(1) reads as follows: "Every patent shall contain a short title of the invention and a grant to the patentee, his heirs or assigns, of the right to exclude others from making, using, offering for sale, or selling the invention throughout the United States or importing the invention into the United States, and, if the invention is a process, of the right to exclude others from using, offering for sale or selling throughout the United States, or importing into the United States, products made by that process, referring to the specification for the particulars thereof."

making or using) the invention, so that the market only has a single seller, which is a market customarily described as a "monopoly." Section 154(b) states that the term of the patent is 20 years from the *filing* of the patent.[3] So while patent law rewards inventors with a legal monopoly, the duration of the monopoly is limited to 20 years from the filing of the patent application. Patent applications must include detailed descriptions of the item to be patented, including engineering drawings and such other technical information as is necessary to fully understand the addition to the scientific body of knowledge germane to the application. Since patent applications that are accepted are public records, the new knowledge provided becomes available to the public, *benefiting society by adding to the body of scientific knowledge.*

Secrecy

In the past, when a patent applicant's submission was rejected by the PTO, the application remained sealed. The thinking was that if society is not rewarding the applicant with a patent, then the applicant should not have to reveal what the applicant invented. Also since patent applications describe the invention in some detail, they are a potential source of trade secrets that could give rival firms advantages. On the other hand, since the United States is the world leader in innovation, it has the world's largest stake in enforcement of legal protection for patents granted. In much of the rest of the world, including Europe with whom we have important patent cooperation treaties, patent applications are made available to the public 18 months after filing, regardless of whether a patent is issued. The U.S. has been pressing other nations to enforce their patent infringement laws more vigorously while the rest of the world has a stake in harmonizing patent application procedures.

American Inventors Protection Act

In 1999, Congress passed the American Inventors Protection Act, which adopts the *European rule* with respect to patent applications. Heretofore, if an applicant for a U.S. patent also files for a patent in a foreign country, the application before the PTO will be published 18 months after filing. Only applicants that do not file their applications with any foreign countries will be assured that their applications for patents will

not be made publicly available if a patent is not issued. The American Inventors Protection Act also changed the U.S. Patent Act in other ways, which are discussed below.

As indicated above, the essence of the bargain struck between inventors and the public is that inventors who invent something new and useful are entitled to exploit their invention as a monopoly for a significant period of time in return for revealing the science and technology of their invention. With this understanding of the basic *quid pro quo* between inventors and society, we can now investigate the requirements inventors must satisfy for their inventions to qualify for patents.

INSTITUTIONAL ASPECTS OF APPLYING FOR PATENTS

Overview
Patent and Trademark Office

Congress created the Patent and Trademark Office (PTO) to make the decisions on patent applications. As the name implies, the PTO also makes decisions regarding trademarks under the Lanham Act (discussion of trademarks takes place in the next chapter). An inventor applying for a patent sends his or her application to the PTO which makes a decision as to whether the invention qualifies for a patent based on the Patent Act, regulations of the PTO, and precedents created by the federal courts.

Court of Appeals of the Federal Circuit

All decisions made by the PTO are subject to review by the federal courts. In 1982 Congress created the Federal Circuit in Washington D.C. to specialize in patent cases (technically the Court of Appeals of the Federal Circuit (CAFC)). All appeals from the PTO and from Federal District Courts go through the CAFC. Appeals from the CAFC are to the U.S. Supreme Court.

Issuance of Regulations

As with most administrative agencies, Congress has given the PTO power to issue regulations consistent with the Patent Act. For example, the Patent Act allows third parties to challenge the validity of a patent by filing a petition for what is known as an "interference". The PTO has issued guidelines for filing an interference which are found in the Code of Federal Regulations (CFR). The PTO guidelines for filing

---

[3]Under the 1999 American Inventors Protection Act, patentees are entitled to a minimum of 17 years as a monopoly if the examination process between filing and issuance of the patent exceeds three years.

an interference are found at the USPTO website (http://www.uspto.gov/web/menu/pats.html). According to this website:

> Interferences are provided for by 35 U.S.C. § 135. The rules governing interferences are found at 37 CFR §§ 1.601–690. Chapter 2300 of *The Manual of Patent Examining Procedure* sets forth the current procedures for the parties of an interference and patent examiners to follow in interferences.

The Patent Act, which Congress enacted, is contained in Chapter 35 of the U.S. Code [of statutes]. Section 135 of the Patent Act specifically deals with "interferences". The rules, or regulations, composed by the PTO that govern interferences are found at Chapter 37 of the Code of Federal Regulations Section 1.601–690. *The Manual of Patent Examining Procedure,* which is also a creation of the PTO, provides additional guidance for parties that desire to file an intereference.

There are, of course, procedural safeguards as well as substantive safeguards regarding the rule-making function of the PTO. Procedurally, the PTO must comply with the Administrative Procedures Act (APA) of 1946 in the issuance of its regulations. So, regulation 37 CFR §§ 1.601–690, as a regulation promulgated by the PTO, must conform to the procedural requirements of the APA.

The APA calls for *notice* of a proposed regulation in the *Federal Register* before the proposed regulation is enacted. In addition, the APA requires the agency to schedule and announce a *hearing* so that interested parties can make their views of any proposal known. If the PTO does not follow the APA *procedural* requirements, any regulation adopted can be challenged by businesses opposed to such regulation. *Substantively,* interested parties can successfully challenge PTO regulations if those regulations are deemed by the federal courts to be contrary to the Patent Act or to be lacking a technical foundation and thus "arbitrary and capricious".

PTO Procedures

The PTO and Internet Assets

Patent applicants must fill out and file a patent application using forms supplied by the PTO. Although, an applicant is not required to obtain the services of an attorney in this endeavor, such services are strongly recommended. In fact, any firm that is engaged in innovation should enlist the services of a patent attorney, or more generally, an intellectual property (IP) attorney,

as protection of IP is a legal quagmire that has the capacity to sidetrack those who do not have access to the latest developments in IP law. The PTO has recently made increasing use of the Internet through its website at www.uspto.gov. At this site, applicants can download the forms required for patent applications and can access a range of helpful information, including listings of IP attorneys. In addition, the PTO provides search engines to assist applicants in determining whether what they are trying to patent has already been patented. There are also well-organized search engines that are made available to the public by corporations, most notably by IBM Corporation (http://www.patents.ibm.com/ibm.html).

Patent Examiner

Once a patent application has been completed, it is submitted to the PTO at which time, generally, the PTO will assign an **examiner** to the application. Efforts are made to assign applications to examiners who are familiar with the discipline of the application. An applicant interested in patenting a new drug or life form would typically be assigned to an examiner with a background in the biological sciences. An applicant whose invention is a new machine for making a product would be assigned to an examiner with training in mechanical engineering or a related field. In recent years, there has been an explosion in patent applications and issued patents that make use of computer software. Not surprisingly, there has been a time lag between developments of what applicants are applying for and the resulting needed changes in the expertise of patent examiners. Rapidly increasing numbers of patent applications involve computer software whereas the traditional training of examiners has been in engineering and the biological sciences.

What Does the Examiner Do?

Unless there is a secrecy order because the patent application involves national security, the patent examiner will act as a *finder of facts*. Patent applicants are required not only to explain what they are trying to patent, but also must submit any relevant information that they possess that may be material to the examiner's decision. For example, articles published in the field that suggest that what the applicant "invented" is actually already known or invented by someone else should be turned over to the examiner by the applicant even though such articles adversely affect the chances of applicant being issued a patent. In fact, a patent issued to an applicant can be revoked if there is good evidence that the applicant deliberately concealed information relevant to the PTO examiner's task.

The PTO examiner can either reject an application or allow it to go forward. If the decision is favorable, a patent will be issued. If the decision is negative, the applicant can amend the patent application and resubmit the amended application. There is a good deal of interaction between the applicant and the examiner, and the examiner will give hints as to the objectionable features of the application. A frequent reason for rejection is the judgment of the examiner that an application claims too much with regard to what the inventor has invented. For example, a patent application for a new vegetable slicer might be acceptable to the examiner if the description of the invention in the application is very narrow and describes the invention with particularity. If the invention is described as a "rotating blade capable of slicing tomatoes and other vegetables", it likely will be rejected by the examiner because that description is too broad—this would be an apt description as well of the capabilities of food processors, which have already been invented.

Patent Applications

Amendments of patent applications are commonplace. Often as a sequel to amendments, the PTO examiner will *allow* the application and a patent will be issued to the applicant. Generally, the result of amendments is

to narrow the scope of the claimed invention so that a relatively modest invention will not block access to creative activity in an entire field. If the PTO examiner continues to reject the application (for reasons discussed below and/or for other reasons) after the applicant amends the application, eventually there will be a *Final Rejection*. Patent applications are typically decided in a time span of 1.5 to 3 years following the filing of the application with the PTO.

Applicants who receive a Final Rejection from the PTO examiner can appeal to the Board of Appeals and Patent Interferences (Board) of the PTO. The Board can reject the decision of the examiner and send the applicant back to the examiner with instructions for reevaluation. The Board can also *affirm* the decision of the examiner in which case an applicant who wants further review must file an appeal in the CAFC in hopes of getting the decision of the PTO reversed. Few applicants appeal beyond the CAFC to the U.S. Supreme Court. Also note that court challenges to the validity of patents can occur after the PTO issues a patent. In infringement suits, in which a patentee alleges that a defendant has made, used, or sold a patented item or process, it is common for the defendant to claim that the patent is invalid. Such suits are necessarily federal suits and begin in federal district courts. If it is decided at district court that the patent is invalid, any appeal must go through the CAFC in Washington rather than to the Court of Appeals in the circuit where the District Court is located.

Congressional Modification of the Judicial Landscape

Imagine that you link yourself up with a friend who is getting a degree in engineering and the two of you form a business. Your friend is always tinkering with electronic appliances and, indeed, he can seemingly fix anything. Suppose that your friend invents a malleable electric screwdriver that is capable of penetrating those hard to reach spots inside electronic appliances. Suppose further that, in spite of a shoestring budget, you manage to obtain a patent from the PTO. You are confident that you have a very valuable product that is even more valuable because, with a patent, no one can duplicate it.

However, suppose a large hardware store chain hears about your invention, copies it, and begins mass distribution selling of an equivalent (knock-off) product. Naturally, you are outraged, you contact your attorney, and you file suit in federal district court against

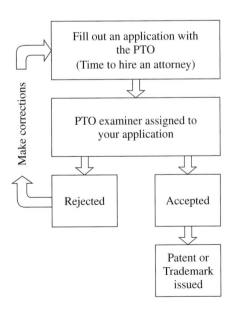

PTO: The Process

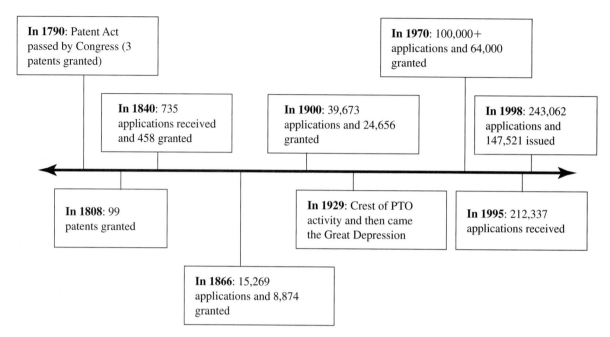

The PTO Historical Time Line

the large hardware chain alleging patent infringement. The hardware chain defends itself by claiming that your patent is invalid. Your parents have mortgaged their home to support you in this endeavor, you obtained your patent from the PTO after considerable negotiation and legal maneuvering that required hefty legal fees, and now the large hardware chain is copying your product with impunity. Suppose you prevail in federal district court, but the defendant appeals. The Court of Appeals in this circuit has an antipatent reputation and declares that your patent is invalid. You scrape together the money to appeal to the U.S. Supreme Court but they decide not to hear the case. At this point, you are without funds to compete and the large hardware store is making sales hand over fist.

Sound far-fetched? This is the situation patentees faced prior to 1982 when approximately 70 percent of the patents challenged for validity were ruled invalid by various Courts of Appeals. Of course there is a huge self-selection bias in the data; defendants would be much more likely to appeal an adverse judgment at the district court level if they thought they would prevail on appeal. It is likely that the weakest patents were challenged on appeal. Still, it is notable that, *subsequent to the creation of the CAFC (Court of Appeals for the CAFC), over 80 percent of the patents*

challenged were upheld. It is particularly notable that those seeking a declaration that a patent is invalid can no longer file a patent interference suit with the PTO and then shop for friendly forums (Court of Appeal Circuits) that are known to be hostile to patentees, because all appeals from the PTO now go through the CAFC.

Historical PTO Data

In 1790, the year the Patent Act was passed by Congress, 3 patents were granted.[4] Data regarding patent applications for that year are not available. In 1808 99 patents were granted by the Patent and Trademark Office, none to foreign countries. In 1840 the first year application data are available, the PTO received 735 patent applications and issued 458 patents, 19 to foreign countries. In 1866 the PTO received 15,269 patent applications and issued 8,874 patents. In 1900 the PTO received 39,673 patent applications, granting 24,656 patents that year. The exponential growth in applications and in the number of patents paralleled the growth of the U.S. economy during that period. The time span between 1865 and 1900 was a

[4]USPTO data are available at their website:
http://www.uspto.gov/web/menu/pats.html.

period of tremendous economic growth for the U.S. economy.

Patent applications crested in 1929 at the beginning of the Great Depression, and then fell dramatically. It was not until 1970 that patent applications topped 100,000, with over 64,000 patents issued that year. By 1995 applications had more than doubled to 212,377. A total of 49,327 *foreign* patents were issued that year. In 1998, the last year for which data are available, 243,062 patent applications were received and 147,521 patents were issued. During that year the PTO received over 17,000 applications for design patents and 720 patent applications for new plants.

Class of Patent

Patents are grouped by numerical class with numbers that rise according to the date that the class was cre-

ated. Class No. 4 includes "Baths, Closets, Sinks, and Spittoons". Class 36 is "Boots, Shoes, and Leggings". As one moves up in number, the classes refer, progressively, to more sophisticated technology. Class 174 is "Electricity: Conductors and Insulators". Class 244 is entitled, "Aeronautics". Continuing with higher classes, it is almost possible to identify dates by looking at the PTO patent classes. The table at the bottom of this page reflects this correlation.

Higher and more recent classes, the 700 series, all deal with data processing and electronic computer devices. Class 705 is "Data Processing: Financial, Business Practice, Management, or Cost/Price Determination". Class 710 is "Electrical Computers and Digital Data Processing Systems: Input/Output". Class 800 is labeled, "Multicellular Living Organisms and Unmodified Parts Thereof and Related Processes". This is the class number for the creation of new life forms.

Class of Patent

Class	Title
307	Electrical Transmission and Interconnection Systems
310	Electrical Generator and Motor Structure
313	Electrical Lamp and Discharge Devices
326	Electronic Digital Logic Circuitry
348	Television
352	Optics: Motion Pictures
355	Photocopying

More Classes of Patents

Class	Title
705	Data Processing: Financial, Business Practice, Management, or Cost/Price Determination
710	Electrical Computers and Digital Data Processing Systems: Input/Output
800	Multicellular Living Organisms, etc.
901	Robots
902	Electronic Funds Transfer
930	Peptide or Protein Sequence

Class 901 is "Robots". Class 902 is "Electronic Funds Transfer". Class 930 is "Peptide or Protein Sequence". Obviously, most of the higher numbered classes refer to technologies that were not even contemplated when the first classes of patents were created.

The PTO has arranged data by class of patent between 1977 and 1999. For the lower numbered classes of patents, the number of patents issued in 1999 as compared to 1977 are about the same or in some cases are far lower. For example, there were 287 patents issued in Class 4 in 1977, but there were 410 patents issued in 1999. For Class 36, 202 patents were issued in 1977 while 258 patents were issued in 1999. Class 51 refers to "Abrasive Tool Making Process, Material, or Composition". In 1977, 75 patents were issued in Class 51, while in 1999, 52 patents were issued. Of course, there is explosive growth in the number of applications and number of patents granted in the higher number classes. For Class 800 (artificial life forms) 5 patents were issued in 1977 while, in 1999, 575 Class 800 patents were issued. In 1977 43 patents were issued for Class 705, but that number had jumped to 713 in 1999. For Class 710 152 patents were issued in 1977, while in 1999 1029 patents were issued in that class.

American Inventors Protection Act, 1999

The American Inventors Protection Act (AIPA) of 1999 reflects the increasing importance of globalization in U.S. patent law. The AIPA also cleans up some loose ends. As a result of the AIPA, inventors awarded a patent are guaranteed at least 17 years to make a profit from their patents. Patentees, particularly in biotechnology, had been loudly complaining that delays by the PTO and the FDA significantly diminished the economic life of their patents. As discussed above, under the AIPA applicants are informed that their applications will be published 18 months after filing with the PTO unless the applicant asserts that it will not file an application with a foreign country.

The AIPA also provides a defense for companies that have constructed inventions more than one year before a filing with the PTO of a comparable invention by another party and have used the inventions prior to the "other" party's filing. This defense, called the *first inventor defense,* applies to situations in which a company with a patentable method of doing business chooses to guard its innovation using trade secret law.

If a patentee subsequently files an infringement suit against the first inventor, the first inventor defense can be asserted. The first inventor defense only applies to methods of doing business (processes) and does not apply to machines, manufactures, and compositions of matter (all of these terms are discussed below).

REQUIREMENTS FOR PATENTABILITY

Novelty

Section 101 of the Patent Act explains that patents are awarded to "Whoever, invents or discovers any new and useful process, machine, manufacture, or composition of matter, or any new and useful improvement thereof, may obtain a patent therefor, subject to the conditions and requirements of this title." A way of analyzing whether an invention is patentable is to examine Section 101 and decide whether the invention falls outside Section 101 and the sections of the Patent Act that are incorporated by reference in Section 101. It is clear from Section 101 that in order to obtain a patent, the inventor must have invented something that is *new.* Reinventing the wheel will not earn the inventor a patent.

Section 102(A): What Is in the Public Domain at the Time of Invention

Section 102 defines newness or novelty according to various criteria, but if the invention is not new, a patent will not be issued. According to Section 102 "a person shall be entitled to a patent unless—

> (a) the invention was known or used by others in this country, or patented or described in a printed publication in this or a foreign country, before the *invention* thereof by the applicant for patent . . . "

The critical date for Section 102(a) is the date of the *invention.* Under patent law, several steps in the inventive process are recognized. An invention is viewed as occurring when the mental steps necessary to construct the invention are *conceived.* If the invention is *reduced to practice,* it is deemed to have been constructed. Returning to our vegetable slicer example, the slicer is invented when it is conceived, not when it is reduced to practice. The slicer is conceived when drawings and plans are laid out with sufficient detail that a person knowledgeable in the industry could transform these plans into an actual slicer. When the actual slicer is constructed, it is "reduced to practice."

Four Disqualifiers in Section 102(a)

Section 102(a) indicates that, if the invention is *known* or *used* by others in this country, there is no more room for a claim of invention of that item or process. Similarly, if the item or process is *patented* in this or in a foreign country, or *described* in a printed publication in this or another country, that item or process cannot qualify for a patent. It is important to link geographic scope with the disqualifier also. The first two disqualifiers are limited geographically to this country, while the last two pertain to events anywhere in the world.

Management Implications

Given the fact that Section 102(a) does not have a "grace" period, it is imperative that firms, involved in innovation that may lead to patents, document what takes place in labs and at staging areas. Priority in the United States (unlike most of the rest of the world) is based on *first to invent* and not *first to file* with the PTO. Priority is established under section 102(a) based on *conception of the invention* so actually building the invention is not the critical factor for establishing a date for Section 102(a) purposes. In order to preserve priority, however, the applicant must be reasonably diligent between *conception* and *reduction to practice* (actually making the patented item or process work). The main lessons of Section 102(a) are that (1) the applicant has to establish that the invention was not known or used before the applicant conceived of the invention and that (2) conception can only be established with adequate documentation. The following case illustrates just how detailed the courts are willing to be in determining whether a prior article describes the patent.

Scripps Clinic & Research Foundation, Revlon, Inc. v. Genentech, Inc.
United States Court of Appeals for the Federal Circuit
927 F.2d 1565; 1991

FACTS AND CASE BACKGROUND

"Factor VIII:C" is a substance found in the human body that aids in coagulation and the research for this method commenced decades ago. The dispute in this case arises from the method to concentrate the substance so that it can be used in medical treatments. The plaintiffs, "Scripps" which includes Drs. Zimmerman and Fulcher, argue that they were the ones to make the big breakthrough in the concentration process and patented it. Prior to the breakthrough by Drs. Zimmerman and Fulcher, Genentech's scientists had been working in the field for years but had not been able to isolate Factor VIII:C in sufficient purity and amount to conduct successful experiments. One of the issues in this case concerns that of prior art in a publication. The defendant, Genentech claims that the patent Scripps claims as novel was in fact described earlier in an article by Dr. Meyer.

OPINION: NEWMAN, CIRCUIT JUDGE

VII. INEQUITABLE CONDUCT BASED ON THE MEYER ABSTRACT

Genentech appeals the district court's grant of summary judgment that Scripps did not engage in inequitable conduct, during examination of the application that led to the '509 patent, based on a reference authored by Meyer, Obert, Zimmerman, and Edgington entitled *Monoclonal Antibodies Specific for Factor VIII from Cellular Hybrids*, No. 395 ("the Meyer abstract").

The district court observed that the Meyer abstract was cumulative to the complete Meyer paper it summarized:

The Meyer abstract was also cited in a paper authored, *inter alia,* by Dr. Meyer herself that was submitted by Scripps to the PTO as reference RS. . . . In contrast to the Meyer abstract, which is only one paragraph long, reference RS is 27 pages in length and much more elaborate in its disclosure. . . .

A reference that is simply cumulative to other references does not meet the threshold of materiality that is predicate to a holding of inequitable conduct.

The Meyer abstract was before the patent examiner who, according to Genentech, discovered it "on his own". When a reference has been considered by the examiner, it is not controlling how it came to the examiner's attention. The complete Meyer paper, and several other references, cited the Meyer abstract. Genentech argues that Scripps should nonetheless have brought the Meyer abstract to the examiner's specific attention, in addition to having listed the complete Meyer paper in Scripps' prior art statement. When a reference was before the examiner, whether through the examiner's search or the applicant's disclosure, it can not be deemed to have been withheld from the examiner.

Genentech presses the argument that the district court erred because the Meyer abstract was a "statutory bar", by which Genentech explains that it was published more than a year before the patent's filing date. Genentech does not explain how this was error, for the district court, like the PTO, treated as prior art both the 27-page Meyer paper and the Meyer abstract. Genentech's argument that the full paper "was not effective prior art" is contrary to law and fact, for it was published before the filing date of Scripps' '509 patent application and Scripps did not attempt to antedate the Meyer paper. It is thus immaterial when the Meyer abstract was published.

Genentech also charged Scripps with inequitable conduct because Scripps originally sought claims to its monoclonal antibodies to Factor VIII:RP, and cancelled these claims after the examiner required Scripps to provide comparative data with the monoclonal antibodies described in

the Meyer abstract and other references. While Genentech argues that obtaining such data was not the burden that Scripps said it was, this is irrelevant to the issue of inequitable conduct. An applicant has the absolute right to decline to do work suggested by the PTO, and to withdraw claims that had been presented for examination, without incurring liability for inequitable conduct.

The district court reviewed the Meyer abstract's content and found, without challenge on this appeal, that:

> The Meyer et al. abstract contains no disclosure of the purification of Factor VIII:C. The Meyer et al. abstract contains no disclosure indicating that any of the monoclonal antibodies could be bound to substrate particles to form an immunoadsorbent for isolation and purification of VIII:C from the VIII:C/VIII:RP complex.

The court concluded: Lacking such disclosure, the Meyer et al. abstract does not appear material to the examination of the claims that were presented in applicants' original application and issued in Patent No. 4,361,509.

QUESTIONS FOR REVIEW

1. The defendant Genentech claims that the reference by Dr. Meyers describes what Scripps received their patent for. What gap in the reference by Dr. Meyers does the court note precludes a claim by the defendant that the article anticipates the patent?

2. The defendant makes reference to inequitable conduct by the plaintiff with respect to the reference written by Dr. Meyers. Does it really make any difference whether the patent examiner found the reference on his own or whether the patent applicant cited the article in the patent application?

3. Is a patent barred by prior art if an expert could describe the thing patented using three or four articles?

Section 102(B): One-Year Rule

Section 102(b) contains four more disqualifying conditions. The text of Section 102(b) reads, [A person shall be entitled to a patent unless]

> (b) the invention was patented or described in a printed publication in this or a foreign country, or in public use or on sale in this country, more than one year prior to the date of the application for patent in the United States . . .

One Year from Filing Date

Again, it is important to keep the geographic scope linked up with the various provisions that create loss of rights to patent a useful invention. The first two conditions apply to the entire world. If the invention has already been *patented* or *described* in a printed publication anywhere in the world, the applicant is not entitled to a patent for the invention if patenting or publication occurs more than one year prior to *filing* of the application with the PTO. The critical date for Section 102(b) is the *filing date,* not the date of conception.

Published or Patented Anywhere in the World

Section 102(b) places a heavy burden on applicants to be aware of patenting and publications anywhere in the world. Fortunately for U.S. inventors, most scientific advances occur in the United States, Europe, and S.E. Asia. This section also places a burden on management to be diligent with regard to public presentations by employees (consider management issue number 1 at the beginning of the chapter). Many times technical employees attend scientific and trade conferences, submit papers, and make presentations. If those papers and presentations describe what the company later submits to the PTO as a patent application, the firm can lose its right to patent the invention if more than one year elapses.

Public Uses or Commercial Sales

Section 102(b) also starts a one-year clock if the patented item is used publicly or sold commercially more than one year before the patent application has been filed. For commercial sales, the one-year limit applies equally to the applicant or to third parties. In other words, if the item that the applicant wants to patent is sold more than one year before filing, either by the applicant or some third party such as a rival in business, the right to patent the product is lost. Quite often, tests of market acceptability or experimental uses or sales of a new product are necessary (management issue number 2 at the start of the chapter). In such cases, the applicant should obtain Non-Disclosure Agreements (NDAs) from participants in the market tests of products that the firm may seek to patent in the future. Note that even an *offer* to sell a

product that the applicant later seeks to patent, can destroy *novelty* under Section 102(b).

Of course, each of the critical descriptive phrases in patent regulations, such as "public use" or "on sale," have been the subject of litigation. In prior cases it has been held that if a "new" machine or process is used to make "existing" goods that are publicly distributed, the one-year clock does *not* begin to run for the machine or process. If the machine or process is producing "new" goods, even if the new goods are not patented, it is a public use for the machine or process and the one-year clock starts. Marketing research with participants who have not signed NDAs has been held to involve products "on sale". Also, distinctive from the situation in the United States, in many European countries, there is no one-year grace period for commercial sales. In that case, once a product is sold commercially the right to patent in some European countries is lost. Because of treaties between the U.S. and European countries, however, if a U.S. patent application is filed before sales in Europe, then the seller can claim the U.S. filing date when subsequently applying for patents in European countries, even after commercial sales have taken place.

Atlantic Thermoplastics Co., Inc. v. *Faytex Corporation*
United States Court of Appeals for the Federal Circuit
5 F.3d 1477; 1993

FACTS AND CASE BACKGROUND

The plaintiffs hold a patent for a shock-absorbing shoe insole and claim that the defendants infringed on that patent. The United States District Court for the District of Massachusetts found that Faytex infringed upon the patent held by Atlantic Thermoplastics, and awarded damages to the patent-holder. The validity of the patent is now contested in the United States Court of Appeals for the Federal Circuit (CAFC) on the basis of the on-sale bar issue.

OPINION: ARCHER, CIRCUIT JUDGE

This case presents several factual disputes which must be resolved

before an ultimate conclusion can be drawn as to the on-sale bar.

B. Atlantic had numerous dealings with a prospective purchaser of the subject innersole prior to the critical date. The parties dispute whether any of three particular events triggers the application of the on-sale bar. On May 3, 1984, an Atlantic salesman met with representatives of Triangle and showed them innersoles made in accordance with the claims of the '204 patent. In a July 9, 1984 letter, Atlantic quoted Triangle a "projected unit cost" of $1.30 to $1.50 per pair of "Product C"—innersoles made in accordance with the claims of the '204 patent. In an August 10, 1984 letter, Atlantic told Triangle that "we now have" the

"products you want" (including Product C) and included an invoice for tooling charges for those products. Although highly probative of whether the product of the claims of the '204 patent was sold or offered for sale, the district court did not evaluate the May meeting or the July or August letters.

In its decision on remand, the district court noted that it had previously "found" that "preliminary negotiations [between Atlantic and Triangle] concerned primarily the necessity of further prototype testing and development" and therefore, those dealings "were for experimental purposes." In so concluding, the district court did not discuss any evidence relevant to the need for or the existence of testing and development of the innersole. A bare "finding" of "prototype testing and development" is inadequate to support the determination of experimental use.

Furthermore, experimental use does not defeat the on-sale bar once the invention has been reduced to practice. In this case, the patentee stated that prior to the critical date a prototype innersole "was made in accordance with the process later described in the '204 patent." Without the benefit of the district court's findings and conclusions regarding reduction to practice, however, we have nothing to review. We will not and cannot take a first look at this important issue on appellate review.

Also unanswered in the district court's opinion is how an innersole similar to one insufficiently developed to trigger an on-sale bar is capable of infringing the claims of the patent. The claims of the '204 patent require that the elastomeric insert have sufficient tack to remain in place in the mold upon the introduction of expandable polyurethane

foam. If displacement occurs, a portion of the foam seeps under the bottom edges of the insert. Atlantic argues in this appeal: "If the insert moved, the innersole would be useless. . . . If the insert were lifted, the open-celled polyurethane would seep under the insert and the result would be unacceptable." Atlantic further argues that the innersole of the '204 patent could not have been on sale prior to the critical date because further innersole testing was required to increase tack and eliminate misplacement, thereby eliminating seepage. Yet Atlantic's representation of the infringing product shows seepage indicating that some displacement occurred during production. Again, however, the district court has not discussed any evidence or made any findings or conclusions in this regard leaving us without a reviewable record.

In Atlantic's first appeal we found the district court's opinion insufficient under Rule 52(a) and remanded the case for specific fact-findings. Without making the necessary fact-

findings based on the record before it, the district court reiterates fact-dependent conclusions as to the on-sale bar just as it did in its original opinion. This is wholly inadequate; Rule 52(a) requires more. We have no choice but to remand this case to the district court a second time. On remand, the district court "shall find the facts specifically and state separately its conclusions of law thereon."

QUESTIONS FOR REVIEW

1. Why is this case being remanded back to District Court? What factual determinations must be made before the District Court can conclude whether the Section 102(b) on sale bar has been failed?
2. For purposes of Section 102(b), what is the critical date?
3. In the second to the last paragraph of this opinion, what does the CAFC find incongruous in the positions taken by the District Court?

Section 102(G): Reasonable Diligence

Under Section 102(g) an applicant is entitled to a patent unless—

> (g) before the applicant's invention thereof the invention was made in this country by another who had not abandoned, suppressed, or concealed it. In determining priority of invention there shall be considered not only the respective dates of conception and reduction to practice of the invention, but also the reasonable diligence of one who was first to conceive and last to reduce to practice, from a time prior to conception by the other.

Abandonment

Section 102(g) establishes priority based on the *date of invention* so long as the invention has not been *abandoned, suppressed, or concealed. Abandonment* has

been defined legally as occurring if an inventor has not been reasonably diligent in the transition from the conception of the invention to the actual building of the invention (generally characterized as *reduction to practice*). Clearly, documentation of the steps taken by the inventor after conception of the invention can prove decisive in determining whether the inventor or firm is entitled to priority and thus a patent. There has been a sizeable volume of litigation over the issue of abandonment. A number of cases have held that a lengthy list of activities does not qualify to excuse lengthy delays between conception and reduction to practice.

Two examples may suffice to give readers an appreciation of what are not legally excusable delays.

1. A university professor conceives of a patentable invention but does not have funding for his graduate assistant during summer. The graduate assistant resumes work on the project during the

fall, but the professor loses priority because a court finds that he has not been reasonably diligent between conception and reduction to practice. The court held in such a situation that the vagaries of university calendars were not its concern.[5]

2. A firm's R&D department discovers a process for dramatically improving the sharpness of laptop monitors. The firm sells laptops and currently has a large inventory. The firm decides to reduce its inventory of existing laptops before pursuing a patent that is likely to make its inventory largely obsolete. Work on making a prototype of the discovery therefore comes to a halt. Can a firm's marketing strategy be used as an excuse for delay in reducing to practice an innovation that clashes with its current sales efforts? Again the courts have looked at this issue and have answered with an emphatic no.[6]

In determining whether the inventor has been reasonably diligent after conception in reducing the invention to practice, courts have taken into account the economic circumstances of the inventor. If the inventor holds a day job and works out of his garage, courts allow greater leeway in defining "reasonable diligence". Again, it is important to have access to an IP attorney for consultation on these issues.

The following case on the next page 224 combines the issues of prior art under Section 102(a) and reasonable diligence between the time when the invention has taken place and the inventor actually reduces the invention to practice. Notice that the claim is that the invention was not new because of prior art (a publication or reference that describes what the applicant is trying to patent) and that the anticipatory reference (or prior art) must be contained in a single reference and not pieced together from several references.

Concealed

An inventor can lose priority if an invention is concealed. Concealment occurs when the invention is protected as a trade secret, which, by definition, must be kept secret to retain its status. Until very recently,

however, an inventor who chose to protect an invention as a trade secret was placed in a vulnerable position because a subsequent inventor could claim priority, based on Section 102(g), which disqualifies an earlier inventor who has *concealed* the invention. Not only could the earlier inventor lose priority, but the subsequent inventor who applied for a patent could then sue the earlier inventor who chose to protect his or her invention as a trade secret.

Congress responded to this dilemma in 1999 by passing the America Inventors Protection Act, which allows those who choose to not to patent their inventions to continue protecting their inventions as trade secrets without becoming vulnerable to an infringement suit by subsequent patentees. The AIPA limits its legal protection (from an infringement suit) to business methods which are invented one year before the patentee files with the PTO. In other words, if a firm makes use of a patentable business method, but chooses instead to protect its new business method through trade secret law, a subsequent patentee of the same invention cannot sue the original inventor for infringement as long as the AIPA conditions are met.

Suppression

In some cases there is evidence that the original inventor deliberately suppressed an invention and tried to prevent it from becoming part of the public domain. When another inventor discovers the same invention and files with the PTO, the original inventor could defeat the priority of the subsequent inventor (by filing an interference claim), unless the subsequent inventor can show that the original inventor *suppressed* the invention. If there was a showing of suppression, Section 102(g) bars the original inventor from being issued a patent.

Section 103: Nonobviousness

Section 103 precludes the issuance of patents for inventions that only trivially advance knowledge in the field.

(a) A patent may not be obtained though the invention is not identically disclosed or described as set forth in section 102 of this title [35 USC § 102], if the differences between the subject matter sought to be patented and the prior art are such that the subject matter as a whole would have been obvious at the time the invention was made to a

---

[5]*Griffith* v. *Kanamaru,* U.S. Court of Appeals, Federal Circuit, 816 F.2d 624 (1987).
[6]*Christie* v. *Seybold,* 55 Fed. 69 (6th Cir. 1893) is an oft-cited case that stands for the proposition that marketing considerations are not sufficient to excuse delays in reducing an invention to practice.

Dr. Sakharam D. Mahurkar v. C.R. Bard, Inc.
United States Court of Appeals for the Federal Circuit
79 F.3d 1572; 1996

FACTS AND CASE BACKGROUND

Dr. Sakharam D. Mahurkar sued the defendant, Mr. Bard, for patent infringement on a medical device called a double-lumen catheter used to help chronic dialysis patients. The court awarded Dr. Mahurkar damages in excess of four million dollars. The case was appealed on the basis of validity and infringement. Mr. Bard argues that the patent is invalid because his work was published in a nationwide catalog, called the Cook catalog, and therefore claims that he should possess the patent rights.

OPINION: RADER, CIRCUIT JUDGE

Section 102(g) of title 35 contains the basic rule for determining priority. Section 102(g) also provides basic protection for the inventive process, shielding in particular the creative steps of conception and reduction to practice. In the United States, the person who first reduces an invention to practice is "prima facie the first and true inventor." However, the person "who first conceives, and, in a mental sense, first invents . . . may date his patentable invention back to the time of its conception, if he connects the conception with its reduction to practice by reasonable diligence on his part, so that they are substantially one continuous act." Stated otherwise, priority of invention "goes to the first party to reduce an invention to practice unless the other party can show that it was the first to conceive the invention and that it exercised reasonable diligence in later reducing that invention to practice."

To have conceived of an invention, an inventor must have formed in his or her mind "a definite and permanent idea of the complete and operative invention, as it is hereafter to be applied in practice." The idea must be "so clearly defined in the inventor's mind that only ordinary skill would be necessary to reduce the invention to practice, without extensive research or experimentation."

* * *

Bard bears the burden of persuasion on the status of the Cook catalog as prior art. Bard must persuade the trier of fact by clear and convincing evidence that the Cook catalog was published prior to Dr. Mahurkar's invention date.

At trial, Dr. Mahurkar offered evidence to demonstrate prior invention in two ways. He offered evidence to show he conceived and reduced to practice his invention before publication of the catalog. He also offered evidence to show that he conceived of his invention prior to the date of publication of the Cook catalog and that he proceeded with reasonable diligence from a date just prior to publication of the catalog to his filing date. Bard, in turn, challenged Dr. Mahurkar's evidence.

With all of the evidence from both sides before the jury, Bard must persuade the jury by clear and convincing evidence that its version of the facts is true. In other words, Bard must persuade the jury that Dr. Mahurkar did not invent prior to publication of the catalog. This is because (1) he did not conceive and reduce his invention to practice before the publication date and (2) that he did not conceive and thereafter proceed with reasonable diligence as required to his filing date. If Bard fails to meet this burden, the catalog is not prior art under section 102(a).

Viewing the evidence of record below in the light most favorable to Bard, this court concludes that no reasonable jury could have found clear and convincing evidence that the Cook catalog was prior art. Dr. Mahurkar testified that he conceived and began work on dual-lumen, flexible, hemodialysis catheters, including the '155 catheter, in 1979. From late 1980 through early 1981, Dr. Mahurkar constructed polyethylene prototype catheters in his kitchen. He bought tubing and various machines for making and testing his catheters.

During this time period, he also tested polyethylene prototypes and used them in flow and pressure drop tests in his kitchen. These tests used glycerine to simulate blood. These tests showed, to the limit of their design, the utility of his claimed invention. Dr. Mahurkar designed these tests to show the efficiency of his structure knowing that polyethylene catheters were too brittle for actual use with humans. But, he also knew that his invention would become suitable for its intended purpose by simple substitution of a soft, biocompatible material. Dr. Mahurkar adequately showed reduction to practice of his less complicated invention with tests which "[did] not duplicate all of the conditions of actual use."

Dr. Mahurkar provided corroboration for his testimony. Dr. Mahurkar confidentially disclosed the catheter prototype tips of his '155 invention to Geoffrey Martin, President of Vas-Cath Inc., in 1981, and Brian L. Bates of Cook, Inc. Mr. Martin testified that he received the polyethylene prototype tips from Dr. Mahurkar in 1981. Dr. Mahurkar also produced a letter from Stephen Brushey, an employee of Vas-Cath, dated April 21, 1981, that described several of his catheters. Additionally, Dr. Mahurkar presented a letter from Brian L. Bates of Cook, Inc., dated October 23, 1981. In this letter, Cook was "impressed with the thought and technology which has gone into the fabrication of the prototype material."

In addition to evidence of actual reduction to practice before publication of the Cook catalog, Dr. Mahurkar also showed reasonable diligence from his conception date through the filing of his patent application. From conception to filing, Dr. Mahurkar continuously sought to locate companies capable of extruding his tubing with the soft, flexible materials necessary for human use.

On this record and with the applicable burden of persuasion, no reasonable jury could have found

that Bard proved the Cook catalog was prior art. Consequently, the court properly granted Dr. Mahurkar's motion for JMOL (Judgement as a Matter of Law) of non-anticipation of claim 1 of the '155 patent.

CONCLUSION

This court affirms the district court's denial of Bard's motion for JMOL under 35 U.S.C. § 102(a) and affirms the district court's grant of Dr. Mahurkar's cross motion.

QUESTIONS FOR REVIEW

1. How does the court define conception for purposes of Section 102(a)?
2. What steps taken by the plaintiff indicated to the court that he was reasonably diligent

between conception and reduction to practice?
3. Notice that a lot of the work in inventing this medical device was undertaken in the plaintiff's kitchen. If the plaintiff was a large corporation, do you think it would have tolerated such a long delay between conception and reduction to practice so that the inventor could find biocompatible material?
4. Examine this case as to the steps that the plaintiff took to document significant events such as conception and reasonable diligence. When did the court consider that the plaintiff's invention has been reduced to practice.

---

person having ordinary skill in the art to which said subject matter pertains. Patentability shall not be negatived by the manner in which the invention was made.

The acid test for Section 103 is whether, at the time of the invention application, the improvement would have been obvious to one skilled in the industry. If the response to the question "Would this improvement be obvious to one skilled in the industry?" is yes, then a patent should not be issued. If evaluating a challenge to an existing patent based on nonobviousness, the courts will look at whether the patent:

a. is a commercial success
b. solves some long-felt but unsolved need or needs
c. was tried by others who failed to solve the problem, and
d. was copied by others in the field.

Courts reason that the nonobviousness test has been passed if the patent is a commercial success, otherwise others would have made the obvious improvement. The fact that others tried to invent the same patent but failed also indicates that the product was not obvious to those skilled in the industry. Given the potentially high cost of being judged an infringer, the fact that a firm copies a patent also indicates that the patent was not obvious to those skilled in the industry.

Obvious Changes

Changes in the form, proportion, degree, or aggregation of old elements have long been held *obvious* and thus not patentable. If old elements are aggregated and produce some synergistic and unexpected results, then it is possible that such an aggregation will survive a challenge based on obviousness. In challenging a patent based on a contention of obviousness, combinations of references in general (scholarly articles, an assemblage of other patents, etc.) are not usable in a skilled combination to show obviousness (see previous case). However, a single reference that revealed the likely outcome of minor changes to a patented item would subject the patentee to an obviousness challenge based on Section 103.

Section 103(c) covers situations in large organizations where, over time, each step in the modification of a machine or process may be obvious given the previous steps in the inventive process. Section 103(c) does not allow an obviousness challenge to a patent where the subject matter of the prior art and the claimed invention were, at the time of the invention, owned by the *same* party. In such situations institutional knowledge cannot be held against the organization for purposes of a challenge based on obviousness, even though the "new" patent applies an obvious next step to assets previously developed by the organization.

In Re Graeme I. Bell
United States Court of Appeals for the Federal Circuit
991 F.2d 781; 1993

FACTS AND CASE BACKGROUND

In 1992 the Graeme Bell and James Merryweather filed for patent protection of "Preproinsulin-Like Growth Factors I and II" involving human nucleic acid molecules, but were denied because of the basis of obviousness. According to the court, "The issue before us is whether the Board correctly determined that the amino acid sequence of a protein in conjunction with a reference indicating a general method of cloning renders the gene prima facie obvious." The PTO denied a patent to the plaintiff based on its view that the invention was obvious to scientists in the field.

OPINION: LOURIE,
CIRCUIT JUDGE

Bell argues that the PTO has not shown how the prior art references, either alone or in combination, teach or suggest the claimed invention, and thus that it has failed to establish a prima facie case of obviousness.

We agree. The PTO bears the burden of establishing a case of prima facie obviousness. "A prima facie case of obviousness is established when the teachings from the prior art itself would appear to have suggested the claimed subject matter to a person of ordinary skill in the art."

The Board supported the examiner's view that the "correspondent link" between a gene and its encoded protein via the genetic code renders the gene obvious when the amino acid sequence is known. In effect, this amounts to a rejection based on the Rinderknecht references alone. Implicit in that conclusion is the proposition that, just as closely related homologs, analogs, and isomers in chemistry may create a prima facie case, the established relationship in the genetic code between a nucleic

acid and the protein it encodes also makes a gene prima facie obvious over its correspondent protein.

We do not accept this proposition. It may be true that, knowing the structure of the protein, one can use the genetic code to hypothesize possible structures for the corresponding gene and that one thus has the potential for obtaining that gene. However, because of the degeneracy of the genetic code, there are a vast number of nucleotide sequences that might code for a specific protein. In the case of IGF, Bell has argued without contradiction that the Rinderknecht amino acid sequences could be coded for by more than 10^{36} different nucleotide sequences, only a few of which are the human sequences that Bell now claims. Therefore, given the nearly infinite number of possibilities suggested by the prior art, and the failure of the cited prior art to suggest which of those possibilities is the human sequence, the claimed sequences would not have been obvious.

Bell does not claim all of the nucleic acids that might potentially code for IGF. Neither does Bell claim all nucleic acids coding for a protein having the biological activity of IGF. Rather, Bell claims only the human nucleic acid sequences coding for IGF. Absent anything in the cited prior art suggesting which of the possible sequences suggested by Rinderknecht corresponds to the IGF gene, the PTO has not met its burden of establishing that the prior art would have suggested the claimed sequences.

This is not to say that a gene is never rendered obvious when the amino acid sequence of its coded protein is known. Bell concedes that in a case in which a known amino

acid sequence is specified exclusively by unique codons, the gene might have been obvious. Such a case is not before us. Here, where Rinderknecht suggests a vast number of possible nucleic acid sequences, we conclude that the claimed human sequences would not have been obvious.

Combining Rinderknecht with Weissman does not fill the gap. Obviousness " 'cannot be established by combining the teachings of the prior art to produce the claimed invention, absent some teaching or suggestion supporting the combination.' " What a reference teaches and whether it teaches toward or away from the claimed invention are questions of fact.

While Weissman discloses a general method for isolating genes, he appears to teach away from the claimed invention by emphasizing the importance of unique codons for the amino acids. Weissman suggests that it is generally advantageous to design a probe based on an amino acid sequence specified by unique codons, and also teaches that it is "counterproductive" to use a primer having more than 14–16 nucleotides unless the known amino acid sequence has 4–5 amino acids coded for by unique codons. Bell, in contrast, used a probe having 23 nucleotides based on a sequence of eight amino acids, none of which were unique. Weissman therefore tends to teach away from the claimed sequences since Rinderknecht shows that IGF-I has only a single amino acid with a unique codon and IGF-II has none.

The PTO, in urging us to affirm the Board, points to the suggestion in Weissman that the disclosed method can "easily" be applied to isolate genes for an array of proteins including peptide hormones. The PTO thus argues that in view of Weissman, a gene is rendered obvious once the amino acid sequence of its translated protein is known. We decline to afford that broad a scope to the teachings of Weissman. While "a reference must be considered not only for what it expressly teaches, but also for what it fairly suggests," we cannot say that Weissman "fairly suggests" that its teachings should be combined with those of Rinderknecht, since it nowhere suggests how to apply its teachings to amino acid sequences without unique codons.

We conclude that the Board clearly erred in determining that Weissman teaches toward, rather than away from, the claimed sequences. Therefore, the requisite teaching or suggestion to combine the teachings of the cited prior art references is absent, and the PTO has not established that the claimed sequences would have been obvious over the combination of Rinderknecht and Weissman.

Finally, the PTO emphasizes the similarities between the method by which Bell made the claimed sequences and the method taught by Weissman. The PTO's focus on Bell's method is misplaced. Bell does not claim a method. Bell claims compositions, and the issue is the obviousness of the claimed compositions, not of the method by which they are made.

CONCLUSION

Because we conclude that the combination of prior art references does not render the claimed invention obvious, we reverse the Board's decision affirming the examiner's rejection of claims 25–46.

QUESTIONS FOR REVIEW

1. What does the court say about the claim of the PTO that an invention can be "obvious" because of the combination of prior articles?
2. What does it mean that a prior reference or article "teaches away" from the invention or vice versa?
3. What is the result of this case in terms of the patent applicant? Why is this patent apt to be quite valuable?

"Frequently Asked Questions about Patents"

Q. What do the terms "patent pending" and "patent applied for" mean?

A. They are used by a manufacturer or seller of an article to inform the public that an application for patent on that article is on file in the Patent and Trademark Office. The law imposes a fine on those who use these terms falsely to deceive the public.

Q. Is there any danger that the Patent and Trademark Office will give others information contained in my application while it is pending?

A. No. All patent applications are maintained in the strictest confidence until the patent is issued. After the patent is issued, however, the Office file containing the application and all correspondence leading up to issuance of the patent is made available in the Files Information Unit for inspection by anyone and copies of these files may be purchased from the Office.

Q. May I write to the Patent and Trademark Office directly about my application after it is filed?

A. The Office will answer an applicant's inquiries as to the status of the application, and inform you whether your application has been rejected, allowed, or is await-ing action. However, if you have a patent attorney or agent of record in the application file the Office will not correspond with both you and the attorney/agent concerning the merits of your application. All comments concerning your application should be forwarded through your attorney or agent.

Q. Is it necessary to go to the Patent and Trademark Office to transact business concerning patent matters?

A. No; most business with the Office is conducted by correspondence. Interviews regarding pending applications can be arranged with examiners if necessary, however, and are often helpful.

Q. If two or more persons work together to make an invention, to whom will the patent be granted?

A. If each had a share in the ideas forming the invention, they are joint inventors and a patent will be issued to them jointly on the basis of a proper patent application. If, on the other hand, one of these persons has provided all of the ideas of the invention, and the other has only followed instructions in making it, the person who contributed the ideas is the sole inventor and the patent application and patent shall be in his/her name alone.

—Continued on page 228

Frequently Asked Questions about Patents" *Continued from page 227*

Q. If one person furnishes all of the ideas to make an invention and another employs him or furnishes the money for building and testing the invention, should the patent application be filed by them jointly?

A. No. The application must be signed by the true inventor, and filed in the Patent and Trademark Office, in the inventor's name. This is the person who furnishes the ideas, not the employer or the person who furnishes the money.

Q. Does the Patent and Trademark Office control the fees charged by patent attorneys and agents for their services?

A. No. This is a matter between you and your patent attorney or agent in which the Office takes no part. To avoid misunderstanding you may wish to ask for estimate charges for: (a) the search, (b) preparation of the patent application, and (c) Patent and Trademark Office prosecution.

Q. Will the Patent and Trademark Office help me to select a patent attorney or agent to make my patent search or to prepare and prosecute my patent application?

A. No. The Office cannot make this choice for you. However, your own friends or general attorney may help you in making a selection from among those listed as registered practitioners on the Office roster. Also, some bar associations operate lawyer referral services that maintain lists of patent lawyers available to accept new clients.

Q. Will the Patent and Trademark Office advise me as to whether a certain patent promotion organization is reliable and trustworthy?

A. No. The Office has no control over such organizations and does not supply information about them. It is advisable, however, to check on the reputation of invention promotion firms before making any commitments. It is suggested that you obtain this information from the Better Business Bureau of the city in which the organiza-

tion is located, or from the bureau of commerce and industry or bureau of consumer affairs of the state in which the organization has its place of business. You may also undertake to make sure that you are dealing with reliable people by asking your own patent attorney or agent or by asking others who may know them.

Q. Are there any organizations in my area which can tell me how and where I may be able to obtain assistance in developing and marketing my invention?

A. Yes. In your own or neighboring communities you may inquire of such organizations as chambers of commerce and banks. Many communities have locally financed industrial development organizations which can help you locate manufacturers and individuals who might be interested in promoting your idea.

Q. Are there any state government agencies that can help me in developing and marketing of my invention?

A. Yes. In nearly all states there are state planning and development agencies or departments of commerce and industry which seek new product and new process ideas to assist manufacturers and communities in the state. If you do not know the names or addresses of your state organizations you can obtain this information by writing to the governor of your state.

Q. Can the Patent and Trademark Office assist me in the developing and marketing of my patent?

A. The Office cannot act or advise concerning the business transactions or arrangements that are involved in the development and marketing of an invention. However, the Office will publish, at the request of a patent owner, a notice in the Official Gazette that the patent is available for licensing or sale. The fee for this is $25.

Source: U.S. Patent and Trademark Office; http://www.uspto.gov/web/offices/pac/doc/general/faq.htm and *General Information Concerning Patents* print brochure.

PATENTABLE SUBJECT MATTER

Section 101 of the Patent Act mentions "process, machine, manufacture, or composition of matter" as statutory subject matter for patent applications. Imagine a tin container of a new pharmaceutical drug. The *process* of making the drug is patentable. The *ma-*

chines that make the drug and the tin are patentable. The tin container may be patentable as a *manufacture*. As long as the drug is not naturally occurring, it also is patentable as a *composition of matter*.

There are several categories of *nonstatutory subject matter,* referring to things that cannot be patented. Perhaps most fundamentally, **ideas** cannot be patented. Patents must be and can only be applied to something that does something rather than to an idea, no matter how clever the idea is. Moreover, patents are applicable to things that are created as opposed to things that are discovered. So, laws of nature and mathematical formulas cannot be patented. Thus, the famous mass/energy conversion equation deduced (discovered) by Albert Einstein, $E = MC^2$ could not be patented but the creation of a nuclear reactor could be. Printed material, functions of machines, mental processes such as Total Quality Management, and compilations of data are not patentable subject matter. Finally, naturally occurring substances cannot in general be patented, but artificial life forms, including genetically altered versions of existing life forms, can be patented. Genetically engineered lab mice have been patented, and the process of cloning is patentable unless the subject matter of the cloning is human.

As with the rest of patent law, each of the foregoing terms have been litigated extensively. Originally, most computer software was considered unpatentable because it was thought to be too close to being a mathematical algorithm. As will be discussed at length in Chapter 10, the patentability of computer software is no longer an issue, either if the software is part of a larger process or as a stand-alone invention that accomplishes some process or task.

BIOTECHNOLOGY: BRAVE NEW WORLD

Overview

Before we traverse the challenges to patent law created by advances in biotechnology, let us note that in several other fields, most notably computer science, broadly defined, technological advances are also challenging and are requiring changes in patent law. What was once thought to be unpatentable is now patentable in many of these fields. Much of Chapter 10 deals with the evolution of patent law as it relates to computer science and information technology. What follows in this chapter is a less extensive foray into biotechnology and consideration of whether the subject matter is patentable.

Basic Distinctions

Section 101 limits patents to "Whoever invents or discovers any new and useful process, machine, man-

ufacture, or composition of matter." Obviously, limitations inherent in Section 101 must be interpreted by the courts because on their face there are few limitations. Is a mathematical formula a process? If so, then we will have to pay royalties to "inventors" of new mathematical techniques. Such a situation is obviously unsatisfactory and so the courts have coalesced to standards that reward inventors but don't choke off innovation for others.

Innovation may be thought of as a continuum that originates with advances in basic science and culminates in improved products for consumers. If the continuum begins at one and ends at ten, patent law rewards inventions in the six, seven, and eight range. Advances in basic science are not rewarded by patent law unless there are specific processes, machines, manufactures, or compositions of matter that are invented as a result. With respect to theoretical advances in science, it could be argued that the advance is not "useful" and thus does not merit a patent. The threat of suppression of science by granting patents too far up the innovation chain is attenuated by the requirement that only inventions or discoveries that are tied to processes etc. are patentable. Still many large companies have been accused of creating a thicket of patents in an area and thus preventing others from innovating. In some cases, thickets of patents have been the basis for antitrust lawsuits as in the case of IBM. In other cases, creation of thickets of patents is part of management strategy, as in the case of the Gillette Company, and has not been subject to legal challenge.

Right to Patent New Life Forms

It is clear that applicants that create or invent new life forms are entitled to patents. In 1980 the U.S. Supreme Court handed down a decision based on an appeal from the Patent Office Board of Appeals by Chakrabarty, who applied for a patent based on the creation of a bacterium that had different characteristics than those found in nature.

Higher Life Forms: Plants

The *Chakrabarty* case dealt with microorganisms, but the pressure to extend patent rights to higher life forms proved irresistible. Since 1985 the PTO has issued patents for seeds, plants, and plant tissues.

Diamond v. *Chakrabarty*
U.S. Supreme Court
100 S.Ct. 2205, 447 U.S. 303 (1980)

FACTS AND CASE BACKGROUND

In 1972 respondent Chakrabarty, a microbiologist, filed a patent application assigned to the General Electric Co. The application asserted 36 claims related to Chakrabarty's invention of "a bacterium from the genus Pseudomonas containing therein at least two stable energy-generating plasmids, each of said plasmids providing a separate hydrocarbon degradative pathway." This human-made, genetically engineered bacterium is capable of breaking down multiple components of crude oil. Because of this property, which is possessed by no naturally occurring bacteria, Chakrabarty's invention is believed to have significant value for the treatment of oil spills. Chakrabarty's patent claims were of three types: first, process claims for the method of producing the bacteria; second, claims for an inoculum comprised of a carrier material floating on water, such as straw, and the new bacteria; and third, claims to the bacteria themselves. The patent examiner allowed the claims falling into the first two categories, but rejected claims for the bacteria. His decision rested on two grounds: (1) that micro-organisms are "products of nature," and (2) that as living things they are not patentable subject matter under 35 U.S.C. § 101.

Chakrabarty appealed the rejection of these claims to the Patent Office Board of Appeals, and the Board affirmed the Examiner on the second ground. Relying on the legislative history of the 1930 Plant Patent Act, in which Congress extended patent protection to certain asexually reproduced plants, the Board concluded that § 101 was not intended to cover living things such as these laboratory-created micro-organisms.

OPINION: BURGER, CHIEF JUSTICE

The question before us in this case is a narrow one of statutory interpretation requiring us to construe 35 U.S.C. § 101, which provides: "Whoever invents or discovers any new and useful process, machine, manufacture, or composition of matter, or any new and useful improvement thereof, may obtain a patent therefor, subject to the conditions and requirements of this title." Specifically, we must determine whether respondent's micro-organism constitutes a "manufacture" or "composition of matter" within the meaning of the statute.

* * *

Guided by these canons of construction, this Court has read the term "manufacture" in § 101 in accordance with its dictionary definition to mean "the production of articles for use from raw or prepared materials by giving to these materials new forms, qualities, properties, or combinations, whether by hand-labor or by machinery." Similarly, "composition of matter" has been construed consistent with its common usage to include "all compositions of two or more substances and . . . all composite articles, whether they be the results of chemical union, or of mechanical mixture, or whether they be gases, fluids, powders or solids." In choosing such expansive terms as "manufacture" and "composition of matter," modified by the comprehensive "any," Congress plainly contemplated that the patent laws would be given wide scope.

* * *

Judged in this light, respondent's micro-organism plainly qualifies as patentable subject matter. His claim is not to a hitherto unknown natural phenomenon, but to a nonnaturally occurring manufacture or composition of matter—a product of human ingenuity "having a distinctive name, character [and] use."

* * *

The petitioner's second argument is that micro-organisms cannot qualify as patentable subject matter until Congress expressly authorizes such protection. His position rests on the fact that genetic technology was unforeseen when Congress enacted § 101. From this it is argued that resolution of the patentability of inventions such as respondent's should be left to Congress. The legislative process, the petitioner argues, is best equipped to weigh the competing economic, social, and scientific considerations involved, and to determine whether living organisms produced by genetic engineering should receive patent protection. In support of this position, the petitioner relies on our recent holding in *Parker* v. *Flook,* and the statement that the judiciary "must proceed cautiously when . . . asked to extend patent rights into areas wholly unforeseen by Congress."

It is, of course, correct that Congress, not the courts, must define the limits of patentability; but it is equally true that once Congress has spoken it is "the province and duty of the judicial department to say what the law is." Congress has performed its constitutional role in defining patentable subject matter in § 101; we perform ours in construing the language Congress has employed. In so doing, our obligation is to take statutes as we find them, guided, if ambiguity appears, by the legislative history and statutory purpose. Here, we perceive no ambiguity. The subject-matter provisions of the patent law have been cast in broad terms to fulfill the constitutional and statutory goal of promoting "the Progress of Science and the useful Arts" with all that means for the social and economic benefits envisioned by Jefferson. Broad general language is not necessarily ambiguous when congressional objectives require broad terms.

* * *

Our task, rather, is the narrow one of determining what Congress meant by the words it used in the statute; once that is done our powers are exhausted. Congress is free to amend § 101 so as to exclude from patent protection organisms produced by genetic engineering. Cf. 42 U.S.C. § 2181(a), exempting from patent protection inventions "useful solely in the utilization of special nuclear material or atomic energy in an atomic weapon." Or it may choose to craft a statute specifically designed for such living things. But, until Congress takes such action, this Court must construe the language of § 101 as it is. The language of that section fairly embraces respondent's invention.

Accordingly, the judgment of the Court of Customs and Patent Appeals is affirmed.

QUESTIONS FOR ANALYSIS

1. What according to the Supreme Court were Chakrabarty's bacteria? Were they a machine, manufacture, composition of matter, or a process?
2. Does this ruling mean that scientists can get a patent for cloning a half-man half-pig, as long as the being does not naturally exist in nature?
3. How did the Supreme Court answer the argument that Congress had not authorized issuing patents for genetically engineered life?

According to the PTO the following are qualified for patenting:

1. A living plant organism which expresses a set of characteristics determined by its single, genetic makeup or genotype, which can be duplicated through asexual reproduction, but which can not otherwise be "made" or "manufactured."
2. Sports, mutants, hybrids, and transformed plants are comprehended; sports or mutants may be spontaneous or induced. Hybrids may be natural, from a planned breeding program, or somatic in source. While natural plant mutants might have naturally occurred, they must have been discovered in a cultivated area.
3. Algae and macro fungi are regarded as plants, but bacteria are not.

Clearly, the PTO is now receptive to plant patent applications for living plant organisms that are asexually duplicated, except for "natural plant mutants" that have been discovered in cultivated areas. Many of the plant patents are issued for genetically engineered foods which has conjured up the notion of "Franken" foods. "Green" movements in both Europe and the United States have begun to press demands for proper labeling of foods so that consumers can determine whether the product is "natural" or genetically engineered.

As controversy in this area continues to heat up, mind-boggling advances in technology continue to confront agribusiness, consumers, and governments with more challenges. To date there are no U.S. requirements to label genetically engineered foods, though the FDA does have authority to step in and pull products off the market if there is evidence that the foods are unsafe. Pressure continues to mount from consumer groups and environmentalists for more stringent government regulation. The estimated value of genetically engineered plant patents should take into account the very real possibility that government regulation may radically reduce their value.

Plant and Animal Progeny

A contentious issue has arisen regarding ownership of the progeny of plants and animals that are patented. The purchaser of a patented machine can make use of the product as he or she sees fit, but in the case of genetically altered plants and animals, the value of the patents is severely compromised if purchasers are allowed to breed and retain the progeny. As patent law stands today, patentees, not purchasers, own the progeny but enforcement is a difficult issue. Patented plants and animals can be cross-bred with nonpatented animals. Patented strains of food products that are imported by other countries that do not allow such patents contravene the Process Patent Act of 1988 (discussed below), but enforcement is an impossible task. Are customs officials really equipped to test imported corn that is produced illegally (from the perspective of U.S. patent law) and imported into the United States?

A possible solution is to genetically engineer patented plants not only to have desirable features, such as resistance to disease or increased yield, but also to make the seed produced sterile so that purchasers would have to go back to the patentee for additional seed. Resistance to this product characteristic among farmers has caused the Monsanto Corporation to back off from negotiations with the company that owns the patent on production of "sterile" seeds.

Patents and Medicines

Third world countries are often desperate for life-saving patented pharmaceutical products but simply cannot afford to pay prices charged by patent owners, the large pharmaceutical companies. Africa is awash in HIV infection and its people are in need of expensive treatments, but the costs of these treatments are utterly beyond the means of these countries. Some of the *patented* products of pharmaceutical companies are naturally occurring compositions of matter that have been produced at much higher volumes or purity levels than what could be obtained from humans, animals, or plants. There are cases that have held that an applicant is entitled to a patent on naturally occurring substances, or the process to produce naturally occurring substances, that are produced in forms that are more concentrated or purified than would occur in nature. In any event, patented, and often high-priced, pharmaceutical drugs are yet another issue that divides the haves from the have nots of the world. In the case of patented medicines, even if a Third World country does not respect patent rights, it generally does not have the facilities to reproduce wanted products in its own country.

Human Genome Project

The Human Genome Project, begun in 1990, is a 13-year effort headed up by the U.S. Department of Energy and the National Institutes of Health (NIH). According to the Human Genome Project (HGP) website (http://www.ornl.gov/TechResources/Human_Genome/home.html), the goals of the project are to:

- *identify* all the 100,000 genes in human DNA,
- *determine* the sequences of the 3 billion chemical base pairs that make up human DNA,
- *store* this information in databases,
- *develop* tools for data analysis,
- *transfer* related technologies to the private sector, and
- *address* the ethical, legal, and social issues (ELSI) that may arise from the project.

It is the view of NIH that patents play a key role in the transfer of technology to the private sector. In 1992 NIH applied for 2,700 patents of human genes and the PTO rejected all of the applications based in part on the lack of a showing that the genes were "useful". According to the HGP, "inventors must:

1. identify novel genetic sequences,
2. specify the sequence's product,
3. specify how the product functions in nature—i.e., its use,
4. enable one skilled in the field to use the sequence for its stated purpose."

According to the HGP website, over three million genome-related patent applications have been filed, but "[Q]uestions have arisen over the issue of when, from discovery to development into useful products, exclusive rights to genes could be claimed."

Gene sequences can be patented as long as they are not naturally occurring, according to the *Chakrabarty* case. When the National Institute of Health (NIH) applied for patents on 2,700 human genes in 1992, they claimed that they were furthering science because, by applying for patents, they allowed scientists who found a use for these genes to profit from subsequent patents. The NIH patent applications did not specify a use for these genes, but they wanted a patent on the genes they had discovered nevertheless. The PTO rejected the patent applications, leaving a controversy that will continue as specific linkages are made between human genes and the functions they serve—thus seemingly eliminating the objection the PTO had to the NIH applications. More recently the PTO has been issuing patents for human genes so long as the patent applicant can show:

1. the gene has been excised and isolated from the form it appears in nature and
2. a new use for the excised gene.

Treating disease is a new use. To date the PTO has issued about 200 patents for human genes, but for each a use must be specified. The PTO is *not* issuing patents for discoveries of human genes.

Frankensteins for the 21st Century

By the year 2000 the functions of specific genes had been discovered and patent applications based on human genes had taken place. President Clinton weighed in suggesting it was unwise to allow individual firms to receive patents based on human genes. Jeremy Rifkin, an iconoclastic scientist known for insisting that ethics and social considerations be more a part of scientific research, applied for a patent on human gene scrambling in 1998.[7] In his application to the PTO, Rifkin, skilled at media manipulation, described a half-man, half-cow artificial life form. The PTO turned down the patent application stating that they would not consider transgenic creations that are partly human. In 1998 the European Patent Organization (EPO) issued a Biotechnology Directive that essentially excludes patenting of both plants and animals, whether or not they are artificially created.[8] Also excluded are any processes that have to do with human cloning. Gene fragments are entitled to patent protection under the EPO, however, as long as they have a specific use. Scientific progress continues to test patent law and more legislation can be expected as human cloning becomes technically feasible.

PATENT CLAIMS AND INFRINGEMENT

What Must Be in a Patent Application

As discussed above, the basic bargain between inventors and society is that patentees are entitled to a legal monopoly for 20 years (minus the time it takes to get the patent approved) in return for disclosure of the scientific or technical advance that their invention incorporates. Firms that obtain patents would, of course, like to have even more protection of their IP rights than the patent bargain provides. So, it is in a firm's interest to avoid disclosing more about an invention than is required, for fear that valuable trade secrets and proprietary information will also be disclosed. One of the most important skills of patent attorneys drafting patent applications is the ability to disclose just enough to the PTO to obtain the patent desired without disclosing too much valuable firm-specific information.

Enablement

In addition to disclosing prior art and references so that patent examiners can determine if the invention is

new and nonobvious, applicants are required to disclose the invention in sufficient detail so that a reasonably skilled practitioner could reproduce that invention. In the case of computer software, the source code does not have to be disclosed if there are several software packages that could accomplish the same tasks. Enablement in this arena means the tasks that the program is expected to accomplish are disclosed. When there are several ways of accomplishing these tasks, the applicant is required to reveal the "best mode". Again the overall criterion is whether the description enables skilled practitioners to determine the best mode.

Infringement

A commercially valuable invention certainly has the capacity to attract imitators, as competitors and potential competitors can be quite eager to share the benefits of innovation. It is claimed that imitation is the most sincere form of flattery. Inventors, however, are generally far more interested in profits from their inventions than compliments. So, court cases based on charges of patent infringement are quite common.

Defenses in Patent Infringement Cases

As stated earlier, a patentee is entitled under Section 154(a)(1) to exclusive right to make, use, or sell the patented invention. Also included under this section of the Patent Act is exclusive right to offer for sale and to sell any product that is made as a result of a patented *process,* including products that are made abroad. Courts have devised several conceptual tests regarding what is and what is not a patent infringement.

Keep in mind that the first line of defense for defendants in infringement cases is to claim that the patent is invalid. We have spent much of this chapter discussing grounds for invalidity of patents. A defendant may argue that

1. A patent is invalid because it was granted in spite of the fact that the knowledge embodied in the patent already existed, or
2. that anything new in the patent is trivial and obvious to one skilled in the industry.

In addition,

3. A patent can be declared invalid if the patentee withheld material information from the examiner.

[7]http://www.linkny.com/~civitas/page58.html.
[8]*Art. 53(b)* of the European Patent Office, section 3.4 reads as follows, "Also excluded from patentability are 'plant or animal varieties or essentially biological processes for the production of plants or animals'."

4. Even if a patent is valid, patentees can lose their patent rights if they *misuse* the patent. This principally occurs if the patentee tries to extend patent monopoly by tying the sale of a patented product to a nonpatented product. Tying contracts involving two products, one patented and the other not, are violations of Section 3 of the Clayton Act, which is one of the antitrust statutes.

Assuming that the plaintiff in a patent infringement case is able to overcome any challenge to the validity of its patent, there are several remaining defenses available to the alleged infringer. At the onset it should be noted that **independent creation is not a defense,** unless the infringer can show that the invention was created prior (more than one year prior to filing) to the patentee's invention and that the infringer employed the invention as a trade secret. Independent creation by itself is not a defense! If the accused infringer's device was invented independently by an inventor in complete ignorance of the existence of the like patented invention, an infringement has still taken place. Finally, if challenges to the validity of the patent or disqualifying conduct on the part of the patentee cannot be shown, the infringer can claim the accused device does not infringe and attempt to prove this with expert testimony on the differences between the plaintiff's device and the defendant's.

Literal Infringement

The most straightforward patent infringement case involves a claim of *literal infringement*. In a literal infringement case the claims made in the patentee's patent application are examined. If the infringing device or process is described exactly in the patent application, the defendant has infringed. If the alleged infringing (accused) device does everything described in the patent application, but also does more, it is also an infringement. An accused device could merit an improvement patent, but the infringer would have to obtain permission of the patentee before applying for the improvement patent.

In the real world, claims made in patent applications are often complicated as the following cases reveal. Let us assume that the patent applicant is applying for a patent based on the process for making a composition of matter. Assumed, simplified claims made in the patent application might take on the following structure.

The composition of matter is composed of a new chemical compound, call it FNR (Ferric nitrous oxide):

Claim   1. FNR is 30 percent ferrous, 25 percent nitrogen, and 45 percent oxygen, and
        2. A catalyst that combines the three.

The process of creating the composition of matter is made in the following claims:

Claim   1. Ferrous is heated to a temperature of 2000 degrees Fahrenheit.
        2. Compressed nitrogen and oxygen are combined.
        3. A catalyst is injected that starts a chemical reaction combining the three.

The following case contains much more complicated claims made by the patentee in his effort to sue alleged infringers. Consideration of these cases requires understanding of the following terms and principles:

Patent Law Terms

The **Doctrine of Equivalents** applies when an accused device performs substantially the same function(s), in substantially the same way, to obtain substantially the same result provided by the patented device. In other words, the accused device or process of the defendant is not literally described by the claims made in the patent application, but the essence of the accused device accomplishes the same thing as the patented device (in a similar way using similar methods). Quite obviously, when the Doctrine of Equivalents applies, the accused device of the defendant generally competes for sales with the plaintiff's patented device.

Rules of the Courts

Courts have devised various "rules" to assist them in making determinations of whether an accused device infringes a valid patent. The **Rule of Exactness** applies to a situation when the claims made in a patent application exactly describe the accused (infringing) creation. The **Rule of Addition** applies when the infringing device is described by the claims in the existing patent application, but the infringing device does even more than is described in the patent application. Both of these rules are applicable when the plaintiff is claiming that the defendant's device has *literally* infringed the plaintiff's patent. The **Rule of Omission** applies when the alleged infringing device lacks one of the essential elements in the assemblage of claimed attributes. For example, an invention that possesses most of the functionality of the patented device, but not all, is not an infringement **unless** the Doctrine of Equivalents applies. The Rule of Omission is applied in the *Pennwalt* case (page 236).

File Wrapper Estoppel

The patent application is the most definitive document delineating what the boundaries are for the patented invention. However, the claims made in patent applications are often ambiguous and infringement cases generally require the testimony of experts in the field to define what the technical words mean within the industry. Also reference can be made to what is called the prosecution history, i.e., the steps taken by the patentee to get the patent application approved. As discussed earlier, the first application submitted to the PTO often is rejected by the examiner because the claims made are too broad, requiring applicants to pare back the extent of their claims to get their applications accepted.

If, after a patent has been allowed, there is subsequent infringement litigation, and literal infringement does not apply because of an imperfect match between the claims ultimately made in the patent application and the characteristics of the defendant's product, patentees often make use of the *doctrine of equivalents*. A patentee pursuing this goal would claim that there are only trivial differences between the patented invention and the accused device (invention). If the court agrees that the differences are trivial, so that infringement has occurred, the scope of the patent-holder's patent is effectively broadened to include the (trivial) additions provided by the infringer's device (invention). On the other hand, if the court concludes that the differences are substantial (non-trivial) and, indeed, if the patentee would not have been awarded the patent if it had claimed what the accused device does, then the doctrine of *file wrapper estoppel* applies. If the patentee was willing to pare back its claims in order to get the patent, then he cannot stretch those claims back far enough to ensnare an accused device on those stretch claims. The Penwalt case on page 236 also illustrates application of file wrapper estoppel.

Doctrine of Reverse Equivalents

Defendants in infringement cases also can make use of the *doctrine of reverse equivalents* if the accused device is literally described in a prior patent application,

but the **use** of the accused device was not envisioned by the patentee. In order for the accused device to escape an infringement claim on this basis, the new use must be a significant and nonobvious improvement.

Pioneer Patents

Not all patents are equal. In spite of the nonobviousness requirement of Section 103, most patents are awarded for incremental improvements to the state of the art in a particular field. There are, however, some patents that open up wholly new fields of science and technology and whose effects are far-reaching. Pioneer patents are likely to be crude and subsequent inventions are quite likely to perform substantially similar tasks, in a substantially similar manner, to accomplish substantially similar results. Pioneer patentees lean heavily on the doctrine of equivalents in attempting to protect their patent turf. It is a judgment call for the courts to decide whether the doctrine applies.

DAMAGES

According to Section 284 of the Patent Act,

> "Upon finding for the claimant [the patentee] the court shall award the claimant damages adequate to compensate for the infringement, but in no event less than a reasonable royalty for the use made of the invention by the infringer, together with interest and costs as fixed by the court. When damages are not found by a jury, the court shall assess them. In either event, the court may increase the damages up to three times the amount found or assessed. The court may receive expert testimony as an aid to the determination of damages or of what royalty would be reasonable under the circumstances."

Section 284 calls for application of a "but for" criterion for determining damages. The question asked is, **"But for** the infringement, what would be the financial position of the patentee?" A number of cases have established, through precedent, the parameters of the "but for" damages test. Among the damages that case law indicates the patentee can recover are:

1. **Lost profits on lost sales.** This damage measure attempts to capture for the patent-holder any profits the patentee would have earned on sales it would have made but for the infringement. This category of damages requires the patentee to show that it would have made the sales that the

Penwalt Corporation v. Durand-Wayland, Inc.
U.S. Court of Appeals for the Federal Circuit
833 F.2d 931 (1987)

FACTS AND CASE BACKGROUND

Pennwalt sued Durand-Wayland for infringing claims 1, 2, 10 and 18 (claims-at-issue) of its U.S. Patent No. 4,106,628 (the '628 patent) on an invention of Aaron J. Warkentin and George A. Mills, entitled "Sorter for Fruit and the Like." Following a non-jury trial on the issues of patent infringement and validity, the district court, on March 22, 1984, issued an opinion concluding that (1) the claims-at-issue were not anticipated by the prior art, (2) the '628 patent had not run afoul of the "on sale" bar of 35 U.S.C. § 102(b) (1982), and (3) the accused devices did not infringe any of the claims-at-issue, either literally or under the doctrine of equivalents. Pennwalt appeals from the district court's holding of noninfringement, both literally and under the doctrine of equivalents, and its award of costs against Pennwalt. Durand-Wayland appeals from the district court's validity holdings and its denial of Durand-Wayland's request for recovery of its attorney fees.

OPINION: BISSELL, CIRCUIT JUDGE

This appeal and cross-appeal are from a judgment of the United States District Court for the Northern District of Georgia, 225 USPQ 558 (N.D.Ga.1984). The district court found that Durand-Wayland's accused devices do not infringe any claim, literally or under the doctrine of equivalents.

* * *

Our disposition of this appeal requires resolution of the single question of whether the district court's finding of no infringement was clearly erroneous.

* * *

The '628 patent claims a sorter. The principal object of the invention is to provide a rapid means for sorting items, such as fruit, by color, weight, or a combination of these two characteristics. The sorter recited in claims 1 and 2 conveys items along a track having an electronic-weighing device that produces an electrical signal proportional to the weight of the item, along with signal comparison means, clock means, position indicating means, and discharge means, each of which performs specified functions. The specification describes the details of a "hard-wired" network consisting of discrete electrical components which perform each step of the claims, e.g., by comparing the signals from the weighing device to reference signals and sending an appropriate signal at the proper time to discharge the item into the container corresponding to its weight. The combined sorter of claims 10 and 18 is a multi-functional apparatus whereby the item is conveyed across the weighing device and also carried past an optical scanner that produces an electrical signal proportional to the color of the item. The signals from the weighing device and color sensor are combined and an appropriate signal is sent at the proper time to discharge the item into the container corresponding to its color and weight.

Durand-Wayland manufactures and sells two different types of sorting machines. The first accused device, the "Microsizer," sorts by weight only and employs software labeled either Version 2 or Version 5. The second accused device employs software labeled Version 6 and sorts by both color and weight through the use of the "Microsizer" in conjunction with a color detection apparatus called a "Microsorter."

I. LITERAL INFRINGEMENT

Pennwalt asserts on appeal that all limitations set forth in claims 1 and 2 and some limitations set forth in claims 10 and 18 can be read literally on the accused devices. Pennwalt contends that the district court erred in interpreting the claims by going beyond the means-plus-function language of a claim limitation and comparing the structure in the accused devices with the structure disclosed in the specification. Such comparison allegedly resulted in the court's reading nonexistent structural limitations into the claims.

* * *

Thus, it was not legal error (as Pennwalt asserts) for the district court to have made a comparison between Durand-Wayland's structure and the structure disclosed in the specification for performing a particular function. The statute means exactly what it says: To determine whether a claim limitation is met literally, where expressed as a means for performing a stated function, the court must compare the accused structure with the disclosed structure, and must find equivalent structure as well as identity of claimed function for that structure.

* * *

We need not determine whether the district court correctly found no equivalency in structure because the district court also found that the accused devices, in any event, did not perform the same functions specified in the claims. For example, the accused devices had no position-indicating means for tracking locations of the item being sorted. The absence of that function negates the possibility of literal infringement.

* * *

II. INFRINGEMENT UNDER THE DOCTRINE OF EQUIVALENTS

Under the doctrine of equivalents, infringement may be found (but not necessarily) if an accused device performs substantially the same overall function or work, in substantially the same way, to obtain substantially the same overall result as the claimed invention. One must start with the claim, and though a "non-pioneer" invention may be entitled to some range of equivalents, a court may not, under the guise of applying the doctrine of equivalents, erase a plethora of meaningful structural and functional limitations of the claim on which the public is entitled to rely in avoiding infringement. . . . Though the doctrine of equivalents is designed to do equity, and to relieve an inventor from a semantic strait jacket when equity requires, it is not designed to permit wholesale redrafting of a claim to cover non-equivalent devices, i.e., to permit a claim expansion that would encompass more than an insubstantial change. (Citations omitted.)

. . . [I]n applying the doctrine of equivalents, each limitation must be viewed in the context of the entire claim. . . . "It is . . . well settled that each element of a claim is material and essential, and that in order for a court to find infringement, the plaintiff must show the presence of every element or its substantial equivalent in the accused device." To be a "substantial equivalent," the element substituted in the accused device for the element set forth in the claim must not be such as would substantially change the way in which the function of the claimed invention is performed.

Pennwalt argues that the "accused machines simply do in a computer what the patent illustrates doing with hard-wired circuitry," and asserts that "this alone is insufficient to escape infringement," citing *Decca Ltd.* v. *United States*. If Pennwalt was correct that the accused devices differ only in substituting a computer for hard-wired circuitry, it might have a stronger position for arguing that the accused devices infringe the claims. The claim limitations, however, require the performance of certain specified functions. Theoretically, a microprocessor could be programmed to perform those functions. However, the district court found that the microprocessor in the accused devices was not so programmed.

After a full trial, the district court made findings that certain functions of the claimed inventions were "missing" from the accused devices and those which were performed were "substantially different." The district court observed that "because the 'Microsizer' uses different elements and different operations (on the elements it does use) than the elements and operations disclosed in the patent-in-suit to achieve the desired results, infringement can only be found if the different elements and operations are the legal equivalents of those disclosed in the patent-in-suit." It is clear from this that the district court correctly relied on an element-by-element comparison to conclude that there was no infringement under the doctrine of equivalents, because the accused devices did not perform substantially the same functions as the Pennwalt invention.

* * *

Second, the district court correctly rejected Pennwalt's assertion that the memory component of the Durand-Wayland sorter which stores information as to weight and color of an item performed substantially the same functions as claimed for the position indicating means. The district court found that a memory function is not the same or substantially the same as the function of "continuously indicating" where an item is physically located in a sorter. On this point the record is indisputable that before the words "continuously indicating" were added as an additional limitation, the claim was unpatentable in view of prior art which, like the accused machines, stores the information with respect to sorting criteria in memories, but did not "continuously" track the location.

Thus, the facts here do not involve later-developed computer technology which should be deemed within the scope of the claims to avoid the pirating of an invention. On the contrary, the inventors could not obtain a patent with claims in which the functions were described more broadly. Having secured claims only by including very specific functional limitations, Pennwalt now seeks to avoid those very limitations under the doctrine of equivalents. This it cannot do. Simply put, the memory components of the Durand-Wayland sorter were not programmed to perform the same or an equivalent function of physically tracking the items to be sorted from the scanner to the scale or from the scale to its appropriate discharge point as required by the claims.

* * *

CONCLUSION

We affirm the judgment based on the finding of no infringement, the award of costs, and the denial of attorney fees to Durand-Wayland. There being no indication that Durand-Wayland's cross-appeal on validity extends beyond the litigated claims or the accused devices found to be noninfringing, we dismiss the cross-appeal as moot and vacate that part of the judgment concerning the validity of Pennwalt's patent.

QUESTIONS FOR REVIEW

1. Why did the CAFC conclude that there had been no "literal" infringement?

2. Why did the CAFC conclude that the doctrine of equivalents did not apply?

3. Even though not designated as such, the CAFC noted that the plaintiff's case ultimately fails because of file wrapper estoppel. Can you find the file wrapper estoppel alluded to by the CAFC?

infringer actually captured and to demonstrate what the profitability of those additional sales would have been.

2. **Price erosion.** A patent grants the patentee a monopoly, which enables the inventor to sell at a higher price than if there is competition. Patentees are entitled to recover, not only for lost profits on lost sales, but also for any reduction in price (hence profits) that occurs on sales that they (the patentees) do make or that the defendant made.

3. **Reasonable Royalties.** Patentees are entitled to recover reasonable royalties on sales made by the infringer that the patentee would not have made. In some cases, patentees cannot show that sales made by the defendant would have been made by the patentee, but for the infringement.

4. **Prejudgment Interest.** Continuing with the "but for" test, but for the infringements, the patentee would have had more money at an earlier date—i.e., at the time sales would have occurred instead of much later when a court award is received. These funds presumably could have been invested and earned a return over that time lapse. Generally, courts are conservative and assume that the money the patentee would have had earlier but for the infringement could have at least earned the interest paid on short term U.S. Treasury obligations—generally considered the safest, most conservative investments possible, or could have earned at statutory "legal" rates of interest.

Adjustments to Court Damages

Section 284 also allows judges to triple the computed "compensatory" damages found by the court or by a jury. Tripling of damages occurs when the conduct of the defendant is judged to be particularly egregious—e.g., in situations where defendants knew they were infringing and continued the illegal conduct. Section 285 of the Patent Act allows the court in "exceptional cases" to award attorney fees to the prevailing party. Exceptional cases are, again, those in which the defendant's conduct is egregious, such as when the defendant is knowingly infringing. It is common in cases in which the plaintiff (patentee) is awarded triple damages for attorney fees to be awarded to the plaintiff as well. Note, however, that Section 285 also contemplates awards of attorney fees to defendants when the plaintiff initiates a clearly nonmeritorious infringement case.

Requirement to Provide Notice and Statute of Limitations

Under Section 287 a patentee forfeits all damages from infringements if the patentee does not provide notice to an infringer, either by placing a sign on the product or on other selling materials, unless the patentee can prove that the infringer was notified of the infringement and continued to sell infringing products. Also under Section 286 there is a six-year statute of limitations on damage claims, which means that the patentee cannot recover damages for infringing sales that took place more than six years prior to the filing of the complaint or counterclaim for damages.

Common Law Defenses

The common law restrictions of laches and estoppel also apply to infringement damage claims. A patentee is guilty of laches if the patentee deliberately delays beginning a suit so that damages are higher. A plaintiff guilty of laches forfeits damages that occurred during the period when he or she was aware of infringement but chose to wait. A patentee guilty of estoppel can lose the right to sue for both past and future infringements. An estoppel can occur if the patentee leads the defendant to believe that its actions do not constitute an infringement but later sues the defendant for infringement. The **estoppel** defense generally arises as a sequel to contract disputes between patentees and licensees. A licensee may complain to a patent-holder that its royalty charges are too high. In response, the patentee may indicate that it is willing to consider a renegotiation of royalty contract, and that the licensee can temporarily waive royalty payments.

Note that in many biotech patent contracts, royalties are paid in two ways: an explicit royalty based on the sales of the licensee and an implicit royalty based on artificially inflated prices of supplies sold by the patentee to the licensee. Such contract agreements are frequently targets for renegotiation. Now, suppose that the renegotiations on royalty rates break down. In this case it is common for the patent-holder to demand full payment for the explicit (past) royalties that were waived while negotiations were under way. Under these circumstances, the defendant is likely to raise the estoppel defense, claiming he was led to believe that payment of royalties was not necessary.

Proof of Damages and the Cost of Litigation

Patent litigation is expensive. In many cases, attorney fees alone on each side can exceed $1 million, with these outlays supplemented by the fees of expensive "experts". In most cases *expert witnesses* are enlisted by patentees to show that they would have made the sales that the defendants did with the accused devices and to establish amounts of profits on projected sales. Defendants counter with their own experts to show that the plaintiffs were incapable of making the sales that the defendants enjoyed and that plaintiff's experts have overstated profitability. Business students know that there are a number of factors that influence sales besides the product itself, such factors including price, place, and promotions. Defendants can claim that they would have made the sales even without using the infringing products or processes. The following case is considered a landmark case because it discusses critical issues in damage computations involving patent infringement.

There also are alternative methodologies for calculating profit rates and, of course, there are significant differences in damage computations if the

---

Panduit Corporation v. *Stahlin Brothers Fibre Works, Inc.*
United States Court of Appeals, Sixth Circuit
575 F.2d 1152 (1977)

FACTS AND CASE BACKGROUND

In 1964 plaintiff Panduit Corp. (Panduit) sued defendant Stahlin Bros. Fibre Works, Inc. (Stahlin) for infringement of Panduit's Walch patent No. 3,024,301, covering duct for wiring of electrical control systems. In 1969 the district court found claim 5 valid and infringed by the "Lok-Slot" and "Web-Slot" ducts made and sold by Stahlin, enjoined Stahlin from further infringement, and ordered an accounting. That judgment was affirmed on appeal.

The duct manufactured by Panduit was invented by its president, Jack Caveney. Panduit began to make and sell the duct in 1955, and Caveney applied for a patent in 1956. In an interference proceeding in the Patent Office, it was determined that Walch, an employee of General Electric, was the first inventor of the duct. A patent issued to General Electric, as Walch's assignee, on March 6, 1962. Panduit then acquired the Walch patent from General Electric and established a firm policy of exercising its right to that patent property, i.e., of the right to exclude others from making and selling the patented duct.

Stahlin began to manufacture and sell the "Lok-Slot" and "Web-Slot" ducts in 1957, and continued to do so after issuance of the Walch patent and its sale to Panduit in 1962. On January 1, 1963, Stahlin introduced a price cut of approximately 30 per cent on its "Lok-Slot" and "Web-Slot" ducts.

Panduit seeks $808,003 as damages for lost profits on lost sales over the period March 6, 1962, the date of first infringement, to August 7, 1970, the effective date of the initial injunction; or, alternatively, a 35 percent reasonable royalty rate yielding $625,940. In addition, Panduit seeks $4,069,000 in profits lost on Panduit's own sales because of Stahlin's price cut.

OPINION: MARKEY, CHIEF JUDGE

The statute, 35 U.S.C. s 284, requires that the patent owner receive from the infringer "damages adequate to compensate for the infringement." In *Aro Mfg. Co.* v. *Convertible Top Replacement Co.*, the Supreme Court stated:

But the present statutory rule is that only "damages" may be recovered. These have been defined by this Court as "compensation for the pecuniary loss he (the patentee) has suffered from the infringement, without regard to the question whether the defendant has gained or lost by his unlawful acts." They have been said to constitute "the difference between his pecuniary condition after the infringement, and what his condition would have been if the infringement had not occurred." The question to be asked in determining damages is "how much had the Patent Holder and Licensee suffered by the infringement. And that question (is) primarily: had the Infringer not infringed, what would Patent Holder-Licensee have made?"

Panduit argues that the district court erred (1) in denying Panduit its lost profits due to lost sales, or, in the alternative, a 35 percent reasonable royalty; and (2) in denying Panduit its lost profits from its own actual sales due to Stahlin's price cut.

Lost Profits Due to Lost Sales

To obtain as damages the profits on sales he would have made absent the infringement, i.e., the sales made by the infringer, a patent owner must prove: (1) demand for the patented product, (2) absence of acceptable noninfringing substitutes, (3) his manufacturing and marketing capability to exploit the demand, and (4) the amount of the profit he would have made.

It is not disputed that Panduit established elements (1) and (3). Regarding (2), the master found that: "The evidence clearly shows the existence of acceptable noninfringing substitute ducts which would have permitted the defendant to retain its customers." That finding, as discussed below, was in error. However, Panduit is not entitled to its lost profits on lost sales in this case because of its failure to establish element (4).

The district court upheld as not clearly erroneous the master's finding that "there was insufficient evidence from which a fair determination could be made as to the amount of profit plaintiff would have made on such sales."

Panduit's Achilles heel on element (4) is a lack of evidence on its fixed costs. Panduit alleges that its omission is overcome by other evidence and by *General Electric Co.* v. *Sciaky Bros., Inc. Sciaky* is distinguishable and therefore not controlling on fixed costs. The accounting presented by *Sciaky's* expert witnesses included some overhead expenses, but omitted others which those witnesses testified were general and "paid by Sciaky during the years in question and would not have been greater if these additional machines had been produced and sold by Sciaky." General Electric (the infringer) disputed that theory, but offered no testimony to contradict it. The court held:

> Whether Sciaky's accounting method was accurate or not was

a matter to be decided on the basis of testimony in the hearing before the Master. This was the specific function of that hearing. We do not believe that this issue can properly be decided as a matter of law before this court on appeal.

On the issue of Panduit's lost profits on lost sales, we affirm the district court.

Stahlin's Price Cut

The district court upheld as not clearly erroneous the master's finding that: "Any loss in (Panduit's) profits due to the price reduction was more than compensated by the gain in profits due to the increase in plaintiff's sales volume because of the price reduction. Thus, the price reduction resulted in a net increase in profit to the plaintiff."

The right to damages caused by price reduction stands on the same ground as that to damages caused by lost sales. Having accepted the master's evaluation, that the testimony of Stahlin's accounting and economic experts was more credible and persuasive than that of Panduit's, we are bound, in the absence of clear evidence to the contrary, to accept as not clearly erroneous the master's finding that the price reduction in this case produced a net increase in Panduit's profits.

We affirm, therefore, the district court's refusal to award damages on the basis of Stahlin's price cut.

Reasonable Royalty

When actual damages, e.g., lost profits, cannot be proved, the patent owner is entitled to a reasonable royalty. A reasonable royalty is an amount "which a person, desiring to manufacture and sell a patented article, as a business proposition, would be willing to pay as a royalty and yet be able to make and sell the patented

article, in the market, at a reasonable profit."

The key element in setting a reasonable royalty after determination of validity and infringement is the necessity for return to the date when the infringement began. In the present case, that date is March 6, 1962. On that date, Panduit possessed the particular property right found to have been infringed by Stahlin. On that date, Panduit had a particular profit margin, and the property right to exclude others from making, using, or selling the patented product. At that point Stahlin chose to continue the making and selling of the patented product.

* * *

The setting of a reasonable royalty after infringement cannot be treated, as it was here, as the equivalent of ordinary royalty negotiations among truly "willing" patent owners and licensees. That view would constitute a pretense that the infringement never happened. It would also make an election to infringe a handy means for competitors to impose a "compulsory license" policy upon every patent owner.

Except for the limited risk that the patent owner, over years of litigation, might meet the heavy burden of proving the four elements required for recovery of lost profits, the infringer would have nothing to lose and everything to gain if he could count on paying only the normal, routine royalty noninfringers might have paid. As said by this court in another context, the infringer would be in a "heads-I-win, tails-you-lose" position.

In determining that a reasonable royalty rate here was 2 1/2 percent, the master found: (1) there were present in the market on the date of first infringement acceptable noninfringing substitutes and competing duct producers, (2) Panduit could not have maintained a high price differential in the face of competition from the substitute ducts, (3) on the hypothetical negotiation date, both Panduit and Stahlin would have been aware of the competitive state of the market, and of the probability of future price cuts, including Stahlin's, (4) the testimony of Stahlin's patent law expert, Scofield, was "more credible and persuasive and more in line with the factual realities of this case" than the testimony of Panduit's patent law expert, and (5) Stahlin's profit on gross sales of all its products for the relevant period was 4.04 percent, and there was "no evidence to indicate that the profit on its duct sales was significantly higher than the profit on its total sales generally." The district court held those findings not clearly erroneous. We disagree.

In adopting the master's report, the district court stated:

The Master based his finding that noninfringing substitutes were available principally upon the additional finding that defendant was markedly successful in switching its customers to noninfringing products when that became necessary. The latter finding is not clearly erroneous, and although defendant was not actually selling the principal noninfringing substitute . . . during the relevant time period, it is not erroneous to conclude that the substitute was available.

The district court also found the master correct in defining an acceptable noninfringing substitute as "a product which customers are willing to buy in place of the infringing product."

Proof of the absence of noninfringing substitutes:

(I)nvolves some of the same evidence as that which was introduced in support of the validity of the patent. The patent owner who had proved a long-felt need for a particular invention has a lighter burden in establishing that his customers, as well as the infringer's customers, were in fact seeking to obtain the patented solution to such need or problem. The other side of the coin involves a strong showing by the infringer that although the patent may have embodied some trifling improvement, which was patentable to a narrow extent, such improvement did not create any preference for the patented product rather than a noninfringing substitute . . .

The prior district and appellate court opinions leave no doubt that the patented product filled a waiting need and met with commercial success due to its merits. Stahlin's own intra-company memo (PX 58), and its $1,788,384 sales of infringing ducts during the period when allegedly acceptable noninfringing substitutes are now said to have been available, leave no doubt that the patented improvement created a substantial customer preference. A product lacking the advantages of that patented can hardly be termed a substitute "acceptable" to the customer who wants those advantages. The post-hoc circumstance that Stahlin, when finally forced to obey the court's injunction, was successful in "switching" customers to a noninfringing product, does not destroy the advantage-recognition attributable to the patent over the prior 15 years. Those preferred advantages were recognized by Stahlin itself, by other infringers, by customers, by the district court, and by this court. That Stahlin's customers, no longer able to buy the patented product from Stahlin, were willing to buy something else from Stahlin, does not establish that there was on the market during the period of infringement a product which customers in general were, in the master's words, "willing to buy in place of the infringing product." Moreover, Stahlin's "switching" occurred years after the date on which the determination of available substitutes must focus, i.e., the date of first infringement.

Hence, the 2 1/2 percent royalty rate recommended by the master and adopted by the district court is clearly erroneous on its face, the master's recommendation having been based in large part on erroneous finding (1), that there were "acceptable" noninfringing substitutes during the relevant period.

In *Georgia-Pacific, supra,* the appellate court affirmed the analysis made by the district court at 318 F.Supp. at 1127, 116 USPQ at 243–44:

CONCLUSION

Elements necessary to the determination of a reasonable royalty in the present case Panduit's actual profit margin in March 1962, and the customary profit allowed licensees in the electrical duct industry, were not determined by the master in his report and cannot be discerned from the record. They therefore must be determined on remand. On remand, the following factors must also be considered: (1) the lack of acceptable noninfringing substitutes, (2) Panduit's unvarying policy of not licensing the Walch patent, (3) the future business and attendant profit Panduit would expect to lose by licensing a competitor, and (4) that the infringed patent gave the entire marketable value to the infringed duct.

For the reasons stated, we reverse the district court's determination of a reasonable royalty, and remand the case for further proceedings consistent herewith.

QUESTIONS FOR REVIEW

1. Why did the court throw out Panduit's recovery for lost profits?

2. What was the basis for the court's determination that Panduit was not entitled to a recovery for the decreased price Panduit received or its sales when it was competing with Stahlin's infringing sales? Does it really make sense that Panduit benefited from price cuts required to meet the competition provided by Stahlin's infringing sales? After all, Panduit could have unilaterally reduced prices if it made them more profits, could they not?

3. What flawed assumption did the master and the district court make in determining that a reasonable royalty was 2 1/2 percent. On what basis did the court conclude that there were no noninfringing substitutes?

plaintiff is able to recover for lost profits on lost sales versus reasonable royalties. For many high-tech patents, particularly software-based patents, profit margins (the difference between the selling price and the cost of production) can be between 50 and 90 percent. Expert testimony from economists and accountants is employed to provide courts and juries with analyses of losses of sales and profits or reasonable royalties. Debates about costing methodologies between plaintiff's economists and/or accountants and those offered by defendant's can leave juries with glazed looks because the discussions are so esoteric.

Reasonable Royalties

In the event that the plaintiff is unable to show lost profits on lost sales, Section 284 explicitly contemplates "expert testimony as an aid to the determination of damages or what royalty would be reasonable under the circumstances." If the plaintiff cannot prove that it would have made the defendant's sales, then juries are asked to imagine a hypothetical negotiation that took place between the defendant and the plaintiff.[9] This is another version of an application of a "but for" test. If the defendant had not infringed, but instead had negotiated with the plaintiff for permission to sell the patented device, what royalty rate would have been charged? Of course, "reasonable" royalties depend on a number of factors, including what is charged in the industry, whether the license is exclusive, renewable, and a host of other factors subject to litigant testimony and, often, expert analysis and testimony.

Other Costs of Litigation

In addition to the out-of-pocket expenses of going to court, paying for attorneys, staff, and expert witnesses,

there are other costs of litigation that may be even more prohibitive. A major expense of litigation is lost executive time. Attorneys on opposing sides typically want to question all of the top corporate officers as well as technical staff. All of these individuals have to devote significant time to preparing for their testimony. During that time (which is accompanied by elevated stress levels for many), management and technical staff are not devoting their time to building better and cheaper widgets. Litigation can sometimes create a "war" mentality that permeates the company. Companies that previously seemed creative, relaxed, and free-wheeling can become hyperconscious of the evidentiary implications of writing and saving memos.

Proactive Management Decisions and Policies

Managers have little choice but to be proactive on litigation issues. Management must understand that if they sue or are sued, significant business disruptions are likely to occur. Adequate executive time must be allocated to prosecute a patent infringement case in addition to doing the other things necessary to make profits for a company. Managers should also recognize, however, that attorneys work for the client, not the other way around. It is also beneficial to be mindful that litigation can inspire a "war" mentality, impeding reasonable settlement efforts. Attorneys are often more objective than clients about their chances of prevailing in court and are better at recognizing attractive settlement offers.

Prudent Document Retention, Storage, and Destruction Policies

Subpoenas requesting documents are highly intrusive and are time-consuming to comply with. E-mails are now targets of information discovery, and there are new questions in the realm of document preservation. At this point, a company that, down the road, is involved in litigation can't expect free reign to destroy

[9]In *Georgia-Pacific, supra,* the appellate court affirmed the analysis made by the district court at 318 F.Supp. at 1127, 116 USPQ at 243–44.

e-mail records, without having their motives for doing so called into question. In other words, questions may be raised as to whether the company is deliberately destroying evidence in anticipation of litigation, which could have serious consequences.

Business document retention and destruction policies are more important than most companies realize until they are in the midst of the "records" wars that commercial litigation brings. Attorneys for litigants in business conflicts can be expected to subpoena all records in a company's possession that have any connection to the issue(s) being litigated. Among a vast assemblage of saved and stored documents, most of which may not have been reviewed or used in any fashion for years, there certainly can be many that, properly interpreted or misinterpreted, give comfort to litigation foes to the detriment of the company producing the records.

In the recent Microsoft antitrust case, a number of embarrassing (to say the least) e-mails were read back to Microsoft witnesses that had the effect of impeaching their pro-Microsoft testimony. Similar impeachment techniques are applied on a regular basis in patent infringement cases. If a company is served with a subpoena for document production, the destruction of documents called for by the subpoena is a crime. Obviously, few managers or attorneys are willing to risk personal jail time for the benefit of a company they work for. It is also illegal to destroy company documents in anticipation of litigation.

It is not illegal or improper, however, for a firm to have a reasonable document storage and destruction policy that effectively keeps long lost memos from creating unpleasant surprises when discovered in the course of litigation. It is likely to be reasonable for a company to set a two, three, or five-year period for document retention, storage, and then destruction. A company memo by the CEO, the CFO, or the CIO (Chief Information Officer) discussing the costs borne by the company in storing documents can provide a reasonable rationale for document destruction. Particular attention should be paid to e-mails. It may not involve immediate out-of-pocket costs to store e-mails on hard drives, but it certainly requires the company to buy more computer equipment in time, if e-mails from the distant past are routinely retained and kept readily accessible. The main point is to provide a rationale for destruction of ancient e-mails if storage of e-mails is costly and may hold unpleasant surprises in the event of litigation.

Other Remedies

The Patent Act provides courts the power to **enjoin** allegedly infringing activities under certain conditions. Section 283 indicates that:

> The several courts having jurisdiction of cases under this title [35 USC §§ 1 et seq.] may grant injunctions in accordance with the principles of equity to prevent the violation of any right secured by patent, on such terms as the court deems reasonable.

An injunction is a court order to cease certain activity. If a firm defies an injunction and persists in the behavior prohibited by the court order, those defying the court order can be sent to jail. If it is clear that a defendant is infringing, then a patentee can go to court and get a temporary restraining order preventing further infringements as long as the patentee can show:

1. That the patentee is likely to prevail when the infringement trial takes place, and
2. That irreparable damages will occur if the defendant's conduct is not stopped.

If the court does not issue an injunction in a situation in which the patentee could not make the sales anyway, the outcome is akin to compulsory licensing. The infringer, if found guilty at trial, will owe the patentee only reasonable royalties, since the patentee cannot get lost profits on sales he would not have made but for the infringement.

Process Patent Act of 1988

Suppose you are the patentee of a process and you have good evidence that your process is being infringed from abroad. That is, you have proof that some company in a foreign country is using your U.S. patented process and is selling the goods produced with that process to retailers in the United States who subsequently sell to U.S. consumers. Suppose, also, that the country in which the company violating your U.S. process patent has erected barriers to a suit brought by you against that company. An immediately obvious question to you since you are a U.S. company is "What can be done to the U.S. retailers who buy, knowingly or unknowingly, from the foreign infringer?" In 1988 Congress addressed this question with passage of the Process Patent Act Amendments.

Section 287(b) of the Patent Act requires a U.S. importer to respond to a U.S. process patentee who suspects that goods produced using its patented process are being imported. Under Section 287(b)(1)(3)(A), the importer has responsibility to obtain written statements from foreign manufacturers that they are not using the patented process in production of the imported products. Section 287 places great weight on the good faith efforts of the importer to honestly try to determine if the goods imported were produced using an infringing process. The verification process required of the importer gets more detailed but provides, essentially, that if the importer complies with the verification procedure it cannot be liable for innocently importing goods into the United States that were manufactured outside the U.S. using an infringing process. If the importer does not act in good faith as defined by Section 287, it is not an innocent importer and is subject to infringement remedies.

Concluding Thoughts about Patents

The previous discussion about patents deals with many important patent issues, but many more were not discussed. Proper management of IP is vital to the health and survival of many companies and all companies should be aware of the parameters of patent law. For the companies involved in innovation and patenting, partnership with competent legal counsel is imperative. Proactive management practices can avoid legal pitfalls that can undermine a company's ability to control its IP. Management and technical staff should know the mistakes made by other firms that have led to invalidity of patents during applications and during litigation. Firms that are not involved in creation of patents can become defendants in patent infringement suits and thus also have a need for acquaintance with patent law. Virtually all firms will become licensees of some patented invention, and the importance and prevalence of patents are likely to increase in the future.

TRADE SECRETS

Overview

As stated above, according to the Uniform Trade Secret Act (UTSA), a trade secret is information that has value because it is kept secret and is subject to reasonable efforts to keep it secret. Other definitions of trade secrets incorporate the following three elements: (1) it is used in business, (2) it gives the

holder a competitive advantage, and (3) it is kept secret. Again, as with patents, once a trade secret becomes part of the public domain, it cannot be taken back into trade secret status. In contrast to patent law standards in an infringement claim, *independent creation* **is** a defense in a *trade secret misappropriation* case. Since 40 states have now ratified the UTSA, that act is a useful guide to trade secret issues.

The Historical Role of Trade Secrets

During the Middle Ages, patent law did not exist in its present form, so there was a much greater reliance on trade secrets to protect inventors. So important were trade secrets that middle class business owners literally went to war at times trying to protect trade secrets. Among the trade secret items that inspired violence were buttons on shirts and seed corn with high productivity. Common law protection for trade secrets was based on differentiating between fair and unfair methods of obtaining such trade secrets. Reverse engineering was considered "fair" while hiring ex-employees to reveal the trade secrets of their former employer(s) was not.

Trade Secret Protection versus Patent Applications

The additional costs of patenting a product, process, etc., can be sizeable while the costs of relying on trade secrets are likely to be already incurred as normal security expenses. Moreover, when a patent is awarded, the application becomes part of the public record, which may reveal more about the company (as well as about the invention) than the applicant desires. There are companies throughout the world that have little respect for IP ownership. These companies seem to view publicly available patent applications as invitations to copy. Patent litigation is an expensive and stressful way of enforcing IP rights. Small firms may not have the resources to finance patent litigation and can be forced to "settle" with large firms that infringe on terms that amount to an involuntary license (remember, the minimum recovery in patent claims is a "reasonable royalty"). For these and other reasons, many firms choose to rely entirely on trade secrets for IP protection, while many other firms rely on trade secrets to protect innovations and inventions until they apply for a patent or a copyright.

Misappropriation of Trade Secrets

Misappropriation of trade secrets is a tort and is prohibited by UTSA. Section 1(2) of UTSA defines misappropriation in the following manner:

(2) "Misappropriation" means:
    (i) acquisition of a trade secret of another by a person who knows or has reason to know that the trade secret was acquired by improper means; or
    (ii) disclosure or use of a trade secret of another without express or implied consent by a person who
        (A) used improper means to acquire knowledge of the trade secret; or
        (B) at the time of disclosure or use knew or had reason to know that his knowledge of the trade secret was
            (I) derived from or through a person who has utilized improper means to acquire it;
            (II) acquired under circumstances giving rise to a duty to maintain its secrecy or limit its use; or
            (III) derived from or through a person who owed a duty to the person seeking relief to maintain its secrecy or limit its use; or
        (C) before a material change of his position, knew or had reason to know that it was a trade secret and that knowledge of it had been acquired by accident or mistake.

Basically, what UTSA prohibits are two actions:

1. Disclosure or use of a trade secret by someone who is not legally authorized to disclose or use the trade secret, or
2. Receipt and use of a trade secret by one who knows or has reason to know that the trade secret was acquired from a source who did what is prohibited in (1).

In plain English, most defendants in misappropriation of trade secret cases are:

A. employees or ex-employees who set up their own firms and compete with their former employer using trade secrets acquired from their former employer, or

B. other employers who obtain the trade secrets from employees or ex-employees of the original employer/possessor of the trade secret(s) or use some other surreptitious means of obtaining another firm's trade secrets.

In addition, consulting firms, law and accounting firms, and their employees have been defendants in trade secret cases. These parties acquire trade secrets in connection with their contracts and work with client firms. Interestingly, these parties are almost always contractually bound by a Nondisclosure Agreement (NDA).

Improper Means of Conducting Business

The UTSA defines "improper means" as "theft, bribery, misrepresentation, breach or inducement of a breach of duty to maintain secrecy, or espionage through electronic or other means." Many of these terms are self-evident. Company A sends an employee to apply (pose) as a secretary for Company B. Company A's employee is trained in espionage and secretly copies plans for a new product that Company B hopes to patent and then market. This is a misappropriation of a trade secret. Many firms have used ingenious schemes to acquire trade secrets from other firms, often even engaging in criminal actions such as trespass, wiretaps, and computer break-ins. Another source of trade secret theft has been visitors at factories, posing as tourists, who come equipped with hidden cameras. Prostitutes have been used to acquire trade secrets from technical employees, particularly in foreign countries.

Trade Secret Misappropriation: Company Policy or Breakdowns in Management

There are companies willing to engage in such nefarious actions simply because the stakes are so high. The advantages conferred by trade secrets may be worth millions or even billions in some situations. Independent creation is a defense in trade secret cases, but research and development is very expensive. It may be cheaper to steal trade secrets rather than go through the hard work of discovering them honestly through hard work. It is also important to recognize that companies are not always fully apprised of the activities of their managers who may be under intense pressure to develop new, innovative products. On-the-job actions of employees are attributable to the company, even if upper management is unaware of, and indeed would not approve of the actions of subordinate managers.

Mid-level managers are often promoted from the ranks of technical staff and often have connections with disgruntled employees from other (competing) companies. Such disgruntled employees may have valuable firm-specific information that they are happy to share. A court may later decide that what was shared was trade secret information. So, while it may be true that in some cases upper management is active in misappropriating trade secrets from other firms, in other cases it is the undetected actions of mid-level managers that generate liability. In still other cases, honest misunderstandings can generate liability, as could be the case when a new employee brings in skills that both the employee and the new company believe to be general skills, but which a court later views differently.

For many products, particularly software products, first mover advantages are so great for the first firm to market that the time taken for other firms to reverse engineer their products is sufficient to gain huge marketing advantages. In many cases first mover advantages enable the innovative firm to establish an industry standard, forcing the rest of industry to incorporate their product features. Unscrupulous firms in such industries are interested in acquiring trade secrets from rivals before the products stemming from those secrets come to market so that they can respond with competitive timing of product introductions or possibly beat their innovating competitor to the market.

Economic Espionage Act of 1996

Congressional awareness of the importance of trade secrets resulted in the passage in 1996 of the Economic Espionage Act. Section 1831 of the Act makes it a federal crime to misappropriate a trade secret "that will benefit any foreign government, foreign instrumentality, or foreign agent, . . ." Under the Act, misappropriation of a trade secret is defined similarly to the language used in the UTSA with a broader scope in terms of what is prohibited. If there is a foreign connection established in the theft (broadly defined) of a trade secret, defendants are subject to a fine of up to $5,000,000 and imprisonment of not more than 15 years. Organizations are subject to fines up to $10,000,000. Section 1832 prohibits the theft of trade secrets using exactly the same language as Section 1831 to define misappropriation. If there is no foreign

entity involved, then defendants stealing trade secrets are subject to 10 years of imprisonment and fines up to $5,000,000. These severe criminal sanctions reflect the seriousness with which lawmakers treat this issue. In addition to federal regulations, most states have their own criminal statutes prohibiting the theft of trade secrets.

Applicable Labor Law

At common law, employees have **fiduciary** duties to their employer. These duties include the duty to be loyal and to put the interests of the employer above those of their own while on the job. Employees are required by the common law to avoid conflicts of interest and must disclose relevant information acquired on the job. At common law, fiduciary duties to employers continue after the employment relationship has terminated, no matter what the reason for termination. Employees are liable to their former employers for revealing trade secrets even after the employment ceases.

On the other hand, general skills developed by employees while working for one employer can be used in subsequent jobs. The courts do not favor employment practices and policies that prevent ex-employees from being able to use their skills, even if the development of these skills was paid for by the former employer. Firm-specific information can generally be protected by trade secret law, but general skills that are known in the industry cannot.

Employment Contracts

Employers in many industries, and particularly in high-tech industries, are often unwilling to rely on common law protection for trade secrets based on fiduciary duty. Such employers generally make use of refined employment contracts that inform employees of actions that the employer considers a breach of contract. Employment contracts will specifically inform employees that their job exposes them to trade secrets and binds them to a nondisclosure agreement (NDA). Employment contracts are often coupled with exit interviews in which the departing employee is reminded of the NDA and what the employer considers to be trade secrets.

Common Law Shop Rights Doctrine

At common law employers can make use of the *shop rights* doctrine which gives employers royalty-free, nonexclusive rights to use any patent or copyright developed on the job by an employee. Employers have been unwilling to accept this common law division of rights. Most typically, employers have used employment contracts to supplement the allocation rights provided under common law. Employment contracts typically require employees to *assign* all IP developed while working for the employer to the employer. Assignment clauses not only give employers title to all patents and copyrights developed on the job, but also to any discoveries that may lead to patents, copyrights, and/or trade secrets. In addition, employers further augment assignment clauses by requiring employees to *notify* the employer of any prospects for patents or copyrights or of any other IP discovered while working for the employer. Under patent law, if an employee is hired to invent things, then the employing company is entitled to file for a patent under the *company's* name.

Limits of Assignment Clauses in Employment Contracts

As with any principle of law, it is possible for employers to go too far in their efforts to claim control of IP created by their employees. Employers do have a legitimate right to any IP developed by employees on the job so long as it relates to their business. That right persists after employment terminates. If an employee makes an employment-related discovery while working for an employer, then quits, and later uses that discovery to apply for a patent, the ex-employer is entitled to that discovery and the resulting patent. However, employers have sought to lay claim to all IP developed by employees during employment, even if the IP was developed away from the job site and had nothing to do with the business of the employer. There have been cases of employers trying to lay claim to the royalties from children's books, written after regular business hours, using the employee's home computer. Several states, including California and North Carolina, as examples, have enacted legislation protecting high-tech workers from overreaching assignment clauses in employment contracts. These state statutes prohibit enforcement of assignment clauses (in employment contracts) that allocate to the employer the right to IP that is unrelated to the employer's business and is not developed using company facilities.[10]

[10]H. Clarke Anawalt, *Ideas in the Workplace,* Durham, N.C.: Carolina Academic Press (1988) at 45.

Covenant-Not-to-Compete Clauses

In addition to requiring notification of all IP employees develop while working for the employer and assignment of all IP developed using company facilities that relates to company business, employers also make use of *covenant-not-to-compete (noncompete) clauses.* These clauses in employment agreements prohibit employees from working for rivals for a period of time. A typical covenant-not-to-compete clause would prohibit an employee from working for another firm in the same industry as that of the current employer for a two-year period. Such clauses are often also geographically limited, and so might prohibit employment with competing businesses anywhere in a surrounding three-state area. Courts do not particularly like noncompete clauses and will refuse to enforce them if they are not reasonable. So, to be enforceable, covenant-not-to-compete clauses must be reasonably limited in time and space. A five-year covenant not to compete is apt to be deemed unreasonable. With the Internet, the geographic area where a company competes is becoming irrelevant. Yet, covenants not to compete have historically had to be limited to the area where the employer actually competes to be enforceable. The following case on page 248 illustrates difficulties with enforcing covenants not to compete.

Covenant-not-to-compete clauses are also used in connection with mergers and acquisitions. A company that is buying another company does not want to risk the threat that the owner of the acquired company will start a new company and compete with his former company.

REMEDIES

Sanctions against Former Employees

In most trade secret misappropriation cases both an ex-employee and a new employer are defendants. In virtually all cases, the assets of the ex-employee are inadequate to justify a suit for damages associated with trade secret misappropriation. Although there may be two defendants, the ex-employee and new employer, the focus of the case from the perspective of the plaintiff (the holder of the trade secret that is claiming misappropriation) is on showing that the new employer knew or should have known that it was receiving a misappropriated trade secret so that a damage award can be obtained from the employing company. Most certainly, if it can be shown that the new employer explicitly paid the ex-employee for the trade

APAC Teleservices, Inc., an Illinois Corporation, Plaintiff, v. *Shawn M. McRae and Access Direct Telemarketing, Inc., an Iowa Corporation, Defendants*
United States District Court for the Northern District of Iowa, Cedar Rapids Division
985 F. Supp. 852; 1997

FACTS AND CASE BACKGROUND

APAC Teleservices, Inc. (APAC) and Access Direct Telemarketing, Inc. (Access Direct) are competitors in the outsource telemarketing industry. In addition to outsource telemarketing, APAC also provides inbound telemarketing services. Access Direct does not currently have an inbound telemarketing operation, but it plans to have one soon. According to Access Direct's Chief Executive Officer, Thomas Cardella, Access Direct had been searching for someone to head up its Inbound department for some time before it hired Shawn McRae as Vice-President in charge of Inbound Telemarketing operations. McRae was working for APAC before he left to take this position with Access Direct.

A simple way of explaining "outsource telemarketing" is that it means that one company makes telephone calls on behalf of another company to generate business. For instance, handling telesales for certain long-distance providers is an example of outsource telemarketing. On the flip side, "inbound telemarketing" means that a company receives incoming calls from customers on behalf of another company. An example of inbound telemarketing is receiving and handling customer services inquiries for another company.

Shawn McRae began working as a technology consultant for APAC in late August or September of 1996. By October, he had moved to APAC's office in Cedar Rapids, Iowa, where he worked in the Information Technology (IT) department as a consultant for a specific project called the "G-Prime Advanced Technology Platform Project for AT&T." In January of 1997 he began working

as a full-time APAC employee, continuing his work in the IT department as one of the head "architects" for the ATP Project for AT&T, and on another project using Computer Telephony Integration (CTI). When he became a full-time employee he signed a nondisclosure agreement, and four months later, in April of 1997, he signed a restrictive covenant which contained a non-competition agreement. In the beginning of September 1997, McRae left APAC to work for Access Direct.

OPINION: MICHAEL J. MELLOY

Most of McRae's work at APAC had focused on these two information technology projects, the ATP and CTI, before he left to work for Access Direct.

As Vice-President of Inbound at Access Direct, McRae asserts that his job is radically different than what he was doing at APAC. At APAC he worked in the information technology department and was primarily focused on outbound telemarketing; at Access Direct, he works in an operations capacity focused exclusively on inbound telemarketing. At APAC he helped to select and adapt off-the-shelf products to meet the joint needs of APAC and APAC's clients; at Access Direct he works with clients to decide what kinds of information the clients need to know and how Access Direct can best forecast their clients' needs and provide information back to them. Instead of testing off-the-shelf products and tailoring those products to meet specific client's needs, now all McRae has to do is to tell the IT department what the Inbound department needs to be able to do, and the IT department has sole responsibility to de-

sign the solution. In addition, in his new job McRae will determine demographic locations, attendance policies, scheduling, financial budgets, and profit margins. He will also work with other departments, such as IT and human resources, to decide how the Inbound department is going to train its staff, and he will hire and fire employees.

* * *

1. PROBABILITY THAT APAC WILL SUCCEED ON THE MERITS

In deciding whether to grant a preliminary injunction, the Court's initial estimation of the strength of the plaintiff's case plays a role, but it is not determinative. The probability of success does not require that the party seeking relief prove a greater than fifty percent likelihood that it will succeed on the merits. *Dataphase Sys. Inc.,* 640 F.2d at 113. Instead of a rigid measuring stick, the Court flexibly weighs the particular circumstances of the case to determine "whether the balance of equities so favors the movant that justice requires the court to intervene to preserve the status quo until the merits are determined." *Calvin Klein,* 815 F.2d at 503, quoting *Dataphase,* 640 F.2d at 113.

* * *

Before this Court even begins to analyze these criteria, however, this Court must examine whether APAC has made the necessary showing to prove that McRae's new position at Access Direct calls his covenant not to compete into question: that is, whether McRae's new job is similar in capacity to his former job at APAC, or whether he is likely to disclose APAC's proprietary information or client information to

Access Direct. If APAC fails to prove that either of these two situations exist, it is unnecessary for this Court to examine whether APAC has otherwise proven each of the next four criteria.

* * *

Even if McRae's job at Access Direct is in a different capacity than what he was doing at his former job APAC could still prove that McRae violated the noncompetition agreement by showing that in his new job, it is likely that he will disclose APAC's proprietary or client information. See Restrictive Covenant Agreement, Pl.'s Ex. 5, Dep. Ex. 8, P 4 ("Employee covenants that . . . [he] shall not . . . assist anyone in the conduct of a business competitive with that of Employer in which Employee is in . . . a capacity in which it is likely that Employee will disclose Employer's Proprietary Information or Client Information"). APAC argues that McRae's job will inevitably lead to such disclosure, while the defendants assert that it will not.

* * *

What appears most useful about McRae's experience with CTI on the inbound side is that he became familiar with various off-the-shelf products

that are currently available on the market. As will be discussed *infra,* McRae would violate both the non-competition covenant and the nondisclosure agreement if he used his technological knowledge to modify these off-the-shelf products to meet the needs of Access Direct's Inbound operation, but that is not what his job at Access Direct entails. In McRae's new job, he will simply tell the IT department at Access Direct what his department needs, and the IT department will have total responsibility to design the solution. While his knowledge of available off-the-shelf products may make him more articulate in expressing his needs to the IT department, ultimately the technological solution will be in someone else's hands.

* * *

The bottom line is that McRae left a technical position in information technology at APAC to assume an operations position for a competitor company. Although McRae lied to both APAC and Access Direct in order to negotiate a good job at Access Direct, APAC has not demonstrated a probability of success on the merits that either (1) McRae or Access Direct is lying about the job responsibilities that McRae's new

position at Access Direct entails, or that (2) McRae's new position will inevitably lead him to disclose proprietary or confidential information.

Accordingly, the court denied plaintiff's request for an injunction preventing McRae from working for defendant, Access Direct, but granted the injunction which prevented him from disclosing plaintiff's trade secrets to Access Direct.

QUESTIONS FOR ANALYSIS

1. The court alludes to the fact that the defendant employee (McRae) lied while working for the plaintiff. Is the court taking into account McRae's lack of honesty when it denies plaintiff's motion to enjoin him from working for his new employer, but does enjoin McRae from disclosing trade secrets?

2. What was the significance of the defendants' (both of them) showing that the McRae's new job was substantially dissimilar from his previous job? Since the job was substantially dissimilar, does that mean that McRae was not violating his covenant-not-to-compete clause in his contract with his former employer?

secrets, liability for misappropriation is established. Such proof is often difficult.

If the new employee is working for an employer and in so doing is breaching a covenant not to compete, liability for that violation is established against the former employee. With such an enforceable covenant not to compete, the job of monitoring for the possible dissemination of trade secrets by ex-employees is lessened as a non-compete suit can be initiated against the former employee immediately.

Injunctions

Since the assets of individual employees rarely provide a damage recovery expectancy that justifies a suit economically, the most effective remedy against

a former employee may be an injunction. For injunctive relief, the former employer would have to show the possibility of irreparable damage and the likelihood of winning an accompanying lawsuit. Both requirements are met when a former employee violates an enforceable covenant not to compete and the employer does not have to show actual misappropriation of a trade secret to bar its ex-employee from working for a competitor. If an ex-employee defies an injunction, he or she can face jail time. In addition, a new employer can be joined in the injunction to prevent appropriation of the trade secret and even to call for dismissal of the employee. Note again, however, that many covenants not to compete have been declared unreasonable and thus not enforceable.

Establishment of Liability

In trade secret suits, direct evidence of misappropriation of trade secrets is often impossible to obtain. Indirect proof often comes in the form of a history, first showing that the defendant had made a number of attempts to solve "the problem" but was unsuccessful, then showing that the alleged misappropriator made significant progress shortly after hiring the ex-employee who had access to the trade secrets. Product comparisons also provide (more direct) evidence on the likely misappropriation of trade secrets. Consider the case of a software firm that contends that another firm is selling a competing software package based on misappropriated trade secret code. Expert analysis in this situation is likely to compare the alternative software packages' code on a line-by-line basis. Finding code that is identical, even down to errors in lines of code, provides strong evidence in support of a misappropriation claim.

Damages and Remedies for Misappropriation of Trade Secrets

According to UTSA, plaintiffs in misappropriation of trade secret suits are entitled to recover both "actual loss caused by misappropriation **and** the unjust enrichment caused by misappropriation that is not taken into account in computing actual loss. In lieu of damages measured by other methods, damages caused by misappropriation may be measured by imposition of liability for a reasonable royalty for a misappropriator's unauthorized disclosure or use of a trade secret." Similarities with damages allowed in patent infringement cases are apparent. Plaintiffs are entitled to recover lost profits if they can show that they would have made sales made by the defendant but for the misappropriation. Plaintiffs are entitled to recover profits of the defendant as long as they can show that those profits are due to the trade secret misappropriation. When all else fails, plaintiffs are entitled to a reasonable royalty for the use of their trade secret that was disclosed or used by the defendant.

A significant problem for proof of damages in trade secret cases is the defense that defendant's profits and sales were not due to the misappropriation of the trade secret. Proving that the defendant made sales because of the trade secret that was wrongfully acquired instead of for other reasons often is a difficult task. Injunctions can be beneficially used in some cases where there is a showing that the trade secret was misappropriated but not disseminated. The defendant can be prohibited from using or disclosing the trade secret, even though proof of monetary damages may be lacking.

Security and Trade Secrets

As has been demonstrated by many sports teams, the best offense may be a good defense. Once a trade secret suit begins, it is difficult to keep the secret under wraps. If a plaintiff claims that the defendant made profits and sales as a result of trade secrets, the jury must have some basis for evaluating that claim. In other words, the jury must be shown proof that the trade secret was indeed valuable and was the cause of the defendant's profits and sales. The UTSA calls for courts to use reasonable means to preserve trade secrets including "granting protective orders in connection with discovery proceedings, holding in-camera (available only to those present in the courtroom) hearings, sealing records of the action, and ordering any persons involved in the litigation not to disclose an alleged trade secret without court approval." In spite of the safeguards provided by the UTSA, many trade secrets no longer are secret after litigation.

As the stakes associated with retention and pilferage of trade secrets have increased, security measures taken by firms to protect trade secrets have similarly escalated. Quite obviously the sophistication of industrial espionage has continued to advance. In 1986 Congress addressed the need for greater protection of proprietary informations with passage of the Computer Fraud and Abuse Act, which makes it a federal crime to break into governmental or financial computer systems.[11] Organizational security has become a major issue not only for private companies but also for governmental and educational institutions. Indeed, an entire industry has sprung up around security and much of the recent growth has been of the high-tech variety.

Security Measures That Firms Have Taken

As we know, trade secrets are protected in law so long as firms take *reasonable security measures* to protect them. The essence of a trade secret misappropriation suit is that the victim firm has taken reasonable means to protect its trade secrets and yet, in spite of those means, another firm has wrongfully uncovered these trade secrets. The tort, then, begs the question, what are reasonable security measures? Clearly if a firm discovers trade secrets of another firm by observing, without the aid of

---

[11]U.S. Code Title 18, 1030.

telescopic lenses and while not trespassing, the courts will not aid the firm with the trade secret because reasonable security measures were not in place. As in other contexts, the term "reasonable" is determined with reference to what is common within the industry, while also taking into account individual circumstances.

Among the measures that firms have taken to try to protect their trade secrets are:

- **Employment contracts with notification, NDAs, assignment, and covenant-not-to-compete clauses.** Also individual counseling with employees may prevent misunderstandings. Explanations of IP, trade secrets, and ownership of same are particularly appropriate at exit interviews.
- **Security experts should be part of the management team.** If security is treated as a "separate" concern, a nuisance to be tolerated, then the chances of security problems escalate. To increase the effectiveness of security systems, management has to "buy into" the systems proposed by security professionals and adhere to the policies of that system.
- **Physical access restrictions.** Computers that contain the company's crown jewels should not be accessible to all employees, but only a select few. Passwords should be changed frequently and consideration given to more sophisticated access devices such as fingerprint and retinal scanners.
- **Don't make it easy for trade secret thieves.** Use document shredders, make sure there are varied locations for trade secrets, check out the credentials of service technicians, especially alleged computer technicians, limit plant tours, and don't allow cameras.

The increasing sophistication of misappropriators makes it imperative that firms, especially firms that rely heavily on computer systems, get professional security assistance. It is also important to recognize that the greatest threats to a company's security are from its own employees. In addition to misappropriation of trade secrets, disgruntled employees have been known to engage in sabotage, particularly of computer systems. Again, many of these issues are human resource management issues that are best resolved with preventive measures. The following case illustrates that, increasingly, the courts are scrutinizing adequacy of the security measures firms are taking in the event of a misappropriation claim.

Carboline Co. v. *Mark Lebeck and PPG Industries, Inc.*
U.S. District Court for the Eastern District of Missouri
990 F.Supp. 762 1997 WL 817353 (E.D. Mo. 1997)

FACTS AND CASE BACKGROUND

Plaintiff Carboline Company manufactures high performance protective coatings. Defendant Mark Lebeck began his employment with Carboline in 1990 as a General Manager of Sales in the power industry division. On May 1, 1990, Lebeck signed an employment agreement requiring him not to disclose confidential information during and after his employment. The Agreement also contained a noncompete provision under which he agreed not to, "either directly or indirectly, go into any business in competition with Employer within the United States for a period of at least two years" after his termination.

With the advent of industry deregulation and a reduction in the construction of new power plants, Carboline's power division sales declined. Carboline downsized the power division and, in the fall of 1996, transferred Lebeck from the power industry division to distribution, with responsibility for the southeast United States. His new position was essentially a sales role, with responsibility for both power industry customers as well as other customers in his territory.

On March 14, 1997, Carboline offered Lebeck a choice between accepting a sales position in Los Angeles, California, or leaving his employment with Carboline. The transfer position did not have a power industry focus, although, like all Carboline sales persons, Lebeck would call on those power customers in his sales territory. Lebeck testified that he initially considered the transfer, although he had earlier expressed reservations about accepting a position, which required relocating his family. In a letter written on April 17, 1997, Lebeck declined the transfer, accepted Carboline's offer of a severance package, and asked to be "totally released" from "any contractual obligations."

On September 19, 1997, Lebeck accepted an employment offer from

PPG for a sales manager position in its high performance coatings division. As a PPG employee, Lebeck has accompanied PPG dealers on calls to customers, many of whom also purchase from Carboline and whom Lebeck had worked with as a Carboline employee. In October, upon hearing of Lebeck's employment with PPG, Carboline notified PPG that it considered Lebeck to be in violation of his noncompete agreement.

Carboline now asks the Court to issue a preliminary injunction restricting Lebeck's employment to preclude him from disclosing or using confidential information, working with specified Carboline customers until April 30, 1999, and working for PPG's recent acquisition, Keeler & Long.

OPINION BY: CATHERINE D. PERRY, DISTRICT COURT JUDGE

In seeking to enjoin a former employee's current work, plaintiff must do more than assert that a skilled employee is taking his abilities to a competitor.

Plaintiff contends that Lebeck was entrusted with trade secrets, including pricing and demonstration strategies, research and development projects, the strengths and weaknesses of Carboline products, upgrade schedules, Carboline's competitive strategy with respect to PPG, customer lists and preferences, and specialized price margins and strategies. In addition, Carboline contends that the documents that Lebeck kept after his termination were all trade secrets. Those documents have all now been returned to Carboline, and Lebeck testified that he retained no copies.

While plaintiff may choose to pursue damages with respect to Lebeck's retention of documents in the first instance, that is a matter for trial, not for preliminary equitable relief.

Plaintiff contends that Lebeck possesses knowledge that he will inevitably disclose to its competitor. Defendants argue that any information that Lebeck possessed was of the sort that quickly becomes stale. For instance, plaintiff submits a power industry marketing plan that Lebeck created for fiscal year 1997, which ended May 30, 1997. Plaintiff has not presented evidence that Lebeck helped compose the 1998 plan. Furthermore, much of the information contained in that plan is readily available in trade publications. Similarly, other documents that Lebeck retained are not conclusively trade secrets: the proposal submitted to Northeast Utility was a group effort, with another firm taking the lead role. The proposal contains no information regarding specific Carboline products.

Plaintiff did not present convincing evidence that it took measures to maintain the secrecy of its documents. Litszinger testified that Carboline maintained strict security measures with respect to computer access. All employees signed the Employee's Agreement containing the confidentiality provision. However, plaintiff did not take more specific measures. For example, the Multi-Gard testing data included results from outside laboratories. Plaintiff did not indicate that it entered confidentiality agreements with these labs. The data sheets were sent to "qualified" customers, but

plaintiff did not indicate how it determined who was qualified nor did it present evidence that it kept track of which customers received the data. The data sheets do not contain a label limiting distribution. Salespeople had access to the data sheets, and plaintiff did not establish that it has in any way restricted their use of the information.

Plaintiff cites *La Calhene, Inc.* v. *Spolyar*, 938 F. Supp. 523 (W.D. Wisc. 1996) to support its assertion that its security measures were sufficient. In *La Calhene*, the Court issued a preliminary injunction against a former employee despite the fact that the employer did not have a formal program for identifying trade secrets. However, the employer there presented its other efforts in far greater detail than what was provided to this Court.

Based on the foregoing, the Court determines that this factor does not support issuing a preliminary injunction.

QUESTIONS FOR ANALYSIS

1. What security measures did the plaintiff take to protect its trade secrets vis à vis Lebeck? Why did the court regard these measures as inadequate?

2. This court was openly skeptical of trade secret value of the information possessed by Lebeck before he left his employment. How valuable is a 1997 marketing plan in 1998? What information that the plaintiff claimed as trade secrets did the court regard as part of the public record?

Presentation of Unsolicited Ideas to Third Parties

The most valuable ideas may sometimes originate from unlikely sources, particularly in high-tech markets. Many very significant ideas have originated from relatively new and independent sources without significant funding or support. At some point, however, there is usually a need by the idea person (inventor) for funding. In order to attract funds, idea people must meet people with money. The two groups, idea people and money people, are not mutually exclusive. Often-times money people are former idea people who have made a lot of money on their ideas and can recognize other good ideas. On the other hand, many money people (venture capitalists, angels, representatives of large firms looking for good ideas to exploit) have a lot of money because they can recognize good ideas.

The numbers associated with the commercialization of technology are brutal. Studies indicate that venture capitalists and others fund about 1 in 100 business plans presented to them.[12] On average, venture capitalists spend about six minutes deciding whether the idea, generally presented to them in the form of a business plan, merits further attention. For every 100 business plans that receive funding, only about 10 will make money. Nine of the 10 proposals that make money will only be moderately successful. Venture capitalists are really looking for that 1-in-100 business idea that takes off and returns triple digit profit rates.[13] Venture capitalists are not the only source of funds for enabling inventors to commercialize their ideas. Often inventors look to established firms known in the industry for innovation and for funding inventors.

Let us assume that both the idea person(s) and the established firm are ethical but also primarily interested in making money. The established firm is willing to pay something for the idea, but only if the idea is truly new, is something that the firm does not already know, or something that is not in the public domain.

Of course, the idea person is reluctant to disclose his or her idea because once that occurs, the idea person has lost his leverage.

Idea people would be well-advised to patent or copyright their idea, if at all possible, *before* they present anything to the established firm. The problem of transmitting ideas in the high-tech world is sufficiently common that a number of firms have developed their own contract forms, which the idea people have to sign before anyone from the established firm will give them an audience to present their ideas. The forms contain waivers that require inventors (idea people) to give up their right to sue the established firm. In some of these forms, inventors waive their right to get paid even if their ideas are used unless the ideas lead to the development of a patent. Idea firms (inventors) should hold out for NDAs that preclude the established firm from disclosing the inventor's idea to others if it isn't exploited. Finally, the inventor should insist on a reasonable royalty if their ideas lead to patents that are used by the established firm.

Many of the forms that companies use and which they require aspiring inventors to sign are so one-sided that inventors would be well-advised not to sign the forms. There are numerous instances of inventors being cheated by money people (established firms, venture capitalists, knowledgeable industry sources) and the converse is also true: many companies have been sued for innovating in an area that a purported inventor claims to have revealed to the firm. Since established firms are generally more aware of the pitfalls of idea transmission, they are the party that draws up the forms signed by the parties before the ideas are presented. Inventors would do well to consult an IP attorney before presenting their ideas to any party with money.

---

[12]L. Downes and Chunka Mui, *Unleasing the Killer App: Digital Strategies for Market Dominance,* Boston, Mass.: Harvard Business School Press Book (4/9/98).
[13]W. D. Bygrave and J. A. Timmons, *Venture Capital at the Crossroads,* Boston Mass.: Harvard Business School Press (1992).

SUMMARY

- Managers of high-tech firms must be equipped to manage IP as well as other assets of their companies.
- *Patents* are a reward to inventors that society is willing to pay in order to encourage innovation. In return for a monopoly for 20 years from filing, an inventor must be willing to reveal what he has invented.
- States protect IP using *trade secret laws,* which make misappropriation of trade secrets illegal.

The American Inventors Protection Act of 1999 provides protections for those who choose not to patent but instead protect their inventions through trade secret laws.
- The Patent and Trademark Office makes patent determinations. A patent application is initially submitted to a PTO patent examiner.
- Ultimately all decisions of the PTO are reviewable by the courts.

- Patents are issued to those whose inventions are *new, useful,* and *nonobvious.*
- Section 102(a) defines what is *new* in terms of what is in the public domain at the time of the invention. If the invention has already been described or patented anywhere in the world, it is not new. Also if the invention was known or used by someone in the United States, it is not new.
- Section 102(b) defines disqualifying acts that take place more than one year before an applicant applies for a patent with the PTO. If the patented item is described in a publication or patented anywhere in the world, used commercially, or sold in the U.S., then the applicant is not entitled to a patent.
- Section 102(g) awards priority to the *first to invent* rather than the *first to file* as long as the invention has not been abandoned, concealed, or suppressed. To maintain priority, applicants must be *reasonably diligent* after invention until the invention is reduced to practice.
- Section 103 denies a patent to anyone whose invention is *obvious to someone skilled in the industry.*
- In order to be patentable, the subject matter must be statutory: *a process, manufacture, machine, or composition of matter.* Ideas, mathematical formulae, and naturally occurring life forms are not patentable.
- Inventors who create new life forms are entitled to patents on those life forms.
- Patenting new life forms has generated heated debate. Among the areas of controversy are: what is a naturally occurring life form, who is entitled to plant and animal progeny, and should life-saving medicines be denied Third World countries because they are poor?
- The Human Genome Project envisioned patenting of human genes, but so far the PTO has resisted issuing patents for human genes unless a specific use is recited in the patent application.
- Patent applications must contain a detailed explanation sufficient to allow one skilled in the industry to reproduce the patented item or process.
- The claims made in the patent application form the basis for infringement suits.
- A *literal infringement* occurs when the claims made in the patent application describe the accused device of the defendant.
- The **Doctrine of Equivalents** applies when the accused device performs substantially the same function(s), in substantially the same way, to obtain substantially the same result provided by the patented device.
- If **File Wrapper Estoppel** applies, the patentee cannot recover for an alleged infringement. File Wrapper Estoppel applies when the patentee is claiming infringement over claims that were withdrawn by the patentee in order to obtain the patent.
- The basic rule governing patent damages is that the patentee should recover enough money to be placed in the same position that would have been enjoyed had the patent not been infringed.
- Patentees can recover for infringement based on lost profits on lost sales, lowered prices as a result of competition from the infringing device, and reasonable royalties on sales made by the defendant that the plaintiff would not have made.
- In order to show lost profits on lost sales, the plaintiff is required to show demand for its product, lack of acceptable noninfringing substitutes, capacity to fill demand, and the revenue and costs evidence that permit lost profits to be determined.
- In some cases plaintiffs are able to recover triple damages based on bad conduct by the defendant. Also in egregious cases the winning party is sometimes awarded court costs and attorney fees.
- Plaintiffs are required to provide notice that their products are patented either on the product or in selling materials.
- The Process Patent Act of 1988 is directed towards imports of products that were made with patented processes for which U.S. patentees do not authorize use. The Act requires importers to take steps to determine whether U.S. Patent law is being violated by the imports.
- A trade secret is information that gives a firm a competitive advantage because it is kept secret.
- Trade secrets protection is based on common law notions of acceptable and unacceptable methods of competing.
- *Misappropriation* of trade secrets occurs when a firm's trade secrets are obtained by the defendant using illegal methods of gaining information or because someone who has confidential information breaches their fiduciary duty to the plaintiff.
- Ex-employees are the main source of trade secret misappropriation.
- Firms have an obligation to use *reasonable methods* to preserve their trade secrets or else the courts will dismiss claims of trade secret misappropriation.

- The Economic Espionage Act of 1996 places severe penalties on anyone misappropriating trade secrets of a U.S. firm on behalf of a foreign entity.
- Preventing misappropriation of trade secrets requires proactive management steps including scrutinizing employment contracts, physical impediments to access to trade secrets, and most importantly, protocols and procedures that limit computer access to trade secrets.
- Employment contracts frequently contain *nondisclosure agreements* and *covenants not to compete.*

Court enforcement of covenants not to compete depends on their reasonableness. Covenants not to compete should be *reasonably limited* in time and space.
- Remedies against trade secret misappropriators include monetary damage claims and injunctions against former employees and competitors.
- Since damages in trade secret cases are difficult to establish, injunctions are often the best hope for effective remedies.

9

INTELLECTUAL PROPERTY II: BASIC COPYRIGHT AND TRADEMARK LAW

T he International Trade Commission estimates that American businesses may be losing as much as $50 million yearly as a consequence of their technology and intellectual property being misappropriated by foreign manufacturers. For individual businesses in the United States, this loss sum may be increased several times over due to misappropriation by other domestic firms. Copyrights and trademarks are legal mechanisms that are intended to provide specific protections for intellectual property and control over its use.

Unconvinced about the financial impact of copyright infringements? Consider the *MP3* case below reported by Yahoo![1]

MP3.com was one of the darlings of the startup 'dot coms' and had a very cavalier attitude towards copyright law. On the other hand, Universal Music Group had perhaps the largest stake in enforcement of copyright laws as they relate to Internet transactions. As we will see later, Napster.com is another Internet startup that basically bet the store on being able to avoid copyright laws. Initial judicial reaction to Napster suggests that their fate may follow that of MP3.com.

---

[1]*San Franciso Chronicle*, Sept. 19, 1996, at B4.

COPYRIGHT OVERVIEW

A copyright is given for "original works of authorship fixed in any tangible medium of expression, . . . from which the work can be perceived, reproduced, or otherwise communicated, either directly or with the aid of a machine or device."[2] The works for which copyrights are awarded include: literary works, including computer software, musical, dramatic, pictorial, graphic movies, sound recordings, and audiovisual performances that have been captured on film.[3] A copyright grants to the author *exclusive* rights to *reproduce* and *distribute* the copyrighted work as well as exclusive rights to prepare *derivative* works. A book about, say, President Clinton, would be an original work of authorship and the medium is the pages in the book.[4] Making a movie from a book is a derivative work.

In the United States *today* copyright law does not require any formalities or notice. In 1988 the U.S. joined most of the rest of the world and became a member of the Berne Convention. A condition of joining the Berne Convention was that the U.S. had to

---

[2]Section 102(a) of the Copyright Act.
[3]Section 102(a) of the Copyright Act.
[4]Section 106 of the Copyright Act.

MP3.com Loses Copyright Case

NEW YORK (AP)—A federal judge ruled Wednesday (Sept. 18, 1996) that the Internet music-sharing service MP3.com willfully violated the copyrights of record companies, and ordered it to pay Universal Music Group $25,000 per CD, or roughly $118 million. U.S. District Judge Jed S. Rakoff said it was necessary to send a message to the Internet community to deter copyright infringement. Rakoff said he could have awarded as much as $150,000 per CD but chose a considerably smaller amount, in part because MP3.com had acted more responsibly than other Internet startups. Universal Music Group, the world's largest record company, had urged a stiff penalty in the closely watched case. "Music is a media and the next infringement may be very different," said Universal lawyer Hadrian Katz. "It may be video or it may be film or it may be books or it may be something very different." Katz had urged the judge to award the record company up to $450 million because MP3.com had copied 5,000 to 10,000 of the company's CDs. The lawyer said such a penalty would cost MP3.com as much as $3.6 billion once the company was forced to pay all the other companies whose copyrights it had violated when it created an online catalog of 80,000 CDs.

Source: Reprinted with permission of The Associated Press.

Additional readings:

http://www.maccentral.com/news/0009/07.mp3.shtml
"MP3.com Loses Copyright Case", September 7, 2000; Brad Gibson, bgibson@maccentral.com.

http://washingtonpost.com/wp-dyn/articles/A23417-2000Sep6.html
"MP3.com Loses Copyright Case", September 6, 2000;David Segal, WashingtonPost Staff Writer.

http://singapore.cnet.com/news/2000/09/07/20000907k.html
"MP3.com Loses Copyright Case; Could Cost US$118m", September 7 2000; Jim Hu and Evan Hansen, CNET News.com.

abandon the requirement in U.S. copyright law that a copyright holder had to *register* the work with the U.S. Copyright Office in order to obtain a copyright. Furthermore the U.S. had to abandon the requirement of *notice* (a © placed next to the copyrighted work) in order for a copyright holder to be able to sue for copyright damages.

Duration of a Copyright

While the expression of an idea can be copyrighted, once the copyright expires that work becomes part of the public domain and cannot be copyrighted again. Currently (for works authored after 1978), a copyright lasts for the life of an author, plus 70 years (the Sonny Bono Act). For joint works, the copyright lasts for the life of the last surviving author, plus 70 years. A work for hire lasts for 95 years from date of publication or 120 years from creation, whichever expires first. A work for hire takes place when an employer hires someone to create copyrighted works, such as a screenplay for a movie, or to write an operating manual for a consumer appliance.

Registration of Copyrighted Work

As indicated above, to become a member of the Berne Convention, the United States was required to give up its tradition of **requiring** registration and notice for enforcement of copyrights. There are still advantages, however, to copyright registration and of providing notice to potential infringers. Under U.S. copyright law, damages attributable to infringement are greater if the copyrighted work has been registered and notice provided to possible infringers. However, even without registration and notice, a copyright holder (someone who creates an original work of authorship that can be fixed in a medium) can sue for copyright infringement. For the damages issue alone it often makes good business sense to register copyrighted material. Registration of copyrighted material is certainly inexpensive, $30 for most registrations, and relatively easy to accomplish, requiring that a copy of the copyrighted work be sent to the Copyright Office in Washington D.C. In law, registration of copyrighted material creates prima facie evidence of validity, even though the Copyright Office does not carefully scrutinize what is submitted to it for registration.

Registration of a copyright does require that the copyrighted material be part of the public record. If there are trade secrets revealed by the public display of the copyrighted material, then these disclosures are an additional, possibly prohibitive, nonmonetary cost of copyright registration that management should consider. For computer software, because disregard for U.S. copyrights is a serious problem and infringement enforcement in some Third World countries is spotty at best, the Copyright Office allows for registration of software code when only the first and last twenty-five pages of code are made available to the public.[5]

SCOPE OF COPYRIGHT PROTECTION

In defining the scope of protection provided by copyright law, it is fundamentally important to *distinguish the expression of an idea* from the *idea itself*. According to Section 102(b) of the Copyright Act, copyrights cannot be used to protect ideas, facts, procedures, processes, concepts, principles, methods of operation, or discoveries. As you may note, **some of what can be protected by patent law is prohibited from copyright protection.** Although patent law cannot be used to protect the discovery of an original idea, it can be used to protect a new and useful process. In general, copyright law cannot be used to protect the *functionality* associated with, say, software. Functionality can only be protected with patent law.

The scope of protection provided by copyright law becomes a particular issue when the subject matter of copyright protection is computer software. In copyright law, computer software is considered a "literary work." A number of cases that illustrate court reasoning have involved software that creates electronic spreadsheets. Over the years, numerous versions of spreadsheets have been copyrighted under trade names that include Visicalc, Lotus, Quattro Pro, and Excel. The formulas and mathematical computations in electronic spreadsheets are examples of the *functionality* of the software and are thus not copyrightable. However, as long as there is more than one way to accomplish an interface with a computer user by which spreadsheets are created and manipulated— i.e., through which the mathematical tasks, the structure, the sequence, and organization of the electronic spreadsheet are created and/or displayed—a particular assemblage of software is copyrightable.

DATABASE PROTECTION

Facts, whether or not they are in the public record, are not protectible under copyright law, but the arrangement of facts can be, as long as the arrangement exhibits some minimal level of creativity. The arrangement of baseball statistics for members of the Hall of Fame is most likely protectible under copyright law. If someone copied baseball statistics and the arrangement of those statistics from a book about baseball Hall of Famers, the copying would be an infringement if it were done without permission. If the only creativity exhibited in the work is an alphabetical arrangement of names (such as in a phone book), copyright law will not protect against the copying of names by rival phone book companies in the same order.[6] Similarly, if the only creativity exhibited in reproducing court cases from the public record is in the creation of a new set of page numbers, that level of creativity is not sufficient to qualify for copyright protection.[7]

In order to qualify for copyright protection, there must be a nontrivial level of creativity exhibited. Certainly many databases do involve sufficient creativity to qualify for copyright protection and receive registration from the Office of Copyright. Court cases are part of the public record and as such, they are not copyrightable. The arrangement of facts from the public record such as court opinions is potentially copyrightable, but there must be some minimal level of creativity or else the material is not copyrightable. The following case deals with the minimal level of creativity necessary to qualify for copyright protection from copying by a rival firm.

European Legal Protection for Databases

The European Union (EU) has historically provided a higher standard of protection for assembled databases than has been available in the United States. In 1995 the EU passed a Directive that imitates U.S. copyright law, which means that arrangements of facts (organization of the database) are protectible under copyright law, but the facts (the contents of a database) are not.[8] The EU Directive remains different from U.S. copyright protection of databases in two respects:

1. The "sweat-of-the-brow" approach rejected, by the Supreme Court in *Feist,* is present in EU law with prohibition on extraction of part or all of the contents of a database for *commercial purposes,* and

---

[5]The presumption is that a copier could not operate the software program by just having access to the first 25 and last 25 pages of code. United States Copyright Office, Copyright Registration of Computer Programs, Circular 61.

[6]*Feist Publications, Inc.* v. *Rural Telephone Service Co., Inc.,* 499 U.S. 340 (1991).
[7]*Bender & Company, Inc.* v. *West Publishing Corporation,* United States Court of Appeals for the Second Circuit, 158 F.3d 693 (1998).
[8]Directive 95/46/EC of the European Parliament of the Council of 24 October 1995 on the "Protection of Individuals with Regard to the Processing of Personal Data and the Free Movement of Such Data," art. 32.

Bender & Company, Inc. v. West Publishing Corporation
United States Court of Appeals for the Second Circuit
158 F.3d 693; 1998

FACTS AND CASE BACKGROUND

In this case the logical plaintiffs and defendants are reversed. The defendant is West Publishing Company, which owns copyrights on federal and state court opinions. The plaintiffs, Bender & Company, Inc., manufacturers and markets CD-ROM disks that cite West compilations of cases. The question at hand is whether the insertions of the citations, called star pagination, into Bender's CD-ROMs is a violation of West's copyright protection. In this case the plaintiffs are seeking a declaratory judgment that copying and otherwise making use of West's star pagination is not a copyright infringement. The United States District Court for the Southern District of New York granted summary judgment to the plaintiff. However, the defendants now appeal with the argument that the star pagination method used by Bender falls under their protected arrangement of cases.

OPINION: JACOBS, CIRCUIT JUDGE

Defendants–appellants West Publishing Co. and West Publishing Corp. (collectively "West") create and publish printed compilations of federal and state judicial opinions. Plaintiff–appellee Matthew Bender & Company, Inc., and intervenor–plaintiff–appellee HyperLaw, Inc. (collectively "plaintiffs"), manufacture and market compilations of judicial opinions stored on compact disc-read only memory ("CD-ROM") discs, in which opinions they embed (or intend to embed) citations that show the page location of the particular text in West's printed version of the opinions (so-called "star pagination"). Bender and HyperLaw seek judgment declaring

that star pagination will not infringe West's copyrights in its compilations of judicial opinions. West now appeals from a judgment of the United States District Court for the Southern District of New York (Martin, *J.*), granting summary judgment of noninfringement to Bender and partial summary judgment of noninfringement to HyperLaw.

West's primary contention on appeal is that star pagination to West's case reporters allows a user of plaintiffs' CD-ROM discs (by inputting a series of commands) to "perceive" West's copyright-protected arrangement of cases, and that plaintiffs' products (when star pagination is added) are unlawful copies of West's arrangement. We reject West's argument for two reasons:

A. Even if plaintiffs' CD-ROM discs (when equipped with star pagination) amounted to unlawful copies of West's arrangement of cases under the Copyright Act, (i) West has conceded that specification of the *initial* page of a West case reporter in plaintiffs' products ("parallel citation") is permissible under the fair use doctrine, (ii) West's arrangement may be perceived through parallel citation and thus the plaintiffs may lawfully create a copy of West's arrangement of cases, (iii) the incremental benefit of star pagination is that it allows the reader to perceive West's page breaks within each opinion, which are not protected by its copyright, and (iv) therefore star pagination does not *create* a "copy" of any

protected elements of West's compilations or infringe West's copyrights.

B. In any event, under a proper reading of the Copyright Act, the insertion of star pagination does not amount to infringement of West's arrangement of cases.

BACKGROUND

West creates "case reports" of judicial opinions by combining (i) certain independently authored features, such as syllabi (which summarize each opinion's general holdings), headnotes (which summarize the specific points of law recited in each opinion), and key numbers (which categorize the points of law into different legal topics and subtopics), with (ii) the text of the opinions, to which West adds parallel citations to other reporters, information about the lawyers, and other miscellaneous enhancements. West then publishes these case reports (first in paperbacked advance sheets, and then in hardbound volumes) in various series of "case reporters." These case reporters are collectively known as West's "National Reporter System," and include (as relevant to this case): the *Supreme Court Reporter*, which contains all Supreme Court opinions and memorandum decisions; the *Federal Reporter*, which contains all federal court of appeals opinions designated for publication, as well as tables documenting the disposition of cases that are unpublished; the *Federal Rules Decisions* and *Federal Supplement*, which contain selected federal district court opinions; and the *New York Supplement*, which contains selected New York State case reports. Cases appearing in West's case reporters are universally cited by the volume and page number of the case reporter series in which they appear. One citation guide recommends—and some courts require—citation to the West version of federal appellate and trial court decisions and New York State court decisions.

Bender markets a series of CD-ROM discs called *Authority from Matthew Bender*. One product in this series—the "New York product"—consists of three elements: (i) "New York Law and Practice" (one disc), which contains New York statutory and treatise materials; (ii) "New York Federal Cases" (three discs), which contains cases from the Second Circuit and New York's federal district courts from 1789 to the present; and (iii) "New York State Cases" (four discs), which contains New York State judicial opinions from 1912 to the present (the New York State Court of Appeals cases begin in 1884). These CD-ROM discs contain published opinions and unpublished opinions and orders from these courts.

Bender obtains the text of the judicial opinions through a license from LEXIS (an on-line database containing legal and non-legal data), and stores the opinions and orders on the discs arranged by court and date, which is also the order in which they would be seen by a user who for some reason browses through the discs without sorting the case reports in a search. For each case that appears in West's case reporters, Bender intends to insert (and in some cases already has inserted) a parallel citation to the West case reporter at the beginning of the opinion and a citation to the successive West page numbers at the points in the opinion where page breaks occur in the West volume.

* * *

Bender's complaint sought a judgment declaring that star pagination to West's case reporters will not copy West's arrangement or infringe West's copyright. HyperLaw intervened seeking the same relief. All parties then moved for summary judgment. The district court granted summary judgment to plaintiffs on the star pagination issue, concluding that the insertion of star pagination to West's volumes on the CD-ROM version of the cases would not reproduce any protectable element of West's compilation. The court noted that "the protection extends only to those aspects of the compilation that embody the original creation of the compiler" and that "where and on what particular pages the text of a court opinion appears does not embody any original creation of the compiler, and therefore . . . is not entitled to protection." The court further ruled that star pagination would be permitted under the fair use doctrine even if West's pagination were copyrightable.

DISCUSSION

West's case reporters are compilations of judicial opinions. The Copyright Act defines a "compilation" as "a work formed by the collection and assembling of preexisting materials or of data that are selected, coordinated, or arranged in such a way that the resulting work as a whole constitutes an original work of authorship." Compilations are copyrightable, but the copyright "extends only to the material contributed by the author of such work, as distinguished from the preexisting material employed in the work." Works of the federal government are not subject to copyright protection, although they may be included in a compilation.

* * *

Under *Feist* [a Supreme Court Decision], two elements must be proven to establish infringement: "(1) ownership of a valid copyright, and (2) copying of constituent elements of the work that are original." Bender and HyperLaw concede that West has proven the first element of infringement, *i.e.*, that West owns a valid copyright in each of its case reporters.

However, as is clear from the second *Feist* element, copyright protection in compilations "may extend only to those components of a work that are original to the author." The "originality" requirement encompasses requirements both "that the work was independently created . . . *and* that it possesses at least some minimal degree of creativity. At issue here are references to West's volume and page numbers distributed through the text of plaintiffs' versions of judicial opinions. West concedes that the pagination of its volumes—*i.e.*, the insertion of page breaks and the assignment of page numbers—is determined by an automatic computer program, and West does not seriously claim that there is anything original or creative in that process. As Judge Martin noted, "where and on what particular pages the text of a court opinion appears does not embody any original creation of the compiler." Because the internal pagination of West's case reporters does not entail even a modicum of creativity, the volume and page numbers are not original components of West's compilations and are not themselves protected by West's compilation copyright. "As a constitutional matter, copyright protects only those constituent elements of a work that possess more than a *de minimis* quantum of creativity."

* * *

The Eighth Circuit in *West Publishing Co.* adduces no authority for protecting pagination as a "reflection" of arrangement, and does not explain how the insertion of star pagination creates a "copy" featuring an arrangement of cases substantially similar to West's—rather than a dissimilar arrangement that simply references the location of text in West's case reporters and incidentally simplifies the task of someone who wants to reproduce West's arrangement of cases. It is true that star pagination enables users to locate (as closely as is useful) a piece of text within the West volume. But this location does not result in any proximate way from West's original arrangement of cases (or any other exercise of original creation) and may be lawfully copied.

Disposition: Affirmed.

QUESTIONS FOR ANALYSIS

1. Briefly explain star pagination. Can a computer arrangement of page numbers constitute creativity sufficient to qualify for a copyright?
2. Does this case stand for the proposition that if a machine creates the copyrightable portion of a copyrighted work, it cannot qualify as a copyright? Don't computer graphic artists make extensive use of computers in creating their work, which is copyrightable?
3. What did the court say was clearly not copyrightable about West Publishing's service? Are facts in the public domain ever copyrightable?

2. Copyright protection of databases lasts for 15 years from the date the database is made available to the public.

Presumably, under the EU Directive, even if a database fails to exhibit a minimal level of creativity, it still is legally protected. So, in spite of the Berne Convention, international fragmentation of copyright law continues to a significant degree. A uniform standard for copyright protection and duration remains elusive with the EU allowing collections of facts that do not pass the minimal creativity test to still be legally protected under EU regulations for 15 years. In Chapter 10 we discuss the Semiconductor Chip Protection Act of 1984 that provides for a different copyright standard for computer chips.

Other Differences in EU and U.S. Copyright Protection of Databases

EU law allows for reproductions of small portions of a copyrighted database for commercial purposes, as long as the source is acknowledged. Also under EU law, if there is no other means of obtaining the facts contained in a database, a reasonable and nondiscriminatory license must be granted to a party that wants to use or republish that database.

More troubling from the mainstream U.S. point of view is EU database **privacy** protection, which is much more extensive than it is in the United States. Notably, the EU requires much more protection of databases that contain information about individuals and also, consistent with the 1995 EU Directive, prohibits sharing database information with countries that do not adhere to the EU standards for the protection of privacy. The U.S. has had to engage in extensive arm-twisting to prevent a cut-off of U.S. businesses' rights to share database contents with their European allies. Database sharing of personally iden-

tifiable *medical* and *financial* records is at the heart of this debate. Essentially, the U.S. approach has been to allow entities to self-regulate on privacy issues while, in the EU, the operative approach has been to have governments establish regulations prohibiting companies that maintain personally sensitive databases from allowing unauthorized secondary use of that information. Recall that rights of privacy, databases, and the Internet were discussed in much more detail in Chapter 6.

COPYRIGHT INFRINGEMENT

Exclusive Rights

Under Section 106 of the Copyright Act, copyright owners have exclusive rights to *reproduce and distribute* copyrighted works subject to various defenses, most prominently, the *fair use* defense. Copyright law also gives owners exclusive rights to distribute and to prepare *derivative* works. Section 106 also states that only copyright holders have the rights:

4. in the case of literary, musical, dramatic, and choreographic works, pantomimes, motion pictures and other audiovisual works, to *perform* the copyrighted work publicly; and
5. in the case of literary, musical, dramatic and choreographic works, pantomimes, and pictorial, graphic, or sculptural works, including the individual images of a motion picture or other audiovisual work, to *display* the copyrighted work publicly.

Proof of Copying

A copyright holder who believes its copyright has been infringed can file suit against the suspected infringer. In such suits, defendants in some instances will admit to copying. In other cases, there is indirect evidence of copying. As an example, in most functioning computer programs there are mistakes in the source code or object code. If the same mistakes that are present in the plaintiff's software are present in the defendant's allegedly infringing software, chances are very high that the defendant copied some of the plaintiff's software. Some computer vendors have been known to insert "dummy" code in their software just for the purpose of making proof of infringement easier in the event of litigation.

In most cases, in order to prove infringement, the copyright holder must show (1) *substantial similarity* between the copyrighted work and the accused work and (2) that the defendant had *access* to the copyrighted work. In copyright law, *independent creation* **is a valid defense.** Hence, it is critically important to show that the defendant had access to the copyrighted work. If the defendant did not have access to the copyrighted work, then it is likely to be concluded that the accused work is an independent creation. A few years ago George Harrison, a former member of the Beatles, was sued for a copyright infringement of the song "He's So Fine", based on Mr. Harrison's song "My Sweet Lord".[9] In order to deflect the independent creation defense, the plaintiffs showed that "He's So Fine" was a hit in England and that Harrison, a close student of music, undoubtedly heard the song many times. Harrison lost the case, though the judge commented that he thought it was an "unconscious" infringement.

Substantial Similarity

A standard ("test") used in determining substantial similarity is that *the similarities are so striking so as to disprove independent creation.* In determining *substantial similarity,* the idea must be separated from the expression of the idea and facts must be separated from the expression of facts. Ultimately it is for the jury (or the judge in his role as finder of facts) to decide whether there is a substantial similarity between the accused work and the copyrighted work. Electronic spreadsheets are composed of ideas and expressions of ideas. Ideas embedded in an electronic spreadsheet are the mathematical formulas that allow users to manipulate standard accounting data in a much more efficient fashion than with paper and pencil. The expressions of the ideas may be the structure,

sequence, and organization of the command structure that appears above the electronic grid lines displayed on a computer monitor. The mathematical formulas are not protectible by copyright laws and neither are the grid lines, but the structure, sequence, and organization of the command structure can be *if* there are other ways of achieving the same functionality.

Computer Software

In the case of computer software, both the literal and nonliteral portions of a software are protectible under copyright law. The literal portions of the program are the computer code, both source code and object code. Object code is only readable by machines, but it is protectible under copyright law. Source code is readable and thus more easily copied, manipulated, or altered by humans. COBOL, Visual Basic, C++, and HTML are all forms of source code. Although source code does not read like a book, it is decipherable by people trained in the programming language and can be altered or copied with relative ease by programmers. Programs are written in the form of source code, then transformed (compiled) into object code before being delivered to customers. So, most computer software is distributed to customers in the form of object code. The transformation of object code back into source code is called *decompilation (or disassembly).*

Decompilation or Disassembly

A source of deep controversy within the software/copyright interface is whether software created through decompilation (disassembly) of a copyrigted program is a copyright infringement. In several cases it has been held that if the purpose of the decompilation is to make the defendant's software products compatible with the plaintiff's operating system, then decompilation is not an infringement.[10] In other cases, where the purpose of the decompilation was *not* to create compatibility between the defendant's products and the plaintiff's operating system or products, but rather reverse engineering, decompilation has been held an infringement. It should be recognized that virtually all software licenses prohibit decompilation, so that decompilation may be a breach of contract as well as a copyright infringement.[11] More extensive discussion of software infringements occurs in Chapter 10. In the following recent case, a number of the issues referenced above are discussed.

---

[9]Cite the *Bright Tunes Music Corp.* v. *Harrisongs Music, Ltd.,* 420 F. Supp. 177, (1976).

[10]*Sega Enterprises Ltd.* v. *Accolade, Inc.,* 785 F.Supp. 1392, (1992).
[11]*Bay State Technologies, Inc.* v. *Harold Bowers, d/b/a HLB Technology,* Case No. 91-40079, jury verdict May 2000.

Sony Computer Entertainment, Inc. v. Connectix Corporation
United States Court of Appeals for the Ninth Circuit
203 F.3d 596; 2000

FACTS AND CASE BACKGROUND

The defendant is the Connectix Corporation, which makes and sells a software program called "Virtual Game Station." The purpose of the Virtual Game Station is to emulate on a regular computer the functioning of the Sony PlayStation console, so that computer owners who buy the Virtual Game Station software can play Sony PlayStation games on their computers. The Virtual Game Station does not contain any of Sony's copyrighted material. In the process of producing the Virtual Game Station, however, Connectix repeatedly copied Sony's copyrighted BIOS during a process of "reverse engineering" that Connectix conducted in order to find out how the Sony PlayStation worked. Sony claimed infringement and sought a preliminary injunction. The district court concluded that Sony was likely to succeed on its infringement claim because Connectix's "intermediate copying" was not a protected "fair use" under 17 U.S.C. § 107. The district court enjoined Connectix from selling the Virtual Game Station or from copying or using the Sony BIOS code in the development of other Virtual Game Station products. Connectix appeals the decision.

OPINION: CANBY, CIRCUIT JUDGE

II. DISCUSSION

To prevail on its motion for injunctive relief, Sony was required to demonstrate "either a likelihood of success on the merits and the possibility of irreparable injury or that serious questions going to the merits were raised and the balance of the hardships tip sharply in its favor." We reverse the grant of a preliminary injunction only when "the district court abused its discretion or based its decision on an erroneous legal standard or on clearly erroneous findings of fact." We review the scope of injunctive relief for an abuse of discretion.

Connectix admits that it copied Sony's copyrighted BIOS software in developing the Virtual Game Station but contends that doing so was protected as a fair use under 17 U.S.C. § 107. Connectix also challenges the district court's conclusion that Sony has established a likelihood that Connectix's Virtual Game Station tarnishes the PlayStation trademark. We consider each of these claims below.

A. Fair use The fair use issue arises in the present context because of certain characteristics of computer software. The object code of a program may be copyrighted as expression, 17 U.S.C. § 102(a), *but it also contains ideas and performs functions that are not entitled to copyright protection.* Object code cannot, however, be read by humans. The unprotected ideas and functions of the code therefore are frequently undiscoverable in the absence of investigation and translation that may require copying the copyrighted material. We conclude that, under the facts of this case and our precedent, Connectix's intermediate copying and use of Sony's copyrighted BIOS was a fair use for the purpose of gaining access to the unprotected elements of Sony's software.

The general framework for analysis of fair use is established by statute, 17 U.S.C. § 107. We have applied this statute and the fair use doctrine to the disassembly of computer software in the case of *Sega Enterprises Ltd.* v. *Accolade, Inc.* Central to our decision today is the rule set forth in *Sega:*

> Where disassembly is the *only way to gain access to the ideas and functional elements embodied in a copyrighted computer program* and where there is a legitimate reason for seeking such access, disassembly is a fair use of the copyrighted work, as a matter of law.

In *Sega,* we recognized that intermediate copying could constitute copyright infringement even when the end product did not itself contain copyrighted material. But this copying nonetheless could be protected as a fair use if it was "necessary" to gain access to the functional elements of the software itself. We drew this distinction because the Copyright Act protects expression only, not ideas or the functional aspects of a software program.

* * *

1. Nature of the copyrighted work Under our analysis of the second statutory factor, nature of the copyrighted work, we recognize that "some works are closer to the core of intended copyright protection than others." Sony's BIOS lies at a distance from the core because it contains unprotected aspects that cannot be examined without copying. We consequently accord it a "lower degree of protection than more traditional literary works." As we have applied this standard, Connectix's copying of the Sony BIOS must have been "necessary" to have been fair use. We conclude that it was.

There is no question that the Sony BIOS contains unprotected functional elements. Nor is it disputed that Connectix could not gain access to these unprotected functional elements without copying the Sony BIOS. Sony admits that little technical information about the functionality of the Sony BIOS is publicly available. The Sony BIOS is an internal operating system that does not produce a screen display to reflect its functioning. Consequently, if Connectix was to gain access to the functional elements of the Sony BIOS, it had to be through a form of reverse engineering that required copying the Sony BIOS onto a computer. Sony does not dispute this proposition.

The question then becomes whether the methods by which Connectix reverse-engineered the Sony BIOS were necessary to gain access to the unprotected functional elements within the program. We conclude that they were. Connectix employed several methods of reverse engineering (observation and observation with partial disassembly)

each of which required Connectix to make intermediate copies of copyrighted material. Neither of these methods renders fair use protection inapplicable. *Sega* expressly sanctioned disassembly. We see no reason to distinguish observation of copyrighted software in an emulated computer environment. Both methods require the reverse engineer to copy protected as well as unprotected elements of the computer program. Because this intermediate copying is the gravamen of the intermediate infringement claim and both methods of reverse engineering require it, we find no reason inherent in these methods to prefer one to another as a matter of copyright law. Connectix presented evidence that it observed the Sony BIOS in an emulated environment to observe the functional aspects of the Sony BIOS. When this method of reverse engineering was unsuccessful, Connectix engineers disassembled discrete portions of the Sony BIOS to view directly the ideas contained therein. We conclude that intermediate copying in this manner was

"necessary" within the meaning of *Sega.*

* * *

CONCLUSION

Connectix's reverse engineering of the Sony BIOS extracted from a Sony PlayStation console purchased by Connectix engineers is protected as a fair use. Other intermediate copies of the Sony BIOS made by Connectix, if they infringed Sony's copyright, do not justify injunctive relief. For these reasons, the district [*610] court's injunction is dissolved and the case is remanded to the district court. We also reverse the district court's finding that Connectix's Virtual Game Station has tarnished the Sony PlayStation mark.
Reversed and remanded.

QUESTIONS FOR ANALYSIS

1. Explain what is fair (and legal) under the fair use doctrine.
2. What limits would Connectix face in the wholesale copying of Sony software for use in its Virtual Game Station product?

DAMAGES WHEN THERE IS INFRINGEMENT: ACTUAL AND STATUTORY

If it is decided that an infringement has taken place, the Copyright Act provides remedies, including monetary damages, to plaintiffs. The successful plaintiff in a copyright infringement suit can opt for either actual damages or *statutory* damages against the defendant. In addition, a defendant can face criminal sanctions for willful violations of the Copyright Act.

Actual Damages

Section 504(b) of the Copyright Act allows a copyright owner to recover for actual damages incurred as a result of an infringement *and, in addition,* the profits the infringer earned as a result of the infringement(s), but qualified by a statutory prohibition on double

counting.[12] Double-counting could occur if the plaintiff was able to recover for its lost profits on sales lost to the defendant plus the profits earned by the defendant *on those same sales.* It is possible, however, that the harm to the copyright owner could far exceed the profits earned by the infringer. In some cases the confusion associated with two parties each claiming to be the rightful copyright owner could foreclose entire markets to the rightful copyright owner and yet the infringer would not profit because the infringer is foreclosed also. Also if a copyright holder is permanently damaged by being foreclosed from a market, part of the damages could be a present value estimation of lost future royalties. An expert witness, generally an economist or accountant, is typically called upon to estimate future royalties in the foreclosed market and to "discount" the projected lost royalties to present

---

[12]Defendants' profits are sometimes referred to as "unjust enrichment."

value using a discount rate that reflects the time value of money as well as market uncertainty/risk. The present value is the current lump sum award that represents compensation for projected future losses.

Burden of Proof

In determining the profits of the infringer, the copyright owner need only identify the gross revenue generated by the infringements. The burden of proof is upon the infringer to show company costs, which are then subtracted from gross revenue. Costs, in most cases, mean *variable* costs without an allocation of fixed costs. Defendants are only entitled to deduct variable costs from gross revenue, while the remainder represents incremental profit damages recoverable by the plaintiff. For much copyrighted material, such as computer software or musical recordings, variable costs are generally trivial in relation to the gross revenue enjoyed by the infringer. In the quantification of damage claims, juries often are treated to a debate between expert witnesses, usually accountants and economists, about what costs are variable (vary according to the number of infringing sales) and what costs are fixed (costs that do not vary with the amount of production).

In defending against damage claims, an infringer is entitled to attempt to show that some of the gross revenue attributable to infringement is due to other factors, such as sales of noninfringing software that is bundled with infringing software. Differing from patent and trade secret law, there is no provision in the Copyright Act for recovery of reasonable royalties from an infringer. The plaintiff in a copyright infringement case does not have to show that but for the infringing sales by the defendant, the plaintiff would have made the sales. If the defendant made an infringing sale and then made a profit, the copyright-holder is entitled to that profit.

In the Alternative: Statutory Damages

Section 504(c)(1) allows plaintiffs in infringement cases to elect, in the alternative, statutory damages "at any time before final judgment is rendered . . ." This section allows "an award of statutory damages for all infringements involved in the action, with respect to any one work, for which any one infringer is liable individually, or for which any two or more infringers are liable jointly and severally, in a sum of not less than $500 or more than $20,000 as the court considers just." This section limits recovery to the amounts listed above for each copyrighted work, *regardless of the number of*

infringements. If the copyright owner possessed a large number of copyrights and each one was infringed by the defendant, then the alternative listed in Section 504(c)(1) may yield greater damages than the "actual damages" provided for in Section 504(b) listed above. In most cases, however, proof of actual damages will yield greater damage awards because actual damages vary according to the number of infringements.

If the court finds that the infringement was willful, meaning that the defendant knew that he was infringing, Section 504(c)(2) allows the court to raise statutory damages to $100,000 for each infringement. On the other hand, if the infringer is successful in proving that his infringements were innocent, in other words, that the infringer did not know and had no reason to know that his actions were infringing the copyright of the plaintiff, the court is entitled to reduce statutory damages to $200.

Additional Remedies and Criminal Liability

Section 505 of the Copyright Act allows for recovery of full costs, including "reasonable" attorney fees to the *prevailing* party. Quite obviously, this section contemplates recovery of the costs of litigation by either side. If the infringement suit by the plaintiff is obviously nonmeritorious, then the defendant could be awarded court costs and attorney fees. Court costs and attorney fees are typically awarded to the plaintiff when the defendant willfully infringed and behaved badly during litigation, such as by failing to provide documents that were named in subpoenas and by providing witnesses who were obviously uncooperative during depositions. Also, at the discretion of the judge, plaintiffs are entitled to recover prejudgment interest—i.e., interest on the damages that occur before final judgment.

As anyone who has rented a video from Blockbuster or other movie rental establishments knows, violations of copyright laws are also criminal offenses. Section 506 says of "Criminal Infringement," "Any person who infringes a copyright willfully and for purposes of commercial advantage or private financial gain shall be punished as provided in section 2319 of title 18." Section 2319 provides for criminal sanctions against willful infringers ranging from fines to incarceration of up to 10 years. Section 506 also provides for *forfeiture and destruction* of "all infringing copies or phonorecords and all implements, devices, or equipment used in the manufacture of such infringing copies or phonorecords."

Focusing on Copyright Defenses

First Sale

A copyright owner has exclusive rights to reproduce the protectible portions of a copyrighted work. Under the Copyright Act, the copyright owner has exclusive rights to distribute, perform, and display copyrighted works. Copyright owners also have exclusive rights to prepare derivative works. Derivative means a transformation or adaptation of protected works. Copyright owners derive their revenue from copyrighted works, primarily by licensing the copyright work. When you buy a CD from a famous musical group, you become a licensee who is entitled to replay the copyrighted work with the CD and a CD player. When you buy a book, you are entitled to read the copyrighted work. In both cases, the purchase of a CD or a book does not entitle you to copy the copyrighted material and resell it to others. However, under copyright law there is a *first sale* exception that allows licensees of copyrighted material to resell the CD or book to friends or others.[13] The first sale exception does not allow a licensee to rent or distribute commercially the copyrighted material.

Using Software and Making Archival Copies

Section 117 of the Copyright Act indicates that owners of a copy of a computer program do not infringe the copyright if they make, or authorize the making of a copy, or an adaptation of the program, provided that making the copy or adaptation:

1. is an essential step in operating the program, or such copy, or
2. is for the purpose of archival copies and that all archival copies are destroyed when the license to the software program ceases.

This section allows licensees or purchasers of software to copy a software program if the copies made are necessary for the running of the program. For example, transferring software from a CD to a hard drive is a reproduction of the computer software program and thus technically, without Section 117, would be an infringement. Similarly, the transfer of a software program from the hard drive to the monitor of a computer is another reproduction of the copyrighted software that is allowed because of Section 117. All of these interme-diate reproductions of copyrighted material are legal.

It is well known that disks, CDs, are sometimes damaged and hard drives have been known to crash. Rather than subjecting licensees to the hassles associated with proving to vendors that their software was damaged or is otherwise inoperable, Section 117 allows licensees to do what is clearly reasonable and prudent: make a backup copy of the software.

Fair Use Exception

The *fair use* exception to the copyright laws allows unauthorized parties to reproduce parts or all of copyrighted works if the reproductions are for purposes of criticisms, commentary, news, teaching or research.[14] The foregoing list is not exhaustive. A copyrighted book can be reviewed by a critic and parts of the book reproduced in connection with the review, without the reproduction involving an infringement (even if the review is exceedingly negative!). The fair use exception is an affirmative defense in a copyright infringement suit, meaning that the burden of proof to qualify for the exception is borne by the defendant. Courts consider a number of factors when determining whether a defendant's copying qualifies for the fair use defense. When all is said and done, however, cases seem to be decided based on whether a defendant's reproductions and distributions *foreclose* sales of the copyrighted material to its market. If the answer is yes, indicating that as a result of the reproductions the copyright holders lose sales, then an infringement is likely to be found.

Factors Used by the Courts in Fair Use Cases

Courts look at several factors in determining whether an unauthorized reproduction or distribution of some or all of a copyrighted work qualifies for the fair use exception.

1. Courts look at whether a claimed infringing use is commercial; if the conclusion is yes, then it is very likely, though not certain, that the use will be deemed an infringement.
2. Courts will also look at the nature of the copyrighted work. If the copying takes place to create compatibility with an operating system or hardware, then it is more likely to be deemed a fair use.

---

[13]Section 109 of the Copyright Act.

[14]Section 107 of the Copyright Act.

3. The more of the copyrighted work is reproduced by the defendant, the more likely the reproductions are to be judged infringements.
4. As stated above, however, the most decisive factor is the market effect. If the market for the copyrighted work for the copyright owner is unaffected by the defendant's actions, it is more likely that fair use will be found.

Types of Infringement

In the next two cases, both of which qualified for the fair use exception, entire copyrighted works were copied. Another factor that courts will examine is whether a device or technique has a noninfringing use. In the *Sony* case, immediately below, the issue was whether time-shifting through the use of video tape recorders (VTRs) is a noninfringing use that qualified for the fair use exception. Notice in the *Sony* case that *direct infringements* took place due to actions of Sony VTR owners. Sony was a defendant by virtue of being a *"contributory infringer"*. For obvious public relations reasons, the networks were not interested in suing their customers. The claim made by the plaintiff (Universal City Studios, Inc. which owned copyrights to TV programs) was that without VTRs sold by Sony, unauthorized reproductions of copyrighted works (the TV programs) would not have taken place. Liability can also be established for infringement based on *vicarious* actions. If the defendant has the right to control the infringer and financially benefits from the infringement, the defendant is vicariously liable to the

plaintiff for an infringement. An example is provided by employers who benefit from infringing actions of employees.

At issue in the *Campbell* case was whether a parody of the Roy Orbison song "Oh Pretty Woman" by the rap group Two Live Crew qualified for the fair use exception. Consistent with the First Amendment, the more vicious the parody, the more likely it is to qualify for the fair use exception. Although Two Live Crew's parody of "Pretty Woman" was quite vicious, it paled in comparison to a parody of a Campari ad by *Hustler* magazine.[15] Featured in the *Hustler* parody of the Campari ad was the Reverend Jerry Falwell who *Hustler* alleged had his first sexual experience with his mother in an outhouse. Falwell sued *Hustler* for defamation, but that suit was thrown out because the U.S. Court of Appeals ruled no one actually believed *Hustler* was alleging the events truly occurred. *Hustler* countersued Falwell when he sent out hundreds of thousands of copies of the *Hustler* parody of the Campari ads in a fund-raising effort. Even though Falwell's intent was undoubtedly commercial, the court threw that suit out also because it ruled that sales of *Hustler* were not harmed by the unauthorized distribution of the Campari parody by Falwell. The court surmised that the overlap between members of the Moral Majority and the universe of *Hustler* customers was very slim, indeed.

[15]*Hustler Magazine, Inc. v. Moral Majority, Inc.,* 796 F.2d 1148 (1986).

Sony Corporation v. Universal City Studios et al.
Supreme Court of the United States
464 U.S. 417; 104 S. Ct. 774; 1984

FACTS AND CASE BACKGROUND

Owners of copyrights on television programs, Universal City Studios et al., sued manufacturers of home video tape recorders, including Sony Corporation, in the United States District Court for the Central District of California, alleging that some individuals had used the recorders to record some of the owners' copyrighted works on television, that these individuals had thereby infringed the copyrights, and that the recorder manufacturers were liable for such infringement because of their sale of the recorders. The District Court entered judgment for the manufacturers, but the United States Court of Appeals for the Ninth Circuit reversed, holding the manufacturers liable for contributory infringement. The United States Supreme Court now decides if the sale of home video tape recorders to the general public constituted contributory infringement of copyrights on television programs.

OPINION: STEVENS, JUDGE

An explanation of our rejection of respondents' unprecedented attempt to impose copyright liability upon the distributors of copying equipment requires a quite detailed recitation of the findings of the District Court. In summary, those findings reveal that the average member of the public uses a VTR principally to record a program he cannot view as it is being televised and then to watch it once at a later time. This practice, known as "time-shifting," enlarges the television viewing audience. For that reason, a significant amount of television programming may be used in this manner without objection from the owners of the copyrights on the programs. For the same reason, even the two respondents in this case, who do assert objections to time-shifting in this litigation, were unable to prove that the practice has impaired the commercial value of their copyrights or has created any likelihood of future harm. Given these findings, there is no basis in the Copyright Act upon which respondents can hold petitioners liable for distributing VTRs to the general public. The Court of Appeals' holding that respondents are entitled to enjoin the distribution of VTRs to collect royalties on the sale of such equipment, or to obtain other relief, if affirmed, would enlarge the scope of respondents' statutory monopolies to encompass control over an article of commerce that is not the subject of copyright protection. Such an expansion of the copyright privilege is beyond the limits of the grants authorized by Congress.

I. The two respondents in this action, Universal City Studios, Inc., and Walt Disney Productions, produce and hold the copyrights on a substantial number of motion pictures and other audiovisual works. In the current marketplace, they can exploit their rights in these works in a number of ways: by authorizing theatrical exhibitions, by licensing limited showings on cable and network television, by selling syndication rights for repeated airings on local television stations, and by marketing programs on prerecorded videotapes or videodiscs. Some works are suitable for exploitation through all of these avenues, while the market for other works is more limited.

Petitioner Sony manufactures millions of Betamax video tape recorders and markets these devices through numerous retail establishments, some of which are also petitioners in this action. Sony's Betamax VTR is a mechanism consisting of three basic components: (1) a tuner, which receives electromagnetic signals transmitted over the television band of the public airwaves and separates them into audio and visual signals; (2) a recorder, which records such signals on a magnetic tape; and (3) an adapter, which converts the audio and visual signals on the tape into a composite signal that can be received by a television set.

* * *

The respondents and Sony both conducted surveys of the way the Betamax machine was used by several hundred owners during a sample period in 1978. Although there were some differences in the surveys, they both showed that the primary use of the machine for most owners was "time-shifting"—the practice of recording a program to view it once at a later time, and thereafter erasing it. Time-shifting enables viewers to see programs they otherwise would miss because they are not at home, are occupied with other tasks, or are viewing a program on another station at the time of a broadcast that they desire to watch. Both surveys also showed, however, that a substantial number of interviewees had accumulated libraries of tapes. Sony's survey indicated that over 80 percent of the interviewees watched at least as much regular television as they had before owning a Betamax. Respondents offered no evidence of decreased television viewing by Betamax owners.

* * *

In summary, the record and findings of the District Court lead us to two conclusions. First, Sony demonstrated a significant likelihood that substantial numbers of copyright holders who license their works for broadcast on free television would not object to having their broadcasts time-shifted by private viewers. And second, respondents failed to demonstrate that time-shifting would cause any likelihood of nonminimal harm to the potential market for, or the value of, their copyrighted works. The Betamax is, therefore, capable of substantial noninfringing uses. Sony's sale of such equipment to the general public does not constitute contributory infringement of respondents' copyrights.

DECISION

Sale of home videotape recorders held not to constitute contributory infringement of television program copyrights.

QUESTIONS FOR REVIEW

1. If surveys showed that the predominant use of Sony VTRs was to acquire libraries of copyrighted programming that would be viewed mujltiple times, would the court's decision have been different? Why do you think it would or wouldn't?

2. How could the use of VTRs result in nonminimal harm to copyright owners?

Campbell v. *Acuff-Rose Music, Inc.*
Supreme Court of the United States
510 U.S. 569; 114 S. Ct. 1164; 1994

FACTS AND CASE BACKGROUND

Acuff-Rose Music, Inc., filed suit against petitioners, the members of the rap music group 2 Live Crew and their record company, claiming that 2 Live Crew's song, "Oh Pretty Woman," infringed Acuff-Rose's copyright in Roy Orbison's rock ballad, "Oh, Pretty Woman." The District Court granted summary judgment for 2 Live Crew, holding that its song was a parody that made fair use of the original song. The Court of Appeals reversed and remanded, holding that the commercial nature of the parody rendered it presumptively unfair under the first of four factors relevant under § 107; that, by taking the "heart" of the original and making it the "heart" of a new work, 2 Live Crew had, qualitatively, taken too much under the third § 107 factor; and that market harm for purposes of the fourth § 107 factor had been established by a presumption attaching to commercial uses. The case was now before the Supreme Court to decide.

OPINION: SOUTER

We think the Court of Appeals was insufficiently appreciative of parody's need for the recognizable sight or sound when it ruled 2 Live Crew's use unreasonable as a matter of law. It is true, of course, that 2 Live Crew copied the characteristic opening bass riff (or musical phrase) of the original, and true that the words of the first line copy the Orbison lyrics. But if quotation of the opening riff and the first line may be said to go to the "heart" of the original, the heart is also what most readily conjures up the song for parody, and it is the heart at which parody takes aim. Copying does not become excessive in relation to parodic purpose merely because the portion taken was the original's heart. If 2

Live Crew had copied a significantly less memorable part of the original, it is difficult to see how its parodic character would have come through.

This is not, of course, to say that anyone who calls himself a parodist can skim the cream and get away scot free. In parody, as in news reporting, context is everything, and the question of fairness asks what else the parodist did besides go to the heart of the original. It is significant that 2 Live Crew not only copied the first line of the original, but thereafter departed markedly from the Orbison lyrics for its own ends. 2 Live Crew not only copied the bass riff and repeated it, but also produced otherwise distinctive sounds, interposing "scraper" noise, overlaying the music with solos in different keys, and altering the drum beat. This is not a case, then, where "a substantial portion" of the parody itself is composed of a "verbatim" copying of the original. It is not, that is, a case where the parody is so insubstantial, as compared to the copying, that the third factor must be resolved as a matter of law against the parodists.

* * *

The fourth fair use factor is "the effect of the use upon the potential market for or value of the copyrighted work." It requires courts to consider not only the extent of market harm caused by the particular actions of the alleged infringer, but also "whether unrestricted and widespread conduct of the sort engaged in by the defendant . . . would result in a substantially adverse impact on the potential market" for the original. The enquiry "must take account not only of harm to the original but also of harm to the market for derivative works."

III. It was error for the Court of Appeals to conclude that the com-

mercial nature of 2 Live Crew's parody of "Oh, Pretty Woman" rendered it presumptively unfair. No such evidentiary presumption is available to address either the first factor, the character and purpose of the use, or the fourth, market harm, in determining whether a transformative use, such as parody, is a fair one. The court also erred in holding that 2 Live Crew had necessarily copied excessively from the Orbison original, considering the parodic purpose of the use. We therefore reverse the judgment of the Court of Appeals and remand the case for further proceedings consistent with this opinion.

DECISION

Denial of fair-use defense to copyright infringement suit held erroneously based on conclusions that commercial song parody (1) was presumptively unfair, and (2) necessarily involved excessive copying.

QUESTIONS FOR REVIEW

1. What was the error made by the Court of Appeals with respect to the importance of the commercial nature of the parody of "Oh Pretty Woman" by Two Live Crew? If a parody of a copyrighted work makes money, does that render the parody a copyright infringement? Isn't the Court of Appeals standard really confining parodies to nonprofit groups?

2. How much of the original work can a parody contain without becoming an infringement? Is there any upward limit according to the Supreme Court?

3. Under what circumstances would a purported parody become a copyright infringement?

Other Defenses

As with patents, the common law defenses of laches, estoppel, and unclean hands apply. Defendants can assert the laches defense when there is evidence that the plaintiff knew about the infringements but delayed a response to the infringement so that damages would be higher. If proof of the laches defense is established, the defendant can escape liability for past infringements for which the defense applies. Also, if the plaintiff was engaging in fraud or some other unethical action, the courts could rule that the plaintiff had unclean hands and refused to enforce infringement remedies. Finally, the doctrine of misuse applies to copyrights also, particularly if the misuse is associated with some form of antitrust violation. So, *tying* together the sale of a copyrighted product (such as software) and a non-copyrighted product can be a misuse of the copyright, disqualifying the copyright holder from infringement remedies.

MUSIC, MP3, AND NAPSTER

The Music Market and Technological Change

There is a sizeable market for popular music, which includes market segments for niche music such as punk, techno, folk, jazz, hip hop, etc. The music market's interface with the Internet has created enormous tension between copyright protection of musical recordings and advances in technology. Everything on the Internet is digitized, including music. When music is digitized, copied recordings are flawless without the diminution in quality that is common in tape recordings. Currently, most musical recordings are purchased from record stores as compact disks (CDs) by young people, many of whom are very adept at transferring digital files and making use of the Internet. A barrier to the downloading of music from the Internet has been the size of the programs necessary to contain a musical recording. Since most modems operate at a 56K capacity or less, the time required to download music was prohibitive. In addition, once a musical recording was downloaded, it was difficult to transfer as only hard drives had the capacity to hold programs the size of a CD download.

Audio Home Recording Act, 1992

Recent technological advancements have broken down barriers to downloading music from the Internet. The MP3 format for compressing large Internet files allows for much faster downloading of programs that contain audio recordings. MP3 is an acronym for MPEG-1 Audio Layer 3, which is compression software that applies an algorithm that enables Internet travelers to download copyrighted audio recordings. In addition to this software, an option now available to computer purchasers is a CD Writer (a digital audio recording machine (DAR)), which has the ability to download musical recordings onto blank CDs. CDs that sell for between $10 and $20 in a record store can be copied and shared among friends for the cost of a blank CD, about $1.00.

In 1992 Congress dealt with this challenge to the Copyright Act by passing the Audio Home Recording Act (AHRA). The AHRA requires sellers of digital audio recording devices (CD Writers) to pay a 2 percent royalty on the sales price of these devices to the Copyright Office. Also sellers of blank CDs have to pay a 3 percent royalty, to be distributed by the Copyright Office to musicians, record companies, composers, and others who have stakes in musical copyrights. The AHRA also requires sellers of digital audio recorders (DARs) to use a serial copy management system (SCMS) so that royalties can be properly allocated.

The AHRA specifically allows for copying of copyrighted CDs for home use, but not for commercial use. In effect, AHRA has created a fair use exception in the case of copying copyrighted works for home use. Realistically, there was no way to stop CD Writers from being used for the benefit (copying copyrighted songs) of a friend. So, in reality, if you want a copy of Sheryl Crow's latest CD and your friend had the CD, you can borrow her CD and burn a copy with your CD Writer. At this evolutionary stage, the commercial threat posed to copyright holders by unauthorized copying among friends is not as ominous to record companies and recording artists as Internet transmissions. Friend-to-friend copying is limited by time and the number of your friends for whom you are willing to break copyright law. With Internet transmissions of digitized music, however, thousands of copies of copyrighted musical recordings can be transmitted to strangers in a short period of time with the copyright owners (musicians and record companies) precluded from collecting royalties on the copies distributed.

Money Makes Strange Allies

The Internet's threats to royalty incomes have joined together traditional adversaries, record companies, and some, but certainly not all, recording artists, in a partnership to do battle against unauthorized access to music without the payment of royalties. Copyright issues on the Internet were fought out in a recent case pitting an association of record companies against a firm that facilitated MP3 recordings of copyrighted material. In the following case, the Ninth Circuit Court of Appeals considered whether a device that can download files that have been compressed by

MP3 software falls within the controls provided by the Audio Home Recording Act of 1992. If you are keeping score on battles between "suits" and the "kids", the kids win round one in the following case. Note that the defendants in this case did not pool recordings, which occurs with Napster technology discussed later.

Recording Industry Association of America v. *Diamond Multimedia Systems, Inc.*
United States Court of Appeals for the Ninth Circuit
180 F.3d 1072; 1999

FACTS AND CASE BACKGROUND

Until recently, the Internet was not a means of concern for copying or distributing music due to the oversized file space and bandwidth required to do so. However, the MP3 algorithm compresses the music files to one-twelfth their original size without compromising sound quality. MP3 makes copying music files from the Internet quick and efficient, and the MP3 download algorithm is free.

The Recording Industry Association of America (RIAA) filed suit against Diamond Multimedia Systems, Inc., the maker of a small device called the "Rio" that makes MP3 downloaded music portable. The question is whether the Rio falls under the guidelines of the Audio Home Recording Act of 1992. RIAA claims that it does, and seeks payment of royalties for music downloaded into the Rio.

OPINION: O'SCANNLAIN, CIRCUIT JUDGE

RIAA represents the roughly half-dozen major record companies (and the artists on their labels) that control approximately 90 percent of the distribution of recorded music in the United States. RIAA asserts that Internet distribution of serial digital copies of pirated copyrighted material will discourage the purchase of legitimate recordings, and predicts that losses to digital Internet piracy will soon surpass the $300 million

that is allegedly lost annually to other more traditional forms of piracy. RIAA fights a well-nigh constant battle against Internet piracy, monitoring the Internet daily, and routinely shutting down pirate web-sites by sending cease-and-desist letters and bringing lawsuits. There are conflicting views on RIAA's success—RIAA asserts that it can barely keep up with the pirate traffic, while others assert that few, if any, pirate sites remain in operation in the United States and illicit files are difficult to find and download from anywhere online.

* * *

The initial question presented is whether the Rio falls within the ambit of the Act. The Act does not broadly prohibit digital serial copying of copyright protected audio recordings. Instead, the Act places restrictions only upon a specific type of recording device. Most relevant here, the Act provides that "no person shall import, manufacture, or distribute any *digital audio recording device* . . . that does not conform to the Serial Copy Management System ["SCMS"] [or] a system that has the same functional characteristics. The Act further provides that "no person shall import into and distribute, or manufacture and distribute, any *digital audio recording device* . . . unless such person records the notice specified by this section

and subsequently deposits the statements of account and applicable royalty payments." Thus, to fall within the SCMS and royalty requirements in question, the Rio must be a "digital audio recording device," which the Act defines through a set of nested definitions.

* * *

The typical computer hard drive from which a Rio directly records is, of course, a material object. However, hard drives ordinarily contain much more than "only sounds, and material, statements, or instructions incidental to those fixed sounds." Indeed, almost all hard drives contain numerous programs (e.g., for word processing, scheduling appointments, etc.) and databases that are not incidental to any sound files that may be stored on the hard drive. Thus, the Rio appears not to make copies from digital music recordings, and thus would not be a digital audio recording device under the Act's basic definition unless it makes copies from transmissions.

* * *

While the Rio can only directly reproduce files from a computer hard drive via a cable linking the two devices (which is obviously not a transmission), the Rio can indirectly reproduce a transmission. For example, if a radio broadcast of a digital audio recording were recorded on a digital audio tape machine or compact disc recorder and then uploaded to a computer hard drive, the Rio could indirectly reproduce the transmission by downloading a copy from the hard drive. Thus, if indirect reproduction of a transmission falls within the statutory definition, the Rio would be a digital audio recording device.

* * *

RIAA's interpretation of the statutory language initially seems plausible, but closer analysis reveals that it is contrary to the statutory language and common sense. The focus of the statutory language seems to be on the two means of reproducing the underlying digital music recording—either directly from that recording, or indirectly, by reproducing the recording from a transmission. RIAA's interpretation of the Act's language (in which "indirectly" modifies copying "from a transmission," rather than the copying of the underlying digital music recording) would only cover the indirect recording of transmissions, and would omit restrictions on the direct recording of transmissions (e.g., recording songs from the radio)

from the Act's ambit. This interpretation would significantly reduce the protection afforded by the Act to transmissions, and neither the statutory language nor structure provides any reason that the Act's protections should be so limited. Moreover, it makes little sense for the Act to restrict the indirect recording of transmissions, but to allow unrestricted direct recording of transmissions (e.g., to regulate second-hand recording of songs from the radio, but to allow unlimited direct recording of songs from the radio). Thus, the most logical reading of the Act extends protection to direct copying of digital music recordings, and to indirect copying of digital music recordings from transmissions of those recordings.

* * *

. . . A device falls within the Act's provisions if it can indirectly copy a digital music recording by making a copy from a transmission of that recording. Because the Rio cannot make copies from transmissions, but instead, can only make copies from a computer hard drive, it is not a digital audio recording device.

* * *

For the foregoing reasons, the Rio is not a digital audio recording device subject to the restrictions of the Audio Home Recording Act of 1992. The district court properly denied the motion for a preliminary injunction against the Rio's manufacture and distribution. Having so determined, we need not consider whether the balance of hardships or the possibility of irreparable harm supports injunctive relief.

Affirmed.

QUESTIONS FOR REVIEW

1. What was the argument that the record companies were making about Rio? Why did they want the court to agree with their contention about the Audio Digital Recording Act?

2. What does the Audio Digital Recording Act prohibit? What are the limitations of the Act that were evident in this case?

3. Does this case enable Rio users to avoid the copyright laws?

Sharing among Your Closest Two Million Friends

Napster is a website (www.napster.com) that has generated a good deal of publicity because it facilitates copying of copyrighted songs. Napster allows visitors to form a huge pool of potentially downloadable MP3 files that contain digitized recordings of copyrighted songs. With Napster and a computer with a CD Writer, a potential customer for music from a popular group such as Metallica can bypass going to a record store and paying $15.00 for one of their CDs by downloading from the library of available songs that is maintained by Napster members.[16] According to Napster,

its copyright policy is partially explained below:

Napster Copyright Policy

Napster is an integrated browser and communications system provided by Napster, Inc., to enable musicians and music fans to locate bands and music available in the MP3 music format. The MP3 files that you locate using Napster are not stored on Napster's servers. Napster does not, and cannot, control what content is available to you using the Napster browser. Napster users decide what content to make available to others using the Napster browser, and what content to download. Users are responsible for complying with all applicable federal and state laws applicable to such content, including copyright laws.

Before the Senate Judiciary Committee in July 2000, the president of Napster claimed that CD sales by recording artists have increased since Napster began

[16]Lars Ulrick, a member of Metallica, has led artists who oppose downloading of their music without payment of royalties. He has been especially critical of Napster.

business. On the other hand, according to Lars Elrich of the heavy metal group Metallica, during a recent two-week period when activity was monitored, his group's music was downloaded more than 1 million times with no royalties received from any downloaded CD. It isn't surprising that Napster is in the midst of court procedures, as discussed below.

More on Music

Digital Performance Right in Sound Recordings Act, 1995

This Act is designed to protect copyrights of owners of sound recordings by adding another copyright exclusive privilege, which is the right to perform their works by digital audio transmissions. Section 106 of the Copyright Act, which elucidates the rights of a copyright owner, was amended with the following additional language added: "in the case of sound recordings, to perform the copyrighted work publicly by means of a digital audio transmission." Potentially, such language, if unqualified, could prohibit Internet radio, which is becoming increasingly popular. Hence, several qualifiers were added to restrict what constitutes an infringement. There are three classes of transmissions listed: subscription, subscription interactive, and nonsubscription (i.e., Internet radio). According to the Act only interactive subscription transmissions are an infringement, which means the structure that enables customers to select transmissions for a fee must be licensed. So, under this Act, interactive subscription services on the Internet that charge a fee must negotiate a license with the copyright owner or else face an infringement charge.

Digital Millennium Copyright Act, 1998

The Digital Millennium Copyright Act (DMCA) of 1998 has been described as the most significant change in copyright law in a generation. It would probably be more accurate to say that for some people, particularly educators and librarians, the DMCA is very significant. A summary of the major provisions of the DMCA by the U.S. Copyright Office divides the DMCA into 5 titles:

Title 1. Implements WIPO (World Intellectual Property Office) Copyright and Performances and Phonograms Treaties Implementation Act of 1998.

Title 2. Creates limitations of liability for service providers for copyright infringement when engaging in certain activity. This is a continuation of a trend that began with several defamation suits in which Internet Service Providers (ISPs) were named as defendants. The courts likened ISPs to bookstores, not publishers, and largely exempted ISPs from liability for making available allegedly defamatory material, unless the ISP is paid a fee for effecting the infringement. The DMCA provides statutory reinforcement for earlier court rulings that insulate ISPs from liability for defamatory material that appear on their servers.

Title 3. Creates an exemption for making copies of computer programs if the copying is for purposes of maintenance or repair.

Title 4. Creates miscellaneous provisions that relate to distance education and exceptions in the Copyright Act for libraries and webcasting of sound recordings on the Internet.

Title 5. Creates a new form of copyright protection for vessel hull designs.

Title 1 makes it illegal to create software or other devices that circumvent technological measures taken by copyright owners to protect their copyrighted works. Thus, software whose sole purpose is to crack encryption mechanisms is illegal. Title 1 also makes illegal tampering with copyright management information, the SCMS referred to above. Both of these provisions are required by World Intellectual Property Organization (WIPO) treaties that the United States has signed and is committed to implementing in order to be a fully functioning member.

In Title 1 a distinction is made between software that enables a hacker to gain illegal *access* to copyrighted work and software that enables the hacker to illegally *copy* the work. Basically, the DMCA makes illegal software that facilitates illegal access to encrypted records, but does not prohibit copying of software that may have anticopying code in it. Thus, it is illegal to develop software whose purpose is to gain unauthorized access to student records at a university. Section 117 of the Copyright Act, however, continues to give owners of copyrighted material the unambiguous right to make archival copies of software as long as their software license is in force.

There are a number of *exceptions* to the prohibitions contained in Title 1 DMCA that refer to the purpose of the circumvention devices. Exceptions are made for:

A. Nonprofit libraries and educational institutions that are making use of circumvention devices for purposes of *determining whether they want to obtain authorized access* to the work, say by the purchase of a subscription.

B. Reverse engineering if the purpose of the reverse engineering is to achieve interoperability with other programs—in other words *to achieve compatibility* with other programs.

C. Encryption research in order to identify flaws in current encryption technology.

D. Protection of minors from objectionable material on the Internet.

E. Personal privacy needs. It is legal if the purpose of the circumvention is to protect personal privacy, such as disabling cookie files.

F. If the purpose of the circumvention measures is to test security systems, it is legal.

Many of the legal issues associated with the DMCA are discussed in the *Napster* case.[17]

[17]The Ninth Circuit Court of Appeals emphatically ruled against Napster and for A&M Records. The Ninth Circuit refused to overturn the findings of the District Court that Napster was both a contributory infringer and a vicarious infringer. *A&M Records, Inc.* v. *Napster, Inc.* 2001 U.S. Ct. of App. LEXIS 5446 (2001).

A & M Records, Inc. v. *Napster, Inc.*
United States District Court for the Northern District of California
54 U.S.P.Q.2D (BNA) 1746; 2000

FACTS AND CASE BACKGROUND

The question before the court is the applicability of a safe harbor provision of the Digital Millennium Copyright Act ("DMCA"), 17 U.S.C. section 512(a). A & M Records, music recording companies, claims that Napster, Inc., a company that makes MP3 music files available via a search system, is involved in alleged contributory and vicarious federal copyright infringement and related state law violations according to the Act. Napster, on the other hand, argues that the Napster system is protected under Section 512(a) which provides an exemption from liability for transmissions of copyrighted material and that A & M Records is therefore not permitted to obtain monetary damages or injunctive relief.

OPINION: MARILYN HALL PATEL, CHIEF JUDGE, UNITED STATES DISTRICT COURT, NORTHERN DISTRICT OF CALIFORNIA

Although the parties dispute the precise nature of the service Napster provides, they agree that using Napster typically involves the following basic steps: After downloading MusicShare software from the Napster website, a user can access the Napster system from her computer. The MusicShare software interacts with Napster's server-side software when the user logs on, automatically connecting her to one of some 150 servers that Napster operates. The MusicShare software reads a list of names of MP3 files that the user has elected to make available. This list is then added to a directory and index, on the Napster server, of MP3 files that users who are logged-on wish to share. If the user wants to locate a song, she enters its name or the name of the recording artist on the search page of the MusicShare program and clicks the "Find It" button. The Napster software then searches the current directory and generates a list of files responsive to the search request. To download a desired file, the user highlights it on the list and clicks the "Get Selected Songs" button. The user may also view a list of files that exist on another user's hard drive and select a file from that list. When the requesting user clicks on the name of a file, the Napster server communicates with the requesting user's and host user's MusicShare browser software to facilitate a connection between the two users and initiate the downloading of the file without any further action on either user's part.

* * *

Napster claims that its business activities fall within the safe harbor provided by subsection 512(a). This subsection limits liability "for infringement of copyright by reason of the [service] provider's transmitting, routing, or providing connections for, material through a system or network controlled or operated by or for the service provider, or by reason of the intermediate and transient storage of that material in the course of such transmitting, routing, or providing connections," if five conditions are satisfied:

1. the transmission of the material was initiated by or at the direction of a person other than the service provider;

2. the transmission, routing, provision of connections, or storage is carried out through an automatic technical process without selection of the material by the service provider;

3. the service provider does not select the recipients of the material except as an automatic response to the request of another person;

4. no copy of the material made by the service provider in the course of such intermediate or transient storage is maintained on the system or network in a manner ordinarily accessible to anyone other than the anticipated recipients, and no such copy is maintained on the system or network in a manner ordinarily accessible to such anticipated recipients for a longer period than is reasonably necessary for the transmission, routing, or provision of connections; and

5. the material is transmitted through the system or network without modification of its content.

* * *

Defendant then seeks to show compliance with these requirements by arguing: (1) a Napster user, and never Napster itself, initiates the transmission of MP3 files; (2) the transmission occurs through an automatic, technical process without any editorial input from Napster; (3) Napster does not choose the recipients of the MP3 files; (4) Napster does not make a copy of the material during transmission; and (5) the content of the material is not modified

during transmission. Napster maintains that the 512(a) safe harbor thus protects its core function—"transmitting, routing and providing connections for sharing of the files its users choose."

Plaintiffs disagree. They first argue that subsection 512(n) requires the court to analyze each of Napster's functions independently and that not all of these functions fall under the 512(a) safe harbor. In their view, Napster provides information location tools—such as a search engine, directory, index, and links—that are covered by the more stringent eligibility requirements of subsection 512(d), rather than subsection 512(a).

Plaintiffs also contend that Napster does not perform the function which the 512(a) safe harbor protects because the infringing material is not transmitted or routed *through* the Napster system, as required by subsection 512(a). They correctly note that the definition of "service provider" under subparagraph 512(k)(1)(A) is not identical to the prefatory language of subsection 512(a). The latter imposes the additional requirement that transmitting, routing, or providing connections must occur "through the system or network." Plaintiffs argue in the alternative that, if users' computers are part of the Napster system, copies of MP3 files are stored on the system longer than reasonably necessary for transmission, and thus subparagraph 512(a)(4) is not satisfied.

Finally, plaintiffs note that, under the general eligibility requirements established in subsection 512(i), a service provider must have adopted, reasonably implemented, and in-

formed its users of a policy for terminating repeat infringers. Plaintiffs contend that Napster only adopted its copyright compliance policy after the onset of this litigation and even now does not discipline infringers in any meaningful way. Therefore, in plaintiffs' view, Napster fails to satisfy the DMCA's threshold eligibility requirements or show that the 512(a) safe harbor covers any of its functions.

* * *

Conclusion

This court has determined above that Napster does not meet the requirements of subsection 512(a) because it does not transmit, route, or provide connections for allegedly infringing material through its system. The court also finds summary adjudication inappropriate due to the existence of genuine issues of material fact about Napster's compliance with subparagraph 512(i)(A), which a service provider must satisfy to enjoy the protection of *any* section 512 safe harbor. Defendant's motion for summary adjudication is DENIED.

Questions for Analysis

1. What type of transmissions are protected by the safe harbor provided by Section 512(a)? Who is the target for this safe harbor? If this safe harbor was not provided, would all ISPs have to shut down?

2. Why did the court conclude that Napster did not qualify for the Section 512(a) safe harbor? What is the difference between what Napster is doing and Rio in the previous case?

No Electronic Theft Act, 1997

This legislation is widely viewed as closing a loophole in criminal law sanctions under the Copyright Act. Until the No Electronic Theft (NET) Act was passed, hackers and mischief-makers who did not **profit** mon-

etarily from their copyright infringing activities did not violate federal criminal copyright law.[18] Thus,

[18]In 1997 the No Electronic Theft (NET) Act again amended section 506 by amending subsection (a) in its entirety. Pub. L. No. 105–147, 111 Stat. 2678.

hackers who sabotage national security by violating posted copyrights were subject to civil sanctions but not criminal incarceration. Since most hackers have few assets, levying financial penalties on them for copyright infringements was not much of a deterrent. The NET Act defines criminal infringers as "Any person who infringes a copyright willfully either—

1. for purposes of commercial advantage or private financial gain, or
2. by the reproduction or distribution, including by electronic means, during any 180-day period, of 1 or more copies or phonorecords of 1 or more copyrighted works, which have a a total retail value of more than $1,000 . . ."

Some concerns have been raised in the academic community that inadvertent copyright infringements can result in criminal sanctions since the NET Act is triggered by *willful* copyright infringements that have a retail value of more than $1,000.[19] Given the wide reach of the Internet, even trivial infringements can pass the $1,000 threshold with relative ease. The NET Act does state that "For purposes of this subsection, evidence of reproduction or distribution of a copyrighted work, by itself, shall not be sufficient to establish willful infringement." A sensible interpretation of *willful* would be there must be a showing of intent to violate the copyright laws before criminal sanctions can be applied.

Moral Rights and Visual Artists Rights Act

Moral rights are rights that authors and artists have that persist even after they assign their rights in copyrighted works to another party. Even though an artist or author assigns "all" of his or her rights to a copyrighted work, that individual still retains certain rights. In the United States, an artist retains the right to prevent distortions that would harm his or her artistic reputation. If a record company speeded up the recording of a musical group, so that they sounded like chipmunks, it would distort their work and harm their reputation. Protection of artists is even more extensive in Europe, where artists generally are allowed to retain the rights of disclosure and attribution in addition to the right of integrity (prevention of distortion), even after a "complete" assignment of rights. Disclosure is required among the movie credits when a recording

artist's songs are used. Attribution would be required when a poster company reproduces a visual work. The artist's name should appear on the poster.

In 1990 Congress passed the Visual Artists Rights Act, which calls for limited rights of attribution and integrity when alterations are made that will harm the reputation or honor of artists. Section 106A of the Copyright Act says that an author of visual art has the right to claim authorship of that work, and to prevent applying his or her name as the author of any work that he or she did not create. Authors of visual art also have the right to prevent distortions of their work that would harm their reputations under this act.

Works for Hire

Under Section 201 of the Copyright Act, the author is the original owner of a copyright. In the case of works for hire, however, the employer of an author who creates a work for hire within his or her *scope of employment* is the copyright owner, unless there is an agreement to the contrary. Actual authors do not have *moral rights* on any creation that is deemed a work for hire. In addition to hiring someone to write a manual for a consumer appliance or other works for hire, Section 101 of the copyright act classifies the following as additional examples of works for hire:

> a work specially ordered or commissioned for use as a contribution to a collective work, as a part of a motion picture or other audiovisual work, as a translation, as a supplementary work, as a compilation, as an instructional text, as a test, as answer material for a test, or as an atlas, if the parties expressly agree in a written instrument signed by them that the work shall be considered a work made for hire . . .

Multimedia Copyright Issues

Multimedia and digitization of film and music creates new opportunities for distortion. Multimedia offers the opportunity to reproduce a film like *Gone with the Wind* and replace the soundtrack with one created using rock or rap music. Some people would consider such a distortion a serious case of artistic blasphemy. An early multimedia conflict surfaced when films that were originally produced in black and white were colorized using computer algorithms. Issues involving claims of distortion will continue to be litigated because the boundaries are not well defined by case law and technological advances are offering new opportunities for distortion.

---

[19]Section 506(a) of the Copyright Act.

Joint Works

Under Section 101, a joint work is a work prepared by two or more authors with the intent that their contributions be merged into a complete, inseparable, unitary whole. Most of the time joint works are the result of consciously joint efforts of composers to produce a joint work. Each author must contribute to the development of the finished product and not just the idea. In these situations it is contemplated from the beginning that the result of the joint efforts will be a joint work, such as software for a video game, composed by more than one programmer.

There are also situations in which joint authorship can occur inadvertently, particularly in software development contracts. If a client collaborates with a consulting software programmer on the development of customized software, the result may be a joint work. If the work is deemed a joint work, then each joint author has the rights of a joint tenant. Any royalties earned by any author must be shared with the other joint author(s) and each author has the right to license the software to licensees. Of course, any issues of inadvertent authorship can be eliminated in advance by anticipating the problem and developing a contract that clearly lays out the rights of the parties.

Copyright Law and the Internet

The Internet provides access to a huge array of copyrighted material even though most of it is not registered with the Copyright Office. In addition to music (discussed above), in the near future both movies and books will be available on the Internet and potentially downloadable. A lot of copyrighted material that does appear on the Internet is being reproduced (uploaded and downloaded) illegally and would not qualify for the fair use defense under copyright law. For copyright owners with valuable copyrights, there is an important question regarding the means by which the wholesale reproduction of their works can be prevented without spending an excessive amount of money on enforcement. Suing individuals who are violating copyright laws will not improve the net worth of copyright owners. Even if statutory damages are sufficient to justify the suit, the defendants are unlikely to have sufficient assets to make the suit worthwhile.

ISPs: Bookstores or Publishers?

Copyright owners look to choke points as a means to collect royalties or enforce copyrights. One choke point is the ISPs. After all, if ISPs did not provide access to the Internet, the illegal uploaders and downloaders could not engage in wholesale infringing activity. It is important to note that there are a lot of ISPs in the world. AOL and Mindspring may have a large market share, but virtually all universities are ISPs for faculty and students. ISP liability for copyright infringement depends on whether ISPs are likened to a bookstore (no liability) or a publisher (liability for copyright infringement). From an economic point of view, it is efficient to allocate liability to parties that present the lowest costs of enforcement. If a bookstore was liable for every copyright infringement contained in the books it sold, it would have a very costly and virtually impossible task of supervising content for each book sold.

Publisher Liability

On the other hand, publishers may have a large portfolio of books, but they have contractual relationships with authors. To require a publisher to supervise the copyrightability of works they publish is not an unfair burden. After all, publishers are already supervising content for purposes of enhancing royalties. Publishers publish authors whom they think will sell well and make them money. To require publishers to scrutinize content for possible copyright violations is not a terrible financial burden, in part because publishers are experts at copyright law anyway. When someone infringes on their copyrights, they are the first to sue!

Bookstore Liability

Copyright violations do not require a showing of intent, though intent to infringe will enable a copyright owner to recover greater damages. Following the technical wording of Section 106 of the Copyright Act would seem to implicate ISPs for copyright violations of subscribers. After some initial false starts, courts recognized that ISPs were more like bookstores than publishers. If ISPs are to be liable for actions of subscribers, they would have to supervise activities of their subscribers. To use a bookstore analogy, imagine if bookstores were liable not only for copyright infringements imbedded in books, but also for infringements that took place postsale. If a customer buys a book, copies it, and then resells it under his or her own name, making bookstores liable for postsale activity would effectively shut them down. Copyright owners sued ISPs on essentially the same grounds, i.e., they were sued for the act of copying copyrighted materials by subscribers to the ISP and for subsequent distribution of that material.

In the following case, the court held that an ISP was not liable unless it knew or should have known that copyright infringements were taking place. The

authors' web pages, which are made available by our employer, NC State University, indicates that these web pages are neither "endorsed, sponsored, or provided" by NC State University. Obviously, based on the next case, NC State University believes that it is not liable for copyright violations that occur on faculty web pages as long as it does not know, or reasonably could know, of such violations. Similar disclaimers are found on the web pages of faculty at other universities.

Religious Technology Center v. *Netcom On-Line Communications Services, Inc.*
United States District Court for the Northern District of California
907 F.Supp. 1361; 1995

FACTS AND CASE BACKGROUND

This case concerns an issue of first impression regarding intellectual property rights in cyberspace. Specifically, this order addresses whether the operator of a computer bulletin board service ("BBS"), and the large Internet access provider that allows that BBS to reach the Internet, should be liable for copyright infringement committed by a subscriber of the BBS. In short, a former minister of the Church of Scientology, Dennis Erlich (defendant), posted copyrighted material on a bulletin board service (BBS). Mr. Erlich used the Usenet newsgroup called alt.relion.scientology (a.r.s) to post his critical views of the church. The BBS gained Internet access from Netcom's online services and the BBS was operated from the home of Thomas Klemesrud (defendant).

The plaintiff seeks to hold Netcom and all other parties involved in posting the material liable for the alleged copyright infringement.

OPINION: RONALD M. WHYTE, UNITED STATES DISTRICT JUDGE

1. DIRECT INFRINGEMENT

Infringement consists of the unauthorized exercise of one of the exclu-

sive rights of the copyright holder delineated in section 106. 17 U.S.C. § 501. Direct infringement does not require intent or any particular state of mind, although willfulness is relevant to the award of statutory damages.

* * *

Netcom cites cases holding that there is no contributory infringement by the lessors of premises that are later used for infringement unless the lessor had knowledge of the intended use at the time of the signing of the lease . . . . Here, Netcom not only leases space but also serves as an access provider, which includes the storage and transmission of information necessary to facilitate Erlich's postings to a.r.s. Unlike a landlord, Netcom retains some control over the use of its system. Thus, the relevant time frame for knowledge is not when Netcom entered into an agreement with Klemesrud. It should be when Netcom provided its services to allow Erlich to infringe plaintiffs' copyrights. It is undisputed that Netcom did not know that Erlich was infringing before it received notice from plaintiffs. Netcom points out that the alleged instances of infringement occurring on Netcom's system all happened prior to December 29,

1994, the date on which Netcom first received notice of plaintiffs' infringement claim against Erlich. Thus, there is no question of fact as to whether Netcom knew or should have known of Erlich's infringing activities that occurred more than 11 days before receipt of the December 28, 1994 letter.

However, the evidence reveals a question of fact as to whether Netcom knew or should have known that Erlich had infringed plaintiffs' copyrights following receipt of plaintiffs' letter. Because Netcom was arguably participating in Erlich's public distribution of plaintiffs' works, there is a genuine issue as to whether Netcom knew of any infringement by Erlich before it was too late to do anything about it. If plaintiffs can prove the knowledge element, Netcom will be liable for contributory infringement since its failure to simply cancel Erlich's infringing message and thereby stop an infringing copy from being distributed worldwide constitutes substantial participation in Erlich's public distribution of the message.

Netcom argues that its knowledge after receiving notice of Erlich's alleged infringing activities was too equivocal given the difficulty in assessing whether registrations are valid and whether use is fair. Although a mere unsupported allegation of infringement by a copyright owner may not automatically put a defendant on notice of infringing activity, Netcom's position that liability must be unequivocal is unsupportable. While perhaps the typical infringing activities of BBSs will involve copying software, where BBS operators are better equipped to judge infringement, the fact that this involves written works should not distinguish it. Where works contain copyright notices within them, as here, it is difficult to argue that a defendant did not know that the works were copyrighted. To require proof of valid registrations would be impractical and would perhaps take too long to verify, making it impossible for a copyright holder to protect his or her works in some cases, as works are automatically deleted less than two weeks after they are posted. The court is more persuaded by the argument that it is beyond the ability of a BBS operator to quickly and fairly determine when a use is not infringement where there is at least a colorable claim of fair use. Where a BBS operator cannot reasonably verify a claim of infringement, either because of a possible fair use defense, the lack of copyright notices on the copies, or the copyright holder's failure to provide the necessary documentation to show that

there is a likely infringement, the operator's lack of knowledge will be found reasonable and there will be no liability for contributory infringement for allowing the continued distribution of the works on its system.

* * *

The court is not persuaded by plaintiffs' argument that Netcom is directly liable for the copies that are made and stored on its computer. Where the infringing subscriber is clearly directly liable for the same act, it does not make sense to adopt a rule that could lead to the liability of countless parties whose role in the infringement is nothing more than setting up and operating a system that is necessary for the functioning of the Internet. Such a result is unnecessary as there is already a party directly liable for causing the copies to be made. Plaintiffs occasionally claim that they only seek to hold liable a party that refuses to delete infringing files after they have been warned. However, such liability cannot be based on a theory of direct infringement, where knowledge is irrelevant. The court does not find workable a theory of infringement that would hold the entire Internet liable for activities that cannot reasonably be deterred. Billions of bits of data flow through the Internet and are necessarily stored on servers throughout the network and it is thus practically impossible to screen out

infringing bits from noninfringing bits. Because the court cannot see any meaningful distinction (without regard to knowledge) between what Netcom did and what every other Usenet server does, the court finds that Netcom cannot be held liable for direct infringement.

* * *

IV. ORDER

The court denies Netcom's motion for summary judgment and Klemesrud's motion for judgment on the pleadings, as a triable issue of fact exists on the claim of contributory infringement. The court also gives plaintiffs 30 days leave in which to amend to state a claim for vicarious liability against defendant Klemesrud, if they can do so in good faith. Plaintiffs' application for a preliminary injunction against defendants Netcom and Klemesrud is denied.

QUESTIONS FOR REVIEW

1. Was the fact that the plaintiff informed Netcom of what it believed was a copyright infringement determinative of this case? Why not?
2. What more would the plaintiff have to have done in order to provide unambiguous evidence of a copyright infringement? Why did the court reject that solution?

Digital Millennium Copyright Act, Title II: Online Copyright Infringement Liability Limitation[s]

The fact that the *Netcom* case shielded ISPs from liability for copyright infringements did not resolve the legal problems as far as ISPs were concerned. Copyright owners could send e-mails or letters to ISPs apprising them of what they believed were copyright infringements, thus satisfying the notice requirement in

Netcom. ISPs could contact the allegedly infringing subscribers who could claim that, in fact, they were not infringing because of the fair use exception or some other defense. ISPs were then put in the position of having to judge whenever there was a claim made to them that a copyright infringement had occurred. Title II of the 1998 DMCA addresses possible legal liability of ISPs and other transactions and transactors on the Internet by creating a number of safe harbors.[20] In this context, a "safe harbor" completely bars a suit for monetary damage as long as a party follows the procedures called for in the DMCA.

E-mails and other Transmissions

Title II of the DMCA adds a new Section 512 to the Copyright Act. Under the DMCA, an ISP is not liable for contributory or vicarious infringement when it is simply performing mechanical routing tasks which allow subscribers to transmit files and messages. Section 512(a) of the DMCA labels this transaction a limitation of copyright liability for "transitory communications." The essence of this limitation is that ISPs are not liable for copyright infringements that may be present in e-mails and other transmitted files as long as the ISP does not have a say in the initiation of the message, the content of the message, and the addressee(s) of the message. This of course is the pigeon hole that Napster tried unsuccessfully to fit into.

Caching

It is common for ISPs to maintain copies of material that have been provided online by someone other than the ISP. ISPs maintain copies of this material rather than going to the original source because it enables ISPs to conserve bandwidth and thus provide more and faster service to subscribers. Caching typically involves subscriber visits to websites of copyright owners. The user visits a website, leaves the site, and then decides to return to the site. If users return to the site in a relatively short period of time, they are not really returning to the site but, rather, to a duplicate copy of the site that has been "cached" by the ISP. Problems arise with caching when the website owner has posted time-sensitive advertising and has installed "counting" software that counts "hits" at the site. Since a copy of the website has been cached, visitors to the site may not see the changed, time-sensitive advertising and their return visit will not be counted as a site "hit."

Technically, ISPs are violating copyright laws by making copies of copyrighted material owned by website owners. Section 512(b) enables ISPs to escape liability if they follow certain procedures. Basically the problem of time-sensitive advertising becoming stale is resolvable if the ISP "refreshes" the cached material

with new material that is up to date. Title II of the DMCA (Section 512(b)) calls for the ISP to refresh the cached material "in accordance with a generally accepted industry data communication protocol."[21] Also the ISP must remove any material that the website owner indicates is out of date and must not interfere in any way with software that counts visitors to the website. As long as an ISP follows these procedures, it will not be liable for copyright infringement to website owners for caching.

Liability for Posting Infringing Material

Without knowledge of possible infringement, ISPs are not liable for posting material that infringes. On the other hand, if an ISP receives financial compensation for infringing actions of a subscriber, it will be liable as a vicarious infringer. If ISPs are not in either of the polar extreme positions posed above, then their liability for posting allegedly infringing material depends in part on their compliance with the DMCA.[22] ISPs are not placed in the category of publisher by the DMCA. However, if ISPs are informed by a copyright owner that they are storing or posting material from a subscriber that the copyright owner alleges infringes their copyrights, then the ISP has several procedures that it must follow to escape liability (qualify for the safe harbor):

1. If the ISP knows the material stored is infringing, then it must take steps to expeditiously remove the material from its server.

2. If the ISP does not know for sure that the material stored is infringing, but receives notice from the copyright owner that:
   a. Identifies the copyright material the owner alleges has been infringed,
   b. Identifies the location of the allegedly infringing material, and
   c. States that the copyright owner in good faith believes the material infringes its copyright, then

the ISP can remove the allegedly infringing material without liability to the subscriber. If the subscriber

---

[20]Title II technically adds a new Section 512 to the Copyright Act.

[21]U.S. Copyright Office Summary, "The Digital Millennium Copyright Act of 1998," December 1998.
[22]The DMCA also states that failure to comply with its designated safe harbors does not mean that the ISP is liable for copyright infringement. Failure to comply with the DMCA just places the ISP in the position they occupied after the *Netcom* decision.

objects to the removal, then the ISP must inform the copyright owner that it is going to reinstate the subscriber's materials unless the copyright owner files suit to obtain a court order against the subscriber's actions. The copyright owner has 10 to 14 days to file suit against the subscriber who has posted the allegedly infringing material, or else the ISP can return the subscriber's material to its accessible presence on the Internet.

Link Law

The power of the Internet allows a browser to move from site to related site by hyperlinks which provide search efficiency that vastly outstrips other means of gaining information or researching a subject. From a legal standpoint the important issue is whether a hyperlinker (the site that provides a link to another site) can be liable for copyright violations by linking to another website. Note that trademark issues may also be involved in linking sites.

It could be argued that by placing a link to another website that the hyperlinker reproduces copyrighted software and displays that are not authorized by the linked website. On the other hand, websites are on the Internet to attract attention. Visitors to a website have implied consent to reproduce what is on the website when they visit the site. Probably the only legal liability for a link to another site that does not infringe on copyrights of a third party occurs when the linked website indicates that it does not authorize links from other websites. In those cases, implied consent to reproduce is negated by clear language to that effect.

Responsibility for Copyright Infringements of a Hyperlinked Site

What if the hyperlinked site is infringing copyrights of a third party? Is the linking site liable to a third party copyright owner as a contributory infringer? This issue is reminiscent of the liability of ISPs for copyright infringement. Section 512(d) of the DMCA "relates to hyperlinks, online directories, search engines and the like."[23] Section 512(d) absolves linkers of liability for linking to sites that infringe the copyrights of third parties as long as the linker does not have *knowledge* of the infringements. If the linker is apprised of copyright infringements, then the same provisions that

applied to ISPs apply to linkers. The linker must eliminate the link or block access to the allegedly infringing website, but must inform the website, which can then contest the action. Again, since there is a possibility that third-party copyright owners may erroneously or fraudulently make such claims, they (the third-party copyright owners) are required to take their claims of copyright infringement to court against the linked site, or the linker is entitled to reinstate the link.

More Link Issues

Deep Linking

Of course, linkers may have less than benign motives when linking their visitors to another website. It may be that linkers enable visitors to their site to visit the linked site in ways that the visitors could not if they were to go directly to the linked website. Suppose the linked website is a travel agency that derives considerable advertising revenue from cross-marketing partners based on the number of visitors to various pages in their website. Suppose that visitors to the travel website seeking low airfares had to click through three web pages that had banners or advertisements of cross-marketing partners of the website. In order to finally get access to the low airfares, website visitors to the travel website had to visit several pages that contained banners for vacation clothiers and American Express travelers checks? Suppose, however, that the linking website enables visitors to its site to go directly to the page on the website of the travel agency that offers the low airfares, effectively bypassing the clothing and traveler check banners. This practice is called "deep linking."

Derivative Works

Alternatively, the linker may alter what visitors to its website see when they linked to another website. If visitors to the linking site were exposed to the linked site by a link that deleted or altered advertisements or banners on their view of the linked site, it could be argued that the altered exposure of the linked site is a derivative work. Of course, the right to make derivative works is exclusively held by the copyright owner of the linked website. In effect, the way linkers channel visitors to the linked website could diminish the commercial value of the linked site relative to a direct visit.

Many linking issues have yet to be addressed by the courts and are beyond the scope of the DMCA. If linking exposes visitors to copyrighted material

[23]U.S. Copyright Office Summary, "The Digital Millennium Copyright Act of 1998," December 1998.

owned by another, usually the links are unauthorized, but generally legal, under the principles of fair use. If the links, however, diminish the value of the linked website or foreclose revenue, then the fair use arguments lose their persuasiveness. Much link law will probably be made on a case-by-case basis as courts analogize what the links are doing in the physical world. If the linker is enabling its visitors to get in the back door of a movie without paying, then the fair use defense would seem to be unavailable. If the linker makes the linked site more valuable, then their maneuvering of website visitors has more justification.

Concluding Thoughts about Copyright Law and the Internet

Virtually everything that appears on the Internet is copyrighted. Virtually everything that appears on the Internet is also regularly uploaded and downloaded without obtaining permission from copyright owners, generally without legal repercussions. That is not to say, of course, that there are no suits by copyright owners against unauthorized reproductions of copyrighted works through the Internet, but litigation is a relative rarity and that is so for good reasons. Much of the downloading would qualify for the fair use exception under the Copyright Act, but much of it would not. So, a large volume of the downloading that takes place is illegal, but involves material for which the stakes are so low that it does not pay copyright owners to pursue the illegal copying that takes place. It is also notable that much of the unauthorized downloading of copyrighted materials takes place innocently; the downloaders may not even be aware of the copyright laws that are being violated.

The rise of the popularity of the Internet has been accompanied by several acts of Congress that are designed to deal with wholesale violations of copyright laws. The interface between copyright law enforcement and the music industry is particularly intense because advances in technology have made pirating copyrighted songs particularly easy. At the time of this writing, major musical groups are losing sizeable flows of royalties because websites are facilitating "sharing" among members that results in perfect digital copies of the same CDs that are available at record stores. Just around the corner, it can be anticipated that movies and other copyrighted material will provide a battleground over the enforcement of copyright law on the Internet.

TRADEMARK LAW

The basic role of a trademark is to identify the source of a product. Consumers are concerned about the quality of goods and, by relying on trademarks, their inspection and search costs can be reduced. When consumers develop trust in a trademarked product, they are thereafter freed from incurring the search and inspection costs they would face if there were no trademarks. The function of trademark law is to prevent consumer confusion by prohibiting sellers from selling their products using trademarks that are **confusingly similar** to another's trademark. By preventing confusingly similar trademarks, U.S. trademark law protects customer *goodwill* built up by companies that work hard to preserve their reputation for quality. Federal trademark law is administered under the Lanham Act, which was originally passed in 1946 and has been amended several times since then.

Trademarks are issued by both state and federal authorities. Federal trademarks are by far more important, but state trademarks convey important legal advantages to holders in many cases. Trademarks are used for tangible, physical goods while *service marks* are used for firms that perform services, including restaurants and consulting firms. According to the Lanham Act, "a trademark includes any word, name, symbol, or device, or any combination thereof", used by a person "to identify his or her goods, including a unique product, from those manufactured or sold by others and to indicate the source of the goods, even if that source is unknown."[24] The Lanham Act definition of *service mark* is similar to that of a trademark. Section 1127: **Construction and Definitions,** indicates that a service mark is any "word, name," etc., that is used "to identify and distinguish the services of one person, including a unique service, from the service of others and to indicate the source of the service, if the source is unknown."

Broadening the Scope of Marks Eligible for Receiving a Trademark

Even though the Lanham Act definition of trademark mentions "word, name, symbol, or device", in recent years, companies have tried with some success to trademark colors, sounds, and smells. The trend among

[24]Section 1127 of the Lanham Act. Constructions and Definitions.

Frequently Asked Questions: Trademarks

Q: Is a federal registration valid outside the United States?

A: No. Certain countries, however, do recognize a United States registration as a basis for registering the mark in those countries. Many countries maintain a register of trademarks. The laws of each country regarding registration must be consulted.

Q: Do I have to be a U.S. citizen to obtain a federal registration?

A: No. However, an applicant's citizenship must be set forth in the record. If an applicant is not a citizen of any country, then a statement to that effect is sufficient. If an applicant has dual citizenship, then the applicant must choose which citizenship will be printed in the Official Gazette and on the certificate of registration.

Source: U.S. PTO; http://www.uspto.gov/web/offices/tac/tmfaq.htm#Basic002.

"What are the benefits of federal trademark registration?"

1. Constructive notice nationwide of the trademark owner's claim.
2. Evidence of ownership of the trademark.
3. Jurisdiction of federal courts may be invoked.
4. Registration can be used as a basis for obtaining registration in foreign countries.
5. Registration may be filed with U.S. Customs Service to prevent importation of infringing foreign goods.

Source: U.S. PTO; http://www.uspto.gov/web/offices/tac/tmfaq.htm#Basic002.

---

judicial opinions has been to broaden the scope of what can be trademarked. On the other hand, if the proposed mark is in any way functional, it cannot be trademarked. The Nike Swirl is legitimately trademarked, but if that swirl appears on the bottom of sneakers and its presence enables athletes to better pivot, then the swirl design could be copied by other shoe companies.

Federal Registration

Registration Formalities

Federal registration of a trademark provides *constructive* notice to other companies that the mark has already been taken. Actual notice can be provided by using the ® symbol on the product or advertising materials. Damages in successful infringement suits are greater if the defendant knew he was infringing, but proceeded with his willful infringement even so. Hence, it makes sense for a company that has a registered trademark to provide notice using the ® symbol.

Registration of a trademark begins with an application, based on interstate sales, or a bonafide

intention to sell in interstate commerce within six months. Applications are submitted to the Patent and Trademark Office (PTO) and assigned to an examiner. The trademark examiner will investigate prior registrations at the PTO that are still in force with an eye toward considering whether the public will be confused by similarities between the applicant's proposed mark and any already registered mark. In the past, a number of firms located in Washington D.C. specialized in conducting trademark searches so that applicants would not waste their time applying for marks that were already in use, or very similar to marks already in force. In recent years, the PTO has developed online search engines that enable firms to conduct preliminary trademark searches without specialized assistance.[25] However, patent applicants should be mindful that exclusive reliance on the PTO's search engines for trademarks is not wise at this time and

---

[25]The search capabilities are very user friendly. Literally users need only submit a word to see if it is a registered trademark. Online searches can be conducted at: http://www.uspto.gov/web/offices/tac/doc/gsmanual/search.html.

that contacting attorneys who specialize in trademarks is still prudent.[26]

Duration of Trademarks and Incontestability

The duration of a trademark is potentially infinite, subject to requirements to pay fees required by the PTO. Initially, a trademark registration lasts for 10 years with a requirement to pay fees between the fifth and sixth years after the trademark is registered. After the fifth year, a mark becomes *incontestable,* which is a misnomer because most potential challenges to the validity of the trademark survive the period after incontestability takes place. For example, if a mark becomes generic (as discussed below) after five years, its validity can be challenged in a subsequent infringement suit. Other potential bases for challenging the validity of a trademark are not lost after five years. A trademark can be lost through nonpayment of fees to the PTO or through nonuse (abandonment).

PTO Decisions, Appeals, and Interferences

As with patent law, there are internal and external appeals procedures if applicants for a trademark or other interested parties disagree with officials of the PTO. Internally, the trademark examiner usually renders a decision within three months of application submission, but amendments are common. A final decision usually occurs within 6 to 18 months after submission. If the examiner turns down the application for a trademark, applicants can appeal to the Trademark Trial and Appeal Board and, if unsuccessful, to the federal courts. If a decision of the Board is appealed, the appeal goes to the Court of Appeals for the Federal Circuit (CAFC).

If the decision of the examiner is positive, the mark is published in the Official Gazette of the PTO, during which time anyone prospectively damaged by federal registration of the trademark can come forth.[27] Those that challenge the soon-to-be-registered trademark file what is known as an "opposition". Since the focus of PTO examiners is on *prior registrations of trademarks by the PTO,* prior, but unregistered, users of the mark or a confusingly similar mark can petition the PTO for priority in the areas where they currently sell the product with the unregistered trademark. Priority in trademark law is based on use, not on the time of filing for registration. If a user of a mark, which is subsequently registered by the PTO to another party, can establish prior use, that party is

entitled to continue selling the trademarked product in its geographic area and line of commerce. Other grounds for an opposition to the registration of a trademark that can be filed by third parties are discussed below.

What Can and Cannot be Registered

A registered trademark carries with it prima facie evidence of validity, which means that challengers, often defendants in trademark infringement suits, have the burden of showing that the "word, name, symbol, or device" adopted by the plaintiff is not eligible to receive a trademark. According to Section 1052 of the Lanham Act, **"No trademark by which the goods of the applicant may be distinguished from the goods of others shall be refused registration on the principal register on account of its nature unless it—. . . ,"** after which the statute lists a number of disqualifying categories as discussed immediately below. The first disqualifying condition occurs when the mark is deemed *generic.*

Generic Marks

Trademarks are supposed to identify the source of a product so that consumer search costs are reduced. If, instead, the mark refers to a class of products, rather than to the products of a particular seller, trademark registration is not performing its economic function. For most people "aspirin" refers to a class of over-the-counter pain relievers that are usually dispensed as little white pills. There are a number of sellers of aspirin and if one of them were able to use "aspirin" as a trademark, the rest would be prevented from describing their products in that manner. To allow generic marks to be registered as trademarks would (1) not identify a particular brand or seller of aspirin and (2) would give monopoly-like advantages to the seller that was able to use that mark to describe its product.

Many generic descriptions of products began as legitimate trademarks. Trampolines, shuttles, and cellophane were all originally trademarked products, but later became generic labels. Both Sanka and Xerox are in danger of becoming generic, i.e., descriptive of a class of goods rather than identifying individual sellers. Firms whose trademarks are possibly dying of "genericide" can spend large sums of money to save their marks from loss of trademark status. Xerox® has spent heavily on advertisements reminding the public, that "there are two R's in the trademark, Xerox®".

---

[26]The PTO makes this same point, namely, that their search engines are not a substitute for attorneys skilled in trademark law.
[27]Section 1063 of the Lanham Act.

A paradox frequently encountered in law is that legal protections and the economic benefits they provide, which are designed to foster product development, can be lost if the product becomes too successful. Copyrighted software that becomes too successful can establish an industry standard and, as a consequence, lose copyright protection for the most successful portions of the product (this issue is discussed extensively in Chapter 10). A very successful product also can become a target for antitrust authorities, as Microsoft has found out. Parallel phenomena occur in trademark law. If a trademark becomes too successful, and the public consequently uses the term to refer to a whole class of goods rather than just to the goods of a particular seller, the trademark can be declared *generic* in a trademark infringement suit. The Parker Brothers Company (owned by General Mills) learned this lesson the hard way when it sued the makers of "Anti-Monopoly" for infringement of its popular board game "Monopoly," and the defendants challenged the validity of the Parker Brothers' trademark in the word, Monopoly.[28] As with the other forms of IP law (patent and copyright), the validity of the mark typically becomes an issue during an infringement suit when the defendant launches an affirmative defense that the mark is generic.

---

[28]*Anti-Monopoly, Inc.* v. *General Mills Fun Group,* 684 F.2d 1316 (1983).

Ale House Management, Inc. v. *Raleigh Ale House, Inc.*
United States Court of Appeals for the Fourth Circuit
205 F.3d 137; 2000 U.S.

FACTS AND CASE BACKGROUND

The plaintiffs, Ale House Management (AHM), have been serving food and ale since 1988 and have built 21 Ale Houses in various cities in Florida. In each city where an AHM Ale House resides the Ale House is named for that city. For example, the AHM Ale House in Orlando is called the Orlando Ale House. AHM filed suit against the Raleigh Ale House for infringement based on the following three marks: (1) the words "ale house," (2) both the exterior and interior appearances of its facilities, and (3) the copyright of its floor plan drawings. The district court rejected Ale House Management's claims and granted Raleigh Ale House summary judgment.

OPINION: NIEMEYER, CIRCUIT JUDGE

Addressing first AHM's claim to exclusive use of the words "ale house," we begin by noting that AHM has not registered "ale house." Nevertheless, it may still seek protection under the Lanham Act, which also protects unregistered marks. To ascertain whether a mark is protected, we must determine whether it is (1) generic, (2) descriptive, (3) suggestive, or (4) arbitrary or fanciful. A generic mark "refers to the genus or class of which a particular product is a member," and such a mark "can never be protected." In this case, because Raleigh Ale House suggests that the term "ale house" is generic and AHM has not registered it, AHM bears the burden of establishing that it is not generic.

Acknowledging that "ale house" may be generic in some applications—such as in reference to a neighborhood English pub—AHM argues that it is not generic in reference to a facility that serves both food and beer, particularly when it has an extensive food menu. AHM has failed, however, to present any evidence that "ale house" does not refer to institutions that serve both food and beer. What it did provide was evidence that AHM facilities are primarily large restaurants that also serve beer and that food sales generate the majority of their revenue.

On the other hand, Raleigh Ale House presented extensive evidence, including citations to newspapers, dictionaries, books, and other publications, that the term "ale house" is generic, referring to several types of facilities.

* * *

AHM has presented no evidence suggesting that "ale house" is not a generic term that can refer to institutions serving both food and alcohol. Indeed, it conceded at oral argument that other Florida food-and-drink facilities incorporate "ale house" in their names. The fact that the facilities referred to by Raleigh Ale House and the various public data do not offer the same menu as AHM and that some focus more extensively on beer and ale does not refute the proposition that "ale house" refers to a "genus or class" of facilities that serve both food and drink.

AHM's response to Raleigh Ale House's unrebutted evidence is that it constitutes inadmissible hearsay, an argument that AHM did not assert below. But, to the extent that

Raleigh Ale House relied on the fact that "ale house" was used or "listed" in public advertising or other media, the evidence was not presented for its truth but for the fact that it was so listed.

In short, we conclude that AHM has no protectable interest in the words "ale house." They are generic words for a facility that serves beer and ale, with or without food, just as are other similar terms such as "bar," "lounge," "pub," "saloon," or "tavern." All serve alcohol alone or both food and alcohol.

Although AHM devotes less attention to its trade dress argument, it nevertheless maintains that Raleigh Ale House violated AHM's rights in its trade dress, both as to the exterior and interior appearance of its facilities. At oral argument, however, when AHM was confronted with the observation that the exterior appearances of its various facilities differed significantly in shape, size, style, color, and materials, AHM appeared to abandon its claim with respect to the exterior and to press only its claim that it had a proprietary interest in the appearance of the interior of its facilities, including its service.

As with generic trade names, the trademark laws do not protect a generic trade dress. Trade dress should be considered generic if "well-known" or "common," "a mere refinement of a commonly-adopted and well-known form of ornamentation," or a "common basic shape or design," even if it has "not before been refined in precisely the same way."

* * *

III

A casual comparison between AHM's various architectural floor plans and Raleigh Ale House's floor plans shows, at most, the imitation of an idea or a concept, but not a copying of the plans themselves. Raleigh Ale House's floor plans are not in the same dimensions or proportions as any of those presented by AHM.

* * *

For the reasons given, the judgment of the district court is AFFIRMED.

QUESTIONS FOR REVIEW

1. Does this opinion mean that the term "ale house" cannot be part of a valid, registered trademark?
2. What other words that are basically synonyms for ale house does the court suggest are also unavailable for trademark registration? Pick a product, any product. Name five ways of describing the product that are so generic that the words could not be trademarked.

"Where can I conduct a trademark search?"

"**S**earches may be conducted on-line at http://www.uspto.gov/tmdb/index.html, or by visiting the Trademark Public Search Library, between 8:00 a.m. and 5:30 p.m. at 2900 Crystal Drive, 2nd Floor, Arlington, Virginia 22202. Use of the Public Search Library is free to the public. Also, certain information may be searched at a Patent and Trademark Depository Library. These libraries have CD-ROMS containing the database of registered and pending marks. (However, the CD-ROMS do not contain images of the design marks.)"

Source: U.S. PTO; Frequently Asked Questions at http://www.uspto.gov/web/offices/tac/tmfaq.htm#Search004.

Other Marks That Are not Eligible for Registration

Other disqualifying conditions are discussed in the order that they occur in Section 1052 of the Lanham Act. Essentially any mark that distinguishes the applicant's mark from others is qualified to be registered, except if it:

(a) Consists of scandalous or immoral matter; or matter which may disparage or falsely suggest a connection with persons, living or dead, institutions, beliefs, or national symbols, or bring them into contempt or disrepute.

Pornography and Celebrity

In general, Congress has prohibited the PTO from aiding pornographers through the federal registration of sex-related products. Under this prohibition, "Old Glory" was denied registration for a condom vendor, though more recently the PTO, perhaps reflecting the times, has allowed registration of words or phrases that were previously considered risqué, such as "Bad Ass". Congress also has prohibited the PTO from registering trademarks based on *unconsented*-to connections with celebrities, national symbols, or other public "icons" that, in fact, are not accurate or tend to tarnish the name of the icon.

> (b) Consists of or comprises the flag or coat of arms or other insignia of the United States, or of any State or municipality, or of any foreign nation, or any simulation thereof.

Flags

Congress has decided that flags within the United States, no matter whether federal, state, or local, are not suitable for trademark registration. Likewise, flags of foreign countries cannot be registered with the PTO.

> (c) Consists of or comprises a name, portrait, or signature identifying a particular living individual except by his written consent, or the name, signature, or portrait of a deceased President of the United States during the life of his widow, if any, except by written consent of the widow.

Living Persons and Past Presidents

At common law it is considered an invasion of privacy to make commercial use of a person's name or likeness without their consent. This subsection adds a statutory prohibition to that practice unless the celebrity has consented in writing to the use of his or her name as a trademark. The same requirements apply to a living ex-President or a deceased President, while his widow is living.

> (d) Consists of or comprises a mark which so resembles a mark registered in the Patent and Trademark Office, a mark or trade name previously used in the United States by another and not abandoned, as to be likely, when used on or in connection with the goods of the applicant, to cause confusion, or to cause mistake, or to deceive: Provided, That if the Commissioner determines that confusion, mistake, or deception is not likely to result from the continued use by more than one person of the same or similar marks under conditions and limitations as to the mode or place of use of the marks or the goods on or in connection with which such marks are used, concurrent registrations may be issued to such marks or the good when they have become

entitled to use such marks as a result of their concurrent lawful use in commerce prior to . . .

Confusingly Similar to Previously Registered Marks

The PTO must consider whether a proposed mark is so similar to previously registered marks that it is likely to cause confusion, mistake, or deception. The criterion used by the PTO is exactly the same that courts use in infringement suits, namely, *confusion of the public*. In making a determination concerning possible confusion of the public, the PTO (like a court) is not bound by what the "majority" thinks. The PTO will deny registration of a mark that so resembles a non-abandoned mark, previously registered, that a **substantial number** of the public is likely to be confused. There are no hard and fast rules concerning whether a proposed mark too closely resembles a previously registered mark, resulting in confusion among the public. At trial, both sides (the trademark registrant and the alleged infringer) often bring in expert witnesses, usually marketing research professors or statisticians, to assist juries in making that factual determination. Demonstrations of confusion among the public, or lack thereof, are provided by results of surveys, time-series analysis of purchasing habits, and focus groups. The trademark owner is not obligated to show that a majority of the public was confused, just a substantial number.

In cyberspace the principles are the same for determining whether a trademark infringement has taken place. In the following case the Ninth Circuit Court of Appeals grapples with consumer confusion in cyberspace.

Proposed marks that are approved by a PTO trademark examiner are published in the Official Gazette of the PTO. Firms that have valuable trademarks often have an employee or a retained attorney routinely examine the Official Gazette for marks that may cause confusion. As discussed above, under Section 1063 owners of registered marks have 30 days after the examiner makes a decision to register a mark in order to oppose registration.

> (e) Consists of a mark which, (1) when used on or in connection with the goods of the applicant is merely descriptive or deceptively misdescriptive of them, or (2) when used on or in connection with the goods of the applicant is primarily geographically descriptive or deceptively misdescriptive of them. . . .

Brookfield Communications, Inc. v. *West Coast Entertainment Corporation*
United States Court of Appeals for the Ninth Circuit
174 F.3d 1036; 1999 U.S.

FACTS AND CASE BACKGROUND

The focus of this case is the application of federal trademark law and unfair competition laws in relation to cyberspace. The plaintiff, Brookfield (holder of the trademark "movie buff"), seeks an injunction to prohibit the defendant from using the trademarked phrase in their domain name and in the metatag for the website. West Coast Entertainment registered the domain name "moviebuff.com," so when Brookfield found the domain taken, they registered "moviebuffonline.com." Brookfield uses the website to sell its computer software called "MovieBuff." West Coast Entertainment is one of the largest video rental stores and it intended to use the website "moviebuff.com" to provide "inter alia", a searchable entertainment database similar to "MovieBuff" software.

OPINION: O'SCANNLAIN, CIRCUIT JUDGE
IV

To resolve whether West Coast's use of "moviebuff.com" constitutes trademark infringement or unfair competition, we must first determine whether Brookfield has a valid, protectable trademark interest in the "MovieBuff" mark. Brookfield's registration of the mark on the Principal Register in the Patent and Trademark Office constitutes prima facie evidence of the validity of the registered mark and of Brookfield's exclusive right to use the mark on the goods and services specified in the registration. Nevertheless, West Coast can rebut this presumption by showing that it used the mark in commerce first, since a fundamental tenet of trademark law is that owner-ship of an inherently distinctive mark such as "MovieBuff" is governed by priority of use.

* * *

V

Establishing seniority, however, is only half the battle. Brookfield must also show that the public is likely to be somehow confused about the source or sponsorship of West Coast's "moviebuff.com" website—and somehow to associate that site with Brookfield. The Supreme Court has described "the basic objectives of trademark law" as follows: "trademark law, by preventing others from copying a source-identifying mark, 'reduces the customer's costs of shopping and making purchasing decisions,' for it quickly and easily assures a potential customer that this item—the item with this mark—is made by the same producer as other similarly marked items that he or she liked (or disliked) in the past. At the same time, the law helps assure a producer that it (and not an imitating competitor) will reap the financial, reputation-related rewards associated with a desirable product."

* * *

The district court classified West Coast and Brookfield as non-competitors largely on the basis that Brookfield is primarily an information provider while West Coast primarily rents and sells videotapes. It noted that West Coast's website is used more by the somewhat curious video consumer who wants general movie information, while entertainment industry professionals, aspiring entertainment executives and professionals, and highly focused movie-goers are more likely to need or to want the more detailed information provided by "MovieBuff." This analysis, however, overemphasizes differences in principal lines of business, as we have previously instructed that "the relatedness of each company's prime directive isn't relevant." Instead, the focus is on whether the consuming public is likely somehow to associate West Coast's products with Brookfield. Here, both companies offer products and services relating to the entertainment industry generally, and their principal lines of business both relate to movies specifically and are not as different as guns and toys. Thus, Brookfield and West Coast are not properly characterized as non-competitors.

Not only are they not non-competitors, the competitive proximity of their products is actually quite high. Just as Brookfield's "MovieBuff" is a searchable database with detailed information on films, West Coast's website features a similar searchable database, which Brookfield points out is licensed from a direct competitor of Brookfield. Undeniably then, the products are used for similar purposes. "The rights of the owner of a registered trademark . . . extend to any goods related in the minds of consumers." The relatedness is further evidenced by the fact that the two companies compete for the patronage of an overlapping audience. The use of similar marks to offer similar products accordingly weighs heavily in favor of likelihood of confusion.

In addition to the relatedness of products, West Coast and Brookfield both utilize the Web as a marketing and advertising facility, a factor that courts have consistently recognized as exacerbating the likelihood of confusion. Both companies, apparently recognizing the rapidly growing importance of Web commerce, are maneuvering to attract customers via the Web. Not only do they compete for the patronage of an overlapping audience on the Web, both "MovieBuff" and "moviebuff.com" are utilized in conjunction with Web-based products.

Given the virtual identity of "moviebuff.com" and "MovieBuff," the relatedness of the products and services accompanied by those marks, and the companies' simultaneous use of the Web as a marketing and advertising tool, many forms of consumer confusion are likely to result. People surfing the Web for information on "MovieBuff" may confuse "MovieBuff" with the searchable entertainment database at "moviebuff.com" and simply assume that they have reached Brookfield's website. In the Internet context, in particular, entering a website takes little effort—usually one click from a linked site or a search engine's list; thus, Web surfers are more likely to be confused as to the ownership of a website than traditional patrons of a brick-and-mortar store would be of a store's ownership. Alternatively, they may incorrectly believe that West Coast licensed "MovieBuff" from Brookfield, or that Brookfield otherwise sponsored West Coast's database. Other consumers may simply believe that West Coast bought out Brookfield or that they are related companies.

* * *

The district court apparently assumed that likelihood of confusion exists only when consumers are confused as to the source of a product they actually purchase. It is, however, well established that the Lanham Act protects against the many other forms of confusion that we have outlined.

* * *

Here, we must determine whether West Coast can use "MovieBuff" or "moviebuff.com" in the metatags of its website at "westcoastvideo.com" or at any other domain address *other than* "moviebuff.com" (which we have determined that West Coast may not use).

* * *

We agree that West Coast can legitimately use an appropriate descriptive term in its metatags. But "MovieBuff" is not such a descriptive term. Even though it differs from "Movie Buff" by only a single space, that difference is pivotal. The term "Movie Buff" is a descriptive term, which is routinely used in the English language to describe a movie devotee. "MovieBuff" is not. The term "MovieBuff" is not in the dictionary. Nor has that term been used in any published federal or state court opinion. In light of the fact that it is not a word in the English language, when the term "MovieBuff" *is* employed, it is used to refer to Brookfield's products and services, rather than to mean "motion picture enthusiast." The proper term for the "motion picture enthusiast" is "Movie Buff," which West Coast certainly *can* use. It cannot, however, omit the space.

VII

As we have seen, registration of a domain name for a website does not trump long-established principles of trademark law. When a firm uses a competitor's trademark in the domain name of its website, users are likely to be confused as to its source or sponsorship. Similarly, using a competitor's trademark in the metatags of such website is likely to cause what we have described as initial interest confusion. These forms of confusion are exactly what the trademark laws are designed to prevent.

Accordingly, we reverse and remand this case to the district court with instructions to enter a preliminary injunction in favor of Brookfield in accordance with this opinion.

Reversed and Remanded.

QUESTIONS FOR REVIEW

1. What was the nature of the consumer confusion that the court was concerned about in this case? Do trademark owners and domain owners have to be competitors for there to be consumer confusion about trademarks and domain names?

2. Beside confusion over trademarks, what other confusion was the court concerned about? Can a firm use a metatag to describe their product when it is the trademark of another firm?

Merely Descriptive and Misdescriptive Marks

A mark that is *merely descriptive* suffers some of the same problems that a generic mark does, namely that it does not identify the source of the good but, rather, simply describes what a product does. Such a mark could convey monopoly-like advantages to the registrant. Consider the term "car starter" as a proposed mark for an automobile battery. The term merely describes in a rather comprehensive way what an automobile battery does. If this term is allowed to be registered, then other sellers of automobile batteries might be hard pressed to describe what use their products have. If one description of an automobile battery is allowed to be registered, then others should be also. In a short period of time, all but a few sellers of car batteries could be prevented from describing what their products do without violating another seller's trademark. If merely descriptive terms are eligible for registration, "body warmer" could be registered as a trademark for coats and "foot protector" for socks. These examples illustrate why a trademark must be more than merely descriptive.

As with most government agencies, the PTO has an interest in preventing fraud. Marks that are deceptively misdescriptive or geographically misdescriptive cannot be registered if there is substantial evidence of deception. A trademark titled "DieselPower" used to sell trucks that are not, in fact, diesel powered would be deceptively misdescriptive. Potatoes grown in Maine but trademarked "Idaho Potatoes" would be geographically misdescriptive.

Fanciful and Suggestive Marks

The concept underlying the existence and use of trademarks is that a trademark (the mark) becomes "distinctive" in the sense that it acquires *secondary* meaning that is important and valuable to the owner(s) of the mark. The **strongest** marks are those that are *fanciful,* having no direct functional or descriptive relationship with the product that is subject to the trademark. Many of these marks make use of distinctive lettering that are well known by the public, not for their literal meaning, but for the products they stand for. The Minnesota Mining and Manufacturing Company is better known for its trademarked 3M® products. America Online and AT&T have trademarks that are combinations of letter-like symbols and distinctive designs that are easily recognizable. None of the foregoing trademarks in any way describe qualities of the products that are sold by these companies.

The PTO does allow for registration of trademarks that are *suggestive* of the qualities of a product. Cool Whip® is a registered trademark of the Kraft® Food Company for a whipped cream product that is refrigerated. Cool Whip® **suggests** the qualities of the product, but it surely has acquired secondary meaning as a registered trademark. Duracell® is another trademark that is suggestive but

not *merely descriptive* of the underlying product. The message that this battery manufacturer/seller is trying to convey is, quite obviously, that its batteries (which are in fact cells) are **durable** and long lived. Coca-Cola® was once challenged as being merely descriptive and then, later, as being misdescriptive as it no longer contained cocaine from coca plants that had been used previously to make the product. Both challenges failed.

The Circular Logic of Trademarks and the Supplemental Register

Trademark law can be described as a continuum or even a circle. The strongest marks are fanciful marks that do not describe product qualities at all. Suggestive marks are weaker but can acquire secondary meaning or distinctiveness as in the cases discussed immediately above (Cool Whip® and Duracell®). Descriptive marks are generally considered weak marks but can acquire secondary meaning. Descriptive marks are typically registered on the Supplemental Register, which gives the registrant fewer rights. If the mark is registered on the Supplemental Register, that registration does not constitute **constructive notice** so that requested injunctions against subsequent users are not automatic.

On the other hand, registrants on the Supplemental Register are entitled to use the ® symbol to provide actual notice to potential infringers. Furthermore, after five years, marks on the Supplemental Register are generally transferred to the Principal Register at which time the mark is entitled to all rights provided by registration. If a mark is *merely descriptive,* it is not considered eligible for registration. A fanciful mark that becomes too strong, however, can become a generic term for a class of products and thus lose trademark registration when challenged in a trademark suit. In such a situation, the generic mark has become **merely descriptive** of a class of goods.

In the *Abercrombie & Fitch* case below, the plaintiff sued based on the defendant's use of the term "safari". The issue in this case is whether the term "safari" was generic.

Duration of Trademarks

As indicated earlier, the initial duration of a trademark is 10 years, subject to renewal for increments of 10 years upon payment of required fees and the

Abercrombie & Fitch Company v. *Hunting World, Inc.*
United States Court of Appeals for the Second Circuit
537 F.2d 4; 1976

FACTS AND CASE BACKGROUND

Abercrombie & Fitch filed a suit against Hunting World for trademark infringement. Hunting World (HW) filed a countersuit claiming that the trademarked words are ordinary, common, descriptive, geographic, and generic. The district court dismissed the case of trademark infringement filed by Abercrombie & Fitch (A&F) and dismissed some of A&F's trademark registrations. The case is now on appeal. The focus of the case is on A&F's registered trademarks using the name "safari" which is used to name A&F's clothing lines.

OPINION: FRIENDLY, CIRCUIT JUDGE
III.

We turn first to an analysis of A&F's trademarks to determine the scope of protection to which they are entitled. We have reached the following conclusions: (1) applied to specific types of clothing 'safari' has become a generic term and 'minisafari' may be used for a smaller brim hat; (2) 'safari' has not, however, become a generic term for boots or shoes; it is either "suggestive" or "merely descriptive" and is a valid trademark even if "merely descriptive" since it has become incontestable under the Lanham Act; but (3) in light of the justified finding below that 'Camel Safari,' 'Hippo Safari' and 'Safari Chukka' were devoted by Hunting World (HW) to a purely descriptive use on its boots, HW has a defense against a charge of infringement with respect to these on the basis of "fair use." We now discuss how we have reached these conclusions.

It is common ground that A&F could not apply 'Safari' as a trademark for an expedition into the African wilderness. This would be a clear example of the use of 'Safari' as a generic term. What is perhaps less obvious is that a word may have more than one generic use. The word 'Safari' has become part of a family of generic terms which, although deriving no doubt from the original use of the word and reminiscent of its milieu, have come to be understood not as having to do with hunting in Africa, but as terms within the language referring to contemporary American fashion apparel. These terms name the components of the safari outfit well-known to the clothing industry and its customers: the 'Safari hat', a broad flat-brimmed hat with a single, large band; the 'Safari jacket', a belted bush jacket with patch pockets and a buttoned shoulder loop; when the jacket is accompanied by pants, the combination is called the 'Safari suit'. Typically these items are khaki-colored.

This outfit, and its components, were doubtless what Judge Ryan had in mind when he found that "the word 'safari' in connection with wearing apparel is widely used by the general public and people in the trade." The record abundantly supports the conclusion that many stores have advertised these items despite A&F's attempts to police its mark. In contrast, a search of the voluminous exhibits fails to disclose a single example of the use of 'Safari', by anyone other than A&F and HW, on merchandise for which A&F has registered 'Safari' except for the safari outfit and its components as described above.

What has been thus far established suffices to support the dismissal of the complaint with respect to many of the uses of 'Safari' by HW. Describing a publication as a "Safariland Newsletter", containing bulletins as to safari activity in Africa, was clearly a generic use which is nonenjoinable. A&F also was not entitled to an injunction against HW's use of the word in advertising goods of the kind included in the safari outfit as described above. And if HW may advertise a hat of the kind worn on safaris as a safari hat, it may also advertise a similar hat with a smaller brim as a minisafari. Although the issue may be somewhat closer, the principle against giving trademark protection to a generic term also sustains the denial of an injunction against HW's use of 'Safariland' as a name of a portion of its store devoted at least in part to the sale of clothing as to which the term 'Safari' has become generic.

A&F stands on stronger ground with respect to HW's use of 'Camel Safari', 'Hippo Safari' and 'Chukka Safari' as names for boots imported from Africa. As already indicated, there is no evidence that 'Safari' has become a generic term for boots. Since, as will appear, A&F's registration of 'Safari' for use on its shoes has become incontestable, it is immaterial (save for HW's contention of fraud which is later rejected) whether A&F's use of 'Safari' for boots was suggestive or "merely descriptive."

* * *

We agree with A&F that footnote 14 was in error in indicating that Safari had become generic with respect to shirts. Since the mark has become incontestable, it is of no moment, on the issue of cancellation, that, as HW urges, the mark may now be "merely descriptive." HW's answer adduces nothing to show that Safari has become the "common descriptive name" for this type of shirt; indeed, HW admits never having advertised its own shirts as such. While HW asserts that "the record is clear that the upper garment of the safari suit is referred to interchangeably as a safari bush jacket and as a safari shirt," the cited pages do not bear this out.

* * *

The petition for rehearing is granted to the extent of striking the word "shirts" from fn. 14 on p. 13 and is otherwise denied.

QUESTIONS FOR REVIEW

1. Can a term be generic for one class of products but not for another? Can a term be generic for particular products within the class of products but not for others?

2. Once a mark becomes "incontestable", can an infringer claim that it is merely descriptive and thus not entitled to be a registered trademark? (Hint: Keep reading for the answer.)

---

provision of verified application of continued use.[29] During the initial period of registration, the registrant must send the PTO an affidavit of continued use between the fifth and sixth year together with fees. There are specific acceptable excuses for nonuse, without the loss of trademark rights, as long as there has been no intent to abandon the mark.

If registration of a mark is refused by the examiner, the applicant has six months to respond and amend the application.[30] If there is no response from the applicant within six months, the application is deemed abandoned. Section 1064 allows for a petition to cancel registration of a mark stating the grounds relied upon, by any person who believes he is or will be damaged by the registration of a mark within five years based on the claim that the mark is *generic,* or that the mark has been *abandoned* or the mark was *fraudulently* obtained. Marks can also be challenged under this section if the petitioner can show that the registrant does not control use of the mark. Amendments to the Lanham Act adopted in 1999 allow for petitioners to challenge a mark that the petitioner believes will *dilute* his mark (Anti-Dilution Legislation is discussed below).

Incontestable Marks

If a mark is registered on the principal register for five years, then the mark is said to be *incontestable*. This designation is really misleading because most of the possible challenges to the validity of the mark still remain in force. The two bases for challenges that are lost once a mark becomes incontestable are the claims that:

1. the mark should not have been registered because it is confusingly similar to a previously registered mark and is likely to cause customer confusion, and

2. the mark is not inherently distinctive and has not acquired secondary meaning.

Registration and Notice

Registration of a mark on the *principal register* at the PTO is *constructive* notice to the world that the mark has been taken. Constructive notice means that potential infringers are deemed legally notified of the mark registration by the fact that they can look up the status of the mark simply by examining the principal register at the PTO. With the advanced search engine technology provided by the PTO, there is really no legitimate excuse for infringers to innocently use a registered mark. Managers who are using trademarks to identify their goods are seriously derelict in their responsibilities if they fail to check whether a proposed mark is already taken. In spite of the ease with which registration of a mark can be checked, Section 1111 of the Lanham Act does not allow a trademark owner to recover profits or damages in an infringement suit unless the owner can show that the infringer had actual notice that the trademark was registered. Quite obviously, owners of registered trademarks should make that fact known by attaching the trademark to goods if possible as well as to advertising material and product packages.

Remedies

Section 1114 of the Lanham Act defines a trademark infringer as, "Any person who shall, without consent of the registrant—

a. Use in commerce any reproduction, counterfeit, copy, or colorable imitation of a registered mark in connection with the sale, offering for sale, etc.

---

[29]Sections 1058 and 1059 of the Lanham Act.
[30]Section 1062 of the Lanham Act.

any goods or services which is likely to cause confusion, mistake or to deceive, or

b. Reproduce, counterfeit, or imitate etc. any registered mark and apply such reproduction to labels, signs, prints, packages, wrappers or advertisements intended to be used in commerce in connection with the sale of goods or services that are likely to cause confusion, mistake, or deception, . . ."

Anyone guilty of infringing ". . . shall be liable in a civil action by the registrant for the remedies provided by the Lanham Act."[31] In ordinary English, a defendant in a trademark infringement suit is liable for using a mark that is so similar to a registered mark that it causes confusion, mistake, or fraud. Under (b) above the registrant cannot recover profits or damages unless the infringement was intentional.

Defenses

As discussed above, when a mark becomes incontestable, it achieves a certain status. According to Section 1115, once a mark becomes incontestable, "the registration shall be conclusive evidence of the validity of the registered mark, the registrant's ownership of the mark, and of the registrant's exclusive right to use the registered mark in commerce." In spite of "incontestability," the section lists eight separate defenses available to defendants in infringement cases including proof that the mark was:

1. fraudulently obtained, or
2. abandoned, or
3. that the mark is being used by the defendant with permission of the registrant, or
4. that the name, term, or device charged to be an infringement is a use of the defendant's name in his own business, or
5. that the mark was in use by the defendant before registration of the registrant's mark took place, or
6. that the accused mark was registered and in use prior to registration of the registrant's mark, or
7. that the registrant's mark was used to violate the antitrust laws, or
8. that the equitable principles of laches, estoppel, or acquiescence are applicable.

This list of defenses is not exhaustive. Notably, as discussed above, genericity remains a defense. Notice in item 8 of the listed defenses that *acquiescence* is a

defense. Acquiescence is claimed to occur when a trademark owner is aware of use of its mark, or a confusingly similar mark, by a third party, but makes no response to that activity within a reasonable time span. The Lanham Act places the burden of policing a mark upon the registrant. A trademark owner's failure to take action when apparent infringement is taking place can result in loss of ability to enforce the mark. In this situation, the registrant not only loses the right to enjoin use of the mark by infringers, but also loses any claims for damages.

Injunctions

A remedy often used in trademark infringement suits is the injunction. An injunction is a court order to cease illegal behavior, in this case, trademark infringement. Trademark owners are often rightly concerned that their reputation for quality can be harmed or lost by infringing sales of products from another seller, which could be of inferior quality. Failure to abide by an injunction is considered contempt of court and can result in jail time. Section 1116 of the Lanham Act allows the court to require a defendant against whom an injunction has been issued to report to the plaintiff the manner in which it has complied with the injunction. Compliance requires cessation of sales with the infringing trademark. In addition, some injunctions require corrective advertising to reduce customer confusion. The injunction or court order could involve publication of statements by the defendant disassociating itself with the plaintiff or the plaintiff's trademarks. Finally, the court order could involve product recalls of sales that were enjoyed using a mark that is confusingly similar to the registrant's mark.

Counterfeit Marks

Penalties are more severe for using a counterfeit mark. Section 1116 defines a counterfeit mark as a counterfeit (copy) of a mark that is registered on the principal register of the PTO, whether or not the defendant knew the mark was registered or a spurious designation that is identical or substantially indistinguishable from a registered mark. For such infringements the statute allows for the court to grant an order to seize the goods sold by the counterfeiter. The seizure of the goods can occur with an ex parte application by the trademark owner, which means that the person whose goods are being seized is not represented before the court to contest the seizure order. In most cases counterfeiters are rip-off artists who would not appear before the court even if summoned. Counterfeiters

---

[31]This is a paraphrase of the language of Section 1114 with redundant language excised.

know what they are doing is illegal and fully expect to be detected, but make their profits during the period between the start of sales and the court order. In many cases, counterfeiters are foreign nationals who are able to evade U.S. jurisdiction, though they may have alliances with U.S. partners.

Court Awarded Damages

Upon a showing that any right of a trademark owner whose mark is registered by the PTO has been violated, the court is entitled to award damages equal to (1) the defendant's profits, (2) the harm to the trademark owner, and (3) costs of litigation.[32] As with copyright law, the plaintiff need only show the defendant's sales and the burden is upon the defendant to show costs. The court can award additional amounts as damages, not to exceed three times *actual damages* incurred by the plaintiff. Again it is possible that the plaintiff can suffer actual damages that are greater than just the profits of the defendant, especially if the plaintiff's reputation or goodwill is harmed. In exceptional cases the court can award attorney fees to the prevailing party, which also indicates that frivolous suits launched by trademark owners could result in the loss of attorney fees to the defendant.

Counterfeit Marks (Knockoffs)

For *intentional use of counterfeit marks,* Section 1117 requires the court to triple damages, defendant's profits or damages to the plaintiff, whichever is greater, together with reasonable attorney fees and possibly prejudgment interest. Again, the targets for intentional use of counterfeit marks are likely to be fly-by-night businesses, many of which are foreign-owned. These businesses are defrauding the public and harming the reputations of the trademark owners. There have been a number of clothing firms that have fraudulently sown in labels of popular designers, such as Calvin Klein and Ann Taylor, on garments that are often of much lower quality than what these designers are known for.

Section 1124: Importation Forbidden of Goods Bearing Infringing Marks or Names

Because of the problem of foreign counterfeiting of U.S. trademarked goods, Section 1124 forbids importation of such goods and actually allows U.S. trademark owners to collaborate with customs officers in stopping these goods at the border. This section allows trademark owners to give to custom officials trademark registration documentation so that, if knockoff goods bearing that trademark appear during a customs examination of imported goods, those goods can be refused entry into the United States or seized.

THE ANTI-DILUTION ACT OF 1996

Dilution and Noncompeting Goods

When an applicant applies for registration of a trademark, the PTO requires identification of the class of goods for which the applicant is seeking the trademarks. There is a U.S. classification of goods and an international classification. Oddly enough, the PTO uses the International Classification (IC) of goods on its website.[33] To determine which class your goods are in, it is necessary merely to go to the PTO website and describe the good. Coats, televisions, computer software, and automobiles are among goods for which trademarks are significant. Coats are in IC 25, Television sets are in IC 9, most Computer Software is in IC 9, and Automobiles are in IC 12. Part of the rationale behind classification of goods is the notion that a similar trademark applied in different classes will not necessarily confuse the public whereas a similar mark within the same class will. For example, the PTO has allowed 34 separate registrations of the term "Bad Ass," many of which have been abandoned. Among the active and concurrent registrants for the Bad Ass® trademark are one seller who sells "sporting goods, namely, wakeboards, wakeboard bindings," etc. in IC 28 and Bad Ass® studios which sells both goods and services for "photographic, video and recording studio (audio and video)" in IC 41.

Federal Antidilution Act

Antidilution legislation is designed to deal with companies that name themselves cleverly, using titles such as McDentists, Buick Beer, or DuPont Shoes. McDonald's, Buick, and DuPont have extremely well-known marks whose value may be *diluted* by sellers of noncompeting goods that could "free-ride" on the goodwill and reputation built up by these better-known sellers. Dilution is also likely to cause confusion among the public as to whether famous trademark owners have actually decided to branch out into new lines of commerce, such as dentistry for the McDonald's corporation.

---

[32]Section 1117 of the Lanham Act.

[33]See http://www.uspto.gov/cgi-bin/gs/gs.cgi?Coats&max=250.

Section 1125 of the Lanham Act was amended in 1996 to deal with the dilution problem at the federal level. Section 1125(a) provides a civil action for anyone who uses in commerce any "word, term, name, symbol or device, . . . which—(1) is likely to cause confusion, or to cause mistake, or to deceive as to the affiliation . . . or (2) in commercial advertising or promotion, misrepresents the nature, characteristics, qualities, or geographic origin of his or her or an-

other person's goods, services, or commercial activities, . . . " This is standard anti-infringement protection for use of marks that are likely to confuse the public.

Famous Marks

Subsection (c) of 1125 was added in 1996. This subsection gives owners of "famous" marks the right to sue for an injunction to stop use of marks that are likely to cause *dilution*. The prohibition only applies

---

"Protect your name"

Added protection for a good domain name—even one that has a registered trademark—is essential to keep copycats and cybersquatters from making trouble with a b-to-b's hard-earned name, advised Rob Smith, director of marketing and sales for idNames, a division of Network Solutions Inc.

Once a domain name has been secured, businesses should register as many permutations of the name as they can, Smith said. He encourages b-to-b operators to register their names using a variety of misspellings and homonyms, inserting hyphens and adding foreign country names at the end. While there are about 110 countries that have restrictions on who can register domain names, there are dozens where no rules apply he said.

"In the b-to-b space, companies need to be aware that their domain name is up for grabs in over 70 countries, including the U.K., South Africa, Israel, Mexico, Russia and Switzerland," Smith warned. "Anybody with a computer and a credit card can register your company's name in those unrestricted countries."

Businesses have more name protection in the U.S. To learn about domain name dispute policies in the U.S., companies can log on to Network Solutions www.domainmagistrate.com. The site explains companies' rights under new legislation passed by Congress last year.

B-to-b operators also should register derogatory versions of their own names to prevent others from doing so, Smith said. Network Solutions has data on the most popular insulting names used and reports that a company's name followed by "sucks" is the hands-down leader in the category.

However, employing that strategy is no guarantee. In a widely reported case, Verizon Communications Inc., the newly named company launched by Bell Atlantic Corp. and GTE Corp., registered "verizonsucks.com" to preempt others from ridiculing it on a similar site.

Online hacker magazine 2600 registered the domain name "verizonreallysucks.com" to poke fun at the company. Angered by the move, Verizon filed a lawsuit against the magazine, alleging 2600's actions posed an infringement on Bell Atlantic's trademark rights under the Anticybersquatting Consumer Protection Act passed by Congress last November. The case is currently in litigation.

Despite the *Verizon* case, Smith said companies should still do all they can to protect their names. "The core question we ask our customers is whether they are willing to lose their Internet identity because they didn't do enough to protect their domain name," he said.

Source: Nemes, Judith, "Domain Names Have Brand Impact"; *B to B,* Aug 14, 2000. Reprinted with permission of B to B.

Additional Readings:
http://www.aspwatch.com/c/199936/d56904EBE5F9511D3ADD500A0C9E95208.asp
"Protecting Domain Names and Trademarks", August 31, 1999; Chris Womack,www.internet.com.

http://www.wirednews.com/news/business/0,1367,36210,00.html
"Real Cybersquatting Really Sucks", May 9, 2000 PDT, *Wired News Report.*

http://www.wirelessweek.com/news/may00/ten515.htm
"Verizon Stockpiles Domains to Protect Its Name", May 15, 2000 issue of *Wireless Week;* By Peggy Albright.

to the use of marks that takes place after the famous mark becomes famous. In amending the Lanham Act, Congress has decided that famous marks deserve special treatment because they are targets for free-riding by much smaller firms that want to associate their products with the famous marks. In determining whether a mark is famous, Subsection (c) directs courts to consider the inherent distinctiveness of the mark, its duration, its geographic scope, its advertising, and so on. For many famous marks such as McDonald's, the courts have a relatively easy time determining whether the mark is "famous".

Remedies: Injunctions and Monetary Damages

Subsection (c) does not allow owners of famous marks to recover monetary damages against the diluter unless there is a showing that there was a willful intent on the part of the diluter to trade on the reputation of the famous mark, in which case the owner of the famous mark is entitled to damages and profits as discussed above. It is difficult to imagine a diluter nonwillfully using a variation of a famous mark but, generally, owners of famous marks just want the diluting activity to stop. Many diluters are small firms with few attachable assets, and showing intent is often difficult.

Anticybersquatting Consumer Protection Act
Internet and Domain Names

Until recently the four important sources of IP have been patents, copyrights, trademarks, and trade secret laws. The explosive expansion of E-Commerce has spawned a new form of IP, domain names, prompting the need for additional protections.

As E-Commerce has gained in significance, the importance and economic value of domain names has increased. As an interesting example of market evolution, the regulation of domain names has actually taken place *privately* (as opposed to by government regulation) and is outside the control of the PTO. For an extended time span, enterprising denizens of the Internet recognized an opportunity and exploited that opportunity by taking (and registering) domain names of famous companies with names that are trademarked. When the Internet was just being discovered and legal rights were uncertain, many large companies were willing to pay $10,000 or more to cybersquatters so that they could remove the confusion and nuisance. The following case illustrates cybersquatting before the Anticybersquatting Consumer Protection Act was passed. Notice that Toys "R" Us may have won the suit, but may wonder if it can collect damages?

Toys "R" Us, Inc. v. Eli Abir
United States District Court for the Southern District of New York
45 U.S.P.Q.2D; 1997

FACTS AND CASE BACKGROUND

Toys "R" Us is a nationwide retail store and owns *a family of* trademarks with varying derivations of the "R" Us phrase. The defendant, Abir, purchased the domain name "toysareus.com" and offered it for sale to the Toys "R" Us company. Abir stated that if the Toys "R" Us Company did not purchase the domain name from him, then he would operate a worldwide toy catalog at the toysareus.com website. A month after the court issued a Temporary Restraining Order against Abir, with respect to the "toysareus.com" do-

main name, plaintiffs allege that they discovered that defendants registered a "kidsareus.com" domain name.

Toys "R" Us claims that the operation of a website "kidsareus.com" will offer irreparable damage to their business and the effect of infringement and dilution is magnified because of the timing with the Holiday Shopping Season.

The plaintiffs seek an injunction to prevent Abir from using the "kidsareus.com" website and a ruling that Abir has violated the Toys "R" US trademark.

OPINION: JOHN G. KOELTL, DISTRICT JUDGE

To prevail on a motion for a preliminary injunction, the party requesting relief must demonstrate: 1) that it is subject to irreparable harm; and 2) either (a) that it will likely succeed on the merits, or (b) there are sufficiently serious questions going to the merits to make them a fair ground for litigation, and that a balance of the hardships tips decidedly in favor of the moving party.

The requirement of irreparable harm is satisfied if the plaintiff can show a likelihood of success in this case. A showing of likelihood of confusion is a required element of trademark infringement and false designation claims. The Second Circuit Court of Appeals has held that such a showing necessarily establishes the requisite irreparable harm in this context. Similarly, the Court of Appeals has also held that a showing of likelihood of dilution, which is a required element under § 43(c) of the Lanham Act, necessarily establishes the requisite irreparable harm with respect to a preliminary injunction in this context.

To prevail on its infringement and false designation of origin claims under §§ 32(1) or 43(a), the plaintiffs must prove that they have a valid mark subject to protection and that the defendants' mark results in a likelihood of confusion. The plaintiffs own federal trademark registrations for marks whose dominant portion is the term, or component, "R" US. The fact that Toys "does not own a registered mark for 'R US' per se, does not prevent the plaintiff[s] from claiming the 'R US' designation as a common component of a 'family of marks.'" Courts have found that the "R" US family of marks is subject to protection under the Lanham Act. Thus, the plaintiffs have satisfied the first prong of their trademark infringement claims.

* * *

First, the "R" US marks have been already adjudicated to be strong marks for purposes of trademark infringement claims, and the record in this case presents no evidence for this Court to find otherwise. The marks are best described as suggestive and thus would be protectable even without proof of secondary meaning. However, other courts have found secondary meaning and the record here supports that finding.

Second, there is a high degree of similarity between the plaintiffs'

Toys "R" Us mark and the defendants' "TOYSAREUS.COM" domain name. "There is no evidence that the composite term 'R US' or the phonetic equivalent 'ARE US' existed before it was coined and extensively used by [Toys] . . . . Any visual differences between plaintiffs' and defendants' marks becomes nonexistent when the marks are spoken."

Third and Fourth, the products at issue in this case—relatively inexpensive toys and other children's items—are identical. As a result, there is no market gap for the defendants to bridge. The distribution channels in this case—cyberspace—are also identical. Further, the cyberspace medium renders it especially difficult for consumers to evaluate any quality differences between the plaintiffs' and the defendants' products.

Fifth, actual confusion is presumed here because the defendants admit they intended to cause confusion and that they acted in bad faith.

Sixth, it is plain that the defendants are guilty of bad faith. Their use of the domain site that copied Toys "R" Us was a deliberate bad faith effort at cyberpiracy.

Seventh, it appears that defendants' products are not thought to be the same quality as the plaintiffs' products.

Finally, it is doubtful that children or parents shopping the Internet for toys are sophisticated buyers.

The defendants are incorrect in suggesting that a disclaimer posted on the "TOYSAREUS.COM" website can cure any possible confusion.

Having established a likelihood of confusion, the plaintiffs have satisfied the second prong of their trademark infringement claims. Thus, the plaintiffs have successfully proven a likelihood of success on the merits of these claims.

"The owner of a famous mark shall be entitled . . . to an injunction against another person's commercial use in commerce of a mark or trade name, if such use begins after the mark has become famous and causes dilution of the distinctive quality of the mark . . . ." To prevail on its dilution claim under § 43(c), the plaintiffs must show that the "R" US marks are famous and that the defendants' use of the "R" US mark in a commercial manner diluted the marks.

For similar reasons discussed above with respect to the strength of the plaintiffs' "R" US marks, it is plain that the marks are famous. Toys has extensively publicized its marks for almost a forty-year period and continues to do so today. No evidence is presented to contradict the plaintiffs' long history and use of the marks. Other courts have specifically found the "R" US family of marks to be protectable under § 43(c) because of the distinctiveness and fame it enjoys. Thus, having established that the "R" US family of marks is famous, to succeed on the merits of this claim the plaintiffs need only show that the defendants are engaged in a commercial use that will cause dilution of the marks.

* * *

Although an injunction will prevent the defendants from using a particular name for their website, it is a name they adopted long after the plaintiffs started to use it. Further, despite the fact that the plaintiffs already had the right to use the name, the defendants intentionally adopted it in order to extort money from the plaintiff or to take advantage of the extensive efforts that Toys expended in developing the name by competing directly against the plaintiffs. Thus, the unclean hands of defendants Abir and Web Site Management tip the balance of the equities strongly against them and in favor of the plaintiffs.

For the foregoing reasons, the plaintiffs' motion for a preliminary injunction is granted. The Court will enter a separate Order incorporating the preliminary injunction. So ordered.

QUESTIONS FOR REVIEW

1. What is the difference between trademark infringement and dilution? What is the principal focus of this case?
2. What other factors weighed heavily in the favor of Toys "R" Us? Was the mark a famous mark? Was there evidence that the defendant was operating in bad faith?

As the Internet became more popular, cybersquatting became more prevalent and it became more and more obvious that cybersquatters were engaged in "shakedown" operations. Congress responded with the Anticybersquatting Consumer Protection Act of 1999, which amends the Lanham Act by providing that any person who, with bad-faith intent to profit from the goodwill of a trademark or service mark of another, registers or uses an Internet domain name that is identical to, confusingly similar to, or dilutive of such a mark, shall be liable in a civil action brought by the owner of the mark.

According to the 1999 Act, "Congress finds that the unauthorized registration or use of trademarks as Internet domain names or other identifiers of online locations (commonly known as 'cybersquatting')—

1. results in consumer fraud and public confusion as to the true source or sponsorship of products and services;
2. impairs electronic commerce, which is important to the economy of the United States; and
3. deprives owners of trademarks of substantial revenues and consumer goodwill."

This Act prohibits the use of domain names or identifiers of online locations that are the trademark of another person, or are sufficiently similar to a trademark so as to cause likely confusion, mistake, deception, or dilution of the distinctive quality of a famous trademark. Note, further, that bad-faith use of domain names can carry criminal penalties as a result of this legislation. In lieu of proof of actual damages from a trademark infringement or dilution, the 1999 Act also allows trademark owners to elect statutory damages which are equal to:

I. not less than $1,000 or more than $100,000 per trademark per identifier, as the court considers just; or
II. if the court finds that the registration or use of the registered trademark as an identifier was willful, not less than $3,000 or more than $300,000 per trademark per identifier, as the court considers just . . .

Concluding Remarks about Trademarks

Trademarks are the third leg of statutory intellectual property protection at the federal level. It is easy to underrate the importance of this branch of IP. The fact that so many companies imitate and counterfeit registered trademarks indicates how high the stakes are in trademark law. Ask yourself whether you would buy any nonbranded computer, car, or golf clubs. The rise of the Internet and E-Commerce has created a rival, nongovernmental source of IP. Clever domain names initially enabled many .com companies to experience exponential growth. Congress has resolved the clash between domain names and trademarks on the side of trademarks.

SUMMARY

- The financial importance of copyright law is enormous. Literally billions of dollars are tied up in copyrighted works and also billions are lost through copyright *infringement* and *piracy*.

- Copyrights are given for original works of authorship fixed in any tangible medium of expression.
- Copyrights do not have to be registered or provide notice as a result of the Berne Convention, which the U.S. became a member of in 1988.

- Copyrights are long lasting: the life of the author plus 70 years for original works not for hire and 95 to 120 years for works for hire.
- Registration of copyrights with the U.S. Copyright Office has benefits if the copyright is infringed because damages are higher and notice is provided to the world.
- Essentially, copyrights protect *expressions* of ideas, not the ideas themselves. Copyright law does not protect the *functionality* of software, only patents can do that.
- Copyrights cannot protect facts, but can protect against copying of the arrangement of facts as long as the author exhibits some minimal level of originality.
- The EU provides greater protection for databases particularly if the databases contain information that is personal and identifies individuals.
- For copyrighted works, copyright law provides the author with *exclusive rights to reproduce and distribute* such works. Also copyright law provides that only authors (or owners of the copyrighted work) can prepare *derivative* works.
- For a claim of infringement, the owner of the copyrighted work must show that the infringer had access to the copyrighted work because independent creation is a copyright defense.
- The test for copyright infringement is whether the accused work and the copyrighted work are *substantially similar*.
- Copyright protects the underlying code, both source and object, of copyrighted software. Also copyright law can protect user interfaces and command structures of copyrighted software.
- Copyright law does not protect against *reverse engineering* of copyrighted software through decompilation or disassembly if the purpose of the reverse engineering is to enhance the interoperability of software.
- A copyright provides for damages in the event of infringement. Actual damages are computed by determining the copyright owner's lost profits on lost sales and the profits of the infringer with a prohibition on double counting. Once the copyright owner establishes lost sales due to infringing sales of the infringer, the burden of proof is upon the infringer to establish costs.
- In the alternative, the Copyright Act provides for *statutory damages*, which range between $200

and $100,000 per infringement depending on the willfulness of the infringer.
- If the defendant's behavior is egregious, courts are empowered to treble damages.
- Copyright law also contains criminal sanctions for willful violations including incarceration for up to 10 years.
- There are a number of exceptions and defenses available to those who reproduce or distribute copyrighted works without authorization. Among those defenses and exceptions are the *first sale exception* which allows purchasers of copyrighted material to resell it to others.
- Purchasers of copyrighted software are entitled to make *archival copies* of the software.
- The *fair use* defense is available to those who copy copyrighted work without permission if the copying is for research, teaching, parody, criticism, and other allowable purposes.
- The determination as to whether an unauthorized copying of a copyrighted work qualifies for the fair use exception depends on a number of factors, but the most important factor is the impact on the market for the copyrighted work. If the market for copyrighted work is negatively impacted, most likely the copier will not qualify for the fair use exception.
- Copyright infringers can be direct infringers, contributory infringers, or vicarious infringers.
- Common law defenses of *laches, estoppel, unclean hands,* and *misuse* also are available to those accused of a copyright infringement.
- The Audio Home Recording Act of 1992 requires sellers of digital audio recording devices to pay royalties to the Office of Copyright and to use serial copy management systems so that royalties can be properly allocated.
- The Digital Performance Right in Sound Recordings Act in 1995 added another exclusive privilege to those of copyright owners, which is the right to perform their works by digital audio transmissions.
- The Digital Millennium Copyright Act of 1998 creates substantial modification of copyright law addressing those who manufacture or distribute products that are designed to circumvent technological measures taken by copyright owners to protect their copyrighted works. Copyright owners are still entitled to make archival copies of their software.

- The No Electronic Theft Act of 1997 was passed to provide criminal penalties for those who for whatever reasons, profit or prank, sabotage computer systems.
- Under U.S. law, artists have limited moral rights of *integrity* and *attribution* when distortions would harm the artists' reputations.
- If an employee creates a copyrighted work on the job, it is a work for hire and ownership of the copyright resides with the employer. When two authors or artists collaborate on the creation of a copyrighted work, the result is a joint work.
- Courts and Congress have decided that Internet Service Providers are more like bookstores than publishers for purposes of copyright law, which means that they are not liable unless ISPs are apprised defamation, in which case the ISP can remove the alleged defamatory material without liability risk if that action is not contested by the content provider. In general, as long as ISPs merely transmit information, they are not liable for the content according to Title II of the Digital Millennium Copyright Act (DMCA).
- The DMCA also absolves ISPs from liability for caching as long as they are commercially reasonable in updating material and follows instructions from content providers when the material is out of date.
- The DMCA provides a procedure for dealing with allegedly infringing material. If the ISP is informed that material it has posted infringes a copyright of a third party, the DMCA provides a *safe harbor* to guide the ISP when there is a dispute as to whether the material does infringe a copyright of a third party.
- In general websites can link with one another without permission or liability for copyright infringement, except if the linker has been warned not to link with another website or the linker distorts what a visitor to its site sees at the linked site.
- Trademark law is based on the Lanham Act which was passed in 1946 but has been amended many times.
- The basic role of a *trademark* is to identify the source of a product. Trademarks represent quality and goodwill and cut down on consumer search costs.
- A trademark includes any word, name, symbol, or device used by a person to identify his or her goods.

- Federal registration of trademarks takes place through the Patent and Trademark Office. Initial duration of a trademark is 10 years, but between the fifth and sixth years fees must be paid. In theory the duration of a trademark can be forever as long as the mark does not become generic and the owner does not abandon the mark.
- Recent decisions by the courts have expanded registered trademarks to include colors, sounds, and other symbols that previously would not qualify for a trademark.
- A mark becomes *generic* when it no longer signifies the origin of product but rather designates *a class of products*. Trampoline, escalator, and aspirin are examples of marks that have become generic.
- Among the other reasons to deny registration to a mark are that the proposed mark is scandalous or immoral, or that the mark disparages persons, institutions, beliefs, or national symbols.
- Flags of this or foreign countries cannot be trademarked.
- Marks that are *confusingly similar* to previously registered marks cannot be registered if there is customer confusion. Customer confusion is not based on the majority of customers but rather on a demonstration that a significant number of customers are confused.
- Registration is denied to marks that are merely *descriptive* or are *misdescriptive*.
- The strongest marks are those that acquire secondary meaning. Marks that are suggestive can acquire secondary meaning, but the strongest marks are fanciful.
- After five years on the principal register a mark becomes *incontestable*. Most challenges remain to incontestable marks but after five years the mark cannot be challenged for being confusingly similar to a previously registered mark or because the mark was merely descriptive.
- The criteria for trademark infringement is that the accused mark is likely to cause confusion among the public or fraud is involved.
- Counterfeit marks are deliberate imitations of registered trademarks. Damages are recoverable for intentional infringements.
- Trademark owners often seek *injunctions* to stop infringers from continuing to sell products that are likely to confuse the public and dilute the

goodwill the owners have built up through their reputation for quality.

- For deliberate infringements trademark owners can seek damages equal to the defendant's profits, the harm to the trademark owner, and in some cases the costs of litigation. For egregious cases damages can be tripled.
- The Anti-Dilution Act of 1996 provides remedies for owners of *famous trademarks,* even if the defendant is selling products not sold by the trademark owner. Again, a violation is likely to be found in court if the defendant's marks are likely to confuse the public.
- The Anticybersquatting Consumer Protection Act of 1999 provides remedies for trademark owners whose trademarks show up as domain names on the WWW. If bad faith is shown, the statute provides for substantial statutory damages, injunctions, and in some cases, criminal sanctions.

INTELLECTUAL PROPERTY III: CREATING, USING, AND PROTECTING SOFTWARE

Arguably, the strength of the U.S. economy in the 1990s has been in large part its superiority in creating software. Virtually every major high-tech advance has either been in the area of software, relies on software for its operation, or has been discovered with the aid of software. Although made possible by some important hardware components, the Internet is essentially a creation of a cauldron of software. Out of this cauldron, E-Commerce has emerged as an exponentially growing part of retail (B to C) and wholesale (B to B) markets and transactions.[1] Internet companies, whose main assets are websites (electronic address software), have at times enjoyed stock market values that defy conventional wisdom gained from analyzing "bricks and mortar" companies. Internet companies have attracted droves of investors even if they have yet to make profits.

The importance of software is illustrated by the fact that Microsoft Corporation, which is quite profitable and is the largest seller of software, has a greater market value than General Motors Corporation does, though it only has a fraction of the physical assets of GM. Quite apparently, popular software represents enormous value in intellectual property that can transcend an accountant's summary of the value of brick and mortar assets. Indeed, in our emerging E-Commerce economy, some authors even suggest that physical assets should be viewed as liabilities rather than assets.[2]

Of course, the importance of software does not end with the Internet. Intranets and networks within companies are transforming intracompany communications. Sales and marketing divisions are linked with operations, accounting, and finance in ways that were unimaginable a few years ago. The same is true of partnering companies (often through Electronic Data Interchange (EDI)) that transact with each other on a continuous basis. Virtual medicine allows doctors to treat patients from remote locations using artificial intelligence that is imbedded in advanced software. The list goes on, but critical to a large share of most of the significant innovations in the United States in the 1990s is advanced software of some kind.

---

[1]"B to C" refers to Business to Consumer, while "B to B" refers to Business-to-Business transactions.

[2]In *Killer Apps*, an influential book for venture capitalists, the author suggests that the physical assets of say, banks and trains, are actually liabilities, *Unleashing the Killer App: Digital Strategies for Market Dominance,* by Larvy Downes, Chanka Mai, & Nicholas Negroponte.

"The Wired Enterprise: Here Come the Intranets"

Please see article at:
www.strategy-business.com/technology/97109/page1.html
January 1997, Lawrence M. Fisher, "the Wired Enterprise: Here Come the Intranets," Strategy & Business.

Additional Readings:
http://www.bizjournals.com/dallas/stories/1998/04/20/smallb4.html
"Intranets and extranets offer some competitive advantages", April 17, 1998; Mellanie Hills,buzjournals.com
http://www.internetnews.ca/archives/web_tech/nov96_intranet.html
"Intranets: The Internet Moves Indoors", Andrew Gray, © Internet News, 1996.
http://cyber.law.harvard.edu/cybercon98/wcm/mennel.html
"Building Strategic Intranets", Cambridge, April 24, 1998; John Mennel and Mary Teichert.

OVERVIEW OF LEGAL PROTECTION FOR COMPUTER SOFTWARE

Given the importance of computer software, it may seem surprising that legal protection of software is ambiguous and problematic. Originally, policy makers envisioned that computer programs would be legally safeguarded by *copyright* law. To that end, amendments to the Copyright Act of 1976 included elements classifying computer programs in the same category as literary works such as novels and screenplays. During the next 10 years, from 1976 to 1986, court protection of computer software through copyright law expanded until the "look and feel" test was developed and used to evaluate possible infringements. The essence of the "look and feel" test is that software programs can be infringed, even though the underlying code (source and object) was not copied, if the software alleged to infringe looks too much like and feels (acts) too much like protected software. During the 1990s, however, court enthusiasm for the "look and feel" test waned, diluting the degree of legal protection provided by copyright law, and prompting software developers to look for alternative means of protecting the IP content of their software programs.

With court decisions that weakened the protection offered by copyrights, it was natural to seek shelter with other existing IP protection devices such as patents. The initial judicial reception to the patentability of software, however, was decidedly negative. In two significant cases the U.S. Supreme Court concluded that the operations of computer software are similar to the solving of mathematical equations,

which the courts labeled "algorithms", and thus are not patentable.[3] The courts have interpreted the Patent Act of 1953 as prohibiting the patenting of *ideas, formulae, laws of nature,* and *naturally occurring substances.*[4] The first contradictory breakthrough in the evolution of court rulings on patent protection of software involved a holding that software could become patentable, but only if the software was part of a larger product or process.[5] Following this concession, it was a relatively short period of time until the patenting of pure software inventions became commonplace. Although controversies remain, **patent law now has become the mainstay of legal protection of software.** Companies continue to use copyright and trade secret law to protect software against copying, but, increasingly, there is recognition that truly innovative software is patentable, and that patent law provides the most comprehensive protection for such IP.

Trade secret law also continues to be an important part of legal protection of software, especially at early stages of development. Virtually all software becomes obsolete in 5 years, either because it is no longer compatible with other software or because rivals have developed products that have more functionality. Software is eternal in the sense that use does not diminish its functionality. So, to sell more product,

---

[3]*Parker* v. *Flook,* 437 U.S. 584 (1978); *Gottschalk* v. *Benson,* 409 U.S. 63 (1972).
[4]In *Diamond* v. *Chakrabarty* the U.S. Supreme Court stated that "The law of nature, physical phenomena, and abstract ideas have been held not patentable. Thus, a new mineral discovered in the earth or a new plant found in the wild is not patentable subject matter." 44 U.S. 303 (1980).
[5]*Diamond* v. *Diehr,* 450 U.S. 175 (1981).

software developers must be continuously upgrading their products. Software development and upgrade plans are crucial to the survival of software firms and parts or all of these plans are known to technical employees who, because of the intensity of demand for their skills, have a great deal of mobility. The threat of trade secret misappropriation suits against former employees and their subsequent employers is another important weapon that firms use in the legal protection of software. However, courts have little enthusiasm for making highly skilled technical employees unemployable by limiting their ability to move from one job to another. Many suits against former employees and subsequent employers have been unsuccessful.

Copyright Protection of Software

The issue of what can be protected by copyright law can best be analyzed by examining what cannot be protected. Section 102(b) of the Copyright Act explicitly prohibits copyright protection for any "idea, procedure, process, system, method of operation, concept, principle, or discovery, regardless of the form in which it is described, explained, illustrated, or embodied in such work." In a word, copyright law cannot be used to protect functional aspects of computer programs, which may be termed "methods of operation." Computer software might also be viewed as a procedure, process, or system, all prohibited by Section 102(b) from copyright protection.

Contrasts with Patent Law

Unlike patents, copyrights are not reserved to those who *significantly* advance the state of the art in a particular field. Those who make even slight improvements over existing copyrighted software are entitled to a copyright as long as the improved version is not "substantially similar." Instead, "[c]opyright protection subsists, . . . in original works of authorship fixed in any tangible medium of expression, now known or later developed, which can be perceived, reproduced, or otherwise communicated, either directly or with the aid of a machine or device."[6] Copyrights are designed to protect authors from unauthorized copies of their creative expressions, but are not intended to grant monopolies. Patent law explicitly grants inventors a legal monopoly, but the requirements for obtaining a patent

are significantly more demanding than those for obtaining a copyright. Unlike copyright registrants, patentees must make a nonobvious (significant) improvement over the state of the art in order to gain their legal monopoly.

What in Software that Copyright Law Cannot Protect?

Copyrights for software can best be viewed as pertaining to those parts of a software program that do not create *monopoly* advantages for the copyright owner. The following would give monopoly-like advantages to a copyright holder of software, and thus copyright law does not protect that part of a computer program that is:

1. An *industry standard.* Copyright protection for that part of the program would give the copyright owner compelling monopoly advantages. Thus, the industry-standard part of a software program *cannot be protected* by copyright law, regardless of whether that part of the program is a user interface, a structure, sequence of commands, or something that considerably improves performance.
2. Necessary to accomplish a *functional* task. Linking copyrighted software with hardware or an operating system accomplishes functional tasks and therefore cannot be protected by copyright law. If there are alternative ways of accomplishing a task, the particular way chosen by the copyright registrant may be protectible.
3. Part of a software program that makes it so popular that it becomes the *industry standard.* As with trademark law, what was once protectible can become unprotectible because it is too successful. The command structure on the top of most application software that begins with *File, Edit,* and ends with *Help* is an industry standard and thus not protectible. Anyone developing software can use that command structure at the top of their software without a royalty obligation.
4. In the *public domain.* Portions of computer software that are in the public domain do not receive copyright protection.
5. Previously *licensed* or *assigned* to an alleged infringer. The portion of a software program that has been licensed to an alleged infringer/licensee can be reproduced by the licensee. That act of reproduction cannot be used by juries to evaluate whether an infringement has taken place.

[6]Copyright Act § 102(a).

"FBI, IRS, Other Agencies Crack Down Further on Software Piracy"

"Globally, piracy is a problem that costs developers of business software more than $11 billion a year and developers of entertainment software nearly $3 billion, according to industry trade groups. These figures include both CD-ROM counterfeiting and other types of piracy.

The FBI, which has stepped up its investigation of software piracy over the past 18 months, currently has 91 cases pending. Last year, FBI investigations led to eight convictions for software piracy.

'I fully expect the statistics will substantially increase,' said Lynn Hunt, chief of the FBI's financial crimes unit. Hunt estimated that the FBI's software piracy investigations have helped recover hundreds of millions of dollars worth of software since 1996.

But as is clear from the wide gap between the number of investigations and number of convictions, and between the lost revenue estimate and the value of the software recovered, law enforcement isn't a magic bullet.

Counterfeit busters say the problem must be attacked on many fronts. Strategies include tougher sentencing guidelines for counterfeiters, stronger enforcement of intellectual property laws by foreign governments and crackdowns on rogue CD-ROM replication facilities.

Software developers are also looking more seriously at copy-protection technology. Among the protection companies pursuing CD-ROM publishers are MLS LaserLock International Inc., Macrovision Corp. (MVSN) and TTR Inc. (TTRE).

'In the last two years there's been a dramatically increased interest in antipiracy technologies from our customers,' said Doug Carson, president of Doug Carson & Associates Inc., which sells equipment used in the production of 80% of the world's CD-ROMs."

Source: Republished with permission of *The Wall Street Journal,* from "FBI, IRS, Other Agencies Crack Down Further on Software Piracy," August 17, 1998. Permission conveyed through Copyright Clearance Center, Inc.

Additional Readings:
http://www.zdnet.com/zdnn/stories/news/0,4586,2393620,00.html
"New Twist on Fight Against Software Piracy", November 15, 1999; Rob Lemos & Lisa M. Bowman, ZDNet News.

http://www.usatoday.com/life/cyber/tech/ct708.htm
"FBI Cracks Down on Software Pirates", 02/28/99; San Francisco, The Associated Press.

http://www.zdnet.com/zdnn/stories/zdnn_smgraph_display/0,4436,2144476,00.html
"White House Orders Crackdown on Software Piracy", October 1, 1998; Maria Seminerio, ZDNN.

This list of limitations can be easily extended but the lesson is clear—copyrights often provide, at best, limited legal protection against unauthorized copying of part or all of a software program.

Object Code and Source Code

Software programs are composed of object code and source code. Object code is sometimes called machine language because it is readable only by machines.[7] Copyright owners may send object code to the Copyright Office for registration, and the resulting copyright will protect against reproduction, distribution, or use of unauthorized copies of the object code. Most software is distributed to users in object code because it is more difficult to copy or alter. Copying object code can be an infringement if the code does not confer monopoly advantages to the copyright owner.

Similarly, source code, which is readable by humans (in languages such as C++ or HTML), can be protected by copyright law. In some cases the Copyright Office will allow for the *registration* of software programs, but not require the entire program to be available to the public. As discussed in Chapter 11 the Copyright Office will allow copyright registration when the first and last 25 pages of code are made available to the public, even when the rest is unavailable. Such registrations are intended to combat software piracy by individuals who deliberately infringe on software copyrights.

Screen Displays and User Interfaces

Object and source codes are what the courts label the *literal* portions of a software program. After loading the literal portions (the code) of a software program into a computer's random access memory, the program provides for the display of information on the computer's monitor. Needless to say, there can be multiple ways to display what a program directs to a computer monitor. Different object and source code, even written in different programming languages,

---

[7]The bar codes on groceries are written in object code.

could be used to generate identical displays on the computer monitor, and very similar code could provide very different screen displays. An immediately apparent question, then, is whether screen displays, which are *nonliteral* components of a computer program, are protectible under copyright law. Screen displays can be classified as user interfaces and as comprising the *structure, sequence,* or an *organization* (SSOs) of the computer program. SSOs have also been labeled by the courts as the *command structures* of software programs.

In the past, several courts have held that user interfaces are akin to visual creations of the author and thus are protectible. If the "look and feel" of a program's user interface could be confused with that of a previously copyrighted program, the vendor of the new program could be found liable for infringement. There are, however, substantial limitations on this copyright protection. A user interface on a computer is a lot like a dashboard on an automobile. In fact, automobile manufacturers tried to copyright dashboards but were denied because the dashboard is essentially *functional* and not aesthetic with many features in common such as speedometers, odometers, and fuel gauges. The argument made by an automobile manufacturer was that there are a number of ways to arrange the instruments on a dashboard, and therefore the particular arrangement selected by a manufacturer ought to be protectible with copyright law. Courts did not accept that argument.

Structure, Sequence and Organization

In several cases brought before the courts in the late 1980s and early 1990s, there was no evidence of copying of object or source code, but screen displays closely resembled the copyrighted work of another. In *Whelan Associates* v. *Jaslow Dental Lab,*[8] the courts first applied the so-called "look and feel" test. To prove that an infringement had occurred, the court ruled that the copyright owner had to show that the two programs were substantially similar. Expert testimony was used to provide relevant evidence as to similarities between SSOs in each program. In this case, the court rejected the argument that only the literal (object and source code) aspects of the software program could be protected by the copyright law and concluded that an infringement occurred if the "look and feel" of the allegedly infringing program closely resembled the copyrighted program. With some qualifiers, the court in *Whelan* held that the look and feel of a computer program, as a whole, was protectible under copyright law as long as the SSO of the program was not the only way to accomplish the functional tasks that the program was designed to accomplish. In a subsequent case a court held that a spreadsheet (VP Planner), which incorporated all of the functional features of Lotus 1-2-3, violated Lotus' copyright because the programs were substantially

[8]797 F.2d 1222 (3d Cir. 1986)

Lotus Development Corp. v. Paperback Software International
United States District Court, D. Massachusetts
740 F.Supp. 37, (1990)

FACTS AND CASE BACKGROUND

At one time in the market for electronic spreadsheets, Lotus 1-2-3 was the dominant product. Paperback Software, the developer of VP-Planner, decided, after lack of success with earlier products that had different user interfaces, to copy the user interface of Lotus 1-2-3. The motivations for copying the familiar, tilted-L-user-interface with spreadsheets was to ensure that users of the

1-2-3 program could transfer their work to VP-Planner software and to reduce user startup time in learning a new spreadsheet. Lotus sued Paperback Software for infringement of their copyrighted user interface.

CASE DECISION: KEETON, DISTRICT JUDGE

The history of copyright law has been one of gradual expansion in the types of works accorded protection,

and the subject matter affected has fallen into two general categories. In the first, scientific discoveries and technological developments have made possible new forms of creative expression that never existed before. In some of these cases the new expressive forms—electronic, music, filmstrips, and computer programs, for example—could be regarded as an extension of copyrightable subject matter Congress had already intended to protect, and were thus considered copyrightable from the outset without need of new legislation. In other cases, such as photographs, sound recordings, and motion pictures, statutory enactment was deemed necessary to give them full recognition as copyrightable works.

Drawing the line too liberally in favor of copyright protection would bestow strong monopolies over specific applications upon the first to write programs performing those applications and would thereby inhibit other creators from developing improved products. Drawing the line too conservatively would allow programmer's efforts to be copied easily, thus discouraging the creation of all but modest incremental advances.

* * *

Since then, congressional and judicial development of the law of copyrightability of computer programs has advanced considerably, and Synercom's central proposition—that the expression of nonliteral sequence and order is inseparable from the idea and accordingly is not copyrightable—has been explicitly rejected by several courts. E.g., Whelan, 797 F.2d at 1240, 1248 ("copyright protection of computer programs may extend beyond the programs' literal code

to their structure, sequence, and organization");

* * *

Of course, if a particular expression of the idea of an electronic spreadsheet communicates no details beyond those essential to stating the idea itself, then that expression would not be copyrightable. The issue here is whether Lotus 1-2-3 does go beyond those details essential to any expression of the idea, and includes substantial elements of expression, distinctive and original, which are thus copyrightable.

* * *

Each of the elements just described is present in, if not all, at least most expressions of an electronic spreadsheet computer program. Other aspects of these programs, however, need not be present in every expression of an electronic spreadsheet. An example of distinctive details of expression is the precise "structure, sequence, and organization," Whelan, 797 F.2d at 1248, of the menu command system.

The fact that some of these specific command terms are quite obvious or merge with the idea of such a particular command term does not preclude copyrightability for the command structure taken as a whole. If particular characteristics not distinctive individually have been

brought together in a way that makes the "whole" a distinctive expression of an idea—one of many possible ways of expressing it—then the "whole" may be copyrightable.

That defendants went to such trouble to copy that element is a testament to its substantiality. Accordingly, evaluation of the third element of the legal test weighs heavily in favor of Lotus.

Taking account of all three elements of the legal test, I determine that copyrightability of the user interface of 1-2-3 is established.

* * *

So, the court ruled that Paperback Software had infringed the copyrightable command structure of the Lotus 1-2-3 spreadsheet.

QUESTIONS FOR ANALYSIS

1. Did the presence of viable substitute spreadsheet programs such as Excel and Visi-Calc aid Lotus in its infringement claim?
2. Does this case mean that any future developers of electronic spreadsheets have to learn a new system? If so, what does this suggest with regard to the market power of Lotus? Does it mean that any future rivals are allowed to make their products compatible with Lotus 1-2-3?

---

similar and there was more than one way for a spreadsheet to operate.[9]

As a postscript to this prominent litigation over market access from just a few short years ago, it is notable that Excel, a Microsoft product, has captured the lion's share of the market for spreadsheets, with Lotus nearly reduced to a mere memory in terms of market share. With the rapid pace of change in software technology, winning a (legal) battle may be of very little

importance in determining the outcome of the war for market share!

INDUSTRY STANDARDS AND FUNCTIONALITY

As soon as the courts latched onto the "look and feel" test, problems with the test began to surface, prompting other courts in subsequent cases to narrow and restrict the test. Essentially, what the courts held is that the "look and feel" test only applied to the parts of the

[9]*Lotus Development Corporation* v. *Paperback Software International*, 740 F.Supp. 37 (1990).

software program that are protectible under copyright law, i.e., only the expressions of the idea, not the idea itself. If the SSO is *indispensable* to accomplish the objective of the software program, then it is not protectible. SSOs are only protectible if it can be shown that the same tasks (or functions) can be accomplished with another SSO so that the copyright owner's SSO is clearly an expression of an idea and not the idea itself.

Another issue that the courts have had to deal with is whether a SSO that is the "market favorite" can be protected. After some initial variability in rulings, courts have decided that if the SSO is the *industry standard,* then it cannot be protected. Court decisions adhering to this principle severely weakened the relevance of the "look and feel" test. In *Borland* v. *Lotus,* the upstart (at the time) Borland sought to make its "Quattro" spreadsheet program completely compatible with Lotus so that Lotus users could switch to Borland and would not have to learn all new commands. Lotus, again, sued for infringement. After several rounds in Court, Borland prevailed.[10] In the words of the court,

> "If Lotus is granted a monopoly on this pattern, users
> who have learned the command structure of Lotus
> 1-2-3 or devised their own macros are locked into
> Lotus, just as a typist who has learned the QWERTY
> keyboard would be the captive of anyone who had a
> monopoly on the production of such a keyboard."

In the Court's view, for an extended period of time, Lotus 1-2-3 held such sway in the market that it had become the *industry standard* for electronic spreadsheet commands. The court concluded that so long as Lotus is the superior spreadsheet—either in quality or in price—there may be nothing wrong with this advantage. The court expressed the view, however, that if a better spreadsheet comes along, it was hard to see why customers who had learned the Lotus menu and devised macros for it should remain captives of Lotus because of an investment in learning made by the users and not by Lotus. Lotus, the court concluded, had already reaped a substantial reward for being first; assuming that the Borland program is now better, good reasons exist for freeing it to attract old Lotus customers: to enable the old customers to take advantage of a new advance, and to reward Borland in turn for making a better product.

The court argued that if Borland has not made a better product, then customers would remain with Lotus anyway.[11]

OTHER LIMITATIONS OF COPYRIGHT PROTECTION OF SOFTWARE

Archival and Other Copies

Section 117 of the Copyright Act guarantees that an owner of a copy of a computer program is entitled to make another copy of the software program ". . . provided: that such a new copy or adaptation is created as an essential step in the utilization of the computer program or that such a new copy or adaptation is for archival purposes only. . . ."

Thus, the Copyright Act firmly establishes the right of owners of copies of copyrighted software to make copies of the software regardless of language that may appear in the licensing agreement between the software vendor and the purchaser. So, per Section 117, owners of copies of copyrighted software are entitled by statute to make copies of that software. Making archival copies is certainly legitimate, but an unscrupulous owner could make copies for surreptitious and infringing distribution. China and other countries have been accused of blatantly ignoring copyright laws with respect not only to software, but also to videos and musical CDs, allowing software pirates to operate with little fear of retribution.

Compatibility and Decompilation

It is common for developers (original equipment manufacturers [OEMs]) of hardware, networks, and operating systems to sell software that is compatible with their hardware (or networks or operating systems) and to aspire to continue selling upgraded software packages to "their" customers. Naturally, such OEMs are concerned with competition from rivals who sell software that is compatible with their hardware. To make this more difficult, an OEM can imbed code in its creations aimed at preventing compatibility with other vendors' software. A number of antitrust cases indicate that OEMs, in fact, quite frequently create intentional technological incompatibilities to thwart substitute software vendors, a practice that the Department of

---

[10]49 F.3d 807 (1995).

[11]*Lotus Development Corp., v. Borland International, Inc.,* 49 F.3rd 807, (Fifth Cir., 1995).

Justice contests when the OEM has significant market power.[12]

Compatibility

The core issue faced in compatibililty cases is whether a rival of the OEM can purchase the hardware and software of the OEM, use those products to figure out how to make their own software compatible with the hardware, and sell their "reverse engineered" software to work with the OEM's hardware. This reverse engineering process may be considerably less costly than original creation of software, and may produce software that can be profitably offered at a lower price than that required by the OEM. Courts have had to deal with the question of whether such a rival, using this procedure, should be permitted to make software that is *compatible* with the OEM's equipment and compete with the OEM for downstream software sales.

Decompilation

Generally, compatibility is accomplished by *decompiling* targeted software. Decompilation occurs when a software developer transforms object code into source code of copyrighted software so that it can find out the secrets of making software developer's software compatible with the hardware or operating system of the other business. The act of decompiling software is an unauthorized reproduction of the software that is an infringement unless decompilation is deemed a *fair use* under the copyright laws.

An issue addressed by the court in the *Sega* case is whether decompilation for purposes of achieving compatibility and competing for sales with the OEM violates the Copyright Act's prohibition on unauthorized reproductions.[13] In this case rival creators of software in the form of cartridges designed to fit into the *Sega* game controller reproduced and decompiled copyrighted software from Sega cartridges to learn the code necessary to make their products compatible. When Sega asked for court protection from this practice, the court answered in the negative stating that "We conclude, based on the policies underlying the Copyright Act, that disassembly of copyrighted object code is a *fair use* of the work if such disassembly provides the only means of access to those elements of the code that are not protected by copyright, and the copier has a

legitimate reason for seeking such access." In other words, decompilation for purposes of achieving compatibility is legal. Other decompilations, such as decompilations to facilitate infringements, are in themselves (per se) infringements.

Following *Sega,* competitors of both equipment OEMs and operating systems producers (such as Microsoft) began using clean room–dirty room techniques to create software that is functionally similar to copyrighted software but does not *infringe.* Remember, copyright law does not protect the functionality of software. In a "dirty" room the target software is cleaned (decompiled) to the point where programmers can separate *ideas* from *expressions of the ideas.* A target *idea* might be a fight scene between some alien beasts and superheroes that users can control to punch and kick. The colors, the scenes, the specific jumps and kicks are the *expressions of the ideas.* The programmers in the "clean" room are then given the ideas from the dirty room and told to create the software program and make it compatible with the hardware or operating system of the OEM. In this process, the software competitor can take elaborate steps to document the clean room–dirty room technique so that it cannot be accused of copying the software of the OEM.

Decompilation also enables rivals to learn the code secrets of copyrighted software programs such as what commands are required by the hardware and what commands links are required to make other parts of the program work efficiently. Such software applications, if discovered through decompilation and reverse engineering, are not protected by copyright law.

Network Externalities and Copyright Protection

In economic jargon, an externality is a cost or benefit that is a side effect of a particular activity. Public education is viewed as having value greater than the value bestowed on an individual because society as a whole benefits from having an educated populace. Similarly, there is widespread agreement that there are external benefits shared by all users of a *network*. Telephone networks provide a familiar illustration of this phenomenon. There is no value to being the only person in an area with a telephone. Telephone networks have value to the extent that there are many in the area that are connected to the network, with the benefits of having a telephone increasing as use becomes more widespread. In fact, for most of the

---

[12]See U.S. v. Microsoft, 84 F.Supp. 2d 9 (1999).
[13]*Sega Enterprises, Ltd.* v. *Accolade, Inc.,* 977 F.2d 1510 (1992).

20th Century, local telephone networks operated as government-regulated monopolies in part because of the benefits of having all users in an area using the same network.

Network software can have similar characteristics. The value of a software network is positively related to the number of users. A consequence of positive network externalities is that in software markets where network externalities are significant, there are likely to be very small numbers of competing suppliers. If software creates a network that enhances compatibility, the value of the network to all participants will increase as the number of users grows, and such networks may grow quite dramatically. In a relatively short time the software that creates a successful network may well become an industry standard, and thus become unprotectible under copyright law. Ironically, copyright law has the capacity to punish good programmers who provide significant and successful improvements that capture markets.

Apple Computer, Inc. v. *Microsoft Corp.*
U.S. Court of Appeals, Ninth Circuit
35 F.3d 1435 (1994)

FACTS AND CASE BACKGROUND

Apple Corporation (Apple) made a significant improvement in computer usability with its icon-based user interface. Their graphical user interface (GUI) was so successful that it was imitated by Microsoft Corporation (Microsoft). When Apple objected, the two corporations negotiated and eventually Apple agreed to license the GUI to Microsoft in the form of Windows 1.0 and also gave Microsoft the right to sublicense derivative works from Windows 1.0. When Microsoft released Windows 3.0 and sublicensed to Hewlett-Packard New Wave software (both with GUIs), Apple objected again and this time they filed suit in federal court claiming infringement.

CASE DECISION: RYMER, CIRCUIT JUDGE

Apple asks us to reverse because of two fundamental errors in the district court's reasoning. First, Apple argues that the court should not have allowed the license for Windows 1.0 to serve as a partial defense. Second, Apple contends that the court went astray by dissecting Apple's works so as to eliminate unprotectible and licensed elements from comparison with Windows 2.03, 3.0 and

NewWave as a whole, incorrectly leading it to adopt a standard of virtual identity instead of substantial similarity. We disagree.

The district court's approach was on target. In so holding, we readily acknowledge how much more complex and difficult its task was than ours. The district court had to grapple with graphical user interfaces in the first instance—and for the first time, with a claim of copying a computer program's artistic look as an audiovisual work instead of program codes registered as a literary work. In this case there is also the unusual, added complexity of a license that arguably covers some or most of the allegedly infringing works. The district court therefore had to cut new paths as it went along; we have the luxury of looking at the case at the end of the trip. From this vantage point, it is clear that treatment of Apple's GUIs, whose visual displays are licensed to a great degree and which are a tool for the user to access various functions of a computer in an aesthetically and ergonomically pleasing way, follows naturally from a long line of copyright decisions which recognizes that works cannot be substantially similar where analytic dissection demonstrates that

similarities in expression are either authorized, or arise from the use of common ideas or their logical extensions.

We therefore hold:

1. Because there was an agreement by which Apple licensed the right to make certain derivative works, the district court properly started with the license to determine what Microsoft was permitted to copy. Infringement cannot be founded on a licensed similarity. We read Microsoft's license as the district court did, to cover visual displays—not the Windows 1.0 interface itself. That being so, the court correctly decided first to identify which visual displays in Windows 2.03, 3.0 and NewWave are licensed and which are not.

2. The district court then properly proceeded to distinguish ideas from expression, and to "dissect" unlicensed elements in order to determine whether the remaining similarities lack originality, flow naturally from basic ideas, or are one of the few ways in which a particular idea can be expressed given the

constraints of the computer environment. Dissection is not inappropriate even though GUIs are thought of as the "look and feel" of a computer, because copyright protection extends only to protectible elements of expression.

3. Having found that the similarities in Windows 2.03 and 3.0 consist only of unprotectible or licensed elements, and that the similarities between protectible elements in Apple's works and NewWave are de minimis, . . . the district court did not err by concluding that,

to the extent there is creative expression left in how the works are put together, as a whole they can receive only limited protection. When the range of protectible and unauthorized expression is narrow, the appropriate standard for illicit copying is virtual identity. For these reasons, the GUIs in Windows 2.03, 3.0 and NewWave cannot be compared for substantial similarity with the Macintosh interface as a whole. Instead, as the district court held, the works must be compared for virtual identity.

QUESTIONS FOR ANALYSIS

1. Given the tremendous sales of subsequent versions of Windows (95, 98, ME, and NT), is it fair to say that much of the success of Microsoft is due to clever lawyering in negotiating the initial license with Apple when the first version of Windows was objected to by Apple?

2. Does the holding in this case mean that a programmer who makes only trivial differences between the Apple GUIs and his or her own is safe from liability for infringement?

"Will Colleges and Universities Become Cybercops?"

" **A**s colleges and universities seek to provide ubiquitous Internet access and other network services for their faculty and students, service provider liability comes to the forefront as a major technology policy topic. Your institution will likely be presented with a liability issue sometime soon, if it has not already.

In recent years some confusion has arisen about whether colleges and universities fall within the same category as commercial Internet Service Providers (ISPs). The precise answer to that question depends on the regulatory and legislative context. The line of analysis used by the Federal Communications Commission for ISPs is long and tortured and is influenced by a historical separation between enhanced service providers and telecommunication carriers (a model endangered somewhat by Internet Protocol telephony). Meanwhile Congress has for the most part defined ISPs very broadly. In

general, colleges and universities appear likely to be swept in with other service providers in any legislation that seeks to affect ISPs.

Two recent congressional actions showcase how colleges and universities may find themselves either (1) receiving beneficial protections from liability or (2) being increasingly drawn into the legal morass of this new communications medium. Both pieces of legislation define the category of network service providers broadly: colleges and universities that provide Internet services appear to fall within the universe of ISPs affected by the legislation."

Source: Sern, Garret "Will Colleges and Universities Become Cybercops?," *Educom Review,* Jul/Aug99, Vol. 34, Issue 4, p. 8, Reprinted with permission.

In the Apple case above, based on the facts presented to it, the Court:

1. rejected the "look and feel" test when most of Apple's program was deemed unprotectible, and

2. indicated that an industry standard is not protectible under copyright law (described as an "aesthetically and ergonomically pleasing way" to access various computer functions"), and

3. indicated that when the "look and feel" test is not appropriate, the test is "virtual identity." Virtual identity means that only unvarnished copying of computer code is protectible under copyright law.

Nonobviousness and Other Limitations

Many commentators believe that court protection of computer software programs through copyright law suffers other fundamental weaknesses. Perhaps most notably among other weaknesses, in contrast to the standard under patent law, there is no nonobviousness requirement for obtaining a copyright. As a result, small changes in software programs are capable of receiving copyrights. Since significant portions of most software programs are not protectible, and the same SSOs and screen displays can be accomplished with a variety of object and source codes, the legal protection provided by copyright laws continues to shrink. Certainly, blatant copying and distribution by rip-off artists are still actionable infringements under the copyright laws even in the *Apple* decision. Yet, a broad range of legal methods of replicating (or nearly replicating) software programs, both the literal and nonliteral portions, clearly passes court muster. The end result is that copyright now provides weak protection against a skilled competitor who is determined to replicate another's software. Because of the limits we have discussed on the effectiveness of copyright protection of software, firms have migrated towards protection of software under other forms of intellectual property law, including patent, trade secret, and trademark law.

Patentability of Software

The Patent and Trademark Office (PTO) will not award a patent to a *scientific discovery*. So, the discovery by Albert Einstein of a relationship between matter and energy ($E = MC^2$) could not give rise to a patent for discovery or application of that relationship. The subject matter of a patent is restricted to the original creation of a *process, machine, manufacture,* or *composition of matter*. A law of nature, a mathematical formula, or an algorithm is not patentable according to the courts and the PTO, no matter how valuable.

A mechanical aid (such as software) that merely solves an equation or yields a solution for a mathematical problem traditionally has been viewed as not patentable. In *Gottschalk* v. *Benson* the Supreme Court upheld the denial of a patent to a software process that converted binary code decimal numbers to equivalent binary numbers. In *Parker* v. *Flook* the Supreme Court denied a patent to a method for computing an alarm limit in connection with a chemical process. The court claimed that the alarm limit was merely a number and thus the process that merely computed that number and generated a warning was an unpatentable algorithm.

Relaxation of Obstacles to Patenting of Software

In a landmark case in 1981, departing from its stance in the *Gottschalk* case, the Supreme Court in *Diamond* v. *Diehr* granted a patent to a *process* that made use of computer software.[14] In *Diehr,* the applicant applied

---

Gottschalk **v.** *Benson* **et al.**
U.S. Supreme Court
409 U.S. 63 (1972)

FACTS AND CASE BACKGROUND

In 1972 the U.S. Supreme Court ruled on whether programming a computer to perform certain tasks was patentable. One way to view computer programs that perform tasks is that they are steps in a mental process of accomplishing a result. As such, they are too dangerously close to an idea for the PTO to issue a patent. The court in *Benson* viewed computerization of mathematical formulae and equations as possibly foreclosing future use of the formulae and equations. This case was decided at the dawn of software and could have posed a significant barrier to patent protection of software. Fortunately, the courts began fashioning exceptions to *Benson* very quickly.

CASE DECISION: DOUGLAS, JUSTICE

The representation of numbers may be in the form of a time series of electrical impulses, magnetized spots on the surface of tapes, drums, or discs, charged spots on cathode-ray tube screens, the presence or absence of punched holes on paper cards, or other devices. The method or program is a sequence of coded instructions for a digital computer.

The patent sought is a method of programming a general-purpose digital computer to convert signals from binary-coded decimal form into pure binary form. A procedure for solving a given type of mathematical problem is known as an "algorithm." The procedures set forth in the present claims are of that kind; that is to say, they are a generalized formulation for programs to solve mathematical problems of converting one form of numerical representation to another. From the generic formulation, programs may be developed as specific applications.

The decimal system uses as digits the 10 symbols 0, 1, 2, 3, 4, 5, 6, 7, 8, and 9. The value represented by any digit depends, as it does in any positional system of notation, both on its individual value and on its relative position in the numeral. Decimal numerals are written by placing digits in the appropriate positions or columns of the numerical sequence, i.e., "unit" ($10<0>$), "tens" ($10<1>$), "hundreds" ($10<2>$), "thousands" ($10<3>$), etc. Accordingly, the numeral 1492 signifies ($1 \times 10<3>$) + ($4 \times 10<2>$) + ($9 \times 10<1>$) + ($2 \times 10<0>$).

The pure binary system of positional notation uses two symbols as digits—0 and 1, placed in a numerical sequence with values based on consecutively ascending powers of 2. In pure binary notation, what would be the tens position is the twos position; what would be hundreds position is the fours position; what would be the thousands position is the eights. Any decimal number from 0 to 10 can be represented in the binary system with four digits or positions as indicated in the following table . . .

* * *

The Court stated in *Mackay Co.* v. *Radio Corp.,* 306 U.S. 86, 94, that "while a scientific truth, or the mathematical expression of it, is not a patentable invention, a novel and useful structure created with the aid of knowledge of scientific truth may be." That statement followed the

longstanding rule that "an idea of itself is not patentable." *Rubber-Tip Pencil Co.* v. *Howard,* 20 Wall. 498, 507. "A principle, in the abstract, is a fundamental truth; an original cause; a motive; these cannot be patented, as no one can claim in either of them an exclusive right." *Le Roy* v. *Tatham,* 14 How. 156, 175. Phenomena of nature, though just discovered, mental processes, and abstract intellectual concepts are not patentable, as they are the basic tools of scientific and technological work. As we stated in *Funk Bros. Seed Co.* v. *Kalo Co.,* 333 U.S. 127, 130, "He who discovers a hitherto unknown phenomenon of nature has no claim to a monopoly of it which the law recognizes. If there is to be invention from such a discovery, it must come from the application of the law of nature to a new and useful end." We dealt there with a "product" claim, while the present case deals with a "process" claim. But we think the same principle applies.

Here the "process" claim is so abstract and sweeping as to cover both known and unknown uses of the BCD to pure binary conversion. The end use may (1) vary from the operation of a train to verification of drivers' licenses to researching the law books for precedents and (2) be performed through any existing machinery or future-devised machinery or without any apparatus.

* * *

We do not hold that no process patent could ever qualify if it did not meet the requirements of our prior precedents. It is said that the decision precludes a patent for any program servicing a computer. We do not so

hold. It is said that we have before us a program for a digital computer but extend our holding to programs for analog computers. We have, however, made clear from the start that we deal with a program only for digital computers. It is said we freeze process patents to old technologies, leaving no room for the revelations of the new, onrushing technology. Such is not our purpose. What we come down to in a nutshell is the following.

It is conceded that one may not patent an idea. But in practical effect that would be the result if the formula for converting BCD numerals to pure binary numerals were patented in this case. The mathematical formula involved here has no substantial practical application except in connection with a digital computer, which means that if the judgment below is affirmed, the patent would wholly pre-empt the mathematical formula and in practical effect would be a patent on the algorithm itself. [7]

* * *

The Supreme Court ruled that Benson could not get a patent on his method of converting binary coded decimals to pure binary form.

QUESTIONS FOR REVIEW

1. Given this holding, could a patent applicant obtain a patent for a new kind of slide rule whose only use was to convert large numbers to logarithms?
2. If Benson had carefully limited his patent claims to specific computer transformations, would that have quelled the concerns voiced by Justice Douglas?

---

for a patent that made use of an equation (the *Arrhenius* equation), that was already well-known and frequently used in connection with rubber-making. In

Diehr, software controlled ovens and molds to keep temperatures at proper limits for curing rubber products. The court claimed that a process does not become unpatentable merely because it makes use of computer software. The court noted that the applicant in *Diehr*

[14]*Diamond v. Diehr,* 450 U.S. 175 (1981).

did not seek to patent or preempt use of the *Arrhenius* equation, but rather the application was for patenting the entire process of curing rubber using a particular software program. According to the Supreme Court in *Diehr:*

> We view D&L's claims as nothing more than a process for molding rubber products and not as an attempt to patent a mathematical formula. We recognize, of course, that when a claim recites a mathematical formula (or scientific principle or phenomenon of nature), an inquiry must be made into whether the claim is seeking patent protection for the formula in the abstract. A mathematical formula as such is not accorded the protection of the patent laws, and this principle cannot be circumvented by attempting to limit the use of the formula to a particular technological environment. Similarly, insignificant post-solution activity will not transform an unpatentable principle into a patentable process.

An Inexorable March Forward

Following the *Diehr* decision, a two-part test became a standard hurdle for patent applications that involve software. The first test issue was whether the applica- tion called for patent protection of software. If the answer was yes, then the courts inquired as to whether the claimed invention as a whole was just a software solution of an algorithm with a little win- dow dressing put on for decoration. If the answer to the second inquiry was yes, then the PTO would deny a patent and courts upheld those decisions. As time passed, however, courts became more receptive to software-related patents. An applicant applied for a patent based on software that transformed speech patterns into waves on an oscilloscope and the court agreed a patent should be issued.[15] In the case below, software that measured heart palpitations of heart at- tack victims and computed a value that was used for medical treatments was also granted a patent. These decisions are at odds with the earlier *Gottschalk* and *Flook* decisions, making it clear that courts have abandoned those earlier decisions in favor of a more welcoming stance towards upholding patents granted to innovations that use or are comprised entirely of software.

---

[15]*In re Alappat,* 33 F.3d 1526 (1994).

Arrhythmia Research Technology, Inc. v. *Corazonix Corp.*
U.S. Court of Appeals, Federal Circuit
958 F.2d 1053 (1992)

FACTS AND CASE BACKGROUND

A critical time for heart attack vic- tims is shortly after the heart attack. Dr. Michael Simson applied for a patent on a device that converted electrocardiogram signals into a for- mula that was used to guide treat- ment. The invention transformed the values of the signals from the heart into a mean square error and based on that figure treatments were prescribed.

CASE DECISION

Whether a claim is directed to statu- tory subject matter is a question of law. Although determination of this question may require findings of un- derlying facts specific to the particu- lar subject matter and its mode of claiming, in this case there were no disputed facts material to the issue.

A new and useful process or ap- paratus is patentable subject matter, as defined in 35 U.S.C. § 101:

> Whoever invents or discovers any new and useful process, machine, manufacture, or composition of matter, or any new and useful improvement thereof, may obtain a patent therefor, subject to the conditions and requirements of this title.

The Supreme Court has observed that Congress intended section 101 to include "anything under the sun that is made by man." There are, however, qualifications to the appar- ent sweep of this statement. Ex- cluded from patentability is subject matter in the categories of "laws of nature, physical phenomena, and ab- stract ideas." A mathematical for- mula may describe a law of nature, a scientific truth, or an abstract idea. As courts have recognized, mathe- matics may also be used to describe steps of a statutory method or ele- ments of a statutory apparatus. The exceptions to patentable subject mat- ter derive from a lengthy jurispru- dence, but their meaning was probed anew with the advent of computer- related inventions. In *Gottschalk* v. *Benson,* 409 U.S. 63, 72, 175 USPQ

673, 676 (1972), the Court held that a patent claim that "wholly pre-empts" a mathematical formula used in a general purpose digital computer is directed solely to a mathematical algorithm, and therefore does not define statutory subject matter under section 101. The Court described the mathematical process claimed in Benson as "so abstract and sweeping as to cover both known and unknown uses of the BCD [binary coded decimal] to pure binary conversion" for its holding that the patentee may not claim more than he has actually invented.

In *Parker* v. *Flook,* 437 U.S. 584, 591, 198 USPQ 193, 198 (1978), the Court explained that the criterion for patentability of a claim that requires the use of mathematical procedures is not simply whether the claim "wholly pre-empts" a mathematical algorithm, but whether the claim is directed to a new and useful process, independent of whether the mathematical algorithm required for its performance is novel. Applying these criteria the Court held nonstatutory a method claim for computer-calculating "alarm limits" for use in a catalytic conversion process, on the basis that "once that algorithm is assumed to be within the prior art, the application, considered as a whole, contains no patentable invention."

Thus computers came to be generally recognized as devices capable of performing or implementing process steps, or serving as components of an apparatus, without negating patentability of the process or the apparatus. In *Diamond* v. *Diehr* the Court explained that nonstatutory status under section 101 derives from the "abstract", rather than the "sweeping", nature of a claim that contains a mathematical algorithm. The Court stated:

> While a scientific truth, or the mathematical expression of it, is not a patentable invention, a

novel and useful structure created with the aid of knowledge of scientific truth may be.

The law crystallized about the principle that claims directed solely to an abstract mathematical formula or equation, including the mathematical expression of scientific truth or a law of nature, whether directly or indirectly stated, are nonstatutory under section 101; whereas claims to a specific process or apparatus that is implemented in accordance with a mathematical algorithm will generally satisfy section 101.

ANALYSIS

Arrhythmia Research states that the district court erred in law, and that the combination of physical, mechanical, and electrical steps that are described and claimed in the '459 patent constitutes statutory subject matter. Arrhythmia Research stresses that the claims are directed to a process and apparatus for detecting and analyzing a specific heart activity signal, and do not preempt the mathematical algorithms used in any of the procedures. Arrhythmia Research states that the patentability of such claims is now well established by law, precedent, and practice.

Corazonix states that the claims define no more than a mathematical algorithm that calculates a number. Corazonix states that in Simson's process and apparatus claims mathematical algorithms are merely presented and solved, and that Simson's designation of a field of use and post-solution activity are not essential to the claims and thus do not cure this defect. Thus, Corazonix states that the claims are not directed to statutory subject matter, and that the district court's judgment was correct.

A. THE PROCESS CLAIMS

Although mathematical calculations are involved in carrying out the claimed process, Arrhythmia Re-

search argues that the claims are directed to a method of detection of a certain heart condition by a novel method of analyzing a portion of the electrocardiographically measured heart cycle. This is accomplished by procedures conducted by means of electronic equipment programmed to perform mathematical computation.

Simson's process is claimed as a "method for analyzing electrocardiograph signals to determine the presence or absence of a predetermined level of high-frequency energy in the late QRS signal". This claim limitation is not ignored in determining whether the subject matter as a whole is statutory, for all of the claim steps are in implementation of this method. The electrocardiograph signals are first transformed from analog form, in which they are obtained, to the corresponding digital signal. These input signals are not abstractions; they are related to the patient's heart function. The anterior portion of the QRS signal is then processed, as the next step, by the procedure known as reverse time order filtration. The digital filter design selected by Dr. Simson for this purpose, known as the Butterworth filter, is one of several known procedures for frequency filtering of digital waveforms. The filtered signal is further analyzed to determine its average magnitude, as described in the specification, by the root mean square technique. Comparison of the resulting output to a predetermined level determines whether late potentials reside in the anterior portion of the QRS segment, thus indicating whether the patient is at high risk for ventricular tachycardia. The resultant output is not an abstract number, but is a signal related to the patient's heart activity.

These claimed steps of "converting", "applying", "determining", and "comparing" are physical process steps that transform one physical, electrical signal into another. The view that "there is nothing necessarily physical about 'signals'" is incorrect. The Freeman–Walter–Abele standard is met, for the steps of Simson's claimed method comprise an otherwise statutory process whose mathematical procedures are applied to physical process steps.

The Simson claims are analogous to those upheld in *Diehr,* wherein the Court remarked that the applicants "do not seek to patent a mathematical formula. . . . they seek only to foreclose from others the use of that equation in conjunction with all of the other steps in their claimed process". Simson's claimed method is similarly limited. The process claims comprise statutory subject matter.

QUESTIONS FOR ANALYSIS

1. As a result of the case, are other physicians precluded from measuring the heart palpitations of heart attack victims and converting those palpitations into mean square errors? If the method of measuring the heart palpitations was different, would that enable other physicians to use the same process for prescribing treatment to heart attack victims?

2. Is the subject matter of this process properly patentable? Why should a doctor in a less developed country have to pay Dr. Simson anything for treating his or her patients in the best possible manner?

1996 PTO Guidelines on Patents and Software[16]

In an attempt to clear confusion regarding the criteria for issuance of software-related patents, the Patent and Trademark Office elucidated formulae in 1996 that were believed to be consistent with court decisions. These Guidelines do not have force of law but, instead, are instructions by the PTO to its own examiners. Courts may or may not abide by these Guidelines, and there are reasons to believe that court standards for patentability of software are even more liberal than these Guidelines. According to the Guidelines,

> . . . , Office personnel will no longer begin examination by determining if a claim recites a "mathematical algorithm." Rather, they will review the complete specification, including the detailed description of the invention, any specific embodiments that have been disclosed, the claims and any specific utilities that have been asserted for the invention.

The Guidelines go on to limit patents to inventions that "possess a certain level of 'real world' value, as opposed to subject matter that represents nothing more than an idea or concept, or is simply a starting point for future investigation or research."[17]

The Guidelines call for examiners to classify each invention as either statutory or nonstatutory and for the invention to be placed in categories within each classification. Thus, if an application is "statutory", it must also be labeled as a process, manufacture, machine, or composition of matter. If the examiner considers the invention nonstatutory, he or she must label whether it is just a mathematical algorithm, an idea, or some other category of nonstatutory invention.

According to the PTO Guidelines, no patents will be issued for what the PTO labels "descriptive" material. Material is *functionally* descriptive if the software "consist of data structures and the computer programs impart functionality when encoded on a computer-readable medium." Essentially what the PTO is saying is that computer data structures are not patentable because they are neither physical things nor statutory processes. To be patentable there must be a relationship between the data structure and other claimed aspects of the invention, which permit the data structure's functionality to be realized. According to the guidelines the computer program itself is not statutory material, meaning it cannot be patented.

When a Physical Product Is also Present

When a computer program is recited in combination with a physical structure in a patent application, it is still deemed a product (manufacture) claim and the issue of subject matter ends at that point. In such cases, the product claim can be evaluated under normal standards for products, even if the product makes use of some software. On other issues involving software, the PTO contends that software can be patented "when a computer program is claimed in a process where the computer is executing the

---

[16]http://www.uspto.gov/web/offices/pac/compexm/examcomp.htm
[17]*Brenner* v. *Manson,* 383 U.S. 519, 528–36, 148 USPQ 689, 693–96 (1966); *In re Ziegler,* 992 F.2d 1197, 1200–03, 26 USPQ2d 1600, 1603–06 (Fed. Cir. 1993).

computer program's instructions . . ." To be statutory, the PTO claims that the computer-related process must either:

- Result in a *physical transformation* outside the computer for which a practical application is disclosed or is obvious to one skilled in the industry, or
- The computer-invention must be limited by language in the claim to a *practical application.*

The *practical application* requirement was satisfied in the *In Re Alappat* case by a computer-driven creation of smooth waveforms in a digital oscilloscope through some computer software. Even though the software transformed pixels on a TV screen in response to input waveform based on the values of a data vector list, the CAFC held that the invention was a statutory (patentable) process because it was a practical application of the principle.[18] The *physical transformation* in the first regulation listed above was satisfied in *Diehr* by the process of making rubber. As discussed above the patent application did not foreclose subsequent use of the *Arrhenius* formula to others, but only the application embodied in the claim.

[18]*In Re Alappat*, 33 F.3d 1526 (1994).

The process resulted in the more efficient curing of rubber.

Recent Patent Protection of Software

The PTO currently faces an avalanche of software-related patent applications. By 1998 over 30,000 software or software-related patents were granted and in force. The traditional training for patent examiners has been in physical sciences or engineering, but an increasing number of patent applications have a significant software component or are entirely software, requiring specialized knowledge for the evaluation of novelty and nonobviousness.

The following case pushed the envelope again on the issue of the patentability of software. This case is notable for several reasons. First, the U.S. Supreme Court threw out what was widely assumed to be an integral restriction of patent law, namely the standard that "business methods" were not patentable. Second, the software at issue in this case does not to appear to be accompanied by any physical transformation. Mathematical values are calculated for investors in a mutual fund. It is very difficult to reconcile this case with *Gottschalk,* although it is possible that the application of this problem-solving algorithm is less far reaching than the invention Gottschalk tried to patent.

State Street Bank **v.** *Signature Financial*
United States Court of Appeals, Federal Circuit
149 F.3d 1368 (1998)

FACTS AND CASE BACKGROUND

Limits are being tested most dramatically in the financial service instruments arena. Financial software that calculated yields to maturity of bonds in a cash management system has received a patent.[19] In the case below, a data processing system for implementing an investment structure in connection with mutual funds was under scrutiny. The District Court held that the software at issue was no more than an unpatentable

[19]*Paine, Webber, Jackson & Curtis, Inc.,* v. *Merrill Lynch, Pierce, Fenner & Smith, Inc.,* 564 F.Supp. 1358 (D. Del. 1983).

algorithm. Also in this case, the CAFC reexamined the business method exception, which was thought to be off limits for patents. According to the Court of Appeals for the Federal Circuit (CAFC), software is patentable if the software produces a useful, concrete and tangible result. This case illustrates how far courts have departed from the Benson decision in 1972.

CASE DECISION: RICH, CIRCUIT JUDGE

The patented invention relates generally to a system that allows an administrator to monitor and record the fi-

nancial information flow and make all calculations necessary for maintaining a partner fund financial services configuration. As previously mentioned, a partner fund financial services configuration essentially allows several mutual funds, or "Spokes," to pool their investment funds into a single portfolio, or "Hub," allowing for consolidation of, *inter alia,* the costs of administering the fund combined with the tax advantages of a partnership. In particular, this system provides means for a daily allocation of assets for two or more Spokes that are invested in the same Hub. The system determines the percentage share that each Spoke maintains in the Hub, while taking into consideration daily changes both in the value of the Hub's investment securities and in the concomitant amount of each Spoke's assets.

In determining daily changes, the system also allows for the allocation among the Spokes of the Hub's daily income, expenses, and net realized and unrealized gain or loss, calculating each day's total investments based on the concept of a book capital account. This enables the determination of a true asset value of each Spoke and accurate calculation of allocation ratios between or among the Spokes. The system additionally tracks all the relevant data determined on a daily basis for the Hub and each Spoke, so that aggregate year end income, expenses, and capital gain or loss can be determined for accounting and for tax purposes for the Hub and, as a result, for each publicly traded Spoke.

* * *

The "Mathematical Algorithm" Exception

The Supreme Court has identified three categories of subject matter that are unpatentable, namely, "laws of nature, natural phenomena, and abstract ideas." Of particular relevance to this case, the Court has held that mathematical algorithms are not patentable subject matter to the extent that they are merely abstract ideas. In *Diehr,* the Court explained that certain types of mathematical subject matter, standing alone, represent nothing more than abstract ideas until reduced to some type of practical application, i.e., "a useful, concrete and tangible result."

Unpatentable mathematical algorithms are identifiable by showing they are merely abstract ideas constituting disembodied concepts or truths that are not "useful." From a practical standpoint, this means that to be patentable an algorithm must be applied in a "useful" way. In

Alappat, we held that data, transformed by a machine through a series of mathematical calculations to produce a smooth waveform display on a rasterizer monitor, constituted a practical application of an abstract idea (a mathematical algorithm, formula, or calculation), because it produced "a useful, concrete and tangible result"—the smooth waveform.

Similarly, in *Arrhythmia Research Technology Inc.* v. *Corazonix Corp.,* 958 F.2d 1053, 22 USPQ2d 1033 (Fed.Cir.1992), we held that the transformation of electrocardiograph signals from a patient's heartbeat by a machine through a series of mathematical calculations constituted a practical application of an abstract idea (a mathematical algorithm, formula, or calculation), because it corresponded to a useful, concrete or tangible thing—the condition of a patient's heart.

Today, we hold that the transformation of data, representing discrete dollar amounts, by a machine through a series of mathematical calculations into a final share price, constitutes a practical application of a mathematical algorithm, formula, or calculation, because it produces "a useful, concrete and tangible result"—a final share price momentarily fixed for recording and reporting purposes and even accepted and relied upon by regulatory authorities and in subsequent trades. For this author the *State Street* decision calls into question whether the PTO Software Guidelines will be respected by the U.S. Supreme Court and thus by extension the CAFC.

As an alternative ground for invalidating the '056 patent under § 101, the court relied on the judicially-created, so-called "business method" exception to statutory subject matter. We take this opportunity to lay this ill-conceived exception to rest. Since its inception, the "business method" exception has merely represented the application of some general, but no longer applicable legal principle, perhaps

arising out of the "requirement for invention"—which was eliminated by § 103. Since the 1952 Patent Act, business methods have been, and should have been, subject to the same legal requirements for patentability as applied to any other process or method.

As Judge Newman has previously stated, [The business method exception] is . . . an unwarranted encumbrance to the definition of statutory subject matter in section 101, that [should] be discarded as error-prone, redundant, and obsolete. It merits retirement from the glossary of section 101. . . . All of the "doing business" cases could have been decided using the clearer concepts of Title 35. Patentability does not turn on whether the claimed method does "business" instead of something else, but on whether the method, viewed as a whole, meets the requirements of patentability as set forth in Sections 102, 103, and 112 of the Patent Act.

We agree that this is precisely the manner in which this type of claim should be treated. Whether the claims are directed to subject matter within § 101 should not turn on whether the claimed subject matter does "business" instead of something else.

Conclusion

The appealed decision is reversed and the case is remanded to the district court for further proceedings consistent with this opinion.

Questions for Analysis

1. After this decision what is left of the limitations on patentability elucidated in *Gottschalk* v. *Benson*?

2. By eliminating the business method exception, does the court allow management methods such as Total Quality Management (TQM) to be patentable? Are business methods only patentable if they are accomplished using software and a digital computer?

Is Innovation Promoted by More Software Patents?

It should be noted that the emerging proliferation of patents applied to software is not an unambiguous leap forward for software innovators. There are two effects of the provision of patent protection to software. On the one hand, patents for software do provide very substantial legal protection for creators of the software. However, as more software become patented, providing broadened and enhanced computing functionality, innovators with fewer resources may be blocked from the creation of marketable competing or derivative works because of their limited ability to cover required license fees. Flippant commentators have suggested that Amazon.com obtained software patents based on a few flicks of customer wrists, precluding others (including potential competitors) from employing the same functionality without paying license fees to Amazon.com.[20] Amazon.com owns patents based on software that is essentially a method for customers to order online using a mouse. Take away the software and ask yourself if companies could patent methods of purchasing in the physical world?

A thicket of patents, and many would add **"obvious"** patents, could result from the liberal granting of patents on software. Consider the Amazon.com thicket of software patents. The following are the names of the patents, with the content of the patent easily inferred from the titles. Keep in mind that this is only a partial list of the patents that Amazon.com has assembled, all of which are associated with ordering a book from Amazon.com online (which is the only way to order a book from Amazon since they do not have bricks-and-mortar outlets).

- Secure method and system for communicating a list of credit card numbers over a nonsecure network.[21]
- Secure method for communicating credit card data when placing an order on a nonsecure network.
- Method and system for placing a purchase order via a communications network.

- Method and apparatus for producing sequenced queries.

The PTO is going to have to deal with the question of when such "business method" software programs are properly subject to challenge under Section 103 of the Patent Act for being "obvious." After all, how else are customers to order books from Amazon except by supplying credit card information and asking questions (queries)? Many courts appear to be narrowly interpreting the scope of software-related patent claims, so that many infringement suits fail because the requirements for literal infringement or for the doctrine of equivalents are not satisfied. Even so, an assemblage of Amazon.com-style patents can have a chilling effect on the emergence of competitors to an Amazon.com. A new online book company that competes with Amazon and Barnes and Noble will have to have a system for its customers to use to order books. For a fledgling .com bookstore, even the threat of a patent infringement suit could scare away investors. These authors believe that new software-related Guidelines from the PTO are likely in the near future as software patents proliferate and threaten to block creativity in software, a potent engine for propelling economic growth in the United States in the '90s and beyond.

TRADE SECRETS

Although litigation related to copyrights and patents protection of software receives a great deal of publicity, most firms continue to rely heavily on common law *trade secret* protection of their software, particularly before it is released for sale. The Uniform Trade Secrets Act defines a *trade secret* as "information," very broadly defined, that:

- derives its economic value from not being generally known or reasonably ascertainable by proper means by people who can obtain economic value from its disclosure or use, and
- is the subject of efforts that are reasonable under the circumstances to maintain its secrecy.[22]

If some aspects of a computer program are used in business and have value because they are kept secret,

---

[20]Amazon.com is the assignee of Patent No. 5,715,399 which is entitled, "Secure method and system for communicating a list of credit card numbers over a non-secure network."

[21]The first sentence of the abstract of Patent No. 5,715,399 describes the patent as "A method and system for securely indicating to a customer one or more credit card numbers that a merchant has on file for the customer when communicating with the customer over a non-secure network."

[22]As with other "uniform" acts, the Uniform Trade Secret Act (UTSA) is state legislation that attorneys and judges prominent in the field have created to iron out state-by-state differences. The authors of the UTSA are the American Law Institute and National Conference of Commissioners on Uniform State Laws. See http://www.nccusl.org/factsheet/utsa-fs.html.

"Electronic Combination Lock Designed to Keep Out Hackers"

"The agency that helped create the world's biggest bombs has now helped create its smallest combination lock, a bit of technology aimed at preventing attacks by computer hackers.

Scientists at Sandia National Laboratories have invented a combination lock the size of a button. The reason for the diminutive size is that the lock is to be placed inside a computer to secure the contents of the hard drive.

Like a standard combination lock, the Sandia invention has mechanical wheels—six of them—that can be turned to the combination that opens the lock. The wheels are microscopic; they are turned with computer commands entered with a keypad, not manually.

Generally speaking, this class of tiny mechanical devices is known as a microelectromechanical system. Practically speaking, this could be an advance in the battle against hackers, said Frank Peter, a mechanical engineer at Sandia who helped design the lock.

When the device is in place, it essentially locks the connection between the hard drive and the rest of the computer. As a result, a hacker would not be able to gain access to the hard drive from the network or even sitting at the computer itself."

Source: From "Electronic Combination Lock Designed to Keep Out Hackers," by Matt Richtel, *New York Times,* October 29, 1998. Copyright © 1998 by the New York Times Co. Reprinted by permission.

Additional Readings:
http://www.us.net/signal/Archive/August99/minuscule-aug.html
"Minuscule Combination Lock, Safeguards Silicon Capital", August 1999;Maryann Lawlor, ©SIGNAL Magazine 1999.

http://www.sciencenews.org/sn arc98/11 14 98/Fob4.htm
"Lock-on-a-Chip May Close Hackers Out", November 14, 1998; P. Weiss, Science News Online.

http://www.sandia.gov/media/hacker.htm
"World's Smallest Combination Lock Promises to Foil Even the Best Computer Hacker, say Sandia Developers", Albuquerque, NM, News Release, October 12, 1998; Sandia National Laboratory.

---

and if that business uses reasonable means to keep the secrets secret, it can sue a misappropriator who wrongfully obtains the software secrets.

The computer software market is highly competitive and innovation is rapid and continuous. Huge financial rewards are *not* provided by "old" software but instead are captured by the latest software. First-mover advantages (the first firm to get to the market) blend nicely with trade secret protection of the innovative aspects of the new software. Patent applications in software typically take two years to execute, by which time the innovative aspects of the program are most likely superceded by yet newer innovations.[23]

Use of trade secrets is not an "either/or" strategy with other forms of IP protection. A firm can use a variety of IP protections. The initial development of software may be protected solely by trade secrets. If the firm sells a product that uses software, the firm may seek to obtain a copyright on the software and a patent on the functional parts of the product. Firms can

continue to use trade secret protection for those aspects of computer software that are not part of the public domain or record. Alternatively, firms can rely solely on trade secrets and copyrights. Patents require detailed disclosure of how the patented software works, prompting many firms to conclude that they would prefer to maintain their secrets, rather than to reveal them in order to obtain a patent. Finally, high-tech firms attach great weight to trademarks on the assumption that a valuable trademark can considerably enhance the value of untested software.

Acceptable and Unacceptable Methods of Competing

Misappropriation of trade secrets is a tort and the damage awards for such actions can be considerable. Discovery and use of another firm's trade secrets is actionable when the taking is wrongful. If a rival firm discovers a trade secret, such as the formula for *Coca-Cola,* through reverse engineering or independent creation, the taking is not wrongful. It is a misappropriation and hence actionable when, for example, ex-employees are induced to reveal trade secrets to rivals. The use of wiretaps, audio bugs, or engineers posing as visitors to learn trade secrets are other acts of misappropriation. Virtually every imaginable

---

[23]A software vendor can put the *patent pending* label on the software as long as the software vendor is applying for a patent. The patent pending label can be a very effective competitive technique, because patent applications are not revealed until the patent is granted. Since the rival has no way of knowing the scope of the claims made in the patent application or its probability of receiving the patent, the patent pending label can be very intimidating.

scheme or artifice has been used by some firm to gain access to the trade secrets of another firm. Although the acceptability of competitive tactics varies from case to case, juries are able to evaluate what seems right and wrong in this area. Courts generally apply a "sweat of the brow" standard in this arena. If the alleged misappropriator *worked* to discover the trade secrets (as in independent creation activities), then the replication is not wrongful, but if the misappropriator stole the secrets or induced employees or ex-employees to breach their fiduciary duties to their employer by revealing such secrets, there is liability.

Reasonable Security Measures

Firms can rely on trade secret protection as long as they use reasonable security measures to protect those trade secrets. What is reasonable varies from case to case. Certainly if a trade secret is readily observable by a rival who is not trespassing or relying on advanced technology to view the premises of a rival, courts would rule that the owner of the trade secrets could not recover for misappropriation of trade secrets by the rival.

What Is at Stake

In the technology arena an arms race has developed between security measures used by firms to guard trade secrets and the inventive tactics of misappropriators who seek to discover such secrets. This arms race, between aspiring good and evil, has been propelled by the huge value of the stakes. Imagine the value to writers of application software who discover the programming secrets used by Microsoft to link their operating system with application software. Every time Microsoft changes its operating system, competing companies have to expend large amounts of programming time to make their software compatible with the latest version of Windows. If they could steal (without getting caught) the compatibility code, vendors of application software would save these resources.

Firm Resources

Reasonable security measures often include combinations of technological and legal measures. The details of the technological measures that firms take to protect their trade secrets are many and varied. The *reasonableness* of security measures is considered in light of the resources of the firm. Courts do not expect small firms to bankrupt themselves guarding their secrets. Firms that have more resources and more valuable

trade secrets are expected by the courts to spend more on security.

Reasonable Measures

Firms with important trade secrets typically restrict physical access to areas from which those secrets could be discovered. Physical access can be controlled with employee badges, logs, locks, guards, and limiting distribution of trade secrets to one person. Note, though, that many high-tech firms rely on programmers and staff who may resent too much security. There certainly is concern that too much emphasis on security can inhibit creativity and innovation.

Computer systems and programs often contain a firm's most important trade secrets. Controlling access to computers within large firms has spawned a vigorous computer security industry. Hackers, of course, try to break into the computers of large corporations and financial institutions, either for amusement and a desire to create havoc, or as paid agents to engage in industrial espionage. There are numerous standard measures employed to avoid unwanted access to computer systems.

Passwords, Access and Cryptography

These include the use of passwords that are frequently changed, restricting access to software programs to company hardware within secure places, and placing phony code in software programs to prove illegal copying. Firms that transfer data over the Internet typically rely on cryptography to protect the transmissions. Cryptography is the science of transforming data to hide its content to prevent unauthorized modification or use. The sender encrypts the data with a key and the recipient decodes it with another key. Obviously, it is very important for the recipient of the transmission not to lose or disclose the decrypting code.

Preventing Penetration: Firewalls and New Means of Identification

As the ingenuity of hackers and industrial espionage agents continues to increase, counter-measures have become increasingly exotic also. Firewalls prevent incoming viruses from outside sources, particularly the Internet. Firewalls block all incoming data that does not have a code authorizing entry. Some of the identification techniques now being used and those contemplated would impress James Bond. It is now possible to restrict access to computers using voice,

All About Cryptography

"There are two types of cryptosystems: secret-key and public-key. In secret-key cryptography, also referred to as symmetric cryptography, the same key is used for both encryption and decryption. The most popular secret-key cryptosystem in use today is known as DES, the Data Encryption Standard. IBM developed DES in the middle 1970's and it has been a Federal Standard ever since 1976.

In public-key cryptography, each user has a public key and a private key. The public key is made public while the private key remains secret. Encryption is performed with the public key while decryption is done with the private key. The RSA public-key cryptosystem is the most popular form of public-key cryptography. RSA stands for Rivest, Shamir, and Adleman, the inventors of the RSA cryptosystem.

The Digital Signature Algorithm (DSA) is also a popular public-key technique, though it can be used only for signatures, not encryption. Elliptic curve cryptosystems (ECCs) are cryptosystems based on mathematical objects known as Elliptic Curves. Elliptic curve cryptography has been gaining in popularity recently. Lastly, the Diffie-Hellman key agreement protocol is a popular public-key technique for establishing secret keys over an insecure channel."

Source: http://www.rsa.com/rsalabs/faq/html/1-3.html.

Additional Readings:
http://www.cs.georgetown.edu/~denning/crypto/Future.html
"The Future of Cryptography", January 6, 1996; Dorothy E. Denning, Georgetown University.

http://www.rsasecurity.com/news/pr/961007.html
"Devon Software Chooses RSA Technology for Authentication Server",—Oct. 7, 1996; Redwood City, CA.

http://www.usc.edu/isd/publications/networker/95-96/Summer 96/feature-encryption.html
"Encryption", Summer 1996, NetWorker; By Wyman E. Miles.

http://www.nortelnetworks.com/corporate/news/newsreleases/1998c/10 06 9898512 RSA.html
"Bay Networks, a Nortel Networks Business Unit, Solidifies Encryption Strategy Through Key Relationship with RSA, Leading Security Software Provider", October 06, 1998; Jeff Young, Nortel Networks.

---

fingerprint, and iris recognition systems. No matter how elaborate the security, however, maximum effectiveness cannot be realized unless management supports the protocols and does not consider the security a nuisance. Of course, even if management buys into the security (this often occurs after the company has been a victim of pilfered trade secrets), the security system is always vulnerable to employees and ex-employees who deliberately violate security protocols, which not infrequently occurs for pecuniary gain.

In spite of the measures taken by companies to protect their software secrets, theft and litigation are common. The following case illustrates that in litigation, when misappropriation of software is alleged, the adequacy of the plaintiff's security will be an issue, even though a defendant has behaved in a clearly unethical manner.

Picker International Corporation v. *Imaging Equipment Services, Inc.*
United States District Court for the District of Massachusetts
931 F. Supp. 18; 1995

FACTS AND CASE BACKGROUND
Plaintiff Picker International Corporation ("Picker") *designs*, manufactures, sells, and services medical diagnostic equipment including the computed tomography scanners ("CT Scanners") involved in this case.

Defendant Imaging Equipment Services, Inc. ("Imaging") is an independent servicing organization ("ISO") which competes with Picker to service Picker-produced CT Scanners. Defendant Thomas J. Quinn is the founder and President of Imaging.

Picker filed suit against Imaging, alleging that Imaging, Quinn, and former employee Leavitt had misappropriated Picker's trade secrets and violated its copyrights in the course of competing to service the Picker CT scanners. Imaging contests the suit of trade secret misappropriation and copyright violation on the basis that Picker did not take adequate measures to protect its information, primarily the service manuals, claiming therefore that the use of such information is not protected.

OPINION: WOLF

There are six factors to consider in determining the viability of a trade secret:

1. The extent to which the information is known outside the plaintiff's business;
2. The extent to which it is known by employees and others involved in the plaintiff's business;
3. The extent of measures taken by the plaintiff to guard the secrecy of the information;
4. The value of the information to the plaintiff and to its competitors;
5. The amount of effort or money expended by the plaintiff in developing the information; and
6. The ease or difficulty with which the information could be properly acquired or duplicated by others.

At the heart of this case is the third factor—the question whether Picker took adequate measures to protect what it now characterizes as its trade secrets. It is axiomatic that: "One who possesses a trade secret and wishes to protect it must act to preserve its secrecy." It is not necessary, however, that an "'impenetrable fortress'" be erected to retain legal protection for a trade secret. Rather, reasonable security precautions are required.

In determining whether reasonable security precautions have been taken:

"Relevant factors to be considered include (1) the existence or absence of an express agreement restricting disclosure, (2) the nature and extent of security precautions taken by the possessor to prevent acquisition of the information by unauthorized third parties, (3) the circumstances under which the information was disclosed . . . to (any) employee to the extent that they give rise to a reasonable inference that further disclosure without the consent of the possessor is prohibited, and (4) the degree to which the information has been placed in the public domain or rendered 'readily ascertainable' by the third parties through patent applications or unrestricted product marketing."

In essence, what is reasonable depends on the circumstances of each case, considering the nature of the information sought to be protected as well as the conduct of the parties. Thus, as circumstances, including the foreseeable risk to information a party deems confidential, change the definition of the security precautions reasonably necessary to protect it may also change.

Significantly for this case, in deciding whether to grant a plaintiff the protection it seeks, "a court should consider the relationship and conduct of the parties," and "it [is] appropriate to balance a plaintiff's conduct in maintaining its security measures against the conduct of a defendant in acquiring the information." Indeed, while a matter may not constitute a trade secret, it may be entitled to protection as confidential business information "against one who improperly procures such information. The law puts its imprimatur on fair dealing, good faith, and fundamental honesty. Courts condemn conduct which fails to reflect these minimum accepted moral values by penalizing such conduct whenever it occurs."

* * *

With regard to the service manuals, Imaging ardently argues that Picker has not taken the required reasonable security measures. More specifically, Imaging contends that Picker has forfeited their protection as trade secrets: by giving Quinn access to service manuals when he was authorized to participate in servicing the Synerview CT Scanner at St. Francis Hospital; by failing initially to place proprietary legends on every binder comprising the manuals; by not stamping each page as proprietary in the manner contemplated by Picker's policy; and by not always keeping the manuals locked-up at customer sites, as also provided by Picker policy. In addition, defendants claim that Picker sold these allegedly proprietary service manuals to its customers, who were free to resell them to Imaging. Each of these contentions is without merit.

In essence, the court finds that Picker initially took reasonable precautions to protect the trade secrets its service manuals represented and that those precautions escalated reasonably as the threat to their confidentiality from Imaging, and perhaps other ISO's, emerged. As discussed in § III.E, *infra,* when Quinn was given access to the service manuals he was reasonably regarded by Picker as an employee of C.A.T. Associates, subject to C.A.T. Associates' obligation to protect Picker's confidential information. At that time, although the manuals did not have Picker proprietary legends on the binders, many of the entries contained such legends, putting Quinn on notice that Picker regarded at least vital parts of the manuals as confidential and that he could not properly use the manuals without Picker's authorization.

As the ISO industry emerged, Picker began placing proprietary legends on each binder that was part of its service manual, and shipped its manuals to its service engineers, rather than to its customers. These later manuals contained even more proprietary legends and copyright notices. They were not, however, marked confidential on each page as one iteration of Picker's policy prescribed. This is not, however, fatal to the characterization of Picker's security precautions as reasonable. Rather, the measures Picker took were sufficient to place Quinn, Imaging, and others on notice that it deemed the manuals to be confidential and that it was not authorizing others to use them or to take them.

The fact that Picker may not always have kept the manuals locked-up at customer sites does not qualify this conclusion. The extent to which Picker employees followed this policy in practice is not clear. Quinn testified that manuals were left unlocked, but he did claim to have personal knowledge about many sites and, more importantly, the court doubts his credibility.

Even assuming, without finding, however, that the allegedly proprietary service manuals were at times not locked-up, in view of all the foregoing facts, denying protection to the Picker's service manuals would, once again, be inconsistent with the obligation of the court to "put its imprimatur on fair dealing, good faith, and fundamental honesty [and] condemn conduct which fails to reflect these minimum accepted moral values by penalizing such conduct whenever it occurs." As described in detail previously, Quinn and Imaging engaged in a

pervasive and relentless campaign of misconduct to misappropriate Picker's trade secrets and violate its copyrights. That misconduct included encouraging Picker customers such as the Leonard Morse Hospital, Monsour Hospital, and Physicians Medical Imaging to refuse to let Picker replace its own copies of the service manuals with the customer versions that did not include Picker confidential information when Picker lost its service contracts with those customers. With regard to its service manuals, Picker clearly regarded them as proprietary and certainly tried, however imperfectly, to protect their confidentiality. The fact that Quinn and Imaging were able to access them as a result of inducing former Picker customers to violate their obligations to return the manuals to Picker, or because Picker employees did not always lock them up, does not mean they lost their status as Picker's trade secrets.

However, even assuming, without finding, that Picker's conduct caused the service manuals to lose their status as trade secrets with regard to an honest competitor, the manuals are entitled to protection as confidential business information against the defendants, who engaged in pervasive misconduct to obtain and use them, without cost, to build and sustain Imaging's business.

* * *

As the foregoing suggests, the court finds to be without merit Imaging's claim that it has the right to use certain of Picker's proprietary service manuals because Imaging purportedly purchased them shortly before trial from the Scanner Corporation. Rather, if Imaging did acquire Picker's proprietary service manuals from the Scanner Corporation,

Imaging's misconduct in the form of misappropriation of trade secrets, conversion, and contributory copyright infringement continued to the eve of trial.

* * *

Picker has prevailed in this litigation. As the remedy for the violations of its right by Quinn and Imaging, Picker requests relief in the form of an order: (1) requiring the return or destruction of all documents and software constituting its misappropriated trade secrets, copyrighted materials, and software; (2) permanently enjoining defendants from violating Picker's copyrights; (3) permanently enjoining defendants from misappropriating Picker's trade secrets; and (4) appointing a monitor to facilitate and ensure compliance with the order . . . Picker is entitled to all of the relief it requests.

QUESTIONS FOR REVIEW

1. Do you think that the plaintiff used reasonable means to protect its trade secrets?

2. Notice that the court indicates that even if the plaintiff's trade secrets lose their status as trade secrets, that the information is still proprietary and thus protectible from the defendants who were trying to thwart the plaintiff's protection in several ways. How effective is the resulting protection provided by the court apt to be?

3. Is the defendant not on weak ground going into this case, in effect, saying, "Yeah, we took something from the plaintiffs that they did not want taken, but they made it too easy for us?"

"Who Really Owns the Products of Our Minds?"

"[A]n invention even may have been developed by the employee on his or her own time, or in an area unrelated to the employment duties, but the employee may have taken advantage of the employer's facilities for construction or testing of the invention. Does the employee/inventor still retain the sole ownership interest? Well, yes and no.

Under such circumstances, the employer acquires only an implied license, called a 'shop right.' The employee keeps the patent rights, but the employer gets a royalty-free, non-exclusive, non-transferable license permitting it to use the invention. This shop right does not amount to an ownership interest (even though the boss gets to take advantage of the employee's idea for free) because only the employee has the right to sue or license others who use the invention.

In at least one instance the fact that a patentable invention embodied a trade secret of the employer was held to override the employee's right to ownership of the invention.

In this case the employer had developed processes and apparatus for specialized welding that were much better than those being used by its competitors. Two former employees were enjoined from any use of those processes or apparatus even though they were undoubtedly inventors of certain patentable aspects thereof.

The court based its decision on the ground that the employees' use of this technology would amount to misappropriation of the trade secrets of the employer."

Source: Waddey, Jack, "Who really owns the products of our minds?" *Nashville Business Journal,* 2/26/96 Supplement Law Journal, Vol. 12 Issue 9, p. 20. Reprinted with permission of Jack Waddey.

Additional Readings:
http://www.lawsch.uga.edu/~jipl/vol3/hershovi.html
"The Trailer Clause and the Rights of Inventive Employees and Their Employers", Marc B. Hershovitz.

http://www.spencerfane.com/publications/IntellectualProp/divvy.html
"Divvying Up Patent Rights in the Workplace", January 4, 2000; Dianne M. Smith-Misemer, Practice Group: Intellectual Property.

http://www.seedandberry.com/steps to take before.htm
"Steps to Take and Issues to Consider before Filing a Patent Application" by Bryan A. Santarelli, Graybeal Jackson Haley LLP and William T. Christiansen, Ph.D. SEED Intellectual Property Law Group PLLC.

THE SEMICONDUCTOR CHIP PROTECTION ACT, 1984

Although protection of intellectual property in the form of code imbedded on semiconductor computer chips would seem to qualify for copyright protection, Congress passed the Semiconductor Chip Protection Act (SCPA) of 1984 because of differences between semiconductors and other copyrighted material. As we will see shortly, in the process, Congress provided copyright protection for functional subject matter that previously had only been protectible under patent law.

Definitions of Terms: Semiconductors and Mask Works

According to the SCPA, semiconductors are defined as (1) "having two or more layers of metallic, insulating, or semiconductor material, deposited or otherwise placed . . . from a piece of semiconductor material in accordance with a predetermined pattern; and (2) intended to perform electronic circuitry functions." SCPA essentially extends protection to a three-dimensional image or pattern formed on semiconductor material, i.e., the topography of the chip. The SCPA defines a "mask" work as a work that (1) has a series of related images representing a predetermined three-dimensional pattern of metallic, insulating, or semiconductor material present and that (2) has a series of images that are related to each other by a pattern of the surface of one form of the semiconductor chip product. In short, the SCPA protects functional topography (of a semiconductor computer chip) that contains intellectual property.

Functional Copyright Protection

Since the topography of a semiconductor chip is functional, it would normally *not qualify* for copyright protection. However, as long as the topography of a semiconductor chip is not *dictated* by an electronic function so that it would be the only topography that could provide the function, it can receive protection under the SCPA. Again, this type of protection extends only to the expression of an idea and does not extend to any *idea,* or *concept*. As with the rest of copyright law, there is no protection for procedures, processes, systems, or methods of operation, regardless of the form in which it is described or embodied in a mask work. So the type of protection that semiconductor chips receive under the SCPA resembles a *copyright,* but the subject matter of the protection is more like that of a *manufacture* under patent law.

The nature of and the rationale for significant qualifiers that prevent certain mask works from achieving SCPA protection are informative. If protection were given to a semiconductor chip whose topography is dictated by a particular electronic function, SCPA protection would become a branch of patent law. Protection of an electronic concept would create a monopoly that would enable the owner to exact an economic rent (monopoly profit) for users of the concept. Under patent law, an invention that created a monopoly for the inventor would *not* be a barrier to issuance of a patent by the PTO. Instead, administration of the SCPA was given to the Copyright Office, which, in general, does not recognize copyright protection for expressions of ideas that create monopoly advantages.

Statutory Requirements

In order to gain protection for a mask work, the author must independently create an "original" work. In the event of two authors creating substantially similar works, as opposed to one party copying the creation of another, independent creation is a defense for the latter work. Under **patent law,** subsequent independent creation is not a defense, but independent creation is a defense under **copyright law** as SCPA again imitates copyright protection. The SCPA goes on to state that there is no protection for a mask work that solely consists of designs that are, " . . . staple, commonplace or familiar in the semiconductor industry, or variations of those designs, combined in a way that, considered as a whole, are not original." The intent is to prevent a party from appropriating and seeking legal protection for concepts, conventions, and expressions that are in the public domain.

In order to receive protection under the SCPA, the owner of the mask work must be one of the following: living in the United States, a U.S. national, a national or domiciliary of a country who has a signed a treaty with the U.S. affording protection to mask works, a stateless person, or the mask work was first commercially exploited in the U.S. Registration of a mask work at the Copyright Office is mandatory if the owner is seeking SCPA protection for the work. Owners of mask works must apply for protection within two years of first commercial exploitation of the work. Priority is to be determined based on the filing date of the work, another similarity with copyright law and contrast with patent law.

Terms of Protection

The SPCA provides for protection of mask works against infringement for a period of 10 years from either the filing date at the Copyright Office or the first commercial exploitation of the work anywhere in the world, whichever occurs first. The SCPA grants owners exclusive rights to:

1. Reproduce a mask work by optical, electronic, or any other means;
2. To import or distribute a semiconductor chip product in which the mask work is embodied;
3. To induce or knowingly to cause another person to do any of the acts described in 1 and 2 above.

The rights of a registered owner of a mask work are limited by an explicit allowance of rivals to reverse engineer the work for purposes of teaching, analyzing, or evaluating the concepts or techniques embodied in the mask work or in the circuitry and so forth.[24] The SCPA allows firms that reverse engineer the chips to incorporate that knowledge in chips they (the rivals) make for subsequent distribution.

The SCPA has a first sale provision that is identical to a provision in copyright law. Purchasers of chips (or books) have the right to resell the chips (or books) as long as they do not reproduce what is on the chip (or in the book). Transfers of rights must be in writing and the usual legal rules apply if the owner of the registered mask work dies (his heirs inherit the rights). Finally, the SCPA allows for protection of trade secrets. If the registrant claims that there is a need to protect sensitive information, certain material may be withheld from deposit at the Copyright Office.

The following case illustrates many of the salient features of the SCPA.

---

[24]Section 906 of the Semiconductor Chip Protection Act.

Brooktree Corporation v. Advanced Micro Devices, Inc.
United States Court of Appeals for the Federal Circuit
977 F.2d 1555; 1992

FACTS AND CASE BACKGROUND

Brooktree Corporation brought suit against Advanced Micro Devices, Inc. (herein AMD) for patent infringement, and infringement of mask work registrations, in connection with certain semiconductor chips used in color video displays. The United States District Court for the Southern District of California entered judgment that the patents were valid and infringed and that the registered mask works were infringed, assessing damages.

OPINION: NEWMAN, CIRCUIT JUDGE

The principal issues on appeal arise under the Patent Act, of which the Federal Circuit has exclusive appellate jurisdiction, and the Semiconductor Chip Protection Act, of which this court's appellate jurisdiction is pendent. Thus for issues of fact and law under the Semiconductor Chip Protection Act we apply the discernable law of the Ninth Circuit, in accordance with the principles set forth in *Atari, Inc.* v. *JS&A Group, Inc.* Judicial consideration of the Semiconductor Chip Protection Act has thus far been sparse, and we have given particular attention to the statute and its history, for the parties dispute significant aspects of statutory interpretation.

This case occasioned a lengthy trial over the course of seven weeks before the jury, in consecutive determinations of liability and damages. The jury verdicts were the subject of duly filed motions for judgment notwithstanding the verdict and for a new trial, which motions were denied by the district court. AMD charges error on issues of mask work infringement and damages, and also on issues of patent validity, infringement, and willfulness. Brooktree cross-appeals certain damages rulings, and the denial of attorney fees under both the Patent Act and the Semiconductor Chip Protection Act.

THE SEMICONDUCTOR CHIP PROTECTION ACT

The Semiconductor Chip Protection Act of 1984 arose from concerns that existing intellectual property laws did not provide adequate protection of proprietary rights in semiconductor chips that had been designed to perform a particular function. The Act, enacted after extensive congressional consideration and hearings over several years, adopted relevant aspects of existing intellectual property law but, for the most part, created a new law, specifically adapted to the protection of design layouts of semiconductor chips.

Chip design layouts embody the selection and configuration of electrical components and connections in order to achieve the desired electronic functions. The electrical elements are configured in three dimensions, and are built up in layers by means of a series of "masks" whereby, using photographic depositing and etching techniques, layers of metallic, insulating, and semiconductor material are deposited in the desired pattern on a wafer of silicon. This set of masks is called a "mask work", and is part of the semiconductor chip product. The statute defines a mask work as:

... a series of related images, however fixed or encoded

A. having or representing the predetermined, three dimensional pattern of metallic, insulating, or semiconductor material present or removed from the layers of a semiconductor chip product; and

B. in which series the relation of the images to one another is that each image has the pattern of the surface of one form of a semiconductor chip product.

(2). The semiconductor chip product in turn is defined as:
    the final or intermediate form of any product—

A. having two or more layers of metallic, insulating, or semiconductor material, deposited or otherwise placed on, or etched away or otherwise removed from, a piece of semiconductor material in accordance with a predetermined pattern; and

B. intended to perform electronic circuitry functions.

* * *

The Semiconductor Chip Protection Act of 1984, . . . would prohibit "chip piracy"—the unauthorized copying and distribution of semiconductor chip products copied from the original creators of such works.

In the evolution of the Semiconductor Chip Protection Act it was first proposed simply to amend the Copyright Act, to include semiconductor chip products and mask works as subject of copyright. However, although some courts had interpreted copyright law as applicable to computer software imbedded in a semiconductor chip, it was uncertain whether the copyright law could protect against copying of the pattern on the chip itself, if the pattern was deemed inseparable from the utilitarian function of the chip. Indeed, the

Copyright Office had refused to register patterns on printed circuit boards and semiconductor chips because no separate artistic aspects had been demonstrated. Concern was also expressed that extension of the copyright law to accommodate the problems of mask works would distort certain settled copyright doctrines, such as fair use.

The patent system alone was deemed not to provide the desired scope of protection of mask works. Although electronic circuitry and electronic components are within the statutory subject matter of patentable invention, and some original circuitry may be patentable if it also meets the requirements of the Patent Act, as is illustrated in this case, Congress sought more expeditious protection against copying of original circuit layouts, whether or not they met the criteria of patentable invention.

The Semiconductor Chip Protection Act of 1984 was an innovative solution to this new problem of technology-based industry. While some copyright principles underlie the law, as do some attributes of patent law, the Act was uniquely adapted to semiconductor mask works, in order to achieve appropriate protection for original designs while meeting the competitive needs of the industry and serving the public interest.

The Semiconductor Chip Protection Act provides for the grant of certain exclusive rights to owners of registered mask works, including the exclusive right "to reproduce the mask work by optical, electronic, or any other means", and the exclusive right "to import or distribute a semiconductor chip product in which the mask work is embodied". Mask works that are not "original", or that consist of "designs that are staple, commonplace, or familiar in the semiconductor industry, or variations of such designs, combined in a

way that, considered as a whole, is not original", are excluded from protection. Protection is also not extended to any "idea, procedure, process, system, method of operation, concept, principle, or discovery, regardless of the form in which it is described, explained, illustrated or embodied" in the mask work.

The sponsors and supporters of this legislation foresaw that there would be areas of uncertainty in application of this new law to particular situations, and referred to "gray areas" wherein factual situations could arise that would not have easy answers. Those areas are emphasized by both parties in the assignments of error on this appeal.

* * *

THE TRIAL

The factual premises of the issues of infringement and AMD's reverse engineering defense were extensively explored at trial, through examination and cross-examination of witnesses, exhibits, displays, and attorney argument. To summarize, AMD argued at trial, and repeats on this appeal, that it did not intend to copy Brooktree's layout, and did not do so. AMD pointed to its "paper trail" of its two and a half years of effort at a cost in excess of three million dollars. AMD stated that if its intent had been to copy the Brooktree layout, it would simply have directed duplication of the circuit layouts, requiring a matter of months, not years. AMD stressed differences between its chips and those of Brooktree, and pointed out its aversion to piracy. According to AMD, this case is not in the gray area where reasonable minds could differ over whether there was reverse engineering or copying. AMD argues that Congress could not have intended that mask work infringement be found in the circumstances of this case, and that this court

should hold, as a matter of law, that AMD did not infringe Brooktree's mask work registrations.

Brooktree, on its part, argued that AMD's cell layout is not original, but was directly copied from Brooktree's SRAM core cell, and repeated 6,000 times. Brooktree stressed AMD's lengthy and expensive failures at designing a layout. Brooktree observed that AMD had incorrectly analyzed Brooktree's chip during its attempts at reverse engineering, and that throughout this entire period of attempted duplication of function, AMD was unable to come close to Brooktree's results. Brooktree pointed to the rapidity with which AMD changed to Brooktree's layout when the error in analysis was discovered, AMD immediately producing, without further experimentation, a substantially identical SRAM cell.

At trial there was extensive evidence of AMD's design efforts, including its full paper trail. Evidence included the following: William Plants, AMD's assigned designer of the SRAM core cell, testified that AMD initiated a project to design a color palette chip in January 1986, based on Brooktree's announcement of such a chip the previous November and introduction of its Bt451 chip in February 1986. In April AMD obtained several Brooktree Bt451 chips. Plants opened up one of the chips and had it photographed, including blow-ups of the SRAM portion, which he said was of particular interest to him. After studying the chip he prepared a "reverse engineering report" in June 1986. Plants incorrectly concluded that the Brooktree chip had eight transistors in each SRAM cell rather than ten. Plants then abandoned his efforts to design an SRAM cell based on six transistors, and attempted, over the next six months, to create an SRAM core cell design based on eight transistors. These attempts were not successful.

There was evidence of increasing pressure to complete the design, including suggestions by AMD supervisors that Plants reexamine the Brooktree chip because the project had gotten "bogged down". Plants did so some time in late January or early February. Plants testified that it was toward the end of January 1987 when he changed to a ten-transistor design in the same arrangement as Brooktree's design. Plants admitted that he did "solve the problem in a week" by adopting the ten-transistor design. Plants denied, however, that he learned of the ten-transistor design from his reexamination of the Brooktree chip, but explained that the design had been suggested to him by a job candidate he interviewed during that period. That candidate did not testify, and an AMD witness said he was dead.

There was extensive exploration at trial of the events during this period, of Plants' design processes, and of the timing and other details of the successful AMD ten-transistor design. For instance, Plants testified that his reexamination of the Brooktree chip was prompted not by pressure from his supervisors, but by a memory flash, like a "bolt from the blue", of something he had seen previously in the Brooktree chip.

In addition, there was extensive testimony and demonstrative and documentary evidence that the similarities in the circuit designs led to the substantial identity between the layouts of the Brooktree and AMD core cells. For example, Plants testified that in laying out the ten-transistor SRAM cell for fabrication in silicon, he never changed the locations of the ten transistors in his design, and never considered alternatives to Brooktree's transistor arrangement. Michael Brunolli, the engineer responsible for the layout of the Brooktree SRAM cell, testified that, in contrast, he had gone through about six changes of transistor layout before he achieved the final design.

Brooktree's expert witness Richard Crisp testified that the layout of the Brooktree SRAM cell was unique and original, and was not a commonplace or staple design. Crisp stated that the most important factor in layout of the SRAM cell is the location of the transistors. Crisp showed the jury exhibits picturing alternative layouts of electrically identical ten-transistor SRAM core cells in other chips, illustrating different layouts of the same circuitry. Plants had agreed that "you could conceivably come up with an infinite number of layouts" for the ten-transistor cell.

Plants admitted that the metal lines connecting the transistors in one layer of his layout were in the same sequence or order as the corresponding lines in the Brooktree chip, although his design had an extra metal line in it. Crisp testified that the extra metal line in AMD's layout did not relate to any function of the SRAM core cell itself. Plants also admitted that he originally included 45-degree angled portions in the polysilicon layer of his initial layout, a feature found in the Brooktree layout. Plants said he later removed the angles at the request of AMD's production engineers because it was incompatible with AMD's process methodology. Brunolli testified that the 45-degree angled portions arose in his design as a result of design rules used at Brooktree, and that he chose the angles to make his cell layout more compact.

Crisp testified that the transistors, which "form the substance of the cell" were "grouped together in the same way" in the AMD and Brooktree layouts. Crisp showed a videotape of the Brooktree and AMD SRAM cells side-by-side and then overlaid. (This tape was shown four times, including once in the jury room.) He stopped the tape at various points to illustrate the similarities in the layout of the two chips, and explained that the differences were primarily the result of AMD's smaller technology and removal of the 45-degree angles. Crisp testified that the differences between the cells were "very minor, trivial, insignificant", and "insignificant electrically", and that "the substance of the cells is the same." Plants had testified that minor differences in design layout would arise because the differing technologies of AMD and Brooktree resulted in each firm having different standard design rules for layout of semiconductor chips.

The standard of review is whether there was legally sufficient evidence whereby a reasonable jury could have reached the verdict reached by this jury. This standard posits that a reasonable jury would have assessed the credibility of witnesses, considered and weighed the evidence presented by both sides, and applied the law in accordance with the court's instructions.

* * *

CONCLUSION

The judgment entered on the jury verdicts, and the district court's rulings, are AFFIRMED.

QUESTIONS FOR REVIEW

1. How credible is the claim by the defendant's engineer that the inspiration for the 10-transistor design was inspired by a "bolt in the sky" rather than reexamination of the plaintiff's chip? How credible is the claim by the engineer for the defendant that the inspiration for the design of the chip came from a job candidate who did not testify at trial?

2. Notice that the court recites the human resource management aspects of this case, the fact that the engineer was under pressure to come up with a workable design and the fact that the engineer had become bogged down prior to reexamining the plaintiff's chip. Juries can themselves become bogged down when listening to engineers argue about various features of chip designs. Is there any doubt that explaining the "human" side of this case provides strong reinforcement for the jury verdict and the court's decision?

3. What motion did the defendant file following the verdict, which was denied by the trial court, and which is the subject of this appeal?

SUMMARY

- Leadership in software is arguably primarily responsible for the surge of the U.S. economy during the 1990s and beyond.
- Given the importance of software, legal protection is surprisingly ambiguous. Much of the content of copyrighted software is not protected by copyright law.
- An "*industry-standard*" part of a software program cannot be protected by copyright law, regardless of whether that part of the program is a user interface, a structure, sequence of commands, or something that considerably improves performance.
- *Functional* aspects of user interfaces are not protectible under copyright law.
- Object code and source code can be copyrighted, but registration means that much of the program may be made available to the public at large.
- The "*look and feel*" test has been used to prove that a copyright infringement has occurred by showing that two programs are substantially similar. The test only applies to the parts of the software program that are protectible under copyright law, and *industry standards* are not protectible.
- The Copyright Act guarantees owners of a legal copy of a computer program the right to make a copy if making the copy is essential to utilize the program, or if it is for archival purposes.
- Software commands that create compatibility with other systems or hardware are not protected copyright law if discovered through decompilation and reverse engineering.
- If software creates a network that enhances compatibility, the value of the network will increase as the number of users grows.

- Neither a *law of nature,* a *mathematical formula,* nor an *algorithm* is patentable or copyrightable.
- The first process patent that made use of computer software was granted by the Supreme Court in 1981.
- Judicial reception for patents based mainly or even entirely on computer software programs has been steadily improving.
- Software that measured heart palpitations of heart attack victims and computed a value that was to be used for medical treatments was granted a patent. (Note the lack of consistent thread among court decisions).
- The PTO contends that software can be patented "when a computer program is claimed in a process where the computer is executing the computer program's instructions . . ."
- The Uniform Trade Secrets Act defines a *trade secret* as information that is valuable because it is not generally known and necessitates *reasonable effort* by the trade secret owner to maintain secrecy.
- Courts generally apply a *sweat-of-the-brow* approach to misappropriation claims. If the alleged misappropriator worked to obtain the trade secret(s), then the appropriation is not wrongful, but if the misappropriator stole the secrets or induced employees or ex-employees to breach their fiduciary duties to their employer, there is liability.
- To protect trade secrets, *reasonable security* precautions must be used. In Internet transactions, cryptography is used to prevent hacking and unwarranted interception. The sender encrypts the data with a key and the recipient decodes it with another key. To prevent incoming viruses,

- firewalls block all incoming data that does not have a code to enter.
- Employees have a fiduciary relationship with their employers and that relationship persists after termination of employment requiring employees to put the interests of the employer above their own.
- To protect employers' IP, employers may require employees to *notify* them as to any IP protection they apply for while employed and for a period thereafter. *Notification clauses* have been ruled legal in several cases even if employers do not have a legitimate claim to all IP developed during employment.
- Reasonable *noncompetition clauses* are enforceable and typically require employees not to work for a rival of their current employer for a period of time in a specific area.
- High-tech firms typically require employees to sign *NDAs,* though common law fiduciary duties would also make disclosure of trade secrets to others firms illegal.
- Under trade secret law a party (a rival of the plaintiff/employer) who knows or should have known that the receipt of information from an ex-employee is a breach of the employee's fiduciary duty is also liable for misappropriation.
- In order to obtain a *temporary restraining order* (TRO), a plaintiff must show that it is likely to prevail in trial and that disclosure of the trade secret will result in irreparable harm.
- A plaintiff can sue for lost royalties but has the burden of proof.
- The Semiconductor Chip Protection Act (SCPA) of 1984 provides copyright protection for functional subject matter that is normally only protectible under patent law.
- The SCPA goes on to state that there is no protection for a mask work that solely consists of designs that are " . . . staple, commonplace or familiar in the semiconductor industry, or variations of those designs, combined in a way that, considered as a whole, are not original."
- The SPCA provides for 10 years of protection of mask works. It grants owners exclusive rights to reproduce a mask work, distribute a chip, and cause another person to reproduce a mask work and distribute it.

BUSINESS ORGANIZATIONS

From peddling newspapers to operating a franchise of a national fast food chain to manufacturing airliners, every business activity is conducted within the framework of a business organization, informal or formal. There are three basic legal forms of business organization which are the *sole proprietorship,* the *partnership,* and the *corporation.* There also are specialized hybrid forms of business organization within these basic categories, with every form having its own special characteristics—rights and obligations. Among the popular forms of hybrids are S corporations, limited liability corporations (LLCs), limited liability partnerships, and limited partnerships.

Among the three broad classes of business organization, sole proprietorships are by far the most numerous, while corporations are by far the dominant form of business organization in terms of "revenues," "profits," and "numbers of owners" (called stockholders). This isn't to say, of course, that sole proprietorships are always very small enterprises. Some sole proprietorships could match size measures with publicly traded companies. The same is true with partnerships, which can range from small operations that only loosely and informally tie two participants together to large, highly structured and formalized organizations

with hundreds or even thousands of "partner" owners. Corporations, some of which are immense (like G.E., with sales revenues greater than many country's gross domestic product), can also be quite small. In fact, in raw numbers the vast majority of corporations are "small" and "closely held."

This chapter provides an overview of the various kinds of business organizations typically encountered in the U.S. economy. For each form of business covered, our review will be particularly concerned with legal issues involved in the formation of the business, the governance of the business once it exists, the legal characteristics of its financing obligations, its life and transferability, and other issues that are characteristic advantages and/or disadvantages of the particular business form. In the next chapter we look at cyber companies and compare and contrast their distinctive features with the traditional business organization reviewed in this chapter.

SOLE PROPRIETORSHIPS

A *sole proprietorship* is a business owned by one person who operates the business for his or her own profit. About three-quarters of all business firms in the

United States are of this simplest form. Sole proprietorships are, by and large, relatively small businesses, operated by an owner, perhaps with a handful of employees. Hair salons, plumbing, electrical and other constructions businesses, car dealerships, and professional practices (doctors, lawyers, accountants, etc.) are a few of many examples of solely owned and operated businesses. Of course, a construction company, a car dealership, and other sole proprietorships can have millions of dollars of annual sales and dozens of employees.

Benefits of Sole Proprietorships

The sole proprietorship form of business has many advantages that make it popular. To begin with, the legal formation of this type of business is very simple as there are virtually no formal business formation paperwork requirements other than, in some instances, registration with local government and the payment of permitting fees.[1] So, there are uniquely low organizational costs involved in starting a sole proprietorship. This form of business is also attractive to the entrepreneurially oriented as, in effect, the owner is the business—he or she makes the management decisions for the firm. The owner has complete freedom to determine whether to operate or shut down, whether to expand or shrink, what products to provide, when to take a vacation, whom to hire and fire, what benefits to pay, etc. As the one owner of the business, the sole proprietor is the recipient of all of the profits the business provides.

Tax Issues and Other Advantages

For income tax purposes, profits of sole proprietorships are reported as personal income (on Schedule C of the personal tax return) and, hence, are taxed just once as personal income (unlike standard corporation income which is subject to "double" taxation). Owners may also shield some portion of their current earnings from taxation by making retirement plan contributions into a Keogh Plan or into an SEP-IRA (two forms of retirement savings vehicles, which can enjoy interest and capital gains growth exempt from taxes). Also, since management knowledge doesn't have to be shared with

anyone else, this form of business has the greatest secrecy (privacy) advantage, though income still has to be reported to the IRS.

Disadvantages of Sole Proprietorships

A major disadvantage of the sole proprietorship form of business is *unlimited liability*—the owner is **personally** responsible for any and all obligations incurred by the business. Hence, an owner's total wealth, personal as well as business, may be taken to satisfy obligations of the business. This disadvantage of unlimited liability for sole proprietors mainly applies to involuntary debts—that is, to tort liability to third parties. A partial respite from unlimited liability is provided by business insurance.

A second major weakness of a sole proprietorship is its limited ability to raise capital. Financing for sole proprietorships is limited to what can be provided from the private funds of the owner or to what can be borrowed. This contrasts sharply with the capacity of corporations to raise capital through the sale of ownership shares (stock) to a broad public financing base.

Closely related to this second weakness is concern for the difficulty of selling ownership interest in a proprietorship. Sales of such businesses are often slow, at prices that reflect significant discounts from what the owner thinks the business is worth, and costly in terms of transactions expenses (advertising, brokerage fees, etc.). In a related vein, continuity of the business in the event of the death or disability of the owner is also an issue. These events result in the dissolution of the business. Even if the business is taken over by and transferred to other family members or someone outside the family, a new proprietorship is established.

Of course, since the sole proprietor owner is the manager, free to make all decisions, he or she also faces the burden of having to be a jack-of-all-trades for the business. This can constitute a third major disadvantage in a technology-driven world as the technical expertise and vision needed to develop successful businesses in today's economy can require the brainpower (intellectual capital) of multiple individuals with an ownership interest in the success of the start-up enterprise. It may also be difficult to hire and retain high quality employees, when the opportunity for advancement (e.g., to a management position) is typically limited.

---

[1] In most cities a business is required to purchase a permit to do business in the city.

PARTNERSHIPS

A *partnership* is formed when two or more owners of a firm decide to join together and operate a business for profit. A partnership, by its very nature, indicates the existence of an *agreement* between or among partners, whether that agreement is *express* or *implied*. Partners are co-owners of a business and, as such, are jointly responsible for managerial control of the firm and are entitled to jointly share in its profits. Partners can agree to whatever terms they want regarding the sharing of responsibility for management decisions, the shares of profits flowing to each partner, the capital contribution(s) of each partner, etc., so long as those terms are not illegal or contrary to public policy. Under their partnership agreement, then, partners are the managers of a firm, fully entitled to participate in all decisions for the firm. In addition, partners are also *agents* of partnership, which means that actions of a single partner legally bind the entire partnership.

The Partnership Agreement

Virtually all states have passed the Uniform Partnership Act (UPA), which defines the rights and duties of partners in the absence of an agreement. In 1992 the National Conference of Commissioners of Uniform State Laws (NCCUSL) enacted the Revised Uniform Partnership Act that has been adopted (by the end of the year 2000) by 26 states and the District of Columbia. In the absence of an agreement to the contrary, the laws governing partnerships are stated in the UPA. The UPA is a codification of common law which applies unless partners agree otherwise. If nothing is otherwise contracted for in a partnership agreement,

1. All partners are entitled to equal shares of profits and losses. Upon dissolution of the partnership, all partners are entitled to equal shares of partnership assets, regardless of who contributed what to the partnership.
2. All partners have an equal say or vote in management decisions. For most management decisions the majority rules, but some decisions involving fundamental change require unanimous agreement.
3. Partnerships have entity status which means they can sue and be sued, as well as own property. A partnership business, however, is not required to pay income tax.

4. Partnerships automatically dissolve upon the death or incapacity of a partner. It is common in many partnerships to have a continuation agreement in which survivors of the deceased partner are entitled to the value of that partner's pro rata share.

Written Partnership Agreements

Except for very small partnerships that are expected to be of limited duration, it is prudent to consult an attorney to draw up a *written* partnership agreement. Partnership agreements drawn up by a competent attorney are particularly useful when a partnership is dissolving, as that is a time when litigation is common. A partnership agreement can be likened to a prenuptial agreement; it determines who gets what in the event of dissolution of the partnership. Quite obviously, partnership agreements deal with a number of other issues such as management of the partnership, transfer of ownership shares, and admission policies for new members. Without a written agreement, those decisions are dictated by the UPA.

Types of Partnerships

Most partnerships, combining two or more business people who decide to join forces and form a business, are *general partnerships*. What we have been describing so far is a general partnership. In this type of business organization, each partner is an owner/manager and each partner has unlimited liability for partnership debts. Each partner is also an agent of the partnership and has the power to bind the partnership by his actions in business. Also each partner in a general partnership owes *fiduciary* responsibilities to put the interests of the partnership above his or her own (aspects of partners' fiduciary responsibilities to each other are discussed below).

The other common type of partnership, to be discussed in some detail later, is a *limited partnership*. A limited partnership has general partners who have management responsibilities as described above and who are unlimitedly liable for partnership debts. Limited partners in a limited partnership, however, are investing partners who do not have management responsibilities. The critically important distinguishing characteristic of a limited partnership is that the limited partners *do not have unlimited liability*. In effect, they are in the same position as shareholders in a corporation. If the corporation or partnership goes bankrupt, creditors cannot pursue the personal assets of the investing limited partners, as long as the limited partners in fact limit their activity to investing and *do not participate in management.*

Advantages of Partnerships

Relative to sole proprietorships, partnerships provide a number of advantages. As a group, partners have more borrowing power with banks and other suppliers of capital. In general, a group also has more of its own capital to contribute than do sole proprietors. With limited partnerships there is increased ability to raise capital without the threat of unlimited liability. Partnerships allow for a pooling of talents and specialization of talents. For all partnerships, profit income earned by partners is still reported as personal income with each partner's profit share entered into his or her personal income tax return.

A partnership is required to file an information return with the Internal Revenue Service (IRS), which reports what profits (or losses) accrued to the partner owners during the tax year, but there is no "business" income tax obligation. Partnerships that make money are virtually forced to distribute this income because such income is attributed pro rata to each partner. If partnership income is not distributed, partners are taxed on income that they have not received.

Disadvantages of Partnerships

Partnerships share the main disadvantages of sole proprietorships, foremost of which is the unlimited liability of the general partners (but not for limited partners). Also, while more ownership participants provide for more financing capacity, the ability of partners to personally fund or borrow for the firm's capital needs is still limited as compared to the fund-raising capacity of a corporation. Ownership in a partnership is also relatively illiquid if a sale is desired, and the rights of individual partners to exit the partnership through a sale of ownership is often strictly limited by the partnership agreement. Partnerships are often simply dissolved when one of the partners dies, which is required if there is not a clause to the contrary in the partnership agreement.

Duties of Partners to One Another

The essence of the obligations of partners to other members in a partnership is called a *fiduciary duty,* required by the *fiduciary relationship* between (among) partners. In a fiduciary relationship, partners must put the interest(s) of the partnership above their own. This requires partners to fully disclose possible conflicts of interest and to refrain from voting on partnership decisions when there is a conflict of interest. If a partner owns real estate that the partnership is considering acquiring, that partner should fully disclose his or her ownership interest and should not vote on whether to acquire the property. Partners should not compete with the partnership nor should partners take money from third parties in connection with their partnership business without fully disclosing that fact. Any monies so received from their business activities is owned by the partnership, not the individual partners.

Many small businesses, including professional businesses, are operated as partnerships. Doubtless, most individuals entering into such business arrangements are not fully informed with regard to problems a partnership can encounter or fully apprised of the obligations borne by members of a partnership. The following case can fill some of those gaps.

Collete Bohatch v. Butler & Binion
41 Tex. Supreme Court J. 308
977 S.W. 2d 543 (Jan. 22, 1998)

FACTS AND CASE BACKGROUND

Collete Bohatch went to work in an office of the Butler & Binion law firm (partnership) in 1986. The managing partner of the office she worked in was John McDonald and that office had one other lawyer, Richard Powers. The office did work almost exclusively for Pennzoil Corporation.

Bohatch became a full partner in February 1990, at which time she began receiving internal firm reports that showed numbers of hours billed by each attorney, the number of hours worked, etc. Upon reviewing these reports, Bohatch became concerned that McDonald was overbilling Pennzoil and discussed this with Powers. On July 15, 1990, Bohatch met with Louis Paine, the overall firm's managing partner, reporting her concerns to him, then described this meeting to Powers.

The following day, McDonald met with Bohatch and informed her that Pennzoil was not satisfied with her work. Bohatch testified that this was the first time she had ever heard criticism of her work for Pennzoil. The next day, Bohatch repeated her concerns in a conference call to a number of Butler & Binion managing partners. Over the next month, the firm engaged in an investigation of the complaint(s). In August, Bohatch was informed that the investigation revealed no basis for her contentions and that she should begin looking for other employment. It was indicated that the firm would continue providing her with office space, a secretary, a monthly draw, and insurance while she conducted this job search.

In January 1991, the firm denied Bohatch a year-end partnership distribution for 1990 and reduced her tentative distribution share for 1991 to zero. In June, the firm paid Bohatch her monthly draw and told her that this draw would be her last. In August, the firm gave Bohatch until November to vacate her office.

By September, Bohatch had found new employment. On October 18, 1991, she filed suit against Butler and Binion for multiple claims including breach of fiduciary duty and breach of partnership agreement. The firm formally voted to expel her from the partnership three days later on October 21, 1991.

The trial court dismissed any claim for wrongful discharge and various other claims and counterclaims. Breach of fiduciary duty and breach of contract claims were tried to a jury. The jury found that the firm breached its partnership agreement and its fiduciary duty to Bohatch as a partner in the firm. It awarded Bohatch $57,000 for past lost wages,

$250,000 for past mental anguish, and $4,000,000 in punitive damages. The trial court reduced the punitive damage award to $237,000. All parties appealed.

The Court of Appeals ruled that the firm's only duty to Bohatch was not to expel her in bad faith, According to the Appeals Court, "'[b]ad faith' in this context means only that partners can not expel another partner for self-gain." Finding no evidence that the firm expelled Bohatch for self-gain, the court concluded that Bohatch could not recover for breach of fiduciary duty. However, the court concluded that the firm breached the partnership agreement when it reduced Bohatch's tentative partnership distribution for 1991 to zero without notice, and when it terminated her draw three months before she left. The court concluded that Bohatch was entitled to recover $35,000 in lost earnings for 1991 but none for 1990, and no mental anguish damages. Accordingly, the court rendered judgment for Bohatch for $35,000 plus $225,000 in attorney's fees.

OPINION: JUSTICE ENOCH

BREACH OF FIDUCIARY DUTY—We have long recognized as a matter of common law that "[t]he relationship between . . . partners . . . is fiduciary in character, and imposes upon all the participants the obligation of loyalty to the joint concern and of the utmost good faith, fairness, and honesty in their dealings with each other with respect to matters pertaining to the enterprise." Yet, partners have no obligation to remain partners; "at the heart of the partnership concept is the principle that partners may choose with whom they wish to be associated." . . . The issue presented . . . is whether the fiduciary relationship between and among partners creates an exception

to the at-will nature of partnerships; that is . . . whether it gives rise to a duty not to expel a partner who reports suspected overbilling by another partner. . . . "[T]he partnership agreement contemplates expulsion of a partner and prescribes procedures to be followed, but it does not specify or limit the grounds for expulsion . . . . Therefore, we look to the common law to find the principles governing Bohatch's claim that the firm breached a duty when it expelled her.

Courts in other states have held that a partnership may expel a partner for purely business reasons . . . . Further, courts recognize that a law firm can expel a partner to protect relationships both within the firm and with clients . . . . Finally, many courts have held that a partnership can expel a partner without breaching any duty in order to resolve a "fundamental schism."

* * *

The fiduciary duty that partners owe one another does not encompass a duty to remain partners or else answer in tort damages. Nonetheless, Bohatch and several distinguished legal scholars urge this Court to recognize that public policy requires a limited duty to remain partners—i.e., a partnership must retain a whistleblower partner . . . because permitting a law firm to retaliate against a partner who in good faith reports suspected overbilling would discourage compliance with rules of professional conduct and thereby hurt clients.

While this argument is not without some force, we must reject it. A partnership exists solely because the partners choose to place personal confidence and trust in one another. . . . [A] partner can be expelled for accusing another . . . of overbilling without subjecting the partnership to tort damages. Such charges, whether true or not, may have a profound effect on the personal confidence and trust essential to the partner relationship. Once such charges are made, partners may find it impossible to continue to work together . . . . We hold that the firm did not owe Bohatch a duty not to expel her for reporting suspected overbilling by another partner.

BREACH OF THE PARTNERSHIP AGREEMENT—The court of appeals concluded that the firm breached the partnership agreement by reducing Bohatch's tentative distribution for 1991 to zero without the requisite notice . . . . [T]he firm's right to reduce the bonus was contingent upon providing proper notice to Bohatch . . .

Accordingly, the court of appeals did not err in finding the firm liable for breach of the partnership agreement. Moreover, because Bohatch's damages [stem from contract breach], and because she sought attorney's fees at trial under [the] Texas Civil Practice and Remedies Code, we affirm the court of appeals' award of Bohatch's attorney's fees.

QUESTIONS FOR ANALYSIS

1. What fiduciary duties do partners owe to other partners?
2. Why did the Texas Supreme Court reason that such duties were not breached in this case?
3. Could another conclusion have been reached depending on the sharing of earnings from Pennzoil work?
4. Would this case make you more or less comfortable becoming a partner in a firm? Explain.

Partnering for a Win–Win Outcome

Once upon a time, there were two consultants who worked for a successful consulting firm. One was six years older than the other and served as head of one of the divisions. The two consultants were a dynamic pair, creating training programs, generating new ideas, and facilitating powerful client sessions. They also deeply enjoyed and were stimulated by each other's thoughts and energy. They became friends, and in the course of working together, decided that they wanted to create their own business. So, they left their old employer and created a new company. Their organization thrived and became known for its creativity, impactive training, and personalized consulting.

Yet, three years later, the friendship was gone, and their relationship was strained, painful, and tense. They split up early in the fourth year, one buying the other out.

What happens to the friendship, the synergy, and goodwill so characteristic at the start of a partnership? What happens to destroy friendships and long-standing relationships, be it in the context of business or personal life?

It turns out that every partnership is actually a crucible in which different personalities, perceptions, needs, and drives are mixed under the pressure and heat of daily interaction, work demands, and the friction of time. The result can be a new level of relationship that is tested and tempered to a higher strength and quality.

Or the results can be more destructive, either shattering the crucible (the partnership) or throwing one or more of the partners out of the mix. The failure to attend to the psychological or emotional quotient issues within the relationship, particularly fear, are almost always the root cause of the disruption and loss.

CARING TO CONFRONT

The main reason that the emotional issues are not addressed is usually due to the failure to clearly state or hear the needs and feelings we have in relation to each other's actions. We give in to our fears of rocking the boat, upsetting the other person, being wrong, getting into a fight, or being judged. We fail to either express ourselves at or to listen to the deeper levels that partnering requires if it is to not only thrive, but also simply survive.

More than 90 percent of the failure is to be found in two areas: a lack of courage to confront, or the inability to access the courage to allow ourselves to be confronted.

Of the two, it is the lack of courage to be confronted by the needs, issues, and insights of the others that does most of the damage. We defend, justify, deny, or even worse, attack by pointing out our critics' shortcomings. This drives them away and creates an undercurrent of resentment, frustration, fear, and mistrust. It takes courage to really listen to, to even invite, the critical feedback about how we are seen and perceived.

The second of the two most common ways that we fail in partnerships, and relationships in general, is in not having the courage to confront each other, or doing it

Continued from page 338

in less-than-effective ways. We either suppress the feelings, feeling tense, anxious, and angry, or we spew them out, dumping our emotions on the other(s). Either way, we create barriers to effective communication, and spoilers of the goodwill and affirmation needed for the maintenance of an effective and robust relationship.

The observations, feelings, and issues in a relationship don't just go away; they will become a painful abscess of unexpressed emotions and needs that slowly poison the mutual respect, trust, and goodwill required if a partnership is to survive over the long haul. The lack of courage to both confront and be confronted destroys the vital "give and take" of a healthy relationship.

For a partnership to thrive over the long term requires attention, focus, and a great deal of work. The work is mostly inner-directed, with manifestations in the ways we listen, confront, invite feedback, and create emotional safety for the expression of "negative" feelings and problematic emotional states.

Let's face it, we all want to be admired and appreciated. The beginning of any partnership usually starts with highly positive interactions. As time goes by, however, and the personality quirks and annoying habits of our "partner" begin to bother us more, we stop giving each other the same level of affirmation and positive attention. Instead, it is easier to dwell on the more negative aspects and traits, especially if we have been storing up our feelings, dumping them on the other, or been unwilling to hear the concerns and complaints of our partner(s).

Over the years, some guidelines for success have become clear. The guidelines have their own logic, but it is the more convoluted and demanding logic of the psyche. These psychological, relationship-focused guidelines have proven over time to offer a greater margin of success. They help to create more satisfying and even joyful relationships.

GUIDELINES FOR EFFECTIVE LONG-TERM PARTNERING

1. Get clarity, in writing, as to the purpose of the partnership. Include its ultimate aim and goals.
2. Make an explicit agreement with each other regarding your inner commitment to the integrity of the partnership and your own "truths" within the relationship, exercising both the courage to respectfully confront and to invite respectful confrontation.
3. Clarify expectations and responsibilities as you see them, and also discuss how you expect them to evolve and change over time. Take the time to write them down and revisit them quarterly.
4. Create agreements and a forum for frequent truth-telling check-ins. This means frequently inviting and encouraging both appreciative and corrective feedback, as well as checking in to how your partner is feeling about him or herself, the partnership, and each other.
5. Agree, up front, on a mutually respected and acceptable "honest broker" to help listen, mediate, and offer perspective when things get tense and it is difficult to internally resolve issues.
6. Negotiate, in advance, how you want to be confronted and addressed when there are problems, particularly when it has to do with how you are behaving or interacting with others.
7. Finally, while you are in a positive frame of mind at the very beginning, create a well-researched and thoughtful legal agreement for the worst case scenario on how to end the partnership fairly and respectfully.

To ensure the greatest likelihood of a long, productive, and enjoyable partnership, make the commitment to pay attention to even your fleeting feelings of discomfort regarding the relationship. Take the time to look within your own heart to find out what is most vital and truthful for you. Be suspicious when you find yourself or your partner justifying or rationalizing anything. Be willing to challenge and invite challenge. If you consciously cultivate, on a daily basis, the courage to both confront and to be confronted, you will find that not only does the partnership prosper, but your self esteem and personal efficacy also flourish.

Source: Reprinted with permission of The Association for Quality and Participation from the May/June 2000 issue of *The Journal for Quality and Participation*, Cincinnati, Ohio. Copyright © 2000. All rights reserved. For more information contact AQP at 513-381-1959 or visit www.apq.org.

Additional Readings:
"Developing World-Class Partnerships"; Rob Faw; *Communications News*, Nokomis; Jul 2000; Vol. 37, Iss. 7; pg. 30, 1 pg.

"Managing Partners is the Next Big Wave"; Stuart Glascock; *Computer Reseller News*, Manhasset; Dec 14, 1998, Iss. 821; pg. 107, 2 pgs.

CORPORATIONS

Entity Status

A *corporation* is a legal creation of state incorporation statutes and in law is a "person" (called *entity status*). By statutory provision, these legal creations (corporations) have powers generally ascribed to individuals—they can own property, can buy and sell, can sue and be sued, and can be parties to contracts. Unlike natural persons, however, the duration of a corporation is potentially infinite; as long as there are shareholders the corporation can continue, even through bankruptcy!

Ownership and Management

The owners of an incorporated business are its stockholders—more specifically the owners of the corporation's *common stock*. The stockholder owners of a corporation hope (expect) to be rewarded by receiving *dividends*—periodic distributions of earnings—and/or by realizing gains in wealth through appreciation of stock prices. The expectation is that these beneficial results will be provided by a firm that has a professional management team—a team of hired managers that works for the stockholder owners of the firm. American business volume is dominated by corporate business transactions, which make up about 90 percent of total business volume reported in the United States. That's probably not surprising as the identities of gigantic corporations—G.E., General Motors, Proctor and Gamble, Microsoft, Sears, Kroger, Home Depot, and a legion of others—are prominent fixtures in the business world.

Advantages and Disadvantages of Corporations

With the large corporation model in mind, we can easily list a number of specific key advantages and disadvantages that characterize the corporate form of business. Perhaps most importantly, corporations are *limited liability* businesses. Stockholders, while they are owners, with rare exception cannot be held responsible for liabilities incurred by the corporation they own. As a legal entity, the corporation has authority to act (as if it were a natural person) and has liability for its actions, separate and apart from the actual persons who are the corporation's owners. Stockholders, then, generally risk a loss of only the amount they have invested in their stock ownership. No party with a claim against the corporation can go after the personal assets of an owner except under the limited circumstances in which the "corporate veil" can be pierced, a prospect that is only of concern to owners of small corporations. The implication of limited liability is that even if it is ultimately decided that Phillip Morris and other tobacco companies have a history of deception that results in massive personal injury and death (tort) claims, tobacco company stockholders will not suffer economic losses other than in the diminished value of their tobacco company stock.

Transferability of Ownership and Indefinite Longevity

Large corporations are distinctively blessed with an ability to attract enormous sums of capital for investment purposes. Anyone interested in buying stock in General Electric has only to call a broker, or make a few computer key strokes, and within minutes (even seconds) will have accomplished that goal. Selling is just as easy. Transacting in either direction is also possible at very low cost (numerous Internet sites offer trades of up to 5,000 shares of stock at less than $10 for the entire trade). So, unlike ownership in partnerships and proprietorships, ownership in a large corporation is readily transferable. This transferability also corresponds to the lack of any natural life of a large corporation. Again, unlike partnerships which technically terminate with the death of a partner/owner, death or incapacity of a stockholder has no impact on the continuation of a corporation. With easy transferability, an unlimited life, and a history of rewarding performance for stockholder owners, corporations attract large volumes of capital in exchange for stock ownership.

Some Disadvantages of Corporate Form

Of course, corporations have distinctive disadvantages also. The formation of a corporation is more demanding, hence more costly, than is the case with other forms of business. Moreover, once formed, these businesses are subject to far greater government oversight (regulation and reporting requirements) than are partnerships and proprietorships. Moreover, the reporting requirements that publicly held corporations face, largely from the Securities and Exchange Commission but also from the need to report performance details to stockholders, prevent the level of secrecy that is available to privately owned businesses.

The corporate form of business is frequently described as subject to a tax disadvantage. Corporations strive to earn profits for the benefit of stockholders. Any such profits earned by a corporation are subject to a corporate income tax (profits tax) levy. From their after-tax profits, if corporations pay dividends to their stockholders, those dividends are subject to personal income tax obligations at the stockholders' individual ordinary income tax rates. Hence, corporate profits (owned by stockholders) are subject to *double taxation*. On the other hand, retained earnings—corporate profits that are not distributed to shareholders—are not subject to double taxation. Retained earnings add to the value of corporate stock and, when this extra value is received at the time of a stock sale, shareholders will likely only be obligated to pay lower capital gains taxes on the additional profits they realize at the time of a sale of stock.

Corporate Formation

Unless a member of the management team has been through the process before, formation of a corporation virtually requires assistance of an attorney. Corporations are a creation of state incorporation statutes and compliance with the statutes is normally required to gain the advantages of being a corporation, namely, limited liability, entity status, and indefinite duration. In order to incorporate, states require that corporate

promoters complete forms that supply information about the name of the corporation, initial financing (classes of stock and par value), and the names of incorporators. If the state incorporation statute is complied with, the incorporators will receive a corporate certificate from state authorities and the corporation is ready to do business. Normally, after the certificate of incorporation is received, incorporators will hold their first corporate meeting at which time stock typically is issued, a board of directors is elected, and corporate bylaws are adopted.

The board of directors (discussed below) is charged with managing the corporation. Corporate bylaws are the rules of the game for managing a corporation. In the corporate bylaws, there will be discussion of possible restrictions on stock transfers, situations in which more than a simple majority of the board of directors is required to approve a change in structure, such as a merger with another firm, and other details of managing the corporation.

De Jure Incorporation

In spite of the assistance of attorneys or perhaps because of the lack of an attorney, a certificate of incorporation occasionally will be issued, even though one of the forms necessary for incorporation has been

Advantages and Disadvantages of the Basic Legal Forms of Business Organization

	Form of Business Organization		
	Sole Proprietorship	**Partnership**	**Corporation**
Advantages	• Owner has complete control • Owner receives all profits • Low organizational costs • Income reported and taxed on owner's personal tax return • Easily dissolved	• More fund-raising ability than a sole proprietorship • More available managerial skills and time • Able to divide managerial tasks • Income reported and taxed on individual partner's tax returns	• Limited liability for owners; can only lose their investment • Ready access to large amounts of capital • Ownership (stock) is easily transferable • Unlimited life • Professionally managed by a large team of executives
Disadvantages	• Owner has unlimited liability; personal wealth fully exposed • Limited ability to raise capital • Owner must have a broad skill set • Staffing difficult with limited advancement opportunities for employees • Continuity at death of owner and transferability are problems	• Owners have complete liability; liability is joint and several • Still limited in ability to raise capital • Partnership likely to dissolve with death (or other withdrawal) of a partner • Difficult to sell or transfer ownership	• Most costly to organize • Subject to more government oversight • Significant public reporting requirements—limits on maintaining secrecy • Overall taxes generally higher because of *double taxation*

improperly filled out. Suppose for example, a mistake was made in stating the par value of stock due to a computational error. Under these circumstances, a question could arise regarding whether limited liability applies, providing investors the expected shielding from unlimited liability? If there is substantial compliance with the state incorporation statutes, the entity will be labeled a *de jure* corporation and all the privileges of incorporation will inhere to the entity, even with a technical deficiency in the incorporation process.

De Facto Incorporation

Even more substantial deviations from the requirements of state incorporation statutes will be tolerated as long as:

1. There is a state incorporation statute,
2. The incorporators have made a good faith attempt to comply with that statute, and
3. The organization has undertaken business under a corporate name.

The three conditions listed above make the organization a *de facto* corporation, and courts will grant limited liability to investor/shareholders. Condition 2 above suggests that the incorporators were not aware of their failures to fully comply with state incorporation law.

Corporation by Estoppel

If third parties deal with a business as a corporation they are estopped from going after the personal assets of the owners of the company. In other words, if the third party bills a corporation that is in fact not a corporation, the third party cannot later sue the owner of the "corporation" for his or her personal assets. The process also works in reverse: if an organization holds itself out as a corporation even though it is not a *de jure* or *de facto* corporation, the organization is estopped from denying its corporation status in court. This issue can arise in cases involving fraud when the defendant fraudulently claims it was doing business as a corporation, when in fact no corporation existed.

Piercing the Corporate Veil

A primary purpose of the corporate form of business is that of protecting stock investor owners from personal liability for obligations of the business. There are, however, circumstances under which courts will allow the *corporate veil of protection to be pierced,* which

means shareholders are personally liable for corporate debts. Generally, corporate "veils" are vulnerable if the business isn't conducted like a corporate business, opening the door to personal liability for owners who may wrongly believe they are protected by corporate status. For this to occur, courts generally require that the corporation is, in fact, controlled by a single shareholder (or a married couple), that this shareholder has engaged in wrongful actions in the course of his control of the business, and that these wrongful actions have resulted in an injury that cannot be satisfied by the corporation. Courts are very likely to rule that corporate status is a veil that obscures the reality of a business's operations under the following circumstances:

1. Corporations must follow *corporate formalities* such as holding shareholders' and directors' meetings, in keeping detailed records of these meetings, and in providing all document filings required by government agencies. In signing documents for a corporation, officers must be careful to sign as corporate officers, not as individuals.
2. Owners must engage in negotiations with vendors and others as corporate officers, not as individuals. If a person dealt with a creditor as an individual, that person cannot later come into court and claim the corporation is liable. A creditor who can convince a court that it believed it was dealing with an individual, not a corporation, can hold the individual liable. This theory of piercing the corporate veil is based on an *estoppel* argument.
3. No matter what an owner's level of ownership in a corporation is, it's important to keep corporate assets and obligations separate from personal assets and liabilities. With any *commingling* of personal and corporate finances, a claim-holder (creditor) can easily argue that it is difficult or impossible to determine what assets belong to whom. The result is likely to be a court decision that makes all (commingled) assets available for paying any obligation. In effect, the corporation is viewed as the *alter ego* of the largest shareholder. If the shareholder does not recognize differences between corporate and personal assets, neither will the courts.
4. If a corporation is *undercapitalized* and lacks reasonable insurance coverage for contingent liabilities, courts are more likely to hold

shareholders personally liable for claims against the corporation. Undercapitalization is a difficult basis for piercing the corporate veil because achievement of limited liability is one of the main reasons the corporate form is chosen. Usually, courts will require additional fraudulent conduct beyond undercapitalization to permit piercing the corporate veil.

Hoskins Chevrolet, Inc. v. *Ronald Hochberg, Individually, and D/B/A Diamond Auto Construction*
Appellate Court of Illinois
294 Ill. App. 3d 550 (1998)

CASE BACKGROUND AND FACTS

Plaintiff Hoskins Chevrolet filed a complaint for breach of contract against the defendant, Ronald Hochberg individually alleging that he personally ordered and received from plaintiff automobile parts valued at $40,198.16, for which he never paid. Defendant Ronald Hochberg filed a motion to dismiss, asserting that at all times relevant to the complaint, he was only the president of a corporation, Diamond Auto Body & Repair, Inc., an Illinois Corporation, and that at no time did he conduct business with the plaintiff in any capacity other than as president of the corporation. Hence, he contended, he had no personal liability for any parts purchased from Hoskins.

Plaintiff filed a motion for summary judgement asserting that at all pertinent times, it had done business with defendant and Diamond Auto Construction, and Diamond Auto Construction was not a corporation nor had it ever been registered with the Illinois Secretary of State as the assumed name of a corporation as required by section 4.15 of the Business Corporations Act of 1983.

Defendant responded that Illinois law provides that a corporation's use of an unauthorized name does not impose vicarious liability upon the corporation's shareholders or officers. He stated that plaintiff knew from the beginning that he represented a corporation and, therefore, was estopped from pursuing him individually on the debt. He denied that he ever did business individually or as Diamond Auto Construction.

After a hearing, the trial court pierced the corporate veil of Diamond Auto Body and Repair, Inc. and found that the defendant, Ronald Hochberg, owed Hoskins Chevrolet $28,198.16 plus costs. It is from this ruling that defendant appeals.

OPINION: JUDGE BUCKLEY

Defendant Ronald Hochberg appeals from an order of the circuit court of Cook County granting summary judgment in favor of plaintiff Hoskins Chevrolet, Inc. Defendant contends that the trial court erred in determining that he was individually liable for a corporate debt.

* * *

Initially, we note that the cases cited by defendant were governed by law in existence prior to the legislative amendment of 1981 which for the first time allowed Illinois corporations to elect to adopt an assumed name if certain prescribed procedures were followed. . . . Where those procedures are not followed, the corporation is required to conduct business under its corporate name. However, the Act provides that a corporation may use the name of a division, not separately incorporated . . . provided the corporation also clearly discloses its corporate name . . . . The use of an assumed name without complying with the Act or disclosing the corporate name neither creates a legal entity nor does it inform creditors of the existence of the parent corporation . . .

In the case at bar, defendant admitted that Diamond Auto Body & Repair, Inc., used the assumed name of Diamond Auto Construction without complying with the filing requirements of the act. Further, the record contains no evidence that while using the assumed name in his dealings with the plaintiff, defendant also disclosed the corporate name as required by . . . the Act . . . . Accordingly, we find no error in the trial court's determination that under the Act, Diamond Auto Construction was neither a corporation nor the assumed name of a corporation for purposes of establishing contract liability in anyone other than defendant.

* * *

. . . [T]he order of the circuit court of Cook County granting summary judgment in favor of plaintiff is affirmed.

QUESTIONS FOR ANALYSIS

1. What lessons does this case teach with regard to the need to conduct business as a corporation in order to have the limited liability protection accorded to corporate ownership and management?
2. Exactly what would Hochberg have had to do differently to avoid the personal liability he ended up facing?

Example of Bylaws

New York State Bar Association
Bylaws of the Corporate Counsel Section (as amended January 27, 1999)

ARTICLE I
NAME AND PURPOSE

Section 1. The Section shall be known as the Corporate Counsel Section of the New York State Bar Association.

Section 2. The Section, alone or in coordination with other sections and committees of the New York State Bar Association (hereinafter referred to as "the Association"), and such other bar associations or related organizations as may be appropriate from time to time, shall (1) plan and conduct such continuing legal education programs; (2) collect, publish and distribute such educational and professional materials; and (3) undertake such other diverse activities authorized from time to time by the Association and the officers and Executive Committee of the Section as are likely to enhance the competence and skills of lawyers engaged as corporate counsel and improve their ability to deliver the most efficient and highest quality legal service to their clients. Its activities also shall be designed to enhance the role of corporate counsel as contributing members and leaders of their communities, the legal profession and the Association, and to provide a medium through which corporate counsel may cooperate with, encourage and assist each other in the resolution of problems common to them and the legal profession, to their mutual benefit and to the benefit of the membership of the Association, the legal profession at large, the substantive body of law in New York, and the general administration of justice throughout the state.

ARTICLE II
MEMBERSHIP

Section 1. Any regular member of the Association who is employed on a full-time basis by a business enterprise to function as legal counsel for such enterprise shall be eligible for regular membership in this Section and shall be enrolled as a regular member of the Section upon application to its Secretary and payment of the dues determined by its Executive Committee. Any regular member who ceases to be employed on a full-time basis by a business enterprise due to retirement shall be eligible to retain the privileges of regular membership upon payment of the dues determined by its Executive Committee.

Section 2. Any member of the Association who has previously been a Regular Member of this Section, but ceases to qualify for Regular Membership because he or she ceases to be employed on a full-time basis by a business enterprise to function as legal counsel for such enterprise, shall be eligible to retain the privileges of Regular Membership for the balance of the calendar year in which his or her qualification ceases plus one additional year. At the expiration of the calendar year in which eligibility for Regular Membership ceases, any such member may qualify for the status of Associate Member by renewing payment of the Section dues payable at that time. Associate Members shall enjoy the same rights and privileges as Regular Members, including the right to serve on committees of the Section, except that Associate Members shall not have the right to vote on any Section matter, including the election of officers of the Section and of the Executive Committee, nor shall they be eligible to serve as a member of the Executive Committee or as an officer of the Section. An Associate Member shall be automatically restored to Regular Membership status upon once again meeting all the qualifications therefor.

Section 3. Despite the limitations in Sections 1 and 2 hereof and Section 1 of Article III, any officer of the Section, other elected members of the Executive Committee and the Section Delegate to the House of Delegates, may continue to serve to the end of his or her respective term of office as such an officer, elected member or Delegate, with all the rights and privileges of a Regular Member regardless of the fact that he or she has during said term ceased to be employed on a full-time basis by a business enterprise to function as legal counsel for such enterprise. For this purpose, "end of his or her term" shall mean (i) in the case of all officers, except the Chairperson-Elect, the Annual Election next following such cessation of employment, (ii) in the case of the Chairperson-Elect, the First Annual Election subsequent to the Annual Election next following such cessation and (iii) in the case of the elected members of the Executive Committee, at the Annual Election at which the member's three-year term expires. In the case of the Delegate to the House of Delegates, "the end of his or her term" shall mean the end of the 31st day of May in the year in which the Annual Election next following such cessation of employment is held.

ARTICLE III
OFFICERS

Section 1. The officers of the Section shall be a Chairperson, a Chairperson-Elect, two Vice-Chairpersons, a

Secretary, and a Treasurer. In order to serve as an officer in the Section, an individual must be an Active Member of the Association, as defined in Article III, Section 1 of the Association's Bylaws.

Section 2. Chairperson. The Chairperson shall preside at all meetings of the Section and its Executive Committee and shall be an ex officio member of all its committees. The Chairperson shall implement such policy directives as may be adopted by the Section's Executive Committee and may submit to it, from time to time, such recommendations as he or she may deem appropriate in promoting the purposes of the Section. In addition, the Chairperson shall perform such other, related duties as ordinarily are incident to the office.

Section 3. Chairperson-Elect. In the absence of or upon the death or resignation of the Chairperson or during the Chairperson's disability, the Chairperson-Elect shall preside at meetings of the Section and its Executive Committee, and shall perform the duties of Chairperson. The Chairperson-Elect also shall attend the meetings of the Section's Committees and coordinate their activities. The Chairperson-Elect shall assist the Chairperson in the discharge of the Chairperson's responsibilities and shall perform such other, related duties as may be assigned to him or her by the Chairperson or the Section's Executive Committee, and as ordinarily as are incident to the office.

Section 4. Vice-Chairperson. The Section shall have two Vice-Chairpersons, each of whom shall be responsible for such matters as will be assigned by the Chairperson, such as supervising the preparation of the Section's newsletter and supervising preparations for the Section's annual and midyear meetings.

Section 5. Secretary. The Secretary shall prepare the minutes of the annual and special meetings of the Section and its Executive Committee, prepare, forward and receive appropriate notices and correspondence, and collect and maintain such other non-financial records, papers and data as may be necessary or appropriate from time to time. The Secretary shall serve as administrative assistant to the Chairperson and shall assist the Chairperson, the Chairperson-Elect and the Section's committee chairpersons in the discharge of their responsibilities. In addition, the Secretary shall perform such other, related duties as may be assigned by the Chairperson or the Section's Executive Committee and as are ordinarily

incident to the office. Immediately upon being succeeded in office, the Secretary shall deliver all Section records, correspondence and other property in his or her possession or control to his or her successor.

Section 6. Treasurer. The Treasurer shall be the custodian of all financial records of the Section, which shall be available during regular business hours to the inspection of any member of the Section, and to the Association's officers, Executive Committee and financial staff. The Treasurer shall prepare the Section's annual budget, except that if a standing financial committee shall be created within the Section, the Treasurer shall prepare the Section's annual budget in cooperation with such committee. The Treasurer shall maintain liaison with appropriate fiscal officers of the Association and shall report upon the Section's finances at each meeting of the Executive Committee, at the Section's annual meeting and at such other times as the Chairperson, the Executive Committee or the President of the Association shall direct. In addition, the Treasurer shall perform such other, related duties as may be assigned by the Chairperson or the Section's Executive Committee and as are ordinarily incident to the office. Immediately upon being succeeded in office, the Treasurer shall deliver all Section records, correspondence and other property in his or her possession or control to his or her successor.

Section 7. Terms. The officers of the Section shall be elected by the regular membership annually at the Annual Meeting of the Section (the "Annual Election"), provided, however, that the Chairperson-Elect, upon completion of the Chairperson's term of office, immediately after the Annual Election, automatically shall succeed to the office of Chairperson.

ARTICLE IV
EXECUTIVE COMMITTEE

Section 1. There shall be an Executive Committee of the Section, consisting of its officers and no fewer than ten nor more than fifteen other members (hereinafter referred to as elected members). To the extent practicable, the Executive Committee shall have at least one representative from each judicial department of the State of New York. The immediate past Chairperson of the Section and the Section Delegate to the House of Delegates (the "Section Delegate") shall be non-voting members of the Executive Committee.

—Continued on page 346

Example of Bylaws

New York State Bar Association
Bylaws of the Corporate Counsel Section (as amended January 27, 1999)   *Continued from page 345*

Section 2. (a) The Executive Committee shall have general supervision and control over the affairs and activities of the Section, subject to any conditions prescribed in the Association's Bylaws and the Bylaws of the Section. It shall be responsible for the authorization of all commitments and contracts, and for the expenditure of all monies collected by the Section or appropriated for its use and purposes. The Executive Committee may adopt its own rules of procedure, including rules as to the number of its members who shall constitute a quorum, the time and place of its meetings, and the manner of providing notices to its members. It may also, by a two-thirds vote of the entire Executive Committee, remove an elected member thereof.

(b) During the period between annual meetings of the Section, the Executive Committee may fill vacancies in the offices of the Section, including its own membership and the position of Section Delegate.

Section 3. Term. The elected members of the Executive Committee shall be divided as nearly as practicable into three classes; the term of office of those of Group 1 to expire immediately upon the next Annual Election; of Group II immediately upon the Annual Election the year thereafter; of Group III immediately upon the Annual Election two years thereafter; and at each Annual Election held after such classification and election, elected members of one group shall be elected by the membership, for a term to expire immediately upon the Annual Election three years thereafter, to succeed those elected members of the group whose terms expire.

ARTICLE V
SECTION DELEGATE

Section 1. The Section shall be represented at meetings of the House of Delegates of the Association by Section Delegate.

Section 2. Term. The Section Delegate shall be elected at the Annual Meeting to serve for a one-year term to commence on June 1 of the year of such Annual Meeting.

ARTICLE VI
NOMINATIONS

Section 1. Not fewer than ninety days nor more than one hundred and twenty days prior to each Annual Meeting of the Section, the Chairperson shall appoint a Nominat-

ing Committee consisting of at least three regular members of the Section, which committee shall make, and report to the Secretary not less than forty-five days prior to the Annual Meeting of the Section, its nominations for the following term for the offices of Chairperson-Elect, two Vice-Chairpersons, Secretary and Treasurer, the position of Section Delegate, and elected members of the Executive Committee, as appropriate. If there shall then exist a vacancy in the office of Chairperson-Elect, the Nominating Committee also shall make and report its nomination for the following term for the office of Chairperson.

Section 2. The report of the Nominating Committee shall accompany the notice of the Section's Annual Meeting. Additional nominations for such offices may be made upon the petition of at least twenty-five regular members of the Section filed with its Secretary not less than fifteen days prior to the Annual Meeting of the Section.

ARTICLE VII
ANNUAL MEETING

Section 1. The Annual Meeting of the Section shall be held in January of each year, on such day and at such place as the Executive Committee may select. Notice of the time and place for holding the Annual Meeting of the Section shall be given by mail to each member of the Section at least thirty days prior to the time fixed for holding said meeting.

Section 2. The Annual Meeting of the Executive Committee of the Section shall be held immediately following the Annual Meeting of the Section.

ARTICLE VIII
COMMITTEES

The Executive Committee of the Section may create such standing committees as it deems appropriate. The Executive Committee or the Chairperson may create such other committees as either may deem appropriate. Section committees shall from time to time make recommendations to the Chairperson or the Executive Committee for such actions as they may deem appropriate, but shall not transmit their views as those of the Section without the approval of the Section's Executive Committee.

ARTICLE IX

MISCELLANEOUS PROVISIONS

Section 1. These Bylaws shall become effective upon their approval by the Association's Executive Committee. These Bylaws may be amended at any meeting of the Section, except that no amendment shall be effective until approved by the Association's Executive Committee.

Section 2. The Executive Committee of the Section shall fix the dues for membership in the Section, subject to approval by the Association's Finance Committee.

Dues shall be payable to the Association's Treasurer, to be held by the Treasurer for the Section. Section funds shall be expended only by approval of the Chairperson and at least one other officer, or by approval of the Section's Executive Committee.

Source: Official Bylaws of the New York State Bar Association. These bylaws can be found on the website location: http://www.nysba.org/sections/corporate/bylaws.html. Reprinted with permission of The New York State Bar Association.

CORPORATE ORGANIZATION AND CORPORATE GOVERNANCE

Management of the Corporation

The typical representation of the organizational structure of a corporation and its linkages to its owners are as illustrated in the diagram below. As shown, the stockholders who own a corporation have the legal right to elect a *Board of Directors* (Board) that, organizationally, is expected to represent the interest of owners in having the corporation managed skillfully for the owners' benefit. In fact, stockholders vote periodically (generally yearly) for a slate of board candidates. Elected by stockholder owners, the Board has ultimate authority to put a senior management team in place and to guide corporate policy. The Board is apt to include key company personnel as well as outside individuals who typically are successful and prominent business people.

A corporation's president or chief executive officer (CEO) is responsible for the day-to-day management of the corporation's conduct of business, presumably in

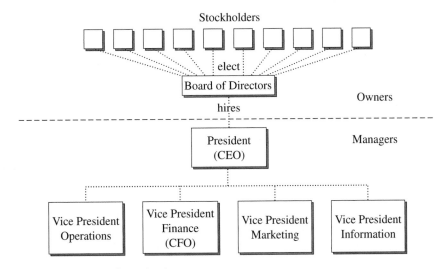

Typical Corporate Organization

conformance with the general policies endorsed by the Board. He is apt to be instrumental in the appointment of a team of senior-level executives and to work closely with that team in directing the activities of the various functional components of the corporation (ranging from operations to finance functions). Note that there is a separation between ownership and management control in the corporate world. While stockholders **own** the corporation, they have little or nothing to do directly with its management. Instead, shareholders elect a Board of Directors who have legal responsibility to manage the corporation for the benefit of those shareholders. The Board delegates actual hands-on management to professional officers of the corporation who are expected to be diligent **agents** for the owners, pursuing the economic interests of those owners.

Fiduciary Duties of Directors and Officers

As with partnerships, both the board of directors and corporate officers have fiduciary obligations to the corporation. These obligations are the same as for partnerships; directors and officers of a corporation have an obligation to place the interest of the corporation above their own personal interests. Both are required not to secretly compete with the corporation, to reveal conflicts of interests, and in the case of directors to refrain from voting on issues when they have a conflict of interest. In addition, directors and officers are legally obligated to protect corporations by not disclosing trade secrets even after their affiliation with the corporation has terminated.

It may be noted at this point that there are business gurus who believe the life of vertically integrated, hierarchically managed enterprises (consistent with the organization chart on page 247), is limited. Their expectation is that successful enterprises in the future will be much "flatter," with more team responsibilities and less direction from the "top" of the enterprise. We'll have more to say about that later.

A PARTNERSHIP HYBRID—LIMITED PARTNERSHIPS

The partnership form of business described most completely above was a *general partnership,* the owners of which are *general partners* in the business. As discussed, the general partners in any partnership arrangement can be personally liable for any debts of the partnership. This risk exposure limits the access to capital from the kinds of investors who would buy common stock, in turn limiting the overall access to capital enjoyed by partnerships. A variant of partnerships, the *limited partnership,* breaks that link between business liability and investor (partner) liability for a specific class of investors described as *limited partners.*

Formalities and Prohibitions

A limited partnership must have at least one general partner and at least one limited partner but, of course, can have many more. A primary objective of limited partnerships is to foreclose limited partners' exposure to the risk of loss of wealth to anything more than the investment the limited partner makes in the partnership (paralleling the situation with common stock in General Motors). Limited partners are not personally responsible for the debts of the partnership as long as they keep their status as limited partners. In contrast, the general partners are personally liable for partnership obligations. Note, however, that most states allow general partners to be corporations, enjoying corporate limits on liability. Unlike a general partnership, a limited partnership must be registered with a state in much the same way that a corporation is. Failure to qualify under the state limited liability act causes limited partners to have unlimited liability.

Common examples of limited partnerships, offered as investments by brokers and financial advisors, include real estate development partnerships and like partnerships involved in a wide range of activities including drilling for oil and gas, owning and leasing airplanes to air carriers, owning and leasing railroad cars to rail shippers, conducting livestock-raising operations, etc. Most of these businesses have an initial period when there are losses on paper to be reported to the IRS, but with large expected gains near the end of the project. Thus, it makes sense to organize such businesses as limited partnerships for tax purposes.

Maintaining Limited Liability

To maintain his or her protected status, a limited partner must be a *passive* investor in the partnership, not a participant in management. An investor can be found to be a general partner, hence presumably liable for partnership obligations, by helping in the control of the partnership, or by engaging in conduct or communications that would cause a third party to believe, reasonably, that the investor is a general partner. Because of the sizeable number of disputes over the line between limited and general partner participation, a 1985 **Revised Uniform Limited Partnership Act** has attempted to clarify what limited partner activities are *not* to be viewed as converting a limited partner into a general partner.[2] The list includes:

1. guaranteeing partnership debt,
2. serving as a consultant to the partnership,
3. acting as an agent of or serving as an employee of the partnership,
4. attending partnership meetings, and even
5. voting on various partnership activities.

Note, however, that if you as a limited partner interact with vendors and/or customers of the limited partnership in a way that would reasonably lead such parties to conclude that you are a general partner, the result is a general partner's liability exposure for you.

Limited partnerships are created by general partners who typically have considerable expertise in this form of business and who have little interest in exposing their personal wealth to significant risk. To limit their personal risk exposure, general partners in a limited partnership sometimes form a corporation to serve as the general partner so that only the assets of the corporation are at risk in the face of claims against the general partner(s). Clearly, the formation of limited partnerships requires technical legal expertise and careful attention to the certification and registration processes with the appropriate state authorities. Failure to adhere precisely to legal formation requirements can bring unexpected, high-magnitude risks for investors in the form of unlimited liability for partnership debts.

Governance

A typical limited partnership will have a small number of general partners and a considerably larger number of limited partners who have provided capital to the partnership. In conformance with the requirements described above, only general partners can be involved in directing the partnership's conduct. Limited partners do have the legal right to be kept informed about the partnership's business and financial condition and performance. Moreover, limited partnership agreements can grant limited partners a significant degree of control over the retention or firing of the general

partner(s). For example, the partnership agreement may allow removal of the general partner(s) by a 70 percent majority vote of limited partners.

Liquidity/Transferability of Ownership

Whether a limited partner can readily transfer an ownership interest to another party is determined by the partnership agreement. Most typically, limited partners are not allowed to sell their interests to other parties unless such a sale is expressly agreed to by the other partners. So, there is no ready secondary market to allow a limited partner to liquidate an ownership interest. However, limited partners are typically allowed to withdraw by turning over their interests to the partnership, with the investor compensated for the *value* of the ownership interest conveyed in a manner determined by the partnership agreement. General partners can also withdraw from a limited partnership (or, on occasion, be dismissed). The limited partnership can continue in business as long as one or more general partner participants are available to continue the management tasks required of such partners.

Taxation

Like a simple general partnership, a limited partnership does not pay income tax. Any earnings generated by the limited partnership flow through to the partners and are taxed (only once) as personal income. Losses from limited partnerships can potentially be deducted against other income of the limited partners. In the event of a sale of a limited partnership, after the payment of sales-related expenses and remaining partnership debts, the proceeds go to the investor partners (in amounts based upon their contributions to the partnership).

Typical Limited Partnership Litigation

As was discussed above, a key feature of the limited partnership form of business is that it offers investors participation in the performance of specific classes of investments, such as rental real estate, free both from the everyday participation in maintenance and management and from a liability (loss) exposure greater than the amount of investment made. Needless to say, at a minimum a limited partner seeks in all cases to avoid liability for debts of the partnership. Whether limited partners have liability exposure for debts of the partnership has been hotly contested in many court cases, including the following one.

---

[2]At this writing, 39 states had adopted the 1976 Uniform Limited Partnership Act with the 1985 Amendments. Forty-nine states have adopted with Uniform Limited Partnership Act of 1976.

Northhampton Valley Constructors, Inc. v. *Horne-Lang Associates*
Superior Court of Pennsylvania
310 Pa. Super. 559, 456 A.2d 1077 (1983)

CASE BACKGROUND AND FACTS

Northampton Valley Constructors built a sewer system on land owned and being developed by Horne-Lang, a limited partnership. After completion of the work, Northampton went unpaid and sued Horne-Lang Associates for breach of contract for its failure to pay for the work performed. Horne-Lang's business was a failure and it was unable to pay.

Horne-Lang was a Pennsylvania limited partnership with a general partner along with 18 limited partners. A key element of Northampton's suit against Horne-Lang was the contention that the 18 investor-partners were really general partners and hence were personally liable for the partnerships' debt. A lower court had dismissed Northampton's suit and Northampton had appealed to the Superior Court.

OPINION: JUDGE MCEWEN

According to judge McEwen, under Pennsylvania law a limited partnership " . . . permits a manner of doing business whereby individuals may invest their money free of the fear of unlimited liability and of the responsibilities of management." According to Pennsylvania's Uniform Limited Partnership Act:

> Sec. 511. Limited partnership defined
>
> A limited partnership is a partnership formed by two or more persons . . . having as members one or more general partners and one or more limited partners. The limited partners as such shall not be bound by the obligations of the partnership . . .

The certificate of the limited partnership we here study contains, pursuant to § 512(a)(1)(vii) [of the Uniform Limited Partnership Act for the state of Pennsylvania], the following provision concerning additional contributions:

> No additional contributions have been agreed to be made. However, additional contributions are required if the General Partner determines that the partnership requires additional funds to meet the obligations of the partnership.

It must be emphasized that this claim against the limited partners is exerted by a creditor of the partnership and not by the partnership. A creditor may pursue a claim against a limited partner as a general partner only in the limited circumstances prescribed by the Act, namely when the limited partner "takes part in the control of the business." Northampton did not, however, allege and does not now argue that the limited partners took part in the control of the business.

This claim . . . is based upon the aforementioned provision of the partnership certificate concerning additional contributions. Northampton contends that, as a result of this provision, the limited partners were *de facto* general partners and argues that, since the general partner could have and should have called upon the limited partners to provide additional capital to the partnership in order to pay the creditors of the partnership, the limited partners are liable to creditors for the debts of the partnership over and beyond their investment. According to Northampton, "the limited partners have committed to make their invest-

ment equal to the obligations [of the partnership] . . . " The premise for this assertion is, however, simply not correct since the limited partners did not commit to make their investments in the partnership equal to the obligations of the partnership; nor does the clear meaning of the plain language concerning additional contributions permit interpretation, let alone allow the inferences urged by Northampton.

Northampton does allege . . . that "the General Partner determined that the partnership required additional funds to meet the obligations of the partnership" and . . . we are obliged to accept that averment as a fact. Nonetheless, whatever liability such a determination by the general partner may have imposed upon the limited partners in favor of the partnership, we are not persuaded that the limited partners thereby became as equally liable to creditors as were the general partner and the partnership.

Order Affirmed.

QUESTIONS FOR ANALYSIS

1. Explain the basis of the court's conclusion that the limited partners did not have to ante up the funds to pay what the partnership owed to Northampton.
2. What particular language in the partnership agreement/certification made Northampton's claims against the limited partners strong enough to get to court (to survive a motion for summary judgment dismissal), in light of the statutory protection of limited partners?

THE CLOSELY HELD CORPORATION

Suppose you and two of your friends have written software that, based on a sophisticated electrocardiogram, allows a quick prediction in an emergency room of heart fibrillation in the hours following a heart attack.[3] You would like to form a company to produce and market this software, but are concerned with the personal liability (for bad predictions) you might face. Your attorney has advised you that a corporate form of business is called for by this risk exposure, but that your state allows closely held corporations to be operated much like a partnership, with advantages that are likely to appeal to the three of you.

As with all corporations, a closely held corporation is owned by shareholders, managed by a board of directors, and operated by corporation officers. Unlike a publicly traded corporation, there is apt to be considerable overlap between shareholders, directors, and chief corporation officers. In the example above, if you and your friends form a corporation, it is likely that you and your friends will own all of the stock, that you and they will be on the Board of Directors, and that you will select yourselves as chief corporate officers. In many cases, a closely held corporation is just a partnership in corporate form. As with any partnership, a closely held corporation should make extensive use of corporate bylaws to break deadlocks and prevent squeeze outs of minority shareholders.

Most broadly, closely held corporations are simply corporations with stock that is not publicly traded on an exchange, but which is closely held (privately held), typically by a small number of shareholders. Most closely held corporations are relatively small businesses, though there are notable exceptions. More narrowly, closely held corporations, or "close corporations", under state laws in about half of the states, have special provisions that provide for a flexible form of corporate structure, while retaining the limited liability advantage of the corporate form of business. The provisions provided are not identical in all states, but generally share a number of important characteristics. Notably, they generally provide that:

1. There is flexibility in the structure of governance and the conduct of company decision making. A standard, publicly traded C Corporation is required to have a governance structure that provides for accountability to public

shareholders. So, such corporations have boards of directors elected by shareholders, published bylaws for the conduct of corporate business with shareholders, extensive public reporting requirements, required annual meetings of shareholders, etc. Those states that provide explicitly for the existence of closely held corporations generally allow such businesses to exist free of many of these requirements.

2. Owners can agree to (contract for) specific protections for individual shareholders' interests and for specific remedies in the event of disputes among shareholders. With regard to shareholder rights (minority interests), the operating agreement can provide whatever degree of protection you and your "partners" deem appropriate. For example, there can be a requirement for unanimous agreement on all decisions made, or for a weaker alternative such as majority rule. Agreements on dispute resolution can require arbitration, can allow for dissolution of the company if demanded by any stockholder, or can provide for any other dispute-solving procedures agreed to by the partner–stockholders.

3. State provisions for closely held corporations permit stockholder chosen restrictions on the transfer of stock. Typically, holders of stock in a close corporation are not allowed to freely sell or otherwise transfer their stock ownership to another party, at least until those shares are offered to the company, often at values defined by agreement of the stockholders at the time of incorporation.

S AND C CORPORATIONS

Congress has sought to encourage the formation of new businesses by providing incentives *to S Corporations*. As the "corporation" component of this label indicates, this form of business organization has the corporate advantage of limited liability for owners. However, like a proprietorship or partnership, an S Corporation is not a taxable entity. For S Corporations, financial benefits, profits or losses, are attributed for tax purposes directly to shareholders. So, an S Corporation has the tax benefits of a partnership that expects initially to have tax losses. Earnings are taxed only once, at the shareholders' tax rate, avoiding the double taxation problem faced by C Corporation earnings.

---

[3]Recall the *Arrythmia* case in Chapter 8.

Any losses carried to a shareholder's tax return can be written off against income from other sources, reducing the shareholder's tax obligations.

What Happens When a Small Corporation Grows Up?

Designed to stimulate small businesses, S Corporation rules can be a disadvantage to successful start-ups that grow significantly. Notably, S Corporations can only issue one class of stock, can have no more than 75 shareholders, must limit stock ownership to only citizens or residents of the United States, and must limit ownership to individuals, estates, or trusts. Most S Corporations convert to C Corporation status as they grow beyond the reasonable bounds permitted by S Corporation rules. It is common for closely held corporations to elect to be operated as an S Corporation, and then as the company expands and increases its number of shareholders, the corporation switches to C Corporation status and also relaxes its restrictive agreements with respect to transfers of stock. Eventually, if the corporation is really successful, its stock becomes publicly traded with few or no restrictions on the transferability of ownership. For many closely held corporations, "success" occurs at the time of an **IPO,** an Initial Public Offering of its stock to the investing public.

LIMITED LIABILITY COMPANIES (LLCs) AND LIMITED LIABILITY PARTNERSHIPS (LLPs)

All 50 states in the United States have either adopted or have proposed legislation authorizing LLCs (Limited Liability Corporations). Like S Corporations, LLCs offer the joint advantages of corporate limited liability and the favorable tax treatment of a partnership, with earnings flowing through to individual LLC owners' personal income for tax purposes. From this point of departure, LLCs differ from S Corporations in a number of advantageous ways. LLCs are permitted to have multiple classes of stock, can have any number of stockholder members, and are not limited in the classes of owners, so they can issue stock that will be owned by corporations and partnerships.

In a number of states, professional service providers (such as doctors and dentists) are not permitted to form LLCs, but are permitted to join together in limited liability partnerships (LLPs). In these states professional codes of ethics require professionals to be unlimitedly liable for malpractice to their clients. As with LLCs, LLPs must be registered with the state in which the organization resides. Operating as an LLP generally provides partners with protection against claims resulting from the malpractice of *other members or employees of the partnership*. This protection is in effect for claims incurred as a consequence of actions and/or events occurring after the formation of the LLP, not for anything that occurred prior to formation of the LLP. In addition, partners generally remain personally liable for general debts of the partnership such as those incurred for rents, repairs, bank loans, etc.

INFORMED CHOICES ON ORGANIZING YOUR BUSINESS

You may recall from Chapter 1 the discussion of the plight of the friends who were struggling to retain or regain control of intellectual property they had shared with a potential benefactor. Perhaps some of their other fellow students had commercializable ideas as well, and managed to keep control of them. In fact, you and a couple of your friends may have such intellectual property, and may be on the threshold of launching a business based on your ideas. If so, you'll have to choose a form of business organization. So, consider the following scenario. You and two friends have created software, usable on the Internet, that will provide "lowest cost" purchasing and transport information for manufacturers who must buy inputs worldwide. You have demonstration software in hand, and need only a few months of further commercial scale development to be ready to market your software to manufacturers anywhere in the world. You've consulted with two corporate attorneys in a law firm that is anxious to work with you and, unfortunately, gotten two very different views on what form of organization you should establish.

Advice of Attorney Number One

A general partnership does not require the services of expensive legal help to protect against risks that are largely irrelevant for young graduates who have few assets to worry about losing. Not only is incorporating expensive, but failure to comply with corporate formalities could forfeit the alleged advantages of incorporating. Instead of hiring an attorney to dress up the organization as a legitimate business, owner/operators can operate with very informal rules and become more formalized and restrictive as the business grows. For those with few assets, unlimited liability is not a significant risk. Furthermore, business insurance can provide protection for all but enormous risks at a very moderate cost. For closely held corporations in their beginning stages, banks will demand personal signatures of owner/operators, so the advantages of limited liability that corporations provide apply mainly to credit supplied by creditors and tort claims of third parties. Most business ideas, including high-tech ideas, fail. Why get suited up for the major leagues when the owner/operators are still in the minor leagues and may abandon the idea if a great employment offer from an established firm comes along.

Advice of Attorney Number Two

The advice of number 2 is, in a word, "Incorporate". The advantages of incorporation are obvious: limited liability, perpetual existence, and a business structure that can grow with the business. If losses are anticipated, election of S Corporation status will generate the tax advantages of a partnership, allowing owners to offset other income with the paper losses that are expected in the first few years of operation for new high-tech start-up. A closely held corporation allows owners to exercise all the powers of a general partnership in terms of restricting ownership, guaranteeing jobs for owner/operators, and structuring dividends. Operating as a corporation negates the inference that the business is a hobby of the owner/operators. Getting corporate stationary and other accoutrements of a corporate form will establish credibility with banks and potential suppliers of capital. Ownership of patents, copyrights, and trademarks are facilitated by a corporate business organization. The goal of many high-tech start-ups is an IPO (initial public offering). IPOs necessitate corporate form, so if an IPO is the goal, why not move things along?

Authors' Thoughts

The choice of business organization for young entrepreneurs who may be working at a "day" job should be determined by a number of factors. The farther along the "idea" [to make millions] is towards a patent or copyrighted software, the more desirable is the corporate form. At the beginning stages of the development of a viable business idea, incorporation does not make much

sense, particularly if finances are tight. If the owners/operators of the high-tech start-up do have significant assets, this factor would encourage corporate formation. Partnerships are easy to operate and the initial partnership agreement need only include the factors that the partners deem important, such as who gets what if the partnership dissolves and how to resolve disputes. Limited partnerships are as complicated as corporations to form and are mainly desirable for tax purposes, i.e., the owner/operators expect an initial period of losses. Owner/operators who have previously been involved in high-tech start-ups are probably savvy enough to radically cut down on legal expenses. Increasingly, legal forms are available online and most of the clerical work can be downloaded without need for attorney assistance. In short, our advice for high-tech start-ups manned by students with few assets is, "It depends!"

OTHER FORMS OF BUSINESS ORGANIZATION

It is likely that any business you might start would take one of the forms described above. However, there are other forms that you likely will have some exposure to in the future, and brief descriptions of the most common of those should provide perspective on their nature and reasons for existence. These alternatives, which include joint ventures, cooperatives, and syndicates, most typically are created to pursue a particular business goal and are not expected to go on indefinitely.

Joint Ventures

Innovations in electronics, biology, and other sciences have spurred a proliferation of technologies that have commercial potential. Many innovations are the brainchild of individuals or small groups of individuals with great ideas, but with limited access to financing and the other inputs needed to transform discovery into commercial products. It is commonplace for large companies, such as Johnson & Johnson in the pharmaceutical industry, to team up in a joint venture with an early stage development company to commercialize a particular technology or even a single product. In addition, large companies, from petroleum exploration and refining giants to automobile manufacturers, can team up for specific projects as well.

As described by the U.S. Supreme Court, a joint venture is a general partnership created for a specific purpose, which has a limited life. Such an arrangement

In the News: Joint Venture

Belo and Time Warner Cable will spend $25 million to launch 2 new 24-hour cable news channels in Houston and San Antonio in 2002. The 50–50 joint ventures are part of a bigger deal that gives TWC retransmission rights to Belo's TV stations and that commits TWC to carrying Belo's existing Texas Cable News channel across its Texas systems. Like the retrans deal, TWC's commitment to carry TXCN has a 10-year term.

The 2 joint-venture news channels have initial 20-year terms.

Source: Excerpt from: "Texas Two-Step"; Steve McClellan; *Broadcasting & Cable,* New York; Oct 2, 2000; Vol. 130, Iss. 41; pg. 34.
Additional Readings:
"Retrans Standoff in Houston"; Richard Tedesco; *Broadcasting & Cable,* New York; Mar 13, 2000; Vol. 130, Iss. 11; pg. 12
"Five Biggest Investors: Paul Allen"; Paula Rooney; *Computer Reseller News,* Manhasset; Sep 20, 1999; Iss. 860; pg. 34.

can be viewed as a partnership between or among firms (generally corporations), with terms of participation spelled out by a joint venture agreement that typically defines the rights and obligations of the participants, including the sharing of any benefits or costs associated with the joint venture's activities. Such an alliance does not result in the creation of an entity that has legal standing (like a corporation) and, hence, the rights of a person. So, a joint venture typically would not be taxable, would not have the right to own property, cannot sue and cannot be the target of a suit. The individual company participants in a joint venture continue their existences with no alteration of status due to their participation in a joint venture.

Joint ventures do share some legal characteristics with partnerships. Each party in a joint venture has the right to mutually direct and govern the venture, profits and losses are shared as in a partnership, and there is a pooling of property, money, skills, and knowledge with respect to the joint venture. With large companies as joint venturers with a small company, it is likely that the large company would draw up the joint venture agreement. In that agreement the large company/partner will seek to limit its downside risk exposure on the project, but typically would provide development funding, without which the small company would have little chance of commercial success.

Cooperatives

A cooperative is an association of individuals or businesses, joined together to provide an economic service to the coop members. Most typically, coops are formed to pool the purchasing power of members to gain bargaining power in the marketplace. In this case, the hope of coop members is that they will receive lower prices by buying in large quantity. Common coops exist in agriculture, in groceries, and in the provision of electricity in rural areas.

Coops can be incorporated or unincorporated. If unincorporated, they generally are treated as partnerships under state law, with members personally and jointly liable for the obligations of the coop. To qualify as a corporation, a coop must adhere to state laws governing the formation and operation of nonprofit corporations. Whatever the legal form of a coop, if it collects revenues that exceed its expenses, the difference is distributed to members with the allocation reflecting the members' value of transactions with (purchases from) the coop. Coops do not have to pay income tax to the extent that their earnings are distributed to coop members, and therefore the coop form of business escapes double taxation.

Syndicates

Syndicates are similar to a joint venture, but often exist for a briefer time span and with a focus on the *financing* of an activity. They are groups of individuals or companies joined together for a specific purpose, such as the financing of a real estate development, the public sale and distribution of a sizeable offering of stock or bonds from a large corporation, etc. As with joint ventures, the details of the agreements among members of a syndicate are spelled out in contractual documents. Syndicates can be organized as partnerships, general or limited, or they can be organized as corporations.

Franchises

Surely every college student feels familiar with franchise operations from having eaten too many meals at McDonald's, Burger King, or Subway, washed down

Tips for Franchising

Entering a franchise agreement is one option to start your own business with minimum risk. Although some franchises offer tried and true plans for business opportunities, prospective franchisees must be wary of franchisers who appear to offer sure-fire methods for success while struggling themselves to stay alive in the market. The mere fact that a business is franchised is not a guarantee of its success. If you are considering entering a franchise agreement, be prepared to do the same research and careful planning that go with any start-up venture.

THINGS TO KNOW BEFORE CHOOSING A FRANCHISE

Before you decide that franchising is right for you, consider several factors. Investigating and closely comparing three or four franchisers will give you an idea of "norms" in the industry. Information about a franchiser and its expectations can be obtained from the franchiser and various governmental and trade organizations. As a prospective franchisee, you should obtain as much information as possible. The list below is far from being all-inclusive; however, it provides a guide for essential questions to ask.

Just as in any business venture, franchised businesses are subject to market fluctuations and economic trends. You should obtain a thorough analysis of an area's demographics to decide if the potential location is prime for such an operation. Just because a restaurant is successful in southern California does not mean it will be successful in Maryland.

Evaluate your knowledge of the franchise business. How much, if any, experience do you have in the area? If you do not have much experience, decide whether the franchiser's training program will compensate for your lack of experience.

Be willing to devote a great deal of time, effort, and money to the operation. Franchisers often require that the franchisee be personally involved in the day-to-day operations of the business and personally guarantee the financial obligations of the business. Do not be deceived. You will not simply negotiate the deal and wait for the profits to roll in.

Find out how many franchises the franchiser owns. Significant franchiser ownership may show the franchiser's confidence in its product and create common interests between he franchiser and franchisee.

The cash needs for franchise operations are similar to any other start-up business. As a franchisee, you must pay a franchise fee in addition to financing the premises, equipment, advertising and operation capital. Franchisers will usually provide an estimate of capital required to start, but it is best to obtain an independent evaluation.

As a franchisee, you will be required to follow the franchiser's operational requirements. Often, such requirements are all encompassing. Therefore, if you an independent person who prefers to do things in your own way, you should evaluate whether you can operate within the structures of the franchise.

Additional readings:
The FindLaw Small Business Center
http://smallbiz.findlaw.com/book/su franchising/articles/11.E..html.
Franchise Online
http://www.franchise.co.nz/buying a franchise/a whats in the agree.html.

---

with Coke or Pepsi products distributed by a local franchised distributor, from having shopped at The Gap, The Limited, and Structure, and from having spent late hours at Kinko's, from driving and riding in cars made in a distant location, but sold through a local franchised dealer, and from having bought gas at a locally owned Exxon or Phillips 66 station. The retail outlets at which the transactions linked to the experiences described above take place may operate as proprietorships, partnerships, corporations, or some other specific form of business—the existence of a franchise does not dictate the form of a franchised business. But, franchising is so common and pervasive in our economy that it deserves discussion in this chapter, even though it is not a separate *form* of business organization. Indeed, over a third of retail sales in our country take place in franchise outlets.

Successful franchise businesses generally have two prominent features. First, they offer a trademark with widespread brand recognition, and second they offer uniformity in the product or service sold. Hence, a Big Mac lover can expect a nearly identical hamburger from a McDonald's, whether it's bought in Vancouver or Virginia Beach. As is typical of franchise businesses, a McDonald's franchisee would operate as a semi-independent business (most often of corporate form), subject to standards and requirements specified by the franchisor (McDonald's Corporation).

To become a franchisee, an applicant generally must make an up-front payment to "buy" the franchise, then must pay annual fees that typically are a percentage of gross sales. Franchisees are also often required to make prescribed payments for participation in coop advertising—national advertising and promotions for all stores in the chain. In exchange, franchise applicants typically expect to receive:

1. use of a trademark, trade dress, and product line that will bring customers in the door,
2. a plan for the successful conduct of business in which the kinks have been worked out in the past, and
3. provision of the inputs (pizza dough, tomato sauce, cheese, etc.) that will insure the uniformity of product that customers demand.

In fact, franchisees are often required to buy their inputs from the franchisor. Franchisees often complain that this allows franchisors the right to levy disguised royalty charges in the form of overpriced inputs, such as paper wrappers, product ingredients, and specialized inputs such as ice cream dispensers.

Franchise Agreement

A *franchise agreement* is a contract between a franchisor and a franchisee that spells out the details of the agreement entered into, including the rights and obligations of both parties. These typically will include strict limits on the use of the franchisor's trademark, trade names and trade dress, the use of the franchisor's operating manual, other instructional and training materials, and even "knowledge" gained from company training programs, identification of the allowable location for a franchised operation, description of the assigned territory acquired by the franchisee, agreements for fee payments, commitments to the company advertising program, and bases and conditions for termination of a franchise agreement.

Franchisee Protection Law

There has been an explosive proliferation of franchising in the last quarter of a century, resulting in an attendant evolutionary development of franchise law. A primary focus of franchise law, both at the federal and state level, has been on protecting franchisees from unscrupulous actions of franchisors. In general, parent companies (franchisors) are much more powerful than franchisees. At the federal level, the Federal Trade Commission imposes disclosure standards in the form of its *Franchise Rule, which* requires that, well before the exchange of any money for franchise rights, a franchisor provide an applicant with documentation that includes the following:

- Names, addresses, and telephone numbers of other franchisees,
- Information on any litigation brought against the company,
- Audited financial statements of the franchisor,
- Information on any bankruptcy proceedings of the franchisor,
- Information on the background and experience of the franchisor's key executives,
- Detailed description of the rights and obligations of franchisor and franchisee,
- A sample set of contracts,
- Estimates of the full amount of likely needed initial investment,
- Information on all fees,
- Any restrictions on the geographic territory available to the franchisee,
- A specific indication of whether or not that territory will be exclusive,
- A listing of what must be purchased from the franchisor,
- The number of franchisees in operation,
- The number of franchises that have gone out of business in the preceding three years.[4]

These requirements are intended to assure the availability of relevant information needed by a prospective franchisee to make a decision regarding a franchise investment. There is no ironclad guarantee regarding the quality of the information provided or the ability of the franchise offeror, in the event of invalid information, to cover any damages incurred as a consequence by a franchisee. A number of states also have extensive franchise statutes that may be stricter than those in place at the federal level. Even so, there are still frequent "bad experiences" with franchise purchases, even though many franchises are very successful.

Termination of the Franchise Agreement

There have been many incidents of hardworking franchisees who have built up a franchise only to have the franchisor find some reason to terminate the franchise

---

[4]The Franchise Rule of the FTC can be accessed at http://www.ftc.gov.

and install a company employee to manage the business and benefit from the franchisee's efforts. States as well as the FTC have passed laws to protect the legitimate expectations of franchisees. Generally, the franchise agreement will contain provisions that specify conditions under which the franchise can be terminated. It is legitimate for the franchisor to expect *quality control* will be maintained by the franchisee, and, in some cases, there are objective measures of quality control. In general, protective legislation requires the franchisor to *notify* the franchisee before any anticipated termination. Some states also require that franchisors state the *reasons* for a termination and provide franchisees an *opportunity to correct* the problem(s). Finally, most franchise agreements have arbitration clauses to enable the parties to get faster resolution of disputes.

Cooper Distributing Co., Inc., a New Jersey Corporation v. *Amana Refrigeration, Inc., a Delaware Corporation*
United States Court of Appeals, Third Circuit
63 F.3d 262., (1995)

CASE BACKGROUND AND FACTS

Defendant Amana Refrigeration, Inc. ("Amana"), a manufacturer of home appliances, appeals a judgment for $9,375,000 in favor of plaintiff Cooper Distributing Co., Inc. ("Cooper"), a distributor of Amana home appliances. After supplying Cooper with its products for approximately 30 years, Amana attempted to terminate its relationship with Cooper. Cooper sued, claiming that the termination and the circumstances surrounding it gave rise to a variety of state law claims.

I. FACTS AND PROCEDURAL HISTORY

Amana began to manufacture home appliances in the 1940's. [References deleted] Currently, Amana is a "full line" home appliance manufacturer: it offers for sale a full set of home appliances, including refrigerators, cooking and laundry appliances, dishwashers, and air conditioners. For many years, Amana employed a two-step process in the distribution of its products. It would sell its products to a network of independent wholesale distributors, who, pursuant to agreements with Amana, would sell to retail dealers located in the wholesale distributors' contractually recognized sales regions. The

retail dealers would then sell the products to consumers.

Cooper began operating as an independent wholesale distributor in 1931. In 1961, Cooper started to distribute Amana products. Cooper and Amana signed an agreement permitting Cooper to distribute Amana's products in New Jersey and New York and have periodically signed new agreements over the years. Their most recent Distribution Agreement (the "Agreement"), which was signed in 1990, allowed Cooper to distribute Amana products in New Jersey, New York, Connecticut, and Pennsylvania. The Agreement stated that it was to be construed "in accordance with the laws of the State of Iowa."

During its relationship with Amana, Cooper operated a showroom/marketing center, first in Newark and subsequently in Englewood Cliffs, New Jersey. Cooper used this facility for Amana product demonstrations, dealer training in Amana products, and dealer open houses. Cooper's sales managers studied the Amana product line, and in turn gave Amana product training to retail dealers. Cooper also placed Amana advertisements in the yellow pages and newspapers, advertised as an authorized Amana servicer,

instructed its servicemen to wear Amana uniforms, distributed promotional items bearing the Amana name, and, pursuant to the Agreement, promised to "use its best efforts to promote sales" of Amana products. Cooper's dealers perceived Amana and Cooper as being one and the same.

In the early 1980's, the marketing of appliances began to change, and by the late 1980's most full-line manufacturers had eliminated the first step in the two-step distribution process. Instead of selling to wholesale distributors, the manufacturers sold directly to retail dealers. Consistent with this trend, Amana started to depart from its previous practice of selling its products to the wholesale distributors. Instead, Amana began to sell directly to certain retail dealers located in the wholesale distributors' sales regions. Amana first sold its appliances directly to "national" retail dealers like Sears.

The Agreement explicitly permitted Amana to make such sales to national retailers. Then, in the summer of 1991, Amana went further. Relying on a provision of the Agreement that reserved for Amana the "right to make sales directly," Amana began to deal directly for the first time with a non-national retail dealer in

Cooper's region, P. C. Richard & Son ("P. C. Richard"). P. C. Richard had a chain of 20 retail stores and represented Cooper's largest account. Amana also sold its products directly to other smaller local retail dealers. Until Amana began selling to the national and local retailers, Cooper had been the exclusive distributor in its region for nearly 30 years.

At the same time that the home appliance industry saw the elimination of two-step distribution, Amana's marketing responsibilities changed. Amana's parent company, Raytheon, which also sold other appliance brands such as Speed Queen and Caloric, decided to consolidate the distribution of its brands. The result was that several of the distributors that sold one but not all of Raytheon's brands were eliminated. In November 1991, Amana terminated its relationship with Cooper pursuant to a provision of the Agreement that allowed either party to terminate the Agreement on ten days written notice. At the same time, Amana also terminated its relationships with 20 of the other 23 remaining Amana wholesale distributors across the country.

In response to its termination, Cooper commenced this action in New Jersey state court alleging, among other things, that Amana had (1) violated section 5 of the NJFPA, N.J.S.A. § 56:10-5, by terminating Cooper's franchise without good cause; (2) breached the 1990 Agreement by selling to the local retailers in Cooper's region; (3) breached the Agreement's implied obligation of good faith and fair dealing; and (4) tortiously interfered with Cooper's prospective economic advantage. In November 1991, the state court issued a temporary restraining order prohibiting termination of or interference with Cooper's Amana distributorship. After the case was removed by Amana to federal court, [Footnotes deleted] a preliminary injunction was entered on February 10, 1992, enjoining Amana "from taking any action whatsoever to limit . . . or in any way interfere with Cooper's activities as a distributor of Amana products."

OPINION: ALITO, CIRCUIT JUDGE
II. NEW JERSEY FRANCHISE PRACTICES ACT

Prompted in large part by the practices of automobile manufacturers and major oil companies, New Jersey enacted the NJFPA in 1971. [References deleted] The Act protects franchisees against indiscriminate termination by providing that "it shall be a violation of this act for a franchisor to terminate, cancel, or fail to renew a franchise without good cause." N.J.S.A. § 56:10-5. A franchise exists under the NJFPA if: (1) there is a "community of interest" between the franchisor and the franchisee; (2) the franchisor granted a "license" to the franchisee; and (3) the parties contemplated that the franchisee would maintain a "place of business" in New Jersey. N.J.S.A. §§ 56:10-3a, -4. Contending that it was not properly held liable under the NJFPA, Amana argues, first, that as a matter of law Cooper was not a "franchisee" under the Act and second, that the district court gave the jury prejudicially erroneous instructions on the NJFPA claim. We will discuss each of these arguments in turn.

* * *

FN3. Amana does not argue that the termination of its business relationship with Cooper was for "good cause," a concept that is "limited to failure by the franchisee to substantially comply with those requirements imposed upon him by the franchise." . . .

* * *

The Act's concern is that once a business has made substantial franchise-specific investments [which are of minimal utility outside the franchise,] it loses virtually all of its bargaining power . . . . Specifically, the franchisee cannot do anything that would risk termination, because that would result in a loss of much or all of the value of its franchise-specific investments. Thus, the franchisee has no choice but to accede to the demands of the franchisor, no matter how unreasonable these demands may be.

* * *

Thus, in order to find a "community of interest," two requirements must be met: (1) the distributor's investments must have been "substantially franchise-specific", and (2) the distributor must have been required to make these investments by the parties' agreement or the nature of the business. In this appeal, Amana has not addressed the second of these requirements, but Amana has strenuously argued that Cooper failed to meet the first of these requirements, i.e., that it failed to show that its investments were substantially franchise-specific.

* * *

Second, and perhaps most important, a reasonable jury could find that one of Cooper's most important assets was franchise-specific goodwill. It is clear that goodwill can constitute a franchise-specific asset. To qualify, however, the goodwill in question must be useful for the alleged franchisee only in the context of its relationship with the alleged franchisor. Moreover, if a distributor sells the products of many manufacturers and creates some goodwill for all or many of these manufacturers, that kind of goodwill "cannot be enough to create a 'community of interest.'"

* * *

Finally, we consider Cooper's investments in tangible assets. The NJFPA protects franchise-specific "tangible capital investments, such as 'a building designed to meet the style of the franchise, special equipment useful only to produce the franchise product, and franchise signs.'" ISI, 614 A.2d at 141 (quoting *New Jersey American,* 875 F.2d at 62). In this case, Cooper introduced evidence showing that it had invested in some tangible items that were of no value outside the Amana-franchise context—for example, the display housing for Cooper's showroom bearing the Amana logo, App. 1034, Amana product literature, App. 1032, and Amana demonstration models.

We do not mean to imply that all of Cooper's investments were Amana-specific. On the contrary, the record shows that Cooper possessed assets that would clearly be useful outside the Amana context. See, e.g., App. 1041 (electronic mail system),

App. 1039-41 (computer system), (repair tools). However, the jury was not required to find that Cooper's investments were entirely franchise-specific but merely that they were "substantial[ly] franchise-specific." ISI, 614 A.2d at 141 (emphasis added). Looking at all of the evidence of Cooper's investments in the light most favorable to Cooper, we hold that a jury reasonably could conclude that Cooper's assets were substantially franchise-specific.

* * *

The court went on to affirm the trial court verdict that the defendant, Amana, had violated the N.J.F.P.A. which requires a showing of good cause before a franchisee is dismissed.

QUESTIONS FOR ANALYSIS

1. Was the defendant arguing that the franchisee (Cooper) deserved to be terminated or simply that Cooper was not a

franchisee? What makes a company a franchisee of another company in New Jersey?
2. What is the goal of the New Jersey Franchise Practices Act? What role does franchise-specific investment play in achievement of the goal of the NJFPA?
3. Termination of long-time franchises is fraught with a sense of betrayal by the franchisee, then later a call to an attorney, resulting in litigation. In the case above, the cost to the franchisor is millions in court-awarded damages plus attorney fees and diverted executive time. As a future manager, possibly of a franchisor, can you think of any measures that you could take to ameliorate franchisee anger and retaliation while still terminating a franchise?

Business Organizations in the Future

Earlier in the chapter, it was suggested that there are many who predict that the structure of business organizations will be significantly different in the near future. Some insight into such predictions can be gained from the following article. You should note that nothing in the following suggests that the legal forms of business we have reviewed will become obsolete or that business will be done without such organizational structures. The arguments are that businesses, no matter what their organizational structures are, will have to function differently to be successful.

Notice that the article "Virtual Corporations" was written in 1994 before the explosion in E-Commerce. Interestingly, most of what the authors predict has taken place in the marketplace. Hierarchical command-based corporate structures have, for many firms, given way to newer, more nimble organizations envisioned in the article.

Creative and energetic individuals, enthusiastic about the prospects for their commercial ideas, are typical of those who start businesses. Most are excited about their plans, and anxious to get going—selling software, manufacturing novel devices, or doing whatever exciting commercial thing has prompted them to start a business. Many have little patience for the detour required for careful **legal** planning. This can be a recipe for sizeable problems in the near future. A careful choice of business organization and careful attention to the details of establishing the form of business chosen are essential. These choices and actions dictate a great deal about the future of the business—how it will be governed (managed), what its tax exposure will be, and what the owners' exposure to personal liability will be. Great businesses may rely primarily on great ideas. Legal decisions can't be far behind in insuring a successful future for your business.

Virtual Corporations: Business in the New Millennium

By Michael Malone and Bill Davidow, May 17, 1994

It says something about the pace of the modern world that an idea, the "virtual corporation," a mere theory on a scrap of paper three years ago, has now become a common phrase in daily business life. In fact, when Bill Davidow and I first came up with the term, we debated whether to use it at all, worried that the audience might be put off by a neologism. Needless to say, just the opposite happened. Yesterday, I heard "virtual" used six times in connection with companies, agencies, towns, and even lifestyles.

Sometimes the term was misused, but that is all part of the development of language. What is especially satisfying is that of the two definitions that competed for prominence—that of similar corporations temporarily joining together into meta-enterprises, and that of manufacturers, suppliers, distributors and even customers linking together in an enduring relationship built on mutual trust—it is the latter, the one we predicted, that has predominated both in language and in application. But new notions, as they expand out into the language, can have side-effects. One of these is imprecision. A term risks becoming a cliche that everyone uses but no one really understands. Worse, sometimes it can come to mean its own opposite, and thus undermine the original purpose.

It is important, then, to occasionally return to first principles; to remind ourselves just exactly where an idea came from. That's what I propose to do in this article: to explain where the notion of a virtual corporation came from. Then, at the end, I want to predict what its implications mean for the future.

CIRCLES OF CHANGE

To fully understand what is meant by the term "virtual corporation," one needs to visualize a number of concentric circles, each emanating outward in a chain of implications from circles it contains.

The center-most circle is the pace of technological change. Living in the middle of it, we forget how extraordinary this development has been. In the fifty years since the warehouse-sized ENIAC computer, integrated circuits have improved computing power, price, size and power consumption by a combined total of 32 orders of magnitude—a jump that literally has no precedent in human history . . . , and shows no sign of stopping . . .

This dynamic makes the next concentric circle possible. These are new products and services—desktop publishing, one-hour eyeglasses, online newspapers, custom automobiles, etc.—these new technologies make possible. We call them virtual products.

VIRTUAL PRODUCTS

"Virtual," as Computer Currents readers know well from virtual memory and virtual reality, is a long-established electronics term that signifies an entity or experience that perpetually adapts to user needs. Virtual products (or services, the two will become increasingly indistinguishable) might be called mass-customized products. They are characterized by high information content and heavy customer participation in their creation. Virtual products may be created at centralized locations (such as Japan's planned customer-designed four-day cars), at hundreds of small manufacturing sites (lens grinding at Pearle Vision and Lenscrafters) or at user desks (examples of this are Actel's or Xilinx's programmable gate-array circuits). In many cases, virtual products, as they're used, gather information about users and modify their functions to match users' needs (as some personal computer software does today). Others, such as ATMs, act as data-gathering nodes and help vendors track usage and improve service.

Virtual products are exciting. They have enormous appeal to consumers and they tend to overrun every market in which they appear. But they're also highly problematic. As many companies are currently discovering, you can't build virtual products without completely transforming every single operation of a company. And that's the next circle:the virtual corporation.

VIRTUAL DEMANDS

You can't just virtualize products overnight because you're likely to be completely unprepared for virtual-product demands placed on your organization. You don't have broadband information-gathering systems in place to learn what you need to about your customer base, and your customers are probably not sufficiently loyal to give you that data. You might not have manufacturing equipment in place or trained personnel, or reliable enough suppliers to create mass-customizable products "anytime and anywhere." And, even if you managed to do all that, your marketing and marketing/communications functions are probably wholly unprepared to deal with the challenge of creating the lifelong customers you'll need.

CO-DESTINY

But most of all, and this is something even well-publicized virtual corporations have yet to reach, you're probably far from the level of deep and mutual trust with employees, partners and customers needed to keep a virtual corporation strong and competitive with increasingly virtual competitors.

What's this new level of trust? A most descriptive term is co-destiny. All players in the process, creation, delivery or use of virtual products must willingly surrender a measure of freedom and mobility in exchange for shared beneficial results.

Take suppliers. A manufacturer cannot move fast enough to create and maintain virtual products unless suppliers can not only meet its needs, but anticipate them as well. This can only occur if the suppliers are privy to a manufacturer's future product plans, market strategies, even financials—a degree of outside access that would scare most modern executives.

Furthermore, to be properly responsive, suppliers will almost have to dedicate production to that one supplier, sometimes even move near that customer, and perhaps also aid that customer in market research. In return for those sacrifices, a supplier will expect sole-sourcing.

Such a relationship, based on co-destiny, will not be possible given the vast supplier pool currently used by many large corporations. As we've seen in electronics, aircraft and automotive industries, supplier rolls are slashed—and only those suppliers with a commitment to common philosophies, information systems and business style survive the cut.

The role of distributors and retailers radically changes as well, as they too assume information gathering responsibilities and narrow their lines and increase their commitment to the remaining manufacturers in exchange for greater exclusivity, more timely deliveries and more access to manufacturers' plans.

There remains one other player in the virtual corporation, perhaps the most important: the consumer. To keep customers for life, manufacturers will have to provide consumers with exactly what they need. The only way they can do this is to enlist customers in a co-destiny relationship as well. And hoping that, in exchange for a better product fit, customers will willingly surrender considerable amounts of personal information. That few of

us would give up such data today to any company is a measure of how far we have yet to go to arrive at true virtual corporations. It also suggests just how obsolete current practices are in such disciplines as marketing, public relations and advertising.

THE GRID

That brings us to the outermost concentric circle: a new society. Just as it is impossible to create a virtual corporation one department at a time, so too is it unlikely that one can build a "virtual" economy one virtual corporation at a time.

What will such a society look like? We already have some clues in such new lifestyles as telecommuters and "Perpetual Motion Executives" (PMXs)—individuals who use a technological tether to conduct their careers either continuously on the move or from remote locations of their own choosing. We also see clues in the extraordinary popularity of the Internet and America Online, as well as the other early manifestations of the Information Superhighway . . . or more properly, the Grid. As important as these online services already are, their real value may lie in their development of a new grammar and vocabulary for life in a virtualized world.

These pioneering institutions also suggest that our society may be reshuffling all of its current alignments, such that Democrat vs. Republican or liberal vs. conservative, urban vs. suburban vs. rural may be no more valid than Whig vs. Democrat was in the Industrial Revolution. New oppositions, even confrontations, such as those between telecommuter and office workers, and between global and blue-collar workers, may pit old allies against one another, while creating new alliances between old enemies.

A similar polarization is also likely to occur between those goods and services offered by the Grid and those that can only be provided (such as groceries) nearby. Companies and individuals that operate in-between (regional services) or at the wrong pole (neighborhood video stores) may soon find themselves in desperate straits.

These sweeping changes are likely to send shock waves through society in the next few years, destroying some industries while establishing others, replacing long-established institutions with relevant new ones, and forcing profound changes on government at every level.

—Continued on page 362

Virtual Corporations: Business in the New Millennium

By Michael Malone and Bill Davidow, May 17, 1994   *Continued from page 361*

If there were doubters just a few years ago, events of the past few months, from giant mergers to the race to the Grid, erase any questions: the Virtual Revolution is the defining business transformation of our generation.

Bill Davidow is the author of two best-selling books: *Marketing High Technology* and *Total Customer Service.* He was senior vice president of sales/marketing for Intel Corp. and a marketing manager for Hewlett-Packard's computer group. He's now a general partner of the venture capital firm Mohr, Davidow Ventures based in Menlo Park.

Michael Malone is the author of *The Big Score,* a respected history of the electronics revolution, and *Going Public: MIPS Computer and the Entrepreneurial Dream.* He's also well known for his interview program, "Malone," which is widely syndicated on public television.

Source: Article By: Michael Malone and Bill Davidow May 17, 1994. No additional sources available.

SUMMARY

- There are three main forms of business organization: *Sole Proprietorships, Partnerships,* and *Corporations.*
- Sole proprietorships are owned by one person who is *unlimitedly liable* for debts of the company. Sole proprietorships are not separate entities from the owner in terms of taxes, liability, and management.
- Sole proprietorships are often at a disadvantage in raising capital because outsiders are generally unwilling to risk money on the life of an individual. Similarly, it is often difficult to sell a sole proprietorship, and diversification is also difficult because of the size of the company.
- Partnerships are formed when two or more partners join together and operate a business for profit.
- Partnership law in the United States is generally subject to the Uniform Partnership Act which has been adopted in 49 states, while 26 states have adopted the Revised Uniform Partnership Act. The UPA and RUPA operate when nothing is said in the partnership agreement regarding a point of law. Partners have great freedom to manage the partnership and divide up profits in just about any way they want.
- There are two types of partnerships: *general* and *limited.* In a general partnership, all partners are unlimitedly liable, while in a limited partnership only the general partners are liable for partnership debts.
- Relative to sole proprietorships, partnerships have a number of advantages including raising capital. Partnerships are more complicated to manage and disputes among partners are sources of litigation. Profits of both partnerships and sole proprietorships are taxed as ordinary income to the partners or owners.
- Partners owe *fiduciary duties* to each other, which means they must put the interests of the partners and partnership above their own.
- Corporations are considered persons in law. They can sue and be sued, must pay taxes, and have potentially infinite duration. Corporations are managed by a Board of Directors who then appoint chief corporate officers.
- Shareholders of a corporation are its owners and benefit from limited liability. Ownership of a corporation is transferable through the sale of corporate shares.
- Corporations are taxed on their income and, if dividends are declared, shareholders are taxed on dividend distributions.
- Both directors and officers are agents of the corporation and as such owe fiduciary duties to the corporation.

- In general, corporations provide shareholder owners with *limited liability,* even if mistakes are made in complying with incorporation statutes. *De jure, de facto,* and corporations *by estoppel* provide shareholders with limited liability.
- Shareholders can lose limited liability if they abuse the corporate form if they fail to comply with corporate formalities, deal with creditors as individuals, commingle corporate and personal funds, or are deliberately undercapitalized.
- *Limited partnerships* must be registered with the state in order to qualify for limited liability for the limited partners.
- Limited partners must refrain from management activity to qualify for limited liability. The line between what limited partners can do and not do to qualify for limited liability is articulated in the Revised Limited Partnership Act.
- Limited partnerships enjoy favorable tax status. Also, transferability of ownership is much easier than for general partnerships.
- *Closely held corporations* share a lot of characteristics with partnerships. The largest shareholders are generally also on the board of directors and are chief corporate officers.
- Closely held corporations are governed by corporate bylaws and shareholder agreements that resemble partnerships. Limits are placed on transferability of ownership stocks, protections are in place to protect minority interests, and there are provisions for resolving disputes.

- *S corporations* are generally smaller than C corporations. S corporations are taxed as if they are partnerships, but there are restrictions that make C corporations the only alternative for corporations with more than 75 shareholders.
- *Limited Liability Companies* and *Limited Liability Partnerships* straddle the advantages of limited liability of corporations and the tax advantages of partnerships. LLCs and LLPs are often selected by professionals to protect themselves from acts of negligence of other professionals while still complying with ethical requirements of state licensing boards.
- *Joint ventures* are like partnerships of two companies or individuals that are organized to accomplish a task but do not generally have a indefinite life. Joint venturers are jointly, severally, and unlimitedly liable for debts of the joint venture.
- *Cooperatives* generally have the legal liabilities of a partnership but distributions of dividends to members are not taxed as income to the coop.
- *Franchises* are a very popular way of retailing products in the United States. Franchises are able to use trademarks of the parent company in return for agreeing to operate the business within the guidelines of the franchise agreement.
- The Federal Trade Commission requires that franchisors disclose to franchisees various risks and provisions of the franchise agreement. Often when a franchise is terminated, there is the potential for litigation.

CYBER COMPANIES AND INTERNET AGREEMENTS

Prior to taking this course, and certainly by now in the course, you likely have become aware of the explosive growth that E-Commerce and E-Businesses have experienced. Even so, a few facts about that expansion may be useful. Before 1990 there was no E-Commerce to speak of. By 1996 there were still fewer than 500 web sites devoted to E-Commerce and total E-Commerce revenue for the year is estimated to have been about $2.6 billion. Expectations are that, by 2001, annual revenue in E-Commerce will have grown by some 100 times to more than $220 billion.[1] According to a March 1999 report, *annual* growth in E-Commerce is estimated at 103 percent, indicating a business volume of $425 billion in 2002.[2] A multitude of other statistics could be cited to illustrate the exponential growth of E-Commerce.

In the service of this exciting era of an electronic revolution, the focus of this chapter is on the legal rights and obligations of cyber companies. This chapter examines primarily the distinctive features of cyber companies, which we define as companies whose primary source of revenue is from E-Commerce. Of course, many of the legal issues faced by cyber companies are also faced by bricks and mortar (B&M) companies that derive most of their revenue from sources other than E-Commerce, but have a presence of some sort on the World Wide Web.

Perhaps the most widely publicized E-Commerce website is Amazon.com. Although Amazon.com originally had almost no physical assets, it recently has been investing in warehouses to facilitate distribution. Amazon.com is most widely known as a seller of books, though it has expanded to include a wide array of other products including music and video. In contrast to Amazon, the Barnes and Noble Company has always maintained a large chain of retail outlets (B&M storefronts) for its products, which are mainly books but also include substantial sales in music CDs and a wide variety of other products. Amazon is a cyber company or, as some would say, a .com (dot-com) company. Even though Barnes and Noble has responded to the Amazon competitive threat by developing a substantial web presence of its own, it is currently a B&M company, though that could change as Barnes and Noble becomes an increasingly popular website.

---

[1] "IDC bullish on E-Commerce growth", Stephanie Mills, *CNET News,* July 22, 1997.
[2] "Global E-Commerce growth estimated at 1–3%, RP Net users seen at 2–3M by 2002", Tessa R. Salazar, *Philippine Daily Inquirer*, March 22, 1999.

E-Commerce Business Models

"Success" in E-Commerce, ultimately, is not different than ordinary business success. Success occurs when profits are made and investors are happy. The route to a successful Internet business, however, may be quite a bit different from that followed by successful B&M companies. A successful business model for Internet companies begins, first and foremost, with a website that generates customer traffic and action. Of course, just getting people to come to your website is not enough; there must be some way of transforming that traffic into revenue. Among the most prominent ways of generating revenue are:

1. **Advertising:** If you have a large volume of customer traffic, you can generate revenue from advertisers who are willing to pay money for exposure on your website, typically with amounts based on the volume of traffic that visits your website. Of course, there is software that counts the number of visitors. The notorious Drudge Report, organized by Matt Drudge, specializes in scandalous stories about politicians but does not have a product to sell. The Drudge Report, however, generates millions of Internet "hits" which makes banners on top of its site very highly sought.

2. **Subscription:** There are a number of businesses that derive significant revenue from subscription agreements. Quite obviously, many porn sites have attracted "members" who pay fees for Internet access to various forms of "adult" entertainment. A very different service provider, *The Wall Street Journal,* targets a subscriber group that spends a lot of their time in front of computers making it convenient to browse the WSJ online rather than reading the paper edition. There are many other subscription businesses on the Internet such as services for investors that allow for potentially quicker and cheaper trades than are possible with traditional brokers. Many special interest groups have been able to create subscription arrangements that benefit members and generate revenue for the website. Subscription members of various cyber clubs get price breaks on products that are made available to members by the company sponsoring the club.

3. **Commerce:** Increasingly, firms are establishing websites to engage in direct retail business sales with their customers. Amazon.com does not have B&M retail outlets. The same is true for Egghead.com, which made a decision to terminate B&M retail outlets and focus its efforts on online sales. Two key factors in the success of E-Commerce websites are a reliable distribution system (supply chain management) and a reliable, secure, and easy-to-use payment system. E-Commerce is expanding in both B2C (Business to Consumer) and B2B (Business to Business) transactions, though the latter is expanding more rapidly.

Similarities between Catalogue Sales and Internet Websites

Online sales can be likened to catalogue sales and some of the challenges and benefits associated with catalogue sales are also challenges and benefits for on-line sales. Critical to the success of catalogue sales is a distribution system that customers view as reliable, easy to understand, and user friendly, particularly if items need to be returned. Also, both online and catalogue sales should have uncomplicated but trustworthy payment systems. At this point in the web's evolution, users' foremost concern appears to be with the reliability and trustworthiness of the payments system.

Website Success

Successful websites have to successfully juggle several balls. They must be able to generate sales, contain costs, reliably fill customer orders, not alienate customers with a complex or unreliable return system, and successfully collect payments for their sales in a manner that satisfies customer's desires for security. Even though investors have exhibited a remarkable willingness to take chances on novel, high-tech forays into E-Commerce, bottom-line or present-value analyses have not been made obsolete. Investors are still motivated by profit and seek those investment opportunities that offer the greatest net present value, adjusted for risk. Quite clearly, there is a sizeable cohort of investors who have an affinity for small, high-tech start-ups that establish a successful web presence as demonstrated by market events—many highly visible examples of web businesses that have gone from paltry revenues and nonexistent profits to multi-billion dollar market valuations in brief periods. There is no escape, however, from present value analysis, and many of the high-flying .com IPOs (initial public offerings) from last year are belly-up and virtually valuless this year. Investors continue to seek businesses that demonstrate a capability for making a profit and for maintaining a competitive advantage.

Engage the Customer

Website success depends on a lot more than just having a good product or service for sale. Computer mice have a lot in common with TV remote controls. A website is vulnerable to being "clicked" off very rapidly by Internet cruisers who have a vast array of other opportunities to surf. In order for a website to be a success, the website should *engage* the customer. One tactic used by successful websites is to act as a web host and offer free web space so that customers can create their own web pages. Such options are available on AOL, an ISP; on Yahoo!, a portal or browser company; and on Xoom.com, an E-Commerce site. In addition to free web space for members, Yahoo! offers auctions, Fantasy Football, local weather, shopping, news, stock quotes, and more. Yahoo! and other modern websites engage visitors and their members. Each of the aforementioned Internet firms offer a wide range of action or interactivity for customers. Other examples of engagement occur when websites offer visitors or members access to unique content products such as access to new CDs before they appear in record stores. Some websites offer members access to valuable databases that may include real estate listings, stock quotes, or used car availabilities.

Creating Cyber Communities

The cyber world has dramatically expanded opportunities for web-surfers to interact with like-minded people, even when they are widely separated geographically. Websites have been able to segment members and create chat rooms that have developed a real sense of a cyber community. Chat rooms enable people throughout the world to meet one another,

but, most importantly, they create *repeat* business. Even though members in the chat rooms make up (sometimes outrageous) names, they develop recognizable personas that they cultivate. Interactivity can be enhanced by contests, sweepstakes, and games. Sony.com, for example, offers members opportunities to compete in cyber games and in contests such as Jeopardy, Trivial Pursuit, and Wheel of Fortune. The website keeps tallies on the highest-scoring contestants, and whole communities are created in connection with the pursuit of these online, interactive games.

Create High Switching Costs

As mentioned earlier, cyber companies have the same basic goals as other companies, i.e., primarily to make money. A part of their strategy to make money is to attract (some would say seduce) Internet travelers to visit their websites. As discussed above, part of fostering repeat visitors' business is providing a website experience that is interactive with the customer, drawing that customer into a cyber community. In addition, websites often do their best to promote repeat customers by deliberately raising costs of switching to other websites. *Information Rules,* a very influential book about the economics of the Internet by Shapiro and Varian, discusses explicit strategies websites can employ to *lock-in* their customers or members.[3] Basic economics suggest that if the expected additional benefits of switching allegiance to a new website are less than switching costs associated with the change, then rational consumers will not make the switch.

Service Provider Switching Costs—Why Aren't You Answering My E-Mails?

A simple but clear example of switching costs involves e-mail. Think of the costs you would bear if, for

---

[3]*Information Rules: A Strategic Guide to the Network Economy,* Carl Shapiro and Hal R. Varian.

Sony.com Game Offerings (as of October 19, 2000)	
Game & Number of People Playing	**Game & Number of People Playing**
JEOPARDY! (889 playing)	Chain Letters (16 playing)
Wheel of Fortune (349 playing)	Napoleon (7 playing)
Trivial Pursuit—registered trademark (188 playing)	Out of Order (28 playing)
Chain Reaction (36 playing)	Take 5 (3 playing)

Free Games

some reason, you could not use your current e-mail address. Say you were a member of AOL, but you had decided to switch to Mindspring. Switching from AOL to Mindspring, you would have to give up your AOL e-mail address. Perhaps the costs to you of switching your e-mail address would simply be the inconvenience and hassle of getting information to all those who communicate with you by e-mail of your new address, but there could also be monetary costs. You might not receive important e-mail that senders assumed you would be receiving at your old e-mail address. In addition to sending "new address" messages to those who communicate with you by e-mail, you might have to change your business cards and purchase new ones, or else be forced to line out your old, out-of-date cards. Certainly, if you operate an E-Commerce business, this would be the case. Suppose you had to change your e-mail address another time? You would have to repeat the process, and, undoubtedly, your friends and business associates would become confused with the potential for missed communications and possible economic losses.

Creating Technological Switching Costs

Changing your e-mail address is just one of the costs of changing servers. There are other costs that websites can impose upon members who have used the website in their e-mail address. In addition to the costs of changing e-mail addresses, Shapiro and Varian discuss several examples of techniques by which websites can lock in their customers or members. Some of the lock-ins are based on technology while others are based on content applications. Using various combinations of software and hardware constraints, websites can create intentional technological compatibilities and incompatibilites with other companies. If the website or company that uses such tactics is "too large" in relation to the industry in which it operates, such lock-in strategies may attract the attention of antitrust authorities at the Federal Trade Commission or Antitrust Division of the U.S. Department of Justice (DOJ). The DOJ antitrust action against Microsoft that began in 1998 focused on deliberate attempts by Microsoft to create an incompatibility between Windows, the Microsoft operating system, and browsers of other companies, particularly the one provided by Netscape, a very successful browser creator which was subsequently acquired by AOL.

On a much smaller scale, some marketing schemes that seek to hook customers are irritants to many, even if they are deemed legal and defensible. In the following case, the plaintiff uses such a scheme to make sales. A "carrot" is offered in the form of shareware that allows a browser to begin playing a game. But, to finish "playing the game," once "hooked" by the shareware, recipients were required to purchase copyrighted software from the distributors of the shareware.

Storm Impact, Inc. v. Software of the Month Club
United States District Court, N.D. Illinois, Eastern Division
13 F.Supp.2d 782 (1998)

FACTS AND CASE BACKGROUND

Storm Impact is an Illinois corporation with an office in Glenview. Its owner is David Alan Cook. Dan Schwimmer worked with plaintiffs designing levels and courses for the games TaskMaker and MacSki which were developed (beginning in 1989) by Cook, Schwimmer and Thomas Zehner (artwork). They produced software and shareware. Cook copyrighted TaskMaker and MacSki and listed himself as sole author.

In October 1993, Storm Impact began selling an upgraded version of TaskMaker "v.2.0." One of the marketing tactics Storm Impact used was to distribute the software as "shareware." Shareware is not a kind of software, it is a way of marketing software as an alternative to retail selling; it is much cheaper than conventional retail methods.

However, Software of the Month Club (SOMC), a California corporation, charges a monthly fee to members in order to receive a CD-ROM containing shareware. SOMC makes profits on the sale of shareware. The question, therefore, is if SOMC has violated fair use rights of the copyrighted material.

OPINION: ZAGEL, DISTRICT JUDGE

The federal government has defined shareware as "copyrighted software which is distributed for the purposes of testing and review, subject to the condition that payment to the copyright owner is required after a person who has secured a copy decides to use the software." Shareware gives the user an opportunity to use the product and try it out before buying it.

There are two common forms of shareware. With the first, the owner of the software makes the complete software available to users without charge for the purpose of evaluation. If users wish to keep the software after a trial basis, they must forward a registration fee to the owner. Shareware programs distributed in this manner rely to a large extent on the honesty of the users. The second form of shareware contains the computer equivalent of a lock on part of the program. The "lock" is a feature built into the software program which disables portions of the program. The user can sample the unlocked portion at no charge, and, if the user likes what he sees, he can buy the "key" in the form of a floppy disk and registration number which enables the user to use the whole program. Storm Impact used this second form of shareware to market TaskMaker.

In September 1994, Storm Impact started selling an upgraded version of MacSki "v.1.5." The MacSki game contained a number of ski runs. The shareware version stopped the user halfway down the ski run. If the user wanted to play the full game, he could register with Storm Impact to purchase the "key." Storm Impact made both TaskMaker and MacSki available on America Online.

Shareware programs typically display a legend that expressly permits the user to try the software before buying it and encourages the user to give unaltered and complete copies of the software to friends, family and associates. The legend customarily contains an express restriction that one cannot charge for copies or try to make a profit from the software or its distribution. The restrictions typically forbid commercial distribution of the software, mass distribution, or its sale for a profit.

Both TaskMaker and MacSki contain express restrictions which appear on their respective screen displays. The Legal sections for both games state:

> Commercial distribution prohibited, as is distribution in exchange for compensation or any other consideration, except that acquisition of download time in exchange for uploading this program onto electronic bulletin boards is allowed. De minimis actual costs incurred in distribution, such as disks and postage, may be recouped. Mass duplication and distribution prohibited, except for uploading to electronic bulletin boards, and then only when no consideration passes except for free download time.

In addition, the MacSki game has an express prohibition against copying the program on CD-ROM, under any circumstances, and further defines mass duplication as "50 or more copies in any 12-month period."

Software of the Month Club [SOMC] is a California corporation with an office in Carlsbad, California. SOMC provides collections of newly introduced shareware to its customers on a monthly basis. SOMC charges an initial fee of $39.95 to become a member. Thereafter, members pay a monthly fee of $24.95 to retain the service and receive a disk or CD-ROM each month.

SOMC has employees scour the online universe for what it thinks is the "latest and greatest" shareware and receives shareware directly at its own website from those who wish to have their products considered for selection by SOMC. SOMC employees then screen through the number of different shareware programs each month and assemble the "best" shareware programs into categories by subject matter, i.e., educational, business, games, etc. About 25 percent of what is examined makes it to the final volume which is then distributed to customers on a monthly basis, but sometimes more frequently. SOMC has 60,000 members and in 1993/94 had about 30,000 members. SOMC sends literature to its customers that recommends that users register with the authors whose work they enjoy.

All of this costs money. SOMC is in business to make profits (and it does) from its labors of searching for and testing shareware and its use of its critical judgment of the popular merits of the shareware. It gets fees from its members and, perhaps, fees from software makers who sell their products through SOMC distribution.

SOMC says it performs a service to authors. Storm Impact strongly disputes this assertion. SOMC clearly does provide a service: it endorses and distributes the works of authors. [Footnote deleted] What Storm Impact means to say is that it does not want the service because it might alienate potential customers, injure its reputation and result in customers being given erroneous technical advice. [Footnote deleted] Storm Impact believes that free shareware is a good distribution technique and does not want to participate in an enterprise where a fee is charged in connection with shareware distribution.

It has been SOMC's policy not to use shareware if it has the restrictions seen on plaintiffs' shareware. Yet, a SOMC employee believed (at a prior time) that if something was shareware, then permission to reproduce was implied. And, before this lawsuit there was a mixed-bag practice of seeking permission to use an author's work at some times and not at others. Apparently, no one at SOMC either read or paid attention to the express restrictions that were on TaskMaker or MacSki, and they never received express permission to put them on SOMC disks. Since the filing of this lawsuit, SOMC now asks all authors for written permission to reproduce their shareware unless the work itself contains permission to reproduce.

The purpose of copyright protection, in the words of the Constitution, is to "promote the Progress of Science and useful Arts." Copyright is based on the belief that by granting authors the exclusive rights to reproduce their works, they are given an incentive to create, and that "encouragement of individual effort by personal gain is the best way to advance public welfare through the talents of authors and inventors." However, for progress to occur, others must be permitted to build upon and refer to the creations of prior thinkers. Thus, there is an inherent tension in the need to protect copyrighted material and to allow others to build upon it.

One device for resolving this tension is the fair use doctrine which creates an exception to the copyright monopoly. The defense of fair use carves out of the exclusive rights conferred by the Copyright Act, and legally empowers a person to use the copyrighted works in a reasonable manner without the consent of the copyright owner. The fair use doctrine requires courts to avoid the rigid application of the copyright statute when it would stifle the very creativity the law is designed to foster.

Fair use allows a second author to make certain uses of the first author's work for the public good. The uses which are deemed fair have a common theme, each is a productive use, resulting in some added benefit to the public beyond that produced by the first author's work. *Id.* As courts have said, the fair use doctrine strikes a balance between the dual risks created by the copyright system: on the one hand, that depriving authors of their monopoly will reduce their incentive to create, and on the other, that granting authors a complete monopoly will reduce the creative ability of others.

This rule was made by judges without benefit of statute until the doctrine was codified at Section 107 of the Copyright Act. This statute does not supersede the common law tradition of fair use. Rather, Section 107 was intended only to restate (and approve) the present judicial doctrine of fair use, not to change, narrow, or enlarge it in any way.

* * *

SOMC argues that shareware per se, and its use of TaskMaker and MacSki, are transformative and therefore within the fair use doctrine. Both of these theories fail. A shareware version of a copyrighted computer program is not transformative within the meaning of fair use. Storm, not SOMC, affected the changes that exist between the original versions and the shareware versions of the two programs. Transformation in the fair use context anticipates transformation by the user, not the copyright holder. Shareware can not be per se transformative because the copyright holder, Storm in this case, limits the program's scope by changing its coding. The user, who claims that the work has been transformed, has done nothing.

* * *

In making its transformation analysis, SOMC compares its use of Storm's shareware to a book review. This analogy also fails. If Storm had simply provided its customers with reviews of new shareware and showed pictures of the games, then the use would be sufficiently analogous to a book review to be transformative. I find, however, that because SOMC copied Storm's products and distributed them for the same purpose Storm designed them, it did not transform TaskMaker and MacSki within the meaning of fair use.

* * *

The fourth fair use factor looks to "the effect of the use upon the potential market for or value of the copyrighted work." Under this concept, courts must consider the extent of market harm caused by the particular actions of the alleged infringer and whether unrestricted and widespread conduct of the sort engaged in by the defendant would result in a substantially adverse impact on the potential market for the original. This inquiry must take account of the harm to the market for derivative works as well as the harm to the original. The Court in *Harper & Row* described this last factor as the single most important element of fair use. "Fair use . . . is limited to copying by others which does not materially impair the marketability of the work which is copied."

SOMC asserts that there is no negative effect upon the potential market for the copyrighted work, but a benefit to both plaintiffs and the public. SOMC claims plaintiffs are benefitted because their sales of the complete software have been greatly enhanced based on the wide distribution of the shareware versions. SOMC also claims the public has benefited as the software market has enhanced access to the best shareware that is available. This argument that increased distribution of an author's work is a benefit to the author has been rejected by the Supreme Court. In *Harper & Row* the Court stated, "any copyright infringer may claim to benefit the public by increasing public access to the copyrighted work. . . . But Congress has not designed, and we see no warrant for judicially imposing, a 'compulsory license'..." to copyrighted works.

Storm Impact and Cook claim that the inclusion of MacSki and TaskMaker among SOMC's mailings has created ill will among potential customers and has interfered with their carefully planned method of distributing MacSki and TaskMaker. Plaintiffs claim they have received numerous complaints from persons who are upset that they have to register and pay them to obtain the "key" after they have already made numerous payments to SOMC. SOMC disputes that any complaints have been made. SOMC claims that customers who use shareware know what it is, that you try before you buy, and cannot possibly believe that they have already paid for the complete software program when they only receive the shareware version. Further, SOMC argues customers are informed when they sign up with SOMC that they are not receiving the complete software program, but are informed that if they like the shareware they may then purchase the "key" from the author.

In order to understand the effect SOMC has had on plaintiffs' work, it is necessary to understand the custom and practice of the shareware market. On the one hand, shareware creators generally give their product away for free and encourage users to give free copies to everyone they

know. At the same time however, shareware creators put restrictions on their products telling users not to sell, mass distribute or charge for copies.

It is also necessary to understand how SOMC fits in within the "of the month club" industry. There seems to be an infinite number of "month clubs," to name only a few: "Book of the Month Club," "Beer of the Month Club," "CD of the Month Club," "Knucklehead of the Month Club," "Fruit of the Month Club," etc. Plaintiffs apparently analogize SOMC to the Book of the Month Club or CD of the Month Club where the customer pays each month to receive a new and complete version of a book or CD. But SOMC is different because it is the free sample of the month club. SOMC's service might be analogized to a newspaper containing movie reviews where a customer buys the paper to read the reviews and see what is playing, but knows she will have to pay again to see the movie. SOMC claims customers know what they are getting and they do not believe they are paying twice to obtain plaintiffs' software.

The effect of SOMC's distribution on Storm's market turns on whether its members knew that they would have to pay more for the full version of Storm's products, whether SOMC gave its consumers bad technical support advice about

TaskMaker and MacSki, and whether either of these factors, if true, adversely affected Storm's future distribution plans. In applying this fourth factor, I note that for-profit defendants, like SOMC, have the burden to show that their conduct falls within fair use. The evidence Storm adduced at trial supports Storm's contention that SOMC's use of the software angered some consumers, that SOMC provided improper technical support, and that SOMC's fee reduced the chance that customers would register with Storm. Therefore, I find that SOMC's use of Storm's product adversely affected the market for Storm's programs and that the fourth factor militates against a finding of fair use.

QUESTIONS FOR ANALYSIS

1. Describe how the plaintiff, Storm Impact, was trying to "hook" customers? How was the defendant, Software of the Month Club, trying to "hook" customers? Why were the plaintiff's customers upset with the defendant's copying of their products?
2. What was the court's response to the claim by the defendant that its copying actually enhanced the market for the plaintiff's products? How does such a claim affect its fair use defense?

An Example of a Technological Lock-in

In a major decision for its future technology base, Bell Atlantic recently invested heavily in AT&T's 5ESS digital switches for operating its telephone network.[4] Before the decision was made to invest in AT&T's switches, Bell Atlantic considered a number of choices including devices offered by Northern Telecom and Siemens. In choosing the AT&T 5ESS switches, Bell

locked itself into a future largely controlled by AT&T. The AT&T 5ESS switches use a proprietary operating system that effectively binds Bell to AT&T for upgrades and for linkages with peripherals.

Following the decision to purchase the 5ESS digital switches from AT&T, Bell Atlantic was not in a position to search the market for peripheral enhancements, for non-AT&T products (upgrades and peripherals) were generally incompatible with AT&T's operating system that was required by AT&T's 5ESS switches. When Bell wanted to upgrade its capabilities

[4]*Information Rules* by Varian and Shapiro.

to recognize toll-free 888 numbers, it had to negotiate with AT&T for the software necessary to make the connections with no meaningful competition from alternative vendors. Bell considered what AT&T demanded for the additional software and hardware necessary to recognize voice dialing to be excessive. According to Bell, which sued AT&T for antitrust violations, AT&T derived 30 to 40 percent of its switch-related revenue from software sales *after* the 5ESS switches are sold.

Content Applications as a Mechanism for Creating High Switching Costs

It is typical for a website to ask and require demographic information from customers or potential members. The information requirements are likely to include names, addresses (real and e-mail), phone numbers, yearly income brackets, education, marital status, and other personal information. Giving out this kind of information takes time and makes people feel uncomfortable because of the potential of identity theft, fraud, and invasions of privacy. Once people are comfortable at one website, they may be reluctant to again give out demographic information to another website that has not earned the trust of the potential customer.[5] There are other lock-ins based on knowledge-based agents (selling or purchasing) that, relying on artificial intelligence, become more efficient as meeting a user's needs based on experience. Skilled website operators know that they should make registration (for membership or preferred customer status) at their website as easy as possible, while simultaneously making subsequent registration at another site as costly as possible once members are signed up at the first website.

Another Example of Switching Costs and Lock-ins

Microsoft sells Windows, a very popular operating system for personal computers. Microsoft also sells application software such as word processing (MS Word) and spreadsheet (Excel). A software firm hoping to get customers to switch to their word processing and spreadsheet products would encounter customer resistance because compatibility is guaranteed between Windows and Microsoft application software, whereas compatibility between application software of rivals and Windows is not assured. Even if compatibility between the current version of Windows and a rival's software products has been tested and guaranteed, there can be no assurance of compatibility between new versions of Windows and the rival's application software. Few purchasers of application software are willing to bear the switching costs of purchasing and learning new application software in addition to buying and learning a new operating system such as Linux. Many users of Microsoft products are unwilling to switch from those products because the entire package from disk to Internet is integrated, seamless, and compatible. These users are locked in to Microsoft.

Attempts to Lock-out Rivals Using Copyright Laws

Many companies have tried to use copyright laws and contract law to lock-in customers and lock-out rivals. In the *Sega* case discussed in Chapter 10, the court held that the copyright laws were not violated if copyrighted software was reproduced through decompilation in order to determine interoperability between an operating system and application software.[6] In *Sega*, the court indicated that copyright law is not designed to give a firm a monopoly and that enhancing interoperability and compatibility among software of rivals benefited the public. In the following case, the court reaffirmed the principle that copyright law was not intended to create or maintain monopoly. The interoperability principle was extended to include making software of a rival compatible with the operating system of another company. The clear lesson from this case is that courts are reluctant to cooperate in a lock-in of customers or a lock-out of rivals based on copyright laws.

Product Differentiation

In economics, product differentiation is viewed as a way of distinguishing the products of one seller from another. Product differentiation can be accomplished by adding special features or functionality to products or by advertising. Without product differentiation, it is typically assumed that there is an inevitable drift

---

[5]Julia Brande Earp and Gale Meyer, "Internet Consumer Behavior: Privacy and Its Impact on Internet Policy", manuscript presented at annual TPRC, September 23–25, 2000. Survey results by Earp and Meyer reveal that there are significant differences between the willingness of Internet travelers to give out personal information to less well-known websites relative to well-known websites with well-known brand names.

[6]*Sega Enterprises* v. *Accolade,* 977 F.2d 1510 (9th Cir. 1992).

DSC Communications Corporation v. *Pulse Communications, Inc.*
United States District Court, E.D. Virginia, Alexandria Division
Cite as: 976 F.Supp. 359 (1997)

FACTS AND CASE BACKGROUND

The plaintiff DSC Communications Corp. sues the defendant Pulse Communications, Inc. for alleged infringement of DSC's digital switching software that operates DSC's Litespan telecommunications system. Litespan customers are primarily Regional Bell Operating Companies (RBOCs). The Litespan uses copyrighted software, which operates through plug-in channel cards to provide residential service known as POTS (plain old telephone service). These POTS cards perform the interface functions necessary to transmit telephone signals to and from the customer.

In 1993, Pulsecom began its efforts to reverse engineer the DSC POTS card. Pulsecom had previously succeeded in the reverse engineering and marketing of POTS and other plug-in cards for use in AT & T (Lucent) digital loop carrier systems. During the 1994–96 period, Pulsecom placed a number of its POTS cards in the testing labs of Ameritech, Bell Atlantic and NYNEX. Pulsecom determined that its POTS cards were being prevented from working in the Litespan system by the lock-out software that had been installed by DSC in certain of these testing labs. In order to determine the reason that the Pulsecom POTS cards were being locked out from the Litespan system, Pulsecom sent a POTS card to NYNEX with a snooper board.

The snooper board was used to identify the memory locations in the Pulsecom boot code which were being accessed by the Litespan system so that Pulsecom could determine how the DSC lock-out was being achieved. Pulsecom was attempting to monitor access to the boot code on Pulsecom's own POTS card so that Pulsecom could find out what portions of the Pulsecom boot code were being read. Pulsecom obtained information from the snooper card at NYNEX that identified the locations in the Pulsecom boot code that the Litespan system was looking at in order to find out if the card was a DSC card or not. These tests did not capture any software from the Litespan, but simply recorded timing and accesses on Pulsecom's own POTS boot code to investigate DSC's lock-out card.

OPINION: HILTON,
DISTRICT JUDGE

Count I of the complaint charged Pulsecom with contributory copyright infringement of DSC's registered POTS-DI software. DSC claims that Pulsecom committed contributory copyright infringement by providing test POTS cards to various RBOCs because during the testing of Pulsecom's POTS cards, the RBOCs download DSC's POTS-DI software onto the Pulsecorn POTS card. DSC claims that this downloading is an unauthorized use and therefore a direct infringement by the RBOCs, and that since Pulsecom provided its POTS card to the RBOCs, Pulsecom was guilty of contributory infringement.

Section 117 of the Copyright Act provides:

> Notwithstanding the provisions of Section 106, it is not an infringement for the owner of a copy of a computer program to make or authorize the making of another copy or adaptation of that computer program provided:
>
> (1) that such new copy or adaptation is created as an essential step in the utilization of the computer program in conjunction with a machine and that is used in no other manner. 17 U.S.C. § 117.

Thus, Section 117 statutorily limits a copyright owner's rights in that it permits the owner of a copy of a computer program to make certain copies of that program without the permission of the program's copyright owner.

* * *

[T]he fact that computer programs are distributed for public use in object code form often precludes public access to the ideas and functional concepts contained in those programs, and thus confers on the copyright owner a *de facto* monopoly over those ideas and functional concepts. That result defeats the fundamental purpose of the Copyright Act to encourage the production of original works by protecting the expressive elements of those works while leaving the ideas, facts, and functional concepts in the public domain for others to build on . . .

The Copyright Act, properly read and interpreted by the case law, allows the fair use defense to copyright infringement for those who have legally acquired the copyrighted work, and who reverse engineer the copyrighted work to understand the functional or unprotected elements of the work. In *Sega* the court found that the record established that the defendant engaged in "wholesale copying" of plaintiff's copyrighted computer program code as part of the development of a competing product, yet found that this copying was fair use. Similarly in this case, where the disassembly and copying of DSC's copyrighted programs was the only way to gain access to the ideas and functional elements embodied in the program, and given Pulsecom's legitimate reason for such access, namely development of a competing POTS card, such copying is fair use as a matter of law . . .

DSC also asserts that Pulsecom is guilty of direct infringement by virtue of inserting a Pulsecorn POTS card into a Litespan machine at the testing labs at Bell South and NYNEX. There is no evidence that the insertion of the Pulsecom POTS card into the Bell South Litespan system was done without the permission of Bell South. Nor is there any evidence that the Pulsecom employee actually inserted a Pulsecom POTS card into the Bell South Litespan system. Regardless of who operated the Litespan machine, Bell South was the legitimate holder of a copy of the POTS-DI software and could authorize the making of a copy of the POTS-DI software on the Bell South machine. Furthermore, the Bell South testing was permissible, because it was merely a test on Bell South's Litespan system to determine how the Pulsecom POTS card was being locked out of the Bell South Litespan.

The Pulsecom POTS card with an attached snooper board was inserted into a Litespan machine at NYNEX. There is no evidence that the card was inserted by Pulsecom. As noted above, the RBOCs have the right under Section 117 to make a copy of the POTS-DI software. Thus any copies of the POTS-DI software that were made by NYNEX in the course of testing the Pulsecom POTS card are protected under Section 117 of the Copyright Act. These tests did not capture any software from the Litespan, but simply recorded timing and accesses on Pulsecom's own POTS boot code to investigate DSC's lock-out card.

* * *

The court determined that it was a fair use for Pulse to disassemble and copy DSC's software if it was for the purpose of preventing DSC from locking Pulse out of the market for interface software.

QUESTIONS FOR ANALYSIS

1. Wasn't Pulse trying to undermine a security system in DSC's software? Why isn't this practice illegal under the Copyright Laws? Would this practice be illegal today, given the Digital Millennium Copyright Act of 1998?

2. Was the purpose of the reverse engineering by Pulse to enable it to reproduce Litespan or was it to tie into the hardware produced by DSC? Do you think that motive should be all-important in copyright infringement cases? Did the track record of the defendant make its claim as to intent more credible? In other words, wasn't the fact that it had done the same thing with respect to AT&T's Lucent products a strong indication that its motive was to compete, not copy?

3. What was the effect of the license agreement that accompanied the software? Does this case support the proposition that license agreements will not be enforced when Section 117 of the Copyright Act is invoked?

towards commoditization of products. Commoditization occurs when consumers view products of different sellers as interchangeable—such close substitutes that there is no preference for a particular manufacturer's product except if it is cheaper. If commoditization occurs with products for which there is competition among several sellers, profit margins will become very low, and sellers forced to look to other avenues for making significant profits (such as in selling services or peripherals). In the opinion of many, PCs have become commoditized and the real profits to be made are in the selling of software, hardware made by component suppliers, and in peripheral sales. In commonplace software, commoditization has taken place too. In the sale of spreadsheets during the 1980s, prices for electronic spreadsheets dropped from $500 for some brands of Lotus spreadsheets at retail outlets to less than $100 as Lotus, VisiCalc, Borland, Microsoft, and others competed for customers.

Brand Awareness

An important part of product differentiation is the creation and maintenance of brand awareness. Quite obviously, legal protection of trademarks plays an important role in protecting brand awareness. Much of the legal activity surrounding E-Commerce has been the result of disputes between trademark owners, particularly large firm trademark owners, and defendants who had applied for domain names that were identical to or closely resembled famous trademarks. The 1999 passage of the Anticybersquatter Consumer Protection Act should reduce deliberate attempts by those engaged in fraud (or near-fraud) from making use of domain names that resemble registered trademarks (this topic was discussed at some length in Chapter 9).

Co-branding and Cross-marketing

Beginning with a website that has legal protection of its brand name (through trademark registration), for any commercial success it is essential to get that brand name in front of a large volume of Internet traffic. Cyber companies and websites like AOL, browsers such as Netscape, and search engines such as Yahoo!, Lycos, Go To and others provide an opportunity for exposure for smaller firms through co-branding and cross-marketing. Co-branding occurs when two companies agree to sell the same product under each of their brand names. Cross-marketing occurs when a website provides the real estate (space on a web page) for the marketing of products of another vendor. Cross-marketing is the activity that is taking place when banners appear at the tops of web pages advertising opportunities to buy products from other firms. Of course, the real estate on high-traffic web

pages is for sale and the costs are directly proportional to the number of visits that are recorded by the host web page. In the case of AOL, there are over 20,000,000 subscribers, and so this website provides a great deal of exposure for banners that are owned by other firms but which are placed on high-profile AOL web pages.

Clearly, cultivating brand awareness and avoiding commoditization are important if websites are to make significant profits on E-Commerce sales. However, for websites that have significant traffic, it is also important to transform the stream of visitors into a revenue stream, which often means co-branding or cross-marketing. Of course, there is intense competition for Internet travelers, so websites cannot afford to be complacent. To achieve this end, many websites involve customers in interactive activities that involve their members and potential customers. Interaction among visitors at a website may be a key to making the website successful, so chat rooms, the provision of free websites, games, contests, and other

---

Popular Opinions

For the past decade or two, much of the world appears to have been taking a page from [Adam] Smith's book. Trade barriers have disappeared; governments have stepped back from steering markets; industries that not long ago appeared to be stable oligopolies have been whipped into a competitive froth. Now there's the Internet, which has the potential to wipe out national borders, demolish barriers to entry in many industries, and render obsolete most of the subterfuges modern merchants use to squeeze money out of their customers. As Bill Gates put it in his 1995 book *The Road Ahead*—after, of course, approvingly citing Smith—the Net "will carry us into a new world of low-friction, low-overhead capitalism, in which market information will be plentiful and transaction costs low. It will be a shopper's heaven." . . .

Of more use is the monopoly explanation of profits. This is what most of the strategy taught in business school is about: finding a way to differentiate your product from competitors' so that it becomes something unique that no one else is able to offer. The technology revolutions of the past few decades have added a new twist: If you can lock customers in to your technology and you're the market leader, profits will come pouring

in. But technological change also seems to have sped up the process of creative destruction, which means such advantages may not last long.

The key is to first build a big customer base, then make it expensive, or at least a hassle, for customers to switch. Microsoft has succeeded at this, so far. So has Cisco. The online companies with the best odds of success are similarly the ones that are hard to get away from. It's easy for an individual to switch his CD-buying from CDnow to Amazon.corn (or vice versa); it's a pain for a company that has moved all its purchasing to an Internet-based system designed and managed by Ariba to switch to another provider. Investors aren't blind to this—they moved in droves from consumer to business-to-business e-commerce stocks last year.

Source: "Profits, Darwinism, and the Internet," Justin Fox, *Fortune,* Mar 6, 2000; Vol. 141, Issue 5, p. F40. Reprinted with permission.

Additional Readings:
"Online Strategies," Victoria Fraza; *Industrial Distribution,* New York; Jan 2000; Vol. 89, Iss. 1; pg. 68.
"The New Digital Galaxy," Steven Levy; *Newsweek,* New York; May 31, 1999; Vol. 133, Iss. 22; pg. 56.

activities are important in the cultivation of repeat business.

Overhead Costs Are Lower on the Internet

In a very important sense, all businesses compete with each other for consumer dollars, even though there are some natural alliances among businesses that make suppression of competition between some businesses efficient. With regard to competitive advantages, websites enjoy one enormous advantage relative to B&M business; it is much cheaper to operate a website than it is to operate a B&M facility. As website businesses grow, it may become efficient for them to add some B&M infrastructure, but reduced overhead promises to continue to be a distinct advantage of E-Businesses. On the other hand, there is certainly more uncertainty associated with operating online. The technology is rapidly evolving and, therefore, virtually by definition, legal rights and liabilities are more uncertain.

Back to the Law

All E-Businesses deal with IP legal issues, especially with copyright and trademark law. All E-Businesses rely extensively on software and, most probably, specialized software developers. So, all E-Businesses have to be familiar with changes in E-Commerce contract law. Of course, they are also affected by cyber-torts and product liability. All of these issues have been discussed in previous chapters. The focus in this chapter is upon the confluence of contracts and arrangements that an E-Business must make with other E-Businesses if it is to maximize its revenue and profit opportunities. By necessity we will be returning to a number of the legal issues that have been discussed in other chapters, though such return engagements will not be in-depth.

LEGAL LIABILITIES ASSOCIATED WITH ESTABLISHING A WEBSITE

Adequacy of Website Development

To be successful, a website must be competent to deliver on what it advertises. A website will be expected to have adequate capacity and service capability levels to meet anticipated consumer demand. If a site is selling high-tech products on which customers are likely to require assistance, there needs to be adequate service technician staffing available, both by telephone and online, to provide a reasonable level of customer service. Failure to provide such infrastructure could be a breach of contract on the sale of such products and allow customers to demand refunds. If Susan buys a Palm Pilot from a website selling these products, she ought to have some reasonable means of communicating with the website if the Palm Pilot does not work properly or some of the components were not shipped. If the phone number associated with the website is always busy and e-mails are not answered within a reasonable time, Susan does not have a reasonable means of communicating with the website or of getting a reasonable level of service.

Clickwrap Agreements

Websites should have *terms of use* agreements with their customers that are available in clickwrap form. The clickwrap agreement should discuss issues such as copyright content, linking policy, privacy policy, dispute resolution procedures, and warranty disclaimers on any of the risks that the website does not want to bear. Extensive discussion of clickwrap agreement was provided in Chapters 3 and 4.

Jurisdiction

When a political entity has **jurisdiction** over a person or company, it means that court decisions within that political entity can affect the subject person or company. If a court in Florida has jurisdiction over a person in New York, it means that a plaintiff in Florida can sue the New York person in Florida courts. If the New Yorker refuses to put up a fight in Florida, he or she will lose by default in the Florida courts. By virtue of the Full Faith and Credit Clause in the U.S. Constitution, the Florida plaintiff can take the court judgment from the Florida court to New York and get a court order from a New York court to levy on the assets of the New York person. Quite obviously a lot is at stake in determining whether the courts in a particular state have jurisdiction over a person or entity. Many suits cannot be justified economically if the plaintiff has to travel to the defendant's state for a lawsuit. From the plaintiff's vantage point, and most plaintiffs are customers of the website, the ideal situation is to sue the defendant in the plaintiff's home state courts.

Website Liabilities

Please see the article:
"Internet Brings Global Liabilities," Carolyn Aldred; *Business Insurance,* Chicago; May 29, 2000; Vol. 34, Iss. 22; pg. 17.

Additional Readings:
"Exposed on the Net: A Comparison of Internet Business Exposures with Standard Business Policies," Greg Nelson; Society of Chartered Property and Casualty Underwriters. *CPCU Journal, Media;* Summer 2000; Vol. 53, Iss. 2; pg. 106.

"If Nothing Else Works, Japan Has the Internet", Arthur M Mitchell; *Global Finance,* New York; May 2000; Vol. 14, Iss. 5; pg. 38.

Minimum Contacts Test for Jurisdiction

In general, state jurisdiction over a person or company is based on geography or contacts between the person or business and the host political entity. For example, if a person is a resident of a state, that state has jurisdiction over that person. If an out-of-state business maintains an office or directs sales agents in a state, that state can exert jurisdiction over that business, based on the "minimum contacts" test. In general, the minimum contacts test is based on the notion that if a business takes advantage of opportunities provided by a state in terms of customers, infrastructure, and enforcement of laws, then the business should be subject to the state's jurisdiction when a resident of the state has a claim against the business. If a business maintains an office and employees in a state, or purposely directs advertising towards that state, court precedents have established that the minimum contacts test is satisfied and the business is subject to the state's jurisdiction.

Limits on the Minimum Contacts Test

State courts have so liberally applied the minimum contacts test that the U.S. Supreme Court and Congress have had to put some limits on the outreach of state jurisdictional rulings. As a result of a famous Supreme Court ruling in the Bella Hess case and, later, an act of Congress, mail order businesses are not subject to the jurisdiction of a state if there is no other physical presence of the mail order business in the forum state.[7] So, interestingly, mail order businesses are largely able to escape out-of-state sales

[7]*National Bella Hess, Inc.* v. *Dept. of Revenue of the State of Illinois,* 386 U.S. 753 (1967).

and income taxes as long as they have no physical presence in the host state and do not violate other parameters set by the minimum contacts tests (more about jurisdiction and taxes a bit later).

A fundamental question for us is whether, for jurisdictional purposes, a website is more like a mail order company or more like a company that has a physical presence within the host state? Cyber space is a different kind of space. Websites are accessible nationally and even internationally with a few clicks of a mouse. If accessibility on the WWW is the criteria for jurisdiction, then all websites would be subject to the jurisdiction of courts in all 50 states as well as in all local governments courts. This situation is clearly unworkable and unsatisfactory as apparently recognized by the court in the *Beer Across America* case on the next page. This case involved the purchase of beer by a minor in Alabama from a website for a business located in Illinois.

Personal Nontax Jurisdiction

In addition to beer sales to minors, e-issues for which a different-state resident might want to sue a website would include fraud, a malfunctioning product, and breach of contract on a service agreement. If the customer has to travel to the home state of the website, the cost of making the journey would typically make a lawsuit uneconomical. With knowledge of this fact plus an expectation of more favorable treatment in their home states, most websites have clickwrap agreements in which customers "agree" to arbitration procedures in the home states of the websites.

Passive versus Active Websites

To date, courts have treated websites that are "passive", those only offering one-way communication

Lynda Butler v. *Beer Across America*
United States District Court, N.D. Alabama
83 F.Supp.2d 1261 (Feb. 10, 2000)

CASE BACKGROUND AND FACTS

The plaintiff in this case is the mother of a minor who the plaintiff alleges purchased an alcoholic beverage from the defendant, Beer Across America, that operates from a website that accepted the credit card of the minor. The plaintiff filed the suit in the Circuit Court of Shelby County, in the State of Alabama. Defendant, an out-of-state corporation, removed the case to Federal District Court based on diversity of citizenship and then moves to have the case dismissed based on lack of personal jurisdiction.

OPINION: HANCOCK, SENIOR DISTRICT JUDGE

The Court has before it the August 6, 1999 motion of defendants Beer Across America, Merchant Direct, and Shermer Specialties (collectively "Beer Across America") to dismiss the present action for lack of personal jurisdiction. Pursuant to the Court's October 8, 1999 order, the motion came under submission on December 17, 1999.

* * *

The burden of establishing personal jurisdiction over a nonresident defendant is on the plaintiff.*** To survive a defendant's motion to dismiss for lack of personal jurisdiction, the plaintiff must demonstrate a prima facie case of personal jurisdiction, which requires the presentation of evidence sufficient to withstand a motion for a directed verdict.*** In considering whether such a showing has been made, the court must accept as true all uncontroverted facts alleged in the complaint and must also draw all reasonable inferences arising from controverted assertions of

fact in the light most favorable to the plaintiff.

Here, the facts are simple. In early April of 1999, plaintiff's minor son, who apparently was left home unsupervised (but with a credit card issued in his name) while his parents vacationed, placed an order for twelve bottles of beer with defendants through Beer Across America's Internet site on the World Wide Web. Under the applicable provisions of the U.C.C., the sale occurred in Illinois. The beer was then shipped to plaintiff's son in Alabama and delivered to the Butler residence by the carrier acting, the entire time, as the agent of the plaintiff's son. The sale was not discovered by plaintiff until she returned home and found several bottles of beer from the shipment remaining in the family's refrigerator. Together, these facts present the following question: whether personal jurisdiction properly may be asserted by a federal court sitting in diversity in Alabama over a nonresident Illinois defendant in an action arising from a sale made in Illinois solely in response to an order placed by an Alabama resident via the Internet?

As one arm of the due process analysis, the court initially must determine whether at least minimum contacts exist between the defendant and the jurisdiction . . . The significant question is whether "the defendant's conduct and connection with the forum State are such that he should reasonably anticipate being haled into court there"? . . . General jurisdiction may be exercised when a defendant's contacts with the forum are sufficiently numerous, purposeful, and continuous, as to render fair an assertion of power over the defendant by that state's courts no matter

the nature or extent of the relationship to the forum entailed in the particular litigation; if general jurisdiction is established, absolutely no connection need be shown between the state and the claim for the defendant to be summoned constitutionally before that forum's courts . . . Regardless of the specific or general nature of the contacts in question, for purposes of satisfying due process, they must be purposeful on the part of the defendant; "it is essential in each case that there be some act by which the defendant purposefully avails itself of the privilege of conducting activities within the forum State, thus invoking the benefits and protection of its laws."

* * *

In addition to minimum contacts, due process mandates a consideration of the fairness in forcing the defendant to litigate in a foreign forum . . . To answer this inquiry into "fair play and substantial justice," the court will examine the nature of the defendant's contacts with the forum in light of additional factors, including the burdens on the defendant of litigating in the foreign forum; the interests of the forum state in overseeing the litigation; the interests of the plaintiff in efficient, substantial relief; the interests of the interstate judicial system in economical dispute resolution; and the joint interests of the states in promoting basic social policies. [Citations deleted] These additional factors may be used to bolster a conclusion that the exercise of personal jurisdiction is actually proper when fewer than the otherwise sufficient number of minimum contacts are present or to defeat jurisdiction in the face of strong evidence of otherwise suffi-cient, purposeful connections be-tween the defendant and the forum state. [Citation deleted] In summary, only if the forum state's laws permit jurisdiction over the nonresident de-fendant and both prongs of the due process inquiry are satisfied may that defendant constitutionally be haled into the forum state's courts. [Cita-tion deleted].

* * *

Regarding the minimum contacts el-ement of due process analysis, plain-tiff asserts that defendants' contacts with the state of Alabama are suffi-cient for either general or specific jurisdiction. To support general ju-risdiction, the plaintiff cites not only the sale to her son but also the defen-dants' sales (in Illinois) to other Alabama residents as well as the sale of beer to defendants by two Al-abama brewers through a non-party Illinois wholesaler. However, the plaintiff has not offered any compe-tent evidence to seriously controvert the defendants' averments that they

are not registered to do business in Alabama; that they own no property in the state; that they maintain no of-fices in the state; that they have no agents in Alabama; that their key personnel have never even visited the state; and that they do not place advertisement with Alabama media outlets (except for what nationally placed advertisements may reach the state) or engage in any other signifi-cant promotions targeting the state, which would rise to such a level as would justify an exercise of general jurisdiction by this state's courts. What plaintiff has offered is simply not sufficient to conclude that Beer Across America can be brought be-fore an Alabama tribunal for any claim that any plaintiff may bring.

QUESTIONS FOR ANALYSIS

1. Does this strongly support the proposition that merely because a website can be accessed in a state does not mean that the website is subject to the jurisdiction of that state?

2. If pornography was offered at a website (say in Illinois), and it was reachable by citizens of a second state that had strict antipornography laws, would the site be subject to criminal prosecution in that second state? Interstate shipment of pornography using the U.S. Mail is clearly illegal. What is the critical difference from the beer sale case?

3. Suppose that the defendants in this case made one trip across the South and into Alabama promoting their products. According to the court in this case, would the "minimum contacts" test be satisfied? Should one promotional trip make that much difference? If one trip does make a difference, then it is clear, is it not, that management should carefully consider whether to promote their products by traveling to states where sales are made?

with customers, as though they were mail order busi-nesses and, thus, not subject to jurisdiction of other states. Illustratively, if the only communication that takes place at the website is orders by customers, courts have treated the website like a mail order busi-ness, with such a website not subject to the jurisdiction of the plaintiff's state courts. The more active and in-teractive the website, the more likely the mail order analogy fails, exposing the more interactive website to an elevated risk of facing jurisdiction in the courts of the plaintiff's state. Among the website "activity" that courts have looked at as establishing minimum con-tacts are e-mails, 1-800 phone numbers, and banners ads targeted to particular geographic locations.

Get the Customer to "Agree" on Arbitration and a Change of Forum

Even if jurisdictional precedents in a state place an out-of-state website under that state's jurisdiction, the website can still avoid having to go out of state to

defend itself from a product liability suit through the use of carefully constructed arbitration clauses and choice of forum clauses in its sales contracts. In order to exert jurisdiction over a website, an out-of-state court would have to rule (1) that the activity of the website was sufficient to pass the minimum contacts tests and (2) that the arbitration and choice of forum clause(s) were, for some reason, unenforceable. Web-sites would do well to avoid activities that clearly place them under the jurisdiction of another state and to supplement that caution with well-written sales agreements that include favorable arbitration and choice of forum clauses.

Jurisdiction and Taxation

In addition to being important for private suits involv-ing E-Commerce, jurisdiction is a prominent issue for the tax-collecting powers of states. With a rapidly growing volume of product and service sales occurring online, states have become increasingly concerned over the volumes of sales tax revenues they are losing by not collecting such taxes on internet sales from outside vendors. States' efforts to remedy the looming tax shortfalls have been largely negated for the immediate future by the Internet Tax Freedom Act of 1998. This Act generally prohibits the imposition of new taxes on websites by states in which the website does not have minimum contacts. The Internet Tax Freedom Act of 1998 treats websites much like mail order business and, thus, frees Internet transactions and E-Commerce sales from out-of-state sales and income taxes. There are a few states that are authorized to tax out-of-state Internet transactions but only if these states can show that they had existing taxes on Internet transactions before the passage of the 1998 Act. Internet tax freedom is scheduled to continue until October 21, 2001. Although candidates from both major political parties have pledged to keep the Internet free from taxation, as E-Commerce grows, the disparity of tax treatment between E-Commerce sales and in-state sales will become more and more difficult to justify. Moreover, with states generally looking for ways to enhance revenues, as E-Commerce expands, it will become an increasingly attractive target for taxation.

A state can also levy taxes on sales from out-of-state websites if the seller has more than the required "minimum contacts" with the host state. There is readily available software that will allow a website to comply with the sales and income tax statutes in all 50 states, allowing for the collection of and payment of any taxes owed. Of course, if a website limits its activities to the point where it does not have minimum contacts in a state, it will be taxed as though it is a mail order catalogue and thus be exempt from that state's out-of-state sales or use taxes. However, if a website targets residents of another state for advertising purposes, engages them in a contest or sweepstakes, or otherwise establishes minimum contacts, it is likely not exempt from the requirement to pay sales tax. For small websites, enforcement of state sales tax undoubtedly is spotty at best. However, a website that is very successful and ends up with a large volume of sales can become a worthwhile target for out-of-state tax authorities to pursue for sales tax collections.

Jurisdictional Paradox

Absent from the discussion above is any attention to issues of international jurisdiction. At present, foreign websites largely escape jurisdiction of states within the United States. In addition, our discussion has paid no attention to the possibility of domestic websites falling under the jurisdiction of foreign countries that are likely to have very different criteria for exerting jurisdiction. It is fair to say that nationally it is clear that, at present, court rulings and the Internet Tax Freedom Act strongly favor E-Commerce sales relative to B&M sales (which certainly are subject to sales tax unless they are mail order business sales to customers in states remote from the mail-order company). Providing more generous jurisdictional authority to states has potentially dire consequences for the fledgling E-Commerce world. Too readily available jurisdiction could result in widespread failures of young E-Commerce businesses as they would struggle to comply with tax and other requirements of 50 different states and innumerable local jurisdictions within the United States.

Federal Regulation Under the FTC—Fraud and Claim Substantiation

The Federal Trade Commission views a website as a business. As such a website is subject to the authority of the FTC to prohibit unfair and deceptive trade practices. The *Geocities* case reviewed in Chapter 6 indicated that the FTC will intervene when a website does not adhere to privacy policies it lists on its own website and, also, if a website collects information from children without the consent of parents. The FTC has more general antifraud authority that relates to advertising, including web-based advertising.

The FTC has authority to prohibit both *unfair* and/or *deceptive* advertising. Most of the time, advertising attacked by the FTC is challenged for being both unfair and deceptive. According to the FTC, "[T]o justify a finding of unfairness the injury must satisfy three tests. It must be substantial; it must not be outweighed by any countervailing benefits to consumers or competition that the practice produces; and it must be an injury that consumers themselves could not reasonably have avoided." Appeals to racial prejudice or coercive practices such as dismantling appliances and refusing to reassemble them unless a purchase is made are examples of unfair trade practices. Collecting information from children or vulnerable groups such as immigrants is an unfair trade practice.

What Is a Deceptive Advertisement According to the FTC?

More pertinent to websites is the FTC authority to prohibit *deceptive* trade practices. According to the FTC, an advertisement is deceptive if it makes material

Internet Taxation

THE FUTURE OF INTERNET TAXATION

Because the various jurisdictions are still attempting to resolve the tax and jurisdiction questions raised by Internet commerce, a definitive answer concerning future taxation is not possible. What is possible, however, is to review the positions of the current actors and the court decisions for clues about which relevant factors will be weighed in, balancing the interests of Internet providers; traditional businesspersons; and Federal, state, and local governments. First, the New York approach advocated by the Department of Finance and Taxation and the Federal courts appears reasonable. The mere appearance of an Internet site on a computer screen should not constitute a sufficient presence or "nexus" with the state or local government to justify taxation. The fact a New York resident has "hit" on an Internet site does not mean the taxing entity has provided any police power benefits to the foreign entity or that a taxable event has occurred. However, where the resident of the state or local government has actually entered into a contract over the Internet for the sale or provision of goods or services, sufficient nexus may be found. It is well settled that states may fairly tax income or profits made in its jurisdiction.

Source: "Taxation of Internet Commerce," by Ken Griffin, *The CPA Journal,* Vol. 68, Issue 1, p. 42. Reprinted with permission from *The CPA Journal,* January 1998, Copyright 1998.

Additional Readings:
"Personal Jurisdiction and the Internet in the New Millennium," Robert Moore; Academy of Marketing Science. *Journal, Greenvale;* Summer 2000; Vol. 28, Iss. 3; pg. 454, 2 pgs.

"Another Alternative View of the Internet," John Cronin; *Accountancy Ireland, Dublin;* Jun 1998; Vol. 30, Iss. 3; pg. 32, 2.

misrepresentation or if it suffers omissions that are likely to mislead consumers generally. There is a second test of deceptiveness which asks whether the misrepresentation or omission is likely to mislead consumers under special circumstances. It is possible that some consumers actually believe that "Danish" pastries are made in Denmark, but advertisers don't need to correct their ads because of the misconceptions of a few extremely gullible observers. On the other hand, there may be situations in which it is recognized that the intended audience as a class is extremely gullible. Representations made to an extremely gullible group such as the elderly, children, or immigrants are not evaluated under an "average" consumer test but, rather, with an average-consumer-within-the-special-group test.

Barry Diller et al., Plaintiffs, v. *Eric M. Steurken et al., Individually, and Doing Business as Thoughts et al., Defendants*
Supreme Court, New York County, New York
712 N.Y.S.2d 311 (2000)

CASE BACKGROUND AND FACTS

Barry Diller is the Chairman and Chief Executive Officer of USAi, a diversified media and E-Commerce company. On January 19, 1999, defendants Steurken and Preisig, using "Thoughts," an assumed business name, registered the Internet domain name "barrydiller.com." They then registered their own domain, "cybermultimedia.com," using another assumed business name, "Cybermul-timedia, Inc." (CMM), and started designing a website. On January 27, defendants incorporated CMM and began to publicize their website one month later.

Defendants essentially established cybermultimedia.com as a domain name brokerage site. They would collect the names of celebrities, register their names as Internet domains, and then attempt to sell them to the celebrities at a substantial profit. From June 1, 1999, until June 22, CMM's site contained numerous uses of Barry Diller's name, one use of his picture, and one use of the name "USA Networks." Defendants never asked Diller for permission to use his name, his picture, or the name "USA Networks" in any manner on the CMM website. On June 10, plaintiffs wrote a letter to defendants demanding removal from the CMM website of all references to

Barry Diller and USAi. Plaintiffs also demanded, inter alia, that defendants transfer "barrydiller.com" to their control. In response to this letter, on June 22, defendants removed Diller's picture and the reference to USAi from the site. However, they did not remove Diller's name and continued to offer the sale of "barrydiller.com" for $10,000,000.

OPINION: CHARLES EDWARD RAMOS

On the issue of injunctive relief, defendants have conceded liability for violation of § 51 of the Civil Rights Law and §§ 349, 350, and 360-k of the GBL by defaulting Section 51 of the Civil Rights Law provides:

> "Any person whose name, portrait, picture or voice is used within this state for advertising purposes or for the purposes of trade. without * * * written consent * * * may maintain an equitable action in the supreme court of this state against the person, firm or corporation so using his name, portrait, picture or voice to *prevent and restrain*

the use thereof" (emphasis added).

Similarly, GBL § 349 (h), which applies to deceptive trade practices, provides that "any person who has been injured by reason of any violation of this section may bring an action * * * to enjoin such unlawful act or practice." The language of GDL § 350 (e) (3), which applies to false advertising, is identical. Furthermore, GBL § 360-1 provides that "likelihood of injury to business reputation or of dilution of the distinctive quality of a mark or trade name shall be a ground for injunctive relief in cases of infringement of a mark registered or not registered or in cases of unfair competition." Consequently, defendants are to be enjoined as a matter of law from using the domain name "barrydiller.com."

In addition to provisions of State law providing plaintiffs with support for an injunction, the recently enacted Anti-cybersquatting Consumer Protection Act ("ACPA") provides for "injunctive relief, including the forfeiture or cancellation of the domain name or *the transfer of the domain name to the plaintiff.*" While the

ACPA was not in effect when defendants registered "barrydiller.com," the Second Circuit has ruled that the ACPA applies retroactively where prospective or injunctive relief is at issue. Moreover, domain name transfer is a remedy of choice in anti-cybersquatting actions. Given the provisions of state law *supra,* the Second Circuit's construction of the ACPA, judicial recognition of domain name transfer as a recognized remedy in anti-cybersquatting actions, and the fact that defendants have indicated a willingness to consent to an injunction in their opposition papers, the court grants plaintiffs' request for injunctive relief and compels defendants to transfer ownership of "barrydiller.com" to the plaintiffs.

QUESTIONS FOR ANALYSIS

1. What kind of tort is the use of someone's name or likeness without permission?
2. Has the plaintiff been defrauded by the actions of the defendant or have customers using the Internet? Does it make sense to allow plaintiff to sue on behalf of customers?

Reasonable Substantiation

Website advertisers that make unsubstantiated claims are subject to an FTC enforcement action, which is likely to be very costly to the advertiser and very public. If successful in its suit, the FTC will obtain a "cease and desist" order from the courts, requiring a halt to the deceptive advertising. To cure earlier misrepresentations, the FTC may seek a court order requiring "corrective" advertisements. In order to avoid FTC enforcement actions, a website should have reasonable substantiation for the claims it makes in its advertisements. If a website product advertisement claims that "doctors recommend its products relative to other products", there must be a survey which conforms to customary practices for survey takers that confirms these claims. If there is a claim that a celebrity endorses a product sold by a website, the website must verify that the celebrity actually uses the product. It is also important to note that other

regulatory bodies can intervene in website advertising. Websites that advertise about the availability or benefits of pharmaceutical products are subject to scrutiny of the Food and Drug Administration (FDA). For other products, additional regulatory agencies may need to be consulted.

IP Protection

Who Owns the Copyright to "Your" Website?

We have previously discussed many of the IP issues that confront E-Businesses. If an E-Business has a website designed by an independent contractor, the copyright to the design is owned by the contractor unless there are provisions to the contrary in the contract between the website and the independent contractor. The contract for website development should include specification of who gets the copyrights to the computer code, artwork, music, and text. Failure to gain agreement on these issues will hamper the website if it decides to use another website developer to upgrade the website. In addition, for material that cannot be protected by either patent or copyright law, there should be NDAs required of the website developer to protect valuable trade secrets of the website owner.

How Can You Use IP Law to Protect Yourself from Imitators?

Components of websites such as text and artwork can be protected from imitation by other websites, but the overall "look and feel" of the website will be difficult to protect under current copyright law, especially if the website is trying to protect its methods of operation. Trademark law could be used to protect the overall "look and feel" of the website because an infringement is based on consumer confusion, which is inherently a "look and feel" test, but trademark law will not protect the functionality of the website. Also, websites that have a distinctive appearance may be able to sue imitators for a *trade dress* infringement, again based on the issue of consumer confusion. Keep in mind, however, if the appearance of the website frequently changes, it will be difficult to claim its appearance is "distinctive." Increasingly, websites are using patent law to protect methods of operation for the website (recall the group of patents that Amazon.com has to protect its method of allowing customers to purchase books online).

Databases or "facts" that are made available on a website are not protectible, though arrangements of those data or facts are protectible under copyright law. Quite obviously, websites should avoid replicating copyrighted material that is owned by third parties, unless they have permission of the third parties. Also, given the number of software patents that have been issued, websites that offer searching or other services should be aware that these methods of operation may infringe the patents of another firm. Finally, suppose that a website makes it clear that it does not like the way you do business. Can Microsoft sue a website entitled, "Microsoftsucks"? The answer is no and that is the unpleasant answer that a number of other famous companies discovered when they encountered "suck" sites. The high regard the courts have for freedom of expression protects "suck" sites from suits even though these sites are using part of the famous site's trademark.

Possible Infringement Suits Against Your Website and Protection of Your IP Rights

Websites should not use the name or likeness of anyone, especially celebrities, without their permission. Posting a name or likeness of a person without their permission is a common law invasion of privacy. A number of states recognize a "right of publicity" which means that the name or likeness of a person can be protected even after death. If you use your own trademark on your website, you have an obligation to provide notice if the trademark is registered at the state or federal level. If you use the trademarks of another firm, you should be careful to ensure that no false association, affiliation, or sponsorship is implied by the use of another's mark and, furthermore, you should avoid using language that could *dilute* the value of a famous mark.

Consider the following situation. You obtain a license to publish an author's work, which you exercise. Then you include the author's work in an electronic database without the author's consent but relying on your license. Have you infringed a copyright? The next case addresses this situation.

Jonathan Tasini et al. v. The New York Times Company, Inc.
United States Court of Appeals, Second Circuit
(1999 WL 753966 (2nd Cir.(N.Y.)))

CASE BACKGROUND AND FACTS

Appellants are free lance writers (individually, "Author" and collectively, "Authors") who write articles for publication in periodicals. Their complaint alleged that certain articles were original works written for first publication by one of the appellee publishers between 1990 and 1993. None of the articles was written at a time when its Author was employed by the particular periodical; nor was any such article written pursuant to a work-for-hire contract. The Authors registered a copyright in each of the articles.

The appellee newspaper and magazine publishers (collectively, "Publishers") are periodical publishers who regularly create "collective works," see 17 U.S.C. 101, that contain articles by free lance authors as well as works created for-hire or by employees. With respect to the free lance articles pertinent to this appeal, the Publishers' general practice was to negotiate due-dates, word counts, subject matter and price; no express transfer of rights under the Author's copyright was sought.*(1)*

As to one article alleged in the complaint, however, authored by appellant David S. Whitford for *Sports Illustrated,* a publication of appellee The Time Incorporated Magazine Company (*"Time"*), a written contract expressly addressed republication rights. We address Whitford's claim separately below.

Appellee Mead Data Central Corp. owns and operates the NEXIS electronic database. NEXIS is a massive database that includes the full texts of articles appearing in literally hundreds of newspapers and periodicals spanning many years. Mead has entered into licensing agreements with each of the Publishers. Pursuant to these agreements, the Publishers provide Mead with much of the content of their periodicals, in digital form, for inclusion in NEXIS. Subscribers to NEXIS are able to access an almost infinite combination of articles from one or more publishers by using the database's advanced search engine. The articles may be retrieved individually or, for example, together with others on like topics. Such retrieval makes the article available without any material from the rest of the periodical in which it first appeared.

We briefly describe the process by which an issue of a periodical is made available to Mead for inclusion in NEXIS. First, an individual issue of the paper is stripped, electronically, into separate files representing individual articles. In the process, a substantial portion of what appears in that particular issue of the periodical is not made part of a file transmitted to Mead, including, among other things, formatting decisions, pictures, maps and tables, and obitu-

aries. Moreover, although the individual articles are "tagged" with data indicating the section and page on which the article initially appeared, certain information relating to the initial page layout is lost, such as placement above or below the fold in the case of *The New York Times.* After Mead further codes the individual files, the pieces are incorporated into the NEXIS database.

Appellee University Microfilms International ("UMI") markets, *inter alia,* CD-ROM database products. Pursuant to an agreement with *The New York Times* and Mead, UMI produces and markets the "NY Times OnDisc" ("NYTO") CD-ROM, which contains the full texts of articles from *The New York Times.* It also produces and markets a "General Periodicals OnDisc" ("GPO") CD-ROM, which contains selected *New York Times* articles and thousands of other articles. Pursuant to its agreement with Mead and *The New York Times,* UMI incorporates the files containing *Times* articles into its NYTO database. UMI uses a somewhat different methodology to incorporate articles from the *NY Times* Sunday book-review and magazine sections onto its GPO CD-ROM. As to these pieces, UMI scans them directly onto "image-based" files. The image-based files are also abstracted and included on the text-based CD-ROM; the abstracts facilitate access to the image-based disk.

The gist of the Authors' claim is that the copyright each owns in his or her individual articles was infringed when the Publishers provided them to the electronic databases. Appellees do not dispute that the Authors own the copyright in their individual works. Rather, they argue that the Publishers own the copyright in the "collective works" that they produce and are afforded the privilege, under Section 201(c) of the Act, of "reproducing and

distributing" the individual works in "any revision of that collective work." 17 U.S.C. 201(c). The crux of the dispute is, therefore, whether one or more of the pertinent electronic databases may be considered a "revision" of the individual periodical issues from which the articles were taken. The district court held that making the articles available on the databases constitutes a revision of the individual periodicals and that appellees' licensing arrangements were protected under Section 201(c).

OPINION: WINTER

We review *de novo* the grant or denial of summary judgment and view the evidence in the light most favorable to the non-moving party. Summary judgment is appropriate only if the pleadings and evidentiary submissions demonstrate the absence of any genuine issue of material fact and that the moving party is entitled to judgment as a matter of law.

The unauthorized reproduction and distribution of a copyrighted work generally infringes the copyright unless such use is specifically protected by the Act. To reiterate, each Author owns the copyright in an individual work and, save for Whitford, has neither licensed nor otherwise transferred any rights under it to a Publisher or electronic database. These works were published with the Authors' consent in particular editions of the periodicals owned by the Publishers. The Publishers then licensed much of the content of these periodicals, including the Authors' works, to one or more of the electronic database providers. As a result, the Authors' works are now available to the public on one or more electronic databases and may be retrieved individually or in combination with other pieces originally published in different editions of the periodical or in different periodicals.

In support of their claim, the Authors advance two principal arguments: first, the Section 201(c) privilege that protects the Publishers' initial inclusion of individually copyrighted works in their collective works does not permit the inclusion of individually copyrighted works in one or more of the electronic databases; and, second, the privilege is not a transferrable "right" within the meaning of Section 201(d) and hence may not be invoked by the electronic database providers. The district court rejected both arguments, reasoning that the privilege is a "subdivision" of a right that is transferrable under Section 201(d)(2), 972 F. Supp. at 815, and that the scope of the privilege was broad enough to permit the inclusion of the Authors' pieces in the various databases, *see id.* at 824–25. We hold that the privilege afforded authors of collective works under Section 201(c) does not permit the Publishers to license individually copyrighted works for inclusion in the electronic databases. We need not, and do not, reach the question whether this privilege is transferrable under Section 201(d).

* * *

The most natural reading of the "revision" of "that collective work" clause is that the Section 201(c) privilege protects only later editions of a particular issue of a periodical, such as the final edition of a newspaper. Because later editions are not identical to earlier editions, use of the individual contributions in the later editions might not be protected under the preceding clause. Given the context provided by the surrounding clauses, this interpretation makes perfect sense. It protects the use of an individual contribution in a collective work that is somewhat altered from the original in which the copyrighted article was first pub-

lished, but that is not in any ordinary sense of language a "later" work in the "same series."

* * *

Second, the privilege set forth in Section 201(c) is an exception to the general rule that copyright vests initially in the author of the individual contribution. Reading "revision of that collective work" as broadly as appellees suggest would cause the exception to swallow the rule. Under Publishers' theory of Section 201(c), the question of whether an electronic database infringes upon an individual author's article would essentially turn upon whether the rest of the articles from the particular edition in which the individual article was published could also be retrieved individually. However, the Section 201(c) privilege would not permit a Publisher to sell a hard copy of an Author's article directly to the public even if the Publisher also offered for individual sale all of the other articles from the particular edition. We see nothing in the revision privilege that would allow the Publishers to achieve the same goal indirectly through NEXIS.

* * *

We emphasize that the only issue we address is whether, in the absence of a transfer of copyright or any rights thereunder, collective-work authors may re-license individual works in which they own no rights. Because there has by definition been no express transfer of rights in such cases, our decision turns entirely on the default allocation of rights provided by the Act. Publishers and authors are free to contract around the statutory framework. Indeed, both the Publishers and Mead were aware of the fact that the Section 201(c) privilege might not protect their licensing

agreements, and at least one of the Publishers has already instituted a policy of expressly contracting for electronic re-licensing rights.

b) Whitford   As noted, Whitford entered into an express licensing agreement with Time. That agreement granted, in pertinent part, to Time:

(a) the exclusive right first to publish the Story in the Magazine:

(b) the non-exclusive right to license the republication of the Story . . . provided that the Magazine shall pay to [him] fifty percent of all net proceeds it receives for such republication: and

(c) the right to republish the Story or any portions thereof in or in connection with the Magazine or in other publications published by [*Time*], provided that [he] shall be paid the then prevailing rates of the publication in which the Story is republished.

Time subsequently licensed Whitford's article to Mead without notifying, obtaining authorization from, or compensating, him.

* * *

CONCLUSION

We therefore reverse and remand with instructions to enter judgment for appellants.

QUESTION FOR ANALYSIS

1. What did the defendants do that the plaintiffs objected to? Did the defendants have a license to publish plaintiff's work?

2. Is this case all about an inadequate license contract drawn up by the *New York Times*? Explain.

Linking to Sites of Third Parties

It is prudent to obtain permission of the other site before linking your site with the website of another business or nonprofit organization. Linking to other websites without permission could imply an affiliation or sponsorship that does not exist and, thus, could be an unfair trade practice under the laws of various states. A small firm selling herbal remedies that links its visitors to a web page of a major pharmaceutical company such as Smith Kline could be sued for an unfair trade practice. Also, if the small firm does some framing (a practice described below) it could be both a copyright and a trademark infringement. Porn sites that provide links to "respectable" sites could also be sued for unfair trade practices. Websites should avoid "deep" links, which allow visitors to skip the home page of another website and link with a page of interest deep within the website. This, too, might be an unfair trade practice or a copyright or trademark infringement.

Privacy Policies

Websites offer a number of advantages relative to B&M establishments. When a person comes into your store, you can observe how he or she is dressed, his or her age, and other characteristics, but you have no idea where (s)he came from or where (s)he is going. Matters are different with a website as, with cookies and other means of extracting information from website visitors, significant information can be obtained from visitors if desired. By the same token, websites are under increasing pressure not to violate privacy rights of visitors to their websites. Quite certainly, it is prudent for a website to post a privacy policy regardless of whether it is collecting information from visitors or members (remembering that 97 percent of websites do collect personal information). In addition, it is important to spell out whether this information will be supplied to third parties. Finally, it is imperative for a website to follow its own privacy policy.

If a website is directed towards children under 13, it must comply with the Child Online Privacy Protection Act, which requires parental permission before collecting information. There are proposals to require mandatory privacy policies at all websites, and, therefore, it is prudent for websites to sign up with TRUSTe or BBBOnLine which require "best practices" in collection and management of personal information from online visitors. Best practices in data collection include the Fair Information Principles of the FTC. Websites that do not adopt a third party certification (such as TRUSTe) of their adherence to industry standards with respect to the collection and management of personal information may be targets for the FTC. Websites are largely insulated from suits based on defamation claims if they republish a defamatory remark in a chat room or other venue. However, since a website is not totally insulated from law suits based on defamation, it should post a Terms of Service agreement that (1) prohibits posting of defamatory material and (2) allows the website to terminate access to any user, member, or subscriber who violates the Terms of Service.

To link or not to link . . .

Companies can get into trouble on the Internet through framing and deep linking, Mendelsohn said. Framing involves lifting content from one website and displaying it on another. Deep linking occurs when a company creates a link from its website to a Web page on another site but bypasses the site's first page. When that happens, a customer may miss important disclaimers or terms of usage on the second site. This ultimately could lead to a lawsuit. "It's like coming in through the back door and missing the security guard," Mendelsohn said.

There is also the possibility that a user who deep links will miss advertising on the second site, which may result in loss of advertising revenue for that company. Often the revenue paid to the owner of the site is tied to the number of visits, or hits, on the page where the advertisement is.

Source: Excerpt from: "Risky Business in Cyberspace" Sally Whitney; *Best's Review,* Oldwick; Jun 2000; Vol. 101, Iss. 2; pg. 143, 4 pgs.

Additional Readings:
"Stay on the Right Side of Copyright Laws"; Susan P Butler; *Macworld,* San Francisco; Aug 2000; Vol. 17, Iss. 8; pg. 105, 3 pgs.

"Laying Down the Cyberlaw"; Carl Sullivan; *Editor & Publisher,* New York; Apr 3, 2000; Vol. 133, Iss. 14; pg. 7, 1 pgs.

Web Hosting Agreements

Creation of a cyber business has some similarities with state incorporation statutes. If a company complies with state incorporation statutes, they derive some very important legal advantages, most notably among them the limited liability of shareholders. In return, state law controls internal governance of corporations including resolutions of disputes between shareholders and the board of directors. Website owners generally must make an agreement with a website host regarding their terms of service. Some of the terms of service are technical such as:

1. Additional disk space, Internet traffic, and e-mail accounts
2. E-mail POP accounts
3. FTP access and anonymous FTP
4. CGI scripting, telnet access
5. Domain name registration, design services
6. Secured credit card transactions

Listed below are some definitions of the acronyms that appear above. Although a lot of what appears immediately above may seem tediously technical, cyber companies should pay detailed attention to these terms. Fortunately, the market provides "turnkey" operations that enable an aspiring cyber company to deal with one company for most of its website preferences. One such company is Webhoster.com. According to webhoster.com, it is,

> "[t]he definitive guide to web hosting! Our mission is to provide the most **objective, accurate** and **non-biased** information pertaining to web hosting. Use the navigation panel on the left to browse the content and the many tools provided. Everyday, thousands of web developers use WebHosters.com to find their host . . . Now it's your turn!"

Companies that wish to establish a website and are unfamiliar with these terms would do well to contact a business lawyer who has E-Commerce experience. For a web-based business, the appearance of its cyber storefront is more important than the storefronts of most B&M operations. It is vitally important for a website to have an agreement with its web host that enables the website to accommodate increased traffic if the website becomes much more popular.

The following are definitions to some of the acronyms that appear above:

Point of Presence—(abbreviation: POP) A site that has a collection of telecommunications equipment; usually refers to ISP or telephone company sites.

File Transfer Protocol—(abbreviation: FTP) An Internet protocol that enables the transfer of files between computers across the Internet. See also anonymous FTP.

anonymous FTP—A service that allows free public access to archived documents, files, and programs via the File Transfer Protocol (FTP). It's not necessary to have a user ID and password when logging into an anonymous FTP site. The user ID "anonymous" bypasses local security checks; often e-mail addresses serve as courtesy passwords. See also File Transfer Protocol.

Common Gateway Interface—(abbreviation: CGI) A standard used by programmers that allows their programs to interact with the World Wide Web. CGI scripts can be written in many computer languages, but Perl and C are the most common.

telnet—A protocol which allows a user to sign onto a remote UNIX computer from another computer located anywhere on the Internet. Telnet access to a remote computer usually requires a user ID and password that is recognized by the remote system.

Other Web Hosting Issues

Many web hosting issues are likely to change substantially as Internet technology continues to evolve. At present, the most pressing issues addressed in web hosting agreements are:

1. **Reliability:** Servers sometimes crash, but if crashes occur too often, they severely interfere with activities conducted on the website. Definitions of reliability should be established in the web hosting agreement.
2. **Domain Name Integrity:** If a host obtains a domain name, responsibility for enforcing trademark infringements should be addressed. If a web host that obtains a domain name for a website, but then fails to prosecute trademark or domain name infringements leaves the website with no legal protection for the domain name.
3. **Site Updates:** A host's responsibilities for updating a website should be described with specificity in terms of frequency and content.

4. **Legality Requirements:** In web hosting agreements, it is common for hosts to require that any website hosted be used only for lawful purposes. Web hosts generally indicate further that:
   a. The host will cooperate with law enforcement,
   b. The host can suspend operation of a website without liability if the host believes that the website is being used for illegal purposes or is creating liability exposure for the host (e.g., because of the publication of defamatory material).
   c. The host will prohibit spamming and impersonations at the website.

5. **IP Prohibitions:** A host's contract will indicate that the host can terminate a website if the website is being used to decompile, disassemble, or reverse engineer web hosting software in order to appropriate trade secrets of the host or create derivative works.

Website Fulfillment with Customers

Even though E-Businesses are conducting much of their business electronically, ultimately an E-Commerce site must deliver product to customers, whether it is a business (B to B) or a consumer (B to C) business. If the website is selling (licensing) software, then fulfillment of the contract with the customer can take place almost instantly, once the customer pays for the software, as the software can be downloaded on line. All warranties and disclaimers become part of the contract by means of a clickwrap agreement, so long as the terms of that agreement are not unconscionable. For physical products delivery, a website can either provide its own supply chain or it can rely on third parties for product conveyance. Typically, websites initially rely on third party common carriers such as the U.S. Post Office or UPS but, as their business volume grows, tend to move toward self-fulfillment. This arrangement becomes increasingly attractive because there are economies of scale in shipping. Not surprisingly, common carriers have responded with their own innovations.

Warranties, Refunds, Shipping and Handling, and Credit

There are numerous state and federal laws that apply to warranties, refunds, shipping and handling charges. Many of the UCC constraints on warranties and disclaimers were discussed in Chapters 2 and 3. There are other laws that regulate acceptable practices on refunds for returned merchandise, packaging, and shipment of ordered goods. The FTC has indicated that required disclosures for websites should be conspicuous, suggesting that a disclosure buried in Legal Notices or in Terms of Agreement are not sufficient.

Ignorance of applicable laws and regulations can result in costly consequences for a website operator. Examples of costly problems are easy to envision. If a website accepts installment payments, it could inadvertently trigger Truth in Lending Act (TILA) requirements, which necessitate a lengthy list of specific disclosures that are not normally provided by websites. According to TILA any payment plan that involves any charge for interest or that requires more than four installments requires TILA disclosures including a boldface listing of the Annual Percentage Rate of interest, even if the interest charge is zero. Timely merchandise shipments can also be a problem for E-Businesses. The FTC's Mail or Telephone Order Merchandise Trade Regulation Rule requires on-time shipment of merchandise when a notice is listed conspicuously, or if there is no time listed, then within 30 days of the date when a buyer places his or her order. If an order cannot be fulfilled within 30 days, the seller must obtain customer consent for the delay or offer an immediate refund.

Faced with intense competition for the attention of Internet travelers, many websites offer game contests and sweepstakes to their site users. These activities should be offered with considerable caution because of the inconsistency of state laws dealing with gaming, gambling, etc. Compliance with the laws of one state (your home state, perhaps) does not ensure compliance with the applicable laws in other states. Many states require disclosures of the odds of winning a contest and some states require registration statements. Some of the required state disclosure and registration requirements are so onerous that it is not worth the effort of meeting the requirements for the volume of web traffic to be gained. Websites that do not comply with the most restrictive state laws regarding sweepstakes should exclude participants from those states.

Electronic Contracts

Websites certainly view the contracts they make with their customers online as binding. For most sales contracts, where the contract payment amount exceeds $500, the UCC requires signatures. States and the federal government have both moved rapidly and forcefully to establish the legality of electronic contracts. Forty states have passed the Uniform Electronic Transactions Act, which grants legal parity between paper and electronic records. Congress and the President enacted the Millennium Digital Signatures Act (MDSA) in 2000. As discussed in Chapter 3, the MDSA makes digital signatures that may be accomplished through passwords, hardware, third party authentication, or encryption fully enforceable.

Having succeeded in making electronic contracts binding, website owners should be aware of the binding obligations they face for honoring outdated offers that remain present at their websites. Such offers might be for out-stock-merchandise or for items listed at prices that are no longer accurate. Unlike advertisements, offers made on a website are binding since acceptances of those offers by website visitors are binding also. Website owners should carefully scrutinize and update offers made at their website on a regular basis.

As discussed in Chapter 3, if website owners use reasonable attribution procedures, they can accept credit card orders and charge the party identified on the credit card. If use of the card is not authorized by the cardholder, that dispute must be resolved between the credit card issuer and the cardholder. On the other hand, if the website does not use a reasonable attribution procedure, then acceptance of an order using a credit card does not bind the cardholder. Given the current state of security, reasonable attribution procedures involve use of encryption to guard against interception of transmitted information. If encryption is not used, then there must be some cross-referencing of information to verify that the cardholder is indeed placing the order. Additionally, in order to cross-reference information on customers, companies must securely store the requisite information to guard against hackers' access to that information. Lack of success in this task will generate liability based on negligence in secure storage.

SUMMARY

- Growth of E-Commerce has been exponential and there is no end of this growth in sight.
- E-Commerce business models make use of the medium to transform web traffic into revenue. Among the most attractive E-Commerce business models are those that are based on selling cyber space real estate to advertisers, signing up visitors on some form of subscription agreement, or engaging directly in E-Commerce.
- Website success is based on the ability of websites to attract traffic. Repeat visitors are attracted to sites that engage customers with games and other intriguing opportunities.
- Frequently, websites are successful in creating cyber communities that generate a lot of repeat business.
- Once a website attracts customers, it often finds ways of creating costs for visitors to switch to rival websites.
- Switching costs can be either technological or content based. In fact, websites seek to "lock-in" their customers and lock-out their rivals through technological incompatibilities.
- Websites recognize that many of their products can be commoditized, and so they seek to differentiate their products when possible. Product differentiation requires cultivation of brand awareness. *Co-branding* and *cross-marketing* are ways of increasing brand awareness.
- A huge advantage that websites have over brick and mortar establishments is that their overhead is much lower.
- Establishing a website entails exposure to a sizeable array of potential legal liabilities. Businesses should be able to fulfill the commitments made on their website. The potential legal liability that is associated with a website often can be limited by clickwrap agreements in which customers and members agree to waive their rights to sue and/or submit to other restrictions.
- An important legal issue is whether a website is subject to the *jurisdiction* of other states. The basic test for establishing jurisdiction is the "*minimum contacts*" test, which looks at whether the website has purposely availed itself of the privileges of operating in the forum state.
- There are two important legal issues associated with jurisdiction: taxation and liability for fraud and and malfunctioning products. If a state establishes jurisdiction, then the website must travel to that forum state to defend itself in any suit, or else lose the pending suit by default.

- The more active a website is, the more likely it is that a court will rule that the website is subject to the jurisdiction of another state. Websites, however, can negate jurisdictional disadvantages by including *arbitration* and *choice of forum* clauses in their terms of service agreements.
- Websites are subject to FTC constraints on unfair and deceptive advertising. The FTC has intervened in a number of website cases to require the website to cease and decease deceptive practices.
- There are important copyright issues associated with websites, including web design and linkages to other websites, especially when the linking distorts the destination website. Also trademark law can be enlisted to provide protection against trademark imitation. If you use a trademark, it is important to designate it as such.
- Linking your website to another site can be an unfair trade practice, depending on the facts of the situation. Among the unfair trade practices associated with linking are framing, deep linking, or linking to a website that makes it clear it does not want to be linked.

- In general, it is prudent to have a *privacy policy* and to adhere to what is said in the privacy policy.
- Web hosting agreements are akin to state charters granted to corporations. The web host creates the terms of trade for the websites that locate on its server.
- Web hosting agreements should discuss reliability, control, and responsibility for domain names, have arrangements with respect to the access that law enforcement has to website files, and provisions for forfeiture of the website in the case of decompilation for the purpose of obtaining trade secrets.
- Website owners should be cognizant of a number of laws that were enacted to protect consumers. Website owners should know when the Truth in Lending Act applies, how the Telephone Order Merchandise Trade Regulation Rule applies to their activities, and when contests are considered sweepstakes.
- E-Commerce was facilitated by the recent enactment of the Millennium Digital Signatures Act of 2000, giving electronic signatures parity with on-paper signatures.

INDEX